Lecture Notes in Computer Science 11462

More information about this series at http://www.springer.com/series/7409

Abdennour El Rhalibi · Zhigeng Pan ·
Haiyan Jin · Dandan Ding ·
Andres A. Navarro-Newball ·
Yinghui Wang (Eds.)

E-Learning and Games

12th International Conference, Edutainment 2018
Xi'an, China, June 28–30, 2018
Proceedings

Springer

Editors
Abdennour El Rhalibi
Liverpool John Moores University
Liverpool, UK

Zhigeng Pan
Hangzhou Normal University
Hangzhou, China

Haiyan Jin
Xi'an University of Technology
Xi'an, China

Dandan Ding
Hangzhou Normal University
Hangzhou, China

Andres A. Navarro-Newball
Pontificia Universidad Javeriana
Cali, Colombia

Yinghui Wang
Xi'an University of Technology
Xi'an, China

ISSN 0302-9743 ISSN 1611-3349 (electronic)
Lecture Notes in Computer Science
ISBN 978-3-030-23711-0 ISBN 978-3-030-23712-7 (eBook)
https://doi.org/10.1007/978-3-030-23712-7

LNCS Sublibrary: SL3 – Information Systems and Applications, incl. Internet/Web, and HCI

This Springer imprint is published by the registered company Springer Nature Switzerland AG
The registered company address is: Gewerbestrasse 11, 6330 Cham, Switzerland

Preface

Edutainment 2018 was the 12th International Conference on E-Learning and Games, which provides an international forum for researchers and practitioners in various disciplines to share and exchange experiences in the emerging research area combining education and entertainment. It took place during June 28–30, 2018, in Xi'an, China. The first event took place during April 15–17, 2006. The previous conferences were held in China (Hangzhou, Changchun, Nanjing, Hong Kong, Taipei, etc.), Canada, Germany, Australia, and the UK. Edutainment has become an international major conference, facilitating the international exchange of the state of the art in academic research and practice. The conference covers all aspects of pedagogical principles, designs and technological issues for education, research, and entertainment.

This year, we received 85 papers, of which 32 papers were accepted as long papers. Five keynote speakers were invited to give their presentation at the conference. Besides, we also organized a Newton Fund Researcher Links workshop, supported by the British Council and the NSF-China – "Health and Wellbeing through VR and AR" – during the conference.

May 2019

Abdennour El Rhalibi
Zhigeng Pan
Haiyan Jin
Dandan Ding
Andres A. Navarro-Newball
Yinghui Wang

Edutainment 2018

28–30 June, 2018
Xi'an, China

Organizer
Xi'an University of Technology, PRC

Co-organizer
Huaiyin Institute of Technology, PRC

Organization

Conference General Co-chairs

Xinhong Hei	Xi'an University of Technology, PRC
Zhigeng Pan	Hangzhou Normal University, PRC
Abdennour El Rhalibi	Liverpool John Moores University, UK

Program Co-chairs

Dandan Ding	Hangzhou Normal University, PRC
Andres A. Navarro-Newball	Pontificia Universidad Javeriana Cali, Colombia
Yinghui Wang	Xi'an University of Technology, PRC

Organization Chair

Haiyan Jin	Xi'an University of Technology, PRC

Organization Co-chair

Jingyang Zhao	Huaiyin Institute of Technology, PRC

Organizing Committee

Rong Fei	Xi'an University of Technology, PRC
Yichuan Wang	Xi'an University of Technology, PRC
Huaijun Wang	Xi'an University of Technology, PRC
Zhaolin Xiao	Xi'an University of Technology, PRC

Workshop Co-chairs

Ruck Thawonmas	Ritsumeikan University, Japan
Feng Tian	Bournemouth University, UK

Publicity Co-chairs

Xun Luo	Tianjin University of Technology, PRC
Yoshihiro Okada	Kyushu University, Japan
Xiaosong Yang	Bournemouth University, UK

Program Committee

Mingliang Cao	The Hong Kong Polytechnic University, SAR China
Fred Charles	Bournemouth University, UK
Yam San Chee	National Institute of Education, Singapore
Antonio Coelho	University of Porto, Portugal
Feng Dong	University of Bedfordshire, UK
Jose Fonseca	Bournemouth University, UK
Christos Gatzidis	Bournemouth University, UK
Martin Goebel	Hochschule Bonn-Rhein-Sieg, Germany
Carlo Harvey	Birmingham City University, UK
William Hurst	Liverpool John Moores University, UK
Marc Jaeger	CIRAD, France
Xiaogang Jin	Zhejiang University, China
Dongwann Kang	Bournemouth University, UK
Kashif Kifayat	Liverpool John Moores University, UK
Hoshang Kolivand	Liverpool John Moores University, UK
Qingde Li	University of Hull, UK
Wei Liang	Xi'an University of Technology, China
Fotis Liarokapis	Masaryk University, Czech Republic
Fuhua Lin	Athabasca University, Canada
Gengdai Liu	Bigo Technology PTE Ltd., Singapore
Yuehu Liu	Xi'an Jiaotong University, China
Ke Lv	University of Chinese Academy of Sciences, China
Katerina Mania	Technical University of Crete, Greece
Tianlu Mao	Institute of Computing Technology Chinese Academy of Sciences, China
Leonel Morgado	INESC TEC/Universidade Aberta, Portugal
Wolfgang Mueller	University of Education Weingarten, Germany
Xiaojuan Ning	Xi'an University of Technology, China
Panagiotis Petridis	Aston University, UK
Edmond Prakash	Cardiff Metropolitan University, UK
Alain Simons	Bournemouth University, UK
Benyue Su	Anqing Normal University, China
Mohdshahrizal Sunar	University Teknologi Malaysia, Malaysia

Mohammad Swash	Brunel University, UK
Wen Tang	Bournemouth University, UK
Dunwei Wen	Athabasca University, Canada
Kevin Wong	Murdoch University, Australia
Zhongke Wu	Beijing Normal University, China
Ning Xie	University of Electronic Science and Technology of China, China
Lihua You	Bournemouth University, UK
Hongchuan Yu	Bournemouth University, UK
Fengquan Zhang	Beihang University, China
Jiulong Zhang	Xi'an University of Technology, China
Xiaopeng Zhang	Institute of Automation, Chinese Academy of Sciences, China
Yinwei Zhan	Guangdong University of Technology, China
Minghua Zhao	Xi'an University of Technology, China

Contents

Virtual Reality and Augmented Reality in Edutainment

Barycentric Shift Model Based VR Application for Detection and Classification on Body Balance Disorders 3
Haiyan Jin, Wentao Lin, Zhaolin Xiao, Huan Liu, Bin Wang, and Xiuxiu Li

Simulating Waiting Hall with Mass Passengers 13
Shaohua Liu, Xiyuan Song, Hao Jiang, Min Shi, and Tianlu Mao

Geospatial Data Holographic Rendering Using Windows Mixed Reality 21
Amira Nasr Eddine and Pan Junjun

Developing an Augmented Reality Multiplayer Learning Game: Lessons Learned 26
Andrea Ortiz, Cristian Vitery, Carolina González, and Hendrys Tobar

Mixed Reality-Based Simulator for Training on Imageless Navigation Skills in Total Hip Replacement Procedures 30
Mara Catalina Aguilera-Canon, Tom Wainwright, Xiaosong Yang, and Hammadi Nait-Charif

Naturally Interact with Mobile Virtual Reality by CAT 35
Shaohua Liu, Tong Zhao, Hongwei Zhang, Xiyuan Song, Haibo Liu, Shijun Dai, and Tianlu Mao

Avebury Portal – A Location-Based Augmented Reality Treasure Hunt for Archaeological Sites 39
Farbod Shakouri and Feng Tian

Gamification for Serious Game and Training

An Analysis of Gamification Effect of Frequent-Flyer Program 53
Long Zuo, Shuo Xiong, Zhichao Wang, and Hiroyuki Iida

A Serious Game for Learning the Conversation Method with Autism for Typically Developing 61
Keigo Yabuki and Kaoru Sumi

User Experience Research and Practice of Gamification for Driving Training 69
Lvjie She, Jinsong Fan, and Mingliang Cao

Affective Interaction Technology of Companion Robots for the Elderly: A Review 79
Jin Wang, Tingting Liu, Zhen Liu, and Yanjie Chai

Gamification Strategies for an Introductory Algorithms and Programming Course 84
Diego Fernando Loaiza Buitrago, Luis Alejandro Álvarez, Carlos Marquez, Diego Fernando Duque, Yana Saint-Priest, Patricia Segovia, and Andres A. Navarro-Newball

Graphics, Imaging and Applications

Structure Reconstruction of Indoor Scene from Terrestrial Laser Scanner 91
Xiaojuan Ning, Jie Ma, Zhiyong Lv, Qingzheng Xu, and Yinghui Wang

A Fast and Layered Real Rendering Method for Human Face Model—D-BRDF 99
Pengbo Zhou, Xiaotong Liu, Heng Wang, and Xiaofeng Wang

A Queue-Based Bandwidth Allocation Method for Streaming Media Servers in M-Learning VoD Systems. 107
Jing Wang, Hui Zhao, Feng Liu, and Jie Zhang

A Hole Repairing Method Based on Edge-Preserving Projection 115
Yinghui Wang, Yanni Zhao, Ningna Wang, Xiaojuan Ning, Zhenghao Shi, Minghua Zhao, Ke Lv, and Liangyi Huang

A Hole Repairing Method Based on Slicing 123
Yanni Zhao, Yinghui Wang, Ningna Wang, Xiaojuan Ning, Zhenghao Shi, Minghua Zhao, Ke Lv, and Liangyi Huang

An Improved Total Variation Denoising Model. 132
Minghua Zhao, Tang Chen, Zhenghao Shi, Peng Li, Bing Li, and Yinghui Wang

Spectral Dictionary Learning Based Multispectral Image Compression 140
Wei Liang, Yinghui Wang, Wen Hao, Xiuxiu Li, Xiuhong Yang, and Lu Liu

Intrinsic Co-decomposition for Stereoscopic Images 145
Xiuxiu Li, Haiyan Jin, Zhaolin Xiao, and Liwen Shi

A Terrain Classification Method for POLSAR Images Based on Modified Scattering Parameters. 149
Shuang Zhang, Lu Wang, Xiangchuan Yu, and Bo Chen

PolSAR Data Classification via Combined Similarity Based Immune Clonal Spectral Clustering 154
Lu Liu, Haiyan Jin, Junfei Shi, and Wei Liang

Game Rendering and Animation

Modeling Emotional Contagion for Crowd in Emergencies. 161
Tingting Liu, Zhen Liu, Yanjie Chai, and Jin Wang

A Semantic Parametric Model for 3D Human Body Reshaping. 169
Dan Song, Yao Jin, Tongtong Wang, Chengyang Li, Ruofeng Tong, and Jian Chang

Dynamic Load Balancing for Massively Multiplayer Online Games Using OPNET 177
Sarmad A. Abdulazeez and Abdennour El Rhalibi

A Slice-Guided Method of Indoor Scene Structure Retrieving. 192
Lijuan Wang, Yinghui Wang, Ningna Wang, Xiaojuan Ning, Ke Lv, and Liangyi Huang

A Deep Reinforcement Learning Approach for Autonomous Car Racing 203
Fenggen Guo and Zizhao Wu

An Improved Bi-goal Algorithm for Many-Objective Optimization 211
Huaxian Pan and Lei Cai

3D Human Motion Retrieval Based on Graph Model. 219
Qihui Wu, Rui Liu, Dongsheng Zhou, and Qiang Zhang

Game Rendering and Animation and Computer Vision in Edutainment

Position-Based Simulation of Skeleton-Driven Characters. 231
Dongsheng Yang, Yuling Fan, and Meili Wang

Parallel MOEA/D for Real-Time Multi-objective Optimization Problems 236
Jusheng Yu, Lu Li, and YuTao Qi

Bearing-Only and Bearing-Doppler Target Tracking Based on EKF. 241
Xiaohua Li, Chenxu Zhao, Jiulong Zhang, and Xiuxiu Li

A Motion-Driven System for Performing Art 245
Zizhao Wu, Feiwei Qin, Shi Li, and Yigang Wang

Latent Topic Model Based Multi-feature Learning for PolSAR Terrain Classification. 249
Junfei Shi, Haiyan Jin, Yinghui Wang, Zhiyong Lv, and Lu Liu

E-Learning and Game

TLogic: A Tangible Programming Tool to Help Children Solve Problems . . . 255
Xiaozhou Deng, Danli Wang, and Qiao Jin

School-Enterprise Cooperative Innovation and Entrepreneurship Courses and Case Library of Emerging Engineering Education 263
Kun Ma, Yongzheng Lin, Kun Liu, Jin Zhou, and Jiwen Dong

The Dilemma and Exploration of the Innovation of Internal Governance in Higher Education Institutions 268
Lei Sun and Chunlin Li

Interactive Web 3D Contents Development Framework Based on Linked Data for Japanese History Education 275
Chenguang Ma, Wei Shi, and Yoshihiro Okada

Collecting Visual Effect Linked Data Using GWAP 284
Shogo Hirai and Kaoru Sumi

E-learning Rhythm Design: Case Study Using Fighting Games. 293
Shuo Xiong, Long Zuo, Zeliang Zhang, Shuo Zhang, and Hiroyuki Iida

A Mobile Learning System with Multi-point Interaction. 303
Jie Zhang, Bingfang Qi, Yingpeng Zhang, Hui Zhao, and Toyohide Watanabe

Research on Mobile Learning System of Colleges and Universities 308
Hui Yu and Zhongqiu Zhang

A Study of Negative Emotion Regulation of College Students by Social Games Design 313
SiQi Xie, MengLi Shi, and Hong Yan

Analysis of College Students' Employment, Unemployment and Enrollment with Self-Organizing Maps 318
Jie Kong, Meng Ren, Ting Lu, and Congying Wang

Hands on Work Game: Neuro-Pedagogical Method to Improve Math Fraction Teaching 322
Manuel Ibarra, Ebert Gomez, Pablo Ataucusi, Vladimiro Ibañez, Eliana Ibarra, and Waldo Ibarra

The Research on Serious Games in Social Skills Training for Children with Autism 327
Tingting Liu, Zhen Liu, Yanjie Chai, and Jin Wang

A WebRTC e-Learning System Based on Kurento Media Server 331
Jie Zhang, Yingpeng Zhang, Bingfang Qi, Hui Zhao, and Toyohide Watanabe

A Plant Growing Game Based on Mobile Terminal and Embedded Technology 336
Jiwang Wang, Xiangyuan Lin, Jixuan Feng, Bin Wang, and Haiyan Jin

Computer Vision in Edutainment

Static Gesture Recognition Method Based on 3D Human Hand Joints 343
Jingjing Gao and Yinwei Zhan

A Combined Deep Learning and Semi-supervised Classification Algorithm for LS Area 352
Xiaofeng Wang, Guohua Geng, Na Wang, Qiannan Song, Ge He, and Zheng Wang

A Novel Feature-Based Pose Estimation Method for 3D Faces 361
Ye Li, YingHui Wang, Jing Liu, Wen Hao, and Liangyi Huang

Humanoid Robot Control Based on Deep Learning 370
Bin Guo, Pengfei Yi, Dongsheng Zhou, and Xiaopeng Wei

Improved Modular Convolution Neural Network for Human Pose Estimation 378
Zhengxuan Zhang, Jing Dong, Dongsheng Zhou, Xiaoyong Fang, and Xiaopeng Wei

Using Face Recognition to Detect "Ghost Writer" Cheating in Examination 389
Huan He, Qinghua Zheng, Rui Li, and Bo Dong

Texture Image Segmentation Based on Stationary Directionlet Domain Probabilistic Graphical Model 398
Zhenguo Gao, Shixiong Xia, and Jiaqi Zhao

Hand Pose Estimation Using Convolutional Neural Networks and Support Vector Regression 406
Yufeng Dong, Jian Lu, and Qiang Zhang

Author Index 415

Virtual Reality and Augmented Reality in Edutainment

Barycentric Shift Model Based VR Application for Detection and Classification on Body Balance Disorders

Haiyan Jin(✉), Wentao Lin, Zhaolin Xiao, Huan Liu, Bin Wang, and Xiuxiu Li

Department of Computer Science and Engineering, Xi'an University of Technology, No. 5 South Jinhua Road, Xi'an 710048, China
jinhaiyan@xaut.edu.cn

Abstract. Virtual reality technology shows serious potential in many fields, such as cinemtic entertainment, professional training, Healthcare and clinical therapies, etc. In this paper, we propose a novel human balance capability evaluation method, which is based on crossing bridge virtual scene and video analysis. We have sampled the crossing bridge movement video of two groups of volunteers with balance ability differences, and then we proposed a balance ability classification algorithm via barycentric shifts model statistical analysis. The small sample experiment shows that our method can accurately identify the possible candidates with balance ability abnormality.

Keywords: Virtual reality · Body balance · Barycentric shift model · Video analysis

1 Introduction

In recent years, there are lots of disabled and half disabled people in the world. People with disorders of balance ability can only have very limited testing and training, and usually it will lead negative repercussions without suitable treatment and training. Therefore, it needs serious to study on the balance capability of the disabled people, the assessment and classification of balance ability is still an opening problem in the training process of disabled people [1].

To address this problem, the researchers are mainly focus on the use of medical equipment and training equipment, which is quite acceptable to general people. However, many people will have natural defects and resistances on traditional medical equipment and treatment [2]. With the recent development of Virtual Reality (VR) technology, some researchers have developed VR training systems suitable for special populations and have achieved good results. Yin et al. [3] present a Virtual Reality-Cycling Training System (VRCTS), which senses the cycling force and speed in real-time, by training the body to enhance their motor coordination. Liau et al. [4] is to develop the human balance assessment system with LabVIEW program interface. 10 healthy adults were enrolled in this study. They were evaluated under four kinds of postures while standing on a 2-axis force platform for 20 s. Lafond et al. [5] compares

A. El Rhalibi et al. (Eds.): Edutainment 2018, LNCS 11462, pp. 3–12, 2019.
https://doi.org/10.1007/978-3-030-23712-7_1

three methods for estimating the mass center in a balanced evaluation. Moraru et al. [6–8] studied the effects of exercising and non-exercising children on balance ability and practice improvement based on virtual reality.

Based on the above works, in this paper, we propose a barycentric shift model based classification method for distinguish people with balance ability disorder from general ones. For this purpose, we have designed a balance ability training system on the VR platform, after sampling the video data of the general and disabled people, when using our system, we calculate the gravity data of the characters by feature extraction, then we detect the balance ability of general and disabled people by using the barycentric shift model based classification.

2 Body Unbalance Posture Modeling

The balanced posture of the human body can have many descriptions, such as the body's swing, shaking. According to the human body's swing, we design a body unbalanced posture model based on the barycentric, as shown in Fig. 1 below.

Figure 1(a) is a non-normal frontal posture model, Fig. 1(b) is an abnormal side posture model and Fig. 1(c) is for the general frontal posture model, Fig. 1(d) is the general side posture model. P_1, P_2 and P_3 are the centroids of the upper and lower body and the center of the human body, θ_1 and θ_3 are the angles of the three centroid points, θ_2 and θ_4 are the angles between the upper and lower centroids, and L is the distance from the center to the center axis.

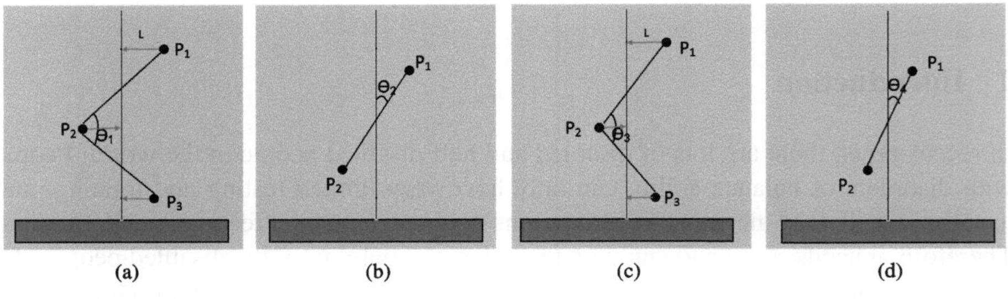

Fig. 1. Body balanced posture model; (a) The positive attitude of abnormal people; (b) Unnatural side view; (c) Normal positive attitude; (d) Normal side profile

In our opinion, if the general person's balance ability is good, the angle θ of the three barycentric will be relatively large and the distance L from the barycentric to the central axis will be relatively small. When a person's gravity angle is relatively large and the distance from the barycentric to the central axis is relatively small, this person's posture will tend to be a line, so we determine that this person is normal and the balance ability is good. The entire model and analysis are based on the Bayesian Probability Rule $P(A|B) = \frac{P(B|A)P(A)}{P(B)}$, $P(A|B) \propto P(B|A)P(A)$, in this formula, A representative of the person's posture is normal or not normal, B represents the barycentric shift angle. In this model, we consider that the factors affecting the balance of human body are the angle of the barycentric, the average of the barycentric of the upper and lower parts and the variance of the barycentric of the upper and lower parts, and the judgment of the balance ability of the human body is as Eq. (1).

$$\partial = \frac{1}{n}\sum_{i=1}^{n} f(p_i) \tag{1}$$

f is the function of the center of gravity p, as in Eqs. (2) and (3). ∂ is the measure for body balance. We assume that the person has a good balance when ∂ is larger than T and bad balance when ∂ is less than T, T is normal and abnormal posture balance threshold. In this paper, we define the balance model as Eq. (2). This formula represents the average distance from the three centers of gravity of the body to the threshold.

$$f(p_i) = |p_i - l| \frac{\sum_{j=1}^{n} \theta_{(p_1, p_2, p_3)}}{180 \bullet n} \tag{2}$$

In Eq. (2) l is the threshold, shown as Eq. (3).

$$l = \frac{1}{n}\sum_{i=1}^{n} p_i \tag{3}$$

where p_i is the coordinates of the three center of gravity points, shown as Eq. (4).

$$p_i = \overline{\sum_{I(x,y)\in\Omega} I(x_i, y_i)} \tag{4}$$

where i represents the threshold of the body posture balance model. Human Body Balance Model as described above, the feature extraction and classification of human body unbalanced pose detection is as follows.

3 Feature Detection and Extraction for Human Unbalanced Posture Classification

The feature extraction and classification of unbalanced posture detection in human body are divided into three parts: Preprocessing of Feature Detection, Unbalanced Posture feature extraction and SVM-based classification of unbalance condition. Image preprocessing will be the main demolition of the video image after the differential and denoised to get people's profile. Image feature extraction is to find the human body barycentric coordinates. Balance classification based on SVM proves the difference between general and abnormal people.

3.1 Preprocessing of Feature Extraction

As shown in Fig. 2, the human is walking in the area divided by two locators. The camera shoots at 0°, 45° and 90° respectively, and the collected training videos are processed as follows.

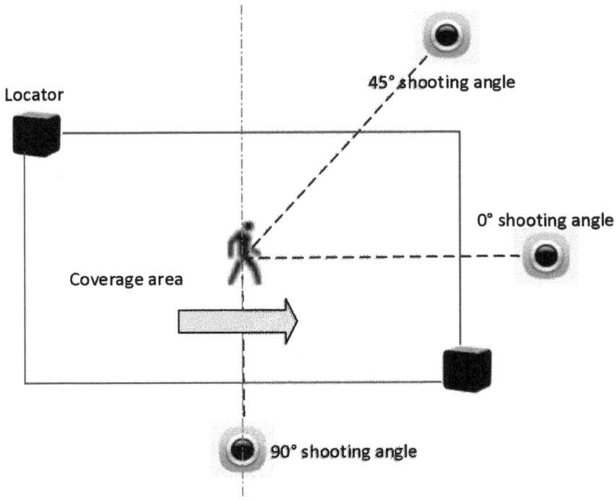

Fig. 2. Experimental scene schematic diagram

1. Opening the frame, take a frame from every two frames to save and wait for processing.
2. The difference, Using Eq. (5) doing differential treatment between the image of someone and the scene without image is processed and the difference image $I_{diff(i)}$ is obtained [9], as shown in Fig. 3(a).

$$I_{diff(i)} = |I_i - I_0| \tag{5}$$

   where I_i represents the image of the ith frame and I_0 represents the reference image with no one in the scene.
3. Denoising, after the difference we can see the image noise from Fig. 3(a), so next the image need denoising [10]. In this paper we use median filter to deal with the image and then image erosion to get human images, as shown in Fig. 3(b). Finally, the image obtained by Fig. 3(b) is binarized to obtain Fig. 3(c).

Fig. 3. Characters denoising figure; (a) Difference; (b) Denoising; (c) Binarization

3.2 Unbalanced Posture Feature Extraction

In Sect. 3.1, the corroded image is obtained. In order to extract the three barycentric of the human body, this paper uses the image moment to extract the center of gravity of image. Extraction steps are as follows:

1. Use the edge detection operator to process the corroded image to get the connected area of the image [11].
2. In order to determine the posture of the target person in the video, this paper uses the moment of the image to extract the center of gravity. The moment of the image sees the image as a flat object, the pixel value of each point is regarded as the density of the point, and the expectation of a point is its moment [12], as shown in Eq. (6).

$$M_{10} = \sum_{i}\sum_{j} i \bullet V(i,j), M_{01} = \sum_{i}\sum_{j} j \bullet V(i,j) \quad (6)$$

When the image is a binary image, $V(i, j)$ only has two values of 0 (black) and 1 (white). M_{10} is the sum of the x-coordinate values of all the white areas on the image. Therefore, the first moment can be used to find the center of gravity of the binary image, as shown in Eq. (7).

$$x_c = \frac{M_{10}}{M_{00}}, y_c = \frac{M_{01}}{M_{00}} \quad (7)$$

According to the above Eq. (7), we can calculate the data of the center of gravity, as shown in Fig. 4. Since each image will get three gravity centers of upper and center and lower parts for the character, we can get the angle information of three points according to the three center points.

(a) (b)

Fig. 4. People focus figure; (a) Normal barycentric map; (b) Abnormal barycentric map

The upper and lower body barycentric variance, shown as Eq. (8).

$$\sigma^2 = \frac{\sum (p_i^t - \overline{p_i^t})^2}{n} \tag{8}$$

where $t \in [1, n]$, P_i^t represented the value of the center of gravity of the upper body or lower body at time t, and $\overline{p_i^t}$ means the average value of the center of gravity.

The pseudocode for feature extraction is as follows.

1 Video feature extraction algorithm

```
function EXTRACTIONALGORITHM(Video)
    capture ← VideoPath
    BlankScene ← Image
    while i = true do
        bSuccess ← Read the video frame
        if bSuccess in NUll then
            cout ← Unable to get video frame
        end if
        imagename ← frame Save the frame image
        ImageDifference(image1, image2, image3)
        Centersrc ← GrayImage
        GrayImage ← ImageCorrosion(GrayImage)
        EdgeDetectionOutput ← EdgeDetection(GrayImage)
        Contours ← FindContours(EdgeDetectionOutput)
        for i = 0 → ContoursSize do
            center1, center2, center3 ← Centroid
            Angel ← TangentAngle(center1, center2, center3)
            Variance ← variance(Angel)
        end for
    end while
    return Angel, Variance
end function
```

3.3 SVM Based Unbalance Condition Classification

To the problem of two kinds of classification SVM (Support Vector machine) is a very effective method. SVM maps input vectors to high-dimensional feature space by some kind of pre-selected nonlinear mapping, constructs linear classification in feature space and determines the final decision function by solving dual problem [13, 14].

In this experiment, we take the human's barycentric coordinates as the input data of SVM. In the experiment of classification, there are 65 training data and 15 test data and the final classification accuracy rate is 86.67%. Table 1 shows the changes of the labels before and after the classification of test data after the SVM classification. In the table, the correct label 1 means the data of the control group and −1 means that the centroid data is the data of the experimental group. It can be get from the table that the barycentric coordinates of the experimental data about human have obvious classification characteristics. Only two groups of data are misclassified in the 15 groups of test data, and other data are classified correctly.

Table 1. Two classification test data and labels

Centroid Coordinates	368	379	383	381	381	384	396	387	313	306	359	360	276	366	355	383
Correctly Labeled	1	1	1	1	1	1	1	1	−1	−1	−1	−1	−1	−1	−1	−1
Test Labeled	1	1	1	1	1	1	1	1	−1	−1	−1	−1	−1	1	−1	1

4 Experiments on Unbalance Classification

4.1 VR Platform with Balance Training Model

As shown in Fig. 5(a) and (b), the system is based on Unity platform and it using HTC VIVE head display device to watch. The whole training system is similar to a game, as shown in Fig. 5(c) and (d). In the game, people will start from one end of the wooden bridge and on the other end is a stone table with fruits and vegetables on top. We request people to walk back and forth from the bridge and pick up the fruit and vegetables at the other end with their handles and the put them in the two well-classified baskets. So on the basis of training balance, but also allow them to have some understanding of life. Secondly, during the walk on the single-plank bridge, we have added some natural climate stimuli such as wind and rain, and some sound stimuli similar to those of nature, making the whole environment closer to reality without becoming dull.

Fig. 5. VR platform with Balance training model; (a) VR scene; (b) Training sence; (c) Front view of wooden bridge; (d) Side view of wooden bridge

4.2 The Angle of Gravity Analysis

When the angle between camera and the target is 0°, we can not see the target body before and after the change. When the angle between camera and the target is 90°, we can not see the changes in the target body around. Therefore, in this paper we select the barycentric angle of 45° video to process. In this experiment, we select the videos with five general subjects and five persons with physical disabilities were trained in the virtual environment. And then extract the characteristics of these videos to get the barycentric angle. We take 20 frames of barycentric data for each video. As shown in Fig. 6.

As shown in Fig. 6, we can notice that the barycentric of general people doing balance training in the virtual environment is centered on 140° and the center of gravity of special people is around 110°. It is shows that the general barycentric training in the virtual environment is higher than the abnormal one. Virtual environment will bring dizziness, irritation and other effects, but the balance ability of normal in the virtual environment is better than the special people.

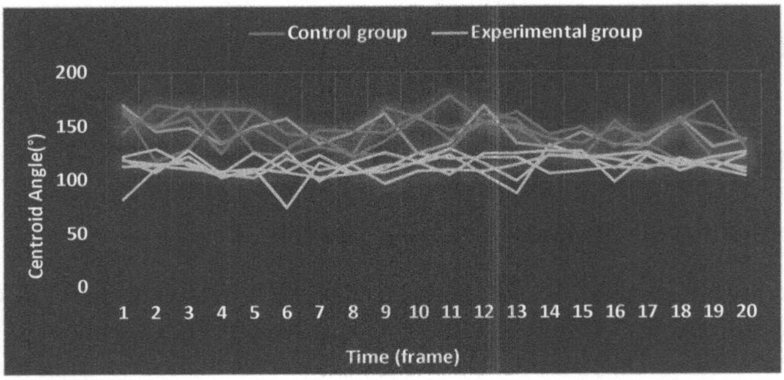

Fig. 6. Center of gravity angle comparison chart

4.3 Barycentric Mean and Variance Analysis

By analyzing the video of five general and five disabled people trained in the virtual environment in the experiment, we got their center of gravity data of upper and lower body. For the processing result, we select an image every 20 frames to make the following table, as shown in Fig. 7.

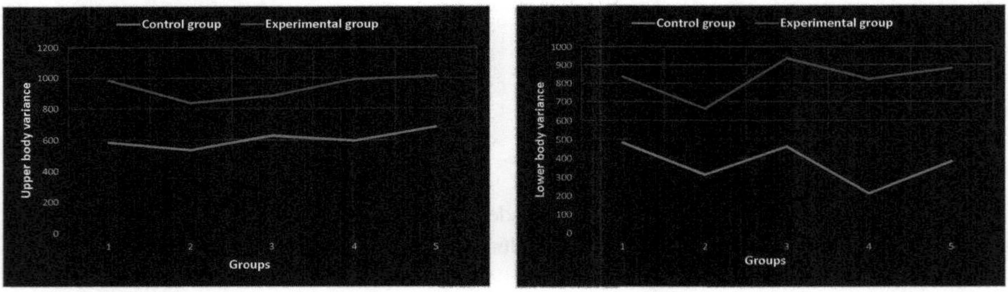

Fig. 7. Variance diagram (a) Upper body variance comparison chart; (b) Lower body variance comparison chart

From Fig. 7, we can draw the conclusion that during the training, the general average upper and lower body center is higher than that of abnormal people, and the upper and lower body center variance is smaller than that of abnormal people. It can be clearly seen from the comparison chart that the general people's upper and lower body center of gravity variance is generally smaller than that of the special people, indicating that abnormal people in the virtual environment training center of gravity fluctuations, significant body shaking and weak balance.

5 Conclusion

There are many factors that determine the balance of the human body, the human body posture is the most obvious one. This paper use the three point of the barycentric angle on human body and the variance of upper and lower body barycentric as the basis for measuring the balance of the body. In the modeling of human equilibrium posture, the general human balance model and the balance of the factors are considered. In the balanced ability training model, we simulate the scenario of crossing the single-plank bridge in reality and add natural scenarios to make the model more vivid and dynamic. After extracting features from the video detection of unbalanced human posture, the simulation analysis of the experimental data shows that there are differences in the balance ability of the general and the disabled. In the process of walking, barycentric angle of general will be higher than the barrier population, the upper and lower center of gravity variance is generally smaller than the obstacle crowd and it is show that the three point of the barycentric angle on general crowd close to the axis and the body is not obvious shaking during walking, balance posture better. In this paper, the classification method based on the center of gravity shift model for the disabled population can effectively judge and distinguish the balance of the human posture. The system of this article may be further used for the recovery of balance ability training.

Acknowledgment. This work is supported in part by the National Natural Science Foundation of China under grant Nos. 61472204, 6150238.

References

1. Ustinova, K.I., Leonard, W.A., Cassavaugh, N.D., et al.: Development of a 3D immersive videogame to improve arm-postural coordination in patients with TBI. J. Neuroeng. Rehabil. **8**(1), 1–11 (2011)
2. Rubin, M.A.: Make precision medicine work for cancer care: to get targeted treatments to more cancer patients pair genomic data with clinical data, and make the information widely accessible. Nature **520**(7547), 290–292 (2015)
3. Yin, C., Hsueh, Y.H., Yeh, C.Y., et al.: A virtual reality-cycling training system for lower limb balance improvement. Biomed. Res. Int. **2016**(1), 1–10 (2016)
4. Liau, B.-Y., Lung, C.-W., Jan, Y.-K.: Development of human balance assessment system with continuous center of gravity tracking. In: Duffy, V.G. (ed.) DHM 2013. LNCS, vol. 8025, pp. 332–337. Springer, Heidelberg (2013). https://doi.org/10.1007/978-3-642-39173-6_39
5. Lafond, D., Duarte, M.F.: Comparison of three methods to estimate the center of mass during balance assessment. J. Biomech. **37**(9), 1421–1426 (2004)
6. Moraru, C., Neculaeş, M., Hodorcă, R.M.: Comparative study on the balance ability in sporty and unsporty children. Procedia - Soc. Behav. Sci. **116**, 3659–3663 (2014)
7. Lloréns, R., Gilgómez, J.A., Alcañiz, M., et al.: Improvement in balance using a virtual reality-based stepping exercise: a randomized controlled trial involving individuals with chronic stroke. Clin. Rehabil. **29**(3), 261–268 (2015)
8. Ferdous, S.M.S.: Improve accessibility of virtual and augmented reality for people with balance impairments. In: 2017 IEEE Virtual Reality, pp. 421–422 (2017)

9. Zhang, B.F., Zhou, J., Zhu, J.C.: Research on three image difference algorithm. In: International Conference on Image Analysis and Signal Processing, pp. 603–606. IEEE (2010)
10. Palaniappan, S.: Image denoising using median filter with edge detection using canny operator. Int. J. Sci. Res. **3**(2), 30–34 (2014)
11. Lin, C.Y., Chai, H.C., Wang, J.Y., et al.: Augmented reality in educational activities for children with disabilities. Displays **42**, 51–54 (2015)
12. Lakhani, B., Mansfield, A.: Visual feedback of the centre of gravity to optimize standing balance. Gait Posture **41**(2), 499–503 (2015)
13. Tarabalka, Y., Fauvel, M., Chanussot, J., et al.: SVM- and MRF-based method for accurate classification of hyperspectral images. IEEE Geosci. Remote Sens. Lett. **7**(4), 736–740 (2010)
14. Ayyaz, M.N., Javed, I., Mahmood, W.: Handwritten character recognition using multiclass SVM classification with hybrid feature extraction. Pak. J. Eng. Appl. Sci. **10**, 57–67 (2016)

Simulating Waiting Hall with Mass Passengers

Shaohua Liu[1], Xiyuan Song[1], Hao Jiang[2], Min Shi[3], and Tianlu Mao[2](✉)

[1] Beijing University of Posts and Telecommunications, Beijing 100876, China
liushaohua@bupt.edu.cn, songxiyuan@ict.ac.cn
[2] Institute of Computing Technology, CAS, Beijing 100190, China
{jianghao,ltm}@ict.ac.cn
[3] North China Electric Power University, Beijing 102206, China
shimin01@ict.ac.cn

Abstract. In this paper, we introduce an integrated framework to simulate waiting halls with mass passengers. We design the framework for the special purpose of passenger safety investigation. It integrates virtual waiting hall environment, mass virtual passengers with heterogeneous behavior and motion, and also editable scenarios to conduct virtual passengers. So that different situations could easily be initialized and simulated to see how they are developed and evolved as time goes on. We also introduce a behavioral decision and execution method which is embedded in our framework. It supports both regular crowded passenger behaviors and emergency passenger behaviors. Results show that simulated passengers have realistic behavior and act heterogeneously in a crowded waiting hall environment under both normal and emergent scenarios.

Keywords: Crowd simulation · Simulating evaluation · Passenger behavior · Safety investigation

1 Introduction

The waiting hall in transportation terminals, such as railway station, airport and shipping wharf, is a place with high passenger density. It's extremely crucial to ensure the passenger flow runs efficiently and safely. The design of passengers' time table and density control measure plays an important role in the passenger safety. And the design of evacuation planning for emergency situations, such as earthquake and fire, is also very important. Therefore, it's necessary to simulate waiting hall with mass passengers in a virtual reality system to deduct possible events and evaluate security.

During the past decades, a series of models and methods have been put forward to study and simulate human crowds. There are some classical and basal models: Optional Reciprocal Collision Avoidance (ORCA) [1], Social Force Model [2], recent Universal Power Law [3] and so on. All of them can simulate pedestrian crowds walking to some given destinations while avoiding collision with each other. Based on these fundamental models, lots of crowd simulation methods are developed to support more complex scenarios, like mass crowds in the annual Hajj pilgrimage [4], crowds with heterogeneous behaviors [5], crowds in egress scenarios [6] and complex evacuation

A. El Rhalibi et al. (Eds.): Edutainment 2018, LNCS 11462, pp. 13–20, 2019.
https://doi.org/10.1007/978-3-030-23712-7_2

scenarios [7], evaluating and optimizing service for crowd evacuations [8], dynamic group behaviors in crowd [9] and so on.

In this paper, we focus on simulating passengers with diversified and heterogeneous behaviors in crowded waiting halls. For such a particular purpose, an integrated simulation framework, along with a behavioral decision and execution method is introduced.

The proposed framework arranges environment data, agent data, simulation and rendering tasks. Its modularized structure supports not only heterogeneous behavior and motion for virtual passengers, but also editable scenarios to conduct virtual passengers. So that time table and facilities in the waiting hall could be changed, different density control measures and evacuation could be carried out. Hence diversified situations could be simulated to see how they are developed and evolved as time goes on.

The proposed behavioral decision and execution method gives sophisticated behavioral station switches and realistic motion execution for passengers according to the time schedule and dynamic scene environment. So that virtual passengers could act and move heterogeneously in a crowded virtual waiting hall, entering the hall, seeking a waiting space, queueing in front of the boarding gate in time, running in emergency and so on.

As shown in Fig. 1 and our video demo, the proposed simulation framework and method have achieved their designed purpose.

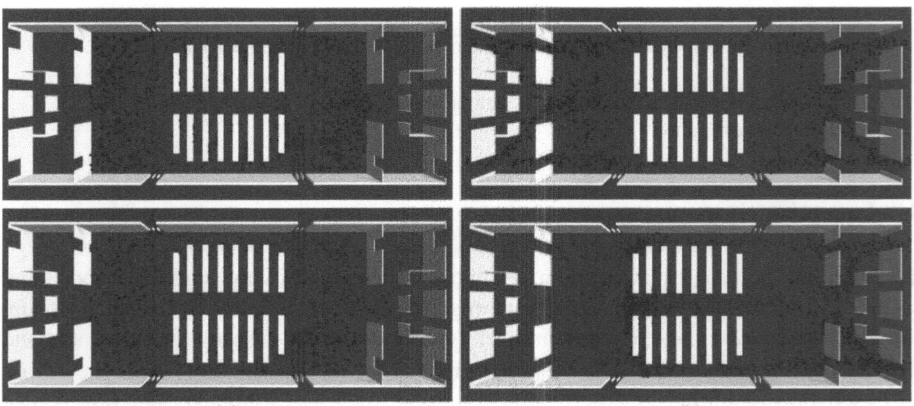

(a) (b)

Fig. 1. Simulation results with our framework. (a) Passengers under different density control measures. (b) Passengers evacuating when gates on both sides available and only gates on one side available.

2 Simulation Framework

The overall framework of our waiting hall simulation is illustrated in Fig. 2. It has four relatively independent layers: environment data, crowd simulation, agent date and rendering engine.

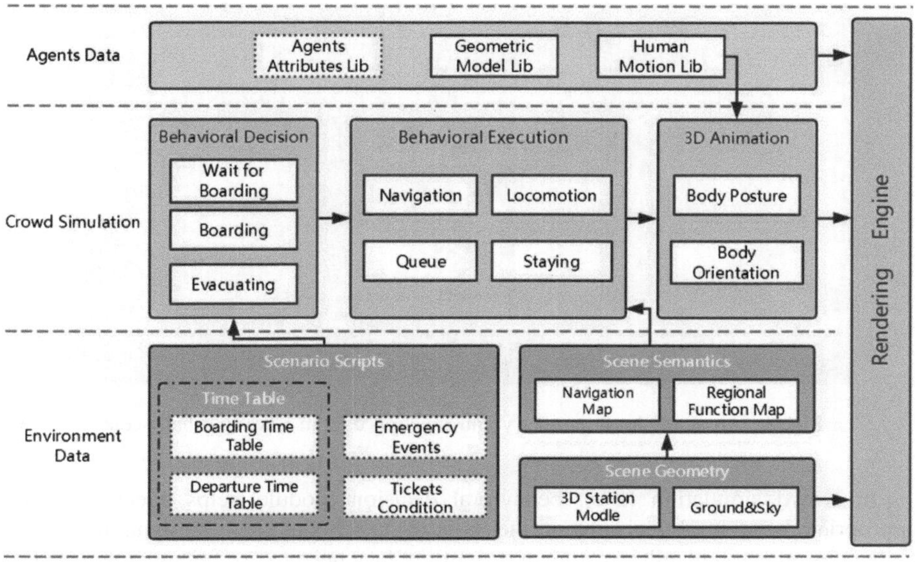

Fig. 2. Simulation framework for a virtual waiting hall system.

Environment data is a basic layer which manages geometry and semantic information of scenes as well as scenario scripts. It also affords an access interface to load a new environment or edit it partly.

Scenario scripts are macroscopic descriptions of the simulated situation, including time table, emergency events and tickets condition. Time table is the schedule for mass virtual passengers and tickets condition reflects the passenger number of every train or flight. They describe the distribution of passengers from the view of time and quantity respectively, determine how many agents and when they will be generated in the simulation. Emergency Events are conditions which could trigger an evacuation, like earthquake and fire. When an emergency event occurs, passengers will stop waiting or boarding and run to the nearest exit doors. By editing scenario scripts, we could apply different scenarios to conduct the simulation as the way we want.

Scene semantic includes navigation map and areas function map. They give the necessary semantical information for the waiting hall environment to support the simulation. Areas function map tells agents if you want to do something where you should go, and navigation map tells agents how to get there more quickly. Figure 3 gives an example of geometry and function data of a waiting hall scene.

The layer of agent data manages attribute, geometry and motion data for simulated agents. Agent attributes lib stores the essential attributes for each agent, such as gender, age, action capability and the train/flight he/she will take. Geometric model lib stores several 3D models of agents. Human motion lib has a variety of motion data for agents in different motion status include standing, walking, running and etc.

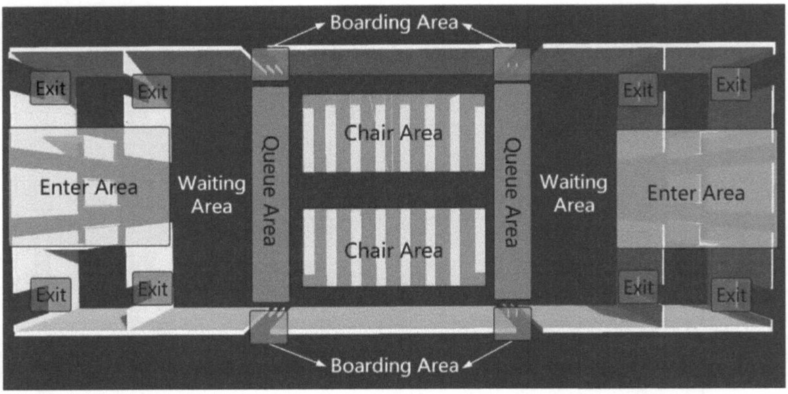

Fig. 3. An example of geometry and function data in a waiting hall scene.

In crowd simulation layer, behavioral decision module helps agents to make appropriate behavioral decisions on the basis of its schedule and the dynamic waiting hall environment, and tells each agent the current task need to do. Behavioral execution module further decomposes the task into a series of operations and realize them step by step, frame by frame. It generates coordinate position for each agent in every simulation step. The details of behavioral decision and behavioral execution will be discussed in Sect. 3. 3D animation is aimed to animate the body orientation and posture of every agent according to the series of positions output by behavior execution.

3 Behavioral Decision and Execution Method

3.1 Decision Model

We design a double layered behavior conversion model, as shown in Fig. 4, to make sophisticated behavioral decisions for passengers in a crowded waiting hall.

In the upper layer, there are three behavior states for agents: *Waiting for boarding* (shortly we call it *Waiting*), *Boarding* and *Evacuating*. Every agent will firstly be in the state of *Waiting* when it enters the waiting hall. If the boarding time comes up, it triggers a switch on behavior state and the passengers belong to this flight/train change state from *Waiting* to *Boarding*. If an emergent event occurs, it will trigger another switch. All passengers in the waiting hall will change their state to *Evacuating*.

The lower layer of our behavior conversion model further decomposes the behavioral states into some sub-states which can be regarded as some small and specific tasks. The sub-states and conditions to trigger them are described in Fig. 4. During the *Waiting* state, every agent will firstly go to a waiting position. Once reaching the waiting goal, agents will stand or sit there and wait for boarding. In the *Boarding* state, agents will firstly leave their original position and go to queues in front of the boarding

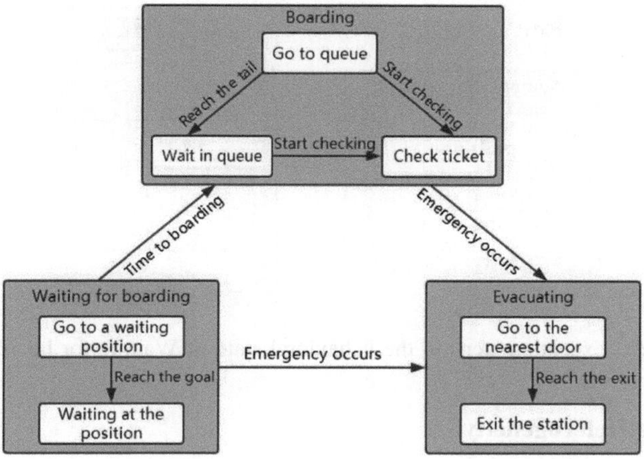

Fig. 4. Double layered behavior conversion model.

gate. If they reach the tail of queue, they will wait in queue. And whenever agents are going to queue tail or waiting in queue, they will move with queue and check tickets if the check door is opened. When emergency events occur, they will change to *Evacuating* state after a short delay which is different from person to person according to its response capability. In *Evacuating* state, agents will go to the nearest door and then exit the waiting hall. In this state, the crowd is mess without queuing behavior.

For the special purpose of passenger safety investigation, our decision model contains limited behavior states as discussed in this section. However, it could be extended with more states, as long as their trigger conditions and tasks are defined clearly.

3.2 Execution Method

According to the characteristics of passenger behaviors, we design a behavior execution method which realize different tasks by combing different series of operations from an operation pool. Here we will further explain it by examples.

After an agent enter the waiting hall, it is firstly in the sub-state of *Go to a waiting position*. As shown in Fig. 5, this task is executed by the following operation sequence: *Select a waiting position*, get the path through *Navigation* operation, use *Locomotion* operation to follow the path and avoid collisions. When the agent reaches its destination, it will switch to the sub-state of *Waiting at the position*. This task could be executed by only one operation, *Staying*. Thus, the agent will wait over there until it behavioral state switches to another state.

If an agent switches into *Boarding* state, it firstly execute the task of *Go to queue* by operations of *Seek the position of queue tail*, *Navigation* and *Locomotion*. Beside above-mentioned basic operations, the operation pool could be extended according to the behaviors need to be demonstrated.

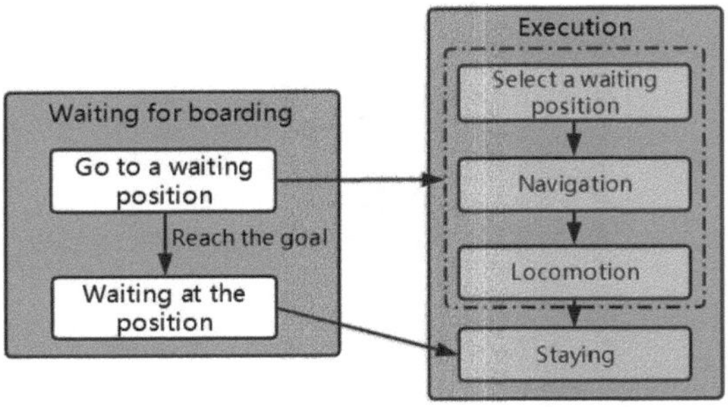

Fig. 5. Execution steps in the behavioral state of Waiting for boarding.

3.3 Simulate Heterogeneity

Passengers are heterogeneous in both behavior and action capability. We modeling such heterogeneity from several aspects.

First, agents are distributed not only in different flight/train number, but also in different age groups and genders. Each category has different action capability. That means different distribution of desired speed in walking and running, and also different distribution of response delay in emergency.

Second, we modeling randomness in both time and space. Agents belong to the same flight/train have different draw in time and boarding time within a certain time span, making their time schedules a little heterogeneous. They also choose different waiting positions before boarding by considering both environment structure and a certain randomness. The further away it from its boarding gate, the lower possibility that the agent will choose it.

4 System Implementation and Simulation Experiment

According to above-mentioned method and framework, we implemented a virtual waiting hall system based on Unity 3D. We designed the 3D scene according to the blueprint of the high-train station in Suzhou, China. As for the basic method of *Locomotion*, we choose ORCA [1]. Figure 6 shows our visualized and editable interface for initializing the simulation. It affords the edit of time table, passenger distribution, evacuation facilities and time preferences of the density control measure. In our experiments we set the departure time table as the real one of Suzhou Station in rush hours. Here we demonstrate simulation results of both normal situations and emergent situations. To investigate situations under different density control measures, we set the earliest time allowed to enter before boarding to 30 min and 45 min respectively. Figure 1(a) shows the results.

In our simulation, if the emergency button is pressed, all agents will evacuate. Figure 7 shows the flow picture of evacuation with gates on both sides are available. Figure 1(b) shows the results of two evacuation, one evacuates from all gates and the other evacuates from gates only on right. In our experiments, emergency occurs at time

8:20 and total amount of passengers in the waiting hall is about 1,200. As a result, evacuation time is about 200 s when one side door is opened and 140 s when both sides door is opened.

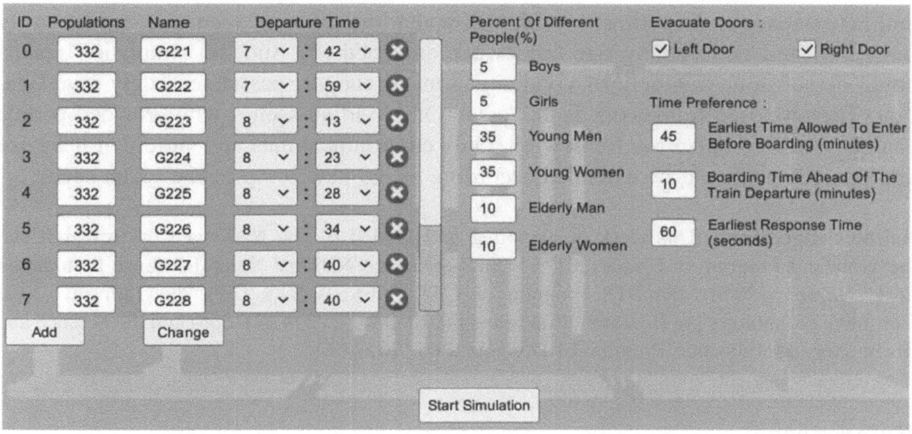

Fig. 6. Visualized and editable interface for initializing simulation.

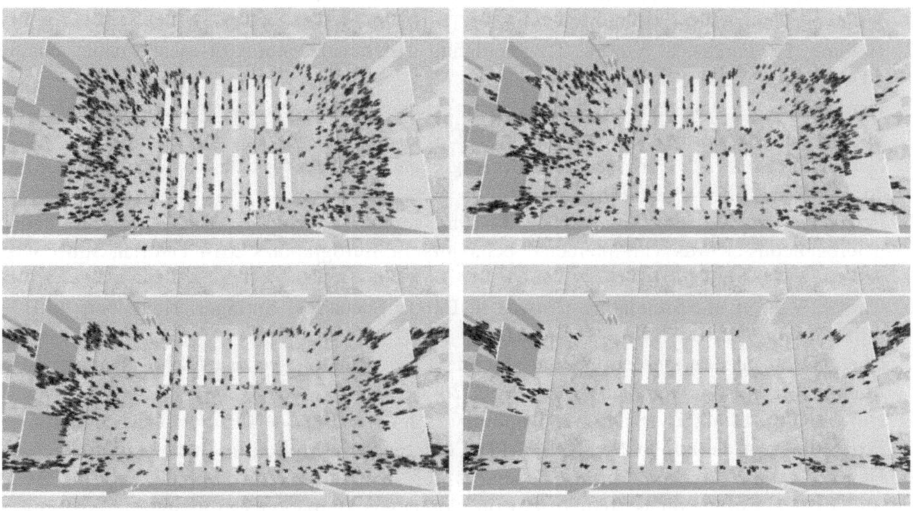

Fig. 7. Flow pictures of evacuation results when both sides evacuation door opened.

5 Conclusion

For the special purpose of passenger safety investigation, we propose an integrated and modularized framework to simulate waiting halls with mass passengers. We also propose a behavioral decision and execution method to make the simulation realistic and heterogeneous. Experiment results show that the different scenarios can be easily initialized and deduced by our framework and method. And 3D simulation results could demonstrate a variety of vivid situations to support passenger safety investigation. The proposed framework is universal. Other virtual scenes with crowded people can be simulated under our framework. Only environment data and variety of behavior and operations should be extended according to the new setup of the given scene.

Acknowledgements. This work is supported and funded by the National Key Research and Development Program of China (2017YFC0804900), the National Natural Science Foundation of China (61532002), the STS Program of CAS (KFJ-SW-STS_155), the 13th Five-Year Common Technology pre Research Program (41402050301-170441402065) and the Science and Technology Mobilization Program of Dongguan (KZ2017-06).

References

1. van den Berg, J., Guy, S.J., Lin, M., Manocha, D.: Reciprocal n-body collision avoidance. In: Pradalier, C., Siegwart, R., Hirzinger, G. (eds.) Robotics Research. STAR, vol. 70, pp. 3–19. Springer, Heidelberg (2011). https://doi.org/10.1007/978-3-642-19457-3_1
2. Helbing, D., Farkas, I., Vicsek, T.: Simulating dynamical features of escape panic. Nature **407**, 487–490 (2000)
3. Karamouzas, I., Skinner, B., Guy, S.J.: Universal power law governing pedestrian interactions. Phys. Rev. Lett. **113**, 238701 (2014)
4. Narain, R., Golas, A., Curtis, S., Lin, M.: Aggregate dynamics for dense crowd simulation. In: ACM SIGGRAPH Asia (2009)
5. Pelechano, N., Kapadia, M., Allbeck, J., Chrysantyou, Y., Guy, S., Badler, N.: Simulating heterogeneous crowds with interactive behaviors. In: Eurographics 2014 Tutorial, Strasbourg, France, 7–11 April (2014)
6. Cassol, V.J., et al.: Simulating Crowds in Egress Scenarios. Springer, Heidelberg (2017). https://doi.org/10.1007/978-3-319-65202-3
7. Chen, D., et al.: Parallel simulation of complex evacuation scenarios with adaptive agent models. IEEE Trans. Parallel Distrib. Syst. **26**(3), 847–857 (2015)
8. Haworth, B., et al.: Evaluating and optimizing level of service for crowd evacuations. In: Proceedings of the 8th ACM SIGGRAPH Conference on Motion in Games (2015)
9. He, L., et al.: Dynamic group behaviors for interactive crowd simulation. In: ACM SIGGRAPH/Eurographics Symposium on Computer Animation Eurographics Association, pp. 139–147 (2016)

Geospatial Data Holographic Rendering Using Windows Mixed Reality

Amira Nasr Eddine(✉) and Pan Junjun

State Key Laboratory for Virtual Reality and Systems,
School of Computer Science, Beihang University, Beijing 100191, China
{amiranasreddine,pan_junjun}@buaa.edu.cn

Abstract. Extracting geographical information from geospatial data has a high priority for all geographic activities which needs powerful tools of visualization. In this paper, a holographic approach is proposed to bridge the gap between mixed reality and virtual world rendering. It envisages the georeferenced raster-based data which are integrated into a virtual world which assembles data from different sources and could be projected them into the real world in order to enhance extracting visually the interesting geographical information. Experiment achieved on the HoloLens. This method will add holographic to improve data observation and to enrich the geographic edutainment.

Keywords: Geospatial · Holographic · Mixed reality · Rendering · Virtual world

1 Introduction

Using geographic information (GI) is always calling such visualization methods. Extracting GI needs exploiting large-scale geospatial data from different sources which data could be draped vividly on the realistic terrain. Since data has been unified and assembled in a virtual globe similar to the real globe, exploring anywhere in this virtual world (VW) is used to extract and learn GI easily. Recent advances in sensors and graphics processing providing a new area of computer inputs which enhance experience perception into the real world as mixed reality (MR) system. Blending VW in the real world can add GI insight. This paper proposes a holographic approach for geospatial data rendering based on Windows MR achieved entirely on the HoloLens smart glasses, which was distinguished by its independent computation running on the embedded operating system (Win10), specifically its holographic processor unit, highly than GPU.

2 Related Work

VWs have mainly integrated all existing data formats. They have explicitly organized data from raster-based data to divers sustainable sources [1]. They granted users to contribute the content by adding and sharing new data. In such a way that input follows explicit ways, mostly support standard formats [2, 3]. Integration, however, has some

A. El Rhalibi et al. (Eds.): Edutainment 2018, LNCS 11462, pp. 21–25, 2019.
https://doi.org/10.1007/978-3-030-23712-7_3

reliance on the WGS 84 system. Else, data should be georeferenced. VWs have modeled the earth's body by triangles strips representations which are gathered together relating to the grid of reference [4]. They focused on massive terrain that covers a large-scale area in a lower pass, based on the successive subdivision of a regular grid [4]. They have visualized terrain by the optimized level of detail (LOD) rendering, using a multiresolution structure based on several view-dependent forms [2, 5].

The main component of our system, the VW as a VR system, was designed with these concepts. We will configure, initialize and visualize it into the real world at a comfortable size, as an AR system, through the HoloLens processing.

3 Preprocessing

To surmount HoloLens low-cost resources, we down-sample data recursively to multi-level of data closely linked to its spatial-resolution that defines the number of LOD. Coarser-finer approach is used to index levels. We subset each level into indexed tiles that are mapped on the rectangular area between the meridian and parallel gridlines of the WGS 84 system. Depending on data format, tiles are grouped into texture-based tiles or elevation-based tiles and stored in a directory hierarchy [6]. We lastly create a file recap processing that contains metadata.

4 Holographic Rendering

Windows MR rendering requires instanced drawing call for holographic rendering. One instance for each eye because the human eye is a binocular field of vision [7] to targets which called a hologram where it has been drawn by the HoloLens device.

For the configuration, the VW has placed forward the HoloLens camera (HC). We adopt a hybrid system to track between inside-out the real-world's objects and outside-in VW's objects. First, attached to moving VW, the HC has been set by default perspective and will be updated by spatial coordinates system of the frame of reference which might be stationary in the real world. The HC's position and orientation guide to take care of the position of the VW. Second, to target VW, the tracking needs creating a virtual camera (VC) which has been set by geographic perspective and will be updated relating to WGS 84 system. The VC can be valued at diverse positions onto the VW.

For initialization, the distance between the HC and the VW is critical [8]. It ranges between 2 and 20 m, guiding as to visualize a world-locked object which is a down-scaled factor to 10^7 guarantying adaptive drawings. At run-time, we load all metadata that ensures the area of interest (AOI). Each metadata switches between two states; on/off demand rendering. When we choose one, its state switches to on-demand, enabling loading its tiles and it becomes VW's object. At program shaders, all inputs are instanced in the vertex shader and they are initialized by the system value *SV_InstanceID* at 0 or 1. Each input must be placed inside the geometry shader unit as a pass-through which leaves the geometry strip unmodified and sets each instance to the render target which identified by the system value *SV_RenderTargetArray* for the left and right display. If the input has been targeted spatially, its vector position P_{xyzw} is determined by the formula 1, else by 2 when it has been targeted geographically.

$$P_{xyzw} = P_{xyzw} * S_{vp}[SV\_InstanceID]. \tag{1}$$

$$P_{xyzw} = G_{wvp} * P_{xyzw}. \tag{2}$$

where S_{vp} is the stereo view-projection matrix of the HC that allows spatial targeting, and G_{wvp} is the world-view-projection matrix of the VC that allows geographic targeting. Switching between formulas 1 and 2 in program shader unit allowing surfing from the outside-in real world to inside-out virtual world, and vice versa.

For visualization, we check the bounding box of AOI and view-dependent to the VW. If they intersect, we create the virtual coarser tiles (VCTs) to request tiles from the location. We spread all extent to create all VCTs for the coarser level. We check frustum culling and keep only the intersected VCT. The VCT is initialized once where it is well paged-in from location and becomes ready to create its shader resource view (SRV) from texture-based tiles and to load its geometry from elevation-based tiles. It can be updated more to the next coarse/fine level when we define whether its size is smaller/larger than the viewport, using hierarchical LOD and out-of-core rendering [9].

However, visualization of textual GI about target position is critical while the device surface does not allow 2D writing. It requires writing the textual GI into SRV which could be loaded on quad-vertices which are constantly positioned in space as real-world's objects without stuttering hologram. Textual GI is extracted in a combination of what the VC is targeting and how to read the target position over everywhere.

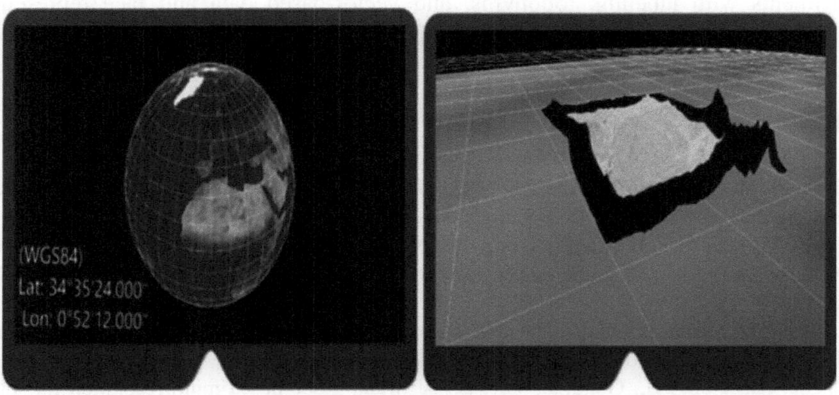

Fig. 1. The virtual world running on the HoloLens emulator.

5 Experiment and Result

The development was done on HoloLens emulator version 10.0.14393 under Visual Studio 2015 Update 3, using Direct3D 11 and HLSL 5. Georeferencing was done on ERDAS Imagine 2014. We used three modalities of data; ASTER to process elevation-based tiles; Landsat ETM+ and a scanned map to process two types of texture-based tiles. Geometry accuracy and visual quality were evaluated and compared with Google Earth framework. For example, Fig. 1, left, shows a VW running in the HoloLens that combines a textured data, WGS 84 gridlines, and textual information, demonstrating the ability to extract GI visually and textually at the same time, where the VW has been attached to the frame of reference at the predicted time.

Figure 1, right, shows a global view of the AOI as a VW's object, using a map draped on a global terrain which slightly extended (in black) and can be exaggerated to bounded metric at several values, from flat to the drastic terrain. The value 4 is well adapted and demonstrates holographically more realistic terrain representation.

6 Conclusion

We have revealed that careful management of geospatial data allows rendering at device frame rates (60 fps). Our approach adds adaptive holographic rendering, can be extracted GI on the desired coordinates, and it is ready to interact with real-world objects using spatial mapping capability. It does not involve installing any particular libraries from additional frameworks. It can be advantageous to all geographic activities whose want to show holographically GI and to enrich the geographic edutainment by another device capacity. Combining VW and the real world can be brought incomparable added value to other geographic-based representation which emotional value can be perceived in exhibition, museum or edutainment. We would like to extend our experiments with labeling, toponyms, and vector-based data and face representing founded on GIS spatial attributes rather than downscaled relatively to the real world.

References

1. Brovelli, M.A., Hogan, P., Prestifilippo, G., Zamboni, G.: Multidimensional virtual globe for geo big data visualization. ISPRS Arch. **41**, 563–566 (2016)
2. Cozzi, P., Ring, K.: 3D Engine Design for Virtual Globes. CRC Press, Boca Raton (2011)
3. Ahlqvist, A.O.: Virtual globe games for participatory GIS. Syst. Cybern. Inform. **8**, 61–63 (2010)
4. Lambers, M., Kolb, A.: Ellipsoidal cube maps for accurate rendering of planetary-scale terrain data. In: Proceedings of the Pacific Graphics Poster Paper (2012)
5. Zheng, X., Xiong, H., Gong, J., Yue, L.: A virtual globe-based multi-resolution tin surface modeling and visualization method. Int. Arch. Photogramm. Remote Sens. Spat. Inf. Sci. - ISPRS Arch. **41**, 459–464 (2016)
6. Lambers, M., Kolb, A.: GPU-based framework for distributed interactive 3D visualization of multimodal remote sensing data, pp. 2–5 (2008)

7. Bimber, O., Raskar, R.: Spatial Augmented Reality Merging Real and Virtual Worlds, vol. 6. A K Peters, Natick (2005)
8. Microsoft: Develop Mixed Reality Apps for Holographic Technology—Microsoft HoloLens (2017). https://www.microsoft.com/en-us/HoloLens/developers
9. Zhang, Z., Zhang, N.: A LOD algorithm based on out-of-core for large scale terrain rendering. In: International Conference on Mechatronic Sciences, Electric Engineering and Computer MEC, pp. 2168–2171 (2013)

Developing an Augmented Reality Multiplayer Learning Game: Lessons Learned

Andrea Ortiz(✉), Cristian Vitery, Carolina González, and Hendrys Tobar

Department of Systems, University of Cauca, Popayán, Cauca, Colombia
{andreaortiz, cvitery, cgonzals, fabian}@unicauca.edu.co

Abstract. In this paper, the design and development of the ARGBL multiplayer game is shown and lessons learned for each of the design and development stages, are stated with recommendations for future ARGBL multiplayer projects.

Keywords: Augmented reality · Multiplayer · Game-based learning · Co-creation

1 Introduction

AR engages people's attention offering the possibility and feasibility of adapting it to solving some educational needs. Social interaction during the game has shown to improve learning and motivation positively. In accordance with studies analyzed, few AR multiplayer games were found [1, 2], however these studies are not focused on learning.

The game's aim is to support student learning about the departments of Colombia and its natural resources. This paper describes the design and development process followed in the construction of "TerraExplora" an ARGBL multiplayer video game. The next section shows a short description of related works. Section 3 refers to the design and development of the application with the lessons learned. Section 4 describes the game and its rules. And finally, Sect. 5 outlines the conclusions and future work.

2 Related Work

The starting point for this project were the results of precedent experience described in [3], in which developed an AR educational video game called (UAPEC) whose learning objective was to identify the richness of the Colombian department of Cauca (geography, tourism, ecology and history). In terms of motivation, UAPEC's results showed that students prefer to learn using the ARGBL game rather than a traditional way. Likewise, the results showed benefits in the learning gains. Nevertheless, there were some shortcomings related to the ergonomics, the amount of text, social interaction, quantity and recognition of markers which were used in TerraExplora's development.

A. El Rhalibi et al. (Eds.): Edutainment 2018, LNCS 11462, pp. 26–29, 2019.
https://doi.org/10.1007/978-3-030-23712-7_4

3 Design and Development Process

This section describes the game design and development process carried out in this project guided by the method Co-CreARGBL [4], which establishes a series of stages divided into activities that guide the design and development of the game taking into account the participation of teachers and the particularities of ARGBL games.

3.1 Training

In this stage, the work team composed of leaders, developers and researchers, adopted the role of instructors introducing ARGBL concepts to teachers, in order to understand their benefits in education. Furthermore, the work team carried out gaming sessions of about an hour to identify different game mechanics that could be taken into account in the videogame design.

The lessons learned during training stage were: (i) teachers training in Augmented Reality games allows showing the potential of this technology applied to school setting. (ii) All the work team, especially teachers new to ARGBL, play AR games and multiplayer games in order to be familiar with the game mechanics currently used and to be inspired to propose the main idea of the game. (iii) The designers should choose carefully the examples of AR experiences and games, from lower complexity board games and digital games with simple mechanics to experiences with higher complexities since they must allow teachers to identify the benefits in education.

3.2 Iterative Design

This stage is composed of four activities: *Specification*, *Analysis*, *Design* and *Development*. During the *Specification* stage, the teachers suggested the main learning objective of the video game, which was to learn about the resources produced in Colombia. The *Analysis* and *Design* activities used the learning objectives defined in the previous stage to construct the main idea of the game with its rules, as well as the story and its characters. The *Development* stage began by identifying the video game requirements exposed by the work team. These requirements are described below, the game must: (i) have a social interaction between players, (ii) address an educational content related to the learning objectives identified and (iii) have the minimum number of physical elements.

Development. The implementation of the video game was planned for two sprints, each one with a duration of two months in which tasks were defined with their respective responsible. The process carried out in each iteration and its results are outlined below.

First Sprint. The first sprint was oriented to the implementation of game mechanics and player's main actions. The prototype was presented to the teachers, which observed the physical elements (board and markers) and indicated some suggestions in terms of usability and teaching. The results showed the need to modify the markers and 3D elements of the game in terms of height and color setting.

Second Sprint. The second sprint was oriented to the integration of main features related like AR and multiplayer mode, as well as the inclusion of power-up cards with AR in the game. Concerning the connection between devices, it was chosen the connection to access point created from one of the devices, which would be the host of the game.

The lessons learned during iterative design stage were: (i) The documentation guide to work team for the fulfillment of its tasks, especially in this project due to the work team is composed of different careers. The documenting in this project is under templates defined by SCRUM [5]. (ii) Marked-based AR was chosen due to that this type allows to player test the game without needing to walk or change position, as well as facilitate multiplayer-AR integration due to not required the mobile data for connection. (iii) The markers must be designed to facilitate their detection due to some external factors such as the inappropriate handling of markers by the children and the limited amount of light. The detection is facilitated through of a design with brightness elements, geometric figures and clear colors that allow creating a recognition pattern. (iv) A multiplayer setting makes the paper-printed markers more prone to be wear by use. For this reason, it is recommended to design a printable document of markers to get them when necessary. (v) For this project, a Wi-Fi hotspot was used to connect the game devices due to the facilities offered by the high-level scripting API that includes Unity, called HLAPI. Nevertheless, the connection can be established via several means such as WLAN, Bluetooth, etc. (vi) The amount of synchronized data (e.g. player's position, completed missions and the used battle cards) needs to be optimized because it could lead to an overload of the connection causing a shutdown of the application.

4 The Game

"TerraExplora" (currently a prototype) is an AR multiplayer video game aimed to support the learning of the departments of Colombia and their natural resources, which must to be find for Players through exploration the map. Each player has the ability to move through the departments of Colombia, explore and collect the resources found. All of these actions have an energy cost and the game is played turn by turn. Players will be affected by several obstacles, such as the opponent player's decisions like power-up cards Fig. 1.

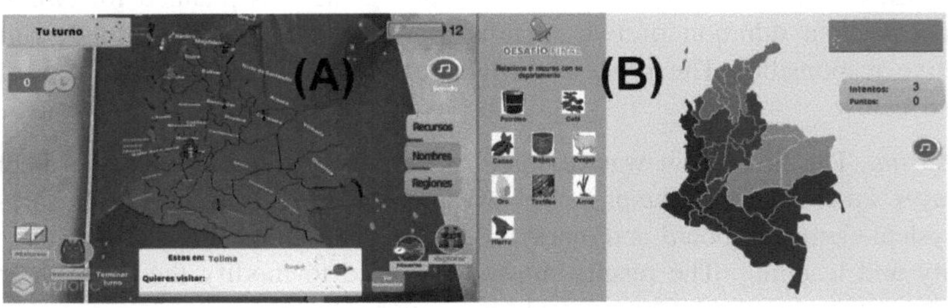

Fig. 1. (A) Main interface. (B) Final challenge interface.

5 Conclusions and Future Work

This paper showed details on the design and development of the game with insights and lessons learned during the process. Among these lessons, we can find that the teamwork with teachers, developers and designers was effective because the suggestions of each member were taken into account, obtaining a product that meets educational and technological needs of the team.

On the other hand, it was identified the importance of carrying out a good design of the markers and minimize elements to synchronize. With respect to the creation of ARGBL multiplayer game, the connection can be established with several ways such as Wi-Fi, Bluetooth, etc. Future research should evaluate the video game "TerraExplora" on real settings guided by an instructional activity to analyze the results and verify how the combination of AR and the multiplayer approach increases learning and motivation.

Acknowledgments. Thanks to the teachers and students who participated on this project. SmartSchool Project. Mobile and Interactive Environment for supporting learning processes. ID. 4565 - University of Cauca.

References

1. Estevez, D., Victores, J., Morante, S., Balaguer, C.: Robot devastation: using DIY low-cost platforms for multiplayer interaction in an augmented reality game. In: Proceedings of 7th International Conference on Intelligence Technology Interactive Entertainment, vol. 15, pp. 1–5 (2015)
2. Oppermann, L., Blum, L., Lee, J.Y., Seo, J.H.: AREEF: multi-player underwater augmented reality experience. In: IEEE Consumer Electronics Society's International Games Innovations Conference IGIC, pp. 199–202 (2013)
3. Tobar-Muñoz, H., Fabregat, R., Baldiris, S.: Capítulo 10. Method for the co-design of augmented reality game-based learning games with teachers (2016)
4. Tobar-Munoz, H., Baldiris, S., Fabregat, R.: Co design of augmented reality game-based learning games with teachers using co-CreaARGBL method. In: Proceedings - IEEE 16th IEEE International Conference on Advanced Learning Technologies, ICALT 2016, pp. 120–122 (2016)
5. Schwaber, K.: SCRUM development process. In: Sutherland, J., Casanave, C., Miller, J., Patel, P., Hollowell, G. (eds.) Business Object Design and Implementation, pp. 117–134. Springer, London (1997). https://doi.org/10.1007/978-1-4471-0947-1_11

Mixed Reality-Based Simulator for Training on Imageless Navigation Skills in Total Hip Replacement Procedures

Mara Catalina Aguilera-Canon[1(✉)], Tom Wainwright[2], Xiaosong Yang[1], and Hammadi Nait-Charif[1]

[1] Faculty of Media and Communications, Bournemouth University, Bournemouth, UK
{maguileracanon, xyang, hncharif}@bournemouth.ac.uk
[2] Faculty of Health and Social Sciences, Bournemouth University, Bournemouth, UK
twainwright@bournemouth.ac.uk

Abstract. Imageless navigation systems (INS) in orthopaedics have been used to improve the outcomes of several orthopaedic procedures such as total hip replacement [1, 2]. However, the increased surgical times and the associate learning curve discourage surgeons from using navigation systems in their theatres [2]. This paper presents a Mixed Reality (MR) simulator that helps surgeons acquire the infrared based navigation skills before performing it in reality. A group of 7 hip surgeons tried the application, expressing their satisfaction with all the features and confirmed that the simulator represents a cheaper and faster option to train surgeons in the use of INS than the current learning methods.

Keywords: Imageless navigation · Holographic · Augmented reality · Mixed reality · Machine vision · Surgical training

1 Introduction

Total hip replacement is one of the most successful and cost-effective surgeries in the orthopaedic field with over 66,000 procedures performed each year in England [3]. Imageless navigation systems (INS) provide an alternative to conventional methods in achieving a more accurate position of the implants [4, 5] minimizing the amount of radiation the patient is exposed to, as well as the risks of leg length discrepancies, dislocation, a higher wear rate and other clinical complications [6].

In order to give the system the right spatial data input and avoid further orientation mistakes intraoperatively, surgeons and trainees must learn to master the skills needed for a proper use of the infrared tracking camera. Unfortunately while surgeons learn to adapt their instrument movements to be recognized by the infrared cameras, surgical times can be extended [5, 7], however this amount of extra can be shorten up to 4.8 ± 3.8 min after significant amount of practice [2].

A. El Rhalibi et al. (Eds.): Edutainment 2018, LNCS 11462, pp. 30–34, 2019.
https://doi.org/10.1007/978-3-030-23712-7_5

Mixed and Augmented reality has been applied into the medical training field due to their standalone nature and spatial understanding capabilities. Among some examples are the company CAE Healthcare [8] and Fundamental VR [9], which have developed holographic interfaces to train medial staff in the use of diagnostic ultrasound, anatomy and surgical approaches. However, to the date and to the best of our knowledge there is no existing MR simulator to help surgeons train in the use of navigation systems without requiring the navigation system itself or cadavers. This paper presents a mixed reality-based simulator, which allows orthopaedic surgeons to practice tool's manipulation skills required in INS based surgery before practicing in real theatres.

2 Materials and Methods

2.1 HoloLens Mixed Reality and PTC Vuforia™ Engine

Our holographic application was designed to train surgeons on the basic skills needed during the calibration stage of INS, namely the awareness of the infrared camera's tracking volume and how to manipulate surgical instruments in hardly to reach places while avoiding targets occlusion. We chose the HoloLens due to its head 6-DoF tracking capabilities and ability to render the digital content according to the spatial understanding information. To optimize development times some of the Mixed Reality toolkit [10] shader libraries and input functions were included during the building stage of the application.

The Vuforia Engine implements machine vision algorithms for real-time tracking of images with certain characteristics folded around different volumes. The desired image-based markers must be pre-processed using the Vuforia *Target Manager* web tool to extract "*sharp, pointed, chiselled detail in the image*" [11] called *features* which will be used to determine the location and orientation of a given target in real time. Two raw images were used as different types of markers and incorporated into the simulator. For both targets high density and uniformly distributed features were used while avoiding repetitive patterns. A plain image target was chosen to help the user locate the surgical scenario on the desired real space coordinates while an image folded as a cylindrical target was chosen for the pointer since its shape provides the camera a continuous projected area at different rotations around its own axis.

2.2 Application Design

During real procedures, the infrared camera (IR) cast rays which are reflected at the surface of some passive spheres attached in a specific position on the surface of a unique mount. To make objects always visible to the camera, this mount has to be pointing in a similar direction as the camera view and inside its tracking volume. In our model each spheres' mount (Fig. 1) has a vector normal to its surface ($\widehat{N}_{tool}$ and $\widehat{N}_{frame}$) and the direction of the camera view is also represented by the vector $\widehat{N}_{camera\,view}$. Once the users anchor the holographic environment in their real-world they ensure that their workplace is inside the camera field of view by modifying the orientation of the camera 3D model thanks to the device's gesture recognition API.

The acquisition of the points or anatomical landmarks on the surface of the pelvis and femur bone are the most important steps during the calibration of INS, since it allows the system to define the anatomical planes in which the angles of resurfacing and acetabular cup implant insertion will be projected. At this stage an important skill to transfer is to be aware of holding the surgical instruments inside the (IR) camera tracking volume and on its field of view. Therefore, in our simulation, the system will be able to register points, only when the angle between the normal vectors of the fixed frame and pointer tool and the camera view are less or equal to 45°.

Finally, the app provides the users an interface of the tools orientation measured on the two anatomic planes calculated from their landmark registration, namely the coronal[1] and sagittal[2] plane. Additionally, a dynamically coloured line is casted from the tip of the reaming tool in the direction D_{tool}, changing its colour according to how close the trainee is to an orientation inside a "safe zone" [4]. A demonstration video is available at http://v.youku.com/v_show/id_XMzQwMzMyNDI4MA==.html.

3 Evaluation

A group of 7 hip surgeons and surgical trainees with previous knowledge about INS were invited to try the simulator. During the study they were asked to set up the surgical scene, adjust the infrared camera field of view and acquire a total of 27 points which were displayed one after another and distributed between pelvic anatomical landmarks, the surface of the acetabulum and femoral landmarks. These high amounts of points enabled learning through repetition, since the simulator would only allow the user to progress in the experience as a new point was acquired, visual and audio feedback were displayed after a successful landmark acquisition, allowing users to quickly understand that the absence of registration success was translated as a wrong instrument manipulation leading them to modify their instrument's pose quickly.

3.1 Results and Discussion

In our study all participants went successfully through all the simulation stages without needing extra help. In addition, all of them agreed that the simulator allows an understanding of the skills needed in INS, furthermore 5 out of the 7 participants believed that the application was easy to use. Moreover, all of them considered that the visual content was attractive and three of them strongly agreed with this affirmation. Finally, for 5 out of the 7 participants, the cylindrical marker was tracked with minimal loss of tracking and one of them reported no loss of tracking at all during the entire experience.

[1] Plane that divides the body into front and back sections.

[2] Plane that divides the body into left and right sections.

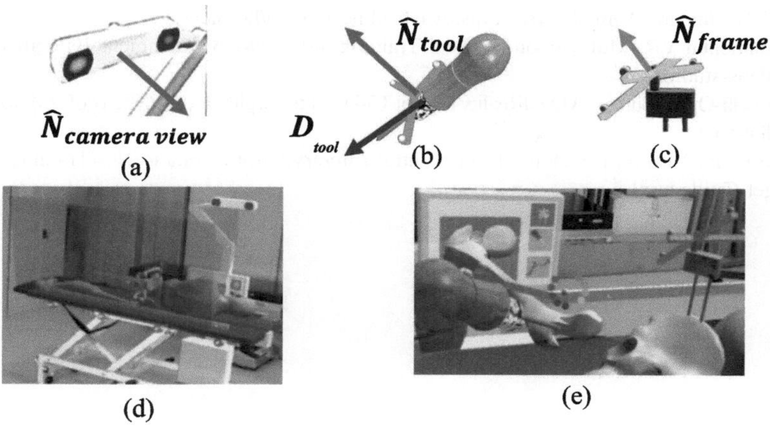

Fig. 1. (a) 3D model of the infrared camera, $\tilde{N}_{camera\_view}$ is the vector normal to the frontal face of the camera. (b) 3D model attached to the cylindrical tracked object, $\tilde{N}_{tool}$ is the normal of the mount surface and D_{tool} a vector in direction of the cylinder's axis. (c) Frame of reference with a vector normal to the surface on which the reflective spheres are supported. (d) Overall view of surgical scene (e) Point registration stage

The simulator represents a valuable practice for both surgeons with some or none previous knowledge about intraoperative navigation systems. We have used game technologies to create a novel proposal of a functional MR based simulator to help trainee surgeons to understand the principles of imageless navigation systems without high-budget investments.

References

1. Snijders, T., Gaalen, S., Gast, A.: Precision and accuracy of imageless navigation versus freehand implantation of total hip arthroplasty: a systematic review and meta-analysis. Int. J. Med. Robot. Comput. Assist. Surg. **13**, e1843 (2017)
2. Thorey, F., Klages, P., Lerch, M., Flörkemeier, T., Windhagen, H., von Lewinski, G.: Cup positioning in primary total hip arthroplasty using an imageless navigation device: is there a learning curve? Orthopedics **32**, 14–17 (2009)
3. National Joint Registry: NJR StatsOnline. http://www.njrcentre.org.uk/njrcentre/Healthcareproviders/Accessingthedata/StatsOnline/NJRStatsOnline/tabid/179/Default.aspx
4. Chang, J.-D., Kim, I.-S., Bhardwaj, A.M., Badami, R.N.: The evolution of computer-assisted total hip arthroplasty and relevant applications. Hip Pelvis **29**, 1–14 (2017)
5. Schnurr, C., Michael, J.W.P., Eysel, P., König, D.P.: Imageless navigation of hip resurfacing arthroplasty increases the implant accuracy. Int. Orthop. **33**, 365–372 (2009)
6. Paprosky, W.G., Muir, J.M.: Intellijoint HIP: a 3D mini-optical navigation tool for improving intraoperative accuracy during total hip arthroplasty. Med. Devices (Auckland, NZ) **9**, 401 (2016)
7. Silvennoinen, M., Helfenstein, S., Ruoranen, M., Saariluoma, P.: Learning basic surgical skills through simulator training. Instr. Sci. **40**, 769–783 (2012)

8. CAE Healthcare: VimedixAR. https://caehealthcare.com/hololens
9. Fundamental VR: Multiperson Medical Training. https://www.fundamentalvr.com/services/hololens-studio/
10. Microsoft-OpenSource: MixedRealityToolkit-Unity. https://github.com/Microsoft-/MixedRealityToolkit-Unity
11. Vuforia, P.: Vuforia Developer Library. https://library.vuforia.com/articles/Training-/Image-Target-Guide.html

Naturally Interact with Mobile Virtual Reality by CAT

Shaohua Liu[1,2(✉)], Tong Zhao[1], Hongwei Zhang[1], Xiyuan Song[1], Haibo Liu[1], Shijun Dai[1], and Tianlu Mao[3]

[1] Laboratory for Cyber-Physical System, School of Electronic Engineering, Beijing University of Posts and Telecommunications, Beijing, China
liushaohua@bupt.edu.cn

[2] Institute of Electronic and Information Engineering in Guangdong, University of Electronic Science and Technology of China, Dongguan, China

[3] Laboratory for Virtual Reality, Institute of Computing Technology, Chinese Academy of Sciences, Beijing, China

Abstract. Traditionally, users used to adopt external device as the controller for the virtual environment. Nowadays we are more interested in natural interaction, such as visual interaction within the virtual reality (VR). More natural human-machine interaction methods would be employed to improve the accessibility of interaction when the user immerses in the virtual or augmented reality. This paper introduces our work on a project called "Collision as Trigger (CAT)" in the mobile virtual reality field, cooperating with a VR helmets vender, a mobile phone manufacturer and a digital entertainment content provider. Our outcomes include stereopsis, motion sensing, scene switching based on collisions as the trigger, as well as some experience improvements on the noise suppression.

Keywords: VR · Visual interaction · Collision as Trigger · Noise suppression

1 Introduction

Human-Machine Interaction, in the long term, has been evolving towards more naturally. To this day, there are still some people who have to sit in front of their PCs because they need the keyboard, mouse or gamepad to interact with the operation system by command lines or GUIs [1]. Recently some new peripherals such as Leap Motion devices were invented to turn hands and fingers into input, which is possible to control the computer by replacing the mouse and keyboard [2]. Nowadays smart mobile phones with the touch screen, which can operate in a relatively comfortable way, are more commonly used than PCs so that you almost see them everywhere. Although the touch screen is more natural than the computer's peripherals, mobile phone users sometimes still feel inconvenient when they hold other things in hand [3].

With technological advancements on human machine interaction, many wearable devices have been brought into the market as potential substitutes for mobile phones [4]. Accordingly, more innovative ways come into effect. For example, some people talk with their phones and use voice as medium to conveniently interact with them [5].

A. El Rhalibi et al. (Eds.): Edutainment 2018, LNCS 11462, pp. 35–38, 2019.
https://doi.org/10.1007/978-3-030-23712-7_6

Accordingly, famous IT companies like Apple, Google and Facebook all show great passions towards the trends of next generation of interaction between human and wearable devices [6]. The Apple watch could become a motion sensing handle for an iPhone. Furthermore, Google Glasses used movement of eyeball to control the device. Nevertheless, if just looking at the appearance of glasses, the touch pad on the right side undoubtedly makes them a little weird due to the asymmetrical structure, which finally leaded Google glasses to a dead end. Suppose that Google removed the touch pad while remain its original function, the smart glasses perhaps attracted more clients [7].

Our team was invited by a digital entertainment content provider into the international collaboration work with a VR helmets vender and a mobile phone manufacturer based on mobile VR headsets using the smart mobile phone's GPU/CPU to power the device and the screen as the display. Our responsibility was to render digital entertainment contents such as their video sources of Formula One motor racing into the mobile VR scenarios. Our research aims to easily launch and transition between VR applications without taking the headset off, really makes the experience magical.

This project developed VR applications that realized a kind of visual interaction called "Collision as Trigger (CAT)". Dispensing with any external handle, a VR mobile device's user could control the virtual character and switch from a program or game scene to another more accurately with the help of noise suppression mechanism.

2 Noise Suppression to Enhance Motion Sensors' Accuracy

The sensors embedded in the mobile phone are widely used into variety applications such as motion games, navigation applications or as a data collection part of human machine interaction process. The accelerate sensor, gyroscope sensor and magnetic sensor are used to detect some simple gestures of the users individually. Motion sensing plays an important role in the VR field and the results of detection from the sensors are directly related to the accuracy of data.

However, the original accuracy of these sensors is not good enough to satisfy more complex motion identification. The noises and errors of signals which are collected from the accelerate sensor and gyroscope sensor impede the accuracy of aggregate motion. This research implemented the integrated algorithm to improve the accuracy by combining Sage & Husa Kalman Filter, Quaternion, Forth-Order Runge-Kutta method, rotation matrix and set some thresholds for the signals from accelerate sensor, gyroscope sensor and magnetic sensor in the handsets to determine complex motions with rotations and obtain their track. As illustrated in Fig. 1, this algorithm can effectively suppress noise so as to alleviate the potential dizziness brought by immersing in VR.

3 Smooth Interaction with Mobile VR by CAT

Based on stereopsis and accurate motion sensing, this project used the collision between the virtual objects in the scene as the trigger, to trigger the certain events. We set a point in the middle of the two cameras as the focus of a ray that represents users' line of sight. When the sight line collides with certain object, the collision will act as the trigger, to trigger the next event. To make it more obvious, a small plane was set near the focus, namely in the middle of the viewport. The plane represents the direction of sight line. When the plane focus on some object, it means the ray collides with that object.

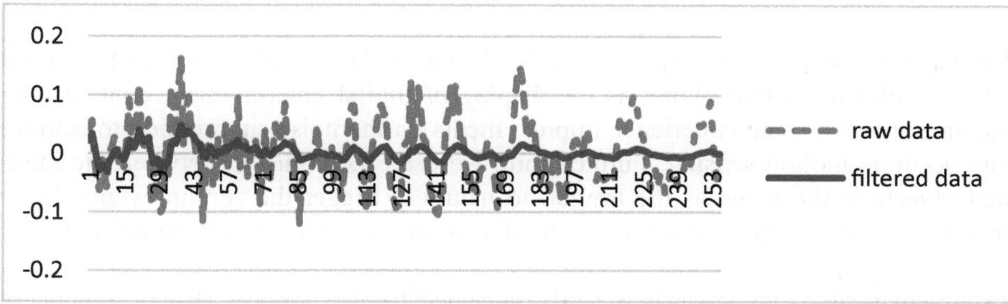

Fig. 1. Noise suppression effectiveness evaluation

As human beings, we simply get two different images through our eyes. Our eyes are at the same height, while there is a short horizontal distance between them. Therefore, the two images will have slight difference. Such slight difference will finally render a three-dimensional scene called stereopsis.

This project used Unity [8] to simulate this effect by artificially presenting two different images separately to each eye by setting a pair of cameras on the proper coordinates [9]. Two cameras were set closely, so that they looked at the same direction at any time. Accordingly, we would receive two slight different images from them. And such two images would render a three-dimensional view as illustrated in Fig. 2.

Fig. 2. Look from two different close cameras' view

When the user turns his/her head, the 3D stereopsis scenes in the VR applications should move as she/he turns accordingly based on accurate motion sensing.

Therefore, this project implemented motion sensing mechanisms that sense the handset movements accurately and track the device's moving trail in the 3D space. The tracked trail could be recognized as a predefined gesture afterwards.

4 Conclusion

This paper introduced our project called "Collision as Trigger (CAT)" based on a VR helmets with the mobile phone as the display of digital entertainment content. Our outcomes involve some experience improvements on the noise suppression to achieve more accurate motion sensing. Furthermore, we used the collision between the interested objects in the scene as the trigger, to naturally trigger the certain events. More accurate motion sensing could reduce the discomfort brought by VR immersion.

Acknowledgments. This research is partly supported by the National Defense Equipment Advance Research Shared Technology Program of China (41402050301-170441402065), and Technological Equipment Mobilization Program of Dongguan (KZ2017-06).

References

1. Nybakke, A., Ramakrishnan, R., Interrante, V.: From virtual to actual mobility: assessing the benefits of active locomotion through an immersive virtual environment using a motorized wheelchair. In: 2012 IEEE Symposium on 3D User Interfaces (3DUI), pp. 27–30 (2012)
2. Cavalcanti, A.F., de Medeiros, F.B.S., Dantas, R.R.: Evaluate leap motion control for multiple hand posture recognition. In: 2017 19th Symposium on Virtual and Augmented Reality (SVR), pp. 341–344 (2017)
3. Sanches, S.R.R., Oizumi, M., Oliveira, C., Damasceno, E.F., Sementille, A.C.: Aspects of user profiles that can improve mobile augmented reality usage. In: 2017 19th Symposium on Virtual and Augmented Reality (SVR), pp. 236–242 (2017)
4. Hodgson, E., Bachmann, E., Waller, D., Bair, A., Oberlin, A.: Virtual reality in the wild: a self-contained and wearable simulation system. In: 2012 IEEE Virtual Reality (VR), pp. 157–158 (2012)
5. Poeschl, S., Doering, N.: Virtual training for fear of public speaking - design of an audience for immersive virtual environments. In: 2012 IEEE Virtual Reality (VR), pp. 101–102 (2012)
6. Aseeri, S.A., Acevedo-Feliz, D., Schulze, J.: Poster: virtual reality interaction using mobile devices. In: 2013 IEEE Symposium on 3D User Interfaces (3DUI), pp. 127–128 (2013)
7. Why the Google glass broke (2015). http://www.nytimes.com/2015/02/05/style/why-google-glass-broke.html?_r=0. Accessed 15 May
8. Jerald, J., Giokaris, P., Woodall, D., Hartbolt, A., Chandak, A., Kuntz, S.: Developing virtual reality applications with Unity. In: 2014 IEEE Virtual Reality (VR), pp. 1–3 (2014)
9. Unity Documentation (2018). http://docs.unity3d.com/ScriptReference. Accessed 30 Jan 2018
10. Naceri, A., Chellali, R.: The effect of isolated disparity on depth perception in real and virtual environments. In: 2012 IEEE Virtual Reality (VR), pp. 107–108 (2012)

Avebury Portal – A Location-Based Augmented Reality Treasure Hunt for Archaeological Sites

Farbod Shakouri(✉) and Feng Tian

Faculty of Science and Technology, Bournemouth University,
Bournemouth BH12 5BB, UK
ftian@bournemouth.ac.uk

Abstract. Many archaeological sites are less popular by visits amongst the younger group and overall less popular than majority of other heritage sites. They are often not enhanced by supporting medium like in museums or historic buildings. Many augmented reality (AR) systems have been developed for archaeological sites and proved to benefit user engagement. However, most result in the superimposition of virtual reconstructions of the site and very little interaction. In this paper, we demonstrate the development of a location-based treasure hunt AR app, Avebury Portal, for the heritage site; Avebury in England. Avebury Portal uses puzzles with the environment to give clues, and a narrative that responds to the user's location. We developed Avebury Portal with Unity Engine and Vuforia to demonstrate the effectiveness of using AR to enhance visitors' experiences on learning.

Keywords: Location-based AR · Archaeological heritage site · Interactive learning · Multimodal interface · Locative narrative

1 Introduction

In 2017, UK Department for Digital, Culture Media & Sport reported that visits to heritage sites of archaeological interest were lower amongst the younger group of 16–24, and overall lower than other heritage sites [1]. A contributing factor may be the lack of exciting mediums used on-site to exhibit the information about archaeological sites when compared to traditional museums, where information is displayed in a controlled environment and enhanced by supporting materials such as signs, photos, videos and even sound systems [2]. One technology recently has shown potential capabilities which help create such environment for outdoor archaeological sites, known as augmented reality (AR).

Augmented reality has become more accessible on mainstream devices like mobile smartphones as they are now capable of providing valuable information from various modes of data like geo-location, touch, etc. People amongst the same age group have shown a rising interest for AR apps like Pokémon Go [3], resulting in researchers finding ways to adopt this technology for productive implications. It is suggested that AR should be adopted in the next few years to provide new and creative ways for teaching, learning and research, according to 55 studies published between 2011 and 2016 [4].

A. El Rhalibi et al. (Eds.): Edutainment 2018, LNCS 11462, pp. 39–49, 2019.
https://doi.org/10.1007/978-3-030-23712-7_7

Many augmented reality systems have been developed and deployed for cultural and archaeological sites where the system had contextual-awareness [5]. However, the focus of these applications was to reconstruct the heritage sites where the systems would visualise 3D models superimposed on their correspondent real-world structures. Ultimately, many of these previous applications did not integrate core framing context like liminal interface or Location Aware Narrative (LAN) to engage the users in a treasure hunt-like experience.

In this paper we propose an augmented reality application for outdoor, location-based treasure hunt called Avebury Portal. Avebury Portal is a mysterious treasure hunt intended to enhance users' engagement with Avebury Henge. The Neolithic stone circle is located in Wiltshire, south west England and serves great importance to contemporary pagans. It was built and altered over many centuries from about 2850 BC until about 2200 BC [6] and is now a part of a village always open to the public for visits. Avebury Portal provides information using contextualised learning which enables users to explore and discover ancient artefacts at the heritage site by walking around with a mobile device to find virtual 'treasures' hidden on-site. The system uses location-aware narrative system to give clues and generate puzzles, and guiding users with the provided 'smart map' that locates points of interest.

2 Related Works

AR applications have been researched and developed for historical and cultural environments. It is often extended to a complete methodology for real-time mixed reality system that features a simulated animation scene, re-enacted by virtual characters [7]. The visitors can observe the animated characters perform in a storytelling drama on the site using mobile mixed reality (MR) glasses in the real-world environment. The solutions have proved to benefit the sensation of presence by generating believable behaviours and interaction between the real and virtual objects.

Earlier solutions have developed sophisticated position and orientation tracking systems with position data given an accuracy of less than 1 m, but in the past, they were often developed for uncomfortable and heavy AR glasses [8]. Smartphone technology comprises multiple components that allow numerous data modalities, enabling the possibility of the same position tracking system made more accessible. Furthermore, the implementation of AR application through industry standard game engines like Unity [Unity3D 2017.30f3], reduces the complexity of development for applications that incorporate such systems and enables the possibility for narrative driven experience completed with real-time visual, haptic, and auditory feedback.

Location-based games can be an experience in which the user and environment are connected through a virtual layer of interactivity. However, games can mediate contextual-awareness, enabling a seamless merge of reality and virtuality. Liminal interface [9] applications can further expand on this experience and create a framing context [10] of which the application takes real life data, merging it with game information so that everyday things can have a new meaning in the context of location-based gameplay, as represented in Fig. 1.

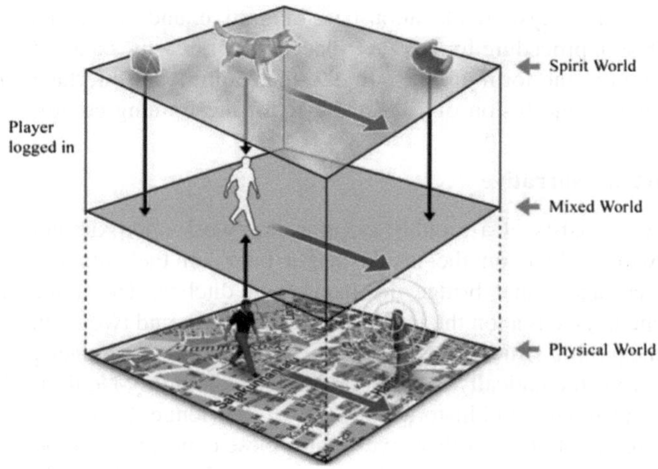

Fig. 1. Frame of game reality [11]

This paper focuses on the development of a location-based application that explores an interactive narrative system to help encourage users to be more engaged with an archaeological site. Subsequently, Avebury Portal investigates appropriate methods for delivering the narrative with appropriate use of multimedia and feedback, in the context of an adventurous game with the element of fantasy.

3 Avebury Portal

Avebury Portal is a fantasy game developed for the age group of 16–24, intended to be used on-site with a smartphone device and the accompanying 'smart map'. It is designed to be an experiential treasure hunt, guiding users around the site looking for clues that lead them to a 'treasure'. At each point of interest (POI), the user is rewarded with a 'treasure' which contains augmented visual, haptic and/or auditory feedback about their location at time. The narrative is driven by the user and their choice of action (e.g. direction of walking). At each POI during the treasure hunt, the user will need to solve a puzzle or riddle to acquire the 'treasure'. The puzzles creatively use the environment to give clues to the user, and often may quiz the user about a previous encounter instead, to ensure the user is engaged.

Avebury Portal uses Unity engine (Unity3D 2017) and the integrated image-based AR recognition technology (Vuforia [Vuforia]). The engine provides the appropriate toolset for a narrative driven application compatible on Android and iOS mobile operating systems. The prototype uses GPS to track user's location and device compass for orientation, incorporated to generate contextual-awareness throughout the user's treasure hunt. The application is designed to be a prototype, showcasing the proof of concept.

Avebury Portal consists of several parts: The Virtual Narrative, Treasure Hunt and the Multimodal Interface. In 3.1, The Virtual Narrative describes the method approached to plan the system's location-based narrative, and in 3.2 Treasure Hunt, we illustrate the design procedure for puzzles, placement of treasures and what information is being delivered in the form of clues. In 3.3, the Multimodal Interface uncovers how the system manages the fusion of GPS and AR for the framing context.

3.1 The Virtual Narrative

Avebury Henge consists of a roughly circular earthwork approximately 1 km in circumference, with a ditch on the inside and a bank on the outside, broken into 4 quadrants by entrances that bridge the banks and ditches. The stone circles inside consisted of one large circle on the inside edge of the ditch and two further inner circles surrounding megalithic structures. Most of these stones are no longer present.

The narrative is thematically inspired by the style of fantasy Neolithic folklores and it explores the spirituality and historical aspects of the Henge. Given that this system is a location-aware narrative, it further investigates these concepts with the corresponding environment and presents the information in small packages called 'clues', with room for the user to have freedom of exploration. However, the system is still required to be easily accessible and safe due to the nature of its interaction. This includes the highlight of key iconic places such as: Southern and northern circle, behind the chapel, the cove, etc. They act as key points throughout the hunt and present themselves as safe places if users get lost.

The POIs have supporting information that act as 'treasures'. The presented 'clues' given at these places are extracted from a handy book [12] found in the site's gift shop, combined with various sources that includes more recent and up-to-date archaeological information [13]. In the system design, we refer to every POI as Node, for narrative planning.

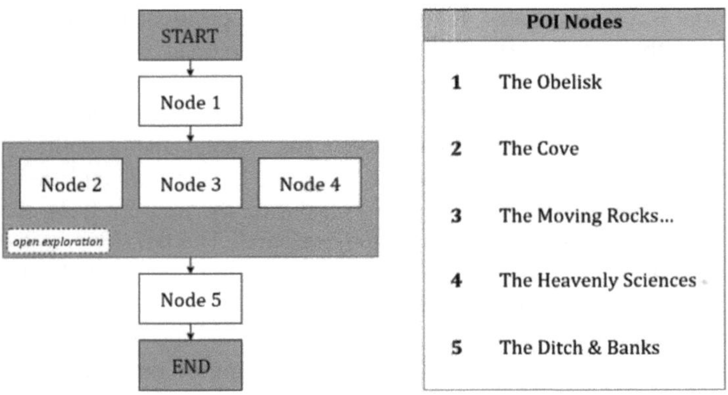

Fig. 2. Treasure Nodes from *Avebury Portal*

The structure of the narrative can be described as a CDP model and a hybrid of a Canyon-Plain-Canyon [14]. The system allows users to have open exploration in between two independent nodes as shown in Fig. 2. This structure guides users through an environment by controlling their beginning and end but allows immersive freedom of exploration in between [15].

3.2 Treasure Hunt

The purpose of this hunt is to use AR to enhance engagement with heritage sites of archaeological type. To retain attentiveness of users and interaction between the user and application, we created a map which indicates POIs, known as the 'smart map'. The 'smart map' is provided alongside the application running on a mobile device, encouraging users to find the 'treasures'. The 'treasures' are at POIs placed on the 'smart map', shown as question marks for users to approach. The map contains marker images that are directly linked to each POI for users to scan when they are prompted, demonstrated in Fig. 3.

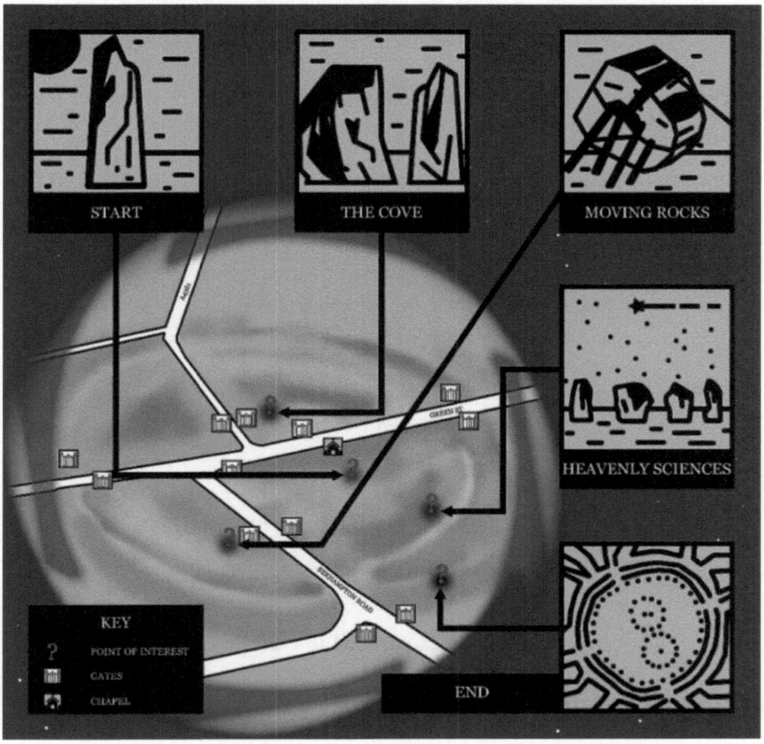

Fig. 3. Smart map printed to be used with *Avebury Portal*

At the start of the application, users are asked to approach the chapel to begin the treasure hunt. Avebury Portal demonstrates how the system works by guiding users through the first 'treasure' next to the chapel, which in a way, acts as tutorial. There are 2 clues attached to each 'treasure' found at each POI about Avebury Henge (Fig. 5.), illustrated through AR animation, sound and static 3D models. The importance of this system is to ensure users remember the clues they gather from each POI and apply them to solve the puzzle of their sequel POI combined with the directed visual clues found in their environment. However, each user's experience can differ from Node 2–4 as this is an open exploration section in the narrative structure. The system enables this structure by storing what POI(s) have been visited using an array of Boolean variables to identify which puzzle to prompt based on the clues they have gathered from previous POI(s). This is illustrated by an example scenario in Fig. 4.

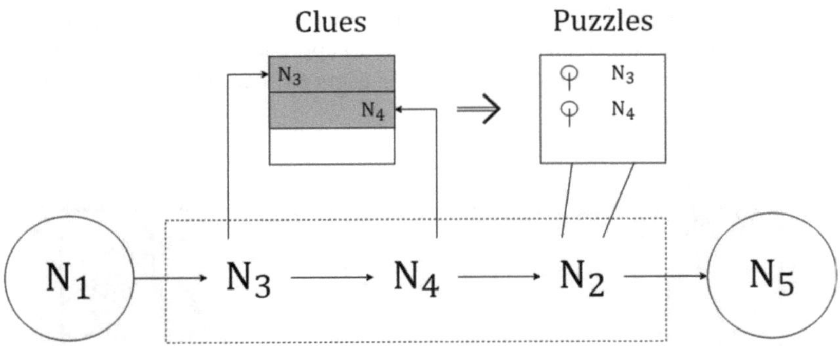

Fig. 4. Example of how clues are collected to be used for the sequel Node.

Node (POI)	Attached Clues
1	**(a)** Age of Avebury **(c)** Obelisk height
2	**(d)** The north circle **(e)** The cove
3	**(f)** South entrance **(g)** Moving rocks
4	**(h)** Cosmic **(i)** Heavenly numbers
5	**(j)** The ditches **(k)** Protecting spirits

Fig. 5. Clues attached to each POI

3.3 Multimodal Interface

Avebury Portal comprises multimodal inputs to contextualise user interaction with the treasure hunt. An example modality is user's position data, measured by the system and discretised as coordinates to locate user's position at a given instance. Avebury Portal takes the position data of the user and calculates the distance to the pre-set POI coordinates. An area of 10 m^2 is created surrounding each POI, except for Node 5 where it's an area of 5 m^2 (for safety precautions). These areas are made to notify the user when they approach the POI. It calculates the distance between two points where φ is latitude, λ is longitude, R is earth's radius (mean radius = 6,371 km).

$$a = \sin^2\left(\frac{\Delta\varphi}{2}\right) + \cos\varphi 1 \cdot \cos\varphi 2 \cdot \sin^2\left(\frac{\Delta\lambda}{2}\right)$$

$$c = 2 \cdot \text{atan2}\left(\sqrt{a}, \sqrt{(1 - a)}\right)$$

$$\text{distance} = R \cdot c$$

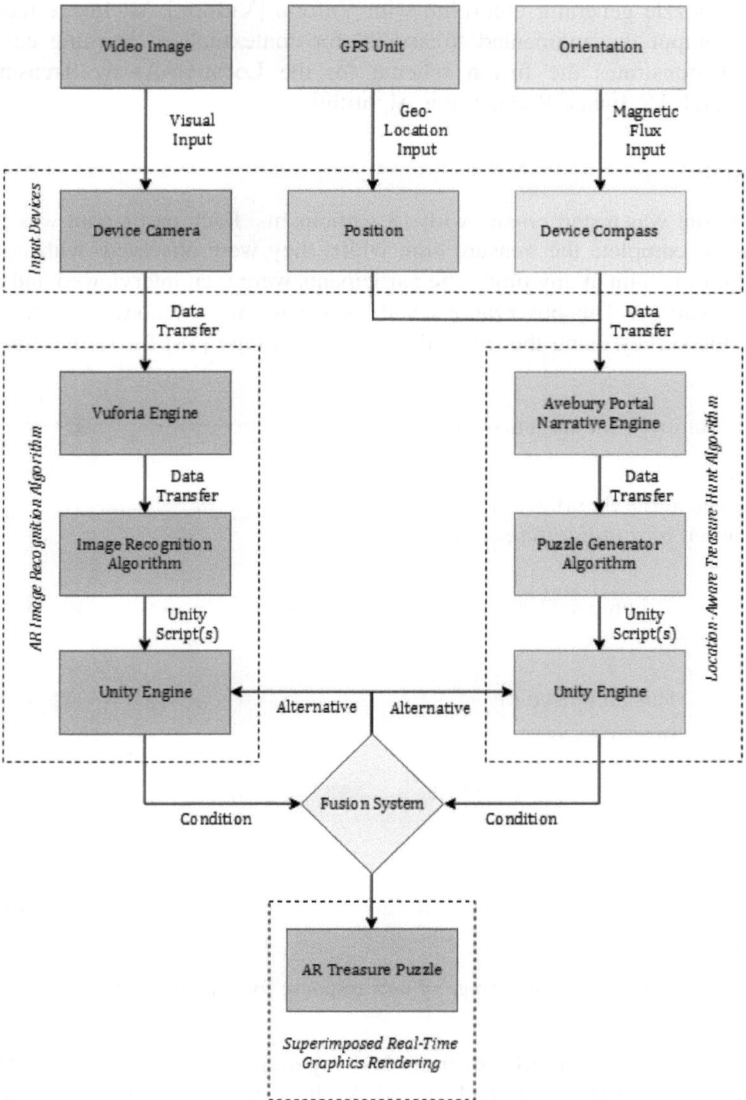

Fig. 6. The fusion scheme for orientation, location, image sensors and algorithms.

Multimodal interface is a method to create an unambiguous format for user interaction by increasing recognition accuracy with data from various modalities, verifying user intention [16]. Multimodal system integration is also referred to as the fusion engine [17]. This idea is expanded further by understanding that modalities with different characteristics may not have obvious ways to connect. Additionally, in [17] Turk concluded, perhaps, the biggest challenge could be the temporal dimension. Some modalities provide information at sparse, discrete points in time (counted) while others generate continuous but less time-specific output (measured).

In Avebury Portal, the use of this method works to fuse the location-aware narrative engine and puzzle generator algorithm with Vuforia [Vuforia] AR image recognition engine, to output the augmented 'treasures' for contextualised learning experience. Figure 6 demonstrates the fusion scheme for the Location-Aware Treasure Hunt Algorithm and AR Image Recognition Algorithm.

3.4 Results

Avebury Portal was tested on-site with 18 participants. Each participant was given up to an hour to complete the treasure hunt whilst they were observed, with notice that they can quit the hunt at any time. The participants were then interviewed and asked to complete a survey. The observations and interviews were recorded to be analysed alongside the survey using the triangulation methodology [18] for further analysis.

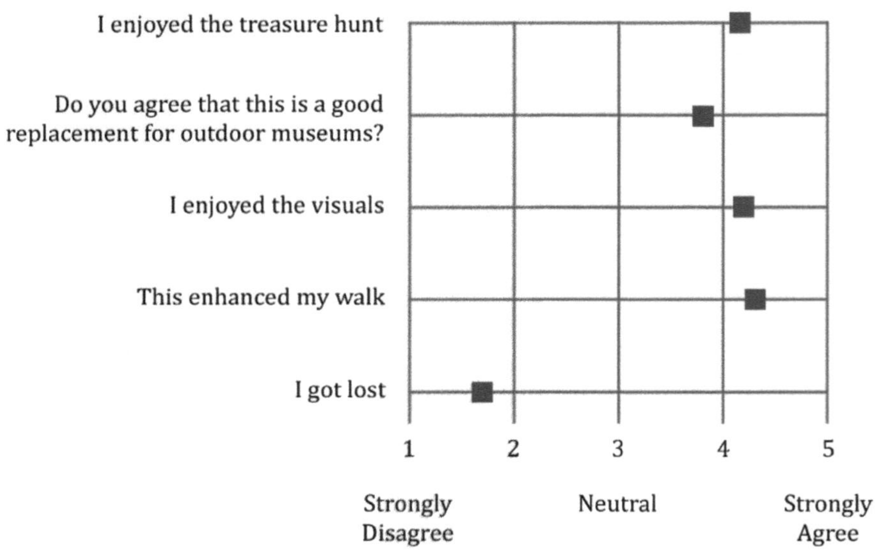

Fig. 7. Mean average of user response for Avebury Portal

The survey results that 50% of users had experienced a location-based AR game, and that 12 of 18 participants had visited Avebury before. 5 participants were also archaeologist who work on-site. The results of the survey also demonstrate the average response for each statement in Fig. 7. Users responded positively to each statement, validated by their actions when observed and backed up by their response in interviews. However, many who responded 1 (Strongly Disagree) to “I got lost” showed some signs of confusion and frustration when they were observed. Perhaps users felt disorientated and confused about their location, suggesting that, they could have been lost (Fig. 8).

Fig. 8. User interacting with Avebury Portal

4 Conclusion and Future Work

In this paper, we manage to design, implement and test a working prototype of a location-based AR treasure hunt that achieves some positive impact on user’s experience during their visit to Avebury Henge. Users praised the augmented visuals, agreed that this encouraged their walk at the site, and most said that they feel this could replace current methods for exhibiting an outdoor heritage site. Some users also mentioned that the haptic feedback for notifying users approaching an area of interest was intuitive and appealing. The information given at each clue was clear to the users and they felt that the animations and the riddles were engaging and informative.

However, some users showed signs of confusion when using the map to locate their position, suggesting that perhaps an alternative would be to completely eradicate the ‘smart map’ and implement in-app navigation system for further guidance of users’ location. The system also needs further work on establishing stable and reliable methods for markerless 3D tracking, which could be integrating together with the location-aware system to create a more seamless virtual dimension for users to interact with.

References

1. UK Department for Digital, Culture Media & Sport: Taking Part Focus on: Heritage. National Statistics, London (2017). https://www.gov.uk/government/uploads/system/uploads/attachment_data/file/655949/Taking_Part_Focus_on_Heritage.pdf. Accessed 13 Jan 2018
2. Bay, H., Fasel, B., Van Gool, L.: Interactive museum guide: fast and robust recognition of museum object. Computer Vision Laboratory, Zurich. https://www.vision.ee.ethz.ch/publications/papers/proceedings/eth_biwi_00394.pdf. Accessed 19 Feb 2017
3. Niantic: Nintendo (2016)
4. Chen, P., Liu, X., Cheng, W., Huang, R.: A review of using augmented reality in education from 2011 to 2016. Smart Learning Institute, Beijing Normal University, Beijing, China (2017). https://pdfs.semanticscholar.org/deaa/5b1ad5a3ecec6a83783e7ac371b2a3970ed3.pdf. Accessed 23 Oct 2017
5. Narciso, D., Padua, L., Adao, T., Peres, E., Magalhaes, L.: MixAR mobile prototype: visualizing virtually reconstructed ancient structures in situ. In: Proceedings of Conference on Enterprise Information Systems/International Conference on Project Management/Conference on Health and Social Care Information Systems and Technologies, CENTERIS/ProjMAN/HCist, 7–9 October 2015
6. English Heritage: History of Avebury Henge and Stone Circles (2002). http://www.english-heritage.org.uk/visit/places/avebury/history/. Accessed 15 Mar 2017
7. Papagiannakis, G., Magnenat-Thalmann, N.: Virtual worlds and augmented reality in cultural heritage applications. In: Baltsavias et al. (eds.) Proceedings of Recording, Modeling and Visualization of Cultural Heritage, January 2006, Abington, pp. 419–430. Taylor and Francis Group, Abington (2006). https://www.researchgate.net/publication/232613064_Virtual_Worlds_and_Augmented_Reality_in_Cultural_Heritage_Applications. Accessed 17 Jan 2018
8. Vlahakis, V., et al.: Archeoguide: an augmented reality guide for archaeological sites. IEEE Comput. Graph. Appl. **22**(5), 52–60 (2002)
9. Nieuwdorp, E.: The pervasive interface: tracing the magic circle. In: Proceedings of Digital Games Research Conference 2005, Changing Views: Worlds in Play, 16–20 June 2005, Vancouver, Canada (2005)
10. Goffman, E.: Frame Analysis. An Essay on the Organization of Experiences. Northeastern University Press, Boston (1974)
11. Mäyrä, F., Lankoski, P.: Player in hybrid reality, alternative approaches in game design. In: de Souza e Silva, A. (ed.) Digital Cityscapes: Merging Digital and Urban Playspaces, 1st edn. pp. 129–146. Peter Lang Publishing, Pieterlen (2009)
12. Francis, E.: Avebury. Wooden Gift Books (2000)
13. Gillings, M., Barker, D., Pollard, J., Strutt, K., Taylor, J.: Squaring the circle? Geophysical survey across part of the southern inner circle of the Avebury (2017)
14. Millard, D.E., Hargood, C., Jewell, M.O., Weal, M.J.: Canyons, deltas and plains: Towards a unified sculptural model of location-based hypertext. In: Proceedings of the 24th ACM Conference on Hypertext and Social Media (2013)
15. Hargood, C., Hunt, V., Weal, M., Millard, D.E.: Patterns of sculptural hypertext in location based narratives. In: Proceedings of the 27th ACM Conference on Hypertext and Social Media. ACM, New York (2016)
16. Kurschl, W., Gottesheim, W., Mitsch, S., Prokop, R., Schönböck, J.: Proposing Usability Patterns for Mobile Multimodal Applications, Hagenberg, Austria (2007)

17. Turk, M.: Pattern Recognition Letters. Multimodal interaction: a review (2013, in press). http://www.cs.ucsb.edu/~mturk/Papers/TurkPRL2013.pdf. Accessed 12 Nov 2017
18. Hsieh, M.C., Lin, H.C.: A conceptual study for augmented reality e-learning system based on usability evaluation. In: Communications in Information Science and Management Engineering (2011)

Gamification for Serious Game and Training

An Analysis of Gamification Effect of Frequent-Flyer Program

Long Zuo[1(✉)], Shuo Xiong[2(✉)], Zhichao Wang[1], and Hiroyuki Iida[1]

[1] School of Information Science, Japan Advanced Institute of Science and Technology, Nomi, Japan
{zuolong,wangzhichao,iida}@jaist.ac.jp

[2] School of Journalism and Information Communication, Huazhong University of Science and Technology, Wuhan, China
xiongshuo@hust.edu.cn

Abstract. This paper explores the benefits of a sales promotion in the aviation industry known as Frequent-Flyer Program. Four well known Chinese FFPs are chosen as a benchmark to assess their gamification effect with a focus on game sophistication and costumer's experience. A data-driven approach is employed to analyze gamification techniques in FFPs such as tiers system and points system. The results show that the degree of game sophistication is relatively low due to its non-game context. The present contribution illustrates how tiers system and points system offer fun-game and serious-game experience respectively. It also shows an advantage of its harmonious combination to attract more potential customers and retain the frequent flyer customers.

Keywords: Gamification · Frequent-Flyer Program · Game experience · Game refinement theory

1 Introduction

Frequent-Flyer Program or FFP in short is a loyalty program offered by airlines, which is considered, from a historical perspective, to be the world's largest gamified service. Many airlines have frequent-flyer programs designed to encourage customers to accumulate points (also called miles or segments), which may be redeemed for air travel or other rewards. FFPs describe how travelers accumulate and redeem their frequent flyer miles, and determine the number of benefits travelers can receive from the program [1]. The history of FFP, considered to have started with the Advantage program, has been characterized by a series of inventions that improved airlines' revenue streams and increased customer recognition [3]. Their purpose was simple: to reward customers for using the airline and to promote future customer loyalty. The concept of gamification has recently been a trend in our modern society to increase people's motivation for more active participation in various non-game contexts. However, only a few studies have empirically investigated the fundamental mechanism of gamified

A. El Rhalibi et al. (Eds.): Edutainment 2018, LNCS 11462, pp. 53–60, 2019.
https://doi.org/10.1007/978-3-030-23712-7_8

systems. We therefore raise a research question: "What are the essential characteristics of FFP and how does it work?" We start by defining the gamification in FFP and then introduce the two fundamental mechanics. Using an assessment methodology, we observe the game experience and game sophistication of these two systems. Finally, we give concluding remarks.

2 Gamification

Gamification employs game design elements which are used in non-game contexts to improve the user's engagement [2]. Gamification is about engaging customers actively by applying game-based thinking through badges, rewards programs and points. Thus we illustrate these three ingredients in this section and offer the strict definition of gamification for the FFP.

Game Elements mean that game designers are trying to build some service that uses the bits and pieces of games. We can see a kind of graphical interface that we typically see in a game and the various kinds of pieces that offer us a game-like experience on the home page of hotel rewards program.

Game Design is the system including points and tiers system in which game elements organized systematically, and a game playing feeling is offered to encourage customers to enjoy the activity.

Non-game Context can be understood as anything other than the game for its purpose where the objective is outside of the game. The players are playing the game for the reasons related to their needs or business.

Gamification in FFP leverages the intrinsic human motivations to keep gathering rewards or miles and build up the users' motivation to ensure that the engagement is continuous [4]. It can be defined as a service quality attribute that consists of two systems: tiers system and points system. Based on the literature review, we give a definition of gamification of FFP.

Definition 1. Gamification of FFP *is the enhancement of service and miles bonus when the customer is promoted to a higher membership status with the well-organized game elements for gameful experiences to retain customer loyalty to the airline brands.*

2.1 Tiers System

One gamification of FFP is the tiers system, which is an application of progression levels or difficulty levels just as in video games. The tiers system is commonly represented by four levels: member, silver, gold and platinum. Different statuses enjoy different levels of rewards, additional points, priority check-in and lounge access, depending on the airline's regulations. We show the membership requirement of tiers system of four Chinese FFPs in Table 1, 2, 3 and Table 4. [1]

[1] All company names, loyalty rewards names, trademarks and pictures are the property of their respective owners.

Table 1. Eastern Miles

Tier	Miles/Segment	Extra bonus
Silver	40,000/25	15%
Gold	80,000/40	30%
Platinum	160,000/90	50%

Table 2. Phoenix Mile

Tier	Miles/Segment	Extra bonus
Silver	40,000/25	25%
Gold	80,000/40	30%
Platinum	160,000/90	50%

Table 3. Sky Pearl Club

Tier	Miles/Segment	Extra bonus
Silver	40,000/20	15%
Gold	80,000/40	30%

Table 4. Fortune Wings Club

Tier	Miles/Segment	Extra bonus
Silver	30,000/20	25%
Gold	50,000/40	50%
Platinum	100,000/80	55%

2.2 Points System

The points system is a type of virtual currency used predominantly within the game world. As a new player, one is offered a "Qualifying Segment" by the system which allows him/her to get fast bonus-point earnings that provide instant gratification. Most, if not all, programs award bonus earnings to premium-cabin passengers and their elite-status members based on tier status. A common bonus for these passengers is to earn an extra 15%–55% of the miles flown on a given flight. Points or miles can be redeemed for air travel, other goods or services, class upgrades and airport lounge access.

3 Assessment Methodology

A measurement of game refinement is employed for the assessment of the degree of game sophistication of a target FFP, which is derived from the game progress model [5]. The "game progress" is twofold. One is game speed or scoring rate, while another one is game information progress with a focus on the game outcome. Game information progress presents the degree of certainty of a game's result in time or steps. Having full information of the game progress, i.e. after its conclusion, game progress $x(t)$ will be given as a linear function of time t with $0 \leq t \leq t_k$ and $0 \leq x(t) \leq x(t_k)$, as shown in Eq. (1).

$$x(t) = \frac{x(t_k)}{t_k}\, t \tag{1}$$

However, the game information progress given by Eq. (1) is usually unknown during the in-game period. Hence, the game information progress is reasonably assumed to be exponential or so. This is because the game outcome is uncertain until the very end of the game in many games. Hence, a realistic model of game information progress is given by Eq. (2).

$$x(t) = x(t_k)(\frac{t}{t_k})^n \tag{2}$$

Here n stands for a constant parameter which is given based on the perspective of an observer in the game under consideration. Meanwhile, we reasonably assume that the parameter would be $n \geq 2$ in many cases like balanced or seesaw games. Thus, the acceleration of game information progress is obtained by deriving Eq. (2) twice. Solving it at the end of the game ($t = t_k$), the equation becomes

$$x''(t_k) = \frac{x(t_k)\ n(n-1)}{(t_k)^n}\ t^{n-2}\ |_{t=t_k} = \frac{x(t_k)}{(t_k)^2}\ n(n-1) \tag{3}$$

It is assumed in the current model that the game information progress in any games is happening in our minds. We do not know yet about the physics in our minds, but it is likely that the acceleration of information progress is related to the force in mind. Hence, it is reasonably expected that the larger the value $\frac{x(t_k)}{(t_k)^2}$ is, the more the game becomes exciting due to the uncertainty of game outcome. Thus, we apply its root square $\frac{\sqrt{x(t_k)}}{t_k}$, as a game refinement measure (say GR).

We show, in Table 5, several sophisticated games including chess and Go from board games, basketball and soccer from sports. We see that sophisticated games have a similar GR value which we recognize a zone value between 0.07 and 0.08. However, there is still less knowledge about the game refinement value of serious game and gamification. In this study we quantify the game sophistication of FFPs. The early works based on the same methodology indicate that the degree of game sophistication in non-game contexts such as hotel loyalty program [8] and language learning platform [10] is relatively lower than boardgames and sports.

Table 5. Measures of game refinement for boardgames, sports and gamified programs

	$x(t_k)$	t_k	GR
Chess [6]	35	80	0.074
Go [6]	250	208	0.076
Basketball [7]	36.38	82.01	0.073
Soccer [7]	2.64	22	0.073
Marriott: Platinum [8]	75	365	0.024
Duolingo: English [10]	55.6	292	0.026

4 Analyzing Gamification Effect

FFP can be defined as a service quality attribute that consists of some redemption of free flight miles and can determine the selection of airlines [1]. So, how do they reward customers? The basic concept is "the more frequently you fly with them, the greater your rewards become." The concept behind FFP is that the airlines want their passengers to maintain the loyalty or finally become the lifetime customers.

Tiers System is an effective and proven way of encouraging repeated business. We determine the game progress model of an FFP based on the action of qualifying segments of membership tiers. The main game progress can be defined by two factors: the number of successful qualifying segments and the total number of segments within a year. Here, we consider the normalized model that the customer can usually get one segment in one day. As the total number of days in a year is 365, the measure of game refinement for the tiers system (say GR_T) is given by Eq. (4), and the results are shown in Fig. 1.

$$GR_T = \frac{\sqrt{Qualifying\_Segments}}{Total\_Segments} \tag{4}$$

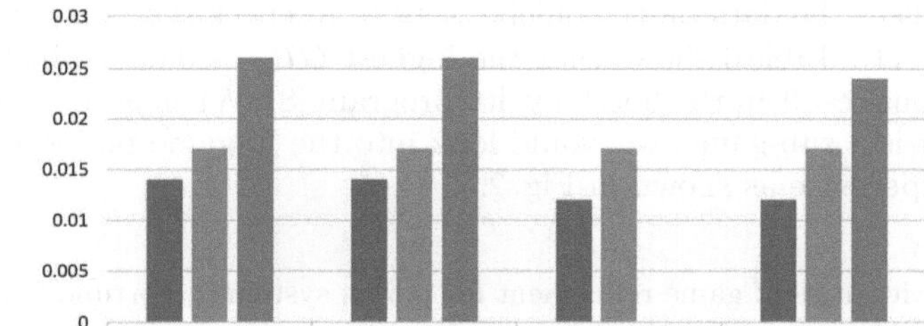

	Eastern Miles	Phoenix Miles	Sky Pearl Club	Fortune Wings Club
Silver	0.014	0.014	0.012	0.012
Gold	0.017	0.017	0.017	0.017
Platinum	0.026	0.026		0.024

Fig. 1. Measures of game refinement for tiers system from four FFPs

Definition 2. Game Experience *is defined as the relationship between the player and the game. Experience includes both the process and the outcomes of the interactions between a player and the game's design. It focuses on the personal challenge that the user experiences from interacting with the application during the entire gaming process.*

Every airline company has almost the same strategy of membership management, with the membership consisting of four tiers, except Sky Pearl Club that has three tiers excluding the platinum tier. Here, maintaining or promoting the status could be considered as tackling a challenge in a game.

Remark 1. The trend of these four FFPs is statistically significant to observe that GR_T tends to increase with the tier promotion, which implies that the tiers system is offering fun-game experience.

Points System describes how travelers accumulate and redeem their miles [9]. In this study, data is collected by considering the flight distance. As game refinement requires the highest level (corresponding to the skillful player) to make the result more objective, we take the most senior membership as a sample to figure out the measurement denoted as GR_P in Eq. (5). Table 1, 2, 3 and 4 show that the higher status customers take, the more miles/points they obtain. Meanwhile, the points for redeeming free segments differ dramatically from the distance, which highlights the consideration on the distance issue when we apply GR_P to the free segments. Thus, we choose three kinds of ranges: short, medium and long. Here, we figure out the impact of a free segment for the highest membership of Fortune Wings Club, considering the distance issue within a year to illustrate game sophistication and game experience.

$$GR_P = \frac{\sqrt{Free\_Segment}}{Qualifying\_Segment} \tag{5}$$

Thus, the total points one can earn within a year with considering the 80 segments (XIY-PVG) of the domestic with the point bonus are about 170,000. Then, we collect the data on the official website to check the points required for a free flight [11]. Table 6 shows that the highest GR_P is 0.045, which is similar to the previous result in the hotel loyalty program [8]. When assuming that each free segment is a sub-game, we would look into the in-game period to illustrate the game experience as shown in Fig. 2.

Table 6. Measures of game refinement for points system in Fortune Wings Club

Segment	Points required	Free flights	Qualifying segment	GR_P
Short (XIY-PVG)	13,000	13	80	0.045
Medium (XIY-NRT)	28,000	6	80	0.031
Long (XIY-CDG)	45,000	3	80	0.022

Remark 2. The more free segments one redeems, the less challenge he/she meets, which implies that the points system is offering serious-game experience.

5 Discussion

The motivation of FFPs all share one goal: to create a close and strong relationship with clients to retain a constant loyalty. Figure 3 demonstrates the relationship between the tiers system and points system. This figure provides an overview of the mechanism as two different kinds of gamified services: tier-based game (red-color path) and point-based game (blue-color path). The tiers system gives customers fun-game experience; this idea gives people the motivation and challenge to promote a higher status or maintain the status. This leads to the

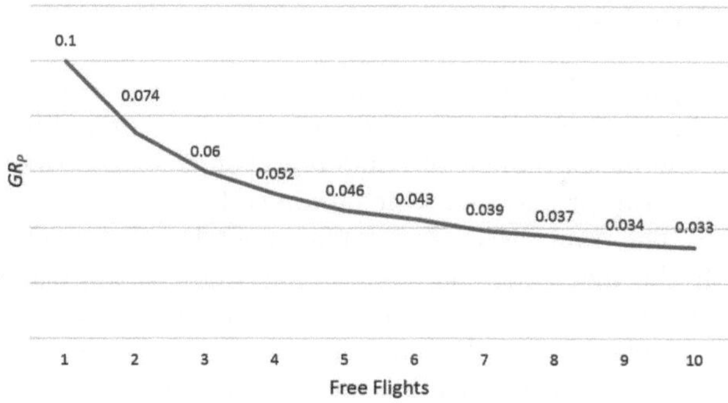

Fig. 2. The trend of GR_P with increasing number of free segment redemption

win-win scenario: customers improve their loyalty and companies increase their revenues. One dimension is the frequency of tiers system which means the sustainability of the frequent customer. Another dimension is the profitability of points system which indicates the popularity of the gamified service, as profit may encourage more customers involved in. The points system concerns about the benefit for customers who may feel serious-game experience (a good balance between customer's capacity and challenge) but related to the popularity. The free ticket is so compelling as everyone desires to enjoy a flight without payment also with the high-level services. Thus, the motivation of these two gamified services organized systematically is to create a program to maintain customer loyalty [12].

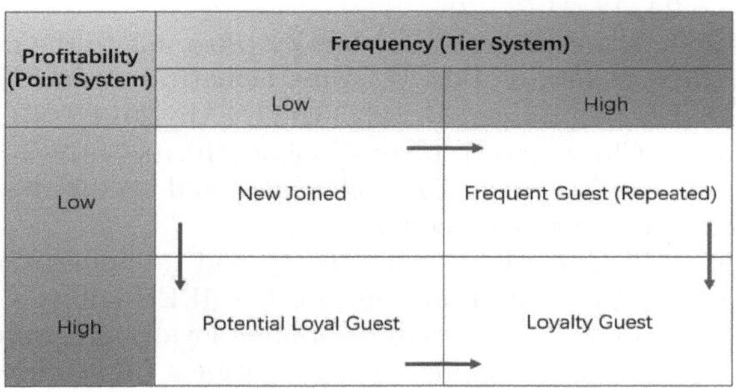

Fig. 3. Interpretation of the relationship between tiers system and points system. Both systems aim to bring customers to Loyalty Guest position in a different path. (Color figure online)

6 Concluding Remarks

In this paper, a game refinement measurement has been used to obtain novel insights into the benefit of FFP with a focus on tiers system and points system. It is observed that the measurement of game refinement for the tiers system tends to increase with the tier promotion, which implies that the tiers system offers fun-game experience. The analysis of game refinement for the points system tends to decrease with the increasing number of free flight redemption. It indicates that the more free segments one redeems, the less challenge he/she meets, which implies that the points system offers serious-game experience.

This paper has shown a promising approach to evaluate the various gamified services such as a sales promotion in the aviation industry known as Frequent-Flyer Program. However, it is nascent, so there is a pressing need for further exploration of a broader range of games including serious games and the investigation of the subjective feelings of some passengers in the future.

Acknowledgement. This research is funded by a grant from the Japan Society for the Promotion of Science, within the framework of the Grant-in-Aid for Challenging Exploratory Research.

References

1. Martín, J.C., Román, C., Espino, R.: Evaluating frequent flyer programs from the air passengers' perspective. J. Air Transp. Manag. **17**(6), 364–368 (2011)
2. Huotari, K., Hamari, J.: Defining gamification: a service marketing perspective. In: Proceedings of the International Academic Mindtrek Conference, pp. 17–22. ACM (2012)
3. De Boer, E.R., Gudmundsson, S.V.: 30 years of frequent flyer programs. J. Air Transp. Manag. **24**, 18–24 (2012)
4. Sanjai, V.: Gamification: taking airline loyalty programs to the next level (2017)
5. Sutiono, A.P., Purwarianti, A., Iida, H.: A mathematical model of game refinement. In: Reidsma, D., Choi, I., Bargar, R. (eds.) INTETAIN 2014. LNICST, vol. 136, pp. 148–151. Springer, Cham (2014). https://doi.org/10.1007/978-3-319-08189-2_22
6. Cincotti, A., Iida, H., Yoshimura, J.: Refinement and complexity in the evolution of chess. In: Information Sciences (2007)
7. Nossal, N., Iida, H.: Game refinement theory and its application to score limit games. In: Games Media Entertainment, pp. 1–3. IEEE (2014)
8. Zuo, L., Xiong, S., Iida, H.: An Analysis of hotel loyalty program with a focus on the tiers and points system. In: The 4th International Conference on Systems and Informatics (ICSAI), pp. 507–511. IEEE (2017)
9. Suzuki, Y.: Airline frequent flyer programs: equity and attractiveness. Transp. Res. Part E: Logist. Transp. Rev. **39**(4), 289–304 (2003)
10. Huynh, D., Zuo, L., Iida, H.: Analyzing gamification of "Duolingo" with focus on its course structure. In: Bottino, R., Jeuring, J., Veltkamp, R.C. (eds.) GALA 2016. LNCS, vol. 10056, pp. 268–277. Springer, Cham (2016). https://doi.org/10.1007/978-3-319-50182-6_24
11. Hainan Airlines (2018). http://www.hnair.com/
12. Laškarin, M.: Development of loyalty programmes in the hotel industry. Tour. Hosp. Manag. **19**(1), 109–123 (2013)

A Serious Game for Learning the Conversation Method with Autism for Typically Developing

Keigo Yabuki(✉) and Kaoru Sumi(✉)

Future University Hakodate, 116-2 Kameda Nakanocho, Hakodate-shi, Hokkaido, Japan
g3119007@fun.ac.jp, kaoru.sumi@acm.org

Abstract. In this study, a serious game was developed to enable typically developing to learn the most appropriate method of conversation with autism. Autism tend to have difficulty with interpersonal relationships because they find it difficult to understand conversational implicatures. As a solution to this problem, we propose a serious game to enable typically developing to learn how to speak to autism in a way they can understand, including how best to convey conversational implicatures. This serious game simulates the experience of autism of being unable to understand conversational implicatures, using conversations based on real life examples, in order to teach players why autism cannot understand what they mean and how they can paraphrase their message. To verify the efficacy of this serious game, an experiment was conducted with 56 students. Experimental results suggested that the system is effective for learning how to speak especially among typically developing who were rarely involved with autism.

Keywords: Conversational implicature · Serious game · Communication support · Autism · Typically developing

1 Introduction

A failure to establish conversation often occurs between autism and typically developing (neurotypical), and this is prone to cause problems in interpersonal relationships. The reason for such failures is that it is difficult for autism to understand the conversational implicatures of ambiguous utterances [1–4]. A conversational implicature is not the literal meaning of an utterance, but the intention behind the utterance [5]. The term ambiguous utterance may refer to an utterance containing expressions suggesting a conversational implicature, such as rhetorical questions, irony, metaphor, demonstrative, pronouns, idioms [3, 4], and indirect speech acts [6]; it may also refer to an utterance that needs a request for clarification [7] or requires a grasp of the relevant context [8]. Furthermore, in corroboration of the notion that these utterance characteristics affect interpersonal relationships, Yamamoto and Kusumoto explain that autism have difficulty with ambiguous situations and interpersonal contexts, because it is difficult for them to understand context [9].

However, another factor in this problem lies in the method of interaction used by typically developing. According to Tanaka and Fujiwara, a typically developing does

A. El Rhalibi et al. (Eds.): Edutainment 2018, LNCS 11462, pp. 61–68, 2019.
https://doi.org/10.1007/978-3-030-23712-7_9

not use abstract expressions, demonstrative and metaphor; by using concrete and straightforward expressions, a speaker can ensure that their message will be properly transmitted, even to autism [10].

Accordingly, this study aimed to support typically developing's ability to convey conversational implicatures to autism. To achieve this purpose, we developed a serious game that can teach them how to speak, conveying the experience of autism in being unable to understand conversational implicatures through the use of real-life examples. According to Prensky, a serious game is a game designed for a primary purpose other than pure entertainment, which aims to solve a social problem, such as one relating to education or medicine [11]. In this case, the target audience for our game is a typically developing who has no expert knowledge and is highly likely to be involved in communicating with autism.

Through the use of the serious game developed by the authors, players learn how to converse with autism in a simple manner by three kinds of utterance including instruction word, utterance including idiomatic expression and utterance with context grasping. In addition, through the use of examples, players can learn that it is difficult for autism to understand conversational implicature. The game is presented in Japanese. The results of an experiment verifying the efficacy of the game [12–14] showed that although the learning effect of this serious game was remarkable among those with low levels of pre-existing expertise, a problem remains with regard to maintaining players' motivation. Therefore, in this paper, we discuss how to improve motivation while maintaining the learning effect.

2 Related Research

Gray proposes comic dialogues representing conversational exchanges as an effective tool to promote conversation between children with autism and their expert therapists and parents [15]. This makes it easy to understand the rapid exchange of information in conversation by visualizing the conversation using line drawings and can provide supplementary support for communication. However, it is not an evidence that autism can be generalized by this technique. Autism have difficulty applying what they learn in an educational setting in real-life situations. In order for individuals with autism to generalize successfully, it is necessary to spend an enormous amount of time facilitating appropriate learning independent of the situation [16]. This approach does not lead to a fundamental solution to the problem.

In research by Yoshii et al., by supporting in stages to a child with autism who was not able to seek clarification of ambiguous instructions, the child learned to voluntarily request such clarification, and was also able to generalize successfully [17]. However, there are severe limitations on who can apply this method, and this research method requires 28 months to enable the child to generalize. This approach also fails to lead to a fundamental solution to the problem.

3 Game Design

The serious game described in this paper simulates a conversation with autism who cannot understand conversational implicatures. The player learns why autism cannot understand the meaning of certain statements, and how to communicate well with autism.

The characters who appear in the game are the player (who plays as a teacher and is the main character); Naresyon, the facilitator; Teina, a typically developing child; and Asuya, a child with autism. A voice synthesizer is used to represent characters other than the player. Additionally, 3D models are used to represent Teina and Asuya.

Figure 1 shows a transition diagram for the serious game and for each chapter, and explains the structure of the serious game. In the prologue, the serious game is explained by Naresyon. The game scenario begins with the assumption that the main character is presenting a lesson on conversational implicature. In Chapters 1, 2, and 3, playing as an elementary school teacher, the player learns through conversation with Teina and Asuya how best to navigate dialogue that may include conversational implicatures. Each chapter consists of three parts: the scenes, a question, and an explanation. First, in the scenes, Teina and Asuya demonstrate that autism cannot understand conversational implicatures. Next, for the question, the player is asked to choose the appropriate way of speaking from three choices; the question is then answered through the subsequent development of the conversation. In the following explanation, the answer given to the question is explained to be correct or incorrect, using an illustration. If the user has made the right choice in response to the question, the system then proceeds to the next conversation; if the user has made a mistake, it

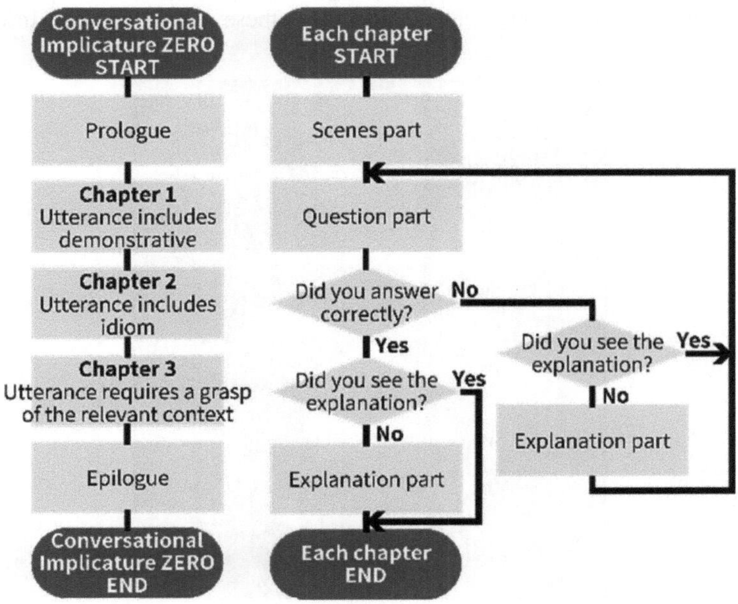

Fig. 1. Transition diagrams for the serious game and each chapter within this

returns to the question so that they can try again. In the epilogue, the serious game is reviewed by Naresyon.

The details of the three kinds of conversation are as follows. In Chapter 1, the initial utterance includes a demonstrative. The context of the conversation is a scene in which Asuya returns a novel to Teina. Specifically, Teina says to Asuya, "How was this novel?" in order to ask for her impression of the novel. Asuya cannot understand the meaning of the demonstrative and is unable to answer appropriately. Therefore, she misunderstands Asuya, and replies "You mean this novel is not interesting, isn't it." In Chapter 2, the initial utterance includes an idiom. The context of the conversation is a scene in which Teina is busy organizing prints. Teina addresses Asuya using an idiom, saying: "I want to borrow the hands of a cat" (a Japanese idiom meaning: "I need all the help I can get") in order to ask for assistance in sorting the prints. Asuya takes the idiom literally and searches for a cat. Chapter 3 illustrates a case in which an utterance requires a grasp of the context in order to be understood. The context of the conversation is that Teina is complaining of a dry throat. Teina then asks Asuya, "Excuse me. Could you please bring me some water?" In response, Asuya brings water, but as the implicature that Teina wants to drink the water is not conveyed, he scoops up water with his hands in order to bring it.

In addition to the dialogue, the most important feature of this serious game is its illustrated commentary, in which the dialogue between Teina and Asuya is visualized so that it can be understood intuitively. Specifically, Teina's utterances and Teina's and Asuya's thoughts are represented using speech bubbles. Additionally, those utterances and thoughts that successfully engage with Asuya's thinking are color-coded green, and those that do not do so are color-coded red. Figure 2 illustrates a case involving idiom, in which Teina makes statements using idioms indicating that she would like help with organizing the prints, while Asuya takes these idioms literally. In this way,

Fig. 2. Illustration of a scenario involving idiomatic expressions (Color figure online)

the illustrated commentary can help people to intuitively understand that there is a discrepancy in the conversation.

The second feature is the animation of the characters. The animations do not merely consist of movements representing each speaker; rather, by making the animations meaningful in relation to the content of the conversation, we allow the player to follow the content of the conversation not only based on the dialogue but also based on the animations, so that it becomes easier to understand and adds fun to the game.

The game was developed using the Unity 5 development environment, and runs on Windows 10.

4 Experimental Design, Methods, and Results

We examined whether this serious game was useful in teaching typically developing how to engage in dialogue by using definite meanings rather than conversational implicatures. The game's learning effects and players' motivation were evaluated. Additionally, this experiment evaluated the usefulness of the meaningful animations used in the serious game.

Participants were 56 typically developing students (35 men and 21 women) from Hakodate Otani College and Future University Hakodate. To accurately verify the game's efficacy, we divided the participants into two groups, consisting of 19 participants who were experienced in communicating with autism (hereinafter referred to as the "relevant group") and 37 participants who were not experienced in communicating with autism (hereinafter referred to as the "not relevant group"). In addition, we allocated 5 participants from the relevant group and 11 participants from the not relevant group to a group who saw animations meaningful to the conversational content (hereinafter referred to as the "meaningful animation group") and allocated the other 14 participants from the relevant group and 26 participants from the not relevant group to a group who saw only simple animations (hereinafter referred to as the "simple animation group").

A pre-test was carried out to measure participants' initial abilities to choose appropriate utterances in cases that could involve conversational implicatures. We prepared two questions, each with three response options, based on cases in which autism have difficulty understanding what is meant. In scoring the test, 50 points were awarded per correctly answered question, with a total possible score of 100 points. After participants had played the serious game, we carried out a post-test that took the same form as the pre-test, and measured the learning effect by comparing pre-test and post-test scores. Finally, a questionnaire was administered, in which participants were asked to respond on a scale of 1 to 5 to the following questions: "Was the game interesting?", "Will it benefit you?", "Do you want to play it again?" and "Do you want to use this serious game in the future?". Possible responses on the 5-point scale and their scores were as follows: "I very much think so" (5 points), "I think so" (4 points), "I cannot say either way" (3 point), "I do not think so" (2 points), and "I do not think so at all" (1 point).

The results were as follows. First, Table 1 shows the results of the pre- and post-tests in percentages. Among participants in the not relevant group, average scores were as follows: those in the simple animation group scored an average of 69.2 points in the pre-test and 98.0 points in the post-test, while those in the meaningful animation group scored an average of 72.7 points in the pre-test and 95.5 points in the post-test. Thus, the average score in both groups rose by more than 20 points.

Table 1. Results of pre-test and post-test

Group		Pre-test result		Post-test result	
		Incorrect answer (%)	All correct answer (%)	Incorrect answer (%)	All correct answer (%)
Simple motion	Relevant	7.10	92.90	0.00	100.00
	Not relevant	57.70	42.30	3.80	96.20
Meaningful motion	Relevant	20.00	80.00	0.00	100.00
	Not relevant	54.50	45.50	9.10	90.90

Next, Table 2 shows the average score and standard deviation for each questionnaire item, and the proportion of participants scoring 4 or more points. To analyze these results, an independent t-test was conducted. First, the difference between the simple animation sub-group and the meaningful animation sub-group of the not relevant group in their responses to the question "Will it benefit you?" was significant at the 5% level, $t(35) = 2.04$, $p < .05$. Next, among participants who had given incorrect answers in the pre-test, the difference between the simple animation group and the meaningful animation group in their responses to the question "Do you want to play it again?" indicated a significant trend at the 10% level, $t(21) = 1.76$, $p < .1$. There were no other significant differences or trends.

Table 2. Result of each questionnaire item

Group		Was the game interesting?			Will it benefit you?			Do you want to play it again?			Do you want to use this serious game in the future?		
		M	SD	4 points or more (%)	M	SD	4 points or more (%)	M	SD	4 points or more (%)	M	SD	4 points or more (%)
Simple motion	Relevant	4.29	0.47	100.00	4.36	0.63	92.90	3.64	1.08	35.70	4.00	0.96	71.40
	Not relevant	3.42	0.90	53.80	3.85	0.92	53.80	2.96	1.04	38.40	3.96	0.82	38.50
Meaningful motion	Relevant	3.20	2.05	60.00	3.20	1.64	60.00	2.60	1.34	40.00	4.60	0.55	100.00
	Not relevant	3.82	0.98	81.80	4.45	0.52	100.00	2.55	1.44	36.40	4.00	0.77	90.90

5 Discussion

As described above, the percentage of participants giving all-correct answers in both the simple animation and the meaningful animation sub-groups of the not relevant group was less than 50% in the pre-test, and 90% in the post-test. Additionally, with regard to average scores, both sub-groups increased their scores by more than 20 points. The large change between pre- and post-test scores among the not relevant group demonstrates that this game induced a very strong learning effect in those who did not have the pre-existing ability to converse with autism. Additionally, with regard to the learning effect, there was no difference between the simple animation and meaningful animation sub-groups of the not relevant group, and learning effects were observed in both groups. Based on this finding, this serious game can be regarded as a useful tool for typically developing to learn how to engage in dialogue that successfully conveys their meaning to others.

However, the results for the questionnaire item “Will it benefit you?” showed that among participants in the not relevant group, the benefits of the learning effect were clearer to those in the meaningful animation sub-group. For this item, the difference between the mean scores of these two sub-groups was found by a t-test to be significant at the 5% level; in other words, the difference between the mean score of 3.85 for the simple animation sub-group and the mean score of 4.45 for the meaningful animation sub-group of the not relevant group can be said to generalize to the population. This indicates that meaningful animation is a more effective means of learning than simple animation for those who are not experienced in communicating with autism.

Additionally, for the questionnaire item “Do you want to play it again?”, the proportion of participants scoring 4 points or more was low in both the simple animation and meaningful animation sub-groups of the not relevant group, and the average score was also less than 3 points, indicating that neither group wanted to play the game again. Furthermore, among participants who had given incorrect answers in the pre-test, the difference between the simple animation group and the meaningful animation group in their responses to this question was found by a t-test to represent a significant trend at the 10% level. In other words, it can be said that the difference between the average score of 3.13 for the simple animation group and the average score of 2.29 for the meaningful animation group is also likely to generalize to the population. However, since a learning effect was observed in the results of the pre and post-tests, the serious game was an effective means of learning for those who had no experience in communicating with autism. That is, in the general population, it is possible for people who do not have the ability to communicate with autism, or knowledge about conversation, including conversational implicatures, before playing this serious game, to learn an appropriate way of conversing with autism in a short period of time.

6 Conclusion

In this study, we attempted to solve the problem of interpersonal relationships between typically developing and autism in relation to conversational implicatures, through the development of a serious game to help users learn the most appropriate way of conversing. As a result, the learning effect of typically developing who are not involved with autism was remarkable. Additionally, by using meaningful animations, we were able to improve the motivation of the typically developing users to play the game.

Acknowledgments. We thank University of Miyagi research associate Yosuke Hashimoto for his cooperation in conducting this experiment and research advice. In addition, we thank the students of Future University Hakodate and Hakodate Otani College who participated in the experiment.

References

1. Uchiyama, T.: Do you know Asperger syndrome?. Tokyo Autistic Association (2002). (in Japanese)
2. Oi, M.: Interpersonal compensation for pragmatic impairments in Japanese children with Asperger syndrome or high-functioning autism. J. Multiling. Commun. Disord. **3**(3), 203–210 (2005)
3. Frith, U.: Unlock the mystery of autism, Tokyo bookscript (1991). (in Japanese)
4. Mitchell, P., Saltmarsh, R., Russell, H.: Overly literal interpretations of speech in autism: understanding that messages arise from minds. J. Child Psychol. Psychiat. **38**(6), 685–691 (1997)
5. Human Academy: Japanese Language Education Textbook Japanese Language Educational Ability Examination Test 50 Order Glossary. Sho sang (2013). (in Japanese)
6. Paul, R., Cohen, D.: Comprehension of indirect requests in adults with autistic disorders and mental retardation. J. Speech Hear. Res. **28**, 475–479 (1985)
7. McTear, M.F., Conti-Ramsden, G.: Pragmatic Disability in Children. Whurr Publishers, London (1992)
8. Baltaxe, C.A.M.: Pragmatic deficits in the language of autistic adolescents. J. Pediat. Psychol. **2**(4), 176–180 (1977)
9. Yamamoto, J., Kusumoto, T.: Development and support of closed-spectrum spectrum disorder. Cogn. Stud. **14**(4), 621–639 (2007). (in Japanese)
10. Tanaka, T., Fujiwara, S.: Books that understand and raise children with Autism Spectrum. Gakken Plus (2016). (in Japanese)
11. Prensky, M.: Digital Game-Based Learning. McGraw-Hill, New York (2001)
12. Yabuki, K., Sumi, K.: A study on serious games that supports conversation including meaning of autism with autistic persons. In: Hokkaido Symposium on Information Processing, pp. 23–27 (2016). (in Japanese)
13. Yabuki, K., Sumi, K.: A study on serious games that supports conversation including meaning of autism with autistic persons. Inst. Word Eng. **53**, 25–44 (2017). (in Japanese)
14. Yabuki, K., Sumi, K.: Conversational implicature ZERO: serious game to learn how to speak properly with autistic people. In: DICOMO 2017, vol. 53, pp. 2–44 (2017). (in Japanese)
15. Gray, C.: Comic Strip Conversation. Future Horizons Inc., Arlington (1994)
16. Japan Autism Spectrum Society (ed.): Autism Spectrum Dictionary. Educational Publishing (2015). (in Japanese)
17. Yoshii, K., Nakano, S., Nagasaki, T.: Support for development of clarification request as a function of restoration of conversation for autistic children - development of clarification requirement expression type, role of joint action routine, functional relationship between expression of clarification request and understanding intention understanding focus. Special Educ. Res. **53**(1), 1–13 (2015). (in Japanese)

User Experience Research and Practice of Gamification for Driving Training

Lvjie She[1], Jinsong Fan[1(✉)], and Mingliang Cao[2]

[1] School of Mechanical and Electrical Engineering, Foshan University, Foshan 528000, Guangdong, China
691784516@qq.com
[2] Guangdong Academy of Research on Virtual Reality Industry, Foshan University, Foshan 528000, Guangdong, China

Abstract. In recent years, with the development of computer science and graphics technology, the Gamification of training industry has become increasingly prosperous. The virtual driving training system in this paper takes the post-90s Chinese youth as the main research object, studies their social environment condition, work habits, cultural background and value identity change trend, using qualitative investigation method and quantitative experimental method, to record and analysis the users' emotional changes. Finally, applying the theory and method of cognitive psychology and situated learning, to make a comprehensive comparison and research on the user demand model and experimental data, and obtained the guidance criteria for the system development and evaluation.

Keywords: Virtual reality · Training gamification · Social cognition · User experience · Cognitive psychology

1 Introduction

Gamification training is a new education method which utilizes game mechanism and game thinking designed to provide professional training and simulation. In the information age, gaming training with the help of the electronic equipment and new media technology, created a sense of relaxed entertainment atmosphere, made the user subtly absorb knowledge in the process and internalized as their value pursuit and code of conduct.

With the development of computer graphics, electronic games have evolved from pixel levels, such as the first generation of Super Mario released by Nintendo in 1985, to the next-generation quality of 3D games, using such as mapping technology and particle system, in order to constantly improve the game's illusion and immersive [1]. In the late 20th century, electronic games on the theme of stimulus and violence began to be challenged. As a result of the widespread negative social impact, it has led people to explore games in a useful way, including serious games of rational education, artistic communication and users' study of aesthetic experience.

The "post-90s" youth group in China is a generation that has grown up with the development of information technology in China. They are available to accept various

A. El Rhalibi et al. (Eds.): Edutainment 2018, LNCS 11462, pp. 69–78, 2019.
https://doi.org/10.1007/978-3-030-23712-7_10

kind of game scenes and their metaphors, and addicted to the fun of the games. For the education and cultural industry, the rapid development of VR technology has also led to new narrative methods in order to gain new vitality. In the field of Gamification training virtual reality is welcomed by the broad audience. This paper mainly carried out related studies as follows:

- A user research, based on social cognitive theory, study their social environment condition, work habits, cultural background and value identity change trend,
- Designing the prototype system of Gamification for driving training, based on the cognitive psychology which characterized by information processing and situated learning,
- An evaluation experiment on the utility of the user experience.

2 Relevant Research Background and Overview

With the development of the living standards of Chinese residents, in 2012 there was an unprecedented peak of the number of driving training learners. After 2012, under the influence of the new syllabus and new standards, traffic congestion, air pollution as well as the bottleneck of driving caused by the pressure of examination, make the number of learners increase slowly. In view of the traditional training model is facing the shortage of space, the difference of teaching level of coaches and the conflict of students' learning time, and so on, the Gamification of driving training as an auxiliary tool has emerged. Guided by the core idea of "Edutainment", through the Gamification of driving training system, students can overcome psychological stress and learn independently from repeated mistakes.

2.1 Development of Gamification Training

The Gamification training follows the historical development of "Education game, Game-based learning, Serious game, Gamification". Since 1994, the United States military has established the world's first Gamification military training institution, they are committed to applying serious games such as the U.S Army to military training to make up for the fact that conventional training cannot simulate reality. Since 80 s of last century, China has begun to explore in related fields of education. After that, with the popularity of video and network, the game elements are more mature. In 2004, China Automobile Association promoted Professional driver as a serious game to popularize traffic safety knowledge.

In September 2017, American Express Company UPS training institutions launched Vive logistics chain training, provided an immersive virtual reality training environment for the driver. Through the Vive simulation training, drivers learn to identify and determine possible road danger in the daily delivery routes. On the other hand, VR create a vivid scene with the enjoyment in game mechanism, to increase the attractiveness of the user and enhance the training effect.

It can be seen that the storyline of the Gamification training with more detailed has won the favor of the users. Simultaneously, based on the real world, and integrating virtual game elements, players can participate in all kinds of alternate reality gaming, representing the latest trend in the development of Gamification training [2].

2.2 Social Cognitive Theory and User Modeling

The construction of cognitive learning path needs to start from the source of users' demands. According to Social Cognitive Theory proposed by famous social psychologist Bandura: There is an interaction between behavior (B), personality (P) and environment (E) [3]. The study of social cognition focuses on the process of social psychology, and with the further study of the integration of structure and process, expected to obtain a more rational explanation of the mechanisms and principles for the generation and development of social psychology [4] (Fig. 1).

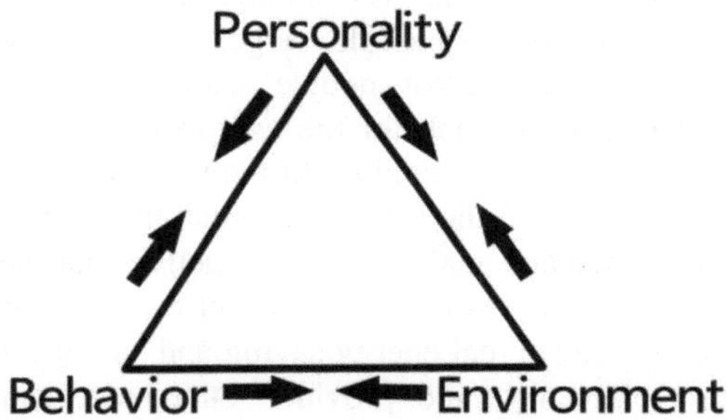

Fig. 1. Social cognition theory based on three elements interaction

China formally joined the Internet in 1994, entered a period of rapid development of information technology from 2000 to 2010. The 13th Five-Year Plan set forth the goal of deepening education modernization, education for all and lifelong education. Against this background, the user modeling of the post-90s in this paper is shown as follows:

- The post-90s' current life is not fully independent, influenced by the homogenization of education, the post-90's peer competition is stressful. In addition, due to the early acceptance of the Internet access to democratic education and the impact of multiculturalism, they have a critical spirit. They live in a period of social industry and economic transition, and more one-child family.
- On the other hand, the post-90s group is in the special period of virtual economic activity, social group differentiation, authoritative class digestion, and traditional cultural status being challenged. Compared with the previous generation's education concept presents multiple complex values [5, 6].
- Under the social environment of pursuit of economic benefits and time cost, the post-90s' demand for pure entertainment is reduced, and the demand for sense of personal achievement and personal identity is rising [7].

High speed development of economy and society, people are eager to be close to each other, but also aware of crisis of the future environment and resources, the post-90s' values is showed: (1) diversity pursue (2) practical and utilitarian (3) contradiction. Nevertheless, the post-90s' dependence on electronic devices is showed (1) the demand for frequent and personalized experience. (2) entertainment and leisure focused more on releasing pressure and relaxed learning atmosphere. (3) eager to interact with others.

Reconstructing the sense of belonging, that is, echoing the humanistic concern of the popular Travel Frog, grasping the emotional sustenance of the user. The above user research is integrated to explore the Gamification training's characteristics of (1) cultural value connotation (2) emotional attraction (3) ease and freedom.

3 System Framework Design

The virtual driving training system in the visual output module simulate the state of the scene module and the sound effect module, target users through the input device (sensor data acquisition) and the control module realize the real-time interaction, the system stores the related data feedback for the user to inquire, so as to discover the problem and achieve the real goal of training. In the process of realizing the function, carried out the main assessment of the training content and extract the key element to design the game, and collected and analyzed the interactive data. Iterative design on the basis of prototype system has a positive effect on optimization design. Virtual reality technology can be used to realize real energy saving and safe driving training, shorten training time, improve efficiency, and provide better safety and civilized driving training for the users (Fig. 2).

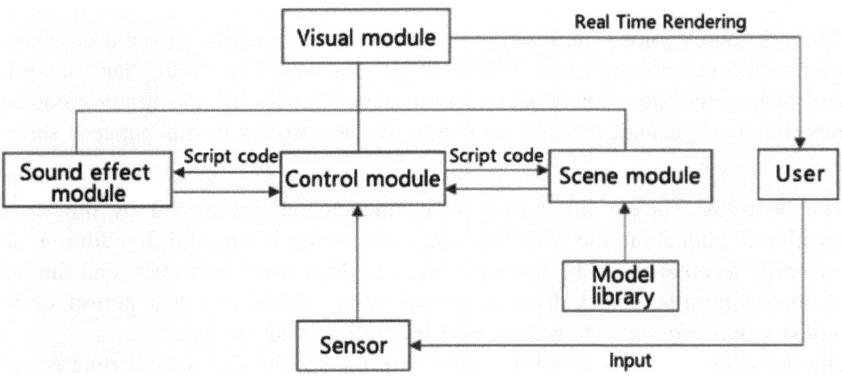

Fig. 2. System framework

3.1 Game Elements

The core of game element design is the mechanism of the game, mainly refers to the process and rhythm of experience, and the rules and logic of the game, it's also the key to creating successful games. The expressions of game element design are in the form of image text, sound effects, and interactive interfaces.

From macro to microcosmic, the conception of game elements is the goal, the content, the scene, the role, etc. Because Gamification training occupies a more fragmented time, the lightweight system design is more user-friendly. In addition, it should be detailed and a little bit uncertainty, brings interests and knowledge, makes the user smile and meet the user's imagination and expectation.

As Kenya Hara mentioned in White that "white" only exists in our perception of feelings. Therefore, we must not try to find "white", but to find a way to feel white [8]. Thus we can understand a kind of artistic conception that "white" conveys to us. It is silence and emptiness. Using this idea in the design of scene elements, we can grasp the subtle emotional changes in the process of users' experience, pay more attention to detail, express the natural emotion and the interest of being close to life in the design, let the user feel in the situation and learn in perception (Fig. 3).

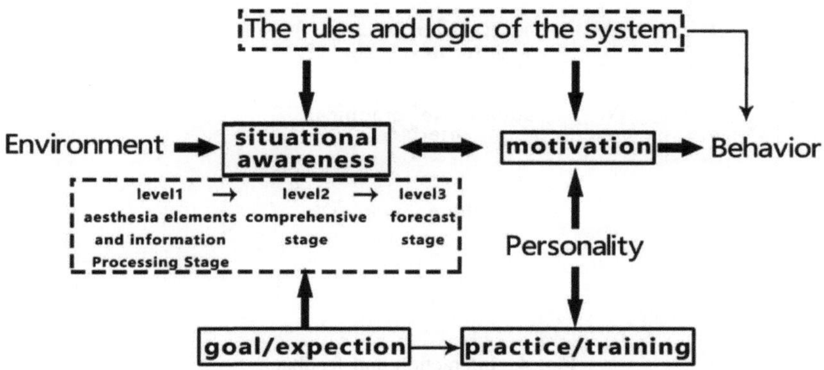

Fig. 3. The natural regression of game elements and the user training system under situational awareness

3.2 Feedback

Compared with the traditional user interface and popular Windows operating, the virtual training mechanism of human-computer interaction is different, in the user's operation, information release, information acquisition and transmission in the process of virtual reality environment experience can also access the third party ports other than the user's direct operation equipment. The interaction can be divided into the entity interaction between the terminal and the user. The user can observe the real-time driving state through the scene output of simulated driving, collide in the training ground, press the line and appear the driving behavior that does not meet the standard the system gives timely feedback, such as the reduction of life value, prompt information, collision sound effect and so on. The user can react through windows, icons, menus, etc. (Fig. 4).

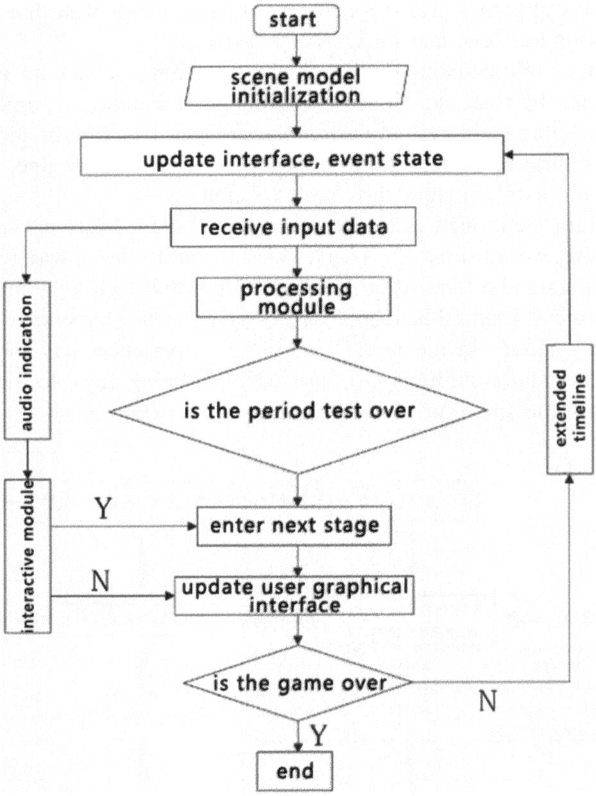

Fig. 4. Interaction and feedback

4 Experiment

The virtual driving training system combines the information tips required by the training function, the training instructions and the relaxed interest of the game. It mainly consists of two venues. The main venue is the training ground, which consists of four driving items in Subject two. Including side parking, right-angle turning, curve driving and reversing, users control the driving and steering of the vehicle through the keyboard, sensing the reference of the site and the distance between the speed and the driveway during the operation. In addition, we set up familiar streets and communities outside the main site for users to relax and explore.

In order to create a natural, relaxed atmosphere, the system has set up the natural birdsong sound, using the particle system to set the weather change from sunny to rainy days, users can see the mist diffuse, then transition to sunny days. Entering the system menu interface, the user can hear lively and exciting background music before starting the game, so as to arouse the user's eager mood and hear the car engine start up at the beginning. The user can simply switch the pause and start state during driving, view the information of improper operation and warning of violation of safe and civilized driving behavior, thereby deepening the user's understanding of driving. Once the training program in the training field is not qualified, the system will end with a pop-up game, and music will be played to encourage users to try the challenge again (Fig. 5).

Fig. 5. Scene: the weather

4.1 Demonstration

To test the system usability and the users' satisfaction and expectations, a corresponding questionnaire survey is made, and through the analysis results for the comprehensive assessment, the experimental results showed that the Gamification of virtual driving training system has a good use effectiveness. The pictures showed below are the users experience of the system in an exhibition center, and four representative user experiences are selected to illustrate (Fig. 6).

Through observation and conversation, the users have a high expectation of participation in the system, when they were told that the system was not racing driving games they were still very willing to try, the majority of the user experience for more than 15 min, easier to get started is one of the reason, the other is that users want to explore all the routes, even "the end of the world" is filled with anticipation, although these expectations deviate from the driving training content itself, but just inspired users explore driving, focus on how to avoid obstacles and go to the specific direction. The majority of users in the process can not help but sigh with emotion, one is a peculiar game scene layout and beyond the imagination of the users, the second reason is the interaction between users and peer cooperation, in originally designed to be relatively flat driving joined the task of human motivation and exploration, so as to attract more people's attention and further strengthen a sense of achievement and driving experience of users.

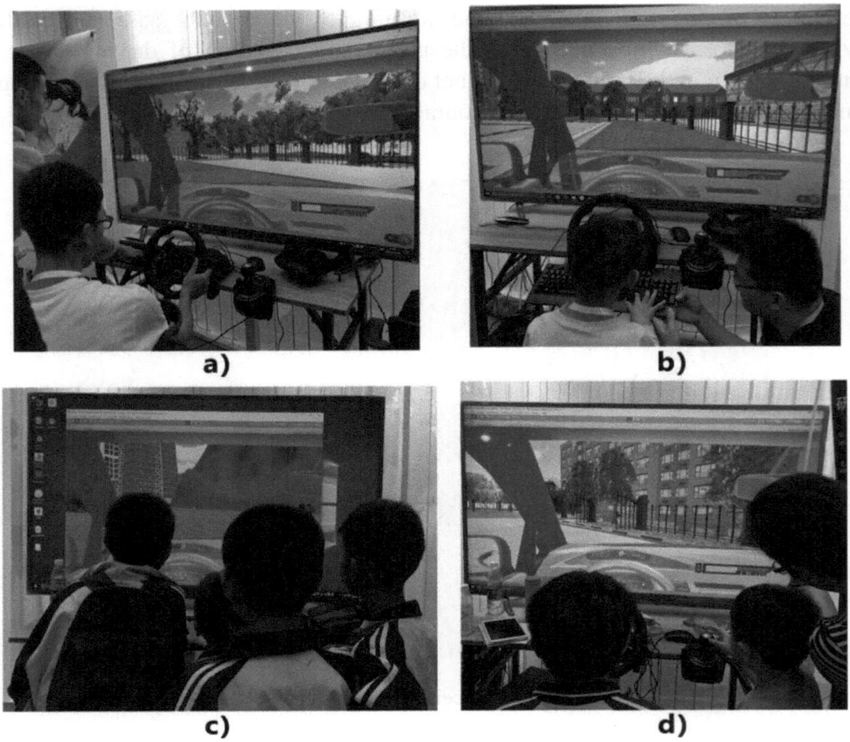

Fig. 6. Users experience of the system

4.2 Experience Assessment

Due to time limitation, only selected seven post-90s to participate in the users questionnaire, through the study of user experience measure [9] found the System Usability Scale (SUS), apply the quantitative evaluation method is more suitable for the test conditions, this method can obtain more accurate conclusions in the sample size of 6–8 people. The following table shows the good utility of the system from this user experience assessment. In addition, the highest score up to an average of 4.57 shows that the user's good impression assessment and the simplification of the system menu hierarchy which can indicate the availability and effectiveness of the system. The lowest two average score shows the users' evaluation of the technical and complexity of the system, which can validate the characteristics in the study of post-90s' growth environment (Table 1).

Table 1. Questionnaire for user experience.

Question	N	M	SD
I think I'm looking forward to using the system	7	4.29	0.756
I think I need technical support to use it	7	3.14	0.9
I found that the different functions in this system are preferably integrated	7	4	0.816
I think most people will soon learn to use it	7	4.29	0.756
I would like to use it again	7	4.14	0.9
The overall response to the system (awful-talent)	7	4	0.577
The overall response to the system (complex-simple)	7	3.86	0.69
The overall response to the system (lack of function-complete function)	7	4	0.816
The overall response to the system (boring-interesting)	7	4.14	0.69
The overall response to the system (stereotype-agile)	7	4.14	0.9
Screen (reading text: difficult-easy)	7	4.43	0.535
Screen (the simplification of the task: no-yes)	7	4.43	0.535
Screen (the organization of information: confusing-clear)	7	4.29	0.756
Screen (the menu hierarchy: confusing-clear)	7	4.57	0.535
Learning (learning of system goals: difficult-easy)	7	4.14	0.9
Learning (explore new feature by trying mistakes: difficult-easy)	7	4.14	0.9
Learning (interaction friendliness: the worst-the best)	7	4	0.816
Learning (tasks and goals: confusing-clear)	7	4.14	0.69
System capability (stability: the worst-the best)	7	4.43	0.535
The emotional experience after using the system tends to (negative-positive)	7	4.43	0.535
The impressions and memories after using the system tends to (fuzzy-clear)	7	4.57	0.535

5 Conclusion and Future Work

China is in a critical period of deepening education reform, applying Gamification to innovation education based on the traditional teaching mode has broad prospects for development. In fact, the Gamification is the integration of game design, game motivation, motivation psychology, behavioral economics, UX/UI, technology platform, and performance driven business systems [10]. Any form of art is not only aesthetic sense, but roots in the deeper implication of the cultural connotation, the cultural connotation will inspire the everlasting emotion in our heart.

Taking the post-90s Chinese as the research object, this paper analyzes and summarizes the user characteristics, value trends and psychological needs of the youth group through social cognitive analysis, and applies cognitive psychology and situational learning theory. A game based virtual driving training system is designed and implemented, and the following guiding principles are obtained:

- Clear system functions and goals;
- Game elements and game mechanism return to nature;
- Strengthening humanistic concern and cultural connotation;

Through the system quantitative evaluation table analysis of SUS, the practical results show that the system has good interactivity and good learning effect.

The natural and intelligent human-computer interaction is the development trend in the future, in the future to improve the validity and accuracy of the existing machine equipment, increase user mobility, make human-computer interaction more humanoid, with the help of computer and virtual display helmet, steering wheel and other external hardware and virtual environment integration for more effective interaction experience, explore the holographic information based on stereoscopic display, improves the intelligence of human-computer interaction, such as machine recognition etc. These will further improve the naturalization and immersion of human-computer interaction.

Acknowledgments. This work is supported by the Characteristics and Innovation Project of Guangdong University from Department of Education of Guangdong, China (No. 2016KTSCX148), and the 2016 Foshan Science and technology innovation project from the Science and Technology Bureau of Foshan, Guangdong, China (No. 2016AG100321).

References

1. Green, C.S., Bavelier, D.: Action video game modifies visual selective attention. Nature **423** (6939), 534–537 (2003)
2. Liu, D., Guo, J.: Review on the training mode of employee training based on game-based thinking. Hum. Resour. Dev. China (02), 89–96 (2017)
3. Bandura, A.: Social Foundations of Thought and Action. Prentice-Hall, Englewood Cliffs (1986)
4. Wang, G.: The first cause of emotion and cognition. Psychol. Dyn. (03), 33–38 (1995)
5. Wang, X.: Research on the network phenomenon of "post-80s and post-90s". Hunan University (2011)
6. Song, Z., Liu, W.: Analysis of China's information development process and its spatial and temporal pattern. Geogr. Sci. **33**(03), 257–265 (2013)
7. Jia, L.: Study on psychological characteristics of "post-90s" college students. South China University of Technology (2013)
8. Hara, K.: White. Guangxi Normal University Press (2012)
9. Albert, B., Tullis, T.: Measuring the User Experience (Interactive Technologies): Collecting, Analyzing, and Presenting Usability Metrics (2013)
10. Du, S: On the media and its significance to esthetic - art. Lit. Rev. 4 (2007)

Affective Interaction Technology of Companion Robots for the Elderly: A Review

Jin Wang[1], Tingting Liu[1], Zhen Liu[2(✉)], and Yanjie Chai[2]

[1] College of Science and Technology, Ningbo University, Yuxiu Road 505, Zhuangshi, Zhenhai, Ningbo 315212, Zhejiang, China
{wangjin2, liutingting}@nbu.edu.cn
[2] Faculty of Information Science and Engineering, Ningbo University, Fenghua Road 818, Jiangbei, Ningbo 315211, Zhejiang, China
{liuzhen, chaiyanjie}@nbu.edu.cn

Abstract. Aimed at the Chinese aging population, companion robots with entertainment and communication functions are popular and useful for the daily life of the elderly. To make robots more reliable and socially acceptable in real scenarios, a better affective interaction with intelligent emotions and adaptive behaviors of companion robots is needed. Through the listed status of human-robot interaction and learning models, the advantages and limitations of companion robots are shown distinctly. In the end, the problems that might exist in technical and ethical at present are proposed, in order to provide references for the further researches.

Keywords: Companion robot · Emotion · The elderly · Affective interaction

1 Introduction

Nowadays China's population is aging at an unprecedented level. As reported, the number of aged 60 or over in China is predicted to be increased into 248 million in 2020 in contrast to 229 million in 2016, which means the aging percentage of total population would grow from 16.6% to 17.2% only in four years [1]. With the intensification of domestic aging, how to accompany daily life of the elderly has become a major issue. In the last few years, the studies of companion robots have gradually become an advanced nursing method to solve the physical and mental health problem of the elderly.

Khosla and Chu proposed the design and implementation of a human-like assistive robot Matilda to improve the emotional wellbeing of the elderly in residential care facilities. Through multimodal communication capabilities, it could provide the elderly sensory enrichment and positively engage them in activities [2]. Gross et al. noticed that by companion of robot Max with health-related instrumental and social-emotional functions in their own homes, the seniors even established emotion with it [3]. With the extended social-force model and a social-aware navigation framework, the robot could deal with real scenarios, which enables it to accompany people for a walk [4].

A. El Rhalibi et al. (Eds.): Edutainment 2018, LNCS 11462, pp. 79–83, 2019.
https://doi.org/10.1007/978-3-030-23712-7_11

2 Interactions Between Human and Robot

To improve the quality of accompany, the interaction between human and companion robots should be attractive, meaningful and reliable.

To attract people's attention and promote their movement capability and spatial awareness, the robot Puffy identified people's gestures, movements, facial expressions, emotions and their relational intentions and provided multi-sensory, engaging experiences [5]. As the interview revealed that the elderly preferred a relative smaller size of humanoid companion robot, Karim et al. suggested to design a robot, which can simulate feeling of closeness to child or friends [6].

Furthermore, the approach proposed by Zsiga et al. indicated, that with the voice in natural language and the touch screen display, the companion robot was acceptable to the elderly even without computer experience before. For the seniors alone at home, the most useful and the most frequently used functions were the verbal communication and entertainment respectively [7].

In order to be more socially acceptable and reliable, robots need to have more social behaviors, such as express intentions and emotions. Compare with human–human interaction, human–animal interaction is much simpler and it has many similarities with human–robot interaction. Lakatos attempted to investigate human–pet interaction by designing robots with pet-like embodiments. The result showed that the dog-inspired social behavior was an effective medium for letting people willingly to attribute inner states and intentions to a robot. Furthermore, with the experiment of dog–robot interaction turned out that the social level in robots was necessary for achieving reliable and socially acceptable behaviors [8].

3 Learning Model of Companion Robots

With various and continuously improved learning models, companion robots are becoming more and more intelligent and adaptive in social behavior and environmental changing.

In order to make the robot behavior more adaptive and personality, Karami et al. referred an architecture with two learning algorithms that learns the preferences of users through their feedback during interaction based on Markov decision process models (MDP). According to the results of experiments with real users, the algorithm with generalization was more time efficient for fine-tuning adaptivity capabilities of the robot compared to the direct algorithm. Specifically, this algorithm tended to generalize the adaptation knowledge obtained from past interaction experiences to first-time users and unknown situations [9].

With a hybrid, deep neural network model consists of CNN and SOM, the neuro-inspired companion robot NICO was able to learn perception of different expressions and person-specific associations between perceived emotions and the robot's facial expressions to adapt to personal nuances [10].

Fear learning has been a forceful source of inspiration to exploit more flexible and adaptive artificial intelligence. Based on fear-learning model of the human brain, Rizzi et al. indicated situation-aware fear learning (SAFEL) model to learn complex temporal patterns of sensed environmental stimuli and create a representation of these patterns. Experiments with a NAO robot using SAFEL revealed that fear-conditioning behavior can be generated with predictive capabilities according to situational information. With the prediction of undesirable or threatening situations according to the past experiences, it would offer robots the opportunity to react and avoid unpleasant even harmful situations. Therefore, the adaptative capability of environmental changing would be increased [11].

4 Emotion Expression of Companion Robots

In order to have a better affective interaction, the accuracy and intelligence of emotion expression with behaviors of companion robots would be important.

Throughout three experiments, Beck et al. proved that body language was an appropriate medium for a robot to display emotions. In order to improve the expressiveness of humanoid robots, an affect space for body expressions would be used. By comparing the interpretation of emotional body language displayed by humans and agents as the first experiment, both interpreted in a similar way according to recognition. The second approach confirmed that the interpretation could be accurately with the expression of the key poses. And the head position expression was especially important to human. The third study indicated the possibility of emotion expression caused by blending key poses along a continuous model of emotions. However, the precise position in the affect space of the generated expressions still demands to be explicitly estimated [12].

For the improvement of the robots' cognitive and behavior systems, Chumkamon et al. proposed a framework of the biologically inspired CONBE robot based on topological consciousness and adaptive resonance theory. Using the TopoART-R as the learning system, the robot could learn autonomously for new patterns of emotion and behavior. The emotion of the robot generated from the motivation modeled by its memory and outside state. Results of experiments showed, that with providing the expressions reflecting its emotional intelligence based on the human's facial expression and affective inner state under face-to-face situation, the interaction between human and robot is natural with social sympathy and empathy functions [13].

5 Affection Towards Companion Robots

With the appropriate emotion expression, the affection between companion robots and the human beings, especially the lonesome seniors, can be easily set up and deserve to be concerned. A companion robot can be human-like or nonhuman-like. As man's best friends, dogs always accompany people by side and are treated as a family member. Companion robots as social partners for people should be treated similarly logically. In fact, peoples' attitude towards companion robots was much more negative than expected according to the research of Konok et al. Most people thought that robots cannot be loved as much as dogs. The mainly reasons are the robots at the moment still have limitations on lifelikeness, emotion expression and social personality. And the perceived dangerousness has also a great influence on people's attitude toward robots. Instead, a household robot was more preferred. Only a minority of participants wanted the humanoid robot because of the language communication. According to the questionnaires, having emotions, personality and showing attachment are the most frequently mentioned advantages of dogs [14]. By avoiding evoking an "Uncanny Valley" experience with the increasingly improved affective interaction, these qualities would be better achieved in a companion robot step by step in the foreseeable future.

Ethically with established intimately relationship between continually evolved companion robots, the elderly would like to have more affective interaction with them, while it can provide more physically and mentally health care as well as a happier and less lonely mood to them. However, it might cause the seniors spending less time on communicating and contacting with the real society. And to a certain extent, a private companion robot might interfere with the privacy and freedom of the elderly more or less. These potential problems should be noticed and solved as far as possible.

6 Challenge and Expectation

All in all, companion robots should have intelligent emotions and social behaviors with learning models that technically more intricately in the years ahead. Although ethically affective interaction between companion robots especially humanoid robots and the elderly still might be a challenge for the moment, the development and the application of human-robot interaction is an unalterable trend. With rapidly developed technology and learning models, the social acceptance will be no doubt increased and companion robots will be widely applicated, particularly for the elderly in the foreseeable future.

7 Conclusion

Based on the summery of the mentioned studies in this paper, it shows a huge demand and research space of companion robots for the elderly those who easily feels lonesome. Companion robots with intelligent emotions and social behaviors can provide mentally console as well as physically healthcare to the elderly through affective interaction. Thus, companion robots with entertainment and communication functions for the elderly as a high-tech with huge social concern, are important in solving aging problem and making contribute to build a harmonious society.

Acknowledgments. This work was sponsored by the project of Medical and Health Science and Technology Plan in Zhejiang (2017PY027).

References

1. Zhiyan Consultancy Group: 2017–2022 Strategic Research Report of Analyzing and Investing in the Status of China's Pension Industry (2016)
2. Khosla, R., Chu, M.T.: Embodying care in Matilda: An affective communication robot for emotional wellbeing of older people in Australian residential care facilities. ACM Trans. Manag. Inf. Syst. **4**, 1–33 (2013)
3. Gross, H.M., et al.: Robot companion for domestic health assistance: implementation, test and case study under everyday conditions in private apartments. In: International Conference on Intelligent Robots and Systems, pp. 5992–5999 (2015)
4. Ferrer, G., Zulueta, A.G., Cotarelo, F.H., Sanfeliu, A.: Robot social-aware navigation framework to accompany people walking side-by-side. Auton. Robots **41**, 775–793 (2017)
5. Gelsomini, M., et al.: Puffy - an inflatable mobile interactive companion for children with Neurodevelopmental Disorders. In: 2017 CHI Conference Extended Abstracts on Human Factors in Computing Systems, pp. 2599–2606 (2017)
6. Karim, H.A., Lokman, A.M., Redzuan, F.: Older adults perspective and emotional respond on robot interaction. In: 4th International Conference on User Science and Engineering, pp. 95–99 (2016)
7. Zsiga, K., Tóth, A., Pilissy, T., Péter, O., Dénes, Z., Fazekas, G.: Evaluation of a companion robot based on field tests with single older adults in their homes. Assist. Technol. **30**, 259–266 (2017)
8. Lakatos, G.: Dogs as behavior models for companion robots: how can human-dog interactions assist social robotics? IEEE Trans. Cogn. Dev. Syst. **9**, 234–240 (2017)
9. Karami, A.B., Sehaba, K., Encelle, B.: Adaptive artificial companions learning from users' feedback. Adapt. Behav. **24**, 69–86 (2016)
10. Churamani, N., Kerzel, M., Strahl, E., Barros, P., Wermter, S.: Teaching emotion expressions to a human companion robot using deep neural architectures. In: 2017 International Joint Conference on Neural Networks, pp. 627–634 (2017)
11. Rizzi, C., Johnson, C.G., Fabris, F., Vargas, P.A.: A situation-aware fear learning (SAFEL) model for robots. Neurocomputing **221**, 32–47 (2017)
12. Beck, A., Stevens, B., Bard, K.A., Cañamero, L.: Emotional body language displayed by artificial agents. ACM Trans. Interact. Intell. Syst. **2**, 1–29 (2012)
13. Chumkamon, S., Hayashi, E., Koike, M.: Intelligent emotion and behavior based on topological consciousness and adaptive resonance theory in a companion robot. Biol. Inspired Cogn. Archit. **18**, 51–67 (2016)
14. Konok, V., Korcsok, B., Miklósi, Á., Gácsi, M.: Should we love robots? – the most liked qualities of companion dogs and how they can be implemented in social robots. Comput. Hum. Behav. **80**, 132–142 (2018)

Gamification Strategies for an Introductory Algorithms and Programming Course

Diego Fernando Loaiza Buitrago[1], Luis Alejandro Álvarez[1], Carlos Marquez[1], Diego Fernando Duque[1], Yana Saint-Priest[1], Patricia Segovia[1], and Andres A. Navarro-Newball[2(✉)]

[1] Universidad Santiago de Cali, Cali, Colombia
{diego.loaiza02, luis.alvarez01, carlos.marquez00, diego.duque01, yana.saint-priest00, pasego}@usc.edu.co
[2] Pontificia Universidad Javeriana, Cali, Colombia
anavarro@javerianacali.edu.co

Abstract. We present a proposal for the application of gamification strategies to an introductory course in algorithms and programming, which is aimed at different university engineering programs. The purpose of the course is that students acquire skills in the development of algorithms and their implementation in a programming language to solve problems in various domains. The activities proposed for the course rely mainly on a platform which allows the presentation and evaluation of these activities. Performance in the field is low, with a rather high failure rate. Our purpose is to propose some gamification strategies in the classroom, based on mechanisms implemented both in the platform and in a mobile application that could serve as support for the course.

Keywords: Gamification · Learning management systems · Algorithms and programming courses

1 Introduction

Gamification, understood as the application of mechanisms and activities of games to environments where entertainment is not the main objective, has matured over the years with its widespread use [1]. It has been extensively used in educational environments or online communities, with some success [2–5]. For example, Khan Academy [2] has a wide offer of online courses, including programming languages. Here, strategies and mechanisms typical of video games are used so that apprentices have feedback on their progress and teachers can create courses in which these mechanisms can be used. One of the most relevant features of the courses in Khan Academy is the continuous feedback: the apprentice can see his/her progress and the proposed learning path, with the option to restart each exercise to accomplish the objectives. The SoloLearn [4] platform works via web and in mobile devices. The platform offers programing courses and code playgrounds where apprentices can tinker with existent code, upload their own codes and get downvotes or upvotes from the community. In these programming courses, the apprentice takes short tests for self-evaluation and receives rewards (badges).

A. El Rhalibi et al. (Eds.): Edutainment 2018, LNCS 11462, pp. 84–87, 2019.
https://doi.org/10.1007/978-3-030-23712-7_12

2 Algorithms and Programming Introductory Course Status

The course is offered to the different programs of the faculty of engineering and is structured around general and specific competences, from which the objectives, activities and evaluations have been built. The content of the course and the different evaluative activities are offered through an LMS (Learning Management System), which requires proper authentication into the platform by the student. In addition to evaluative activities, short training evaluations that serve as preparation are offered. To date, no course of the faculty of engineering has implemented gamification strategies in the LMS or outside it.

Some main thematic areas have been proposed, and the course is structured in such a way that the complexity of the concepts increases as the course progresses and revolves around the competences that the students must acquire, so they can be graded with the evaluations. The course is evaluated through some exams performed in the LMS, with some short practice tests taking place once or twice in each week, therefore, the use of the platform is important. In a model based on credit hours, the course demands at least 6 h per week of autonomous work from the student, much of which is offered in online material through the LMS.

Based on the course's teachers own studies, there is data on the averages and the reprobation rate in the periods from 2012A to 2017A, which shows that during the 2016A period there is a peak in the latter indicator, with a downward trend in the 2017A period. There is no data on the rate of failure from the 2012 to 2013B period. However, it can be noted that the average of grades shows a decrease in the 2016B period, even though the rate of reprobation presents a tendency to the low. Although there is no accurate data on the dropout rate, the teachers of the course say that it is around 50%, which is significantly high. The LMS offers up-to-date statistics of the student's accesses to the platform. Here, it's been evident that students usually spend only a couple of hours per week in the platform, including reading of the material and tests preparation.

3 Design and Implementation of the Gamification Strategies

User studies were carried out through focus groups and one online survey (90 students sample), to obtain some important aspects of the learning process, such as the causes of the scarce participation in the activities in the LMS. Two focus groups were used, with 8–12 students in each one, in one and hour and a half sessions. The key questions were: Do you consider important the learning of algorithms and programming languages for your career? Do you spend enough time in the LMS platform to review the material and make the training tests? Do you consider the way the course is structured in the LMS helps you to learn the material, achieve the learning objectives and finally get a good grade?

The answers showed that students consider the course important but can't find a connection with their disciplines. Most of them don't consider the platform engaging enough to spend time in it. They state that feedback of most of the activities is neither clear nor "useful" to them. It can be deduced that activities must be focused in problem solving, with richer content that favors student engagement. Finally, the feedback frequency and quality must be improved.

Besides that, the survey shows that 71.4% of students spend from 0 to 2 h weekly playing videogames, 18.7% spend from 3 to 10, and 9.9% spend more than 10 h. Regarding genre preferences, the survey shows that 25.3% prefer action and adventure-themed games, 17.6% strategy games, 14.3% casual games, 4% puzzle-like games and the rest prefer simulation games, MMORPG, shooter and other genres. Only 4% say they don't play at all. Survey also shows a significant tendency to use videogames to socialize and share, in a greater extent, and to compete and improve their own abilities.

About the use of additional technology in the classroom, the survey shows that 56% use it to reinforce class material, 93% of these technologies correspond to video tutorials, 37% use online forums, discussion groups and social networks and 52% use additional teaching material, like downloadable material.

As a b-learning course, the algorithms and programming introductory course is supported on independent work, so the strategies suggested cover both the use of the LMS and a mobile app for the in-the-classroom and out-the-classroom activities, taking advantage of some technologies not offered in the LMS such as streaming and richer content as videogames. All of them are oriented to the engagement and motivation of the student, with a strong component of meaningful feedback to allow them to track their progress and help them to achieve the learning objectives.

The gamification strategies proposed look forward to accomplishing the objectives of the course and are based on the course performance data extracted from the LMS, the evaluations and supported by the results obtained from the survey. One of the objectives is to increase the engagement of students with the activities proposed on the platform. According to [6], in the design of optimal environments for learning, some of the characteristics to be considered, together with the subjective experience that supports them are: meaningful and timely feedback to help the perception of learning and the construction of skills, added to a clearer statement of the goals in order to help the student to focus his/her efforts, and mechanisms that help build positive relationships with the peers and teachers. These characteristics will serve to implement mechanics such as: (1) "clues" that clarify the student the task to be performed; (2) constant feedback of the result of the executed task, for example, users should know when the task has been completed and that the feedback is in accordance with the expectation [7] (e.g. a reward system related to the level of difficulty); (3) use of "avatars" and "characters" that guide the experience and help the student handle more emotional responses to the mechanics [7]; (4) recognition for participation in the forums, interaction with peers and leadership boards, which help to exploit the social characteristic present in the players.

Since the main purpose is to implement most of the strategies in the LMS platform, we will use the open standard OpenBadges for handling mechanics such as badges [8], and the SCORM standard (Sharable Content Object Reference Mode) to create interactive content for the different activities of the course, whether they involve evaluation or not. Similarly, given that this standard allows communication with the LMS via JavaScript, the possibility of using HTML 5 for the development of this interactive content is being studied. Additionally, for some independent and complementary activities, we will develop a mobile application for mechanics such as videogames, content sharing, chats or social-network-like features that are difficult to implement in the LMS platform due to technical limitations.

4 Discussion and Future Work

Despite no game mechanics were implemented on the initial user studies, we believe it is important to include more dynamic content (e.g. video games and multimedia) to increase the student's participation in the independent and in-classroom activities through a mobile app and the LMS. We also believe that through timely and constant feedback, the proposed system may allow reach the proposed learning objectives.

Acknowledgements. This project is funded by the Universidad Santiago de Cali (project internal code DGI-COCEIN-N°. 613-621116-A08).

References

1. Zicherman, D., Cunningham, C.: Gamification by Design, 1st edn. O'Reilly Media, Sebastopol (2011)
2. Khan Academy. https://www.khanacademy.org/
3. Code.Org. https://code.org/
4. SoloLearn. https://www.sololearn.com/
5. Bartle, R.: Hearts, clubs, diamonds, spades: players who suit MUDs. J. MUD Res. **1**, 19 (1996)
6. Shernoff, D.: Optimal Learning Environments to Promote Student Engagement. Springer, New York (2013). https://doi.org/10.1007/978-1-4614-7089-2
7. Allanwood, G., Beare, P.: Design of User Experience, 1st edn. Bloomsbury, London (2015)
8. Prakash, E., Rao, M.: Transforming Learning and IT Management Through Gamification. Springer, Heidelberg (2015). https://doi.org/10.1007/978-3-319-18699-3

Graphics, Imaging and Applications

Structure Reconstruction of Indoor Scene from Terrestrial Laser Scanner

Xiaojuan Ning[1(✉)], Jie Ma[1], Zhiyong Lv[1], Qingzheng Xu[2], and Yinghui Wang[1]

[1] Institute of Computer Science and Engineering, Xi'an University of Technology, Xi'an, China
fly-snow2001@163.com
[2] College of Information and Communication, National University of Defense Technology, Xi'an, China

Abstract. Indoor scene reconstruction from point cloud data provided by Terrestrial laser scanning (TLS) has become an issue of major interest in recent years. However, the raw scanned indoor scene is always complex with severe noise, outliers and incomplete regions, which produces more difficulties for indoor scene modeling. In this paper, we presented an automatic approach to reconstruct the structure of indoor scene from point clouds acquired by registering several scans. Our method first extracts different candidate walls by separating the indoor scene into different planes based on normal variation. Then the boundary of those candidate walls are obtained by projecting them onto 2D planes. We classify the walls into exterior wall and interior wall by clustering. After distinguishing the 3D points belonging to exterior walls, a simple strategy is generated to refine the 3D model of wall structure. The methodology has been tested on three real datasets, which constitute of different varieties of indoor scenes. The results derived reveal that the indoor scene could be correctly extracted and modeled.

1 Introduction

Three-dimensional reconstruction of indoor scenes has received more attention due to its wide applications in building information modeling, indoor mapping and navigation, robot route planning, and managing building maintenance [1–4]. Compared with other scenes, 3D modeling of indoor scenes of buildings can be applied to fire rescue, secret-chamber exploration and archaeological excavation. However, in recent years, due to the existence of all kinds of occlusion objects or dramatic illumination changes in the buildings indoor scenes, interior scenes reconstruction has become a challenging problem.

As the geometry of indoor scene often differs from the original plans, it is a common need to reconstruct an accurate 3D model of the interior scene. Such reconstruction is often a manual or semi-automatic time-consuming process. It is necessary to provide an automatic process to reconstruct the indoor scene. Indoor scene can be collected by terrestrial laser scanning (TLS). The TLS scanner is normally equipped onto a tripod to scan a portion of the indoor scene on each

A. El Rhalibi et al. (Eds.): Edutainment 2018, LNCS 11462, pp. 91–98, 2019.
https://doi.org/10.1007/978-3-030-23712-7_13

Fig. 1. 3D indoor scene in point clouds from Berkeley dataset

station. Therefore, a large scene can be covered by a set of scanning from different viewpoints. It provides a large amount of accurate data in a very fast way and with a high level of detail, as shown in Fig. 1.

In this paper, we provide a simple and fast modeling pipeline for recovering the structure of indoor scene. Our pipeline considers as input data a set of 3D point clouds and produces as output a set of polyhedra representing the boundaries of the rooms in the environment. Our work is mainly to reconstruct the structure of indoor scene without considering the details (e.g. windows, small cavities and protrusions in the walls).

Our pipeline contains two main stages: (1) **Detection of planar regions** The indoor scene is first decomposed into planar regions to determine the candidate wall, ceiling and ground. (2) **Boundary-based structure modeling**. The candidate wall is first detected and the boundary of each candidate wall between point cloud is analyzed accurately, and then a method of structure reconstruction of indoor scene point cloud is proposed.

In this paper, a state of the art of the process which consists in the modeling the indoor scene from point clouds is analyzed in Sect. 2. In Sect. 3, we detail the full description of the proposed pipeline which considers indoor point clouds as input. The pipeline is presented and the two parts of the approach, namely the detection of planar elements point clouds and the 3D reconstruction of walls are detailed. The assessment of our approach is then considered in Sect. 4. Datasets and efficiency used for the assessment are presented and results of both parts of the approach are shown. Finally, the future works are proposed and new trends for further indoor scene modeling are discussed in Sect. 5.

2 Related Work

In recent years, the acquisition technology of point cloud data has been changing rapidly, from Kinect of small range scanning to laser scanner which can quickly scan large areas. Because of its ability to guide and facilitation for human production activities, 3D reconstruction has been widely concerned in researchers [5]. The building area measurement based on three-dimensional laser scanning technology can greatly reduce the complexity and error of manual measurement. In contrast to the outdoor scene reconstruction, indoor scene reconstruction should be more precise to provide more help which is particularly significant. Many researchers have studied the reconstruction of scene interiors and exteriors from image [6], RGBD [7], range image [8] and point cloud data [2]. In this paper, our work mainly focused on the modeling of indoor environments from point clouds. It requires other methods and involves more challenges to overcome. Moreover, existing buildings can present numerous occlusions which disturb the modeling.

Indoor scene reconstruction has also attracted plenty of research interest recently [6,7,9,10]. Chen et al. [11] learned the contextual information to perform RGB-D data reconstruction. Oesau et al. [12] proposed an automatic reconstruction of permanent structures of indoor scenes. This reconstruction work mainly focuses on the primary structures, such as walls, floors and ceilings. Nan et al. [13] introduced a search-classify scheme for indoor scene modeling, which assumes that all objects are placed upward on the ground floor. Wang et al. [14] proposed a pipeline that employs a decomposition-and-reconstruction strategy to create the indoor structural elements on the floor plan. Ochmann et al. [15] presented an automatic approach for the reconstruction of parametric 3D building models from indoor point clouds. In contrast to pure surface reconstructions, this representation allows more comprehensive use. Wang et al. [16] introduced a functional part-guided modeling method for cluttered indoor scenes.

However, although the aforementioned algorithms have advantages, they are always complex and time-consuming. In this paper, we proposed a simple and efficient approach by segmentation of the planar region, perspective of boundary detection, and final generation of the polyhedron structure model.

3 Methodology

The methodology starts by decomposing indoor scene into different planar clusters. Through selecting the optimal seed point for growing clusters in the indoor scene from point clouds. Then, the candidate wall clusters are located and isolated from other objects (e.g. ground, ceiling and other objects). The boundary of each candidate wall is extracted based on alpha-shape based method and the interior and exterior wall is classified and the further 3D linear model is generated. Figure 2 shows the workflow of the methodology.

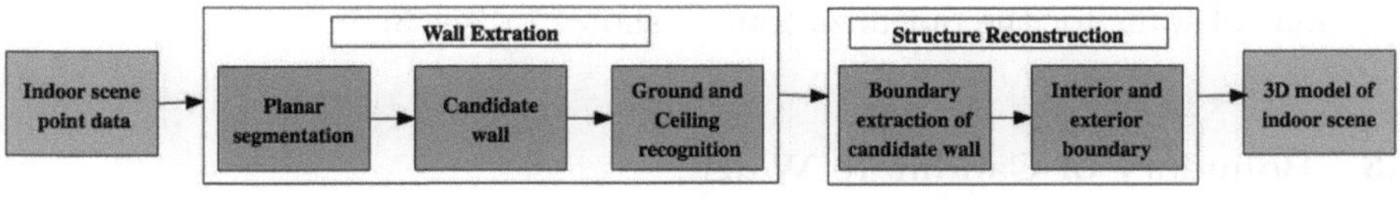

Fig. 2. Workflow of the methodology.

3.1 Planar Segmentation

Geometric features are critical elements to distinguish those points that belong to one planar cluster. Therefore the local geometrical features are essential for planar segmentation. Given scanned outdoor scene data $\mathrm{P} = \{p_0, p_1, p_2, \ldots, p_\mathrm{n}\}$, the k neighboring points of a point p_i be $q_j = (x_j, y_j, z_j)\,(j = 1, 2, \ldots, k)$. The covariance matrix of point p_i is constructed as $M = \frac{1}{k}\sum_{i=1}^{k}(p_i - \overline{p})(p_i - \overline{p})^T$, where k is the number of outdoor data P, $\overline{p}$ is the centroid point of P. The eigenvalues are positive and ordered as $\lambda_0 \geq \lambda_1 \geq \lambda_2$. According to the eigenvalues, the normal vector N_i, i.e. (n_x^i, n_y^i, n_z^i) of point p_i can be determined by the eigenvector corresponding to λ_0.

As we all known, most of the walls can exhibit planarity, and the wall is always planar and different walls of indoor scene should have different normal vector. Also the points in a wall cluster should have a smooth surface. i.e. the angle between two normal vectors does not vary too much. Points on a plane may share the same normal of orientation, therefore the normal vector can be utilized to extract the walls existed in scene. To achieve this we define an angle threshold θ, which is used to restrict the normal of points in the same wall.

Assigning the points to the region that current seed point belongs to if they are within θ. If no more seed point can be determined, the indoor scene data have been segmented completely. Meanwhile we remove those planar regions with minor point number. After this process, we could obtain the planar segmentation results of indoor scene.

3.2 Candidate Wall Clusters

After planar segmentation, we will distinguish the candidate wall clusters from those planar clusters based on the feature analysis.

(1) From those planar clusters, we can select the cluster which has minimum z coordinate as ground, and select the cluster which has maximum z coordinate. In order to visualize the segmentation results of the indoor scene, we remove the ceiling part.
(2) For other planar clusters, to obtain more optimal candidate wall elements from vertical surfaces observed in the scans. They constitute possible locations of walls for the optimization, as shown in Fig. 3.

3.3 Boundary of Candidate Walls

Boundary points of candidate walls from point cloud data can be determined by projecting the original wall clusters onto its representative plane, and then an alpha-shape based boundary detection algorithm is used to extract accurate set of boundary points. The alpha shape algorithm has been widely used in determining the boundaries of the point clouds especially the boundaries of outdoor buildings. The process contains:

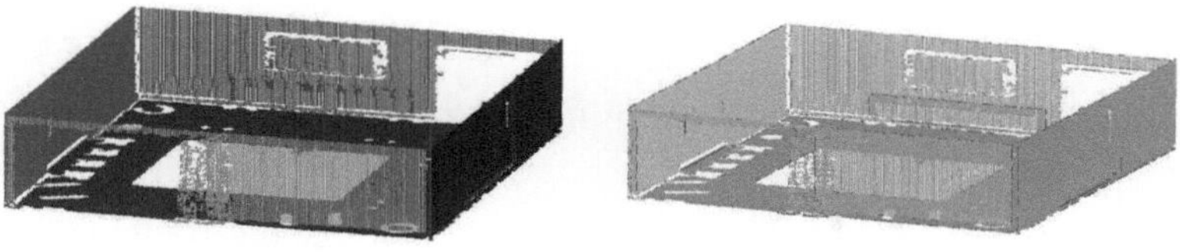

(a) (b)

Fig. 3. Candidate wall detection for scene 1. (a) planar segmentation result, (b) boundary extraction of individual wall. (Color figure online)

(1) Project each wall clusters onto their optimal local fitting planes and obtain 2D projection data.
(2) Let p be one point in original point cloud P, search for all its k (k varies from 10 to 20) neighboring points (within distance $2 * r$) set $Q = q_1, q_2, \ldots, q_k$. Select any point q_i from Q, and we can compute a circle center C according to the two points p, q_i and a radius r (defined by user, for most of the data $r = 1.0$).
(3) If point p is a boundary point then all its neighboring points are not within the circle, i.e. the distance to C is larger than r.

After the aforementioned steps, we can obtain the boundary points (in red color) from original point cloud data, shown in Fig. 3(b). We remove the ceiling part from the whole data in order to see the scene inside.

3.4 Interior and Exterior Walls Classification

It is important to classify the boundary of the wall into two kinds, namely, the interior boundary, which is the boundary of the wall and the exterior boundary, which is the boundary of each hole on the wall. The classification procedure starts from the clustering by searching for their neighboring points. The process is as follows:

(1) Based on the boundary points, we could order the boundary points by searching for the nearest neighboring points.
(2) The ordered boundary points can be clustered if the searching distance is within $2 * r$. If no suitable point is found after searching, more neighboring points should be obtained given a constraint of distance and number. If it does not work, then a new cluster is generated and the process restarts from another point without labeling in the remaining points.
(3) We repeat the aforementioned process until all the boundary data are labeled. Afterwards, we calculate the convex hull of the classified boundary. The larger one would be the exterior boundary and the other ones are interior boundary.

In this paper, we just utilize the exterior boundary to locate the shape of wall, the interior boundary will be used to further determine the detail of wall which would be our further work. The convex hull of the exterior wall boundary can be used to represent the linear model, as shown in Fig. 4.

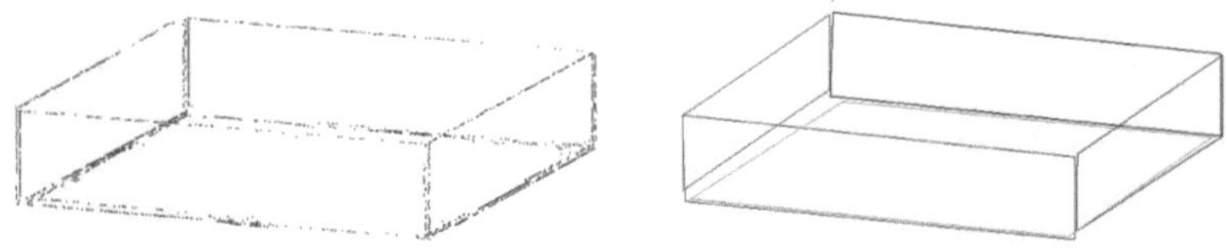

(a) (b)

Fig. 4. Reconstruction of scene 1. (a) exterior boundary, (b) linear model of scene 1.

4 Experimental Results

We experimentally evaluate our method primarily using scanned point cloud contain various categories of rooms. A gallery of indoor scene is chosen from Berkley Dataset. We first describe the experimental setting of our method and then demonstrate the results using our method.

Our method is implemented using C++ and run on a desktop PC with an Intel I7-6700 CPU (quad core, 3.4 GHz) and AMD Radeon R5 340X graphics card. For our experiments, we use the Berkley 3D Point Cloud Dataset.

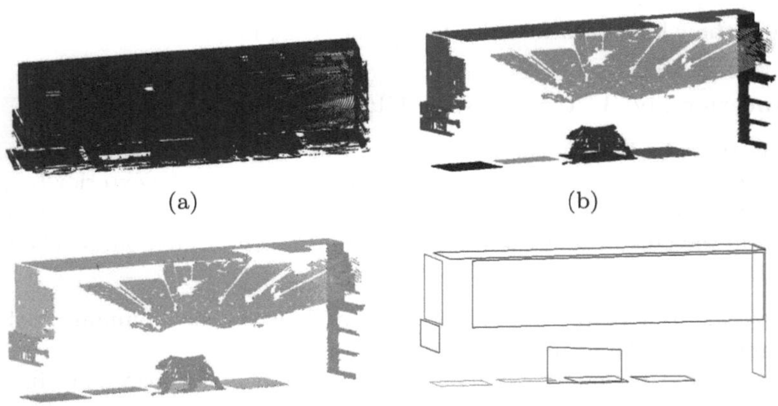

(a) (b)

(c) (d)

Fig. 5. Reconstruction of scanned indoor scene 2; (a) input point cloud, (b) planar region decomposition, (c) extracted boundary points, (d) final linear model.

Figure 5 shows all methodology phase applied to the data of scene 2. After planar segmentation, the scene 2 is segmented into different planar regions (Fig. 5(b)). The boundary extraction of individual walls in Fig. 5(c). Figure 6 show the results for a complex indoor scene with multiple room in scene 3. The result demonstrate the structure of the whole scene could be reconstructed.

The results shown above could demonstrate the visualization of scene structure modeling from laser scanned raw data. We provide some quantitative results to investigate the effectiveness of our algorithm. The running time of three scene dataset are respectively 33.206 s, 52.949 s, 67.487 s with 372778, 584407, and 522429 point number. We have removed the ceiling point from original data during boundary extraction, therefore the running time of scene 2 is lower than that of scene 3.

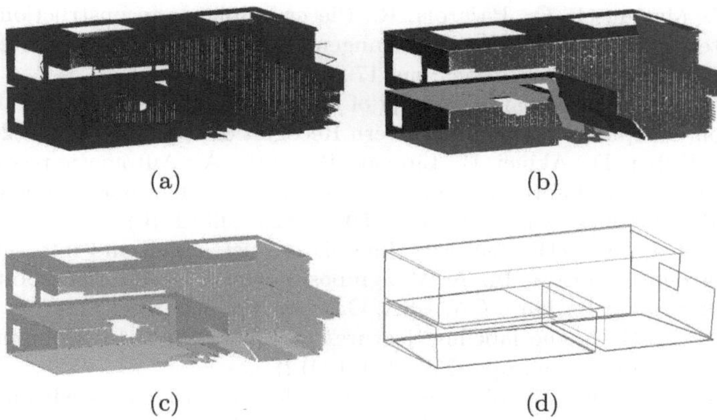

Fig. 6. Reconstruction of scanned scene 3; (a) input point cloud, (b) planar region segmentation, (c) extracted boundary points, (d) final linear model.

5 Conclusions

In this paper, we proposed a pipeline for indoor scene modeling represented by point cloud data, which consists of (1) detection of candidate wall, ground and ceiling using the consistency of normal vector, (2) boundary representation of candidate wall clusters and separation of the interior and exterior walls, and (3) the structure of the indoor scene is represented by linear model. Experimental results demonstrated the proposed algorithm can obtain promising result in representing individual wall. For future work, we plan to integrate the more detailed information including windows, doors, and protrusions in the walls in order to develop more robust indoor scene information results. More geometric features could be explored with the goal of improving scene modeling result.

Acknowledgments. This work was supported in part by the National Natural Science Foundation of China (No. 61871320,61872291); in part by China Postdoctoral Science Foundation (2014M552469); in part by Key laboratory project of Shaanxi Provincial Education Department (17JS099); in part by Shaanxi Postdoctoral Science Foundation (434015014); in part by Shaanxi Natural Science Foundation (2017JQ6023).

References

1. Mura, C., Mattausch, O., Villanueva, A.J., Gobbetti, E., Pajarola, R.: Robust reconstruction of interior building structures with multiple rooms under clutter and occlusions. In: International Conference on Computer-Aided Design and Computer Graphics, pp. 52–59 (2013)
2. Xie, L., Wang, R.: Automatic indoor building reconstruction from mobile laser scanning data. ISPRS - Int. Arch. Photogramm. Remote. Sens. Spat. Inf. Sci. **XLII-2/W7**, 417–422 (2017)
3. Mura, C., Mattausch, O., Pajarola, R.: Piecewise-planar reconstruction of multi-room interiors with arbitrary wall arrangements. In: Pacific Conference on Computer Graphics and Applications, pp. 179–188 (2016)
4. Armeni, I., et al.: 3D semantic parsing of large-scale indoor spaces. In: IEEE Conference on Computer Vision and Pattern Recognition, pp. 1534–1543 (2016)
5. Tang, P., Huber, D., Akinci, B., Lipman, R., Lytle, A.: Automatic reconstruction of as-built building information models from laser-scanned point clouds: a review of related techniques. Autom. Constr. **19**(7), 829–843 (2010)
6. Izadi, S., et al.: KinectFusion: real-time 3D reconstruction and interaction using a moving depth camera. In: ACM Symposium on User Interface Software and Technology, Santa Barbara, CA, USA, October, pp. 559–568 (2011)
7. Fox, D.: RGB-(D) scene labeling: features and algorithms. In: Computer Vision and Pattern Recognition, pp. 2759–2766 (2012)
8. Du, H., et al.: Interactive 3D modeling of indoor environments with a consumer depth camera. In: International Conference on Ubiquitous Computing, pp. 75–84 (2011)
9. Henry, P., Krainin, M., Herbst, E., Ren, X., Fox, D.: RGB-D mapping: using depth cameras for dense 3D modeling of indoor environments. In: The International Symposium on Experimental Robotics, pp. 647–663 (2013)
10. Macher, H., Landes, T., Grussenmeyer, P.: From point clouds to building information models: 3D semi-automatic reconstruction of indoors of existing buildings. Appl. Sci. **7**(10), 1030 (2017)
11. Chen, K., Lai, Y.K., Wu, Y.X., Martin, R., Hu, S.M.: Automatic semantic modeling of indoor scenes from low-quality RGB-D data using contextual information. ACM Trans. Graph. **33**(6), 208 (2014)
12. Oesau, S., Lafarge, F., Alliez, P.: Indoor scene reconstruction using feature sensitive primitive extraction and graph-cut. ISPRS J. Photogram. Remote Sens. **90**(90), 68–82 (2014)
13. Nan, L., Xie, K., Sharf, A.: A search-classify approach for cluttered indoor scene understanding. ACM Trans. Graph. **31**(6), 1–10 (2012)
14. Wang, R., Xie, L., Chen, D.: Modeling indoor spaces using decomposition and reconstruction of structural elements. Photogram. Eng. Remote Sens. **83**, 827–841 (2017)
15. Ochmann, S., Vock, R., Wessel, R., Klein, R.: Automatic reconstruction of parametric building models from indoor point clouds. Comput. Graph. **54**(C), 94–103 (2016)
16. Wang, J., Xie, Q., Xu, Y., Zhou, L., Ye, N.: Cluttered indoor scene modeling via functional part-guided graph matching. Comput. Aided Geom. Des. **43**(C), 82–94 (2016)

A Fast and Layered Real Rendering Method for Human Face Model—D-BRDF

Pengbo Zhou[1], Xiaotong Liu[2], Heng Wang[2], and Xiaofeng Wang[2](✉)

[1] School of Art and Communication, Beijing Normal University, No. 19, XinJieKouWai Street, HaiDian District, Beijing 100875, China
[2] Information Science and Technology, Northwest University, Xi'an 710127, China
xfwang@nwu.edu.cn

Abstract. Accurate rendering a real-world object has been a long-standing challenge in computer graphics area. The most popular method is BRDF, it is valid for opaque materials, such as metals, but it fails for translucent materials, such as skin. In order to render human skin faster and better, we propose a layered method D-BRDF, which divides the face model into three layers: sebum, epidermis and dermis, and combines the ambient light, specular reflection of sebum, diffuse reflection of the epidermis and subsurface scattering of the dermis to get the sum of light intensity and the final rendering effect. We experiment on several models, and the results show that it is more effective and faster than BRDF working on translucent models. The effects are downy and transparent, especially in the ear, cheek and other details. And it can be widely used in other related areas.

Keywords: Rendering · Layered method · D-BRDF · Translucent materials · Face model

1 Introduction

Rendering a real-world object accurately has been a long-standing challenge in the computer graphics research. So now a great deal of research work on describing the scattering of light from materials. One of the most popular methods is measuring the bidirectional reflectance distribution function (BRDF), which assumes that light enters and leaves an object at the same position, so it is valid for opaque materials, such as metals, but it fails for translucent materials [1], such as skin, marble, milk, cloth, etc., which exhibits significant transport below the surface.

According to translucent materials, many materials have layered biological structures such as skin, flower petals, etc. The modeling of light interaction with human skin is relevant in a variety of fields such as realistic image synthesis, the cosmetics industry, and so on. Understanding the way of light absorbing and propagating in skin tissues can assist generating realistic and predictable images of skin tissues. Creating believable images of human beings is usually an art entirely to designers and animators. Artists currently model skin by carefully adjusting rendering parameters such as textures and colors. It can also assist the design of superior cosmetics.

A. El Rhalibi et al. (Eds.): Edutainment 2018, LNCS 11462, pp. 99–106, 2019.
https://doi.org/10.1007/978-3-030-23712-7_14

In this paper, we present an improved BRDF algorithm for rendering the translucent materials, named D-BRDF, here D means the Depth of surface layer. And for the sake of simplicity, the paper uses the skin model with three layers' structure.

2 Related Works

The BRDF was first defined by Fred Nicodemus around 1965 [2]. It described how light is reflected at an opaque surface, and employed both in the optics of real-world light, computer graphics algorithms, and computer vision algorithms. In computer vision, it is necessary to model, represent and process the material characteristics and scatter behavior in order to perform higher level semantic analysis of scenes captured using image based methods or accurate reconstruction of 3D shapes. It is very important for rendering, so many researchers put forward the application and improvement of BRDF model in different directions. Tongbuasirilai [3] used the Projected Deviation Vector parameterization to improve the effect of BRDF method on sampling and reduce RMS errors, but its performance on diffuse materials is poor. Nielsen [4] proposed a novel mapping of the BRDF space that allows descriptive principal components to be extracted from the measurement database and solves the problem of reconstructing data from a limited number of samples. Collin [5] proposed a Vector Radiative Transfer Equation (VRTE) solution to the problem of subsurface scattering. However, the VRTE solver is complete, but slow. At present, the BRDF method is mainly applied to the reconstruction of remote sensing image [6], the reconstruction of geographical environment [7] and the rendering of three-dimensional model [8]. It is widely used in the render engine for it is fast. However, BRDF ultimately assumes that light scatters at one surface point and it does not model subsurface transport from one point to another in the model, so it fails for translucent materials. So some researchers have proposed a new method, named bidirectional surface scattering distribution function (BSSRDF) [1], but the author [1] proved that the BRDF image was rendered in 7 min, but the BSSRDF image was in 17 min. So BSSRDF is slower than BRDF.

Now there are some new research on the rendering area. Jimenez [9] presents two different separable models: the first one yields a high-quality diffusion simulation, while the second one offers an attractive trade-off between physical accuracy and artistic control. Jakob [10] improved the approach with Fisher scattering, and an approximate multiple surface-scattering correction for rough interfaces. Tanaka [11] described a method for recovering appearance of inner slices of translucent objects. The outer appearance of translucent objects is a summation of the appearance of slices at all depths, where each slice is blurred by depth-dependent point spread functions (PSFs). Corso's technique [12] was the first one including interactive transport of emergent light from deformable translucent objects. Van Leeuwen [13] showed that the contribution of skin to the distinct appearance of veins primarily results from Rayleigh scattering occurring within the papillary dermis. Chen [14] had done some work about hyperspectral modeling of skin appearance. So rendering is a very important work in the world.

In this paper, we are trying to use the benefit—fast speed of BRDF to solve rendering problem in translucent materials. So we propose an improved BRDF method for rendering human skin, with a thickness of surface layer parameter, which makes rendering human face faster and more effective.

3 Faster and Layered Real Rendering Method—D-BRDF

In order to model the scattering quickly and simply, the paper improves the BRDF and proposes the method D-BRDF, D means depth. The method divides the model into three layers: sebum, epidermis and dermis. Specular reflection happens in the sebum layer, and diffuse reflection arises in the second epidermis layer, and subsurface scattering arises in the third dermis layer. The method mainly combines the ambient light, specular reflection of sebum, diffuse reflection of the epidermis and subsurface scattering of the dermis to get the sum of light intensity and the final rendering effects. The details are shown as follows:

Step1: Prepare face model, which includes: 3D face model, diffuse reflection texture of face model, normal texture of face model and skin detail texture.

Step2: Get the sum of four kinds of light intensity, and then export the sum to face model, and get the final render effect by formula (1). The four light intensities are ambient light I_{am}, specular reflection of sebum I_{sp}, diffuse reflection of the epidermis I_{hdiff} and subsurface scattering of the dermis (I_{R2}, I_{G2}, I_{B2}).

$$\mathrm{I} = I_{am} + I_{hdiff} + I_{sp} + (\mathrm{I_{R2}}, \mathrm{I_{G2}}, \mathrm{I_{B2}}) \tag{1}$$

Among the formula (1),

$$\mathrm{I_{am}} = \mathrm{k_d} \cdot \mathrm{globalAmbient} \tag{2}$$

$\mathrm{k_d}$ is reflection coefficient, $0 < \mathrm{k_d} < 1$, globalAmbient is ambient light intensity.

The model use "Half Lambert" to simulate the diffuse reflection on the epidermis. "Half Lambert" lighting is a technique firstly developed in the original Half-Life. It is designed to prevent the rear of an object losing its shape and looking too flat.

The Lambert equation is:

$$I_{diff} = K_d I_l (N \cdot L) \tag{3}$$

I_l is the power of the incident light, about 100 lx–130 lx. K_d is reflection coefficient. N is the surface's normal vector, and L is pointing from the surface to the light source.

And, Half Lambert equation is:

$$\mathrm{I_{hdiff}} = \mathrm{I_{diff}} * 0.5 + 0.5 \tag{4}$$

Its effect is enhancing the diffuse reflection of object's surface.

The specular reflection on the epidermis is:

$$I_{sp} = k_s\sqrt{1-(L\cdot T)^2\sqrt{1-(V\cdot T)^2}-(L\cdot T)(V\cdot T)}^{n^s} \quad (5)$$

k_s is specular reflection coefficient, the value is about 0.3. n^s is highlight coefficient, the value is about 1.3. L is direction of incident light. V is direction of viewer. T is tangent of the point, and its value is crossing N and V.

For the purpose of simulating scattering light on the dermis, we set a new light named I_{pl} that its power is less than the incident light I_l. And because there are red blood cells, melanin, etc. in the dermis, so I_{pl} transmitted into skin seems to be red. In order to show the red, we make component R—$I_{pl,r}$ accounted for 90% of the total power of I_{pl}, and G and B component $I_{pl,g}$ and $I_{pl,b}$ accounted for 10% of the power. So the method separately calculates R, G, B component of reflected light on the dermis:

$$\mathrm{I_{R2}} = K_d I_{pl.r}(\mathrm{N_1}\cdot\mathrm{L_1}) \quad (6)$$

$$\mathrm{I_{G2}} = K_d I_{pl.g}(\mathrm{N_1}\cdot\mathrm{L_1}) \quad (7)$$

$$\mathrm{I_{B2f}} = K_d I_{pl.b}(\mathrm{N_1}\cdot\mathrm{L_1}) \quad (8)$$

And $\mathrm{N_1} = \mathrm{N}+\mathrm{N}*\mathrm{D}$, D is depth of dermis. $\mathrm{L_1} = \mathrm{L}+\mathrm{L}*\mathrm{D}$.

$$I_{pl} = 0.9I_1 - I_{lose} \quad (9)$$

$$I_{lose} = I_1\cdot e^{-ad\left(\frac{1}{\cos\theta_i}+\frac{1}{cos\theta_r}\right)} \quad (10)$$

θ_i is the angle that light source I_1 enters the dermis layer. θ_r is the angle light source I_1 away from dermis layer. I_{lose} is lost light intensity when I_1 enters the dermis by θ_i and away from it by θ_r, I_1 is light intensity of I_1, d is the thickness of the dermis, unit is mm, the value is about 4 mm, a is absorption coefficient, the value is 0.03–0.07, I_1 is incident light.

We can get vertex normal vector on subsurface N_1 and direction of incident light L_1.

$$N_1 = N+N*\mathrm{D} \quad (11)$$

$$L_1 = L+L*D \quad (12)$$

N is vertex unit normal vector of face model. L is unit vector from the vertex of the face model directing to the light source. D is facial cortex thickness, and the value is about 1 mm.

4 Experiments and Result Analysis

We have implemented our D-BRDF method in a number of face models, and in this section we will present a series of comparisons of the traditional BRDF rendering method with our D-BRDF rendering method from effects and time spent. The simulation experiments use Unity3D for model rendering (Fig. 1). All simulations have been done in 3.40 GHz i7-3770 CPU and NVIDA GT630 environment.

FPS (Frames Per Second) is an important index valuating the effect. The value of FPS is higher, the picture looks smoother. Figure 2 shows the FPS value of two methods, we can find that when rendering the same model D-BRDF has a higher FPS value than BRDF. The computing time of occupation CPU and render thread are shown in Table 1. We can find that the CPU time and render thread used in D-BRDF are all lower than BRDF, which all show that D-BRDF method outperforms the BRDF.

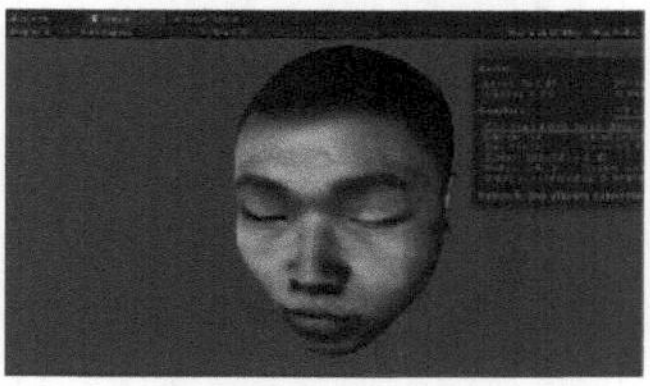

Fig. 1. Rendering statistics window

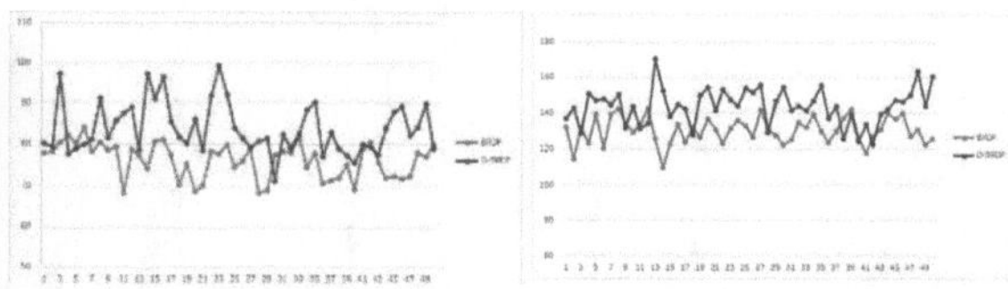

(a) model 1 (b) model 2

Fig. 2. Two methods are compared when the values of FPS changes in the two models

Table 1. The parameters value when rendering on the three models.

Model number	Parameter	BRDF	D-BRDF
1	FPS	76.25 fps	83.92 fps
	CPU	10.6 ms	10.2 ms
	Render thread	0.4 ms	0.3 ms
2	FPS	130.16 fps	143.81 fps
	CPU	10.2 ms	9.8 ms
	Render thread	0.3 ms	0.3 ms
3	FPS	77.04 fps	80.74 fps
	CPU	12.8 ms	12.5 ms
	Render thread	0.6 ms	0.5 ms

We show the effects of the rendering methods in Fig. 3. Among them (1) and (2) are the whole models. Through the comparison of the rendered models, we found that the faces rendered using the BRDF method are stiff and their ruddy skin rendering level is not obvious, but rendered using D-BRDF method have a softer appearance. Figure 3 (3) to (5) shows the details of the models mainly from the ear, facial wrinkles, cheeks and other high-scattering simulation parts. It is clearly found that the D-BRDF method is more realistic than the BRDF method. Here, the absorption by blood is particularly noticeable as the light scatters redder in the depths of the skin. Compared to the BRDF method, the D-BRDF method can show the sense of blood color hierarchy better and more delicate in details of human skin. So the D-BRDF rendering method can render human skin more real than the BRDF method.

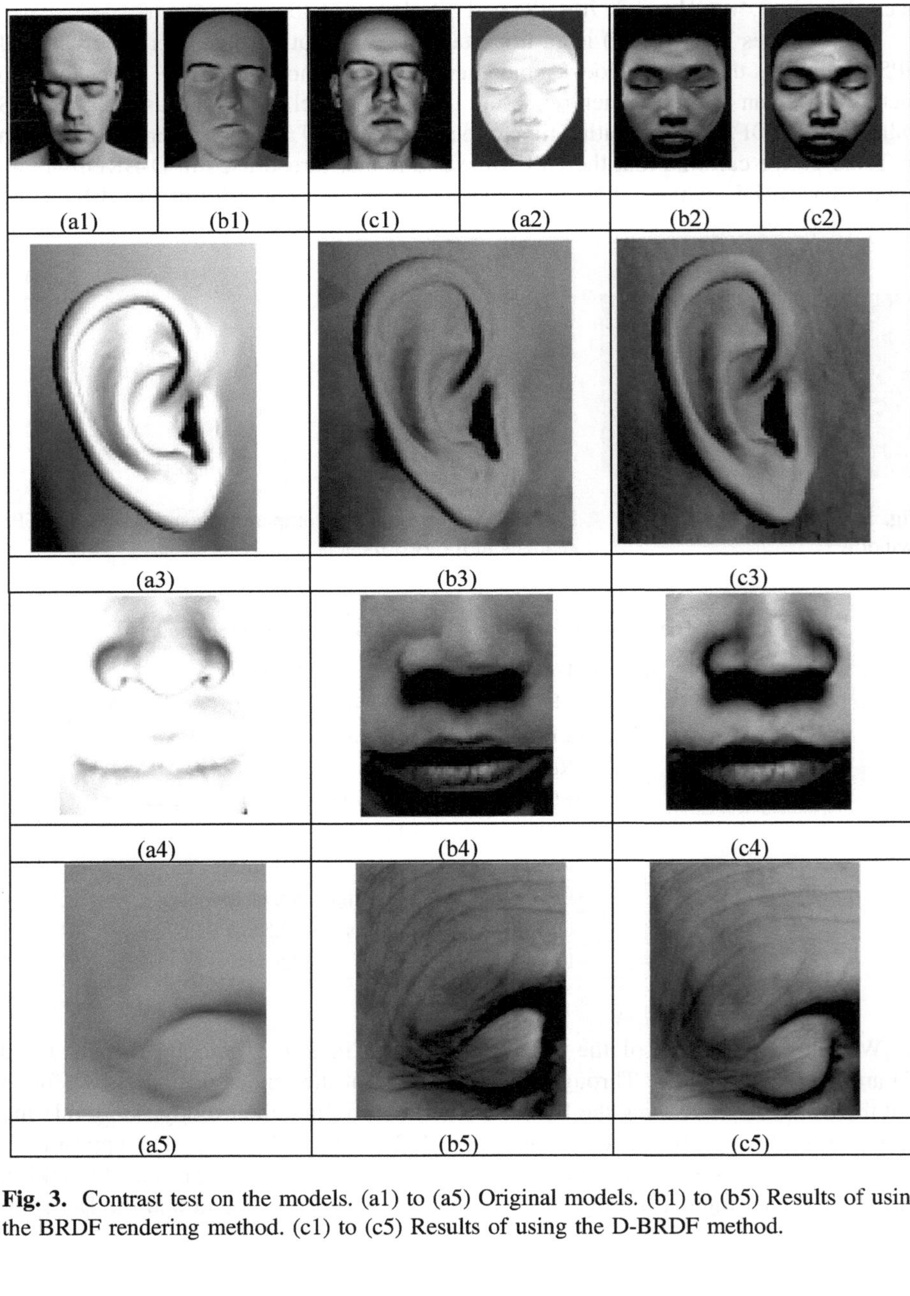

Fig. 3. Contrast test on the models. (a1) to (a5) Original models. (b1) to (b5) Results of using the BRDF rendering method. (c1) to (c5) Results of using the D-BRDF method.

5 Conclusion

In order to render human skin more fast and real, we present a new method D-BRDF, which simulates the scattering light in the algorithm. We do some experiments on several models, and the results show that it has better performance and faster than BRDF, so it can be used successfully on human face rendering process. In computer area the BRDF is the main rendering method in mainstream rendering engine for it is fast. But now our method D-BRDF get better effect and faster speed than BRDF, so it has good potential in rendering engine and other similar area. Now in the method, the parameter D is a constant but on the face the different places have different depth, so it is the next work we plan to work.

Acknowledgments. We thank the National important Research Development Program (2017YFB1002702), National Natural Science Foundation of China (Number: 61602380, 61731015, 61673319, 61772421, 61802311).

References

1. Jensen, H.W., Marschner, S.R., et al.: A practical model for subsurface light transport. In: Proceedings of SIGGRAPH, pp. 1–8 (2001)
2. Nicodemus, F.: Directional reflectance and emissivity of an opaque surface. Appl. Opt. **4**(7), 767–775 (1965)
3. Tongbuasirilai, T., Unger, J., Kurt, M.: Efficient BRDF sampling using projected deviation vector parameterization. In: IEEE International Conference on Computer Vision Workshops (ICCVW), Venice, Italy, pp. 153–158 (2017)
4. Nielsen, J.B., et al.: On optimal, minimal BRDF sampling for reflectance acquisition. ACM Trans. Graph. **34**(6), 1–11 (2015)
5. Collin, C., et al.: Computation of polarized subsurface BRDF for rendering. In: Graphics Interface Canadian Information Processing Society, pp. 201–208 (2014)
6. Bachmann, C.M., et al.: Inverting a radiative transfer model for sediment density retrieval from hyperspectral BRDF data. In: IEEE International Geoscience and Remote Sensing Symposium (IGARSS), pp. 1477–1479, Fort Worth, TX (2017)
7. Jensen, D.J., Simard, M., et al.: Imaging spectroscopy BRDF correction for mapping louisiana's coastal ecosystems. IEEE Trans. Geosci. Remote Sens. **99**, 1–10 (2017)
8. Kim, S., Kyung, M.H., et al.: Thread-based BRDF rendering on GPU. In: 18th Pacific Conference on Computer Graphics and Applications, Hangzhou, pp. 54–61 (2010)
9. Jimenez, J., Jarabo, A., Wu, X.C., et al.: Separable subsurface scattering. Comput. Graph. Forum **34**(6), 188–197 (2015)
10. Jakob, W., D'Eon, E., et al.: A comprehensive framework for rendering layered materials. ACM Trans. Graph. 1–14 (2014)
11. Tanaka, K., Mukaigawa, Y., et al.: Recovering inner slices of translucent objects by multi-frequency illumination. In: IEEE Conference on Computer Vision and Pattern Recognition (CVPR), Boston, MA, pp. 5464–5472 (2015)

12. Corso, A.D., Frisvad, J.R., Mosegaard, J., et al.: Interactive directional subsurface scattering and transport of emergent light. Vis. Comput. 1–13 (2016)
13. Van Leeuwen, S.R., Baranoski, G.V., et al.: Identifying the optical phenomena responsible for the blue appearance of veins, 14 (2017). https://doi.org/10.1117/12.2274560
14. Chen, T.F., Baranoski, G.V.G., Kimmel, B.W., Miranda, E.: Hyperspectral modeling of skin appearance. ACM Trans. Graph. **34**(3), 1–14 (2015)

A Queue-Based Bandwidth Allocation Method for Streaming Media Servers in M-Learning VoD Systems

Jing Wang[1], Hui Zhao[1(✉)], Feng Liu[1], and Jie Zhang[2]

[1] Xidian University, Xi'an 710071, Shaanxi, China
{wangjing,hzhao}@mail.xidian.edu.cn, liufeng@stu.xidian.edu.cn
[2] Xi'an University of Technology, Xi'an 710048, Shaanxi, China
jiezhang1984@xaut.edu.cn

Abstract. Nowdays, VoD (video-on-demand) has become a wide-used technology in m-learning. In m-learning VoD systems, we need to allocate appropriate bandwidth for streaming media servers with the aim of optimizing the user experience and reducing the service cost. In this paper, a queue-based bandwidth allocation method for streaming media servers in m-learning VoD system is proposed. Firstly, it analyzes the user historical learning logs to mine the user behavior characteristics. Secondly, it utilizes the queueing theory to establish a bandwidth resource allocation model for streaming media servers. Thirdly, it predicts the user arrival rate in real-time, allocates appropriate bandwidth resource dynamically by the bandwidth resource allocation model, so as to solve the bandwidth resource allocation irrationality problem. Finally, the simulation results have proved the correctness and effectiveness of the proposed bandwidth resource allocation method, which can improve the bandwidth resource utilization and reduce the service rejection rate.

Keywords: Bandwidth allocation · Queueing theory · Streaming media servers · Video on demand · M-learning

1 Introduction

With the rapid development of mobile Internet and smart devices, mobile learning (m-learning) has become a fundamental and hot research topic in the next generation e-learning. Generally, m-learning systems offer a great deal of course videos to online learners, and VoD (video-on-demand) technology is widely used in m-learning systems. Due to the particularity of m-learning and the heterogeneities of networks and smart devices, m-learning can be regarded as a large-scale VoD with special user behaviors. The m-learning VoD systems have to allocate bandwidth resource to the streaming media servers appropriately and efficiently, so as to serve large number of demands concurrently, optimize the user experience, and reduce the service cost. In m-learning systems, how to solve

A. El Rhalibi et al. (Eds.): Edutainment 2018, LNCS 11462, pp. 107–114, 2019.
https://doi.org/10.1007/978-3-030-23712-7_15

the problem of allocating appropriate bandwidth resource for streaming media servers is still a challenge.

There have been some resource allocation methods for server cluster, and they can be divided into three types: the methods based on control theory [1,2], the methods based on performance model [3,4] and the methods based on workload prediction [5,6]. For example, Dutreilh et al. [1] developed a management framework that can automatically allocate resource for virtualization applications. Leboucher et al. [3] proposed a swarm intelligence method to determine the server resource allocation and job scheduling. Ardagna et al. [5] predicted the future workload of each application as well as the future performance of each machine, and then they allocated appropriate resources for each application. However, the exiting resource allocation methods did not take into account the user behavior in m-learning VoD systems, and they cannot be applied directly to the streaming media servers with continuous resource utilization.

In this paper, we propose a queue-based bandwidth allocation method for streaming media servers in m-learning VoD system. Firstly, it analyzes the user historical learning logs to mine the user behavior characteristics, including the average user request arrival rate, the video playing time distribution, and the video popularity distribution, etc. Secondly, it utilizes the queueing theory to establish a bandwidth resource allocation model for streaming media servers. With the model, it can train the bandwidth requirement under different cases. Thirdly, it predicts the user arrival rate in real-time, allocates appropriate bandwidth resource dynamically by the bandwidth resource allocation model, so as to solve the bandwidth resource allocation irrationality problem. Finally, we evaluate our bandwidth allocation method with the metrics of bandwidth resource utilization and service reject rate. The simulation results prove the correctness and effectiveness of our bandwidth allocation method, which can improve the bandwidth resource utilization and reduce the service rejection rate.

2 User Behavior Analysis in M-Learning VoD Systems

Generally, VoD service process can be described as a queueing system [7], shown in Fig. 1. To get all the parameters of queueing theory, we need to analyze the historical user behavior logs and mine user behavior characteristics.

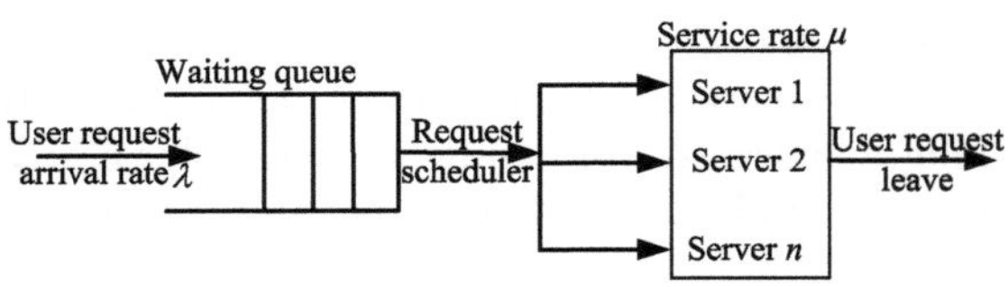

Fig. 1. The process of VoD.

In this paper, we use the logs of our m-learning system, SkyClass [8,9], to analyze the user behavior. We select all the logs (about 0.98GB) generated from

December 1, 2014 to January 31, 2015. After data preprocessing, there are 92632 logs, which cover 5142 courses.

The Average User Request Arrival Rate: We select VoD logs of several days to count the number of arrival user requests every one minute, and calculate the probability of user request arrival rate. Figure 2(a) shows the distribution of statistical user request arrival rate. It can be seen that the distribution is similar to the Poisson distribution [10], that is $P(X=i)=\frac{\lambda^i}{i!}e^{-\lambda}, i=0,1,2,\cdots$.

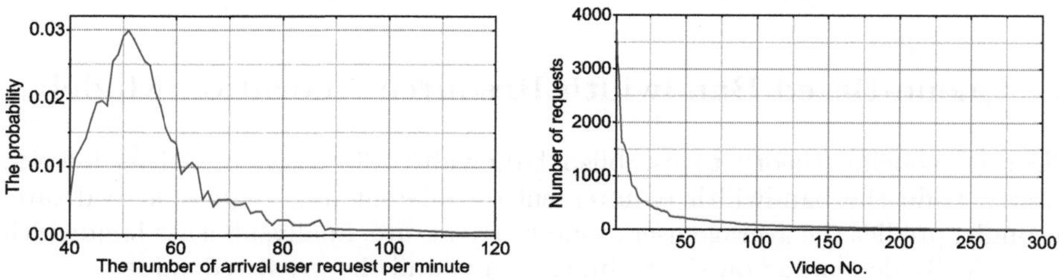

(a) The user request arrival rate (b) The video popularity

Fig. 2. The distribution of the user request arrival rate and the video popularity.

The Video Popularity Distribution: The video popularity refers to the probability of requesting a video in a certain time interval. Generally, the video popularity distribution follows Pareto's law (20/80), as shown in Fig. 2(b). Some related researches used Zipf-like distribution [11] to formulate it as: $p_i=\frac{s_i}{S}=\frac{1}{i^\theta * \sum_{i=1}^{M} i^{-\theta}}$. Here p_i denotes the popularity of video i; s_i is the request number of video i; S is the total request number of all videos; M is the total video number; θ is the distribution parameter.

The Distribution of Service Time (Video Playing Time Distribution): The service time is the interval from the user's request arrival time to the user leaving time. The distribution of service time is some statistical roles of the service time. We assume the service time is video playing time in this paper. The distribution of service time of some courses is shown in Fig. 3. Since the service times of different courses are independent, it can be described by general distribution $G(t), t \geq 0$, that is, the user's service time is independent, and the average service time is $0 < t = 1/\mu = \int_0^\infty t dG(t)$.

The Bandwidth Requirement of a Single Request: The average bandwidth requirement of a video streaming can be expressed as: $R=E[r_i]$. Here, r_i is the bit rate of video i.

The Average User Waiting Time: The user waiting time is the length of time between user request arrival time and the service beginning time. In this paper, the average user waiting time is a known constraint.

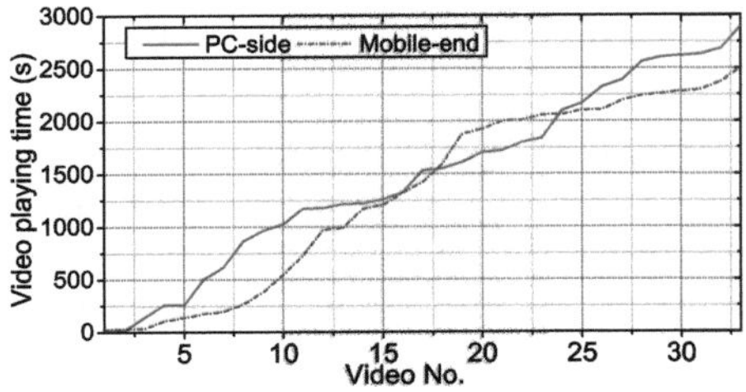

Fig. 3. The distribution of video playing time.

3 Queue-Based Bandwidth Resource Allocation Model

We use queueing theory to establish bandwidth allocation model as follows. Firstly, train the bandwidth requirement of different user request arrival rate; secondly, predict the average user request arrival rate; finally, allocate bandwidth dynamically depending on the training results and the predicted value.

3.1 Bandwidth Resource Allocation Training

We suppose the user arrival requests of m-learning VoD system obey the Poisson distribution with the average user request arrival rate λ, the service rate is μ, the request time follows a general distribution with mean $1/\mu$, the average bandwidth requirements of a request is R, and the average waiting time is T, then we can calculate the bandwidth requirement using above parameters. The M/G/n queueing theory [12] can be used to solve this problem, the corresponding waiting probability of user request is:

$$P_Q = \frac{(n\rho)^n}{n!(1-\rho)} * \left[\sum_{k=0}^{n-1} \frac{(n\rho)^k}{k!} + \frac{(n\rho)^n}{n!(1-\rho)} \right]^{-1} \tag{1}$$

The average number of waiting requests in the queue (queue length) is:

$$N_Q = \frac{\rho \overline{X^2}}{2\overline{X}^2(1-\rho)} * P_Q \tag{2}$$

where $\rho = \lambda/(n\mu)$, n is the streaming server parallelization capability; $\overline{X^2} = [{t_i}^2] = \sum p_i \cdot {t_i}^2$ denotes the variance of request service time. The average waiting time in the queue is $T = N_Q/\lambda$.

Given parameters of the M/G/n queueing model, we can calculate the streaming server parallelization capability n_s by using step-by-step approximation method respectively. As the average bandwidth requirement of a request is R, the required bandwidth resource will be $B = n_s \cdot R$.

3.2 User Request Arrival Rate Prediction

We use the secondary exponential smoothing method to predict the user request arrival rate. Let $F_t^{(1)}$ and $F_t^{(2)}$ denote the linear exponential smooth value and the secondary exponential smooth value. They are calculated as follows:

$$F_t^{(1)} = \alpha Y_t + (1 - \alpha) F_{t-1}^{(1)} \tag{3}$$

$$F_t^{(2)} = \alpha F_t^{(1)} + (1 - \alpha) F_{t-1}^{(2)} \tag{4}$$

where Y_t denotes the user request arrival rate at time t, α is the smoothing coefficient ($0 < \alpha < 1$). If we get the linear and secondary exponential smooth values at t, then we can calculate the predicted value at $t + \Delta t$ by:

$$F_{t+\Delta t} = a_t + b_t \Delta t \tag{5}$$

where $a_t = 2F_t^{(1)} - F_t^{(2)}$, and $b_t = \alpha(F_t^{(1)} - F_t^{(2)})/(1 - \alpha)$.

3.3 Dynamic Bandwidth Resource Allocation

If the user request arrival rate continues to increase and reaches a certain level, then additional bandwidth resource should be added into the streaming media servers. If the user request arrival rate continues to decrease and the bandwidth resource utilization decreases, then the streaming media servers need to cut down the bandwidth. The algorithm is shown in Table 1.

Table 1. Dynamic bandwidth resource allocation algorithm

Algotithm: Dynamic Bandwidth Resource Allocation

```
while true do
    cur_max_rate = get_rate(Q_n, ART);
    pre_max_rate = get_rate(Q_{n-1}, ART);
    cur_rate = list(n); // Get current user request arrival rate
    if cur_rate >= cur_max_rate/2 or cur_rate <= pre_max_rate then
        Predict next_rate by Equation (4);
        if next_rate < cur_rate then
            Reduce bandwidth resource;
        else
            Predict future_rate by Equation (5);
        endif
        if future_rate >= cur_max_rate then
            Add bandwidth resource;
        endif
    endif
    Update list Q_n;
endwhile
```

4 Simulations

In the simulations, we evaluate our bandwidth allocation method with the metrics of bandwidth resource utilization and service rejection rate.

(1) Bandwidth resource utilization is expressed as follows: $U_b = b/B$. Here, b is the used bandwidth resource; B is the total bandwidth resource.
(2) Service rejection rate (RR) is the ratio of the number of rejected requests to the total number of requests in m-learning VoD. The service rejection occurs when the request waiting time in the queueing list is longer than the maximum limitation T_{wait}. RR is calculated by: $RR = n_{reject}/n_{total}$.

4.1 Bandwidth Resource Allocation Model Training

In the first experiment, we set the request waiting time as 5 s, then we train the bandwidth requirement by using the queueing theory in different user request arrival rates (the number of arrival user requests per second). The results are shown in Fig. 4(a). In the second experiment, we set the user request arrival rate as 1/s, then we train and get the bandwidth requirement with the average waiting time varying from 1 s to 59 s, the results are shown in Fig. 4(b). It can be seen from Fig. 4(a) and (b) that the bandwidth resource gradually increases as the user request arrival rate increases, and the bandwidth resource gradually decreases as the average waiting time grows.

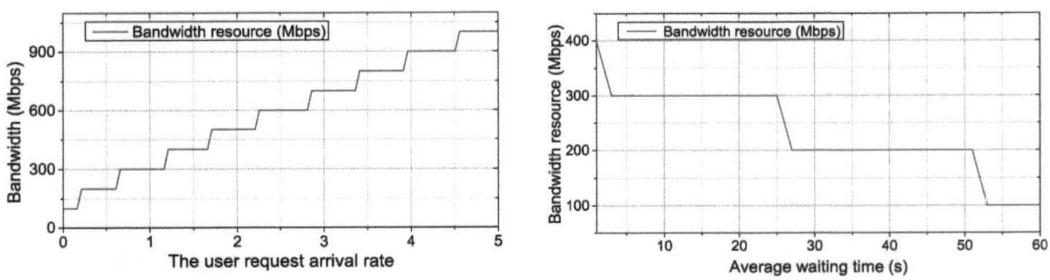

(a) The user request arrival rate (b) The user average waiting time

Fig. 4. The bandwidth allocation under different user request arrival rates and the average waiting times.

4.2 Dynamic Bandwidth Resource Allocation Results

The number of arrival user requests changes great with time, thus the streaming media servers need to allocate bandwidth dynamically to adjust the real-time user request arrival rates. Figure 5(a) shows the variety of bandwidth resource with the changes of the user request arrival rate in 50 h, and Fig. 5(b) shows the corresponding service rejection rate and bandwidth resource utilization.

It can be seen from Fig. 5(b), the service rejection rate is basically low with the changes of user request arrival rate, while the average bandwidth resource utilization is over 60%. The rejection rate and bandwidth resource utilization are around 1% and 80%. This shows the correctness and effectiveness of the proposed bandwidth resource allocation method. When the user request arrival rate continuously increases and decreases 3 times, the allocated bandwidth resource has the same trend as the user request arrival rate shows. Please note that the bandwidth resource utilization reaches 100% 3 times, at the same time, the service rejection rate is about 10%. That is because when the user request arrival rate continues to grow, but the new allocated bandwidth resource is not added to the servers in time. Similarly, when the user request arrival rate continues to decrease, the resource utilization and service rejection rate are relatively low, because excessive bandwidth resource is not recycled in time.

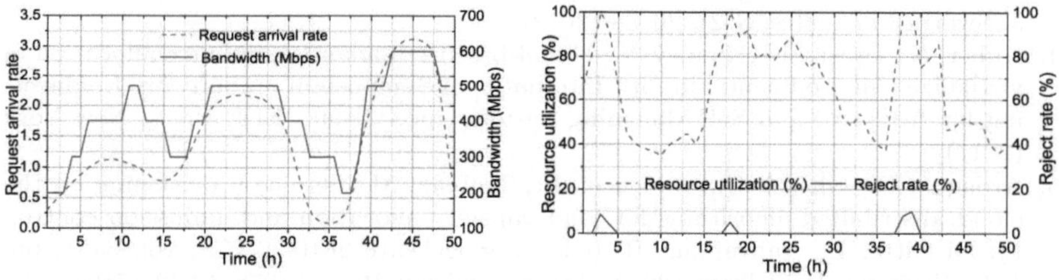

(a) The bandwidth resource allocation

(b) The bandwidth resource utilization and service rejection rate

Fig. 5. The dynamic bandwidth resource allocation results.

5 Conclusion

A queue-based bandwidth resource allocation method for streaming media servers in m-learning VoD is proposed in this paper. The method analyzes the user's historical learning logs, mines user behavior characteristics, and uses the queueing theory to train the bandwidth resource allocation model. Then, it predicts the user request arrival rate and allocates bandwidth resource dynamically. Finally, we use the bandwidth resource utilization and service rejection rate to evaluate the correctness and effectiveness of the proposed method. However, it did not analyze behaviors for mobile users. As for the future work, we intend to further mine the characteristics of the mobile users and improve our bandwidth resource allocation method.

Acknowledgments. This research was mainly supported by the National Natural Science Foundation of China (61702400) and the Fundamental Research Funds for the Central Universities (JB190308, JB180306, JB170307). It was also supported by Shaanxi Key R&D Program (2019ZDLGY13-07), the Science and Technology Projects of Xi'an (201809170CX11JC12), Ningbo Natural Science Foundation (2018A610051), the Projects of International Cooperation and Exchanges NSFC (61711530248) and the National Natural Science Foundation of China (61702409, 61702394, 61702395, 61802294, 61702409).

References

1. Dutreilh, X., Rivierre, N., Moreau, A., et al.: From data center resource allocation to control theory and back. In: 3rd IEEE International Conference on Cloud Computing, pp. 410–417. IEEE Press, New York (2010)
2. Pan, W., Mu, D., Wu, H., et al.: Feedback control-based QoS guarantees in web application servers. In: 10th IEEE International Conference on High Performance Computing and Communications, pp. 328–334. IEEE Press, New York (2008)
3. Leboucher, C., Chelouah, R., Siarry, P., et al.: A swarm intelligence method combined to evolutionary game theory applied to the resources allocation problem. Int. J. Swarm Intell. Res. **3**(2), 20–38 (2012)
4. Huber, N., Brosig, F., Kounev, S.: Model-based self-adaptive resource allocation in virtualized environments. In: 6th International Symposium on Software Engineering for Adaptive and Self-Managing Systems, pp. 90–99. IEEE Press, New York (2011)
5. Ardagna, D., Ghezzi, C., Panicucci, B., Trubian, M.: Service provisioning on the cloud: distributed algorithms for joint capacity allocation and admission control. In: Di Nitto, E., Yahyapour, R. (eds.) ServiceWave 2010. LNCS, vol. 6481, pp. 1–12. Springer, Heidelberg (2010). https://doi.org/10.1007/978-3-642-17694-4_1
6. Khan, A., Yan, X., Tao, S., et al.: Workload characterization and prediction in the cloud: a multiple time series approach. In: IEEE Network Operations and Management Symposium, pp. 1287–1294. IEEE Press, New York (2012)
7. An, X., He, Y., Guan, L.: Queueing model based resource optimization for multimedia cloud. J. Vis. Commun. Image Represent. **25**(5), 928–942 (2014)
8. Zheng, Q., Zhao, H., Zhang, W.: A mobile learning system for supporting heterogeneous clients based on P2P live streaming. In: 2012 ACM/IEEE ICDSC, pp. 1–6. IEEE Press, New York (2012)
9. Zhao, H., Zheng, Q., Zhang, W.: Demo: SkyClass: a large-scale mobile learning system for heterogeneous clients. In: 2012 ACM/IEEE ICDSC, pp. 1–2. IEEE Press, New York (2012)
10. Ling, Q., Zhang, Y., Yan, J., et al.: Construction and application of users' behavior model in the video on demand system. J. Chin. Comput. Syst. **34**(3), 548–552 (2013)
11. Iullo, D., Martina, V., Garetto, M., et al.: How much can large-scale Video-on-Demand benefit from users' cooperation? In: IEEE INFOCOM, pp. 2724–2732. IEEE Press, New York (2013)
12. Cao, Y., Hu, W.: Customer service representative staffing based on after-sales field service queuing approximation M/G/m model. J. Chongqing Normal Univ. (Nat. Sci.) **4**, 36–40 (2010)

A Hole Repairing Method Based on Edge-Preserving Projection

Yinghui Wang[1,2], Yanni Zhao[1,3(✉)], Ningna Wang[4], Xiaojuan Ning[1], Zhenghao Shi[1], Minghua Zhao[1], Ke Lv[5], and Liangyi Huang[6]

[1] Institute of Computer Science and Engineering, Xi'an University of Technology, Xi'an, China
feifei6513@163.com
[2] Shaanxi Key Laboratory of Network Computing and Security Technology, Xi'an, China
[3] Department of Computer Science, Shannxi Vocational and Technical College, Xi'an, China
[4] Booking B.V., Herengracht 597, 1017 CE Amsterdam, Netherlands
[5] Institute of Automation, Chinese Academy of Sciences, Beijing, China
[6] School of Engineering and Applied Science, George Washington University, Washington, D.C., USA

Abstract. A point cloud hole repairing method based on edge-preserving projection is proposed in order to maintain sharp features of holes. First, the hole boundary points are acquired by quadrants and angles, then connections among 3D hole boundary points are projected onto the two-dimensional plane using the edge-preserving projection. Secondly, the two-dimensional region obtained from projection is subjected to point collectivization for obtaining filling points, at the same time, the radial-basis interpolation mapping technique is used to construct the hole surface according to the 3D hole boundary point. Finally, the two-dimensional filling points are reflected onto the surface of the constructed hole to complete hole repairing. Experimental results show that our method can effectively repair the hole of the point cloud and restore the sharp features of the hole.

Keywords: Edge-preserving projection · Boundary point · Hole repairing · Sharp features

1 Introduction

The repairing of three dimensional point cloud holes is important to ensure the integrity of data. However, since point cloud is a discrete set of 3D data points which do not have explicit topology, there are some problems during the process of repairing, such as unsatisfactory fusion between holes and neighborhood points, inability to maintain the sharp features of the holes and inaccuracy of recovering complex hole surface. Therefore, it is a challenging task to detect, extract and repair holes in a robust way.

At present, there are two main methods for repairing the point cloud hole: hole repairing method based on grid model [1, 2] and hole repairing method based on point cloud model [3], both of these approaches have done a great deal of research on how to maintain sharp features in hole repairs.

A. El Rhalibi et al. (Eds.): Edutainment 2018, LNCS 11462, pp. 115–122, 2019.
https://doi.org/10.1007/978-3-030-23712-7_16

(1) Hole repairing method based on grid model

The hole repairing method based on the grid model is to mesh the point cloud model and then repair holes. Pfeifle [4] realizes the fusion between hole and original grid by optimizing the hole triangle. Zhang [5] establishes the feature surface of the space hole polygon to maintain the sharp features of the hole. Liu [6] adopts feature enhancement processing aimed at the sharp features of the hole boundary. Liu [7] introduces the energy optimization method and the plane cluster method to restore the sharp features near missing holes in the model. Van Sinh [8] uses the hole boundary point cutting plane to repair the holes and maintain the sharp features. All above methods must be meshed with three dimensional point cloud model, and the grid requires a relatively accurate spatial distribution of points cloud, a little "irregular" point cloud can cause inaccuracy or even failure of the grid, especially if the point cloud data is very complex or noisy, it is not possible to ensure that it can be meshed. The limitation of grid model makes many scholars turn their attention to the hole repairing method based on point cloud. For point cloud repairing, it is unnecessary to create complex grids, and the filling efficiency can also be improved.

(2) Hole repairing method based on point cloud model

The hole repairing method based on point cloud model is to directly repair holes in point clouds. Chalmovianský [9] proposes a nearest neighborhood repairing method for holes. Due to the continuity characteristic between the hole and the surrounding surface. Qiu [10] uses the surrounding points to construct the local patches in the hole position and fill them. Sharf [11] relies on the neighborhood similarity principle to match the feature of hole area and other regions in order to find the most similar regions for repair. Pernot [12] uses the newly increased patches to repair holes under the minimum curvature of the hole-filled area and its adjacent area. All of above methods are not ideal for complex holes with high curvature or sharp features.

In order to maintain the sharp features of the hole, Wu [13] proposes a hole filling method for scattered point sets based on boundary extension and boundary convergence. Yang [14] introduces different constraints in surface reconstruction. Lin [15] divides holes into feature holes and non-feature holes, and adopts the tensor voting algorithm for non-feature hole filling. Wang et al. [16, 17] design a method based on ridge and valley point for the sharp features of hole surface. These methods can do a better job maintaining the sharp features of holes, but if large portion of point cloud data is missing, the repaired holes can not ensure the rationality of its sharp feature.

In this paper, a projection strategy with edge-preserving is introduced for preserve the sharp feature on the hole, radial-basis interpolation mapping technology is used to construct holes and surfaces, so as to achieve hole repair.

2 Overview

The overall idea of our method consists of two steps: the first step is the extraction and connection of hole boundary, and the second is the repair of hole. Which is shown in Fig. 1.

(1) Based on the angle and quadrant distribution of point clouds, the boundary points of holes are extracted and the boundary points are connected.
(2) By using the edge-preserving strategy, the connection among hole boundary points in the three-dimensional space is projected onto the two-dimensional plane, and the two-dimensional filling points are obtained by point collectivization processing of two-dimensional region.
(3) According to the hole boundary points, the radial basis function interpolation mapping technique is used to construct the hole surface.
(4) The two-dimensional filling point is reflected on structured hole surface, and the repairing of the hole is completed.

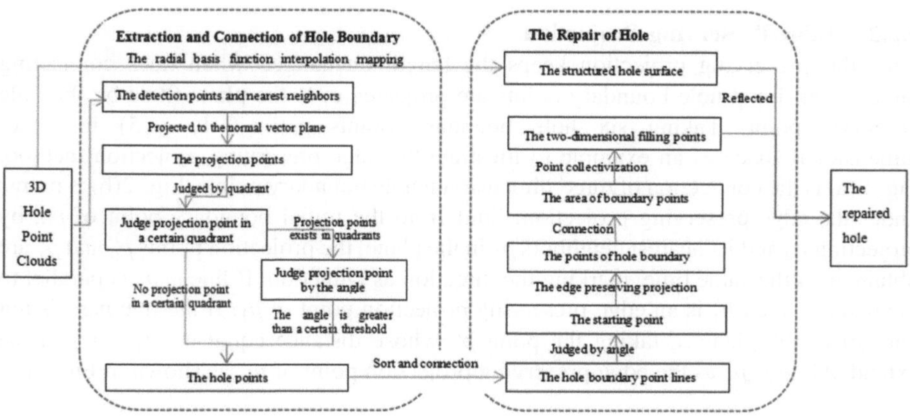

Fig. 1. The profile of our method

3 Methodology

3.1 Boundary Extraction of the Hole

When extracting the hole boundary, the detection points and nearest neighbor points are projected to the normal vector plane where points are located. Taking the detection point as the origin point of coordinate, the local coordinate system is established and the boundary of holes are judged by projection points. If the nearest neighbor of a point has no projection point in certain quadrants, then that specific point is the hole boundary point. If the projection points exists in all four quadrants, then the angle of line connecting between the query point and its nearest neighbor point is calculated. If the angle is greater than a certain threshold, then the point is also considered as the boundary point of holes.

3.2 Hole Boundary Point Projection

In this paper, the hole boundary points are projected on two dimensional plane and following with point collectivization. The filling points of collectivization set are reflected onto the surface formed by the boundary point of the three-dimensional hole to obtain the repairing point.

3.2.1 Initial Boundary Point Determination

The defined hole boundary points are sorted and connected to boundary lines in turn. First, an arbitrary hole boundary point is taken as a query point, find the first nearest neighbor point of it and connect, then use the nearest neighbor point as a new query point to find its neighbors, continue searching until the entire boundary point is traversed, a polygon obtained by the connection of the hole boundary points. The angle corresponding to each vertex of the polygon is calculated, and the boundary point corresponding to the minimum angle is selected as the starting boundary point.

3.2.2 Edge-Preserving Projection

The edge-preserving projection keeps the length unchanged when lines connecting three-dimensional hole boundary points are projected onto the plane fitted by the hole boundary point. Taking six hole boundary points $p_i(i = 0, 1, \cdots, 5)$ in three-dimensional space as an example to illustrate the edge-preserving projection method, Fig. 2(a) is the connection of three-dimensional hole boundary points, Fig. 2(b) is points under the edge-preserving projection. Start from the initial boundary point of p_0, by projecting p_0 and its nearest neighbors p_1 in the plane, the projection points p_0' and p_1' are obtained, at the same time, marking the direction as Direction. If line p_0p_1 is parallel to the plane S, then p_1' is an edge-preserving projection point of p_1, If the line p_0p_1 is not parallel to the plane S, taking the point p'' whose distance equal to $d(p_0, p_1)$ in the extended line $p_0'p_1'$ as the edge-preserving projection point of p_1, as shown in Fig. 2(c).

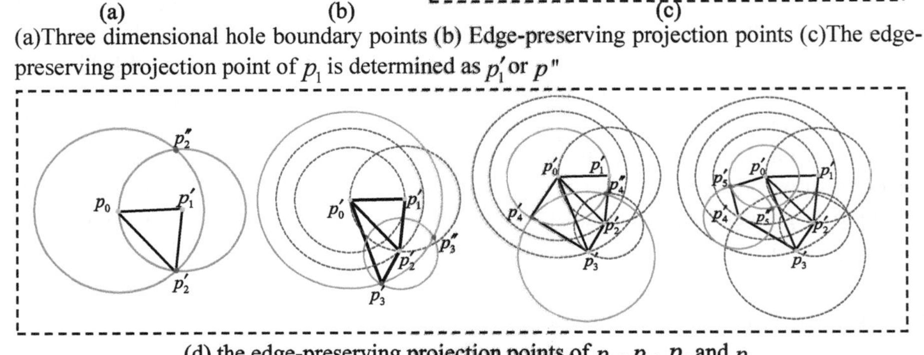

Fig. 2. The process of obtaining edge-preserving projection points

The projection point p_2 is determined as follows, take p'_0 and p'_1 as the center of circle respectively, and draw circles with radius $d(p_0, p_2)$ and $d(p_1, p_2)$, then the intersection of two circles are p'_2 and p''_2, select p'_2 as the projection point of p_2 according to the marked Direction. According to this method, the edge- preserving projection points p_3, p_4 and p_5 are determined as p'_3, p'_4 and p'_5, which shown in Fig. 2(d).

3.3 Hole Repairing

The point collectivization is carried out in the area surrounding by the boundary points of two-dimensional plane which is projected through the process of edge-preserving projection. As shown in Fig. 3(a), the interior of area is filled with a certain number of points. Firstly, the average density of points in the two-dimensional projected plane is calculated, that is to say, the boundary point and its k nearest neighbors are all projected onto two-dimensional plane to form the point set, and then to solve the density of the point set as *avg*. It should be noted that the difference between this projection and the previous projection is that, the previous projection is the projection of edge-preserving projection and only projected by hole boundary points, this projection is the projection of holes and its neighbor points, and also does not require the edge-preserving projection. Secondly, the regional decomposition is performed to find the center of gravity of the two-dimensional hole. According to the density, the length of the hole and the center of gravity are equally divided in order to determine the coordinates of each point, and so as to determine the position coordinates of these vertexes, as shown in Fig. 3(b). Finally, the point collectivization of boundary is carried, which means the area of boundary point is filled with the point whose density is *avg*, the effect shows in Fig. 3(c).

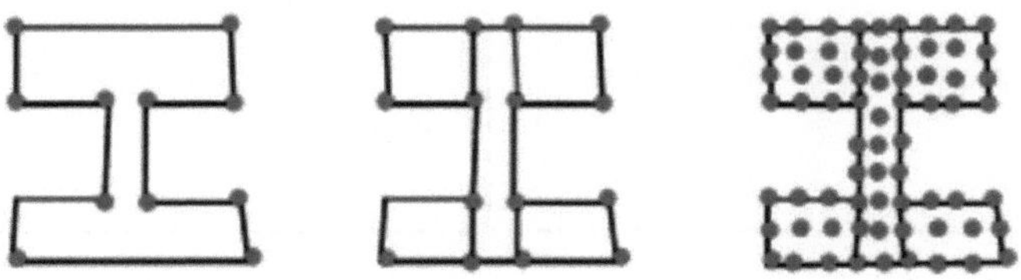

(a) (b) (c)
(a)Area of Boundary point(b)The regional decomposition (c)Point collectivization of boundary

Fig. 3. Boundary line point collectivization

The hole boundary points and the k-nearest neighbor points in the three-dimensional space are considered as constraints, using radial-basis interpolation mapping technique to construct hole surface. Then the two-dimensional grid filling point obtained above is reflected on the hole surface structure and formed to repair three-dimensional holes, thus completing the hole repairing.

4 Experimental Results Analysis

In this paper, the Bear model and the Desk model are used to show the repairing results. Digging a hole in the left foot of the Bear model with sharp features and a hole in a sharp corner of the Desk model, as shown in Fig. 4.

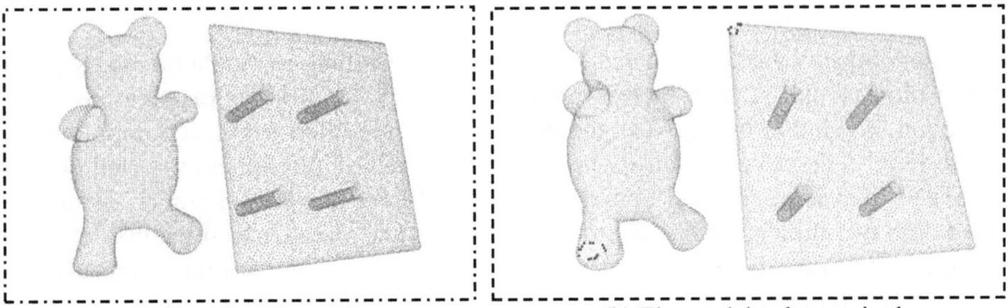

(a) The original model (b) The model to be repaired

Fig. 4. The model of Bear and Desk model

Based on the quadrant and the angle size, the extraction result of hole boundary point shows in Fig. 5(a). Figure 5(b) is a result of the connection among hole boundary points.

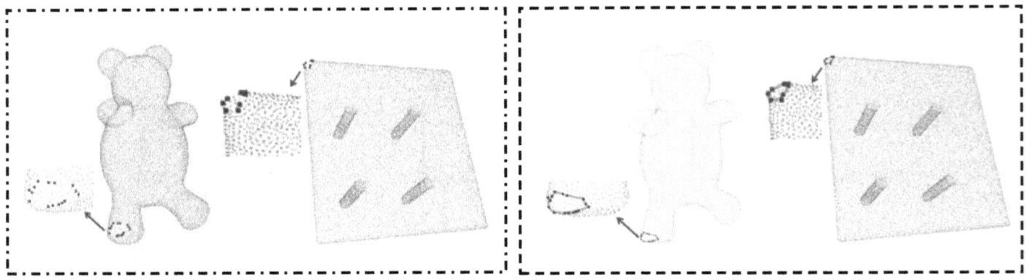

(a) Hole boundary points (b) The connection of hole boundary points

Fig. 5. Hole boundary point extraction and connection of Bear and Desk model

Three-dimensional hole boundary points are project to two-dimensional plane by edge-preserving, the result is shown in Fig. 6(a), the red points in green line indicate the connection of the original hole boundary points, the green points in red line indicate the connection among hole boundary points mapped to the plane by the edge-preserving. The two-dimensional area obtained by the projection is collectivized to obtain the filling points, as shown in Fig. 6(b). Among them, red points are hole boundary points, green points are edge-preserving projection points, blue points are filling points.

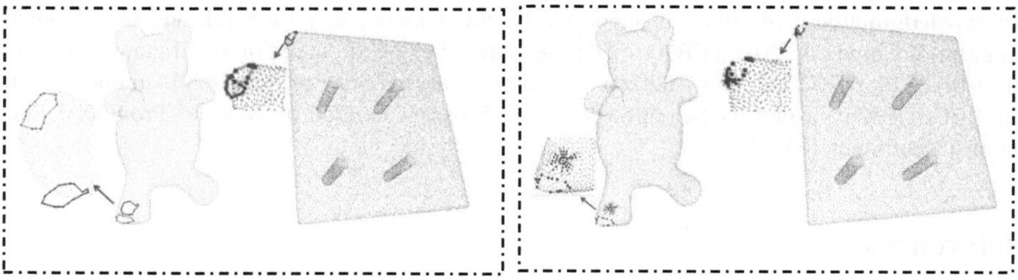

(a) Edge-preserving projection (b) Point collectivization

Fig. 6. The Edge-preserving projection and point collectivization of Bear and Desk model (Color figure online)

The two-dimensional filling points are reflected on the hole surface of the structure, and the final repairing result is shown as Fig. 7. It can be seen that the hole repairing method in this paper based on the edge-preserving projection is maintaining sharp features of the holes while effectively completing the hole repairing.

Fig. 7. The repairing results of Bear and Desk model

5 Conclusions

To solve the problem of preserving sharp features of holes, this paper introduces an edge-preserving strategy to repair holes. The idea of extracting hole boundary points based on quadrant and angle is more reasonable and effective for extracting the boundary points. The projection method of the edge-preserving ensures the uniqueness and shape invariance of the hole boundary point projection on the two-dimensional plane, as to achieve the effective restoration of sharp features in hole boundary points. The filling points as average density achieves better fusion of the hole boundary point and surrounding neighborhood points. Therefore, the method of this paper can effectively repair the holes while maintaining the sharp features of the holes.

Acknowledgments. This study is supported by the National Key Research and Development Program of China No. 2018YFB1004905; the Nature Science Foundation of China under Grant No. 61472319, 61872291, 61871320; and in part by Shaanxi Science Research Plan under Grant No. 2017JQ6023; in part by Scientific Research Program Funded by Shaanxi Provincial Education Department 18JS077.

References

1. Altantsetseg, E., Khorloo, O., Matsuyama, K., Konno, K.: Complex hole-filling algorithm for 3D models. In: Computer Graphics International Conference (CGI 17), p. 10. ACM, June 2017. https://doi.org/10.1145/3095140.3095150
2. Attene, M., Campen, M., Kobbelt, L.: Polygon mesh repairing: an application perspective. ACM Comput. Surv. **45**(2), 1–33 (2013). https://doi.org/10.1145/2431211.2431214
3. Guo, X., Xiao, J., Wang, Y.: A survey on algorithms of hole filling in 3D surface reconstruction. Vis. Comput. 1–11 (2016). https://doi.org/10.1007/s00371-016-1316-y
4. Pfeifle, R., Seidel, H.P.: Triangular B-splines for blending and filling of polygonal holes. In: Proceedings of Graphics Interface 1996, Toronto, Canada, pp. 186–193 (1996)
5. Zhang, L.Y., Zhou, R.R., Zhou, L.S.: Research on the algorithm of hole repairing in mesh surfaces. J. Appl. Sci **20**(3), 221–224 (2002)
6. Liu, G., Bailin, L.I., Chaoming, H.E.: Polygon models holes filling for preserving sharp features. Manuf. Technol. Mach. Tool **17**(5), 59–62 (2011)
7. Liu, Z.: Recovery of Sharp Features in Mesh Models. University of Science & Technology China (2015)
8. Van Sinh, N., Ha, T.M., Thanh, N.T.: Filling holes on the surface of 3D point clouds based on tangent plane of hole boundary points. In: Symposium on Information and Communication Technology, pp. 331–338. ACM (2016)
9. Chalmovianský, P., Jüttler, B.: Filling holes in point clouds. In: Wilson, M.J., Martin, R.R. (eds.) Mathematics of Surfaces. LNCS, vol. 2768, pp. 196–212. Springer, Heidelberg (2003). https://doi.org/10.1007/978-3-540-39422-8_14
10. Qiu, Z., Song, X., Zhang, D.: Reparation of holes in discrete data points. J. Eng. Graph. **25** (4), 85–89 (2004)
11. Sharf, A., Alexa, M., Cohen-Or, D.: Context-based surface completion. ACM Trans. Graph. (TOG) **23**(3), 878–887 (2004)
12. Pernot, J.P., Moraru, G., Véron, P.: Filling holes in meshes using a mechanical model to simulate the curvature variation minimization. Comput. Graph. **30**(6), 892–902 (2006)
13. Wu, X., Chen, W.: A scattered point set hole-filling method based on boundary extension and convergence. In: Intelligent Control and Automation, pp. 5329–5334. IEEE (2015)
14. Yang, L., Yan, Q., Xiao, C.: Shape-controllable geometry completion for point cloud models. Vis. Comput. **33**(3), 1–14 (2016)
15. Lin, H., Wang, W.: Feature preserving holes filling of scattered point cloud based on tensor voting. In: IEEE International Conference on Signal and Image Processing, pp. 402–406. IEEE (2017)
16. Tang, J., Wang, Y., Zhao, Y., Hao, W., Ning, X., Lv, K.: A repair method of point cloud with big hole. In: IEEE International Conference Proceedings on Virtual Reality and Visualization, ICVRV 2017, Zhengzhou, China, 21–22 October 2017 (2017)
17. Wang, Y., Jing, T., Zhao, Y., Hao, W., Ning, X., Lv, K.: Point cloud hole filling based on feature lines extraction. In: IEEE International Conference Proceedings on Virtual Reality and Visualization, ICVRV 2017, Zhengzhou, China, 21–22 October 2017 (2017)

A Hole Repairing Method Based on Slicing

Yanni Zhao[1,3], Yinghui Wang[1,2(✉)], Ningna Wang[4], Xiaojuan Ning[1], Zhenghao Shi[1], Minghua Zhao[1], Ke Lv[5], and Liangyi Huang[6]

[1] Institute of Computer Science and Engineering, Xi'an University of Technology, Xi'an, China
wyh_925@163.com
[2] Shaanxi Key Laboratory of Network Computing and Security Technology, Xi'an, China
[3] Department of Computer Science, Shannxi Vocational and Technical College, Xi'an, China
[4] Booking B.V., Herengracht 597, 1017 CE Amsterdam, Netherlands
[5] Institute of Automation, Chinese Academy of Sciences, Beijing, China
[6] School of Engineering and Applied Science, George Washington University, Washington, D.C., USA

Abstract. The repairing of 3D point cloud holes has an important meaning to ensure the integrity of cloud data. We present a slice-based repairing method for 3D point cloud in this paper. Firstly, the model is horizontal sliced and each slice is projected on a two-dimensional plane, then the band-shaped points obtained during projection are clustered to select boundary points of the hole. Combined with optimal fitting points, the hole repairing point sets in the projection layer are re-sampled based on the cubic B-spline curve to fit boundary points. Finally, all hole repairing point sets in the projection layer are combined in 3D space to finish the entire hole recovery. The experimental results show that the proposed method can effectively repair complex holes for various point cloud models.

Keywords: Slicing · Hole repairing · Curve fitting · Boundary point

1 Introduction

Three-dimensional point cloud models have been widely studied and applied in varied fields. However, due to the defect of models as well as the occlusion and reflection of measurement methods [1, 2], it is unavoidable that cloud data is incomplete and holes exist at the surface of point cloud model. Therefore, the repairing of holes for point cloud model is the key step of identification and reconstruction of 3D model.

At present, there are mainly two methods of hole repairing for point cloud: hole repairing method based on mesh model [3, 4] and the hole repairing method based on point cloud model [5]. The hole repairing algorithm based on mesh model is to repair the model by converting the point cloud model into mesh [6]. So far, there are many mesh-based methods of hole repairing at home [7] and abroad [8–10]. However, mesh model has relatively high requirements on the spatial distribution rules of point clouds, which means a little "irregular" point clouds will lead to inaccuracy or even failure.

A. El Rhalibi et al. (Eds.): Edutainment 2018, LNCS 11462, pp. 123–131, 2019.
https://doi.org/10.1007/978-3-030-23712-7_17

In particular, if the point cloud data is complex or noisy, it is not possible to ensure that it can be meshed correctly. Therefore, our paper focuses on repairing of holes directly from point cloud model.

Generally, the hole repairing method of point cloud model mainly achieved through curve fitting based on some characteristics of point cloud. Chalmovianský [11] proposed the nearest neighbor hole repairing method. According to certain continuous features between holes and its surrounding surface, QIU [12] utilized surrounding points around holes to regenerate local patch and refill for hole repairing. Chen [13] adopted k-d tree to extract the boundary points of holes from the incomplete point cloud, and the radial basis function is used for surface fitting to repair holes. This feature-based curve fitting method is good for low complexity holes, however for higher complexity, especially those hole areas containing variety of surfaces, the repairing result is not satisfactory.

To solve above problems, researchers also proposed slicing techniques based on point cloud to repairing complex surfaces. He [14] proposed a hole repairing method based on self-adaptive slice, which divided point cloud data according to feature data block and then performed slicing and repairing. Meng [15] made adaptive slicing of the whole point cloud while maintaining local characteristics of point cloud, and after slicing, total least squares fitting is applied to achieve point cloud repairing. The limitation of these two methods is that if the accuracy of feature extraction of point cloud will affect the subsequent slice processing and hole repairing effect. Wang [16] introduced the bi-directional slicing technology for complex hole repairing by cutting point cloud with certain direction and certain criteria. After generating hole boundary points, the slice processing and repairing operation are carried out. In this case, the accuracy of the hole boundary point location directly affects the follow-up operation. Also, the bi-directional slice of this method is limited to the X axis and the Y axis, which means the flexibility needs to be further improved.

In our paper, a slice-based repairing method of 3D point cloud hole model is proposed in order to repair complex holes, especially the absence of broken holes around hole areas, the direct cutting on the point cloud model is implemented. Our method provides better hole repairing result without feature extraction or boundaries finding in advance, which avoids the influence of feature extraction and the accuracy of boundary point positioning on subsequent operations.

2 Overview

The overall idea of our method is consists of two steps: the hole extraction and the hole repairing. Which is shown in Fig. 1.

(1) The point cloud model is cut in the direction of vertical *Z* axis, and the cutting point set is projected on the middle plane parallel to the upper and lower cutting surfaces to obtain a band-shaped point set;
(2) The clustering algorithm is used to extract the band-shaped point set from projection. That is to say, the band-shaped point set is divided into *n* clusters, and cluster centers are clustered in each cluster to replace surrounding points;

(3) The center of mass for each cluster is sorted according to the distance, also boundary points and adjacency points of hole are selected;
(4) The optimal fitting points is calculated, the cubic B-spline curve fitting is used to fit the repairing points of the cutting layer and achieve the repairing result of single-layer holes;
(5) The repair of the whole holes is obtained and the complete repair of the 3D hole model is finished.

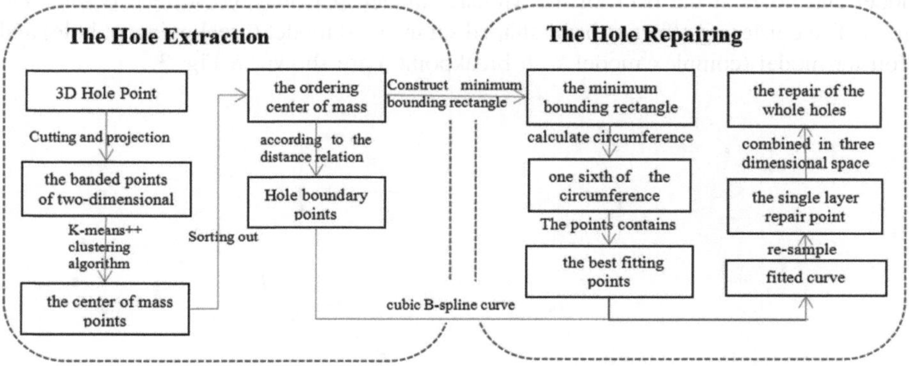

Fig. 1. The profile of our method

3 Methodology

3.1 Slicing and Clustering

The 3D point model is assumed to be vertical and perpendicular to *XOZ* plane. If the normal vector direction of the model is not parallel to the *Z* axis, the rotation will first applied to the model. Then the 3D point cloud model is partitioned into h number of horizontal slices along the vertical *Z* axis such as slices shown in Fig. 2. Thereby two-dimensional band-shaped points can be obtained.

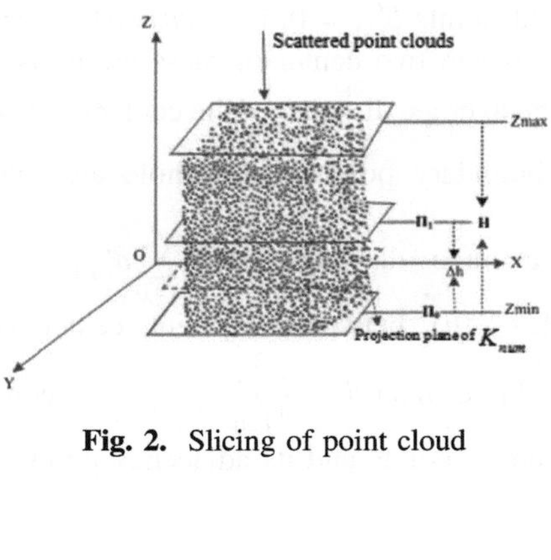

Fig. 2. Slicing of point cloud

In the paper, the clustering algorithm is used to abstract model's core skeleton from band-shaped points. *k-means* ++ clustering algorithm is used to divide the band-shaped point set into n clusters. In each cluster, the cluster center point (center of mass) is calculated by *k-means* ++ clustering method to replace surrounding points. And the boundary point of hole based on the center of mass point set is obtained.

According to shape and complexity, holes are divided into three types: simple hole, broken hole, complex hole with breakpoints. In order to prove the efficiency of our method of repairing of complex holes, we dig holes in the middle of palm for the Hand model and holes at the back of the Monster model in which the surface is sags and crests. The clustering effect of band-shaped set in Hand model (breakpoints at hole) and Monster model (complex model with breakpoints) are shown in Fig. 3.

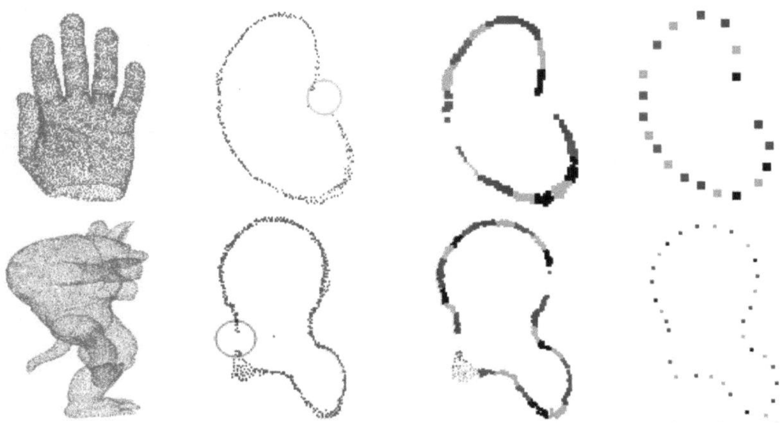

(a) Original point cloud (b) Cut projection point cluster (c) Clustering point set (d) Each cluster center of mass

Fig. 3. The process of clustering center of mass for Hand and Monster model.

3.2 Boundary Extraction of the Hole

The center of mass set $S_i(i = 0, 1, \cdots, n)$ is ordered according to the distance between points to generate ordered points $S'_i(i = 0, 1, \cdots, n)$. At the same times, the distance $d'_{i(i+1)}(i = 0, 1, \cdots, n)$ between two center of mass points is calculated according to $S'_i(i = 0, 1, \cdots, n)$, and the average distance of the center of mass points is calculated as $\overline{d'} = \frac{1}{n}\sum_{i=0}^{n} d'_{i(i+1)}$. Then boundary points of the hole are selected according to the distance relation, the average distance $\overline{d'} = \frac{1}{n}\sum_{i=0}^{n} d'_{i(i+1)}$ is compared with the distance $d'_{i(i+1)}(i = 0, 1, \cdots, n)$ between adjacent center of mass points, when $d'_{i(i+1)}(i = 0, 1, \cdots, n)$ is larger than $\overline{d'} = \frac{1}{n}\sum_{i=0}^{n} d'_{i(i+1)}$, it is considered as a hole, at the same time, the hole boundary points and its adjacency points are found.

3.3 Hole Repairing

According to the optimal fitting points, cubic standard B-splines is used for curve fitting, and the sampling points of filling hole are obtained in the corresponding layer.

3.3.1 Optimal Fitting Points

The cubic B-spline curves are fitted based on optimal fitting points, so the selection of the optimal fitting points directly affects the effect of hole repairing. If the size of selected points is too small, it will reflect the trend of the missing part, on the other side, if too much, it will increase the fitting time and reduce the efficiency. In this paper, the optimal fitting points are determined by distance, which firstly construct the minimum bounding rectangle in the cutting projection layer after clustering model, then calculate the circumference of the minimum external rectangle. A large number of experiments show that when the distance is one sixth of the circumference, which contains a number of points in the distance as the optimal fitting points, fitting is the best result.

Figure 4 shows the experimental results obtained from the Hand model and the Monster model, which proves that optimal fitting points determined by this method are more accurate. The numbers of points N around the holes are taken as 2, 4, 6, 8 and 10 respectively. From experiment, it can be seen that when the number of points around the hole is 10 in Hand model and 6 in Monster model, which are one sixth of the circumference, the fitting curve is gradually approaching the trend of the surface around the hole. When the number of points increases, the fitting curve will not change much. It is reasonable that the larger the number of points, the better the fitting curve, but at the same time, the execution time of the model is also longer in order to fit the curve. Therefore, adopting the optimal fitting points determined in this paper can not only ensure the fitting effect but also take into account the fitting efficiency, and recover the structural features of the projection layer with high cutting complexity.

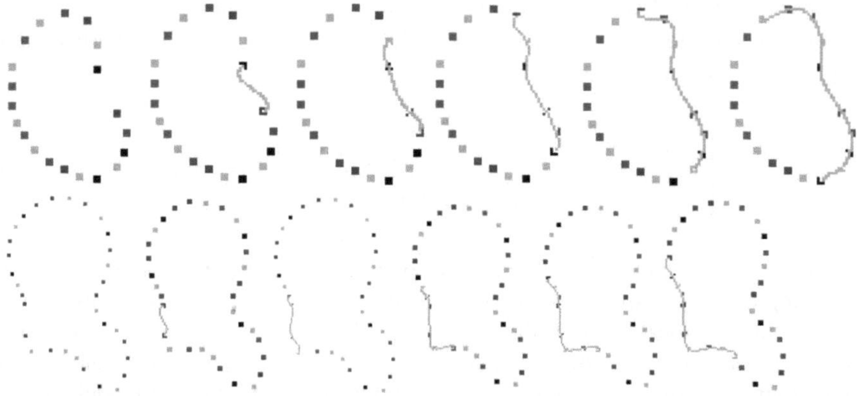

(a) Single-layer (b) N=2 (c) N=4 (d) N=6 (e) N=8 (f) N=10

Fig. 4. Curve fitting diagram of Hand model and Monster model

3.3.2 Curve Fitting for Single Layer

The hole repairing point on the projection layer can be obtained by re-sampling the fitted curve according to the average density of the original model. The point at the non-hole in the original model and the point at the re-sampled hole form a new model that completes the overall hole repairing, which also keeps the distribution density of points at the hole consistent with that at the non-hole. The example of single layer cutting projection hole repairing are shown in Fig. 5.

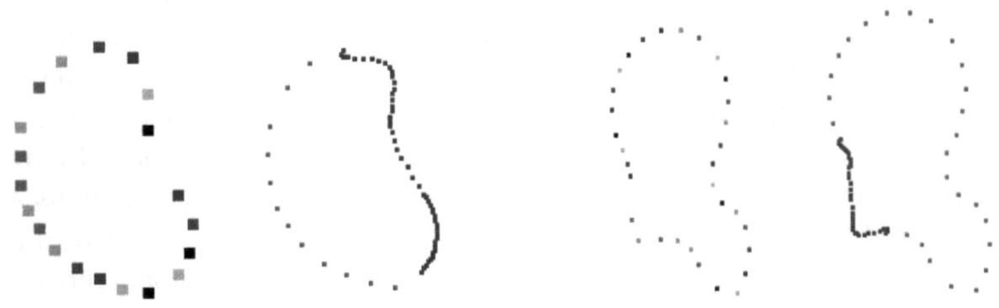

Fig. 5. The diagram of hole layer sampling point of Hand and Monster model

3.3.3 Repairing of Holes

The cubic B-spline curve is used to fit and re-sample boundary points and adjacent points of the hole as to repair single-layer holes. Next, repaired points are combined in three-dimensional space to complete the repair of holes.

The repairing method is to project the point set obtained during cutting onto the middle plane which is parallel to the upper and lower cutting planes. And according to the *Z* value of the initial cutting layer, the number of points needed to be reinserted into the cutting plane, the *Z* value corresponding to each cutting thickness layer can be calculated.

Suppose a layer of coordinates is $P(x_{i_{Knum}}, y_{i_{Knum}}, z_{i_{Knum}})$, The coordinates of a point converted into a three dimensional space is $P'(x'_{i_{Knum}}, y'_{i_{Knum}}, z'_{i_{Knum}})$, The corresponding coordinate conversion relationship is:

$$\begin{cases} x_{i_{Knum}} = x'_{i_{Knum}} \\ y_{i_{Knum}} = y'_{i_{Knum}} \\ z_{i_{Knum}} = z'_{i_{Knum}} = h_0 + n * \Delta d \end{cases} \quad \mathrm{i} \in (0, \mathrm{k}) \text{ and } \mathrm{z}'_{i_{Knum}} \le h_1 \tag{1}$$

In order to restore the single layer repair points in the three-dimensional space, *n* is the re-sampling layer number between the upper and lower cutting surfaces in which the cutting layer is located, Δd is the step length of the sampling point and $\Delta d = \Delta h / n$, Δh as the thickness of the slice and $\Delta h = (Z_{\max} - Z_{\min}) / layernum$, $Z_{\max}$ and $Z_{\min}$ are the maximum and minimum value of a three-dimensional point cloud model along the direction of the *Z* axis, *layerNum* is the number of layers that cut the 3D point cloud model, The coordinates of the Z axis with the cutting surface under the slice are $h_0 = Z_{\min} + (K_{num} - 1) * \Delta h$, the coordinates of the *Z* axis of the cutting surface on the slice are $h_1 = h_0 + \Delta h$. The current cutting layer number is K_{num}.

4 Analysis of Experimental Results

The repairing experiments of Hand and Monster models are carried out in this paper as Fig. 6, the original model shows in figure (a), the model to be repaired in figure (b), the repair results in figure (c).

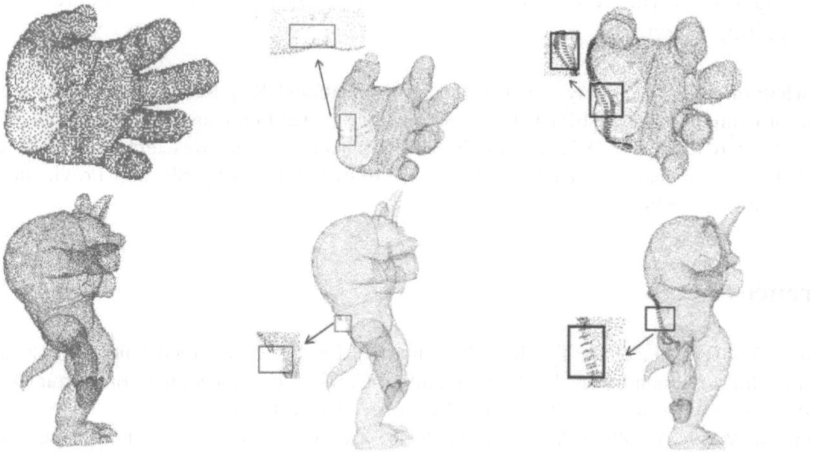

(a)The original model (b)The model to be repaired (c)The repair results

Fig. 6. The repair result of Hand model and Monster model

According to the analysis of experimental results, the hole repair method based on slicing can achieve better fusion of holes and its surrounding areas because of the average density of the original model. A direct cutting method based on slicing is relatively simple and can avoid downsides of other factors, so the repair result is more reasonable. It can be seen that the method proposed in this paper is not only suitable for general holes or holes with low complexity, but also for higher complexity models with plenty missing points, such as broken model after cutting like the Hand model and complex hole with breakpoints like the Weapon model. Points corresponding to these shapes on the cut plane can also be found and well repaired.

5 Conclusions

In this paper, a slice-based repair method of 3D point cloud hole model is presented, which directly cutting on the point cloud model without the need of feature extraction or hole boundary location in advance. The method is relatively simple and can avoid the effect of feature extraction and accuracy of boundary point on subsequent operations. Optimal fitting points are selected by distance, which avoids the difference of density due to different density fitting points generated by various methods. And the method can not only repair holes with lower complexity, but also obtain better repairing and maintain the distribution consistency for the missing points of models with higher complexity, such as broken holes, complex holes with breakpoints.

When the method is used for curve fitting, optimal fitting points are taken at the direction of left and right to repair the single-layer hole, and then the whole three-dimensional hole is repaired. But in fact, the trend of missing points is not only related to the left and right points, but also related to the top and bottom points. Therefore, in the next stage of work, we're planning to take all these points into consideration for a better repairing effect.

Acknowledgments. This study is supported by the National Key Research and Development Program of China No. 2018YFB1004905; the Nature Science Foundation of China under Grant No. 61472319, 61872291, 61871320; and in part by Shaanxi Science Research Plan under Grant No. 2017JQ6023; in part by Scientific Research Program Funded by Shaanxi Provincial Education Department 18JS077.

References

1. Wang, Y., Tang, J., Zhao, Y., Hao, W., Ning, X., Lv, K.: Point cloud hole filling based on feature lines extraction. In: IEEE International Conference Proceedings on Virtual Reality and Visualization, ICVRV 2017, 21–22 October 2017 (2017)
2. Tang, J., Wang, Y., Zhao, Y., Hao, W., Ning, X., Lv, K.: A repair method of point cloud with big hole. In: IEEE International Conference Proceedings on Virtual Reality and Visualization, ICVRV 2017, 21–22 October 2017 (2017)
3. Attene, M., Campen, M., Kobbelt, L.: Polygon mesh repairing: an application perspective. ACM Comput. Surv. **45**(2), 1–33 (2013)
4. Altantsetseg, E., Khorloo, O., Matsuyama, K, Konno, K.: Complex hole-filling algorithm for 3D models. In: Computer Graphics International Conference, CGI 2017, p. 10. ACM, June 2017
5. Guo, X., Xiao, J., Wang, Y.: A survey on algorithms of hole filling in 3D surface reconstruction. Vis. Comput. 1–11 (2016)
6. Liepa, P.: Filling holes in meshes. In: Proceedings of the 2003 EUROGRAPHICS/ACM SIGGRAPH Symposium on Geometry Processing (SGP 03), pp. 200–205, June 2003
7. Zhang, L.Y., Zhou, R.R., Zhou, L.S.: Research on the algorithm of hole repairing in mesh surfaces. J. Appl. Sci. **20**(3), 221–224 (2002)
8. Tran, M.H., Nhan, B.C.: A complete method for reconstructing an elevation surface of 3D point clouds. REV J. Electron. Commun. **4**(3-4), 91–97 (2015)
9. Quinsat, Y.: Filling holes in digitized point cloud using a morphing-based approach to preserve volume characteristics. Int. J. Adv. Manuf. Technol. **81**(1-4), 411–421 (2015)
10. Van Sinh, N., Ha, T.M., Thanh, N.T.: Filling holes on the surface of 3D point clouds based on tangent plane of hole boundary points. In: Symposium on Information and Communication Technology, pp. 331–338. ACM (2016)
11. Chalmovianský, P., Jüttler, B.: Filling holes in point clouds. In: Wilson, M.J., Martin, R.R. (eds.) Mathematics of Surfaces. LNCS, vol. 2768, pp. 196–212. Springer, Heidelberg (2003). https://doi.org/10.1007/978-3-540-39422-8_14
12. Qiu, Z., Song, X., Zhang, D.: Reparation of holes in discrete data points. J. Eng. Graph. **25**(4), 85–89 (2004)

13. Chen, F., Chen, Z., Ding, Z.: Filling holes in point cloud with radial basis function. J. Comput.-Aided Des. Comput. Graph. **18**(9), 1414–1419 (2006)
14. He, G.: Hole patching of adaptive slicing based on feature-data segmentation. J. East China Jiaotong Univ. (4), 95–99 (2014)
15. Meng, Q.: Research on the holes repairing method based on the total least squares slicing method. Geospatial Inf. **15**(6), 47–50 (2017)
16. Wang, Y.G., Yan-Jun, X.U., Lin, H.R.: Research about point cloud hole- repairing based on bidirectional slice method. Geomat. Spat. Inf. Technol. **10**, 218–220 (2015)

An Improved Total Variation Denoising Model

Minghua Zhao(✉), Tang Chen, Zhenghao Shi, Peng Li, Bing Li, and Yinghui Wang

School of Computer Science and Engineering, Xi'an University of Technology, Xi'an 710048, China
mh_zhao@126.com

Abstract. Total variation denoising model is vulnerable to the influence of the gradient and often loses the image details. Aiming at this shortcoming, an improved total variation denoising model is proposed to recover the damaged additive Gaussian noise image. First, guided filtering and impulse filtering are used to preprocess noisy images; second, the adaptive norm parameter is selected by the edge detection operator; third, the horizontal and vertical weight values are selected by adaptive method; Finally, the image processed by non-local means filter replaces the noisy image to modify the fidelity term in the method. Experiments show that the improved total variation denoising model can remove the noise and can keep the texture and edge of the image better as well.

Keywords: Image processing · Image restoration · Image denoising · Total variation

1 Introduction

Image denoising is to estimate the original image from the contaminated noise image, and retain important image features such as edge and texture. Image denoising technology has been widely used in the fields of scientific research, military technology, agricultural production, medicine, meteorology and astronomy.

In 1992, Rudin, Osher and Fatemi proposed a denoising method based on total variation (TV, Total Variation) model [1], referred to as ROF (Rudin, Osher, Fatemi) model. It has a significant drawback that it is easy to produce ladder effect, that is, the flat region of the image produces false boundaries. In order to solve this problem, many improved methods were put forward, which can be divided into model improvement and numerical calculation. In terms of model improvement, Esedogl divided the TV model into the isotropic TV model and the anisotropic TV model according to the regular term [2]. Song proposed a generalized total variation denoising model based on L1+p norm [3]. The model could overcome the false edge generation, but the objective selection of different image p had a great impact on the image denoising effect. Buades et al. proposed an nonlocal method [5]. The nonlocal variation item was used to replace the total variation item of the TV model and better denoising effect was obtained. In terms of numerical calculation, the gradient descent method used characteristic of the negative gradient direction as the fastest descent direction to determine the new search

A. El Rhalibi et al. (Eds.): Edutainment 2018, LNCS 11462, pp. 132–139, 2019.
https://doi.org/10.1007/978-3-030-23712-7_18

direction of each iteration [6]. But the final speed is low. Amir Beck et al. combined the well-known gradient projection and fast gradient projection method to solve the slow speed of the TV model, which accelerated the convergence rate [7]. Tai improved the two steps penalty method to obtain the augmented Lagrange method [8]. However, the selection of parameter β had a serious influence on the convergence effect. Model improvement methods are more sensitive to noise and lose some important texture information, while numerical calculation methods are low convergence.

In order to overcome the shortcomings of these methods, we improved the total variation model and an adaptive weighted total variation image denoising model is presented in this paper. The model has several steps. First, the guided filtering method is used to remove the image noise and the impulse filtering method is used to enhance the edge information of the image; next, the adaptive selection paradigm parameters and weight size are established based on the edge detection of the preprocessing image; finally, the original denoised image in the fidelity term is modified by the image obtained by the non-local mean filter.

2 Total Variation Image Denoising Model

The total variation image denoising model [1] is shown as Eq. (1).

$$\min_{u} \frac{\lambda}{2} ||u_0 - u||^2 + \int_{\Omega} |\nabla u| \tag{1}$$

In Eq. (1), u is the real image, u_0 is the observed image, Ω represents the image interval and λ is the Lagrange factor, which balances regular and fidelity items and satisfies $\lambda > 0$. The first item is the fidelity term, which mainly retains the original image characteristics and reduces the image distortion. The second term is the regular term, which mainly plays a smoothing role. The total variation model will diffuse along the edge when denoising and effectively maintain the edge. However, it is easy to produce the ladder effect in the smooth region [5].

3 An Adaptive Weighted Total Variation Image Denoising Model

In order to overcome the obvious ladder effect of TV denoising model and improve the denoising effect, by using the edge detection operations to choose the adaptive parameters based on the preprocessed images [9], an adaptive weighted total variation image denoising model, as shown in Eq. (2), is proposed in this paper.

$$\min_{u} \frac{\lambda}{2} ||u_{NL} - u||^2 + \frac{1}{g(\mathrm{i,j})} \int_{\Omega} \mathrm{W(i,j)} |\nabla u|^{g(\mathrm{i,j})} \tag{2}$$

In Eq. (2), u_{NL} is the denoising image obtained by means of non-local means filtering; W(i, j) is used to reduce the weight parameters of the texture and edge and its adjacent pixels between horizontal and vertical differences; $g(\mathrm{i},\mathrm{j})$ is an adaptive normal form parameter, which controls the diffusion behavior so that the TV denoising model based on L1 norm is in the edge. The improved total variation model shown as Eq. (2) preserves the edge region effectively when the noise is removed, while the total variation model shown as Eq. (1) blurs the edge region. This method can be divided into the steps of edge detection, adaptive norm setting, weight setting and image initializing.

3.1 Edge Detection

In order to reduce the sensitivity of the adaptive parameter $g(\mathrm{i},\mathrm{j})$ in Eq. (2) to noise, the parameter u_0 of the noisy image in Eq. (1) is preprocessed by the guided filtering [10] and the impulse filtering [11]. The guided filtering is used to smooth the Gaussian noise and impulse filtering is used to enhance the edge of the image. That is, the preprocessing can enhance the edge of the image while smoothing the noise.

Four edge detection operations d_θ (size as 6×6) are introduced in this process [12]. For $\theta = 0$, $d_0 = \begin{bmatrix} & O_1 & \\ O_2 & M & O_2 \\ & O_1 & \end{bmatrix}/12$, where $M = \begin{bmatrix} 1 & 2 & 2 & 1 \\ -1 & -2 & -2 & -1 \end{bmatrix}$, $O_1 = \begin{bmatrix} 0 & 0 & 0 & 0 & 0 & 0 \\ 0 & 0 & 0 & 0 & 0 & 0 \end{bmatrix}$ and $O_2 = \begin{bmatrix} 0 \\ 0 \end{bmatrix}$. Other operators d_θ can be obtained by bicubic interpolation and rotation angle θ, as shown in Fig. 1 and the rotation angle range is set as $\Theta = \left\{\frac{\pi}{4}, \frac{\pi}{2}, \frac{3\pi}{4}\right\}$.

3.2 Adaptive Parameter Setting

According to the definition of the edge detection operator d_θ shown as Sect. 3.1, the adaptive parameter $\mathrm{g}(\mathrm{i},\mathrm{j})$ in the adaptive weighted total variation model is defined as Eq. (3).

$$g(\mathrm{i},\mathrm{j}) = 1 + \frac{1}{1 + \sqrt{\sum\limits_{\theta \in \Theta} (\mathrm{d}_\theta \otimes y)^2}} \quad 1 \le g \le 2 \tag{3}$$

In Eq. (3), $\Theta = \left\{0, \frac{\pi}{4}, \frac{\pi}{2}, \frac{3\pi}{4}\right\}$, y is the preprocessed image and $\otimes$ is convolution operator.

In the smooth region of an image, $\sum\limits_{\theta \in \Theta} (\mathrm{d}_\theta \otimes \mathrm{y})^2$ is close to 0 in Eq. (3), therefore the adaptive parameter $\mathrm{g}(\mathrm{i},\mathrm{j})$ is close to 2. In this way, the denoising model is close to the isotropic diffusion denoising model based on the L2 norm. The regularization term, as shown in Eq. (4), can obtain better smoothing effect and avoid the ladder effect.

$$\int_{\Omega} \mathrm{W(i,j)}|\nabla u|^{g(i,j)} = \int_{\Omega} \mathrm{W(i,j)}|\nabla u|^{2} = \sum_{i=1}^{m-1}\sum_{j=1}^{n-1}\sqrt{w_1(\mathrm{i,j})(\mathrm{x}_{i,j}-x_{i+1,j})^2 + w_2(i,j)(\mathrm{x}_{i,j}-x_{i,j+1})^2}$$
$$+\sum_{i=1}^{m-1}\mathrm{w}_1(\mathrm{i,n})|\mathrm{x}_{i,n}-x_{i+1,n}| + \sum_{j=1}^{n-1}\mathrm{w}_2(m,j)|\mathrm{x}_{\mathrm{m},j}-x_{\mathrm{m},j+1}| \tag{4}$$

In Eq. (4), W(i, j) is the weight parameter, w_1 is horizontal weight and w_2 is the vertical weight, $g(i,j)$ is the adaptive parameter, m and n are the number of pixels along the horizontal and the vertical direction and ∇u is gradient.

In the edge region of an image, $\sum_{\theta\in\Theta}(d_\theta \otimes y)^2$ is close to ∞ in Eq. (4), therefore the adaptive parameter $g(i,j)$ is close to 1. In this way, the denoising model is close to TV denoising model based on L1 norm. The regularization term, as shown in Eq. (5), can better preserve the details and texture information in the image.

$$\int_{\Omega} \mathrm{W(i,j)}|\nabla u|^{g(i,j)} = \int_{\Omega} \mathrm{W(i,j)}|\nabla u| = \sum_{i=1}^{m-1}\sum_{j=1}^{n-1}\{w_1(\mathrm{i,j})|\mathrm{x}_{i,j}-x_{i+1,j}| + w_2(\mathrm{i,j})|\mathrm{x}_{i,j}-x_{i,j+1}|\}$$
$$+\sum_{i=1}^{m-1}\mathrm{w}_1(\mathrm{i,n})|\mathrm{x}_{i,n}-x_{i+1,n}| + \sum_{j=1}^{n-1}\mathrm{w}_2(m,j)|\mathrm{x}_{\mathrm{m},j}-x_{\mathrm{m},j+1}| \tag{5}$$

In Eq. (5), W(i, j) is the weight parameter, w_1 is horizontal weight and w_2 is the vertical weight, $g(i,j)$ is the adaptive norm parameter, m and n are the number of pixels along the horizontal and the vertical direction and ∇u is gradient.

In Eqs. (4) and (5), the boundary values are set as Eq. (6).

$$\mathrm{x}_{\mathrm{m}+1,\mathrm{j}} - x_{\mathrm{m,j}} = 0, \mathrm{x}_{i,n+1} - x_{i+1,n} = 0, \forall i. \tag{6}$$

3.3 Weight Setting

In order to reduce the difference between the special pixel (texture and edge) and its adjacent pixels, and to prevent the texture and edge over smoothing, the weight parameter W(i, j) is defined as Eqs. (7) and (8).

$$\mathrm{w}_1(\mathrm{i,j}) = 1 - \mathrm{a}|\mathrm{EM(i,j)} - \mathrm{EM(i+1,j)}| \tag{7}$$

$$\mathrm{w}_2(\mathrm{i,j}) = 1 - \mathrm{a}|\mathrm{EM(i,j)} - \mathrm{EM(i,j+1)}| \tag{8}$$

In Eqs. (7) and (8), $a \in [0,1]$ and EM is the edge image obtained by the edge detection algorithm shown in Sect. 3.1. In the image texture and edge regions, pixels change greatly and $|\mathrm{EM(i,j)} - \mathrm{EM(i+1,j)}|$ will be larger. In this way, in certain cases of a, W(i, j) will have smaller values in texture and edge regions than other regions, thus can suppress smoothness and keep edges better.

3.4 Image Initializing

In the total variation model shown as Eq. (1), the fidelity term is calculated by means of the difference between the noised image and the processed image. The Euler Lagrange equation of Eq. (1) is shown as Eq. (9).

$$div\left(\frac{\nabla u}{|\nabla u|}\right) + \lambda(\mathrm{u_0} - \mathrm{u}) = 0 \tag{9}$$

The evolution function of the time evolution parameter is obtained by the gradient descent method, shown as Eq. (10).

$$\begin{cases} u_t = div\left(\frac{\nabla u}{|\nabla u|}\right) + \lambda(\mathrm{u_0} - \mathrm{u}) \\ u|_{t=0} = u_0 \\ \lambda = \frac{1}{\sigma^2|\Omega|}\int\limits_{\Omega} div\left(\frac{\nabla u}{|\nabla u|}\right) + \lambda(\mathrm{u} - \mathrm{u_0})\mathrm{d}\Omega \end{cases} \tag{10}$$

In Eq. (10), $|\Omega|$ is image area, λ is global scale factor. It can be seen from Eq. (10) that there exists a problem in the evolution function of the fidelity term in the TV model. σ^2 and λ are inversely proportional to each other and the value of λ is small when the original image has a large noise, as a result of which, the evolution function is mainly determined by the solution of regularization term $div\left(\frac{\nabla u}{|\nabla u|}\right)$. It's easy to appear a ladder effect when dealing with edges in this situation and the larger the image noise is, the more obvious the ladder effect will be.

The noise variance needed to calculate λ is determined by $\mathrm{u_0}$ and $\mathrm{u_0}$ will cause larger error when the noise is large, as a result of which, the starting point of solving the above problem is $\mathrm{u_0}$ in the fidelity term. Equation (11) is used to estimate the denoised image $\mathrm{u_0}$ from the noisy image $\mathrm{u_{NL}}$ [7], which is widely used in image processing applications [13].

$$\mathrm{u_{NL}(i)} = \frac{\sum_{\mathrm{j}\in \mathrm{S_j}} \mathrm{w'(i,j)u_0(j)}}{\sum_{\mathrm{j}\in \mathrm{S_j}} \mathrm{w'((i,j))}} \tag{11}$$

In Eq. (11), $\mathrm{S_j}$ is a neighborhood window with pixel j as the center, and $\mathrm{w'(i,j)}$ is the similarity weight between pixel j and pixel i.

4 Experiments and Analysis

4.1 The Visual Performance of Our Proposed Method

Lena image, Cameraman image and Barbara image are used to evaluate the effectiveness of the proposed image denoising method and the size of the test images are set as 256 × 256. TV model [1], ZTV (Zhang total variation) model [4] and our proposed method are used to denoise the image, and the denoising results are shown in Fig. 1. In Fig. 1, column (a) shows the original images, column (b) shows the noisy images, and column (c) shows restoration results using the TV model, column (d) shows the restoration results using the ZTV model, and column (e) shows the restoration results of our proposed method. In the experiment, the Gaussian noise with standard deviation of 15 is added on the Lena image, the Gaussian noise with standard deviation of 30 is added on the Cameraman image, and the Gaussian noise with standard deviation of 30 is added to the Barbara image. It can be seen from the experimental results that compared with the other two denoising methods, the proposed method has better visual effect with different intensity of Gaussian noise.

4.2 Objective Performance of Our Proposed Method

The denoising performance of our proposed method is evaluated by PSNR (Peak Signal to Noise Ratio). Gaussian noise with standard deviation of 15 and Gaussian noise with standard deviation of 30 are added to Lena image, Cameraman image and Barbara image. The PSNR values of the restoration results to noise images using the TV model, ZTV model and our proposed method are shown in Table 1. It can be seen from Table 1 that, comparing with the TV model and the ZTV model, the PSNR values improved by 0.43 dB–0.86 dB and 0.23 dB–0.41 dB respectively with our proposed method, which means that the proposed method can effectively remove noise.

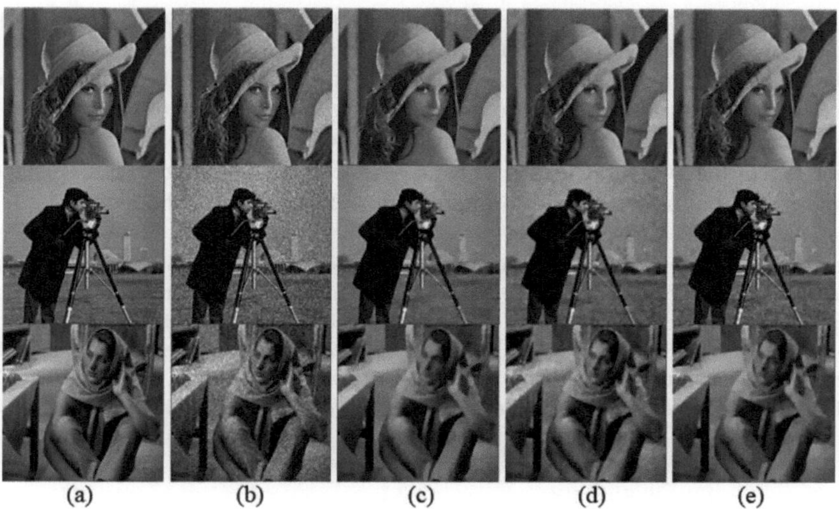

Fig. 1. Image denoising results (a) The original images (b) The noisy images (c) Denoised by the TV model (d) Denoised by the ZTV model (e) Our method

Table 1. PSNR values of restoration images with different methods

Gaussian noise	Image	PSNR values			
		Noisy	TV	ZTV	Our method
$\sigma = 15$	Lena	24.09	29.15	29.45	29.71
	Cameraman	24.61	29.58	29.92	30.33
	Barbara	24.63	28.09	28.58	28.95
$\sigma = 30$	Lena	18.06	26.10	26.36	26.59
	Cameraman	18.58	26.49	26.72	27.02
	Barbara	18.57	25.39	25.61	25.89
$\sigma = 45$	Lena	14.53	23.70	24.01	24.29
	Cameraman	15.06	23.77	23.99	24.25
	Barbara	15.10	23.04	23.39	24.66

5 Conclusions

An adaptive weighted total variation image denoising model is proposed in this paper. The proposed method has three main contributions. First, in order to inherit the advantages of isotropic and anisotropic processing, L1 norm is selected in the texture region and the edge region to avoid smooth transition, L2 norm is selected in the smooth region in order to smooth noise with better; second, the horizontal and vertical weight parameters are introduced to reduce the difference between the texture and the edge and its adjacent pixels, so as to avoid the over smoothing of the texture and edge; third, the fidelity items in the algorithm are modified by using non-local means filter images instead of original noisy ones. Experimental results show that the model can reduce the ladder effect, and can retain the details and texture structure information of the image as well. That is, denoising performance is improved with our proposed method.

However, global regularization parameter is used in our proposed method, which cannot reflect the structural features of images well to some degree. Local adaptive parameter will be further studied to improve the effectiveness of the model.

Acknowledgements. This work was supported by the National Natural Science Foundation of China (No. 61401355, No. 61472319, No. 61502382), the Key Laboratory Foundation of Shaanxi Education Department, China (No. 14JS072), Science and Technology Project Foundation of Beilin District, Xi'an City, China (No. GX1621) and the Science and Technology Project of Xi'an City, China (No. 2017080CG/RC043 (XALG011), 2017080CG/RC043 (XALG021)). The authors also thank anonymous reviewers for their valuable comments.

References

1. Rudin, L.I., Osher, S., Fatemi, E.: Nonlinear total variation based noise removal algorithms. In: Eleventh International Conference of the Center for Nonlinear Studies on Experimental Mathematics: Computational Issues in Nonlinear Science: Computational Issues in Nonlinear Science, pp. 259–268. Elsevier North-Holland, Inc. (1992)
2. Esedoglu, S., Osher, S.J.: Decomposition of images by the anisotropic Rudin-Osher-Fatemi model. Commun. Pure Appl. Math. **57**(12), 1609–1626 (2004)
3. Song, B.: Topics in variational PDE image segmentation, inpainting and denoising. University of California (2010)
4. Zhang, H.Y., Peng, Q.C.: Adaptive image denoising model based on total variation. Opto-Electron. Eng. **33**(3), 50–53 (2006)
5. Buades, A., Coll, B., Morel, J.M.: A review of image denoising algorithms, with a new one. SIAM J. Multiscale Model. Simul. **4**(2), 490–530 (2006)
6. Palsson, F., Sveinsson, J.R., Ulfarsson, M.O.: A new pansharpening algorithm based on total variation. IEEE Geosci. Remote Sens. Lett. **11**(1), 318–322 (2014)
7. Liao, F., Coatrieux, J.L., Wu, J., et al.: A new fast algorithm for constrained four-directional total variation image denoising problem. Math. Probl. Eng.
8. Tai, X.-C., Wu, C.: Augmented lagrangian method, dual methods and split Bregman iteration for ROF model. In: Tai, X.-C., Mørken, K., Lysaker, M., Lie, K.-A. (eds.) SSVM 2009. LNCS, vol. 5567, pp. 502–513. Springer, Heidelberg (2009). https://doi.org/10.1007/978-3-642-02256-2_42
9. Liu, Y.D., Zhou, K.F., Wang, J.L., et al.: Adaptive total variation denoising algorithm based on curvature differential. Comput. Eng. Appl. **52**(16), 167–170 (2016)
10. He, K., Sun, J., Tang, X.: Guided Image Filtering. IEEE Computer Society (2013)
11. Osher, S., Rudin, L.I.: Feature-oriented image enhancement using shock filters. SIAM J. Numer. Anal. **27**(4), 919–940 (1990)
12. Almeida, M.S.C., Almeida, L.B., et al.: Blind and semi-blind deblurring of natural images. IEEE Trans. Image Process. A Publ. IEEE Sig. Process. Soc. **19**(1), 36–52 (2010)
13. Feng, R., Zhong, Y., Wu, Y., et al.: Nonlocal total variation subpixel mapping for hyperspectral remote sensing imagery. Remote Sens. **8**(3), 250–270 (2016)

Spectral Dictionary Learning Based Multispectral Image Compression

Wei Liang(✉), Yinghui Wang, Wen Hao, Xiuxiu Li, Xiuhong Yang, and Lu Liu

School of Computer Science and Engineering, Xi'an University of Technology, No. 5 Jinhua South Road, Xi'an 710048, China
wliang@xaut.edu.cn

Abstract. Multispectral image encoding/decoding methods using spectral dictionary learning and sparse representation to fully exploit spectral features are proposed. In the scheme, K-SVD is first adopted for training a redundant dictionary from typical similar spectra. Then the sparse representative coefficients of each spectrum are obtained by the dictionary for spectral redundancy removal. Finally the equivalent nonzero sparse coefficients are quantified and stored. Experimental results show the superior spectral reconstructed performance compared with sample principal component analysis (PCA) and classical adaptive PCA at the same or even lower bit rates. Besides, the spectral dictionary learning can also be combined with compressed sensing or spatial decorrelation technologies to further expand its application.

Keywords: Multispectral image compression · Spectral redundancy · Dictionary learning · Sparse representation

1 Introduction

Multispectral images (MSIs) record spectral reflectance of observed objects under specific illumination. Compared with traditional color images, MSIs reflect more optical properties of the scene. Therefore, MSIs have not only been widely used in remote sensing but also gradually applied to textile, medical imaging, high-fidelity color reproduction and other fields [1–4]. However, MSI are too huge to be handled. Targeted and effective data compression must be carried out first.

At present, MSI compression are all based on reduction of spectral and spatial correlation, and then formed by quantization and coding. Correlation removal quality always determines compression performance [4]. For spatial redundancy removal, two-dimensional discrete cosine transform (2D-DCT) and 2D discrete wavelet transform (DWT) are widely used. For eliminating spectral redundancy, Karhunen-Loeve transform (KLT), 1D-DWT, 1D-DCT are frequently utilized. DWT and DCT are based on the established mathematical models. Although they are universal for various signals, they often cannot achieve optimal sparsity. KLT is the statistical optimal method for second-order correlation removal. The corresponding principal component analysis (PCA) is also considered to be the optimal linear spectral dimensionality reduction method. The algorithm has certain adaptability but it comes at a cost of high

A. El Rhalibi et al. (Eds.): Edutainment 2018, LNCS 11462, pp. 140–144, 2019.
https://doi.org/10.1007/978-3-030-23712-7_19

computational complexity [4]. In recent years, a complete dictionary obtained by dictionary learning can provide adaptive basis selection based on various inputs, which can be utilized to describe a MSI with better sparsity [5].

To solve the problem of insufficient spectral redundancy removal and weak adaptivity in the existing compression, we propose an efficient MSI compression algorithm based on spectral-dimension dictionary learning. Firstly, we perform proper dictionary learning on a variety of natural scenes and colorful spectra. Then according to different MSIs, we find the best transform domains for their spectral-dimension and gain the sparse representations. Finally, we quantify the sparse coefficients. Experimental results show the superior performance of our proposed method.

2 Spectral Dictionary Learning Based MSI Compression

A MSI $\boldsymbol{F}$ could be constituted by the sub-spectral images taken in L bands and also could be made up of $M \times N$ sub-spatial images $\boldsymbol{F}(x,y) \in R^L, x = 1,2\cdots M$; $y = 1,2\cdots N$. This paper utilizes strong spectral redundancy among pixels of sub-spatial images, and treats $\boldsymbol{F}$ as 2D spectral matrix formed by $\boldsymbol{F}(x,y)$. Based on these, we design a MSI compression scheme as shown in Fig. 1.

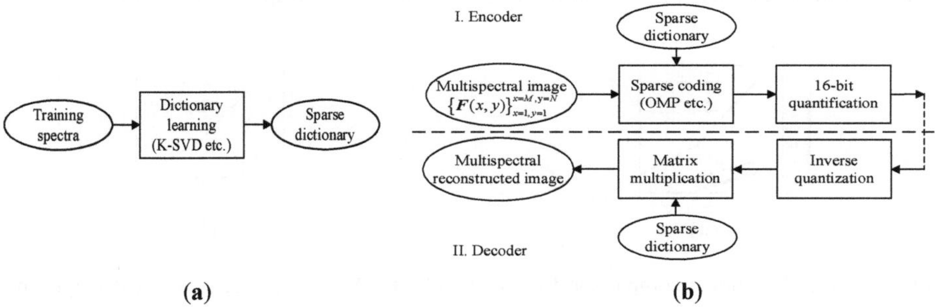

Fig. 1. MSI compression scheme. (a) MSI dictionary training; (b) Flow chart of MSI codec.

Dictionary Training for Sparse Representation. As shown in Fig. 1(a), to compress generic natural MSIs, such as nature scene, color patches, person, etc., our training data is chosen from spectra of standard color patches, various fruits, flowers, skin and so on. Owning to good description of various spectra, the learned dictionary is then considered as the sparse dictionary for the subsequent data compression and decompression. In the paper, we apply K-SVD to obtain satisfied dictionary.

Spectral Sparse Dictionary Based MSI Compression. (1) Reorganization: we form MSI matrix $\boldsymbol{F}$ by listing $\{\boldsymbol{F}(x,y)\}_{x=1,y=1}^{x=M,y=N}$ in a certain order such as column-major or row-major. (2) Sparse coding: we obtain sparse representation matrix for $\boldsymbol{F}$ utilizing OMP. (3) Quantization: the sparse represented non-zero values on the supported set are quantified with 16 bits, and all elements of the support set are binary coded.

Decompression. Sparse represented coefficient matrix is first obtained by inverse quantization. Then the matrix is multiplied by the sparse dictionary to rebuild MSIs.

3 Results and Discussion

To verify the superiority of our method, we make a comparative analysis of different methods by two typical MSIs. Figure 2 shows bands of colorchecker and jellybeans.

(a) (b)

Fig. 2. Test images: 31 bands, 16 bpppb, 256 × 256. (a) colorchecker: 5th; (b) jellybeans: 22th.

Performance Comparison for K-SVD and Sample PCA Based Compression. Each K-SVD dictionary is denote as the form of Dic_*k*4_*m*32, which represents the dictionary with 4-sparsity and 32 atoms. Figure 3 displays comparison results.

(a) (b)

Fig. 3. Spectral accuracy comparison for reconstructed MSIs. (a) colorchecker; (b) jellybeans.

As shown in Fig. 3, at the same sparsity, the RMSE for each MSI reconstructed by the K-SVD dictionaries is much lower than that of the PCA sample dictionaries. For two test MSIs, Dic_*k*4_*m*64, Dic_*k*4_*m*128, and Dic_*k*4_*m*256 have RMSEs with 4 nonzero coefficients that are close to or less than the RMSEs with the PCA sample basis with 8 components. In actual codec, we retain 6 components for sample PCA, and let 4-sparsity for our compression. It is known that when $m \leq 256$, our algorithm has the same or even lower bits. In this case, the RMSE with 4-sparsity and less than 256 atoms are significantly lower than that of the sample PCA with 6 components. So we obtain that at the same or lower bit rates, our algorithm has strong superiority.

Performance Comparison for K-SVD and Adaptive PCA Based Compression. We utilize PCA basis generated by each MSI as the adaptive dictionary. In this experiment, we choose the first 6 components as PCA basis and set $k = 4$, $m \leq 256$ in our method. Table 1 tabulates the performance comparison.

Table 1. Reconstruction performance comparison.

Test MSIs	Average spectral error (RMSE)				
	Spectral K-SVD dictionary based compression				Adaptive PCA
	Dic_*k*4_*m*32	Dic_*k*4_*m*64	Dic_*k*4_*m*128	Dic_*k*4_*m*256	PCA_6
Colorchecker	0.007870	0.006613	0.006362	0.006327	0.006766
Jellybeans	0.011540	0.009148	0.008716	0.008047	0.013612

Table 1 shows that for colorchecker, the RMSE of our compression is 0.0011 higher than that of adaptive PCA only when m is 32, but the bit rate of the PCA algorithm is 14.34% higher than that of Dic_*k*4_*m*32. When m is 64, 128 and 256, the RMSE is gradually reduced and all are lower than that of PCA. It should be noticed that the Dic_*k*4_*m*256 based compression has the largest decreasement of 0.000439 at 0.0015 bpppb lower bit rate, which is reduced by 6.49% compared with adaptive PCA, reflecting its optimum spectral reconstruction performance. Similarly, for jellybeans, the RMSE gradually decreases when m is increasing. Compared with adaptive PCA, the bit rate of our compression decreases by 0.3886 bpppb, 0.2595 bpppb, 0.1305 bpppb and 0.0015 bpppb, meanwhile the RMSE of our algorithm is reduced by 0.0021, 0.0045, 0.0049 and 0.0056 respectively.

4 Conclusion

We have proposed a novel approach to remove spectral redundancy sufficiently using an adaptive and flexible sparse representation. And inspired by transform coding, we have presented a new dictionary learning based MSI compression algorithm. In this paper, spectral redundancy is first removed by the redundant dictionary, and sparse representation coefficients of each sub-spatial image are then obtained. Finally, the equivalent sparse representation coefficients are quantified stored. Experimental analysis indicates that for MSI sub-spatial images, sample K-SVD dictionary with 4-sparsity can reach the represented accuracy of the 8-component sample PCA. In comparison with classical adaptive PCA, our method can achieve better reconstructed spectral accuracy at lower bit rates. In addition, this algorithm can be combined with spatial decorrelation as well as compressed sensing to achieve higher performance.

Acknowledgments. This work is supported by Scientific Research Project of Shaanxi Provincial Education Department (17JK0535); Dr. Start-up Fund of Xi'an University of Technology (112-256081503); National Science Foundation (NSF) (61602373, 61472319, 61502382); and Xi'an BeiLin Science Research Plan (GX1615).

References

1. Valsesia, D., Boufounos, P.T.: Universal encoding of multispectral images. In: IEEE International Conference on Acoustics, Speech and Signal Processing 2016, ICASSP, pp. 4453–4457 (2016)
2. Hagag, A., Hassan, E.S., Amin, M., El-Samie, F.E.A., Fan, X.: Satellite multispectral image compression based on removing sub-bands. Optik-Int. J. Light Electron Opt. **131**, 1023–1035 (2017)
3. Shinoda, K., Murakami, Y., Yamaguchi, M., Ohyama, N.: Lossless and lossy coding for multispectral image based on sRGB standard and residual components. J. Electron. Imaging **20**(2), 023003–023012 (2011)
4. Liang, W., Zeng, P., Xiao, Z., Xie, K.: Multispectral image compression methods for improvement of both colorimetric and spectral accuracy. J. Electron. Imaging **25**(4), 043026 (2016)
5. Ülkü, İ., Töreyin, B.U.: Sparse coding of hyperspectral imagery using online learning. Signal Image Video Process. **9**(4), 959–966 (2015)

Intrinsic Co-decomposition for Stereoscopic Images

Xiuxiu Li[1(✉)], Haiyan Jin[1], Zhaolin Xiao[1], and Liwen Shi[2]

[1] Xi'an University of Technology, Xi'an 710048, China
{lixiuxiu, jinhaiyan, xiaozhaolin}@xaut.edu.cn
[2] China Life Data Center, Shanghai 201201, China
shiliwen@e-chinalife.com

Abstract. An intrinsic co-decomposition model is presented for stereoscopic images. To build the correlation of inter-image or intra-image, the sparse subspace clustering in superpixel level and K-mean clustering in pixel level are implemented. With the constraints on correlation, stereoscopic images are decomposed simultaneously and the reflectance components with more details and higher contrasts are obtained for the edge-preserving of superpixel and the local reflectance correlation of pixels. Experiments show that the reflectance components of co-decomposition are clearer visually. Furthermore, information entropy and standard deviation of reflectance components of co-decomposition are calculated to validate the effectiveness quantitatively of the co-decomposition.

Keywords: Intrinsic decomposition · Stereoscopic images · Sparse subspace clustering

1 Introduction

In stereoscopic vision, the color difference among images would affect the further usage of stereoscopic images. To solve it, intrinsic image decomposition is used to get the reflectance components. In stereoscopic vision, there exist many same scenes, so co-decomposition is necessary.

In co-decomposition, building correlation among images is critical. In [1, 2], the sparsity constraint are used to build correlation. In [1], a non-local sparsity constraint is used to build correlation of intra-images and inter-images. In [2], the sparse reflectance gradients and optical flow are used to derive temporal constraint. In [4], RGB images are decomposed with the relation of surface normal, reflectance and the incident illumination from the processed object. In [3], a balanced quad-tree is used to establish super-pixel level correspondence for stereoscopic images. In [5], dense optical flow and K nearest neighbors are used to establish the correspondence.

In this paper, an intrinsic images co-decomposition model is proposed for stereoscopic images. In this model, global and local correlations are acquired with two-level clustering, which benefits the details and contrast are preserved in co-decomposition.

A. El Rhalibi et al. (Eds.): Edutainment 2018, LNCS 11462, pp. 145–148, 2019.
https://doi.org/10.1007/978-3-030-23712-7_20

2 Co-decomposition Model

According to Retinex theory, each image I can be represented the product of the reflectance components R and the shading components s:

$$I = sR \tag{1}$$

Refer to [6], the reflectance component $R(x, y)$ of a pixel (x, y) is written as:

$$R(x,y) = r(x,y)\vec{R}(x,y) \tag{2}$$

Where $\vec{R}(x,y) = I(x,y)/\|I(x,y)\|$, then $s(x,y) = \|I(x,y)\|/r(x,y)$.

To get the reflectance component of stereoscopic images simultaneously, an objective function is constructed:

$$E = \omega_s E_s + \omega_R E_R + \omega_{cl\_F} E_{cl\_F} \tag{3}$$

Where ω_s, ω_R and ω_{cl_F} are the weights of constraints terms. r is the only unknown variable in the co-decomposition model.

E_s is a local smoothness term which assumes the shading is smooth at the local area. The Laplacian smoothing term of all the pixels are used as following:

$$E_s = \sum_i \|\nabla^2 s(x,y)\| \tag{4}$$

E_R is an Retinex constraints term, in which large change in intensity attribute to reflectance changes, while small change is given to the shading variations. So E_R is:

$$E_R = \sum_{(x,y)} \sum_{(x',y') \in N(x,y)} (R(x,y) - R(x',y')\alpha \cdot (I(x,y) - I(x',y')))^2 \tag{5}$$

Where (x', y') is in (x, y)'s neighbor $N(x, y)$(the 4-connected neighbor.); and β is a weight to measure the derivative between $I(x, y)$ and $I(x', y')$:

$$\beta = \begin{cases} 1 & if |v(x,y) - v(x',y')| > \tau_v \& |c(x,y) - c(x',y')| > \tau_c \\ 0 & else \end{cases}$$

Where $v(x, y)$, $c(x, y)$, $v(x', y')$ and $c(x', y')$ are the intensity and chromaticity of pixel (x, y) and (x', y'). τ_v and τ_c is the corresponding derivative thresholds.

E_{cl_F} is an global and local correlation term among the different areas and pixels. The definition is in Sect. 3.

3 Correlation Term

Let $SP = \{sp_{i,n} | i = 1,\ldots,nSP_n, n = 1,\ldots,n\,\mathrm{Img}\}$ be the superpixels set of stereoscopic images, where $sp_{i,n}$ is the ith superpixel in the nth image, nSP_n and $n\mathrm{Img}$ are the number of superpixels in the nth image and the number of images respectively. The according feature set is $F = \{f_{i,n}, f_{i,n} \in R^D\}$ and each feature is composed with the histogram of chromaticity $h_{i,n}$ and texture spectrum $T_{i,n}$.

In stereoscopic images, some features in F can be denoted sparsely with same features bases for the redundancy. So the sparse subspace clustering is used to cluster the features in F [7], and the clustering result *cluster_F* is obtained.

According to *cluster_F*, the superpixels in the same class are called correlated superpixels *con_sp*. To ensure the contrast of images, K-means is used to cluster pixels in *con_sp*, which have the same reflectance component. Therefore E_{cl_F} is defined:

$$E_{cl\_F} = \sum_{con\_sp \subset cluster\_F} \; \sum_{ssp_{i,n} \in con\_sp} \; \sum_{(x,y) \in sp_{i,n}} \left(R(x,y) - \tilde{R}_{\alpha(x,y)}\right)^2 \tag{6}$$

Where $\tilde{R}_{\alpha(x,y)}$ is the center of cluster α which the pixel (x, y) belongs to.

4 Experiments

Some results are showed in Fig. 1. In (a), a pairs of input images are presented. The co-decomposition result in [1] are showed in (b) and (c), and the result of this model are showed in (d) and (e). By comparisons visually, more details and higher contrast are contained in the reflectance components (Fig. 1(d)) than in Fig. 1(c).

(a)Input images (b)The reflectance components with method in [1] (c)The shading components with method in [1] (d)The reflectance components with this model (e)The shading components with this model

Fig. 1. The co-decomposition result

In Table 1, some quantitative comparisons are presented. The 1-D entropy and 2-D entropy are calculated to measure the amount of information on pixel value distribution and the distribution of pixel value variation respectively. Mutual entropy is to measures the information that different view share. It's obvious that the 1-D entropy, 2-D entropy and mutual entropy with the co-decomposition in this paper is higher than the result in [1].

Table 1. Entropy and Std of the co-decomposition result

		View	Entropy			Standard deviation (Std)	
			1-D entropy	2-D entropy	Mutual entropy	Std for single image	Std for images
"House"	Input	L	6.8599	5.3535	1.3457	73.3745	73.3333
		R	6.8650	5.3599		73.2938	
	Reflectance in [5]	L	6.2428	4.8933	1.2429	32.6318	32.6843
		R	6.2611	4.9172		32.7365	
	Reflectance in this paper	L	7.0514	5.5134	1.3499	64.5851	64.4464
		R	7.0672	5.4928		63.3044	

Std (standard deviation) is used to measure the contrast of singe image and image pair. In the Table 1, the Std of the reflectance components are higher in this paper than in [1], that means more detailed images are obtained with the co-decomposition in this paper.

5 Conclusion

An intrinsic co-decomposition model is presented in this paper. In this model, the sparse subspace clustering in superpixel level is used to build the global correlation among images, and K-mean clustering in pixels is used to build the local correlation. The edge-preserving of superpixel and the reflectance correlation of local pixel keep more details and higher contrast in co-decomposition. Experiments show the reflectance component of co-decomposition in this paper is superior to the method in 1 in visual effect and numerical analysis.

Acknowledgment. This work has been partially supported by the National Natural Science Foundation of China under grant Nos. 6150238, 61501370, 61703333.

References

1. Dai, H., Feng, W., Wan, L., Nie, X.: L0 Co-intrinsic image decomposition. In: International Conference on Multimedia and Expo, pp. 1–6 (2014)
2. Bonneel, N., Sunkavalli, K., Tompkin, J., Sun, D., Paris, S., Pfister, H.: Interactive intrinsic video editing. ACM Trans. Graph. (TOG) **33**(6), 1–10 (2014)
3. Kang, J., Jiang, B., Chen, J., Liu, X.: Stereoscopic image recoloring via consistent. In: International Conference on Virtual Reality and Visualization, pp. 272–277 (2014)
4. Hachama, M., Ghanem, B., Wonka, P.: Intrinsic scene decomposition from RGB-D images. In: IEEE International Conference on Computer Vision, pp. 810–818 (2015)
5. Xie, D., Liu, S., Lin, K., Zhu, S., Zeng, B.: Intrinsic decomposition for stereoscopic images. In: IEEE International Conference on Image Processing, pp. 1744–1748 (2016)
6. Barron, J.T., Malik, J.: Shape, illumination, and reflectance from shading. IEEE Trans. Pattern Anal. Mach. **37**(8), 1670–1687 (2015)
7. Elhamifar, E., Vidal, R.: Sparse subspace clustering: algorithm, theory, and applications. IEEE Trans. Pattern Anal. Mach. Intell. **35**(1), 2765–2781 (2013)

A Terrain Classification Method for POLSAR Images Based on Modified Scattering Parameters

Shuang Zhang[1](✉), Lu Wang[1], Xiangchuan Yu[2], and Bo Chen[3]

[1] School of Automation and Information Engineering, Xi'an University of Technology, Xi'an, People's Republic of China
shzhang_work@163.com
[2] ZTE Trunking Technology Corporation, Beijing, People's Republic of China
[3] China Academy of Electronic and Information Technology, Beijing, People's Republic of China

Abstract. In this paper, improved scattering parameters of polarimetric synthetic aperture radar (POLSAR) image based on spatial information and Bayes rule is proposed. The spatial information of scattering parameters is introduced by using an adaptive weight window. Bayes rule is used to improve the performance of the scattering parameters. Experiments on real AIRSAR L-band fully POLSAR data are carried out, and the efficacy of the improved scattering parameters is verified.

Keywords: Terrain classification · Polarimetric synthetic aperture radar · Target decomposition · Scattering mechanisms

1 Introduction

The polarimetric synthetic aperture radar (POLSAR) image classification is one of the most important steps in image interpretation. It can not only output the classification results directly, but also provide the features for the later target recognition.

The features used for POLSAR image classification can be divided into two categories: statistical feature, such as Wishart distance [1] and physical scattering feature [2–5]. The physical scattering features have the advantages of clear physical meaning and simple calculation. The scattering parameter is derived from eigenspace of the second-order statistical matrix of POLSAR data [2]. The scattering parameter uses the eigenvalues to characterize the type of scattering mechanism, i.e., single-target scattering, double-target scattering, and random-target scattering. The scattering parameters are nonnegative, rotational invariant and good at the terrain classification of SAR images. However, the same scattering eigenvectors are used for all the pixels in the process of decomposition, and it's not good to obtain the dominant scattering parameters. Meanwhile, the features are greatly affected by noise.

Aiming to the above problems, this paper proposes weighted scattering parameters based on Bayes rule. The weight values are derived from the classification results based on initial scattering parameters. The Bayes rule is used to get the modified scattering

A. El Rhalibi et al. (Eds.): Edutainment 2018, LNCS 11462, pp. 149–153, 2019.
https://doi.org/10.1007/978-3-030-23712-7_21

parameters. The experiments demonstrate the validity of modified scattering parameters in terrain classification of POLSAR images.

2 Modified Scattering Parameters

In the backscattering system, if the POLSAR data satisfy the reciprocity theorem, the multi-looks POLSAR images can be represented as a 3 × 3 coherency matrix T, and the eigenvalue decomposition of the coherency matrix is shown as:

$$\langle [T] \rangle = U \cdot \Sigma \cdot U^{*T} = \sum_{i=1}^{3} \lambda_i u_i \cdot u_i^{*T} \tag{1}$$

Where Σ contains three real eigenvalues $\lambda_1, \lambda_2, \lambda_3$ and $\lambda_1 \geq \lambda_2 \geq \lambda_3 \geq 0$. U is composed of three corresponding eigenvectors.

According to reference [2], three different cases of the scattering mechanism in one cell are defined. (I) Single-target scattering–one scattering mechanism is present in the resolution cell, (II) Double-target scattering–the echo contains two scattering mechanisms with equal amplitudes, (III) Random-targets scattering–three scattering mechanisms exist with equal amplitudes in one cell.

The scattering eigenvectors V_s, V_d and V_r are defined as $V_s = [1 \quad 0 \quad 0]^T$, $V_d = [1/2 \quad 1/2 \quad 0]^T$, and $V_r = [1/3 \quad 1/3 \quad 1/3]^T$ respectively. p_s, p_d and p_r are the corresponding parameters, i.e. single-target scattering coefficient, double-targets scattering coefficient and random-targets coefficient. The coherency matrix is decomposed as $p_s \cdot V_s + p_d \cdot V_d + p_r \cdot V_r = [\lambda_1 \quad \lambda_2 \quad \lambda_3]^T / (\lambda_1 + \lambda_2 + \lambda_3)$. p_s, p_d and p_r are solved as $p_s = p_1 - p_2$, $p_d = 2(p_2 - p_3)$ and $p_r = 3p_3$, where $p_i = \frac{\lambda_i}{\lambda_1 + \lambda_2 + \lambda_3}$, $i = 1, 2, 3$.

Local spatial information can improve the performance of the scattering parameters, and the square window is the widely used method to extract the local spatial information. The square window in this paper (window size is 5 × 5) is shown as follows:

c	c	c	c	c
c	b	b	b	c
c	b	a	b	c
c	b	b	b	c
c	c	c	c	c

(a)

2	2	2	2	3
1	1	1	2	3
1	1	1	2	3
2	2	1	3	3
2	2	1	1	1

(b)

Fig. 1. Square window. Size is 5 × 5. a ≥ b ≥ c ≥ 0, and a + 8b + 16c = 1. The position of 'a' is the center of the window in (a).

The pixels in Fig. 1(a) may be in the different classes, and averaging the all pixels in the window will reduce the performance of the scattering parameters, therefore, an adaptive weighted window method is used by distinguishing the same class. In Fig. 1(b), '1', '2' and '3' stand for the pixel is classified into single-target scattering class, double-targets scattering class and random-targets scattering class respectively. For the center pixel in Fig. 1(b), the weight of single-target scattering class $\boldsymbol{W}_{\mathrm{s}}$ is a + 4b + 5c, the weight of double-targets scattering class $\boldsymbol{W}_{\mathrm{d}}$ is 3b + 7c, and the weight of random-targets scattering class $\boldsymbol{W}_{\mathrm{v}}$ is b + 4c.

The Bayes rule is defined as follows:

$$p(y|x) = \frac{p(x|y)p(y)}{p(x)} \tag{2}$$

$p(y)$ is a priori probability, $p(x|y)$ is class-conditional probability, and $p(x)$ is total probability of x. $p(x)$ can be omitted in computation.

$$p(y|x) \sim p(x|y)p(y) \tag{3}$$

In this paper, we used Bayes rule to improve the scattering parameter. The center pixel in the window is x, and the $p(y)$ is priori probability of x. $\boldsymbol{W}_{\mathrm{s}}$, $\boldsymbol{W}_{\mathrm{d}}$ and $\boldsymbol{W}_{\mathrm{v}}$ are alternative $p(y)$. $p(x|y)$ stands for the probability that x belongs to class y. Therefore the improved scattering parameters, i.e., single-target scattering coefficient f_s, double-targets scattering coefficient f_d and random-targets coefficient f_r are shown as:

$$\begin{aligned} f_s &= p_s \cdot W_s = (p_1 - p_2) \cdot W_s \\ f_d &= p_d \cdot W_d = 2(p_2 - p_3) \cdot W_d \\ f_r &= p_r \cdot W_d = 3p_3 \cdot W_r \end{aligned} \tag{4}$$

3 Experiments and Discussions

In order to prove the effectiveness of the proposed parameters, comparative experiments are performed on L-band data from the AIRSAR system of JPL/NASA shown in Fig. 2(a). The incident angle range is 5°–60°, the resolution is 10 m × 10 m, the number of look is 4, and the size is 700 × 600. There are three major types of features, i.e., sea, city, and forest.

The experimental results of the proposed parameters, initial scattering parameters [2], Freeman-Durden decomposition [4], an improved Freeman-Durden decomposition [6], and three scattering mechanisms [3] are shown in Fig. 2(b)–(f). The image is classified into three classes, i.e., sea, city and forest, indicated by blue, red and green. The result of proposed parameters in Fig. 2(b) is the best, the initial scattering parameters in Fig. 2(c) and the improved Freeman-Durden decomposition in Fig. 2(e) give the better results. In contrast, most of the original Freeman-Durden decomposition in the middle and lower parts of Fig. 2(d) are misclassified into forest. The three backscattering mechanisms in Fig. 2(f) are misclassified the part of the urban area as forest, and the forest area in the upper left part is almost completely misclassified as ocean.

Fig. 2. Classification results of AIRSAR data. (a) Original image, (b) Proposed parameters, (c) Initial scattering parameters, (d) Original Freeman-Durden decomposition, (e) Improved Freeman-Durden decomposition, (f) Three scattering mechanisms. (Color figure online)

In order to compare the efficacy of the improved scattering parameters with the initial scattering parameters [2], three regions are selected in Fig. 2(a), called Zone1, Zone2 and Zone3. The size is all 50 × 80 pixels. Table 1 listed the improved scattering parameters f_s, f_d, f_r and initial scattering parameters p_s, p_d, p_r in the three zones. From Table 1, the proposed modified scattering parameters f_s, f_d, f_r are all better than initial scattering parameters p_s, p_d, p_r.

Table 1. Scattering parameters in three zones

	Initial scattering parameters			Improve scattering parameters		
	p_s	p_d	p_r	f_s	f_d	f_r
Zone1	0.9393	0.0110	0.0497	**0.9992**	0.0001	0.0006
Zone2	0.2588	0.4988	0.2425	0.1318	**0.8509**	0.0173
Zone3	0.1850	0.1800	0.6350	0.0092	0.0243	**0.9665**

4 Conclusions

In this paper, the modified scattering parameters are used to measure the variety of scattering mechanisms in a cell. The spatial information is considered by an adaptive weighted window, and Bayes rule is also used to improve the scattering parameters. The efficacy of proposed scattering parameters is proved by testing on NASA/JPL AIRSAR L-band data.

References

1. Lee, J.S., Grunes, M.R., Kwok, R.: Classification of multi-look polarimetric SAR imagery based on complex Wishart distribution. Int. J. Remote Sens. **15**(11), 2299–2311 (1994)
2. Zhang, S., Wang, S., Chen, B.: Classification method for fully PolSAR data based on three novel parameters. IEEE Geosci. Remote Sens. Lett. **11**(1), 39–43 (2014)

3. Van Zyl, J.J.: Unsupervised classification of scattering behavior using radar polarimetry data. IEEE Trans. Geosci. Remote Sens. **27**(1), 36–45 (1989)
4. Freeman, A., Durden, S.L.: A three-component scattering model for polarimetric SAR data. IEEE Trans. Geosci. Remote Sens. **36**(3), 963–973 (2014)
5. Lee, J.S., Grunes, M.R., Pottier, E.: Unsupervised terrain classification preserving polarimetric scattering characteristics. IEEE Trans. Geosci. Remote Sens. **42**(2), 722–731 (2004)
6. An, W., Cui, Y., Yang, J.: Three-component model-based decomposition for polarimetric SAR data. IEEE Trans. Geosci. Remote Sens. **48**(6), 2732–2739 (2010)

PolSAR Data Classification via Combined Similarity Based Immune Clonal Spectral Clustering

Lu Liu(✉), Haiyan Jin, Junfei Shi, and Wei Liang

School of Computer Science and Engineering, Xi'an University of Technology, Xi'an 710048, China
{lucie0613,jinhaiyan,shijunfei,wliang}@xaut.edu.cn

Abstract. Traditional spectral clustering (SC) employed *k*-means to find the cluster centers, which leads to the problem of sensitive to initialization and easily falls into local optimum. To address this issue, a novel superpixel-based immune clonal spectral clustering (ICSC) method in the spatial-polarimetric domain is proposed for PolSAR data classification. Firstly, the proposed method divides PolSAR image into superpixels, which not only considers the region homogeneity but also reduces the computational complexity. After that, combined manifold distance measures in the spatial-polarimetric domain are used to construct the similarity matrix. Finally, immune clonal algorithm (ICA) is substituted for *k*-means to obtain global optimum solution with large probability. Experiments results show the feasibility and efficiency of the proposed method.

Keywords: PolSAR image classification · Immune clonal clustering · Spectral clustering

1 Introduction

Polarimetric SAR (PolSAR) image can provide a good opportunity for more detailed land cover classification. Most previous classification methods cannot make full use of the information involved in polarimetric data.

In recent years, spectral clustering (SC) method is utilized to the PolSAR image classification [1]. Anfinsen [2] has effectively addressed the problem that asymmetric Wishart distance cannot be directly applied to SC. Inspired by the proposed symmetric revised Wishart distance, Ersahin has presented spectral graph partitioning (SGP) [3] framework for PolSAR classification. In [4], Wishart-derived distance measure and polarimetric measure are combined to form the affinity matrix, which sufficiently considering the spatial and polarimetric relations between pairwise pixels.

Although these approaches can receive promising results, there are still two shortcomings. First, in the traditional SC, *k*-means algorithm is sensitive to initial partition and easily get trap into local optimum results. Secondly, SC is difficult to deal with large-scale PolSAR data for its high computational complexity.

In this paper, a novel superpixel-based immune clonal spectral clustering (ICSC) model has been introduced to handle these difficulties. First, we introduce the Simple

A. El Rhalibi et al. (Eds.): Edutainment 2018, LNCS 11462, pp. 154–158, 2019.
https://doi.org/10.1007/978-3-030-23712-7_22

Linear Iterative Clustering (SLIC) algorithm [5] to over-segment the PolSAR image. And then, ICSC in the spatial-polarimetric domain is employed to obtain the final results, which combines the complementary advantages of SC and ICA. Experiments results show the feasibility and efficiency of the proposed method.

2 Methodology

In this paper, 15-dimensional commonly used polarimetric characteristics were extracted. Two common texture features are employed in this paper. A 16-dimensional GLCM features, such as the angular second moment (ASM), contrast (CON), entropy (ENT) and correlation (COR), were selected in four orientations. Six orientations and six center frequencies were chosen to receive a 36-dimensional Gabor feature matrix. In addition, a 128-dimensional Scale Invariant Feature Transform (SIFT) feature is acquired as spatial features. LE is used to reduce the dimension of feature matrix, which has mapped the feature matrix to obtain a 10-dimensional feature matrix F.

ICA [10] is extremely effective to accomplish the clustering analysis for the PolSAR data. Nevertheless ICA is less than ideal for tackling the classification of data sets with higher dimension due to it is based on antibody encoding. To address this issue, ICSC in the spatial-polarimetric domain is proposed for PolSAR image classification.

In order to make full use of the spatial-polarimetric information of PolSAR image, we introduce the Markov Random Field (MRF) potential function to construct the manifold distance based similarity matrix of SC [6].

$$\Delta^{SRW}(i,j) = \begin{cases} D^2_{SRW}(T_i, T_j) & D_{SRW}(T_i, T_j) \le t_1 \\ t^2 + 2t(D_{SRW}(T_i, T_j) - t) & D_{SRW}(T_i, T_j) > t_1 \end{cases} \tag{1}$$

$$\Delta^{F}(i,j) = \begin{cases} D^2_{F}(F_i, F_j) & D_{F}(F_i, F_j) \le t_2 \\ t^2 + 2t(D_{F}(F_i, F_j) - t) & D_{F}(F_i, F_j) > t_2 \end{cases} \tag{2}$$

$$\Delta(i,j) = \Delta^{SRW}(i,j) \times \Delta^{F}(i,j) \tag{3}$$

The similarity matrix is constructed as follows:

$$S(i,j) = \begin{cases} 0 & i = j \\ \frac{1}{1+\Delta(i,j)d(i,j)} & i \ne j \end{cases} \tag{4}$$

After constructing the similarity matrix, the improved immune clonal clustering is used to overcome the disadvantages caused by SC used the k-means clustering. The essence of ICC is to increase convergence rate and search space, and prevent premature and local optimum. Some crucial operations of ICC are described subsequently.

Self-adaptive Antibody Encoding. If the cluster center k_i is encoded by antibody p_i in D dimensional space, then the length is expressed as $Len_i = k_i \times D$, where $k_i \in [2, k_{Max}]$, $k_{Max} = \sqrt{n}$, n is the number of total clustering data.

Antibody Affinity. PBM-index is selected as antibody affinity. The larger values of PBM-index represent better classification performance.

$$Affinity\ (p_i) = PBM = \left[\frac{1}{k}\frac{E(1)}{E(k)}D_m(k)\right]^2 \tag{5}$$

Where k is the number of clusters, n is the number of total classes.

3 Experiment

The PolSAR data in this experiment was acquired by AIRSAR over Flevoland, with a size of 300 × 270. Pauli RGB image and the ground truth map are shown in Fig. 1(a) and (b). The area contains six types of crops: wheat, potato, bare soil, beet, peas and barley. Four comparison methods are: pixel-level ICSC (PL-ICSC), random sampling based SC (RS-SC), ICSC based on Wishart-derived distance measure (WT-ICSC), ICSC based on Euclidean distance measure of feature vector (FE-ICSC) (Table 1).

Classification results are evaluated by overall accuracy (OA), average accuracy (AA) and Kappa coefficient. To verify the validity of the SLIC, superpixels result are visualized in Fig. 1(c).

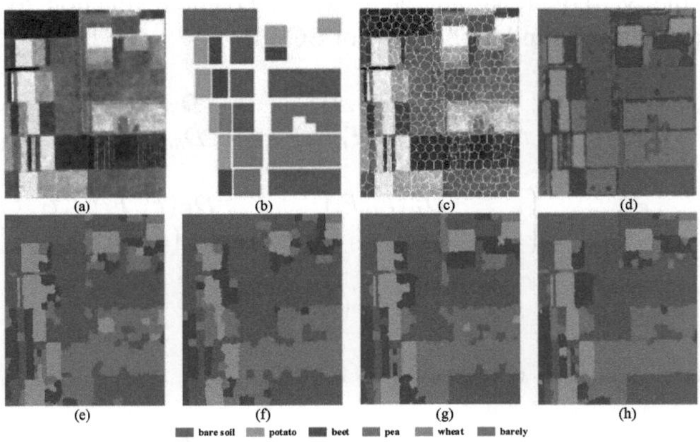

Fig. 1. Classification results: (a) Pauli RGB image, (b) Ground truth, (c) Superpixel result, (d) Pixel-level ICSC, (e) RSSC, (f) TW-ICSC, (g) FE-ICSC, (h) Proposed method.

Table 1. Classification accuracy comparison

Method	OA	Kappa coff.	AA	Accuracy					
				Bare soil	Potato	Beet	Barely	Wheat	Pea
PL-ICSC	0.9386	0.9287	0.9298	0.9481	0.9159	0.9124	0.9385	0.9008	0.9784
RS-SC	0.8980	0.8682	0.8385	0.9490	0.9989	0.4954	0.9825	0.7860	0.8298
WT-ICSC	0.9110	0.8852	0.8658	0.9734	0.7780	0.6609	0.9935	0.8910	0.8894
FE-ICSC	0.9513	0.9483	0.9278	1.0000	0.9890	0.7070	0.9954	0.9335	0.9193
Proposed	0.9684	0.9594	0.9369	1.0000	0.9997	0.7255	0.9960	0.9340	0.9655

Figure 1(d)–(h) illustrates that all the five methods can achieve a satisfactory partition of bare soil. The proposed method which has initialized by superpixel partition, is superior to pixel-level ICSC and achieves notable improvement in region connectivity, uniformity and robustness. Compared with RN-SC, our method get a higher OA for adopting ICC instead of k-means during the clustering process of SC. At the same time, Table 2 represents that the OA of the proposed method achieves 96.84%. As reflected in the confusion matrix, our method has remarkably reduced the misidentification rate and prominently improved the classification performance.

Table 2. Confusion matrix of the proposed method

Class	Bare soil	Potato	Beet	Barely	Wheat	Pea
Bare soil	1.0000	0.0000	0.0000	0.0000	0.0000	0.0000
Potato	0.0	0.9997	0.0000	0.0003	0.0000	0.0000
Beet	0.0	0.0000	0.7255	0.0122	0.2623	0.0000
Barely	0.0002	0.0000	0.0020	0.9960	0.0000	0.0018
Wheat	0.0000	0.0	0.0480	0.0180	0.9340	0.0000
Pea	0.0	0.0	0.0006	0.0329	0.0010	0.9655

4 Conclusions

In this paper, a novel ICSC method is proposed for PolSAR data classification, which combines the complementarity advantages of SC and ICA: (1) the dimensionality reduction of SC reduces feature dimension, improves the efficiency of ICA to find global optimization solution obviously consequently; (2) ICA can obtain global optimum solution with large probability and improve the classification results. Future work will focus on analyzing the sensitivity of the relevant parameters in ICSC, so as to select the best parameters to further promote the classification effect of PolSAR data.

References

1. Ersahin, K., Cumming, I.G., Yedlin, M.J.: Classification of polarimetric SAR data using spectral graph partitioning. In: IEEE International Conference on Geoscience and Remote Sensing Symposium, pp. 1756–1759. IEEE Press, Denver (2006)
2. Anfinsen, S.N., Jenssen, R., Eltoft, T.: Spectral clustering of polarimetric SAR data with the Wishart-Derived distance measures. In: Proceedings of POLinSAR, Frascati, vol. 7, pp. 1–9 (2007)
3. Ersahin, K., Cumming, I.G., Ward, R.K.: Segmentation and classification of polarimetric SAR data using spectral graph partitioning. IEEE Trans. Geosci. Remote Sens. **48**, 164–174 (2010)

4. Liu, L., Wang, R., Jiao, L., Shi, J.: Combined similarity based spectral clustering ensemble for POLSAR classification. J. Xidian Univ. **42**, 48–53 (2015)
5. Achanta, R., Shaji, A., Smith, K., Lucchi, A.: SLIC superpixels compared to state-of-the-art superpixel methods. IEEE Trans. Pattern Anal. Mach. Intell. **34**, 2274–2282 (2012)
6. Liu, L., Shi, J., Jiao, L., Jin, S.: An improved spectral clustering ensemble algorithm for POLSAR land cover classification. Int. J. Earth Sci. Eng. **8**, 937–943 (2015)

Game Rendering and Animation

Modeling Emotional Contagion for Crowd in Emergencies

Tingting Liu[1], Zhen Liu[2(✉)], Yanjie Chai[2], and Jin Wang[1]

[1] College of Science and Technology, Ningbo University, No. 505, Yuxiu Road, Zhuangshi, Zhenhai, Ningbo, Zhejiang, China
{liutingting, wangjin2}@nbu.edu.cn

[2] Faculty of Information Science and Engineering, Ningbo University, No. 818 Fenghua Road, Jiangbei, Ningbo, Zhejiang, China
{liuzhen, chaiyanjie}@nbu.edu.cn

Abstract. Due to the serious situation of the public security in China, it has important practical meaning to make contingency plans for emergencies in advance. During the emergency evacuation, crowd will be in a non-rational state. The characteristics of the crowd aggregation are different from the usual crowd movements and easily lead to emotional contagion. However, the research on emotional contagion in crowd animation is still rare in the existing studies. From the perspective of psychology, this paper discusses the related concepts, parameters, and methods of measurement for emotional contagion, and summarizes the work of using computer vision technology in obtaining the crowd parameters. Based on these, a model of emotional contagion has been proposed. The experimental results show that the proposed model can well represent the crowd evacuation behavior and can be a new method for crowd emergency management.

Keywords: Emergencies · Crowd · Emotional contagion · Behavior

1 Introduction

Increasing emergencies have a negative impact on the stability of the society. It is of great practical significance to formulate contingency plans for various extreme situations and to improve the emergency response capability. An efficient 3D visualization platform can deduct extreme situations visually and will greatly improve the efficiency of decision making.

Through surveillance videos of fires in recent years, it is easily to find that people often fall into a panic state in emergencies. For example, herd behavior can be observed in the fire evacuation. This paper will take crowd evacuation behavior in a large supermarket as an example and try to analyze the possible consequence of crowd aggregation from the perspective of social computing. As fire is always accompanied by smoke, people's sight will be blocked during the evacuation. Limited vision will then cause panic, which will spread in the crowd. Without adequate and effective information, people will distribute unevenly. Some navigation areas may not be used, and some may be crowded by lots of people. In this case, convergence will occur.

A. El Rhalibi et al. (Eds.): Edutainment 2018, LNCS 11462, pp. 161–168, 2019.
https://doi.org/10.1007/978-3-030-23712-7_23

In the existing crowd models, the cellular automaton model and the social force model are two representative models. However, these models treat people as a "particle". They do not take full account of human psychological and emotional factors. With these models, it is difficult to accurately describe the behavioral characteristics of the crowd in emergency situations. Moreover, most of the crowd behavior data that support existing theories and experiments are obtained from the crowd in non-emergencies or daily exercises. These data cannot reflect crowd's real behavior in emergencies. Based on ethical considerations, it is impossible to let people experience real disasters or accidents to obtain their behaviors. Therefore, simulating people's behavior with behavior rules learned from real emergency videos will be a good solution to deduce extreme consequences. The topic has become one of the hot topics in social computing.

This paper will carry out computational experiments to simulate the crowd evacuation behavior from the perspective of the emotional contagion. Individuals will be regarded as agents with limited rationality. Their behaviors and decisions will be influenced by the surrounding people. The paper considers the effect of personality, navigation information and emotional contagion in an uncertain environment and provides a new perspective for crowd evacuation.

2 Crowd Behavior Modeling

Based on the individual animation, earlier crowd animation uses rule-based approach to simulate crowd movement. Algorithms for this method are simple and can simulate daily movement of urban crowd. Based on this method, Musee et al. guided the movement of people with constructed semantic information [1]. After that, a crowd autonomous navigation algorithm has been proposed. Shao et al. set up the data structure of the virtual scene and gave the individual a cognitive structure. Individuals can be navigated by querying the scene data [2]. Similarly, Paris et al. proposed a crowd cognitive model that can simulate crowd's natural behavior [3]. Due to the randomness of individual motion, it is difficult to control the motion for each individual in an emergency by specifying rules. In order to accurately describe the continuous variations in the movement of the crowd, it is necessary to use physical methods to characterize the movement of the crowd. In this regard, Helbing's social force model (SFM) is still a classic model for simulating crowd behavior. The model abstracts various phenomena in the movement of the crowd into various forces and can reproduce the congestion near the exit [4]. However, the formula of the SFM still needs to be improved. With the collision forces between individuals, the crowd simulated with SFM may jitter at the bottleneck.

In recent years, SFM has been continuously improved. Saboia et al. applied mobile grids to the SFM [5]. Pelechano et al. simulated the emergency evacuation crowd with the improved SFM [6]. Huang et al. applied steering force to reduce the jitter [7]. Hu also simulated the crowd through an improved SFM [8].

With the deepening of research on crowd animation, the problem of crowd navigation has begun to attract attention. In the area of global navigation, Treuille proposed a collision detection method between crowd and dynamic objects [9] and Jin proposed a crowd navigation method with [10]. In recent years, research on crowd animation has become a multi-disciplinary study. Durupinar et al. proposed an OCEAN personality model from the perspective of psychology to improve the credibility of the crowd animation [11]. They updated the model in 2016, giving each agent a personality to make different agents behave differently [12]. Haciomeroglu et al. put forward a motion model to simulate the crowd in the city. The model could automatically extract the required data structure from the spatial analysis and navigation information. Thereby a method based on random distribution of motion individuals can be implemented [13].

Crowd collision detection is a key technique in the crowd animation. In recent years, a local collision detection algorithm Reciprocal Velocity Obstacles (RVO) has attracted wide attention [14]. However, crowd simulated with the RVO may still jitter during the movement. In recent years, people began to improve the crowd collision detection algorithms with the psychology. For example, Park et al. analyzed various behavioral paths of the crowd from the perspective of psychology and provided a theoretical basis for avoiding collision between agents [15].

3 Emotional Contagion

The concept of emotional contagion originally came from the field of psychology and was proposed by Hatfield et al. In 1996 [16]. They defined emotional contagion as a process that individuals automatically and continuously mimic the facial expressions, sounds, gestures, movements, and behaviors of others in their interactions with the group. However, in the field of crowd behavior modeling, the crowd emotional contagion has not been concerned about until the last few years.

In many emergencies, the panic emotion will lead to overcrowding and will cause casualties during evacuation. The agglomeration and herding that caused by emotional contagion can be observed in both scientific experiments and real emergencies. Altshuler designed an experiment to observe ants' evacuation behavior in an emergency [17]. They drive ants to escape by dripping irritating liquid into a round container. Although two exits are completely symmetrical, the ants' choice of them is not symmetrical. The experimental result showed that most of the ants evacuate from the left exit. Similar phenomenon can be observed in the mouse experiment that carried out by us. In our experiment, mice aggregated together in emergencies. While in the surveillance video about the fire in the Dancing King Club, Shenzhen, 2008, overcrowding can be observed (Fig. 1). Due to the sudden fire and the lack of organization, most of the people rushed to the front door (left side of Fig. 1) with panic. The overcrowding resulted in 43 deaths and 65 injuries.

The above cases showed that the emotional contagion will have a huge impact on the crowd evacuation. If the panic emotion can be controlled in time, a lot of injuries will not happen.

Fig. 1. The screenshot of surveillance video about the fire evacuation in the Dancing King Club, Shenzhen.

In the process of emotional contagion, the emotional influences between individuals are mutual. The individual that affect others' emotions will also be influenced by others. Barsade called this phenomenon as "ripple effect" [18] while Walter et al. called the phenomenon as "spiral effect" [19].

There are some models have been proposed for emotional contagion. Bosse proposed a computational model with the parameters between the sender and receiver of emotion [20]. Yin et al. studied the individual emotional model in a crowd from the perspective of social psychology. The model suggested that the interaction between crowd and individuals is related to three factors: the personality, attention of the individual and the size of the crowd [21]. Liu et al. put forward an emotional model to describe the panic behavior of the crowd on the footbridge [22]. After that, they studied people's behavior in a crowded railway station platform. The idea of agent is used to describe individual's behavior under the influence of emotions. In this model, the emotions of the crowd are related to the presence of managers. The model is used to simulate three-dimensional scenarios of emotional contagion, avoidance and falls in the crowd. The results showed that the negative emotions of the crowd are not only related to crowd's initial emotions, but also to the number and distribution of managers [23].

4 Multi-agent Based Emotional Contagion Modeling

In this paper, an individual is regarded as an agent with quick response ability. The cognitive model of the agent has the modules of perception, memory, motivation, goal, behavior, emotion, action and social parameters. Among them, the perception module has a mechanism of attention. It can perceive the time and spatial information through the visual and auditory perceptron. The emotion module contains an emotion trigger and an emotional contagion sub-module. The former is used to trigger a specific emotion based on the information from the perception module and the latter is used to affect surrounding individuals' emotions. The social module contains parameters that can reflect the real word. For example, social identity (manager, rescuer, etc.) will guide agent's behavior in the emergency and each party's priority coefficients in the encountering will be used to simulate social interactions among people.

From the perspective of safety management, emotion can be divided into three catalogues: positive emotion (such as calm), negative emotion (such as panic), and unstable state (transitional state between positive emotion and negative emotion). With the positive emotions, crowd can move orderly and avoid chaos. With the negative emotions, crowd will have disorderly movement and stampede will happen.

In emergencies, the emotional contagions of the crowd usually have the following characteristics:

(1) Emergencies will evoke an individual's emotions. If the intensity of the emotion exceeds a certain threshold, the individual will be in an emotional state (such as changing the speed of movement).
(2) Individual's emotional behaviors (through physical exercise, etc.) will affect others surround it. The area of emotional contagion is a circular area centered on the individual's location and with the radius of the affected area.
(3) The process of emotional contagion can be divided into two stages. In the first stage, some individuals are in their emotional state and cause emotional changes in their surrounding individuals while the distant individuals are not affected. In the second stage, with the movement of the people in the emotional state, the emotional contagion spreads from the local to the whole crowd, and the crowd is in chaos. At this stage, crowding events are likely to occur.
(4) Individual's speed changes with the emotion. When determining the speed of the next step, an agent's speed planning will be affected by its current panic value. An agent with high panic value will prefer the speed of the large rate, which may cause collision and fall; while an agent with low panic value will be more conservative in its choice of speed.
(5) Administrators can reduce individual's panic and navigate the crowd.

While calculating the emotional contagion of the crowd, every agent's emotional value needs to be determined firstly. The value is related to the distance from the agent to the event and the size of the event. Then the average emotional value in each agent's perception area (circle) will be calculated. If an agent's emotion value is larger than the average value, it will not be affected by the emotion of the surrounding agent. Vice versa, it will be affected by the surrounding agents' emotions. It is possible to formulate a formula for calculating the amount of change in the emotion of the agent after being influenced by the surrounding agent, thereby calculating the emotional infection of the emotion.

5 Visualization of Emotional Contagion

To visually present the crowd's emotional contagion, this paper proposes a color-based rendering method. In Fig. 2, cylinders with different colors represent agents' different emotional states. The red cylinders refer to the agents that have been emotionally affected, the yellow cylinders refer to the agents that will be emotional affected and the white ones refer to those that are not been affected. In emergencies, an agent will be affected by neighboring agents. In the case of a fire, some agents that are close to the fire will perceive the risk before others. Their emotion will then change to a state of panic, and will trigger the emotional contagion. With graphical display, emotional contagion can be reproduced vividly. People can visually observe the impact of the emotional contagion on the evacuation crowd. It can be a reference for setting the position and quantity of managers.

Fig. 2. The emotional contagion in a shopping mall fire. (Color figure online)

The OCEAN model is used to describe the personality of the agent. In this model, each of the traits has two poles. Agents with type-O and type-C personalities will have strong subjective awareness, and agents with type-E personality are extroverted. They will have self-conscious and will not be easily affected by other. While agents with type-A and type-E personalities are more susceptible to the emotions of others.

When Type-A and Type-N agents increase their emotional perception ability, they are much more easily to be affected by the panic emotion and the number of affected agents in the crowd will be increased. In this circumstance, the number of agents at the exit is relatively volatile and there may arise situations in which only one exit is passed by a large number of agents and other exits are not used effectively.

The experimental results showed that:

(1) Emotional contagion can cause "herding". Most of the people will follow others to evacuate and will form a group.
(2) Emotional contagion can exacerbate the panic among the crowd. People will gather at the bottleneck and may cause congestion.

6 Conclusion

This paper summarizes typical achievements of crowd modeling and affective computing, and analyzes the shortcomings of the existing research. As not taking the emotional contagion in to account, the existing crowd models did not thoroughly discuss the extreme consequences of the emotional contagion and could not simulate the crowd evacuation behavior in emergencies very well. Furthermore, most of the crowd data that support these studies are empirical data and are not suitable for describing crowd behaviors in emergencies.

After analyzing crowd's behavior in emergencies, we propose a cognitive model for the agent and put forward some formulas for emotional contagion. In order to observe the emotional contagion in the crowd vividly, we use different colors of cylinders to represent agents in different emotional states. The experiment showed that the perception ability will influence the emotional contagion level of the crowd and will lead to different crowd movements. To further improve the model, crowd density and other information will be integrated into the proposed emotional contagion model in our future work.

References

1. Musse, S.R., Thalmann, D.: Hierarchical model for real time simulation of virtual human crowds. IEEE Trans. Vis. Comput. Graph. **7**(2), 152–164 (2001)
2. Shao, W., Terzopoulos, D.: Autonomous pedestrians. Graph. Models **69**(5–6), 246–274 (2007)
3. Paris, S., Donikian, S.: Activity-driven populace: a cognitive approach to crowd imulation. IEEE Comput. Graph. Appl. **29**(4), 34–43 (2009)
4. Helbing, D., Farkas, I., Vicsek, T.: Simulationg dynamical features of escape panic. Natrue **407**, 487–490 (2000)
5. Saboia, P., Goldenstein, S.: Crowd simulation: applying mobile grids to the social force model. Vis. Comput. **28**(10), 1039–1048 (2012)
6. Pelechano, N., Badler, N.: Modeling crowd and trained leader behavior during building evacuation. IEEE Comput. Graph. Appl. **26**(6), 80–86 (2006)
7. Huang, P., Liu, Z.: Study on improved social force model for crowd simulation. J. Syst. Simul. **24**(09), 1916–1919 (2012)
8. Hu, Q.M., Fang, W.N., Guo, B.Y., Nong, Z.L.: 3-D simulation of crowd evacuation based on a pedestrian movement model. J. Beijing Jiaotong Univ. **33**(4), 34–37 (2009)
9. Treuille, A., Cooper, S., Popovi, Z.: Continuum crowds. ACM Trans. Graph. **25**(3), 1160–1168 (2006)
10. Jin, X.G., Xu, J.Y., Wang, C.L., Huang, S.S., Zhang, J.: Interactive control of large-crowd navigation in virtual environments using vector fields. IEEE Comput. Graph. Appl. **28**(6), 37–46 (2008)
11. Durupinar, F., Pelechano, N., Allbeck, J., Gudukbay, U., Badler, N.: The impact of the OCEAN personality model on the perception of crowds. IEEE Comput. Graphics Appl. **31**(3), 22–31 (2011)
12. Durupinar, F., Gudukbay, U., Aman, A., Badler, N.: Psychological parameters for crowd simulation: from audiences to mobs. IEEE Trans. Vis. Comput. Graph. **22**(9), 2145–2159 (2016)
13. Haciomeroglu, M., Laycock, R.G., Day, A.M.: Distributing pedestrians in a virtual environment. In: International Conference on Cyberworlds, CW 2007, pp. 152–159. IEEE Press, New York (2007)
14. van den Berg, J., Lin, M., Manocha, D.: Reciprocal velocity obstacles for real-time multi-agent navigation. In: IEEE International Conference on Robotics and Automation, pp. 1928–1935. IEEE Press, New York (2008)

15. Park, J.H., Rojas, F.A., Yang, H.S.: A collision avoidance behavior model for crowd simulation based on psychological findings. Comput. Animat. Virtual Worlds **24**, 173–183 (2013)
16. Hatfield, E., Cacioppo, J.T., Rapson, R.L.: Emotional Contagion. Cambridge University Press, Cambridge (1994)
17. Altshuler, E., Ramos, O., Nunez, Y., Fernandez, J., Batista-Leyva, A.J., Noda, C.: Symmetry breaking in escaping ants. Am. Nat. **166**(6), 643–649 (2005)
18. Barsade, S.G.: The ripple effects: emotional contagion and its influence on group behavior. Adm. Sci. Q. **47**(4), 644–675 (2002)
19. Walter, F., Bruch, H.: The positive group affect spiral: a dynamic model of the emergence of positive affective similarity in work groups. J. Organ. Behav. **29**(2), 239–261 (2008)
20. Bosse, T., Duell, R., Memon, Z.A., Treur, J., van der Wal, C.N.: A multi-agent model for emotion contagion spirals integrated within a supporting ambient agent model. In: Yang, J.-J., Yokoo, M., Ito, T., Jin, Z., Scerri, P. (eds.) PRIMA 2009. LNCS (LNAI), vol. 5925, pp. 48–67. Springer, Heidelberg (2009). https://doi.org/10.1007/978-3-642-11161-7_4
21. Yin, Y.J., Tang, W.Q., Lin, W.Q.: Emotion model of virtual individual based on emotional contagion. Comput. Simul. **30**(8), 216–220 (2013)
22. Liu, Z., Huang, P.: Study of panic behavior model for crowd on pedestrian bridge in emergent event. J. Syst. Simul. **24**(09), 1950–1953 (2012)
23. Liu, Z., Jin, W., Huang, P., Chai, Y.J.: An emotion contagion simulation model for crowd events. J. Comput. Res. Dev. **50**(12), 2578–2589 (2013)

A Semantic Parametric Model for 3D Human Body Reshaping

Dan Song[1], Yao Jin[2], Tongtong Wang[1], Chengyang Li[1], Ruofeng Tong[1(✉)], and Jian Chang[3]

[1] State Key Lab of CAD&CG, Zhejiang University, Hangzhou, China
trf@tju.edu.cn

[2] College of Information Science and Technology, Zhejiang Sci-Tech University, Hangzhou, China

[3] NCCA, Bournemouth University, Bournemouth, UK

Abstract. Semantic human body reshaping builds a 3D body according to several anthropometric measurements, playing important roles in virtual fitting and human body design. We propose a novel part-based semantic body model for 3D body reshaping. We adopt 20 types of measurements in regard of length and girth information of body shape. Our approach takes any number (1–20) of measurements as input, and generates a 3D human body. Firstly, all missing measurements are estimated from known measurements using a correlation-based method. Then, based on our proposed semantic model, we learn corresponding semantic body parameters which determine a 3D body from measurements. Our model is trained using a database of 4000 registered body meshes which are fitted with scans of real human bodies. Through experiments, we compare our approach with previous methods and show the advantages of our model.

Keywords: Semantic human model · 3D body reshaping · 3D body reconstruction · Imputation

1 Introduction

3D human body modeling has been researched for about 20 years in computer graphics and animation, and has various applications in movies, computer games and virtual fitting. Parametric human body models represent 3D body through deforming a template body mesh with a series of parameters, and can be classified into edge-based models and vertex-based models. Edge-based models [1,2] capture the shape deformation as edge deformations relative to template mesh, usually with a 3×3 matrix. Vertex-based models [3] treat the shape deformation as vertex displacements with a 3-dimensional vector. Our proposed semantic model is a vertex-based model.

There are several ways to create 3D human bodies using parametric models, such as reconstructions from scans, images and anthropometric measurements.

A. El Rhalibi et al. (Eds.): Edutainment 2018, LNCS 11462, pp. 169–176, 2019.
https://doi.org/10.1007/978-3-030-23712-7_24

Anthropometric measurements (e.g., height, chest size, waist size, etc.) provide semantic and intuitive controls towards body shapes, so in this paper we propose a semantic parametric model using body measurements to create or edit 3D human bodies.

We review existing related approaches, and conclude the state-of-the-art framework of 3D body reshaping with anthropometric measurements. First of all, a database containing various 3D body shapes with a similar standing pose is prepared and a set of measurements are defined. Then the state-of-the-art framework consists of the following three steps: (1) Using the known measurements, the number of which is not limited, to estimate the missing measurements; (2) Learning a 3D body shape with all measurements; and (3) Optimizing the body shape with the original known measurements as constraints. Zhang et al. [4] use such a framework, while the others [5–7] only put emphasis on part of the framework.

For step 1, most works [1,6,7] take all the defined measurements as input while Zhang et al. [4] and Zeng et al. [5] can take any number of measurements as input, which relaxes the restriction on the input and is user-friendly to body creaters. Zhang et al. [4] propose a correlation-based method and Zeng et al. [5] use MICE (Multivariate Imputation by Chained Equations [8]) to estimate missing data from the known one(s). In Sect. 3.1, we compare their methods, KNN (K-Nearest-Neighbor) and a matrix completion method. The method we use for step 1 in our approach is similar to [4] with minor revisions.

For step 2, existing methods map the defined measurements to body parameters which determine a 3D body shape. There are various types of body parameters, such as weights of PCA bases and affine transformations of mesh triangles. Some works [7,9] map the measurements to the weights of PCA bases performed on the whole body shape, which control vertex displacements relative to the corresponding vertices of template mesh. Some researchers [5,6] map the measurements to the triangle deformations relative to the corresponding triangles of template mesh. We propose a vertex-based semantic model consisting of part-based semantic bases which control deformations according to measurements, and whole body non-semantic bases that make the whole body shape coherent. In Sect. 3.2, we compare our method with the two common-used approaches, and our method achieves the best performance for body reshaping while obtaining comparative reconstruction error.

The time-consumption and result quality of step 3 rely on the quality of the body reconstructed from step 2. How to further refine the learned body shape with original known measurements is out of the scope of this paper.

We use MPII database [10] which contains 4301 registered bodies to train and test our approach. The experiment results show that our novel body model can: (1) perform semantic controls towards body shapes, (2) better satisfy the measurements requirement for body reshaping, and (3) keep the whole body shape coherent.

The paper is organized as follows. In Sect. 2, we firstly give an overview of our method, and then introduce measurements estimation and our proposed semantic model. Experiments are conducted and analyzed in Sect. 3. Section 4 concludes the paper.

2 Method

2.1 Overview

Figure 1 shows the overview of our approach, which contains the online process and the offline process. The online process experiences three stages: (1) estimating all measurements from given limited input, (2) predicting body parameters using all measurements, and (3) reconstructing 3D body shape according to body parameters with our proposed model. The offline process is based on a public database [10] of 4000 3D registered bodies which are fitted with human scans. The following subsections introduce each online stage and corresponding offline preparations.

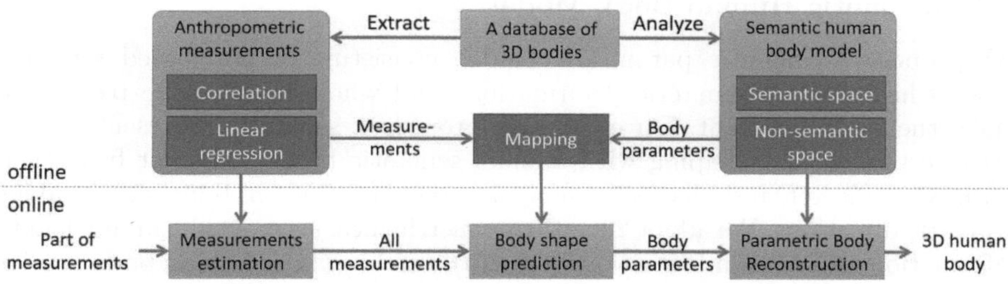

Fig. 1. Overview.

2.2 Measurements Estimation

The anthropometric measurements we use are shown in Fig. 2(a), and we compute the measurements of 4000 3D bodies. How to compute measurements can be found in [11]. Based on the dataset of 4000 sets of measurements, we compute the Pearson's correlation coefficient and train the linear relationship for any two measurements.

We use a correlation-based method similar to [4] to estimate missing measurements from known ones. Given a subset of 20 anthropometric measurements, which is denoted as S_{in}, we want to get the subset (S_{out}) of unknown measurements. We set a step value s ($s = 0.04$ in our implementation) and iteratively expand S_{in}. Suppose current iteration is $iter$, for measurement i in S_{out}, if there exists any measurement j in S_{in} and the correlation coefficient of i and j is larger than $1 - iter \times s$, we use the trained linear relationship to predict the value of measurement i from measurement j. If there are more than one measurements in S_{in} satisfying the condition, we will compute the weighted average value of predicted values, where the weights are decided by the correlation coefficients.

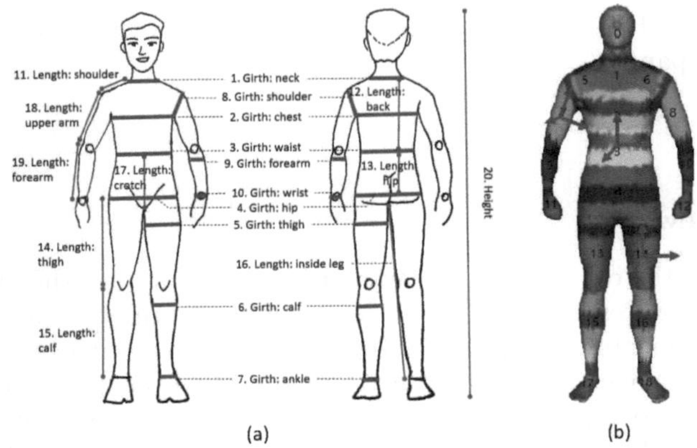

Fig. 2. 20 anthropometric measurements and body partitions. (Color figure online)

2.3 Semantic Human Body Model

We propose a semantic parametric model, consisting of part-based semantic bases which control semantic deformations and whole body shape bases that make the body coherent. Du et al. [12] propose a semantic representation of 3D face model for reshaping with manual semantic bases. Different from their work, we train semantic bases by analyzing the variations of body shapes along semantic directions. We adopt 20 anthropometric measurements including length information and girth information (Fig. 2(a)), and segment human body into 19 partitions in accordance with these measurements (Fig. 2(b)). The vertices of darken area of each partition in the figure are used for girth calculation.

Equation 1 illustrates our model, where $\boldsymbol{\theta}$ and $\boldsymbol{\beta}$ are body parameters. $\boldsymbol{V}$ is a $3N$-dimensional vector denoting the positions of body vertices, and $\hat{\boldsymbol{V}}$ represents the corresponding vertex positions of template body. N is the number of vertices, and P is the number of body partitions. $\boldsymbol{B}_i^l$ represents semantic length bases, $\boldsymbol{B}_i^g$ represents semantic girth bases, and $\boldsymbol{U}$ denotes non-semantic bases, the training of which is introduced in the following two paragraphs.

$$\boldsymbol{V}(\boldsymbol{\theta}, \boldsymbol{\beta}) = \hat{\boldsymbol{V}} + \sum_{i=1}^{P} (\boldsymbol{B}_i^l \boldsymbol{\theta}_i^l + \boldsymbol{B}_i^g \boldsymbol{\theta}_i^g) + \boldsymbol{U}\boldsymbol{\beta} \tag{1}$$

We train $\boldsymbol{B}_i^l$ and $\boldsymbol{B}_i^g$ separately for each part and $\boldsymbol{U}$ for the whole body. For each part, we firstly represent vertices using local coordinate whose x-z plane is parallel to girth plane (marked with red arrows in Fig. 2(b)) and y axis corresponds to length direction (marked with purple arrows in Fig. 2(b)). Secondly, we compute the rigid transform from training sample shape to template shape, and let each transformed shape subtract the template shape. Thirdly, we separately perform PCA on the y positions and on the x and z positions to gain semantic bases $\boldsymbol{B}_i^l$ and $\boldsymbol{B}_i^g$ respectively. We should mention that $\boldsymbol{B}_i^l$ is a $3N \times L$ matrix, $3N - N_p$ rows of which are set to zero. $\boldsymbol{B}_i^g$ is a $3N \times G$ matrix, $3N - 2N_p$

rows of which are set to zero. Here N_p is the number of vertices of the part and L and G represent the number of bases.

For training non-semantic bases of the whole body, we firstly represent each training sample only with semantic bases. Then we make each training sample subtract corresponding semantic represented one, and perform PCA on the vertex residuals of all training samples to obtain non-semantic bases $\boldsymbol{U}$ (a $3N \times W$ matrix, where W is the number of bases).

2.4 Body Shape Prediction

For each one of 4000 bodies in the training database, we have its body measurements M and body parameters $(\boldsymbol{\theta}, \boldsymbol{\beta})$ as a training example. For each measurement, we learn a linear relationship between the measurement and its corresponding body parameter. The body parameter is L-dimensional for length measurement while G-dimensional for girth measurement. We also train a linear relationship between the semantic parameter $\boldsymbol{\theta}$ and the non-semantic parameter $\boldsymbol{\beta}$.

In online process, given 20 anthropometric measurements, we firstly estimate the semantic parameter according to measurements and then predict the non-semantic parameter. Finally, we reconstruct the 3D body shape with body parameters $(\boldsymbol{\theta}, \boldsymbol{\beta})$ using formula 1.

3 Experiment Results

3.1 Measurements Estimation Error

We prepare 301 testing samples using MPII database [10], which have no overlaps with training samples. The 20 anthropometric measurements are computed for every testing sample. We randomly miss a number of measurements and estimate the missing data from known one(s) using correlation-based method, KNN, SoftImpute [13] with BiScaler [14] and MICE [8]. The correlation-based method is implemented as we describe in Sect. 2.2, and the other three methods are based on the fancyimpute code [15].

Figure 3 shows the mean absolute error of estimated measurements with different numbers of known measurements. Overall, correlation-based method performs best. When we know more than 12 measurements, KNN achieves less estimation error. For the results displayed in Fig. 3, the training and testing samples contain both male and female bodies. If we train separate models for male and female, we will get slightly less error, but the trends and comparisons of these methods are the same.

3.2 Evaluation of Semantic Body Model

In this section, we compare our approach, which predicts 3D body shape as introduced in Sect. 2.4, with two common-used approaches. One maps measurements to the weights of whole body PCA bases (abbr. PCA weight mapping),

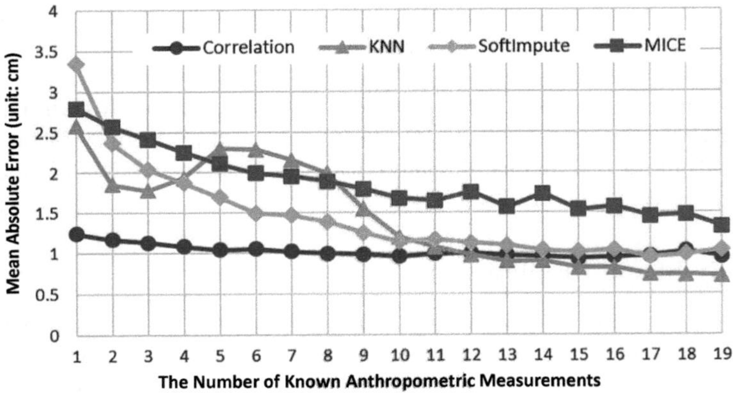

Fig. 3. Measurements estimation error with different numbers of measurements as input.

and the other maps measurements to the triangle deformations (abbr. triangle deformation mapping). PCA weight mapping method is adopted by many researchers such as [7] and [9], which learns the linear relationship between measurements and the weights of PCA bases. Triangle deformation mapping method [5,6] learns the linear relationship between the affine deformation and the corresponding measurement for each triangle. After obtaining the affine transformation for each triangle, we adopt the vertex formulation proposed by [16], which satisfies the shared vertex constrains, to solve the positions of vertices.

We take the 20 anthropometric measurements of 301 testing samples as input to predict 3D bodies using these three methods, and Table 1 compares the mean absolute vertex-to-vertex error in x/y/z direction. Our approach achieves comparative reconstruction accuracy with PCA weight mapping method, while triangle deformation mapping method falls behind.

Table 1. Reconstruction error of different methods (unit: mm)

Method	X direction	Y direction	Z direction
Our method	2.82	3.56	2.40
PCA weight mapping	2.80	3.54	2.37
Triangle deformation mapping	5.12	5.44	6.40

We further compare the performance of these three methods for body reshaping by changing sizes. Figure 4 shows examples of the shape changes when we adjust chest size to 80 mm more or waist size to 50 mm less. We measure the increment of chest size or the decrement of waist size for these three methods. We also compute the absolute vertex-to-vertex distance between the shape before adjustment and that after adjustment, and show the distance with colors. The blue color denotes smaller distance while the red color illustrates far distance.

The shape deformation performed by our method is the closest to the requirement, while triangle deformation mapping method barely changes the shape. Triangle deformation mapping method maps measurements to the triangle deformations relative to the corresponding triangles of template body mesh. The vertex positions of triangles affected by the adjusted size rely on the positions of neighboring triangles controlled by the unchanged sizes, so this method cannot get required shape change when we only adjust partial sizes. Our method and PCA weight mapping method use vertex-based human body models, and learn vertex displacements relative to the corresponding vertices of template mesh. Compared with PCA weight mapping method, our method achieves better size changes, and we suppose that it owes to the part-based semantic bases which improve the expressive ability of model for local deformations.

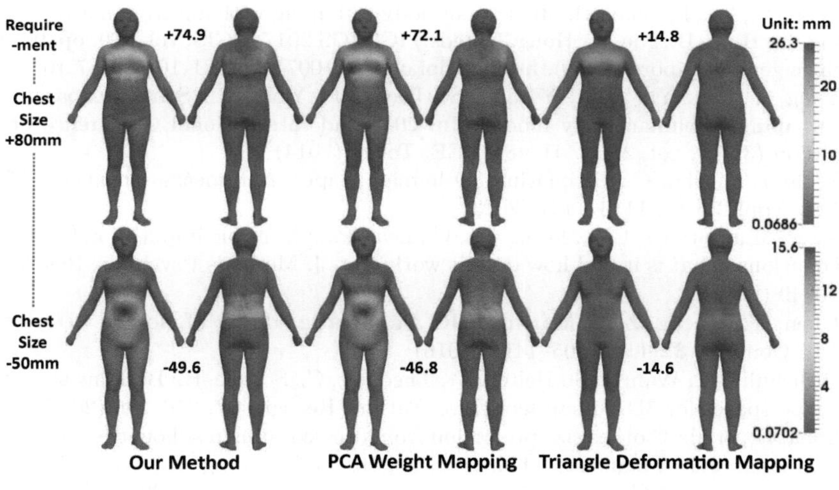

Fig. 4. Shape changes when we adjust chest size to 80 mm more or waist size to 50 mm less. (Color figure online)

4 Conclusion

We propose a novel semantic parametric model for 3D human body reshaping. Our model contains part-based semantic bases which control deformations according to measurements, and whole body non-semantic bases that make the whole body shape coherent. The experiment results show that we obtain comparative reconstruction accuracy, and can perform desired shape deformations with sizes changing.

Acknowledgments. The research is supported in part by NSFC (61572424, 61832016) and the Science and Technology Department of Zhejiang Province (2018C01080). Yao Jin is supported in part by Zhejiang Provincial Natural Science Foundation of China(LY17F020031).

References

1. Hasler, N., Stoll, C., Sunkel, M., Rosenhahn, B., Seidel, H.P.: A statistical model of human pose and body shape. Comput. Graph. Forum **28**(2), 337–346 (2009)
2. Anguelov, D., Srinivasan, P., Koller, D., Thrun, S., Rodgers, J., Davis, J.: SCAPE: shape completion and animation of people. ACM Trans. Graph. (TOG) **24**(3), 408–416 (2005)
3. Loper, M., Mahmood, N., Romero, J., Pons-Moll, G., Black, M.J.: SMPL: a skinned multi-person linear model. ACM Trans. Graph. (TOG) **34**(6), 248 (2015)
4. Zhang, Y., Zheng, J., Magnenat-Thalmann, N.: Example-guided anthropometric human body modeling. J. Vis. Comput. **31**(12), 1615–1631 (2015)
5. Zeng, Y., Fu, J., Chao, H.: 3D human body reshaping with anthropometric modeling. In: Huet, B., Nie, L., Hong, R. (eds.) ICIMCS 2017. CCIS, vol. 819, pp. 96–107. Springer, Singapore (2018). https://doi.org/10.1007/978-981-10-8530-7_10
6. Yang, Y., Yu, Y., Zhou, Y., Du, S., Davis, J., Yang, R.: Semantic parametric reshaping of human body models. In: 2014 2nd International Conference on 3D Vision (3DV), vol. 2, pp. 41–48. IEEE, Tokyo (2014)
7. Wuhrer, S., Shu, C.: Estimating 3D human shapes from measurements. J. Mach. Vis. Appl. **24**(6), 1133–1147 (2013)
8. Azur, M.J., Stuart, E.A., Frangakis, C., Leaf, P.J.: Multiple imputation by chained equations: what is it and how does it work? Int. J. Methods Psychiatr. Res. **20**(1), 40–49 (2011)
9. Chen, Y., Cheng, Z.Q., Martin, R.R.: Parametric editing of clothed 3D avatars. Vis. Comput. **32**(11), 1405–1414 (2016)
10. Pishchulin, L., Wuhrer, S., Helten, T., Theobalt, C., Schiele, B.: Building statistical shape spaces for 3D human modeling. Pattern Recogn. **67**, 276–286 (2017)
11. Song, D., et al.: Clothes size prediction from dressed-human silhouettes. In: Chang, J., Zhang, J.J., Magnenat Thalmann, N., Hu, S.-M., Tong, R., Wang, W. (eds.) AniNex 2017. LNCS, vol. 10582, pp. 86–98. Springer, Cham (2017). https://doi.org/10.1007/978-3-319-69487-0_7
12. Du, J., Song, D., Tang, Y., Tong, R., Tang, M.: "Edutainment 2017" a visual and semantic representation of 3D face model for reshaping face in images. J. Vis. **21**(4), 649–660 (2018)
13. Mazumder, R., Hastie, T., Tibshirani, R.: Spectral regularization algorithms for learning large incomplete matrices. J. Mach. Learn. Res. **11**(Aug), 2287–2322 (2010)
14. Hastie, T., Mazumder, R., Lee, J.D., Zadeh, R.: Matrix completion and low-rank SVD via fast alternating least squares. J. Mach. Learn. Res. **16**, 3367–3402 (2015)
15. https://github.com/iskandr/fancyimpute
16. Sumner, R.W., Popović, J.: Deformation transfer for triangle meshes. ACM Trans. Graph. (TOG) **23**(3), 399–405 (2004)

Dynamic Load Balancing for Massively Multiplayer Online Games Using OPNET

Sarmad A. Abdulazeez[(✉)] and Abdennour El Rhalibi[(✉)]

Department of Computer Science, Faculty of Engineering and Technology, Liverpool John Moores University,, Liverpool, UK
Sarmadalrawi17@gmail.com, A.Elrhalibi@ljmu.ac.uk

Abstract. In recent years, there has been an important growth of online gaming. Today's Massively Multiplayer Online Games (MMOGs) can contain millions of synchronous players scattered across the world and participating with each other within a single shared game. Traditional Client/Server architectures of MMOGs exhibit different problems in scalability, reliability, and latency, as well as the cost of adding new servers when demand is too high. P2P architecture provides considerable support for scalability of MMOGs. It also achieves good response times by supporting direct connections between players. In this paper, we have proposed a novel dynamic load balancing for massively multiplayer online games (MMOGs) based this hybrid Peer-to-Peer architecture. We have divided the game world space into several regions. Each region in the game world space is controlled and managed by using both a super-peer and a clone-super-peer. The region's super-peer is responsible for distributing the game update among the players inside the region, as well as managing the game communications between the players. However, the clone-super-peer is responsible for controlling the players' migration from one region to another, in addition to be the super-peer of the region when the super-peer leaves the game. We have designed and evaluated the dynamic load balancing for MMOGs based on hybrid P2P architecture. We have used OPNET Modeler 18.0 to simulate and evaluate the proposed system. Our dynamic load balancer is responsible for distributing the load among the regions in the game world space. The position of the load balancer is located between the game server and the regions. The results, following extensive experiments, show that low delay and higher traffic communication can be achieved using dynamic load balancing for MMOGs based on hybrid P2P system.

Keywords: MMOGs · Client/Server · Peer-to-peer · OPNET Modeler

1 Introduction

Massively Multiplayer Online Games (MMOGs) have the possibility to support hundreds of thousands of synchronised players scattered across the world and participating with each other within a single shared game. The increase in the number of players in MMOGs has led to some issues with the demands for servers which generates a significant increase in costs for the game industry and impacts on the quality of service offered to players. With the rapidly increasing player numbers, servers still need to

A. El Rhalibi et al. (Eds.): Edutainment 2018, LNCS 11462, pp. 177–191, 2019.
https://doi.org/10.1007/978-3-030-23712-7_25

work efficiently under heavy load. Generally, the game server of MMOG is responsible for handling massive numbers of game players, as well as providing the indispensable consistency in order to provide the same feeling for all the game players in the same game world [1]. In real online games, when a specific game server becomes overloaded to the other games servers in the game world, it is caused by many players preferring to play in a specific region of a game world; the game server can become unsteady. This problem can be caused by an increase in network delay, traffic send and received and bandwidth.

Massively multiplayer online games (MMOGs) are readily becoming one of the most significant form of entertainment and a major mechanism of learning. Many researchers have started to use MMOGs for an educational aspect. However, there is a rarity of research on the authentic culture/cognition of MMOGs gameplay, despite its necessity for sound theory and viable design. We can used our hybrid P2P architecture in addition to the dynamic load balancing in the aspect of learning to encourage the students to understand more about the game network in an easy way using OPNET Modeler.

There are several research works to balance the load of the game server [2–4] but most of the researches in this area are based on the client-server architecture. In this paper, we have proposed and designed a new dynamic load balancing technique for MMOGs based on hybrid P2P architecture [5].

2 Research Background

2.1 Load Balancing in P2P MMOGs

Load balancing can be defined as the process of effectively distributing processing requirements of applications across a number of various servers [6] and is the main concern for all distributed systems. In other words, load balancing technique is linked to the mechanism to distribute the load of processing that occurs when the peers join and leave the system. Actually, the scalability problem in MMOGs based on Client/Server architecture is intrinsically related to load balancing [7]. However, when applying load balancing for MMOGs' infrastructure, it must be implemented in an effective way to avert essential resources over-supplying on the server side. The basic method to load balancing is to migrate nodes from heavily loaded to the other lightly loaded and then to redistribute the load across the nodes. However, this load balancing approach is far from straightforward in a peer-to-peer system. In P2P architecture, there are two main issues. Firstly, how to determine that the node is overloaded or under-loaded. Secondly, how to find an appropriate partner node where to redistribute the load [8]. In [9], Naaz et al., presented three essential parameters which generally define the strategy a particular load balancing algorithm will employ. These parameters are the maker of the load balancing decision, the information used to make the load balancing decision, and the time of the load balancing decision being made. Load balancing can be categorised into two main types: static and dynamic.

2.2 Load Balancing Techniques

Load balancing techniques are primarily used for balancing the workload in distributed systems. The load balancing can be classified into two main types: "static load balancing" and "dynamic load balancing". These kinds of load balancing are explained in the next sections. The main objective of load balancing techniques is to improve the level of performance by redistributing the load between available server nodes. Dynamic load balancing techniques react to the current state of the system, while static load balancing techniques rely on just the average system behaviour in order to achieve the load balancing of the system, transfer decisions are separated from the actual current state of the system. This situation makes the dynamic technique more complicated than static one. However, dynamic load balancing policies have the possibility to achieved the best performance compared to static load balancing [10]. The performance of different load balancing techniques is measured by several parameters such as fault tolerant, centralised or decentralised, scalability, reliability, stability, migration, resource utilization, and responsiveness [11].

2.2.1 Static Load Balancing

Static load balancing algorithm works statically without the need of the present state of nodes. Static load balancing algorithm basically depends on the information about the average of the system work load without the need for the actual current system status. The performance of the processors is specified during the compilation time. Then according to their performance, the master processor is responsible for assigning the work load. However, the slave processors are responsible for calculating their assigned work and submitting the result to the master processor. A task is always implemented on the processor to which it is allocated, that is static load balancing algorithms are non-pre-emptive. The static load balancing algorithms work to distribute load according to a fixed group of rules, and these rules are linked to the kind of load, such as CPU power requirement and memory requirement [12]. All the prior information of the system is previously known, such as CPU power, memory availability, performance as well as data about node's requirements for instance bandwidth. Static load balancing algorithm works with less complex situations, the reason is it does not need the information relating to the present state of the system [13]. This type of load balancing has serious disadvantages when the sudden failure happens in the system resources, tasks cannot be moved during its implementation for the load balancing. Round robin is considered one of the models of static load balancing algorithm which divides the traffic evenly between servers. However, there are several problems appearing in round robin algorithm, in order to cope with these problems, a new load balancing algorithm is proposed called Weighted Round Robin [13]. The major idea for this algorithm is that each server has been allocated a weight, therefore the servers that have the highest weight will receive more connections. The main objectives of static load balancing algorithm are to decrease the execution time of the processes and reduce the communication delay [11]. However, the main disadvantage of this technique is the algorithm does not check the load of other nodes in the network. Thus, they cannot guarantee whether they balance up or not. This leads to decrease the performance of the system.

2.2.2 Dynamic Load Balancing

In this approach, the processes are assigned to different processors based on the new information collected [14]. Dynamic load balancing allocates processes dynamically when one of the processors becomes under loaded. Dynamic load balancing can provide a considerable improvement in performance when compared with static load balancing technique. The static load balancing algorithms are more stable compared to dynamic algorithms. When one of the processors becomes under loaded, dynamic algorithms can be allocated processes dynamically [15]. However, this approach provides an efficient load balancing but with additional cost for collecting and maintaining load information, thus it is significant to maintain these overheads within sensible limits [14]. This method is suitable for MMOGs because of the changing resources of the game world, also changes in avatar behaviour.

Dynamic load balancing algorithms work on present state of node and distribute the load between the nodes at run time. The decision of balancing is taken according to the present status of the system. Dynamic load balancing is implemented, when the load of the system and processes number is probably to change at run time. In this situation, there is a need for permanently monitoring the load of the system. This case will increase the overhead and makes the system more complicated compared to the static policies [16]. Substantially dynamic load balancer is used to track real time load distribution across the system, and all the decisions will be taken dependent on the system wide load. It also makes sure that the load is evenly distributed across all nodes.

One of the key purposes of dynamic load balancing is to decrease the load produced from the game by equally controlling and real time monitoring the loads between servers (super-peers) in the game world. In other words, the load balancing is used to distribute load among a number of nodes in order to improve the benefit of the computation capability of each node, as well as to achieve optimum resource utilization which maximises throughput and minimises the task response time. Load balancing is very fundamental in MMOGs in order to improve the quality of service by dealing with continuous changes of the load over time which leads to improvement of the performance of the system. The load balancing leads to a reduction in the overall waiting time of the resources and averts too much loading on the node's resources. The main advantages of using load balancing is to increase the availability of resources, improve the performance of the system by increasing reliability, increase the throughput, maintain and increase the level of stability, optimize resource utilization and provide fault tolerance ability [10].

There are two main methods for dynamic load balancing: distributed and non-distributed [16]. In the distributed dynamic load balancing, the load balancing is done for all nodes in the system and the load balancing task is shared between them in the network system. Every node communicates with all the other nodes in the system. This leads to a high level of internal process communication. The benefit of using this method is to give a good fault tolerance for the system. When one or more nodes in the system fail, it will not affect the whole load balancing process. This can improve the performance of the system.

However, in non-distributed dynamic load balancing, either one node or a set of nodes do the load balancing task. It can be described in two forms: centralised and semi-distributed. In centralised form, just one master node implements the load balancing in the whole system such as central node (server). The other remaining nodes communicate just with the master node. However, in semi-distributed form, all system nodes are divided into several clusters. Each cluster is working in centralised form. Election technique is used to select a central node for each cluster. The load balancing of the system is implemented by using the centralised nodes. Obviously, the dynamic load balancing is more complex compared to the static technique, but the dynamic technique has a priority rather than static technique due to the better level of performance that is provided by the dynamic load balancing. Also the interaction between nodes to achieve load balancing can be divided into two main types: cooperative interaction and non-cooperative interaction [16]. The cooperative nodes interaction are working side-by-side to achieve the load balancing. The main goal is to improve the overall level of system performance. However, in a non-cooperative interaction, each node in the system works independently to achieve its own goals. This methods is used to improve the response time of a local task

3 Literature Review

Recently, there has been a new technical challenge emerging in the gaming industry which focused on the possibility of managing the resources of game servers for massively multiplayer online games (MMOGs).

Denault et al. [18] introduced a dynamic load balancing mechanism that takes into consideration both the load related to game actions in addition to the load incurred by interest management. In this research, hybrid techniques have been used to split the main tasks the game's logic has to perform. Firstly, interest management (IM) and secondly, state update dissemination. The main concept is to partition the game world into small triangles that take into account the world geometry such as walls. A cell consists of many triangles connected with each other within the virtual world. There are two factors considered in this technique: the load associated with performing game actions and the load incurred over interest management [18]. The load balancing is achieved in two ways. The first way is called cell load model. In this model, when players and objects are equally distributed across the game world, the servers have the same cell size. However, it is uncommon that objects are equally distributed; also, most players resort to the most interesting zones in the game world. Thus, servers holding the heavily populated tiles have to do more processing for IM. The IM for each player has to be determined, and a large number of players in the cell. Therefore, the calculating load of the server is based on two components: the number of players into server's cell and the number of objects and players the server has subscribed [6]. The second way is called cell load distribution. When the cell skips the threshold value and become overloaded, it tries to move some of its tiles to a neighbouring cell. It is quite important to select the tiles to be transferred. To do this, the cell calculates a priority value as follows; if the tiles neighbours and all members of the same cell, the priority is low such as 0. Otherwise, the priority is calculated according to the number of edge hops between this tile and the nearest tile of priority 0 [18]. However, the limitations of this technique are the authors did not mention the obvious criteria to calculate the threshold value for each player, and this research is based on the client-server system and it need more servers to cope with the increasing number of players. This causes the high cost for adding a new server to the game world.

Bezerra et al. [19] proposed a new mechanism for dividing the game world space into small regions based on kd-tree and achieves the load balancing of servers by repeatedly adjusting the split coordinates stored in its nodes. The important benefits for using kd-tree are: making this partitioning to allow a fine granularity to distribute the load and the readjustment of the regions becomes simpler. The load balancing approach is based on two main criteria: first, considering the servers as heterogeneous. It means each server may have a different quantity of resources. Second, the loads of the servers are not related to the numbers of players, but to the amount of bandwidth required to send state update messages to them. Because the number of messages sent by the players to the server will be growing linearly with the increase of player numbers, the number of state update messages sent by the server may not be good due to lack of bandwidth in the server. In this approach, using kd-tree with two dimensions, each node in the tree represents a region of the space and the node stores a split coordinate. Each node has two children and represents a subdivision of the region represented by the parent node. One of them represents the sub-region but has the parent node representing the region before the split coordinate. The region of the space is represented by the leaf node, which stores the list of avatars who are currently in that region. Ultimately, every leaf node is connected to the server of the game. When a server is overloaded, it performs the load balancing by using the kd-tree to modify the split coordinates that define its region, in addition to reduce the amount of content managed by the server. Also, each node in the tree stores two values: capacity and load of the sub-tree. The calculation of the load and capacity of a non-leaf node are equal to sum of the load of its children. However, the leaf nodes have the same values of the server connected to each one of them. The calculation of the load is dependent on the way of distributing the players among the regions. The players are deployed between the servers according to the bandwidth for each server. However, this method is not optimal when the number of messages transmitted between players is large. Using a brute-force method for calculating the loads by calculating the number of messages that should be obtained by each player by unit of time [19]. This architecture does not support the scalability, therefore this is not suitable for the MMOGs with high numbers of players.

Lu et al., [6] presented a load balancing technique based on clustered server to achieve scalability. Allowing servers to transfer player actions to each other, however the responsibility for processing players' actions remains with the server to which they are initially earmarked. The system consists of two main levels: the application level and the database level. Firstly, the player connects to the server cluster through a load balancer, and he/she is then linked to a particular server in the application level. Application level is dedicated to meet the runtime requirements of game play. Through the database level, an application server can have access to the virtual world constructs and players' statistics via the load balancer that exists between application level and the database level [6]. But, this method is ineffective because the load balancer has not enough resources to cope with the increase of player numbers. Also, the cost of providing a large number of servers is very high as well as the cost of maintenance.

Usually zone size in MMOGs is fixed, but there are some techniques that cope with dynamic region size using for instance Voronoi diagrams. Most of these techniques do not have load-handling mechanisms. The problem is the difficulty to predict player density or deploy the players before the start of a game. Thus, the server cannot share its resources with surrounding region servers. This approach, presented a load balancing mechanism where region shapes are not predefined. Consider a system with a number of masters/servers with a large single region in the game world, the players can join and leave the game over time and at first only one server is involved. In this method [20], the game is divided dynamically depending on players' logical position and interaction pattern. Consequently, the zone shapes are not uniform. The bisection algorithm is used to divide a region into two sub-regions of roughly equal load while attempting to reduce the communication cost, such as the number of links crossing logical boundaries. Depending on the bisection methods, at the first time, the region is divided into one dimension to produce two sub-regions. Other partitions are made repeatedly in the new sub-regions if necessary [20]. However, this method is not efficient when the number of players is too large because we need extra servers to manage the load, then the cost of provide servers is high; furthermore, the maintenance

4 Design Dynamic Load Balancing Technique for MMOGs

Dynamic load balancing techniques rely on recent system load information in addition assigning the job for each server node at run time. The load balancing decisions are dependent on the current system state. Thus allowing the workload to dynamically shift from an overloaded node to the light-load node in order to increase the response time of server nodes. The main advantage of using the dynamic load balancing is the capability of responding to difference in the system. We have designed a new dynamic load balancer for MMOGs based on hybrid P2P system. Our load balancing system measured the load of each super-peer in the game world space in order to find out the availability for each region. The measurement of the load is based on the node resources such as power of the CPU, memory available, bandwidth, disk space as well as stability and reactivity. When the first player joins the game for the first time, it must be registered in the game server. The server will assign this player as a super-peer for the region. After that, each player wanting to join the game must be registered in the game server. The game server sends the ID of the player to the dynamic load balancer to find the suitable region to connect to it. The load balancer is responsible for sending a message to the super-peer of the region to inform him that a new player will join the region. When the player joins the second time or subsequent times, it should join the game through the game server in order to find the appropriate region to allocate to it. However, in the case of a player leaving the game, it should inform the super-peer or clone-super-peer of the region about that. The super-peer is responsible for informing both the dynamic load balancer and the game server. The dynamic load balancer updates the load of each region when the new player joins the game or when the player leaves the game. When the super-peer of the region leaves the game, it must inform both the game server and the clone-super-peer of the region about that. The clone-server will become the super-peer of the region and assign a new clone-super-peer for that region. All the information will be updated in the game server and the dynamic load balancer. If all the regions in the game world space are overloaded, the load balancer will inform the game server to create a new region in order to handle the work load of the players. While, if there are regions that do not contain any players, the dynamic load balancer will work with the server to destroy the region and allocate the super-peer and clone-super-peer of that region to another convenient region in the game world space. The dynamic load balancing algorithm is explained in the next section.

4.1 Dynamic Load Balancing Algorithm

Each player must be registered in the game server at the beginning of the game. The first player will be assigned as the super-peer of the first region in the game world space. However, the second player will be allocated as the clone-super-peer of that region. All the information of the super-peer and clone-super-peer will be sent to the load balancer in order to inform it. After that, each player will be assigned as a normal player in the region by sending all the players from the game server to the super-peer through the load balancer. When the first region is full, the load balancer is responsible for informing the game server about that in order to create a new region and assign both super-peer and clone super-peer for that region. If the normal player wants to leave the game, he/she will inform the super-peer of the region about that leaving. The super-peer turn to inform both load balancer and the game server to update the load of this region. However, if the player decides to migrate to another region, he/she will inform the clone-super-peer and send the region ID. The clone-super-peer will check the availability and the possibility of that region to join the player through the load balancer. If the new region is available and possible to accept the player, the load balancer is responsible for allocating the player to that region and update the load information for the two regions. All the updated information is sent to the game server and the super-peers of the regions concerned. As for the leaving or migration of the super-peer of the region, he/she will send a notification the game server, load balancer and clone-super-peer of the region. The clone-super-peer will be assigned as the super-peer of this region and he/she has the possibility to allocate a new clone-super-peer for the region. All the updated information is sent to the game server and the load balancer. However, if the clone-super-peer leaves or migrates the game, he/she will inform the super-peer of the region to assign new clone-super-peer of the region. All the updated information is sent to the load balancer and the game server.

4.2 Simulation of Dynamic Load Balancing

In order to design the simulation for dynamic load balancing for MMOGs, we have fail all the nodes of players before the simulation. It will help us to start the game from the base. We have used the deterministic technique for generating failures and recoveries for each node (peer) in the game world space. All the nodes will start to recover according to the specific time that will be given to each node in the game world space.

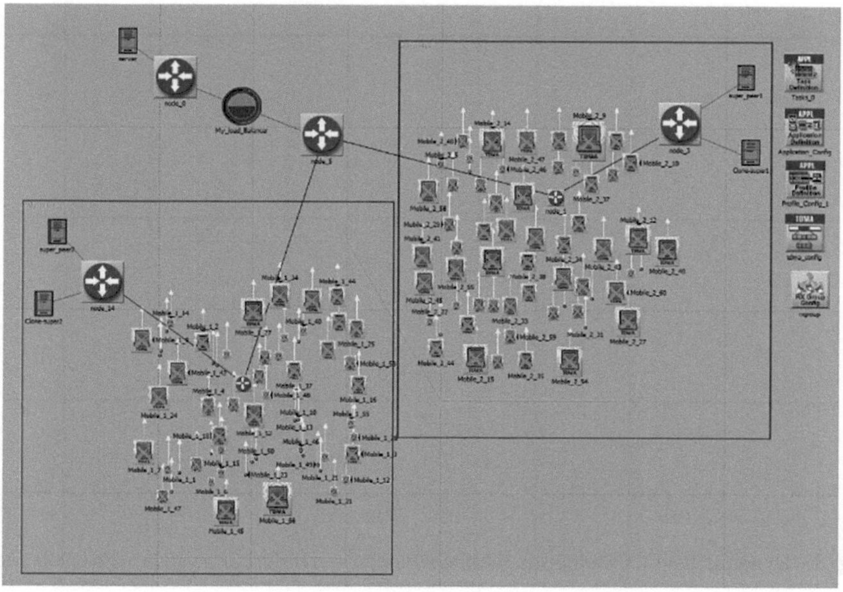

Fig. 1. Dynamic load balancing for MMOGs based on hybrid P2P system with 125 peers

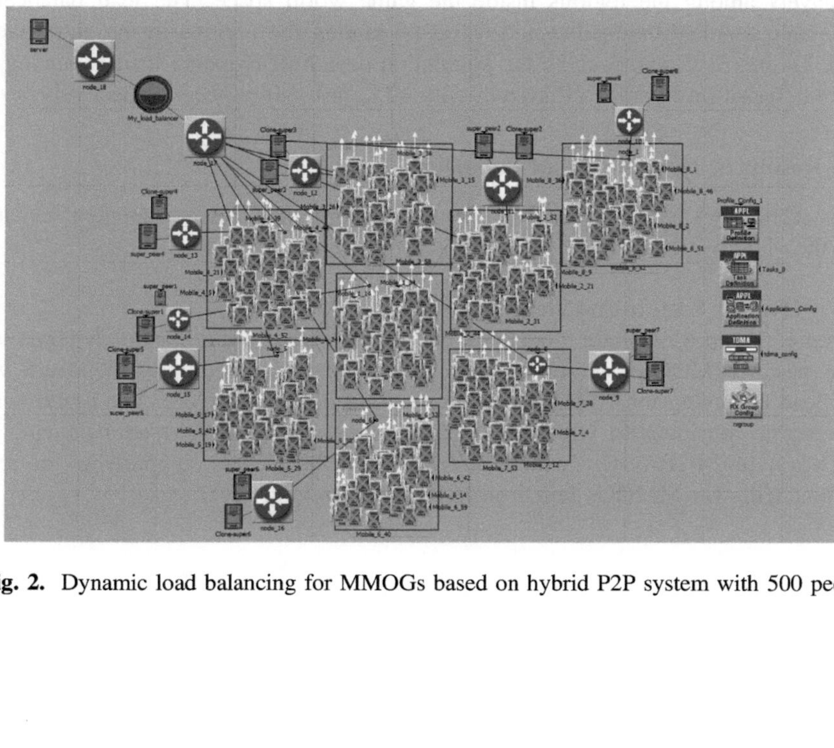

Fig. 2. Dynamic load balancing for MMOGs based on hybrid P2P system with 500 peers

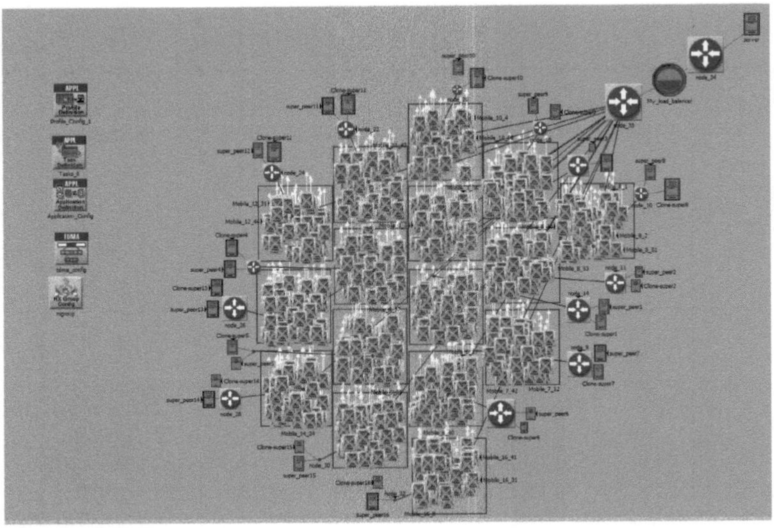

Fig. 3. Dynamic load balancing for MMOGs based on hybrid P2P system with 1000 peers

After the player's node recovers, it will start the game by registration in the game server. The game server is responsible for creating a profile for each player and sends this information to the load balancer in order to enable the load balancer to distribute the players among the regions inside the game world space. The load balancer is responsible for distributing the nodes (peers) among the regions in the game world space. Figures 1, 2, and 3 show the simulation design of dynamic load balancing for MMOGs based on hybrid P2P system with 125, 500, 1,000 peers respectively.

4.3 Results of Dynamic Load Balancing

In this section, we have analysed the network performance under simulation scenarios from the view of two primary parameters.

4.3.1 Overall End-to-End Delay

Figures 4, 5, and 6 illustrate the overall end-to-end delay results for the dynamic load balancing for MMOGs based on hybrid P2P architecture and compare the results with static load balancing for MMOGs based on hybrid P2P architecture. The figure below illustrates a considerable variation of delay when using static load balancing for MMOGs hybrid P2P system with 125, 500, and 1,000 players compared to the static load balancing for MMOGs based on hybrid P2P architecture.

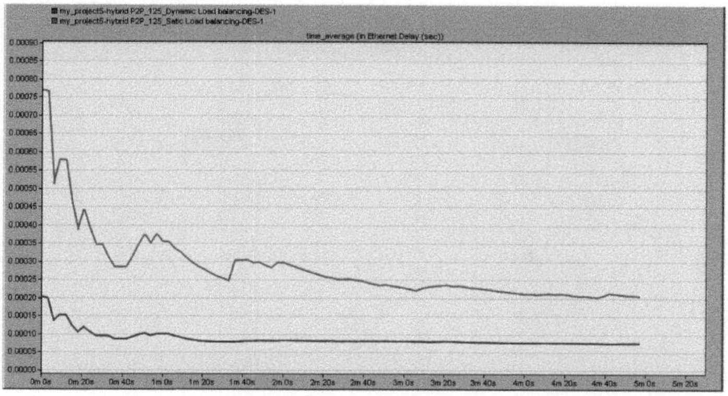

Fig. 4. Overall delay for dynamic load balancing for MMOGs with 125 peers

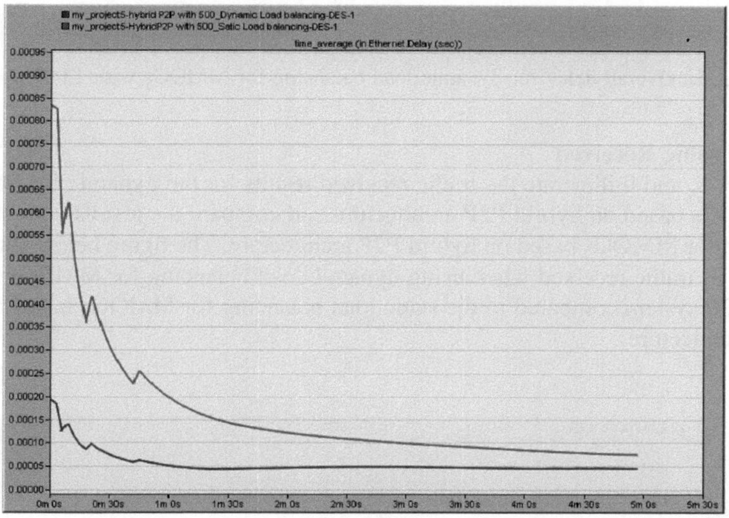

Fig. 5. Overall delay for dynamic load balancing for MMOGs with 500 peers

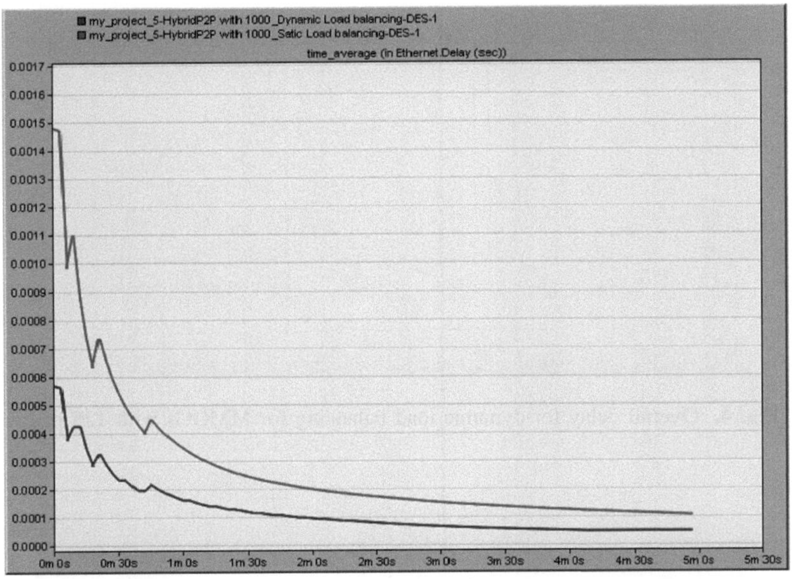

Fig. 6. Overall delay for dynamic load balancing for MMOGs with 1,000 peers

4.3.2 Traffic Received

Figures 7, 8, and 9 illustrate the traffic received results for the dynamic load balancing for MMOGs based on hybrid P2P architecture and compare the results with static load balancing for MMOGs based on hybrid P2P architecture. The figure below shows a big variation of traffic received when using dynamic load balancing for MMOGs based on hybrid P2P system compared to the static load balancing for MMOGs based on client-server architecture.

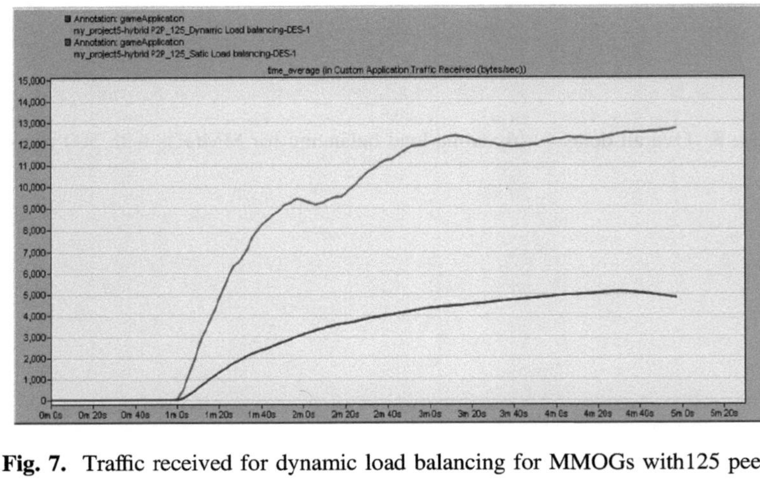

Fig. 7. Traffic received for dynamic load balancing for MMOGs with125 peers

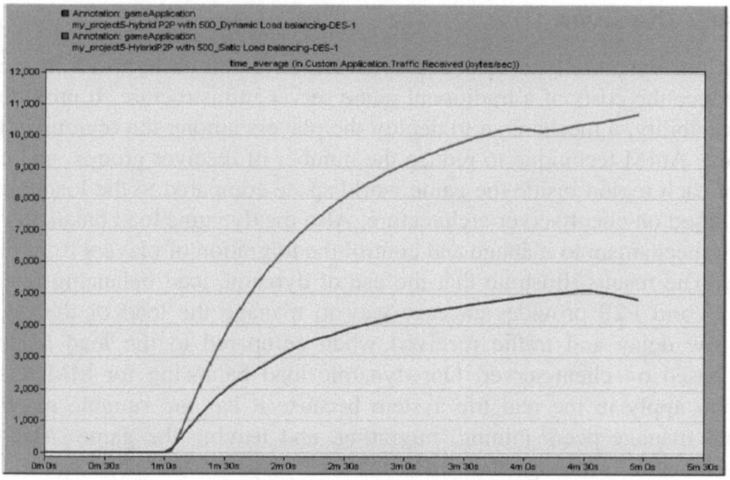

Fig. 8. Traffic received for dynamic load balancing for MMOGs with 500 peers

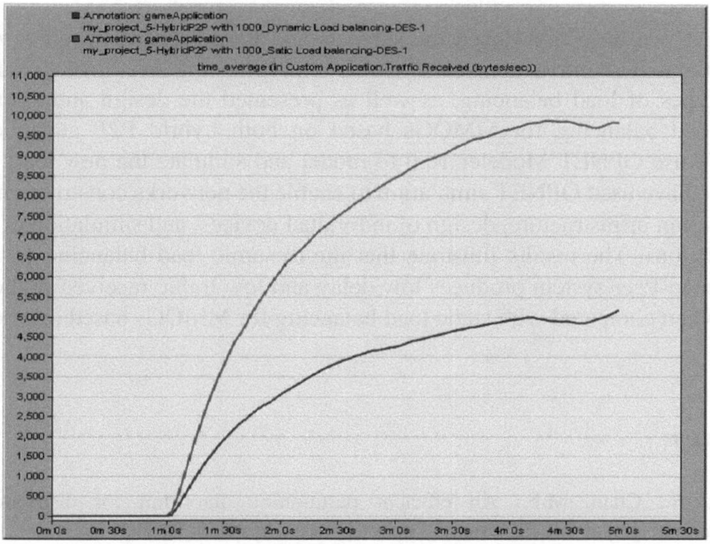

Fig. 9. Traffic received for dynamic load balancing for MMOGs with 1,000 peers

5 Discussion

This section discusses the different results of the dynamic load balancing evaluation. Starting with the limitations that influence the results of the evaluation which are illustrated in the previous sections. Followed by the evaluation findings of the dynamic load balancing simulation.

5.1 Results Discussion

In general, our dynamic load balancer for MMOGs based on hybrid P2P architecture aims to reduce the costs of a traditional game server infrastructure. It provides a good level of scalability, a mechanism to deploy the players among the regions in the game world space, AoIM technique to reduce the number of receiver groups, and control of the load of each region inside the game world space compared to the load balancer for MMOGs based on client-server architecture. Also the dynamic load balancing provides an efficient mechanism to manage and control the migration of players from one region to another. The results illustrate that the use of dynamic load balancing for MMOGs based on hybrid P2P provides an easy way to manage the load of the regions and provides low delay and traffic received when compared to the load balancing for MMOGs based on client-server. Our dynamic load balancing for MMOGs has the flexibility to apply in the real life system because it has the suitable mechanism to control and manage peers joining, migrating, and leaving the game. Also, it has a robust mechanism to manage the AoIM for each player in the game world.

6 Conclusion

In this paper, we have introduced the subjects and issues related to our research and explained the main contributions for dynamic load balancing. We have also introduced the main types of load balancing, as well as presented the design and simulation of dynamic load balancing for MMOGs based on both hybrid P2P and client-server system. We use OPNET Modeler 18.0 to model and simulate the new load balancing system. We have used OPNET simulation to enable the networks construction, study of communication infrastructure, design of individual devices, and simulation of protocols and applications. The results illustrate that the dynamic load balancing for MMOGs hybrid Peer-to-Peer system produces low delay and low traffic received in the network topology when compared with static load balancing for MMOGs based on client-server system.

References

1. Lui, J.C.S., Chan, M.F.: An efficient partitioning algorithm for distributed virtual environment systems. IEEE Trans. Parallel Distrib. Syst. **13**(3), 193–211 (2002)
2. Deng, Y., Lau, R.W.H.: Dynamic load balancing in distributed virtual environments using heat diffusion. ACM Trans. Multimed. Comput. Commun. Appl. (TOMM) **10**(2), 1–20 (2013)
3. Jiang, H., Iyengar, A., Nahum, E., Segmuller, W., Tantawi, A., Wright, C.P.: Design, implementation, and performance of a load balancer for SIP server clusters. IEEE/ACM Trans. Netw. **20**(4), 1190–1202 (2012)
4. Zhou, S.: A dynamic load sharing algorithm for massively multiplayer online games
5. Abdulazeez, S., El Rhalibi, A., Merabti, M., Al Jumeily, D.: Survey of solutions for peer-to-peer MMOGs. In: 2015 IEEE International Conference on Computing, Networking and Communications (IEEE ICNC), California, USA (2015)

6. Lu, F., Parkin, S., Morgan, G.: Load balancing for massively multiplayer online games. In: Proceedings of 5th ACM SIGCOMM Workshop on Network and System Support Games, NetGames 2006, p. 1 (2006)
7. Chertov, R., Fahmy, S.: Optimistic load balancing in a distributed virtual environment. In: Proceedings of 2006 International Workshop on Network and Operating Systems Support for Digital Audio and Video, NOSSDAV 2006, p. 1 (2006)
8. Link, C., Vu, Q.H., Ooi, C., Rinard, M., Tan, K.: Histogram-based global load balancing in structured peer-to-peer systems (2014)
9. Naaz, S., Alam, A., Biswas, R.: Load balancing algorithms for peer to peer and client server distributed environments. Int. J. Comput. Appl. **47**(8), 17–21 (2012)
10. Garg, A.: A comparative study of static and dynamic load balancing algorithms. IJARCSMS **2**(12), 386–392 (2014)
11. Wadhwa, D., Kumar, N.: Performance Analysis of Load Balancing Algorithms in, vol. 4, no. 1, pp. 59–66 (2014)
12. Rajani, S., Garg, N.: A clustered approach for load balancing in distributed systems, vol. 2, no. 1, pp. 1–6 (2015)
13. Mishra, N.K.: Load balancing techniques: need, objectives and major challenges in cloud computing- a systematic review. Int. J. Comput. Appl. **131**(18), 11–19 (2015)
14. Malik, S.: Dynamic load balancing in a network of workstations. 95.515F Research Report
15. Sharma, S., Singh, S., Sharma, M.: Performance analysis of load balancing algorithms. World Acad. Sci. Eng. Technol. **38**, 269–272 (2008)
16. Alakeel, A.M.: A guide to dynamic load balancing in distributed computer systems. IJCSNS Int. J. Comput. Sci. Netw. Secur. **10**(6), 153–160 (2010)
17. Soundarabai, P.B., Rani, A.S., Sahai, R.K., Thriveni, J., Venugopal, K.R., Patnaik, L.M.: Comparative study on load balancing techniques in distributed systems. Int. J. Inf. Technol. Knowl. Manag. **6**(1), 53–60 (2012)
18. Denault, A., Canas, C., Kienzle, J., Kemme, B.: Triangle-based obstacle-aware load balancing for massively multiplayer games. In: 2011 10th Annual Workshop on Network and Systems Support for Games, pp. 1–6, October 2011
19. Bezerra, C.E.B., Comba, J.L.D., Geyer, C.F.R.: A fine granularity load balancing technique for MMOG servers using a KD-tree to partition the space. In: 2009 VIII Brazilian Symposium on Games and Digital Entertainment, pp. 17–26 (2009)
20. Ahmed, D.T., Shirmohammadi, S.: Uniform and non-uniform zoning for load balancing in virtual environments (2010)
21. OPNET. http://www.riverbed.com/products/performance-management-control/opnet.html. Accessed 21 Jan 2018

A Slice-Guided Method of Indoor Scene Structure Retrieving

Lijuan Wang[1,2], Yinghui Wang[1,3](✉), Ningna Wang[4], Xiaojuan Ning[1,3], Ke Lv[5], and Liangyi Huang[6]

[1] Xi'an University of Technology, South Jinhua Road no. 5, Xi'an 710032, China
wyh_925@163.com

[2] Xi'an Technology University, Mid Xuefu Road no. 2, Xi'an 710021, China

[3] Shaanxi Key Laboratory of Network Computing and Security Technology, South Jinhua Road no. 5, Xi'an 710032, China

[4] Booking.Com, B.V. Vijzelstraat 66-80, 1017HL Amsterdam, Netherlands

[5] Institute of Automation, Chinese Academy of Sciences, Beijing, China

[6] School of Engineering and Applied Science, George Washington University, Washington DC 20052, USA

Abstract. The structure information of indoor scene is necessary for a robot who works in a room. In order to achieve structure of an indoor scene, a slice-guided method of indoor scene structure retrieving is proposed in this paper. We present a slicing based approach that transforms three-dimensional (3D) segmentations into two-dimensional (2D) segmentation and segments different kinds of primitive shapes while keeping the global topology structure of the indoor scene. The global topology structure is represented by a graph. The graph is compared with the given indoor scene template. The matched objects and the topology relation between them are finally presented. Our experiment results show that the proposed method performs well on several typical indoor scenes, even if some data are missing.

Keywords: Indoor scene · Structure · Primitive shapes · Global topology structure

1 Introduction

Retrieving structure information of the indoor scene is necessary for a robot working in a room. Segmentation of indoor scene objects and acquiring the relation between them are needed in indoor scene structure analysis. To face this issue, many methods are proposed, including learning-based methods [1–4] and context-based methods [5–9]. In these methods, machine learning is often needed, and the objects extraction result highly depends on training data sets. Objects arrangements are also required to meet specific rules.

Based on the observation of indoor scene, it can be concluded that most of objects consist of primitive shapes, and the spatial relation between these shapes is stable, which could be used to infer the structure of an indoor scene.

A. El Rhalibi et al. (Eds.): Edutainment 2018, LNCS 11462, pp. 192–202, 2019.
https://doi.org/10.1007/978-3-030-23712-7_26

In this paper, a slice-guided method of indoor scene structure retrieving is proposed. During the method, three-dimensional (3D) segmentation of indoor scene is simplified into two-dimensional (2D) segmentation by slicing. 2D features of indoor scene primitive shapes are analyzed. The features are then used to segment the primitive shapes. Meanwhile, the global topology structure of indoor scene is constructed. The constructed topology structure is compared with the given template using graph matching. Finally, the matched objects and the relation between these objects are presented. The novelty of the proposed method is that primitive shapes and the global topology structure of an indoor scene are obtained simultaneously.

2 Relate Work

The existing indoor scene structure retrieving methods mainly include learning-based methods [1, 2], context-based methods [5, 6, 9] and topology-structure-based methods [10–12]. Compared with other two methods, the topology-structure-based methods did not require a large amount of data for training. It also doesn't rely on the objects arrangement. However in most of existing topology structure based methods [10–12], only the local topology structure of the indoor scene can be acquired. Although in a few methods (e.g. method [10]), the global topology structure of the indoor scene could be achieved, primitive shapes of the indoor scene can't be acquired simultaneously. In the proposed method, overall indoor scene is sliced, and 2D projection features of all scenes parts are obtained simultaneously. Then, 2D features are utilized to segment the all the 3D primitive shapes of the scene. At the same time, the global topology structure of the indoor scene is constructed. By comparison with the indoor scene template, the indoor scene objects and the global topology relation between them can be recognized simultaneously.

3 Methodology

The proposed method has three steps:

(a) Extract indoor scene primitive shapes.
(b) Construct the topology structure templates of indoor scenes.
(c) Construct the topology structure for an input scene; match the topology structure graph with indoor scene template.

3.1 Extraction of Primitive Shapes

Indoor scene objects are designed by human beings and could be approximated by primitive shapes such as plane, cylinder, sphere and so on. A slicing-based primitive shapes extraction approach is proposed.

Firstly, the indoor scene is sliced along a specific direction. The slicing procedure in paper [13] is adopted and 2D segments are produced. The 2D segment $\{p_i\}_{i=1}^{N}$ may be a line or an arc. According to the method [14], the eigen vector and eigen values of the covariance of point set $\{p_i\}_{i=1}^N$ are computed. If the minimum eigen value is less than a threshold, the point set $\{p_i\}_{i=1}^N$ is a line, otherwise, it is an arc.

Secondly, three following primitive shapes are defined.

(1) Horizontal plane. The horizontal plane is parallel with slicing plane. Normal of the points that belong to a horizontal plane is orthogonal to normal of the slicing plane.
(2) Vertical plane. A vertical plane is composed of a set of parallel lines that lie on different slices. Two lines on neighboring slice meet the following necessary constraint.

Constraint 1:

$$\mathrm{dis}(line1, line2) < threshold_l \tag{1}$$

$$\mathrm{angle}(avgnormal\_P_{line1}, avgnormal\_P_{line2}) < threshold_{\theta\min} \tag{2}$$

$dis(line1, line2)$ is the spatial distance between two line segments. It is computed by the distance between a point belongs to a line and another line. $avgnormal\_P_{line1}$ is the average normal of all points in a point set P_{line1}. P_{line1} is 3D points set corresponding to $line1$. $avgnormal\_P_{line2}$ and P_{line2} have the similar meaning. $\mathrm{angle}(avgnormal\_P_{line1}, avgnormal\_P_{line2})$ denotes the intersect angle of the two normal.

(3) Cylinder. Cylinder is composed of a set of adjacent arcs on different slices. Two arcs of neighboring slices should meet the following necessary constraint.

Constraint 2:

$$\mathrm{dis}(O_1, O_2) < threshold_o, R_1 \approx R_2 \tag{3}$$

O_1 and O_2 is the centers of the two arcs respectively. $dis(O_1, O_2)$ denotes the Euclidean distance between O_1 and O_2. R_1 and R_2 denote the corresponding radius respectively.

Finally, merge the lines and arcs on neighboring slice into primitive shapes according to Constraint 1 and Constraint 2.

3.2 Construction of Indoor Scene Topology Structure Template

A core insight is that a scene (e.g. an office room, a reception room) could be represented by a tree topology structure. For example, an office room can be expressed as a tree topology structure graph (see Fig. 1). Figure 1 includes three kinds of nodes. The dark blue nodes denote the horizontal plane. The light blue nodes denote the vertical plane. The green nodes denote the cylinder. In the tree topology structure, each horizontal plane and its' vertical plane sub-nodes or cylinder sub-nodes constitute an object. The root node has two vertical plane nodes, i.e. a table is composed of a horizontal plane and two vertical planes. Each dark blue sub-node have a light blue sub-node and four green nodes, which means a chair has a vertical plane back and four-cylinder legs. The edge between the horizontal plane and the vertical plane or the cylinder denotes the topology relation between them. The global topology relation between objects is represented by the edge between the dark blue nodes.

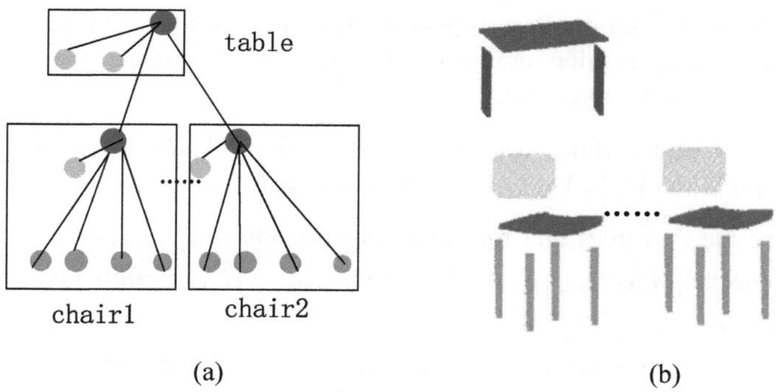

Fig. 1. An indoor scene. (a) Tree topology structure graph, (b) indoor scene objects. (Color figure online)

Given a topology graph structure G, the node attribution, A_V has two items, i.e. the shape type and size. There are three types of primitive shapes as mentioned above. For horizontal plane the size means its' area. For cylinder, the size means its' height. The edge attribution A_E has two items, i.e. the symmetric edge numbers and the intersect angle between these edges, as shown in Fig. 2.

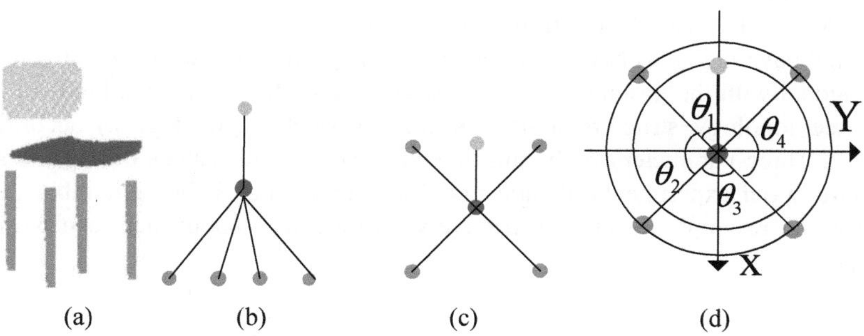

Fig. 2. Topology relation between parts of indoor scene objects. (a) chair, (b) topology graph of a chair, (c) projection of topology graph, (d) intersect angle between projected topology graph edges.

3.3 Construction and Matching of Indoor Scene Topology Structure Graph

The tree topology structure graph $G = (V, E, A_V, A_E)$ of an indoor scene is constructed as the following steps:

(1) Acquire the centroids of primitive shapes. Centroids are taken as nodes and colored according to their shape types.
(2) Construct the orientation bounding box (OBB) for each horizontal plane. The vertical plane and cylinder that belong to an OBB of a horizontal plane will be sub-nodes of the horizontal plane node.
(3) Order the horizontal plane parts according to their z-value. The horizontal planes that have same z-value are ordered clockwise. Construct the tree topology structure according the order.

The tree-to-tree matching between template $G_t = (V_t, E_t, A_{Vt}, A_{Et})$ and a scene structure graph $G = (V, E, A_V, A_E)$ is performing as following.

(1) Traverse the two trees, get root node objects $object_{temp\_root}$, $object_{root}$, and sub-node objects $\{object_{temp\_child\_i}\}_{i=1}^{N}$, $\{object_{child\_j}\}_{j=1}^{M}$ respectively.
(2) Match $\{object_{child\_j}\}_{j=1}^{M}$ with target $\{object_{temp\_child\_i}\}_{i=1}^{N}$ and the $object_{root}$ with $object_{temp\_root}$ respectively by the method [15], and label the matched objects.
(3) If root node objects and some sub-node objects have been matched successfully, the two topology graph is considered as matched globally. The matched objects and the topology relation between them are given.
(4) If only some sub-node objects have been matched successfully, then two topology graphs are matched partially. The matched object is detected.

4 Experiments

The experiments have been done on four indoor scenes, and results have been shown in Figs. 4, 5, 6 and 7. The data is from the reference [1]. In the experiments, orthogonal planes that have big areas have been viewed as the ground and wall. The direction that is orthogonal with the ground is selected as the slicing direction. Two kinds of indoor scene tree topology structure templates are constructed (see Fig. 3.) according to Sect. 3.2. Three parameters N, h, and d need to be set with values during the slicing procedure in our experiments. Parameters N, h, and d denotes slicing numbers, slicing step size and resample distance respectively. More details about them can be seen in paper [13].

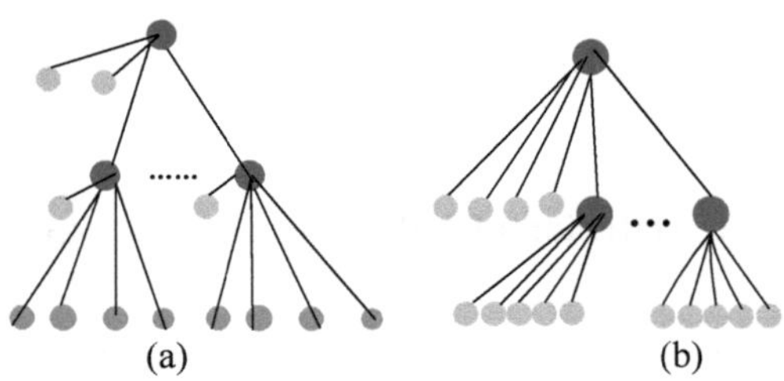

Fig. 3. Scene topology structure templates. (a) Template 1, (b) template 2.

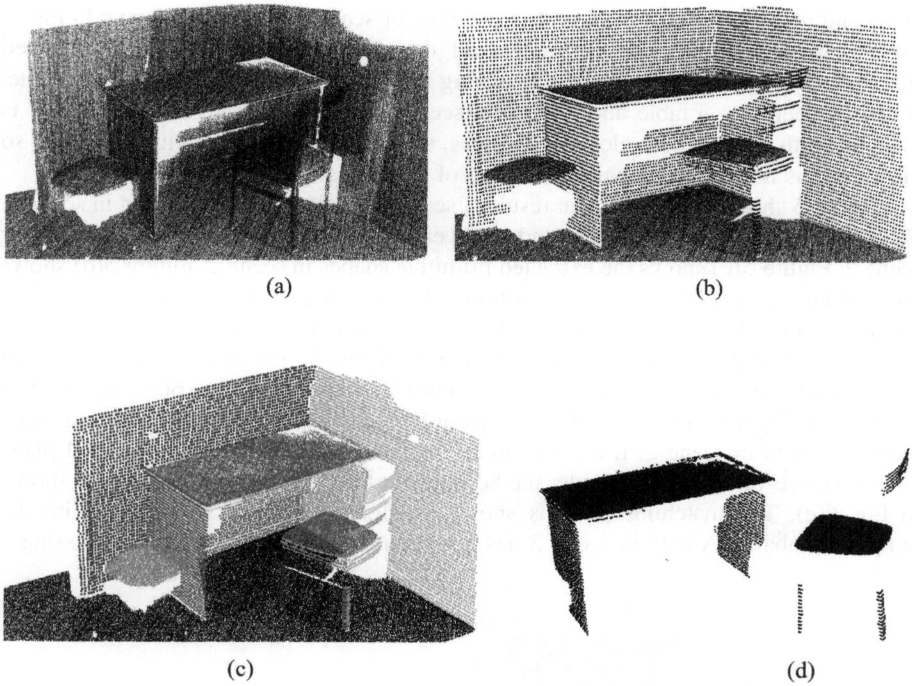

Fig. 4. Results of scene1. (a) Point clouds of scene1, (c) slicing procedure results of scene1 with N = 60, h = l, d = 0.04, (c) parts of scene1, (e) indoor scene structure.

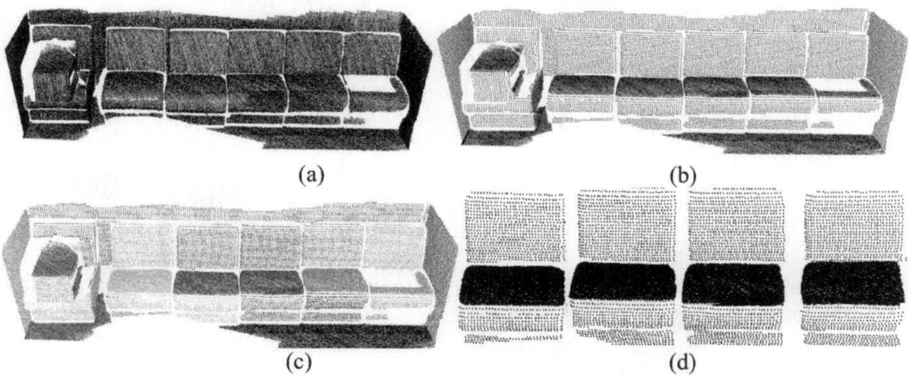

Fig. 5. Results of scene2. (a) Point clouds of scene2, (c) slicing procedure results of scene2 with N = 60, h = l, d = 0.5, (c) parts of scene2, (e) indoor scene structure.

The experiment result of scene1 is shown in Fig. 4. A table and a set of chairs are included in scene 1. The table includes three primitive shapes, i.e. a horizontal plane and two vertical planes. The chair has six parts, i.e. a horizontal plane and a vertical plane and four cylinders. Template 1 is selected for scene 1. Scene 1 is shown in Fig. 4 (a). It can be seen from Fig. 4(c) that all the parts in indoor scene1 is extracted successfully. Figure 4(d) shows the matching result between scene 1 and the template. It can be seen that a table and a chair in scene is extracted successfully. Scene 1 is matched with the template globally. Besides, some data is missing in indoor scene, so the chair has not been recognized because of data missing.

Figure 5 shows the experiment result of scene 2. A set of sofas are listed in scene 2. Each sofa has a horizontal plane and two vertical planes. Template 2 is selected for scene 2. Figure 5(c) shows the extracted primitive shapes in scene 2. Figure 5(d) shows the matching result. It can be seen that four sofas have been extracted. The matching is partial. A sofa of scene 2 is not extracted because of data missing.

The test result of scene 3 is shown in Fig. 6. Scene 3 includes a table and a set of sofas. Template 2 is choose for scene 3. Scene 3 is shown in Fig. 6(a). The sofa in scene 3 has been scanned completely. Accordingly, sofas in scene 3 have four more parts than sofa in scene 2. It has two more vertical planes above the horizontal plane and two more vertical planes under the horizontal plane. The extracted parts are shown in Fig. 6(c). The matching result is shown in Fig. 6(d). Scene 3 matched with the template globally. A sofa in scene 3 has not been detected because of data missing.

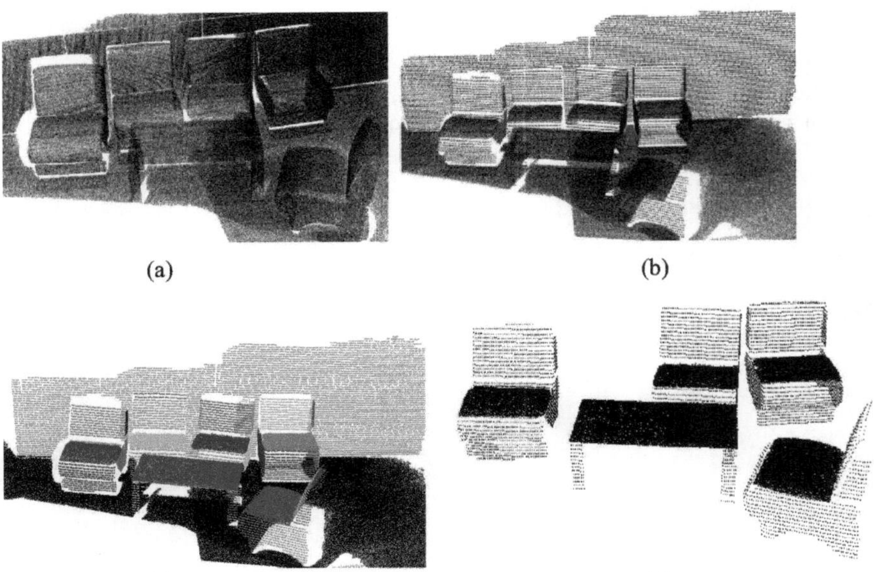

(a) (b) (c) (d)

Fig. 6. Results of scene3. (a) Point clouds of scene3, (c) slicing procedure results of scene3 with N = 60, h = 1, d = 0.5, (c) parts of scene3, (e)indoor scene structure.

The result of scene 4 is shown in Fig. 7. There are some chairs in scene 4. Each chair has six parts, i.e. a horizontal plane, a vertical plane and four cylinders. Template

1 is taken for scene 4. Scene 4 is shown in Fig. 7(a). The extracted parts are shown in Fig. 7(c). The matching result is shown in Fig. 7(d). Scene 4 matched with the template partially.

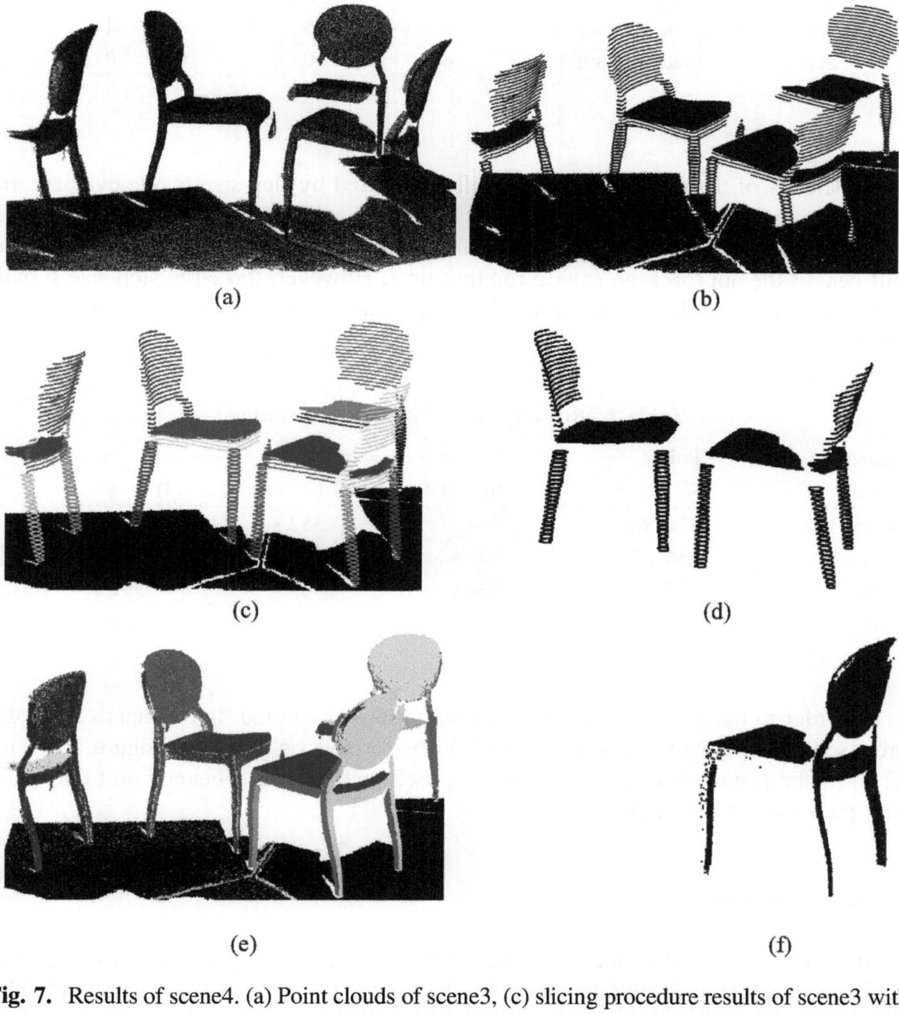

Fig. 7. Results of scene4. (a) Point clouds of scene3, (c) slicing procedure results of scene3 with N = 60, h = l, d = 0.04, (c) parts of scene3, (e) scene structure extracted by the proposed method, (f) scene structure extracted by the method [10].

Table 1 shows a quantitative evaluation of the structure retrieving results for the scene point clouds of the proposed method. The columns show matching results, number of actual counted objects, and detected objects.

Table 1. The indoor scene matching result

Scene	Template	Matching result	Target objects			Extraction objects		
			Chair	Table	Sofa	Chair	Table	Sofa
Scene 1	Template 1	Global	2	1	0	1	1	0
Scene 2	Template 2	Partial	0	0	6	0	0	4
Scene 3	Template 2	Global	0	1	5	0	1	4
Scene 4	Template 1	Partial	4	0	0	2	0	0

Efficiency of the proposed method will be affected by step size h. We evaluate the computing cost of the proposed method by setting with different values for h. The running time of the proposed method is shown in Table 2. It shows a bigger step size will benefit the approach on saving running time. However, too large step size h may result in the missing detection of primitive shapes. In our experiments, step size h is not larger than 1.2 * l.

Table 2. Running time of the proposed method

Scene	Points	Times(s) (N = 60)		
		(h = 0.8 * l h = 1.0 * l h = 1.2 * l)		
Scene 1	374492	404 s	382 s	357 s
Scene 2	356580	404 s	385 s	346 s
Scene 3	604582	434 s	403 s	352 s
Scene 4	492306	412 s	392 s	360 s

In order to demonstrate advantage of the proposed method, the comparison of the proposed method with the method [10] is performed on scene 4. Figure 7(d) and (f) show the results. It can be seen the proposed method gets a better result due to its well parts extraction result.

5 Conclusion

A slice-guided method of indoor scene structure retrieving is proposed in this paper. In the method 2D projection features of indoor scene primitive shapes are extracted by slicing the point clouds. The 2D projection features are then used to retrieve indoor scene primitive shapes. Meanwhile, the method can maintain the global topology structure of the indoor scene. The topology structure graph is matched with the template. The objects of matched indoor scene and the topology relation among them could be obtained.

The experiment results show that the proposed method could detect different kinds of objects and preserve the topology relation among them. Some object could be detected even when data is missing. There are some limits in the method. Although most indoor scene parts could be approximated by primitive shapes defined in the proposed method, some parts could not. Segmentation of the non-primitive shape parts and using them to represent the indoor scene will be done in our future work. Besides, the slicing direction impacts on retrieving results. Different slicing direction will lead into different results. In this paper, all the indoor scene objects are assumed to be placed upright. Under this circumstance, the direction that is orthogonal to the floor is selected. If there are some objects is located abnormal, how to decide the direction will be done in our future work.

Acknowledgement. This study is supported by the National Key Research and Development Program of China No. 2018YFB1004905; the Nature Science Foundation of China under Grant No. 61472319, 61872291, 61871320; and in part by Shaanxi Science Research Plan under Grant No. 2017JQ6023; in part by Scientific Research Program Funded by Shaanxi Provincial Education Department 18JS077.

References

1. Nan, L.L., Xie, K., Sharf, A.: A search-classify approach for cluttered indoor scene understanding. ACM Trans. Graph. **31**(6), 1–10 (2012)
2. Silberman, N., Hoiem, D., Kohli, P., Fergus, R.: Indoor segmentation and support inference from RGBD images. In: Fitzgibbon, A., Lazebnik, S., Perona, P., Sato, Y., Schmid, C. (eds.) ECCV 2012. LNCS, vol. 7576, pp. 746–760. Springer, Heidelberg (2012). https://doi.org/10.1007/978-3-642-33715-4_54
3. Socher, R., Huval, B., Bhat, B., et al.: Convolutional-recursive deep learning for 3D object classification. In: Neural Information Processing Systems Conference and Workshop, NIPS, Nevada, pp. 665–673 (2012)
4. Xu, K., Huang, H., Shi, Y., et al.: Auto scanning for coupled scene reconstruction and proactive object analysis. ACM Trans. Graph. **34**(6), 177 (2015)
5. Xiong, X.H., Huber, D.: Using context to create semantic 3D models of indoor environments. In: British Machine Vision Conference, BMVC 2010, Aberystwyth, UK, pp. 1–11 (2010)
6. Anand, A., Koppula, H.S., Joachims, T., et al.: Contextually guided semantic labeling and search for 3D point clouds. Int. J. Robot. Res. **32**(1), 19–34 (2011)
7. Jiang, Y., Koppula, H., Saxena, A.: Hallucinated humans as the hidden context for labeling 3D scenes. In: Computer Vision and Pattern Recognition, pp. 2993–3000, IEEE press, Portland (2013)
8. Savva, M., Chang, A.X., Hanrahan, P., et al.: SceneGrok: inferring action maps in 3D environments. ACM Trans. Graph. **33**(6) (2014)
9. Zhang, Y., Xu, W., Tong, Y., Zhou, K.: Online structure analysis for real-time indoor scene reconstruction. ACM Trans. Graph. **34**(5), 159 (2015)
10. Wang, J., Xie, Q., Xu, Y., et al.: Cluttered indoor scene modeling via functional part-guided graph matching. Comput. Aided Geom. Des. **43**(C), 82–94 (2016)
11. Hao, W., Wang, Y.H.: Structure-based object detection from scene point clouds. Neurocomputing **191**, 148–160 (2016)
12. Schnabel, R., Wahl, R., Wessel, R., et al.: Shape recognition in 3D point-clouds, vol. 272, no. 1, pp. 512–520. Václav Skala - UNION Agency (2008)

13. Wang, Y., Wang, L., Hao, W, et al.: A novel slicing-based regularization method for raw point clouds in visible IoT, pp. 1–9 (2000)
14. Guru, D.S., Shekar, B.H., Nagabhushan, P.: A simple and robust line detection algorithm based on small eigenvalue analysis. Pattern Recogn. Lett. **25**(1), 1–13 (2004)
15. Leordeanu, M., Hebert, M.: Unsupervised learning for graph matching. Int. J. Comput. Vis. **96**(1), 28–45 (2012)

A Deep Reinforcement Learning Approach for Autonomous Car Racing

Fenggen Guo and Zizhao Wu(✉)

School of Media and Design, Hangzhou Dianzi University, Hangzhou, China
wuzizhao@hdu.edu.cn

Abstract. In this paper, we introduce a deep reinforcement learning approach for autonomous car racing based on the Deep Deterministic Policy Gradient (DDPG). We start by implementing the approach of DDPG, and then experimenting with various possible alterations to improve performance. In particular, we exploit two strategies: the action punishment and multiple exploration, to optimize actions in the car racing environment. We evaluate the performance of our approach on the Car Racing dataset, the experimental results demonstrate the effectiveness of the proposed approach.

Keywords: Deep reinforcement learning · Policy gradient · Autonomous driving

1 Introduction

Reinforcement learning is considered to be a strong AI paradigm which can be used to teach machines through interaction with the environment and learning from their mistakes. Recently, with the success of Deep Learning [9] on vision tasks, significant progress for autonomous driving has been made by combining the reinforcement learning with deep learning. The mixture of reinforcement learning and deep learning, which is also referred as deep reinforcement learning (DRL), has been demonstrated to be one of the most promising techniques in handling with the case, where an agent aims to learn an optimal behavior through trial-and-error interactions with a dynamic environment. Well-known works include playing Atari games [11] and playing Go games [14].

In reinforcement learning tasks, the agent's action space may be discrete, continuous, or some combination of both. In our case, car racing control requires us to consider continuous action spaces and many physical factors, which are pointed out to be more challenging [10]. Many researches have studied these problems by suggesting many approaches, one of the most typical approaches is the Deep Deterministic Policy Gradient (DDPG) [10], which presents an actor-critic, model-free algorithm based on the deterministic policy gradient that can operate over continuous action spaces.

There are some publicly datasets have been provided for evaluation of DRL based approaches, including the Car-Racing Dataset [1], the Stanford Drone Dataset [13], and so on. We note that some virtual environments, like games, can be seen as ideal framework to demonstrate and measure the performance of developed DRL systems as

A. El Rhalibi et al. (Eds.): Edutainment 2018, LNCS 11462, pp. 203–210, 2019.
https://doi.org/10.1007/978-3-030-23712-7_27

they provide a way to quickly iterate on the algorithm and model in a controlled and reproducible environment.

In this paper, we present a DDPG based approach for autonomous car racing, we exploit two strategies: the action punishment and multiple exploration, to optimize the original results of DDPG, which lead our model more reasonable to generate actions. We have evaluated our model on the car-racing dataset. As a result, we are able to obtain an average reward of 781 over 100 episodes, with a maximum value of 932 in score.

2 Related Work

Over the past years, reinforcement learning with deep learning [9] has emerged as a powerful tool to produce fully autonomous agents that interact with their environments to learn optimal behaviors. Deep Q-Network (DQN) [11] is perhaps the first well-known deep reinforcement learning method proposed by DeepMind, which uses deep neural networks to represent the Q-network, and has achieved human-level (or even super-human level) control in many of Atari games [11] and Go games [14].

In reinforcement learning tasks, the agent's action space may be discrete, continuous, or some combination of both. While DQN solves problems with discrete and low-dimensional action spaces, which cannot be straightforwardly applied to continuous domains.

Instead, policy search methods do not need to maintain a value function model but directly search for an optimal policy. Typically, once a parameterized policy is chosen, the parameters of which are updated to maximize the expected return using either gradient-based or gradient-free optimization [4]. Neural networks that encode policies have been successfully trained using both gradient-free [5, 8] and gradient-based [6, 10] methods.

It is possible to combine discrete value functions with an explicit representation of the policy, resulting in actor-critic methods. The actor (policy) learns by using feedback from the critic (value function). In doing so, these methods tradeoff variance reduction of policy gradients with bias introduction from value function methods [7].

3 Deep Deterministic Policy Gradient

Since our algorithm is based on the DDPG, in this section, we present a brief introduction to the DDPG [4].

Mathematically, the continuous control reinforcement learning can be modeled a Markov decision process (MDP), which consists of a state space S, an action space A, an initial state s_0, and the corresponding state distribution $P_0(s_0)$, a stationary transition distribution describing the environment dynamics $p(s_{t+1}|s_t, a_t)$ that satisfies the Markov property, and a reward function $r(s, \alpha) : S \times A \rightarrow R$ for every state S and action A.

Starting from an initial state, an agent follows a policy to interact with the MDP to generate a trajectory of states, actions, and rewards $s_0, a_0, r_0, \cdots, s_T, a_T, r_T$,. The goal of an agent is to maximize the return from a state, defined as the total discounted reward $R_t = \sum_{i=0}^{\infty} \gamma^i r(s_{t+i}, \alpha_{t+i})$, where $\gamma \in (0, 1]$ is the discount factor describing how much we favor future reward over those at current.

To describe how good it is being in state s under the policy μ, a state-value function $V^{\mu}(s) = \mathbb{E}_{\mu}[R_t | s_t = s]$ is defined as the expected return starting from state s, following the policy μ, interacting with environment dynamics, and repeating until the episode terminates. An action-value function: $Q^{\mu}(s, \alpha) = \mathbb{E}_{\mu}[R_t | s_t = s, \alpha_t = \alpha]$, which describes the value of taking a certain action, is defined similarly, except it is the expected return starting from state s after taking an action α under policy μ.

DDPG is devised to combine a state-action value function (the critic) and policy function (the actor) based on the actor-critic architecture [12] within one framework to deals with continuous control tasks. In DDPG, both the critic and the actor are approximated by deep neural networks, where an actor network learns a policy to make actions and a critic network estimates the actor-value function, and criticizes decisions made by the actor. The actor with policy $\mu_{\theta}(s)$ and the critic with $Q^{\mu}(s, \alpha)$ are trained simultaneously.

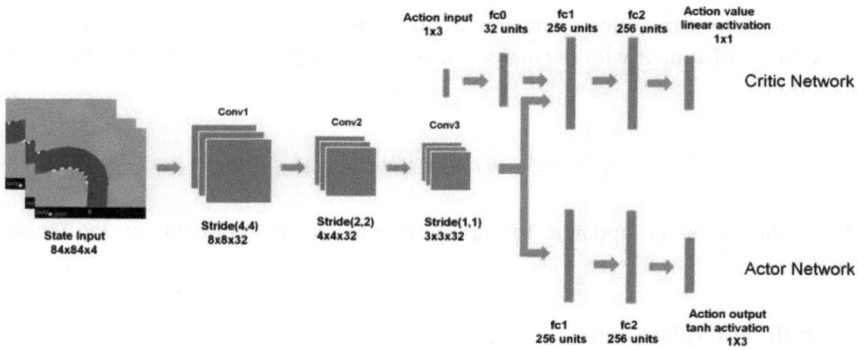

Fig. 1. The network structure of our algorithm, which consists of two sub-networks: the critic network and the actor network. Both of them share the convolutional layers with ReLU activations.

4 Our Optimization

In this section, we present our optimization on DDPG, which consists of the action punishment and the multiple exploration.

4.1 Action Punishment

In the original DDPG [10], the loss function of the critic network is defined to be:

$$L = \frac{1}{N} \sum_i (y_i - Q(s_i, \alpha_i))^2 \tag{1}$$

where $y_i = r_i + \gamma Q'(s_{i+1}, \mu'(s_{i+1}))$, the policy gradient is defined in a chain rule manner:

$$\nabla_\theta J \approx \frac{1}{N} \nabla_a Q(s,a)|_{s=s_i,a=\mu(s_i)} \nabla_\theta \mu(s)|_{s_i} \tag{2}$$

Theoretically, the above equation is used for gradient ascent to the actor network, which is equivalent to update the parameter θ^μ to increase the value of $Q(s, \mu(s))$, so as to optimize the output action of the network. In fact the gradient is not correct and is monotone at the earlier training, which often leads to an extreme value when updating the action. As a result, the error probability of an agent will increase in the form of running out of track.

To address this, we suggest an action punishment strategy to limit the action output in appropriate range. So the training will be stable at early stage. The action punishment is defined to be:

$$P(\alpha) = (\alpha - \alpha_0)^2, \tag{3}$$

where α_0 is the mean action, which is a smoothing strategy to the acceleration. We combine the punishment with the action-value function $Q(s, \alpha)$ to optimize the gradient computation:

$$\nabla_\theta J \approx \frac{1}{N} \nabla_a (Q(s,a) + \lambda P(a)|_{s=s_i,a=\mu(s_i)} \nabla_\theta \mu(s)|_{s_i} \tag{4}$$

Then the actor is updated by applying the policy gradient to the network parameters.

4.2 Multiple Exploration

In the later period of training procedure, the scale of exploration noise is small, which cause the generated actions are those actions appeared before, other actions are hard to be learned. As a result, the training process in the later period is hard to learn new actions, which is unreasonable, since there is the probability that the un-sampled value is more appropriate than the pre-sampled values.

To alleviate this problem, we suggest the multiple exploration. Specifically, after performing the first exploration for learning, we have achieved some policies with parametrized networks. When the system needs to learn for the multiple times, we suggest to directly load the former network. This strategy will lessen the training time, and help to generate more reasonable actions for the actor network.

5 Results

In this section, we present our results by describing the environment, the implementation details, as well as the results.

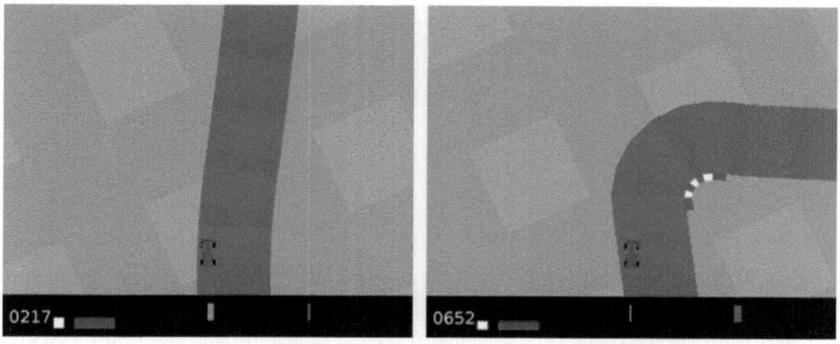

(a) Straight road (b) Curved road

Fig. 2. The CarRacing-v0 simulation environment of OpenAI Gym, which uses different colors to represent the entities including road, checking belt, car, and so on.

5.1 Environment

We used OpenAI Gym [1] as the simulation environment for our autonomous vehicle. OpenAI Gym features many built-in environments for evaluation of learning algorithms. Their driving environment is an open-source 2D driving simulator.

Figure 2 illustrates the environment. Values of direction, acceleration, and brake will be computed for an agent to control the car, these values are −1, 0, and 1. For example, one can control the direction of wheels based on the value from −1(left) to 1 (right), and control the acceleration based on the real value between 0 and 1, and control brake value of the car based on the value between 0 and 1. After initialization, a ring track can be generated, which includes N track tiles, once the car has successfully passed the tile, there will generate a reward value of 1000/N when the number of track tiles are N. Otherwise, the reward value will set to be −0.1.

5.2 Implementation

We have implemented our model in Python using the Keras library [2] for some functions of commonly used, and the TensorFlow library [3] for some functions of user defined.

To reduce the computational cost, we have pre-processed the original $96 \times 96 \times 3$ RGB images to gray images with 84×84 resolution. In addition, in order to perceive the velocity and acceleration of a car to our agent, we stack the last 4 images to a batch as the input to our agent.

The chosen of hyper-parameters are based on [10], the learning rate of actor network and critic network are set to 1e−4 and 1e−3 separately, the size of replay buffer is set to 100,000. In our experimental, we set the value of λ to −4.0 in the Eq. 4. The network structure we adopted is illustrated in Fig. 1, which contains actor network and critic network. The convolutional layers in each network are shared between these networks.

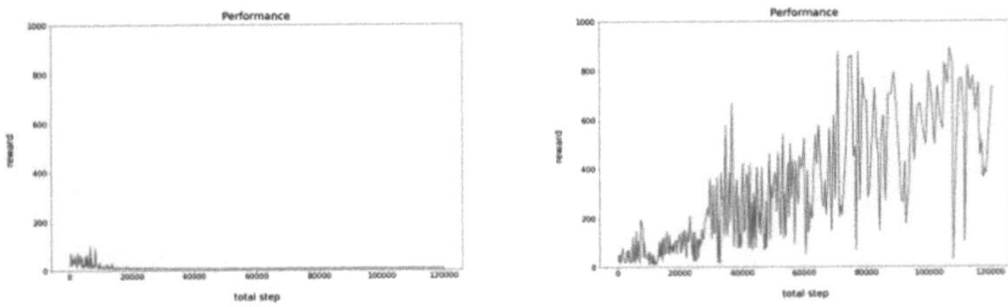

(a) Without optimization (b) With the action punishment

Fig. 3. The reward curves based on the standard DDPG algorithm and our optimized algorithm. We have conducted 100,000 training steps for the evaluation.

5.3 Results

We conduct experiments using both the standard DDPG algorithm and our optimized algorithm. We have recoded the reward values over 100,000 training iteration steps. Figure 3(a) shows the results. As can be seen from the figure, after training 100,000 steps, the highest reward value is 160 at the early stage, and is declined to 0 in the later. This means that our agent is failure to learn some meaningful strategies. Instead, based on our optimized algorithm with action punishment, we achieve the results shown in Fig. 3(b). We can note that the reward values are higher than 900 for many times.

We further analysis the internal reasons that causing the reward data various. In Fig. 4, we characterize actions of the agent, where the x-axis denotes the time step of an interaction between the agent and the environment, and the y-axis represents the action values to control steering, acceleration, and brake of the car. As can be seen from Fig. 4(a), the standard DDPG algorithm will output the maximum value for any state of the environment, which shows they are limited to local optimization. As a comparison in Fig. 4(b), our optimized algorithm achieves varying values of actions, which is supposed to be more reasonable.

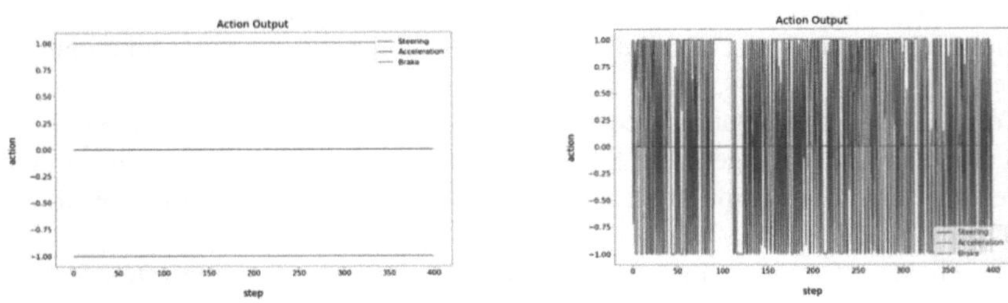

(a) Without optimization (b) With action punishment

Fig. 4. The action values using variants of DDPG: original DDPG algorithm (a), and DDPG with action punishment in (b).

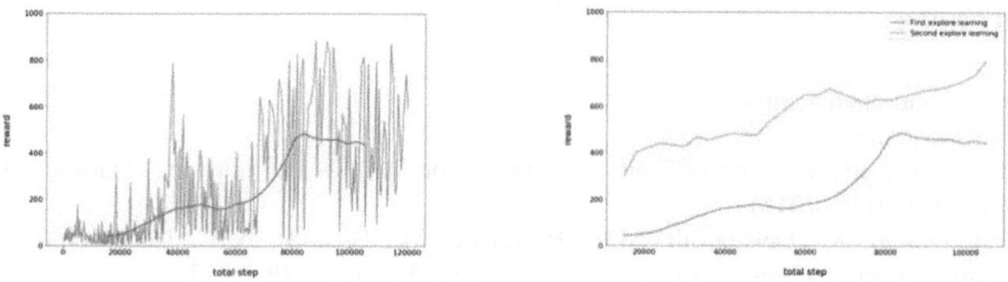

(a) Without multiple exploration (b) With multiple exploration

Fig. 5. The left figure shows the reward curves for the original DDPG based algorithm, the right figure shows the algorithm with our multiple exploration optimization. As a comparison, we can see from (b) that by applying multiple exploration, our method achieves higher reward values.

Figure 5 exhibits the training performance of the standard algorithm and the algorithm using the multiple exploration optimization. As can be seen from this figure, multiple exploration optimization will enhance the network performance in terms of the reward values, which means the actor network will output more reasonable action of the agent, when comparing to the standard algorithm.

6 Conclusion

In this paper, we have presented a deep reinforcement learning for autonomous car racing based on the DDPG, we make two contributions to the original DDPG, they are: action punishment and multiple exploration. We show in the results that our method can achieve better results than the original DDPG, which lead to more reasonable action of an agent to perform.

We notice that four frames of images have been employed as the input to our network in order to perceive the information of speed, accelerations, and so on. This strategy may have limitations as the former status will affect the decision at present, but it is hard to be perceived by the network. To alleviate this issue, in the future, we plan to employ the Long Short-Term Memory (LSTM) network to handle with this problem, which has been demonstrated of great success in handling with the time series data.

Acknowledgments. This work was supported in part by the National Natural Science Foundation of China (No. 61602139), the Open Project Program of State Key Lab of CAD&CG, Zhejiang University (No. A1817), and Zhejiang Province science and technology planning project (No. 2018C01030).

References

1. https://gym.openai.com/
2. https://keras.io
3. Abadi, M., et al.: TensorFlow: a system for large-scale machine learning. CoRR abs/1605.08695 (2016)
4. Arulkumaran, K., Deisenroth, M.P., Brundage, M., Bharath, A.A.: Deep reinforcement learning: a brief survey. IEEE Sig. Process. Mag. **34**(6), 26–38 (2017)
5. Gomez, F., Schmidhuber, J.: Evolving modular fast-weight networks for control. In: Duch, W., Kacprzyk, J., Oja, E., Zadrożny, S. (eds.) ICANN 2005. LNCS, vol. 3697, pp. 383–389. Springer, Heidelberg (2005). https://doi.org/10.1007/11550907_61
6. Heess, N., Wayne, G., Silver, D., Lillicrap, T.P., Erez, T., Tassa, Y.: Learning continuous control policies by stochastic value gradients. In: Advances in Neural Information Processing Systems 28: Annual Conference on Neural Information Processing Systems 2015, Montreal, Quebec, Canada, 7–12 December 2015, pp. 2944–2952 (2015)
7. Konda, V.R., Tsitsiklis, J.N.: Onactor-critic algorithms. SIAM J. Control Optim. **42**(4), 1143–1166 (2003)
8. Koutnik, J., Cuccu, G., Schmidhuber, J., Gomez, F.J.: Evolving large-scale neural networks for vision-based reinforcement learning. In: Genetic and Evolutionary Computation Conference, GECCO 2013, Amsterdam, The Netherlands, 6–10 July 2013, pp. 1061–1068 (2013)
9. Krizhevsky, A., Sutskever, I., Hinton, G.E.: ImageNet classification with deep convolutional neural networks. In: Advances in Neural Information Processing Systems 25: 26th Annual Conference on Neural Information Processing Systems 2012, pp. 1106–1114 (2012)
10. Lillicrap, T.P., et al.: Continuous control with deep reinforcement learning. CoRR abs/1509.02971 (2015)
11. Mnih, V., et al.: Human-level control through deep reinforcement learning. Nature **518** (7540), 529–533 (2015)
12. Peters, J., Vijayakumar, S., Schaal, S.: Natural actor-critic. In: Gama, J., Camacho, R., Brazdil, Pavel B., Jorge, A.M., Torgo, L. (eds.) ECML 2005. LNCS (LNAI), vol. 3720, pp. 280–291. Springer, Heidelberg (2005). https://doi.org/10.1007/11564096_29
13. Robicquet, A., Sadeghian, A., Alahi, A., Savarese, S.: Learning social etiquette: human trajectory understanding in crowded scenes. In: Leibe, B., Matas, J., Sebe, N., Welling, M. (eds.) ECCV 2016. LNCS, vol. 9912, pp. 549–565. Springer, Cham (2016). https://doi.org/10.1007/978-3-319-46484-8_33
14. Silver, D., et al.: Mastering the game of go with deep neural networks and tree search. Nature **529**(7587), 484–489 (2016)

An Improved Bi-goal Algorithm for Many-Objective Optimization

Huaxian Pan[1] and Lei Cai[2](✉)

[1] Xing Zhi College of Xi'an University of Finance and Economics, NO. 57 Dizhai Road, Xi'an 710038, Shaanxi, China
panhuaxian@outlook.com

[2] Faculty of Computer Science and Engineering, Xi'an University of Technology, NO. 5 South Jinhua Road, Xi'an 710048, Shaanxi, China
caileid@gmail.com

Abstract. In this paper, an evolutionary algorithm based on bi-goal is proposed for many-objective optimization. We first provide a new proximity estimation, ensuring the convergence of algorithm. Afterwards, a new sharing function with a novel discriminator is employed to improve the diversity. The dominance-based environmental selection is applied in bi-goal space, which is expected to archive a good balance between convergence and diversity. The experimental results show that the proposed method can work well on most instances considered in this study, demonstrating that it is very competitive for solving many-objective optimization problems.

Keywords: Many-objective optimization · Aggregation-based method · Proximity · Diversity · Bi-goal evolution

1 Introduction

Many-objective optimization problems (MaOPs), typically referring to the task of optimization with four or more objectives, has attracted great attention in recent years. The boom of these researches on MaOPs is inspired from two aspects: First, the optimization problems with high number of objectives frequently appear in various real-world applications. e.g. software engineering [10] and industrial scheduling problems [13]. Second, the Pareto-dominance based methods, which shown excellent performance on the problems with two or three objectives, deteriorate their search ability noticeably when solving MaOPs. Thus, it is not surprising that the MaOPs can be considered as a substantial challenge in artificial intelligence (AI) [9].

In order to overcome the obstacle caused by the high dimensional curse, researchers have proposed various many objective optimization algorithms (MOEAs). Based on the key ideas used, these methodologies can be broadly classified into three categories. The first and most direct attempt is the development of relaxed dominance based algorithms. Since the Pareto-dominance based

A. El Rhalibi et al. (Eds.): Edutainment 2018, LNCS 11462, pp. 211–218, 2019.
https://doi.org/10.1007/978-3-030-23712-7_28

methods have a long heritage. It is natural to propose some methods to alleviate the drawbacks of these methods, which lies in the difficulty of providing selection pressure in high-objective space. Generally, some of these methods try to enlarge the dominated area of a solution, it has a high change to be dominated by other ones [7,12]. Despite these methods usually involve some extra parameters and the setting of them is problem-dependent, they can increase the selection pressure towards Pareto Front (PF) to some extent. The second avenue for solving MaOPs is the indicator based methods, taking advantage of a indicator metric to guide a whole optimization. As an representative algorithm, hypervolume estimation algorithm (HypE) is theoretically well-supported, and it has been proved that maximizing the hypervolume is equivalent to approximate the PF [2]. Nevertheless, the computation cost of this method grows extremely high when solving higher objective problems. Thus, some researchers trying to estimate the hypervolume in more efficient ways [2,11].

The third alternative way is the aggregation-based method, which aggregates the objectives of an MOP into a scalar value depending on the uniform weight vectors. As a typical method, MOEA/D (A multi-objective evolutionary algorithm based on decomposition) can improve the efficiency of both variation and selecting offspring for the next generation [14]. However, MOEA/D struggles to maintain a good diversity for MaOPs. Besides, some dominance-based methods partially borrow the idea of aggregation-based method as well. For example, as a hybrid algorithm, NSGA-III designed a diversity emphasis method, which is aided by a set of reference points initialized in advance, to handling high objective optimization problems [6].

Besides above mentioned methods, it is worth noting that some meta-objective optimization algorithms also obtain a good performance on MaOPs. On account of two ultimate goals of MaOPS (convergence and diversity) directly, the Bi-Goal Evolution (BiGE) is implemented by using two separated methods for estimating solution's performance (proximity and crowding degree) [9]. According to that, all solutions in the objective space have been embedded into a bi-goal space. In the process of environmental selection, BiGE using classical Pareto non-dominated sorting method, iteratively selects an offspring for next generation via these two final goals. It has been experimental validated that the BiGE is able to alleviate the loss of selection pressure in many-objective space.

However, the proximity estimate in BiGE is simply acquired by summing the value in each objective, which may degrade the search ability of the algorithm. Inspired by the mechanism of BiGE and aggregation-based method, we propose an improved BiGE (iBiGE) and introduce two innovations, involving a proximity estimation based on aggregation function, and designing a new discriminator for the crowding degree estimation. In addition, another contribution of this paper lies in the experimental aspect. We provide an extensive comparison between the proposed method with other state-of-the-art algorithms on 9 test problems. The results indicate that the proposed iBiGE is a very promising method for MaOPs.

The rest of paper is organized as follows. Section 2 is devoted to the description of our proposed algorithms for MaOPs. Experimental results are presented and discussed in Sect. 3. Finally, conclusions are drawn in Sect. 4.

2 Method

Basically, there are two ultimate but often conflicting goals for MaOPs. The first is *convergence*, which means that a MaOPs need to find a set of solutions that can approximate the PF. The second goal is to maximizing the distribution of solution set along the whole PF (i.e. *diversity*). Thus, the basic idea of BiGE is to consider bi-goals instead of original many objectives as final metrics for Pareto-dominance comparison [9]. Taking this idea in mind, we propose a variant of BiGE based on the aggregation-based method.

Algorithm 1. The proposed improved Bi-goal evolution

Require: H (The number of divisions)

$P_0 \leftarrow initializePopulation(H)$
$\boldsymbol{\Lambda} \leftarrow weightVectorsGenerator(H)$
$\mathbf{z}^* \leftarrow initializeIdeaPoint(P_0)$
$t \leftarrow 1; P_t \leftarrow P_0$
while termination criterion not fulfilled **do**
    $proximityEstimation(P_t, \boldsymbol{\Lambda}, \mathbf{z}^*)$
    $crowdingDegreeEstimation(P_t, \boldsymbol{\Lambda})$
    $\hat{P}_t \leftarrow mattingSelection(P_t)$
    $Q_t \leftarrow variation(\hat{P}_t)$
    $R_t \leftarrow P_t \cup Q_t$
    $\mathbf{z}^* \leftarrow updateIdealPoint(Q_t)$
    $P_{t+1} \leftarrow environmentalSelection(R_t)$
    $t \leftarrow t + 1$
end while

Compared the original BiGE with the proposed algorithm (Algorithm 1), the differences manly lies in the initialization and two operators of estimations. Prior to the aggregation-based method, some weight vectors are supposed to created in advance. In this work, the method developed by Das and Dennis is introduced [5] and two-layers approach is used for the objectives over seven [3]. The ideal points set, defined as the best scalar for each objective in current state, update iteratively in the process of evolution.

In addition, there are two key operators in BiGE: *proximity estimation* and *crowding degree estimation*. In this study, the main process of these two operators has been modified significantly. In the following two subsections, the detailed implementation of these two operators will be illustrated.

2.1 Proximity Estimation

The original BiGE estimates the proximity of a solution $\mathbf{s}$ simply by summing its scalar value in each objective

$$f_p(\mathbf{s}) = \sum_{k=1}^{m} F^k(\mathbf{s}) \tag{1}$$

where $f_p(\mathbf{s})$ is the objective value of solution $\mathbf{s}$, and m denotes the number of objectives. By using this simple method, the accuracy of the estimation can be influenced by the shape of PF, and the search ability might degrade when dealing with the problem with scaled objectives. Although these two issues can be alleviated by introducing the second goals and using normalization method respectively, they still affect the efficiency of evolution. In order to solve these issues, we propose a new proximity estimation method based on aggregation function. Specifically, for a solution s with specific weight vectors w_j, its aggregation function value can be obtained by Eq. (2).

$$\mathcal{F}_j(\mathbf{s}) = \max_{k=1}^{m}\{\frac{1}{w_{j,k}}|F_k(\mathbf{s}) - z_k^*|\} \tag{2}$$

where $w_{j,k} \geq 0$ for $k \in \{1, 2, \ldots, m\}$. This convergence ability of using this modified Tchbycheff function has been reported both analytically and experimentally in some exacting studies [3,4].

Next, we need to determine which weight vector could be chosen as the best reference for calculation of aggregative value. In this work, the weight vector which is close to the current solution $\mathbf{s}$ is selected. More specifically, the vector with minimum perpendicular distance $d^{\perp}$ to current $\mathbf{s}$ is considered as the best weight vector for the proximity estimation. This perpendicular is calculated as follows:

$$d^{\perp}(s, \mathbf{w}_j) = \mathbf{F}(s) - \frac{\mathbf{w}_j^T \mathbf{F}(s)}{\mathbf{w}_j^T \mathbf{w}_j}\mathbf{w}_j \tag{3}$$

2.2 Crowding Degree Estimation

In original BiGE, niching techniques is used for measuring the crowding degree for a solution in the population. We still use this method yet with a different mechanism for enhancing discrimination. To be more specific, Using Eq. (4), the crowding degree of a solution $\mathbf{s}$ in population P is defined as follows [9]:

$$f_c(\mathbf{s}) = (\sum_{\mathbf{s} \in P, \mathbf{s} \neq \mathbf{q}} sh(\mathbf{s}, \mathbf{q}))^{1/2} \tag{4}$$

where $sh(\mathbf{s}, \mathbf{q})$ is sharing function. In this work, a new sharing function with modified discriminator is used as follows:

$$sh(\mathbf{s},\mathbf{q}) = \begin{cases} (0.5(1-\frac{d(\mathbf{s},\mathbf{q})}{r}))^2 & \text{, if } d(\mathbf{s},\mathbf{q}) < r, d^{\perp}_{\min}(\mathbf{s}) < d^{\perp}_{\min}(\mathbf{q}) \\ (1.5(1-\frac{d(\mathbf{s},\mathbf{q})}{r}))^2 & \text{, if } d(\mathbf{s},\mathbf{q}) < r, d^{\perp}_{\min}(\mathbf{s}) > d^{\perp}_{\min}(\mathbf{q}) \\ rand() & \text{, if } d(\mathbf{s},\mathbf{q}) < r, \\ 0, & \text{otherwise} \end{cases} \quad (5)$$

where r here is the radius of a niche, which is adaptively calculated by $r = 1/\sqrt[m]{N}$.

After describing the details of crowding degree estimation, we would like to discuss the main similarities and differences between the proposed estimation and the original one. For the similarities, both of them use niching technology to get crowding degree. But they differ in the implementation of discriminator. The previous method use the proximity to assign different weight parameters for two individuals. And the individual with a better proximity can obtain a lower crowding degree. In contrast to that, the proposed crowding degree estimation considers the perpendicular distance as an evaluator. The solution, which is closer to its nearest weight vector, would assign a lower weight parameters. Since the pre-defined weight vectors have been distributed assigned in the objective space, the new discriminator could emphasize the diversity of the final population.

3 Experimental Studies

In order to test the effectiveness of the proposed iBiGE, A well-known continuous benchmark WFG1-9 [8], is involved for the empirical studies. The number of objectives for each problem is set as $m \in 3, 5, 8$. Besides, we set the number of decision variables $n = 24$, and the position-related parameter is $m - 1$.

In this paper, we use hypervolume (HV) as comparison criterion. It can measure both convergence and diversity of solution set, and larger value means better quality. The setting of reference point follows the recommendation in [4]. As for the compared algorithm, three state-of-the-art algorithms are considered as the peer algorithms: BiGE [9], IDBEA [1], and MOEA/D [14]. In order to evaluate the differences of two compared algorithms, Wilcoxon signed-rank test at a 5 % level is applied for analysis.

The comparative results on all test instances are shown in Table 1. As can be observed from that, the proposed iBiGE is particularly competitive to other algorithms in the scope of WFG 4-9. Aided by the weight vectors, iBiGE can archive a relatively good performance when the PF is regular. Compared with original BiGE, the proposed method achieves an obvious improvement in 3 and 5 objective problems. For 10-objective instances, iBiGE fails to show better performance than BiGE, but still more effective than other methods. These results verity that the new proximity and crowding degree estimation is comparable with or even better than other peer algorithms.

To describe the distribution of different algorithms in high dimensional objective space. Figure 1 plots the obtained solutions in a single run on 8-objective WFG6 problem by parallel coordinates. Form inspection of Fig. 1, the five algorithms perform differently in terms of diversity. iBiGE and IDBEA have good

Table 1. Performance comparison on WFG1-9 problems with respect to the average HV values

Problem	obj.	iBiGE	BiGE	IDBEA	MOEA/D
WFG1	3	0.818471	0.831623	0.814436	**0.911308**
	5	0.740980	**0.878223**	0.607277†	0.847980
	8	0.607239	**0.777652**	0.603437	0.686077
WFG2	3	**0.940325**	0.900192†	0.933089†	0.926123†
	5	**0.993992**	0.978326†	0.971927†	0.957989†
	8	0.951251	**0.989944**	0.971344	0.989272
WFG3	3	0.688815	0.557293†	0.691348	**0.705539**
	5	**0.674258**	0.632776†	0.559460†	0.584767†
	8	0.480311	**0.634179**	0.448554†	0.485826
WFG4	3	**0.715548**	0.683045†	0.714557†	0.698283†
	5	**0.854308**	0.840454†	0.807338†	0.744254†
	8	0.875565	**0.946372**	0.876145	0.822711†
WFG5	3	**0.688840**	0.588898†	0.686875†	0.675991†
	5	**0.822458**	0.766534†	0.778726†	0.712879†
	8	0.829129	**0.895539**	0.843161	0.757722†
WFG6	3	**0.687656**	0.581300†	0.685041†	0.672674†
	5	**0.809044**	0.777931†	0.774312†	0.704609†
	8	0.829627	**0.897013**	0.838566	0.758439†
WFG7	3	0.709475	0.638440†	**0.710764**	0.704927†
	5	**0.853929**	0.815360†	0.790510†	0.736929†
	8	0.894219	**0.944928**	0.884670†	0.811058†
WFG8	3	**0.677863**	0.617905†	0.672118†	0.667656†
	5	**0.787475**	0.741178†	0.739919†	0.664497†
	8	0.711604	**0.838614**	0.728450	0.676467†
WFG9	3	**0.676669**	0.614475†	0.671675	0.675983
	5	**0.832703**	0.773733†	0.690830†	0.712429†
	8	0.740505	**0.870058**	0.753428	0.777175

"†" means that the result is significantly outperformed by iBiGE.

diversity than MOEA/D. Besides, it seems that IDBEA can be outperformed by BiGE, which means that BiGE has a clear advantage over IDBEA on this test instance. Overall, it is clear that iBiGE and BiGE are able to find a good approximation of the PF, whereas MOEA/D can only converge to a portion of the PF.

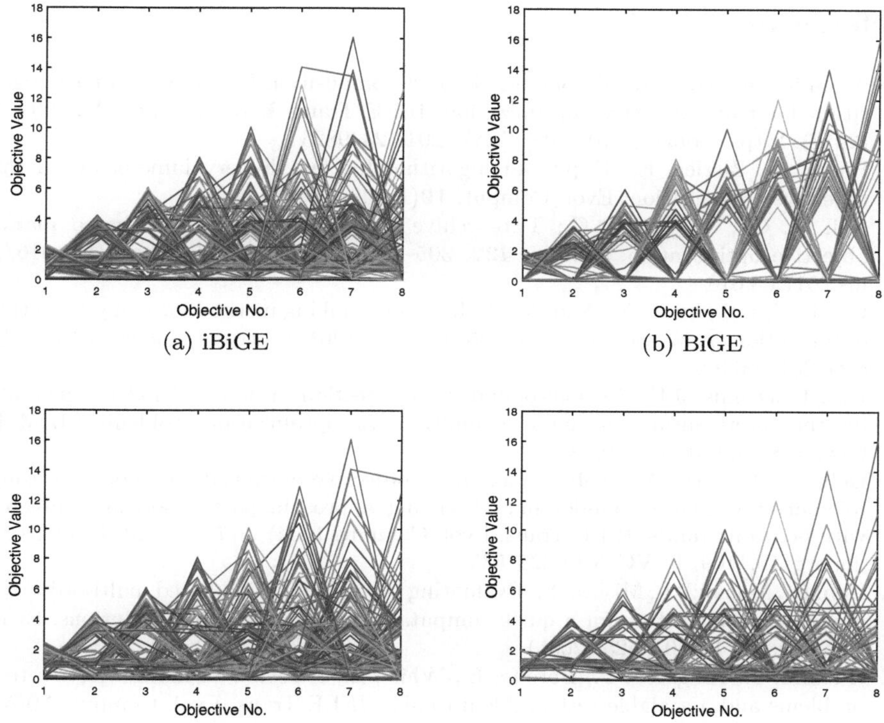

(a) iBiGE (b) BiGE

(c) IDBEA (d) MOEA/D

Fig. 1. The final solution set of the four algorithms on the 8-objective WFG6 instance, shown by parallel coordinates.

4 Conclusion

In this paper, a novel Bi-goal based algorithm is proposed for MaOPs. The proposed method, namely iBiGE, employs two new estimations on proximity and crowding degree. Experimental results on WFG1-9 with 3, 5 and 8 objectives indicate that the proposed algorithm is competitive compared with state-of-the-art algorithms. Although the overall performance of iBiGE is promising, some deeper insight into the search behavior of iBiGE need to be carried out in the future. Moreover, it has been observed that the iBiGE is outperformed by BiGE in the most 10 objective problems, thus it would be interesting to further extent iBiGE to solve more instances with higher objectives.

References

1. Asafuddoula, M., Ray, T., Sarker, R.: A decomposition based evolutionary algorithm for many objective optimization. IEEE Trans. Evol. Comput. **PP**(99), 1 (2014). https://doi.org/10.1109/TEVC.2014.2339823
2. Bader, J., Zitzler, E.: HypE: an algorithm for fast hypervolume-based many-objective optimization. Evol. Comput. **19**(1), 45–76 (2011)
3. Cai, L., Qu, S., Cheng, G.: Two-archive method for aggregation-based many-objective optimization. Inf. Sci. **422**, 305–317 (2018). https://doi.org/10.1016/j.ins.2017.08.078
4. Cai, L., Qu, S., Yuan, Y., Yao, X.: A clustering-ranking method for many-objective optimization. Appl. Soft Comput. **35**, 681–694 (2015). https://doi.org/10.1016/j.asoc.2015.06.020
5. Das, I., Dennis, J.E.: Normal-boundary intersection: a new method for generating the pareto surface in nonlinear multicriteria optimization problems. SIAM J. Optim. **8**(3), 631–657 (1998)
6. Deb, K., Jain, H.: An evolutionary many-objective optimization algorithm using reference-point-based nondominated sorting approach, part i: solving problems with box constraints. IEEE Trans. Evol. Comput. **18**(4), 577–601 (2014). https://doi.org/10.1109/TEVC.2013.2281535
7. Deb, K., Mohan, M., Mishra, S.: Evaluating the ε-domination based multi-objective evolutionary algorithm for a quick computation of pareto-optimal solutions. Evol. Comput. **13**(4), 501–525 (2005)
8. Huband, S., Hingston, P., Barone, L., While, L.: A review of multiobjective test problems and a scalable test problem toolkit. IEEE Trans. Evol. Comput. **10**(5), 477–506 (2006). https://doi.org/10.1109/TEVC.2005.861417
9. Li, M., Yang, S., Liu, X.: Bi-goal evolution for many-objective optimization problems. Artif. Intell. **228**, 45–65 (2015). https://doi.org/10.1016/j.artint.2015.06.007
10. Praditwong, K., Harman, M., Yao, X.: Software module clustering as a multi-objective search problem. IEEE Trans. Softw. Eng. **37**(2), 264–282 (2011). https://doi.org/10.1109/TSE.2010.26
11. While, L., Bradstreet, L., Barone, L.: A fast way of calculating exact hypervolumes. IEEE Trans. Evol. Comput. **16**(1), 86–95 (2012)
12. Yang, S., Li, M., Liu, X., Zheng, J.: A grid-based evolutionary algorithm for many-objective optimization. IEEE Trans. Evol. Comput. **17**(5), 721–736 (2013). https://doi.org/10.1109/TEVC.2012.2227145
13. Yuan, Y., Xu, H.: Multiobjective flexible job shop scheduling using memetic algorithms. IEEE Trans. Autom. Sci. Eng. **12**(1), 336–353 (2015). https://doi.org/10.1109/TASE.2013.2274517
14. Zhang, Q., Li, H.: MOEA/D: a multiobjective evolutionary algorithm based on decomposition. IEEE Trans. Evol. Comput. **11**(6), 712–731 (2007). https://doi.org/10.1109/TEVC.2007.892759

3D Human Motion Retrieval Based on Graph Model

Qihui Wu, Rui Liu(✉), Dongsheng Zhou, and Qiang Zhang(✉)

Key Laboratory of Advanced Design and Intelligent Computing, Dalian University, Ministry of Education, Dalian 116622, China
{liurui, zhangq}@dlu.edu.cn

Abstract. Motion retrieval has important practical value for the reuse of motion capture data. However, it is a challenging task to represent the motion data effectively due to the complexity of the motion data structure. As graph models is an effective way to represent structured data. This paper proposes a new method for human motion retrieval based on graph model. First, a method of graph model constructing based on Maximum Range of the Distance (MRD) is proposed. The MRD is used to select the joint pairs that are deemed important for a given motion, and different motions have different graph model structures. After that, similar motions can be retrieved by matching the similarity of the attributes of graph model. In the process of motion retrieval, cosine similarity is defined to measure the similarity of graph models. The experimental results show that the method proposed in this article is better than the previous methods of motion retrieval in many ways.

Keywords: Motion capture · Retrieval · Graph model

1 Introduction

The technology of motion capture has been widely used in computer animation, film and television special effects, virtual reality, computer games, sports training and so on [1]. However, it is well known that motion capture devices are expensive, and generating new motion data takes a lot of time and effort. In addition, there are already many large human motion capture databases available for free. Hence, there is an increasing need that how to deal with a large number of data and apply the existing motion capture database effectively. So human motion retrieval is a hot topic in the field of motion data reusage [2]. Although there have been important research contributions in the past few decades, motion retrieval is still a challenging issue due to the complex structure of human movement [3].

The graph plays an important role in the modeling of complex structural data [4]. But few researchers have considered using graphics for human motion data retrieval. Li et al. [5] proposed a novel graph construction method which connected the joints that were deemed important for a given motion, and used Adaptive-Graph Kernel (AGK) to measure the similarity of two adaptive graphs, inspired by Li's work, this paper uses the Maximum Range of the Distance (MRD) between the joints as the description of human motion, and propose a novel graph model based on the MRD. The graph model

A. El Rhalibi et al. (Eds.): Edutainment 2018, LNCS 11462, pp. 219–227, 2019.
https://doi.org/10.1007/978-3-030-23712-7_29

can preserve the complex spatial structure between joint pairs, and different motions result in different graph structures. Hence, the graph model is discriminating. Then, the cosine similarity is used to match the similarity between the attribute of graph model, and the similar motion can be retrieved step by step. The human motion data used in our experiments are from the Carnegie Mellon University Motion Capture Database [6] and HDM05 database [7]. The framework of the method is shown in Fig. 1.

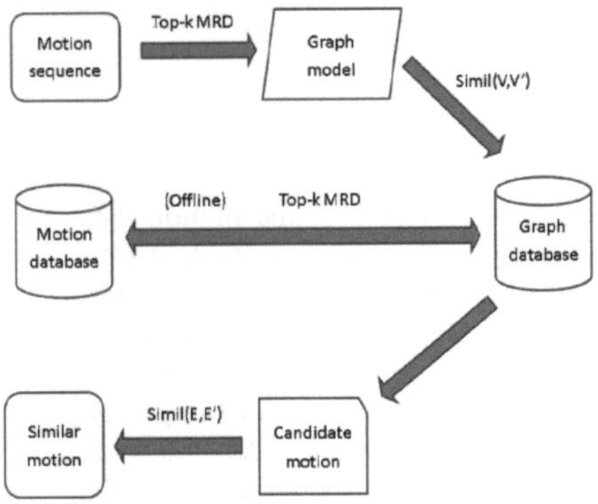

Fig. 1. The framework of the method

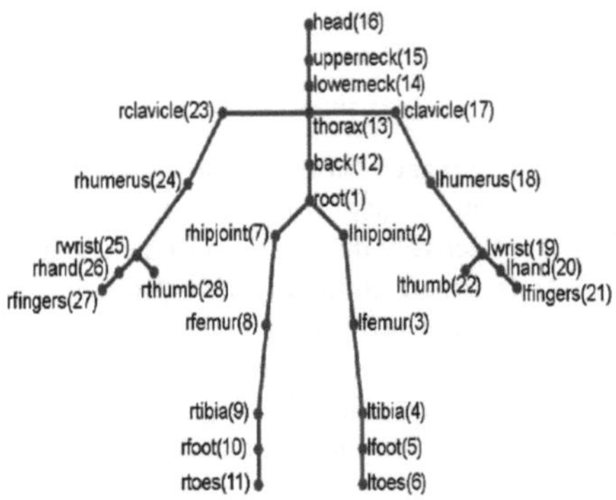

Fig. 2. Human model

2 Related Work

In recent years, Content based retrieval methods have been widely used in the retrieval of human motion capture data. A lot of methods have been proposed for human motion retrieval. Muller et al. [8, 9] proposed a motion template for automatic recognition and retrieval of human motion capture data, the essence of the method is that the same kind of motion can be extracted by a characteristic matrix with clear representation. Chen et al. [10] present an effective method based on relative geometry features to support partial similarity human motion retrieval. While these approaches can be efficient search in large databases, their feature descriptor can only represent the geometric relationship of some points between the key frames. As a result, their movement descriptor cannot complete describe the human motion data with complex space-time structure.

In addition to consider the relationship between the key points, some scholars also pay close attention to the relation of the whole frame sequence. Dynamic time warping (DTW) method is an effective method for matching different lengths of time series, and widely used in time series processing and signal processing field. Liu et al. [11] retrieved similar motions by two-phase approach with normalization similarity and DTW average distance. However inter-frame information of motion sequence can't reflect the spatial and temporal variations of key relationships, which makes these methods are not able to describe the complete sequence of movement effectively.

Graph is an effective tool for modeling complex structured objects [12], there are also some researchers construct the graph model for 3D human motion capture data. Xiao et al. [13] constructed a graph model to represent the relationship between two human movements, then Kuhn–Munkres (KM) algorithm was used to solve maximum matching problem of weighted graph. Celiktutan et al. [14] proposed the hyper-graph model to represent the human movement, and derived an efficient exact minimization algorithm by dynamic programming approach. In this article, a graph model based on Top-k MRD is constructed to represent motion sequence, and the cosine similarity measure is used to measure the similarity between graph models. Based on these two methods, the 3D human motion retrieval is realized. Compared with the previous method, the retrieval effect is improved.

3 Motion Representation

3.1 The Maximum Range of the Distance

For a motion sequence with T frames can be denoted as $M = \{F_1, F_2, \ldots, F_T\}$, in which $F_t = \{J_1(t), J_2(t), \ldots, J_N(t)\}$ represents the t-th frame. And $J_i(t) = \{x_i(t), y_i(t), z_i(t)\}$ is the i-th $(1 \leq i \leq N)$ joint in the t-th frame. There are N = 28 joints in the human model as shown in Fig. 2.

In each frame of motion data, any two joints constitute a pair of joints, and there are $C_{28}^2 = 378$ joint pairs in each frame. The distance between any two joint points is calculated by Euclidean distance. The greater the range change of the distance, indicated that the joint pair has a larger contribution for the movement. The maximum range of the distance is used to characterize the motion and named it as MRD.

The MRD of the $\langle i,j \rangle$ joint pair can be formulated as:

$$\begin{aligned} MRD(i,j) = & \max\{d_{L_2}(J_i(1), J_j(1)), d_{L_2}(J_i(2), J_j(2)), \cdots, d_{L_2}(J_i(T), J_j(T))\} \\ & - \min\{d_{L_2}(J_i(1), J_j(1)), d_{L_2}(J_i(2), J_j(2)), \cdots, d_{L_2}(J_i(T), J_j(T))\} \end{aligned}$$

Where T is the total number of frames in a motion. The value of MRD is used to measure the importance of each joint pair in the motion description. For a joint pair, the greater the MRD value is, the more important the joint pair is. The distance between two hands in clapping motion is shown in Fig. 3.

In Fig. 3, the joint points of the two hands were marked as 20 and 26, a, b, c are three moments of motion. The $\mathrm{d}_{L_2}(J_{20}(t_a), J_{26}(t_a))$ represents the maximum distance, and the $\mathrm{d}_{L_2}(J_{20}(t_c), J_{26}(t_c))$ represents the minimum distance in the motion sequence. Hence, the Maximum Range of the Distance between the two joints $(20, 26)$ formulated as:

$$MRD(20, 26) = \mathrm{d}_{L_2}(J_{20}(t_a), J_{26}(t_a)) - \mathrm{d}_{L_2}(J_{20}(t_c), J_{26}(t_c))$$

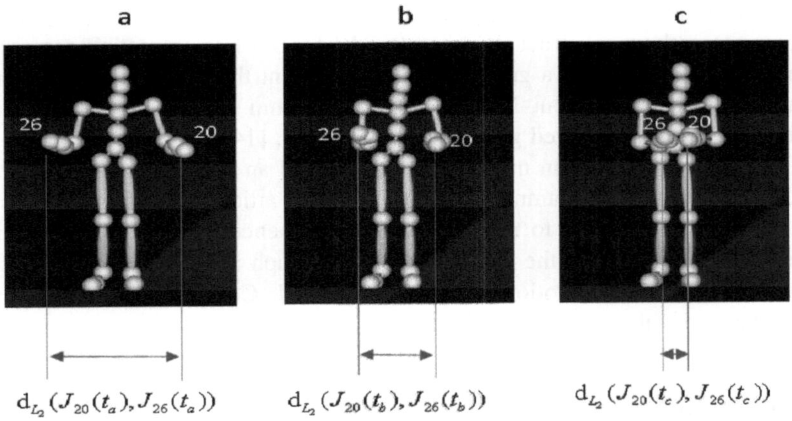

Fig. 3. The distance between the two hands joint in clapping

3.2 Graph Construction

According to the motion M, the graph model of the motion can be constructed based on MRD. The graph can be denoted as $G = (E, V)$, where E is the edge set consisting of joint pairs (each joint pair represents one edge, 378 edges in total), and V is the vertex set consisting of joint points. The maximum k values in MRD are selected as top-k MRD (in this paper k = 50). If the corresponding MRD value of joint pair (i,j) belongs to top-k MRD, set $E(i,j) = 1$, otherwise $E(i,j) = 0$. Then, the attribute E can be represented by a one-dimensional array which consists of 0 and 1. The formulas are as follows:

$$\underset{1 \leq i < j \leq N}{E(i,j)} = \begin{cases} 1 & \textit{if } MRD(i,j) \in top - k\ MRD, \\ 0 & \textit{otherwise.} \end{cases}$$

$$E = \{E(1,2), E(1,3), E(1,4), \cdots, E(i,j), \cdots, E(27,28)\}\ (1 \leq i < j \leq N)$$

The E attribute of graph for several motions based on top-50 MRD are shown in Fig. 4. It can be seen from the chart that the joint pairs selected by MRD are different in different motion, and basically the same in the same motion.

The V attribute denoted as $V = \{v_1, v_2, \ldots, v_N\}$, in which v_n indicates the number of the n-th joint point appearing in the top-k MRD. The formula is as follow:

$$v_n = \sum_{i=1}^{n-1} E(i,n) + \sum_{j=n+1}^{N} E(n,j)$$

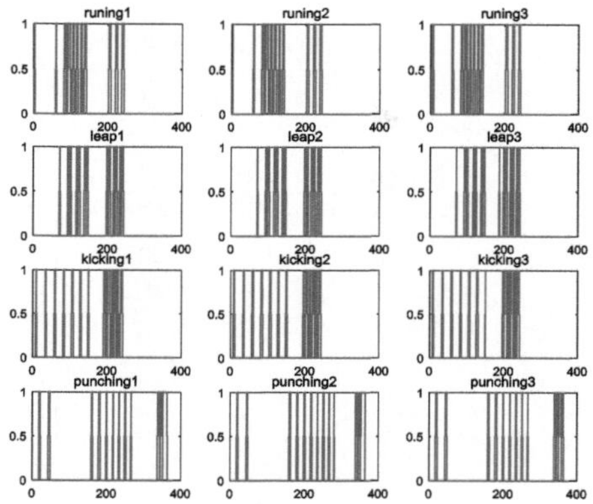

Fig. 4. The E attribute of graph for several motions based on top-50 MRD. Where the abscissa represents the sequence number of the joint pairs, and the ordinate represents the value.

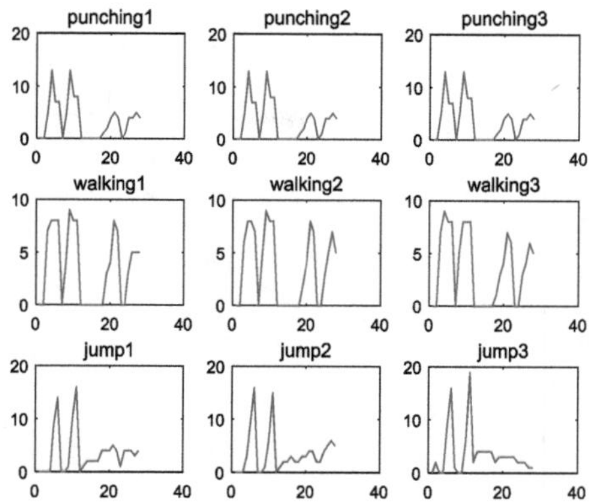

Fig. 5. The V attribute of graph for several motions. The abscissa represents the serial number of the joint point, and the ordinate represents the value.

The V attribute of graph model for several motions are shown in Fig. 5. It can be seen from the diagram that the V attribute features of different types of motion are also different. But compared with the attribute E, the attribute V has a lower degree of distinction between motions. But the data dimension of the V attribute is much smaller than the E attribute, therefore, matching the similarity of V attribute can reduce the retrieval time and improve the retrieval efficiency. The time cost to match the similarity by V attribute and E attribute is shown in Fig. 6. Therefore, in order to ensure the efficiency and accuracy of the motion retrieval, in the retrieval process, this paper first retrieve the similar motion according to the attribute V, and then retrieve the similar motion accurately according to the attribute E.

3.3 Retrieval

Motion retrieval requires not only accuracy but also efficiency. Based on the above analysis, a retrieval method is proposed in this paper. First, graph model based on top-k MRD is used to represent the motion data. Given two motions M and M', $G = (E, V)$ and $G'(E', V')$ represent their graphs respectively. Second, the similarity of the V attributes is calculated to retrieve the candidate motion sets and eliminate most of the different movements. At last, the similarity of the E attributes is calculated to retrieve the similar movements from the candidate motion sets. Because of both the E attributes and the V attributes are one-dimensional arrays, which can be treated as vectors in high dimensional space. The similarity of E and V can be calculated by the cosine similarity. The formulas are as follows:

$$simil(V, V') = \cos(V, V') \qquad simil(E, E') = \cos(E, E')$$

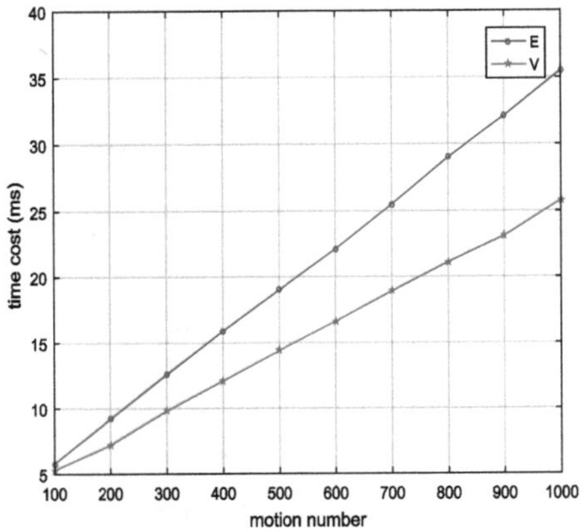

Fig. 6. The time cost to match the similarity by V and E attributes

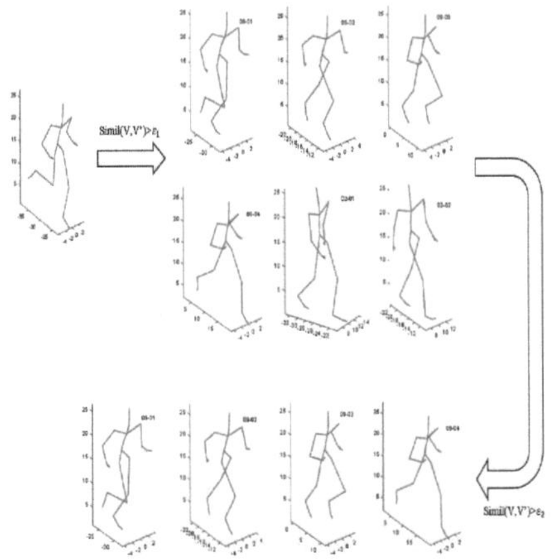

Fig. 7. The retrieval process of running motion

It is easy to see from the formula that the range of similarity is between $[0, 1]$. The closer the cosine similarity is to 1, the more similar the two motions are. Therefore, two thresholds ε_1 and ε_2 are set during retrieval. When $simil(V, V') > \varepsilon_1$, it is considered that M and M' are potential similar movements, when $simil(E, E') > \varepsilon_2$, it is considered that they are similar movements. Through the above steps, the 3D human motion retrieval is realized. The retrieval process of running motion is shown in Fig. 7. Through a large number of experiments, it is found that the similarity of graph model attributes is almost above 0.9 for the same type of motion. So in this experiment, the threshold parameters are set as follows: $\varepsilon_1 = 0.9$ and $\varepsilon_2 = 0.92$, which can be fine-tuned according to the actual retrieval.

4 Experiments and Analysis

In order to verify the effectiveness of the method mentioned in this paper, some experiments have been carried out. All the experiments were executed on a desktop computer with Intel(R) core(TM) i3-4160 CPU @ 3.60 GHz processor. The motion retrieval method is carried out in the Matlab simulation environment. The motion data used in this paper comes from the Carnegie Mellon University Motion Capture Database and HDM05 database which contains rich motion data. In order to verify the effectiveness of the algorithm, different kinds of human motion are selected to build our experimental database that include running, walking, jumping, right foot kicking (rfkicking), punching, sitting down, rotating right arm (rrarm), right hand boxing (rhboxing), hopping and throwing, The scale of the experimental database is shown in the Table 1.

Table 1. The scale of the experimental database

Motion	Number	Motion	Number
running	150	sitdown	105
walking	154	rrarm	86
jumping	96	rhboxing	72
rfkicking	67	hopping	120
punching	90	throwing	60

The partial retrieval results of several motion are shown in Figs. 8 and 9.

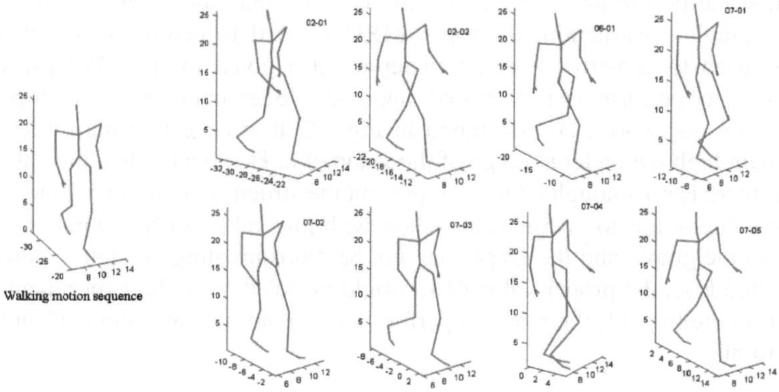

Fig. 8. Partial retrieval results of walking motion

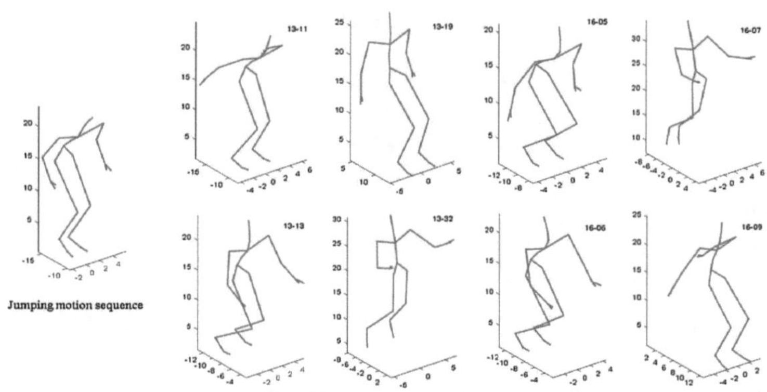

Fig. 9. Partial retrieval results of jumping motion

The recall ratio and precision are two important indexes that reflect the validity of the motion retrieval method. We generate the average precision–recall curves to compare the retrieval performance of our approach with other works [9, 15]. Precision is defined as the ratio of correctly retrieved motions (denote as N_c) to the total number of retrieved motions (denote as N_t), and recall ratio is defined as the ratio of correctly retrieved motions (N_t) to the total number of relevant motions in the motion database (denote as N_r). Their formulas as follows:

$$\Pr ecision = \frac{N_c}{N_t} \qquad \text{Recall ratio} = \frac{N_c}{N_r}$$

The average precision–recall curves are shown in Fig. 9. From these curves, it can be seen that the performance of our method is better than the other two methods.

In the graph construction, the top-k MRD is used to determine which k edges should be used to construct a graph to represent a given motion. We use different values of k to perform our proposed approach to examine the influence of the parameters on our works. As illustrated in Fig. 10, it is clear that the retrieval accuracies remain high over a large range of the value of k. However, when the value of k is too small, there is not enough edges to represent the structure of the joint pairs in MRD. When the value of k is too large, some edges with low values of MRD may be selected to construct the graph, and the graph may not be discriminating enough to describe the actions. Therefore, the proper value of k should be selected in the experiment. As can be seen from the Fig. 11, the retrieval performance is optimal and stable when k ranges from 40 to 80.

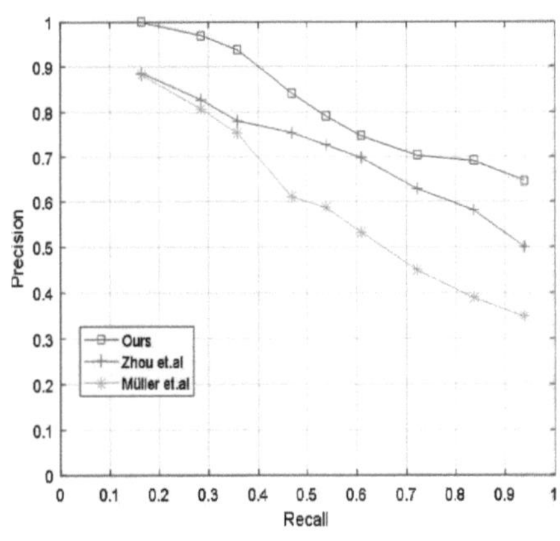

Fig. 10. The precision–recall curves of our method and other methods Müller et al. [9], and Zhou et al. [15]

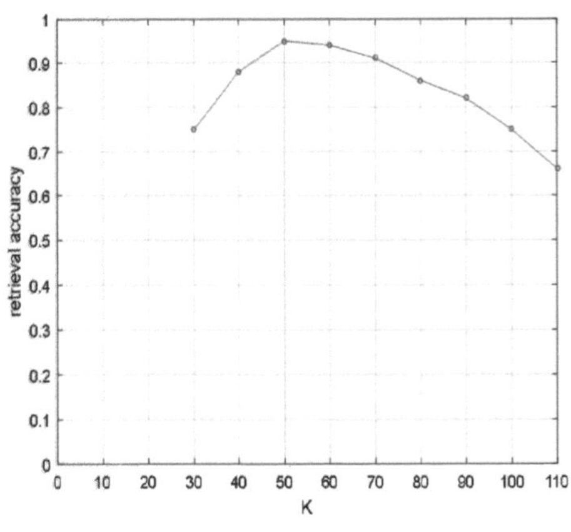

Fig. 11. The average retrieval accuracy with different values of k

5 Conclusions

In this paper, a method of 3D human body retrieval based on graph model is proposed. First, a discriminative graph model based on top-k MRD is constructed to represent the human motion. The graph model has two attributes V and E, the E attribute represents the set of joint pairs, and the V attribute represents the number of joint point appearing in the top-k MRD. Then, cosine similarity is used to match the similarity of the graph model. Finally, two attributes of the graph model are matched respectively to realize the retrieval of the similar motion. The experimental results show that our method has superior performance compared with other classical methods.

Acknowledgement. This work is supported by the National Natural Science Foundation of China (Nos. 61402164 and 61751203), Program for Changjiang Scholars and Innovative Research Team in University (No. IRT_15R07), Program for the Liaoning Distinguished Professor, by the Science and Technology Innovation Fund of Dalian (No. 2018J12GX036), and by the High-level talent innovation support project of Dalian (No. 2017RD11).

References

1. Varkey, J.P., Pompili, D., Walls, T.A.: Human motion recognition using a wireless sensor-based wearable system. Pers. Ubiquitous Comput. **16**(7), 897–910 (2012)
2. Xiao, J., et al.: Sketch-based human motion retrieval via selected 2D geometric posture descriptor. Sig. Process. **113**, 1–8 (2015)
3. Chen, C., Liu, K., Kehtarnavaz, N.: Real-time human action recognition based on depth motion maps. J. R.-Time Image Process. **12**(1), 155–163 (2016)
4. Li, M., Leung, H.: Graph-based approach for 3D human skeletal action recognition. Pattern Recognit. Lett. **87**, 195–202 (2017)
5. Li, M., et al.: 3D human motion retrieval using graph kernels based on adaptive graph construction. Comput. Graph. **54**, 104–112 (2016)
6. CMU Graphics Lab Motion Capture Database. http://mocap.cs.cmu.edu/
7. Mocap Database HDM05. http://resources.mpi-inf.mpg.de/HDM05/
8. Muller, M., Roder, T., Clausen, M.: Efficient content-based retrieval of motion capture data. In: International Conference on Computer Graphics and Interactive Techniques, vol. 24, no. 3, pp. 677–685 (2005)
9. Muller, M., Roder, T.: Motion templates for automatic classification and retrieval of motion capture data. In: International Conference on Computer Graphics and Interactive Techniques (2006)
10. Chen, S., et al.: Partial similarity human motion retrieval based on relative geometry features. In: Fourth International Conference on Digital Home (2012)
11. Liu, X.M., Zhao, D., Hao, A.M.: Human motion data retrieval based on dynamic time warping optimization algorithm. Pattern Recognit. Artif. Intell. **25**(2), 352–360 (2012)
12. Liu, L., Lu, Y., Suen, C.Y.: Retrieval of envelope images using graph matching. In: International Conference on Document Analysis and Recognition (2011)
13. Xiao, Q., Wang, Y., Wang, H.: Motion retrieval using weighted graph matching. Soft. Comput. **19**(1), 133–144 (2015)
14. Celiktutan, O., et al.: Fast exact hyper-graph matching with dynamic programming for spatio-temporal data. J. Math. Imaging Vis. **51**(1), 1–21 (2015)
15. Zhou, L., et al.: Spatial temporal pyramid matching using temporal sparse representation for human motion retrieval. Vis. Comput. **30**, 845–854 (2014)

Game Rendering and Animation and Computer Vision in Edutainment

Position-Based Simulation of Skeleton-Driven Characters

Dongsheng Yang, Yuling Fan, and Meili Wang(✉)

College of Information Engineering, Northwest A&F University, Yangling 712100, China
wml@nwsuaf.edu.cn

Abstract. The rise of skeletal skinning technology has provided great convenience for animators. At the same time, it improves the efficiency of animation production. However, the deformation resulting from this technology suffers from some undesirable effects, which require manual improvement. In this paper, we propose an approach addressing the problem of creating believable mesh-based skin deformation. In this approach, the skin is first deformed with a classic linear blend skinning approach, which usually lead to artifacts like the candy-wrapper effect or volume loss. Then we enforce the geometric constraints which displace the positions of the vertices to mimic the behavior of the skin and achieve effects like volume preservation. At last, we adopt the finite element method to handle large deformed elements which could accelerate the system's convergence rate. This approach is easy to implement and has a high skinning efficiency without affecting the simulating effect.

Keywords: Skinning · Deformation · Tetrahedral generation · Position-based dynamics · Finite element method

1 Introduction

In computer graphics, simulating human and animals has always been a challenging issue. Modeling vivid skin deformations is difficult and computational. The rise of skeletal animation skinning technology has made animation more efficient. It has been widely adopted in real-time applications such as games for its computational efficiency [3]. However, the traditional skeletal based deformation techniques suffer from several kind of artifacts like the candy-wrapper effect and volume loss [6], which need the animators to repair manually.

This paper present a simple skinning technique for animating human or animals. In order to simulate the behavior of the skin a tetrahedral mesh is generated from a triangle mesh. The tetrahedral meshes help to preserve the total volume of the character body [2]. In this method, the deformation of the character is decoupled in three steps. First, we apply linear blend skinning (LBS) to the given character. Then we enforce geometric constraints which could displace the positions of the vertices to mimic the behavior of the skin and achieve effects like volume preservation. This step is based on the position-based dynamics (PBD). At last, we use the finite element method (FEM) to

A. El Rhalibi et al. (Eds.): Edutainment 2018, LNCS 11462, pp. 231–235, 2019.
https://doi.org/10.1007/978-3-030-23712-7_30

update the vertices again, which can make the simulation result more believable. It could accelerate the convergence rate at the same time.

The main contribution of this paper is that it combines the position-based dynamics (PBD) and finite element method (FEM) to handle the deformation of the virtual characters. The result proves this method is effective and stable. This method could produce similar results while maintaining the simplicity of the PBD method.

2 Related Work

Position-based dynamics can handle general constraints formulated via constraint functions. With the position based approach it is possible to manipulate objects directly during the simulation [1]. The final positions are determined by minimizing the distance between the reference shape and the deformed shape of a model.

Nadine and Marco proposed a two-layered approach addressing the problem of creating believable mesh-based skin deformation [2, 3]. Being based on Position-Based Dynamics guarantees efficiency and real-time performances while enduring robustness and unconditional stability. But their method is dependent on the time step and iteration count of the simulation.

Jan and Matthias made a survey, it focused on a popular and practically relevant subset of approaches [7]. It shows that the geometrically motivated techniques are not force-driven and particularly appropriate in interactive applications due to their versatility, robustness, controllability and efficiency.

Miles and Matthias introduced a simple extension to PBD that allows it to accurately and efficiently simulate arbitrary elastic and dissipative energy potentials in an implicit manner [5]. However, the animation result is depend on the parameter. Similar to PBD, low iteration counts that terminate before convergence will result in artificial compliance.

Jan and Dan present a novel fast and robust method for the simulation of two- and three-dimensional solids that supports complex physical phenomena [4]. Their approach combines continuum mechanical material models with a position-based energy reduction. This method can handle complex physical effects of lateral contraction.

Kim and Pollard proposed an approach relying on the finite element method (FEM) to simulate the skin deformation, able to handle both one-way and two-way simulations within a unified framework [8].

3 Implements

3.1 Delaunay Tetrahedral Partition

The inputs of our method are triangle meshes representing the skin of the character. We generate tetrahedral mesh from the triangle mesh using the open source software Tetgen. The generated tetrahedral is used for defining the geometric constraints [2].

This step is a pretreatment, there is no need to take this step anymore in the following steps (Fig. 1).

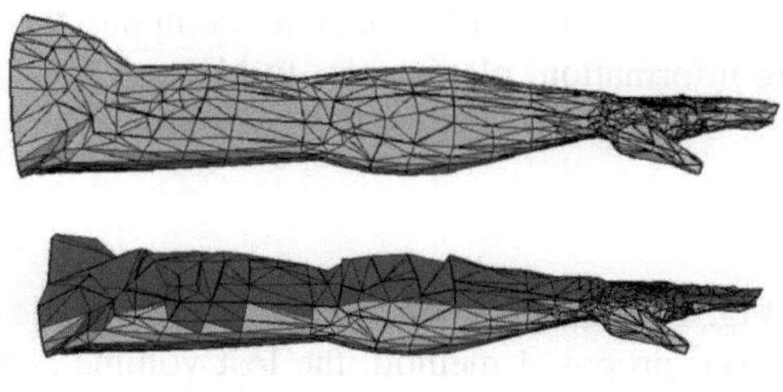

Fig. 1. The result of the Delaunay tetrahedral partition.

3.2 Position-Based Dynamics

The most popular methods for simulating dynamics are force based. Force based method computes the accelerations based on Newton's second law of motion [1]. With the position based approach it is possible to control the integration directly thereby avoiding overshooting problems in connection with explicit integration.

The PBD method defines several non-linear constraints $C(p) = 0$ which indicate asset of geometric relationships between the particles, where p is the vector of all the positions of the particles [2]. The set of constraints is composed by non-linear equality and inequality equations such that:

$$C_i(p) \succ 0, i = 1, \ldots, m. \tag{1}$$

where m is the number of constraints. Each constraint is solved independently through Gauss-Seidel iterations [3]. For a single constraint we find a correction Δ_p by solving the following equation:

$$C_i(p + \Delta p) \approx C_i(p) + \nabla_p C_i(p) \cdot \Delta_p = 0. \tag{2}$$

3.3 Energy Constraint

Position-based dynamics could not model the inner structure of the model skin, so we choose to use the finite element method (FEM) to optimize the result. In finite element method, the deformation of a body is described by a continuous displacement field u [4]. This displacement field is used to define the deformation function:

$$\phi(x) = X + u = x. \tag{3}$$

where x and X denote the positions of a point in the material after and before deformation respectively. The deformation gradient is defined by the Jacobian of the deformation mapping:

$$F = \frac{\partial \phi(X)}{\partial X}. \tag{4}$$

We choose Saint Venant-Kirchhoff model to compute the elastic forces from deformation. For more information, please refer to [4].

4 Results

As we can see from Fig. 2, after LBS, the elbow has lost some volume, it makes it unreal. After applying our proposed method, the lost volume is compensated. PBD's behaviour becomes more stable and believable as the iteration count increased, while the behaviour of our method is consistent regardless of iteration count. It proves that our method has a faster convergence rate.

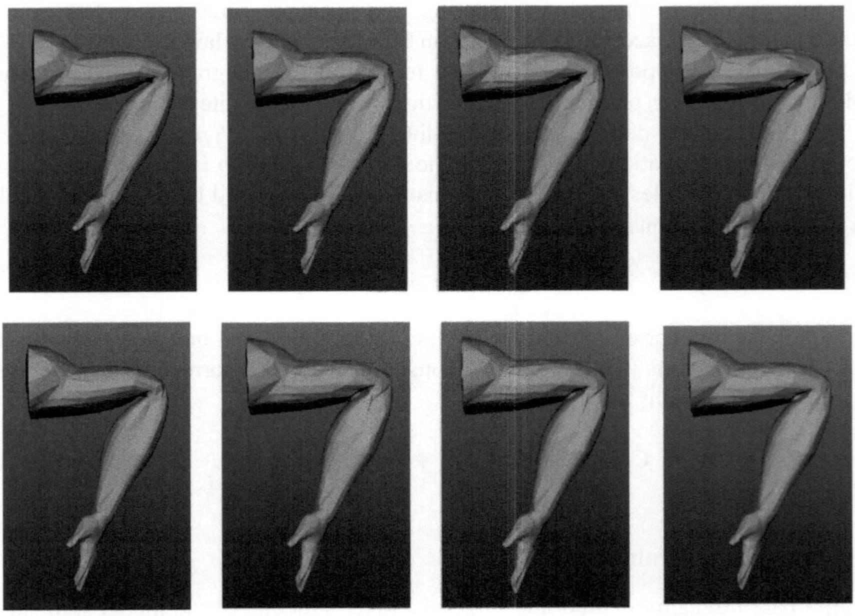

Fig. 2. An arm with 0, 5, 20, and 40 iterations respectively (left to right). Top row: PBD, Bottom row: Our method.

We compared the performance impact of PBD with our method and find that the two methods almost have the same time cost. Please refer to Table 1 for more detail.

Table 1. Per-step simulation time (ms) for a deformed arm at varying iteration counts.

Iterations	0	5	20	40
PBD	0	0.33	1.31	2.56
Our method	0	0.40	1.45	2.60

5 Conclusion

We have presented a simple skinning method for skeleton-driven deformations of virtual characters. Our method combines the position-based dynamics with the finite element method. During the animation process, the volume of the deformed model can be preserved. The FEM step accelerate the convergence rate of PBD, it also helps providing satisfactory results.

References

1. Müller, M., Heidelberger, B., Hennix, M., Ratcliff, J.: Position based dynamics. J. Vis. Commun. Image Represent. **18**(2), 109–118 (2007)
2. Rumman, N.A., Fratarcangeli, M.: Position based skinning of skeleton-driven deformable characters. In: Spring Conference on Computer Graphics, pp. 83–90. ACM, Slovakia (2014)
3. Rumman, N.A., Fratarcangeli, M.: Position-based skinning for soft articulated characters. Comput. Graph. Forum **34**(6), 240–250 (2015)
4. Bender, J., Dan, K., Charrier, P., Weber, D.: Position-based simulation of continuous materials. Pergamon Press, Inc. (2014)
5. Chentanez, N., Chentanez, N.: XPBD: position-based simulation of compliant constrained dynamics. In: International Conference on Motion in Games, pp. 49–54. ACM, Burlingame (2016)
6. Rumman, N.A., Fratarcangeli, M.: State of the art in skinning techniques for articulated deformable characters. In: The International Conference on Computer Graphics Theory and Applications, Rome (2016)
7. Bender, J., Müller, M., Otaduy, M.A., Teschner, M.: Position-based methods for the simulation of solid objects in computer graphics. In: EUROGRAPHICS 2013 State of the Art Reports, Girona (2013)
8. Kim, J., Pollard, N.S.: Fast simulation of skeleton-driven deformable body characters. ACM Trans. Graph. **30**(5), 1–19 (2011)

Parallel MOEA/D for Real-Time Multi-objective Optimization Problems

Jusheng Yu, Lu Li, and YuTao Qi(✉)

School of Computer Science and Technology, Xidian University, Xi'an, China
18234121638@163.com, 1562009225@qq.com,
ytqi@xidian.edu.cn

Abstract. There are a large number of multi-objective optimization problems in real-world applications, like in games, that need to be solved in real time. In order to meet this pressing need, we suggests a method of parallelizing the multi-objective evolutionary algorithm based on decomposition (MOEA/D). Furthermore, a novel task decomposition strategy and scalarizing method without the ideal point are proposed for meeting the requirements of real-time and precision of the game. By combining the novel scalarizing function and GPU-based CUDA technology with the MOEA/D, a parallel MOEA/D for real-time multi-objective optimization problems is developed, namely P-MOEA/D. Experimental studies on ZDT and DTLZ benchmark problems suggest that the P-MOEA/D algorithm is efficient and fast.

Keywords: Real-time multi-objective optimization · Evolutionary multi-objective optimization algorithm · Parallelization · Scalarizing function

1 Introduction

Many games involve more than one conflicting objective to be optimized simultaneously that requires real-time solution [1]. Such problems are commonly referred to as multi-objective optimization problem (MOP) [2]. Unlike single-objective optimization problems, MOPs may have multiple trade-off solutions based on multiple conflicting criteria. These multiple tradeoff solutions are known as Pareto optimal solutions (PS). The image set of all the PS in the objective space is termed as the Pareto optimal front (PF).

Multi-objective evolutionary algorithm based on decomposition has been considered by many as a competent solver for MOPs [3]. Through a set of evenly weight vectors, MOEA/D first converts a target MOP into a series of scalar optimization subproblems by employing a single scalarizing function. Then, the decomposed subproblems are solved simultaneously in a collaborative manner by using an evolutionary algorithm. However, the biggest limitation of MOEA/D is its time-consuming so that it is difficult to meet the real-time requirements of games. Therefore, this paper studies the parallelism of MOEA/D.

To achieve parallelism of MOEA/D, there is an important technical problem to be solved in MOEA/D for decomposing a MOP into a set of simple multi-objective optimization subproblems. That is a global ideal point to dominate all the

A. El Rhalibi et al. (Eds.): Edutainment 2018, LNCS 11462, pp. 236–240, 2019.
https://doi.org/10.1007/978-3-030-23712-7_31

non-dominated solutions on PF, which determines the coverage of the solutions, is needed. The population that solves MOP subproblems needs to share their estimated ideal point in real time and adjust their own search scope according to the current global ideal point. To solve this problem, this paper suggests a new scalarizing function which is independent of ideal point. With the above design, Parallel MOEA/D for real-time multi-objective optimization problems (P-MOEA/D) is developed. Experimental results have shown the effectiveness of P-MOEA/D.

2 The Proposed P-MOEA/D

Through a set of weights vectors $\{\lambda^1, \lambda^2, \ldots., \lambda^N\}$ and a reference point z^r specified by the decision maker in the objective space, the reference point based scalarizing function decomposes the target MOP subproblems into a series of scalar optimization subproblems. The subproblems associated with weight vector λ^i can be formulated by the following Eqs. (2–4):

$$\min_{x\in\Omega} g^R\left(\mathbf{x}|\lambda^i, \mathbf{z}^i\right) = \min_{x\in\Omega} g^R\left(\mathbf{x}|\mathbf{z}^i\right). \tag{1}$$

$$g^R\left(\mathbf{x}|\mathbf{z}^i\right) = \max_{1\leq j\leq m}\left\{\left(f_j(\mathbf{x}) - z_j^i\right)\right\} + \rho\sum_{j=1}^{m}\left(f_j(\mathbf{x}) - z_j^i\right). \tag{2}$$

$$\mathbf{z}^i = \mathbf{z}^r + \alpha\lambda^i. \tag{3}$$

It is worth paying attention to that Eq. (2) is different from the Tchebycheff function in that it does not use the ideal point z^* and the parameter ρ is fixed at 10^{-6}. Instead, a new set of reference points derived from the original reference point (provided by the decision makers), are used. Each of these new reference points $\{\mathbf{z}^1, \mathbf{z}^2, \ldots, \mathbf{z}^N\}$(where $\mathbf{z}^i = \left(z_1^i, z_2^i, \ldots, z_m^i\right)^T$, $i = 1, 2, \ldots, N$) can be generated by shifting the reference point z^r along the direction of λ^i by a distance of $\alpha(\alpha > 0)$, as described in Eq. (3).

$$\mathbf{z}^i = \mathbf{z}^r - \alpha\lambda^i. \tag{4}$$

Through further research, we found that Eqs. (3) and (4) represent different decomposition principles.

The shape of the preferred region for the two objectives problems is the same, just like what is shown in Fig. 1(a), i.e. A = B. However, the different decomposition principles are completely opposite to the preferred regions of the three objectives problem. As shown in Fig. 1(b), the decomposition principles in Eq. (4) corresponds to the preference region of the positive triangle (A in Fig. 1(b)). On the contrary, the preferred region of inverted triangle is formed (B in Fig. 1(b)) is formed.

By combining the novel scalarizing function and GPU-based CUDA technology with the MOEA/D algorithm [3, 4], P-MOEA/D is developed. P-MOEA/D recursively generated a series of uniformly distributed reference points in the first. Then start

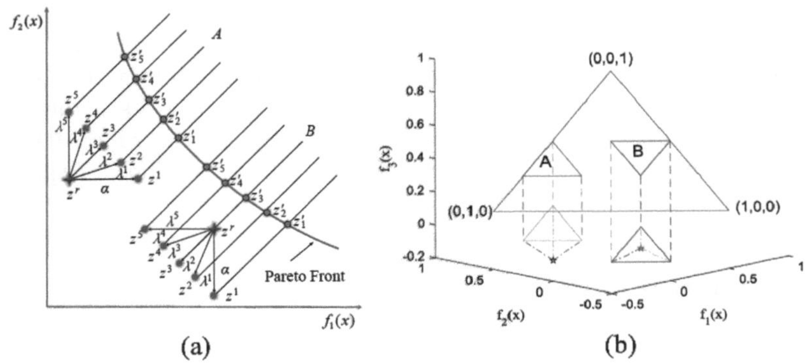

Fig. 1. A novel scalarizing function for two objectives and three objectives problems.

multiple threads and each thread to complete the evolution of a reference point. The evolutionary process is completed by GPU.

3 Experimental Results

In this section, P-MOEA/D is compared with two other algorithms MOEA/D-M2M [5] and NSGA-III [6]. Experiments are conducted on bi-objective and tri-objective benchmark functions including ZDT and DTLZ test suites, to demonstrate the effectiveness and superiority of the proposed algorithm.

3.1 Comparative Studies on MOPs

We set the subpopulation size S = 100 for P-MOEA/D and MOEA/D-M2M with all test instances. The population size is 100 and 300 for bi-objective and tri-objective instances in NSGA-III. According to the MOEA/D-UDM [7], we can construct the weight vectors with arbitrary amount. The number of reference points and evolutionary generation are K = 8 and gen = 2000 on bi-objective problems, K = 64 and gen = 8000 on DTLZ1, K = 256 and gen = 3000 on DTLZ2. The inverted generational distance (IGD) metric [8] is employed to evaluate the performances of the compared algorithms. The results of comparison are based on the population size of NSGA-III, the population size are 100 and 300 on bi-objective and tri-objective problems, respectively. For a uniform sampling of the results of P-MOEA/D and MOEA/D-M2M, we draw out 100 or 300 individuals to be fair. The parameter α is set to 0.1 for all test instances.

Figure 2 takes the bi-objective ZDT1 problems and the tri-objective DTLZ1 problems as an example to illustrate the effectiveness of the P-MOEA/D algorithm. As shown in Fig. 2, P-MOEA/D makes good use of the complementarity between preferred regions and reduces the overlap between preferred regions. From the above experimental results, we can come to the conclusion that P-MOEA/D can well cover the entire PF with appropriate α.

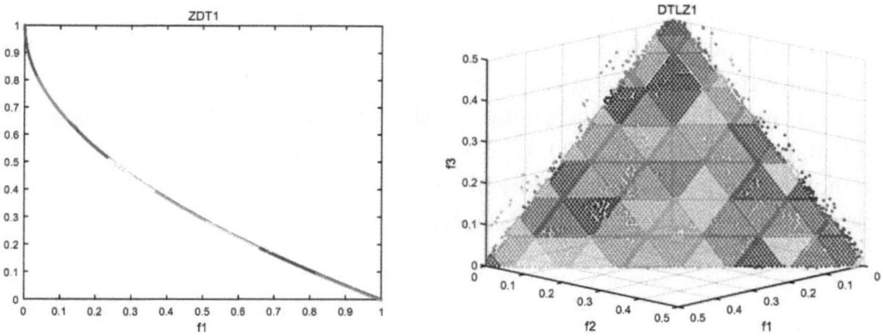

Fig. 2. Effectiveness of the P-MOEA/D algorithm.

Table 1. Performance comparisons on problems.

Problems	P-MOEA/D	MOEA/D-M2M	NSGA-III
ZDT1	1.89e−2	2.19e−2	**1.83e−2**
(2Obj)	(4.40e−3)	(5.26e−3)	(2.314e−3)
ZDT2	**2.213e−2**	2.342e−2	2.46e−2
(2Obj)	(7.62e−3)	(1.70e−3)	(3.393e−2)
ZDT3	**1.89e−2**	1.90e−2	3.305e−2
(2Obj)	(1.70e−3)	(1.89e−2)	(2.57e−2)
DTLZ1	2.572e−3	**2.304e−3**	2.840e−3
(3Obj)	(9.37e−4)	(1.70e−3)	(1.736e−3)
DTLZ2	**1.065e−2**	1.234e−3	2.595e−2
(3Obj)	(1.27e−3)	(2.0e−3)	(1.578e−4)
Wins/total		3/5	4/5

The average and standard deviation of IGD for the 30 runs are summarized in Table 1. Table 1 compare the performances of P-MOEA/D with MOEA/D-M2M and NSGA-III on bi-objective and tri-objective problems. The mean and standard deviation of the metric values are presented, where the best results are highlighted in bold. It can be seen from Table 1 that, P-MOEA/D performs better than MOEA/D-M2M and NSGA-III in 3 and 4 out of 5 comparisons. Such comparison results indicate that P-MOEA/D outperforms MOEA/D-M2M and NSGA-III according to IGD. Clearly, P-MOEA/D outperforms MOEA/D-M2M and NSGA-III on both the bi-objective and tri-objective problems.

4 Conclusions

Many multi-objective optimization problems in the game need to be solved in real time. However, there are two main flaws in the current EMO algorithm. One of them is its time-consuming so that it is difficult to meet the real-time requirements of games. The other is that need share their estimated ideal point in real time and adjust their own search scope according to the current global ideal point. This paper has proposed a novel scalarizing method without the ideal point that makes use of a series of new reference points derived from a reference point specified by the decision maker. By combining the novel scalarizing function and GPU-based CUDA technology with the MOEA/D algorithm, P-MOEA/D is developed. Experimental studies on ZDT and DTLZ benchmark problems have been conducted. The results have validated the superiority and effectiveness of the P-MOEA/D.

References

1. Zhen, J.S., Watson, I.: Neuroevolution for micromanagement in the real-time strategy game StarCraft: brood war. In: Cranefield, S., Nayak, A. (eds.) AI 2013. LNCS (LNAI), vol. 8272, pp. 259–270. Springer, Cham (2013). https://doi.org/10.1007/978-3-319-03680-9_28
2. Deb, K.: Multi-Objective Optimization Using Evolutionary Algorithms. Wiley, Hoboken (2001)
3. Zhang, Q., Li, H.: MOEA/D: a multi-objective evolutionary algorithm based on decomposition. IEEE Trans. Evol. Comput. **11**(6), 712–731 (2007)
4. Li, H., Zhang, Q.: Multi-objective optimization problems with complicated Pareto sets, MOEA/D and NSGA-II. IEEE Trans. Evol. Comput. **13**(2), 284–302 (2009)
5. Liu, H., Gu, F., Zhang, Q.: Decomposition of a multi-objective optimization problem into a number of simple multiobjective subproblems. IEEE Trans. Evol. Comput. **18**(3), 450–455 (2014)
6. Deb, K., Jain, H.: An evolutionary many-objective optimization algorithm using reference-point based non-dominated sorting approach, part I: solving problems with box constraints. IEEE Trans. Evol. Comput. **18**(4), 577–601 (2014)
7. Ma, X., Qi, Y., Li, L., et al.: MOEA/D with uniform decomposition measurement for many-objective problems. Soft Comput. - A Fusion Found. Methodol. Appl. **18**(12), 2541–2564 (2014)
8. Zitzler, E., Thiele, L., Laumanns, M., Fonseca, C.M., Da Fonseca Grunert, V.: Performance assessment of multi-objective optimizers: an analysis and review. IEEE Trans. Evol. Comput. **7**(2), 117–132 (2003)

Bearing-Only and Bearing-Doppler Target Tracking Based on EKF

Xiaohua Li[1(✉)], Chenxu Zhao[2], Jiulong Zhang[1], and Xiuxiu Li[1]

[1] School of Computer Science and Engineering, Xi'an University of Technology, Xi'an 710048, China
lxhxy2009@163.com

[2] National University of Defense Technology, Changsha 741200, China

Abstract. According to the characteristics of underwater target tracking, extended Kalman filter (EKF) algorithm was applied to underwater bearing-only and bearing-Doppler non-maneuverable target tracking problem. EKF is recursive Bayesian filter algorithm based on the linearization of the nonlinearities in the target state and the measurement equations. To ensure the observability in passive target tracking, we use single maneuvering observer. The simulation results show the suitability and effectiveness of the EKF algorithm to the single non-maneuverable target.

Keywords: Targets tracking · Extended Kalman filter · Bearing-only · Bearing-Doppler

1 Introduction

Because of the extensive application prospects on the military and civilian fields, underwater target tracking problem has gained wide concern by the society [1, 2]. Even so, there are many annoying problems need to be resolved at present, such as the convergence, robustness, accuracy and real-time performance of the filter algorithm.

In this paper, we consider the single non-maneuverable target in two-dimensional (2D) space [3, 4]. One of the most important parts in target tracking is filtering algorithm. The bearing-only and bearing-Doppler target tracking systems are nonlinear, for which the Kalman filter [5] can be unstable and divergent especially in highly nonlinear conditions [6]. Therefore, the nonlinear filtering becomes very important in target tracking problems. And the extended Kalman filter (EKF) has shown promise outperforming. Based on the principle of Bayesian filtering, the EKF algorithm is one of the most well-known method to deal with nonlinear problems [7].

The other challenging problem for bearing-only target tracking is that the target state is not fully observable [8]. The observability issue can be solved by using two or more observers if only the target does not move on the line of the multiple observers. By introducing Doppler frequency measurement information, the passive tracking system can be observable on the condition of without the observer's maneuvering moving. In this paper, we investigate the performance of the recursive EKF algorithm on the single target tracking based on bearing-only measurements and bearing-Doppler measurements for the cases of the single maneuvering observer.

A. El Rhalibi et al. (Eds.): Edutainment 2018, LNCS 11462, pp. 241–244, 2019.
https://doi.org/10.1007/978-3-030-23712-7_32

2 System Model

The target's state is $\mathbf{x}(t) = [x(t), y(t), \dot{x}(t), \dot{y}(t)]^{\mathrm{T}}$, where $[x(t), y(t)]$ is target's location, and $[\dot{x}(t), \dot{y}(t)]$ is target's velocity. Similarly, the sth observer's state is defined as $\mathbf{x}_s(t) = [x_s(t), y_s(t), \dot{x}_s(t), \dot{y}_s(t)]^{\mathrm{T}}$, where $[x_s(t), y_s(t)]$ is the sth observer's location, and $[\dot{x}_s(t), \dot{y}_s(t)]$ is s^{th} observer's velocity.

The target's discrete-time state equation is

$$\mathbf{x}(t) = \mathbf{F}(t)\mathbf{x}(t-1) + \mathbf{w}(t) \tag{1}$$

where t is the time, and the $\mathbf{w}(t)$ is zero mean white process noise with variance $\mathbf{Q}(t)$, and $\mathbf{F}(t)$ is a deterministic transition matrix.

The sth measurement equation for bearing-only target tracking problem is given by

$$z_s(t) = \arctan\left(\frac{x(t) - x_s(t)}{y(t) - y_s(t)}\right) + v_s(t) \tag{2}$$

where $v_s(t)$ is zero-mean independent Gaussian noise.

The bearing-Doppler target tracking system can get the targets' redial velocity. Combine the bearing measurements and targets' velocity, the system can get targets' position. Take no account of the measurements noise, the Doppler frequency $f_s(t)$ of the sth observer is given by

$$f_s(t) = \left[1 - \frac{(\dot{x}(t) - \dot{x}_s(t))\sin\theta_s(t) + (\dot{y}(t) - \dot{y}_s(t))\cos\theta_s(t)}{c}\right] f_0 \tag{3}$$

The measurement equation for bearing-Doppler system is

$$\mathbf{z}_s(t) = \begin{bmatrix} \arctan\left(\frac{x(t)-x_s(t)}{y(t)-y_s(t)}\right) \\ \left[1 - \frac{(\dot{x}(t)-\dot{x}_s(t))\sin\theta_s(t) + (\dot{y}(t)-\dot{y}_s(t))\cos\theta_s(t)}{c}\right] f_0 \end{bmatrix} + \begin{bmatrix} v_\theta(t) \\ v_f(t) \end{bmatrix} \tag{4}$$

where $v_\theta(t)$ and $v_f(t)$ are bearing measurement noise and Doppler frequency noise, respectively.

3 Simulation

The conditions of simulation are as follows. The total sampling time is 200 s with 1 s sampling interval, and 100 Monte Carlo runs were performed. The target's location is (900, 1700) m, velocity is (25, −30) m/s. And the initial distance from target to origin of coordinate is 2000 m, the origin of target bearing is 30°, and the origin of target speed and target course are 40 kn and 140°, respectively. The target's radiation frequency is 385 Hz. The single observer's initial location is (0, 1000) m with velocity (0, 6) m/s. In the middle time of experiment, the observer is turning with velocity

(6, 6) m/s. The measurement noise and process noise were modeled as Gaussian distributions. And the bearing noise covariance is 3°, the Doppler noise covariance is 5 Hz.

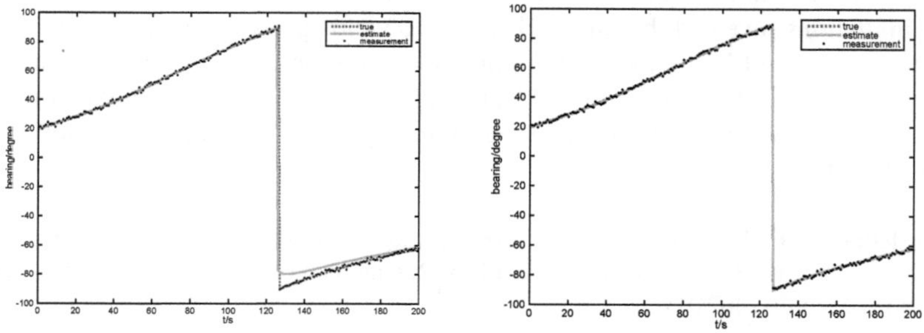

(a) bearing-only (b) bearing-Doppler

Fig. 1. The target's bearing: true value, estimate value and measurement. (a) bearing-only, (b) bearing-Doppler

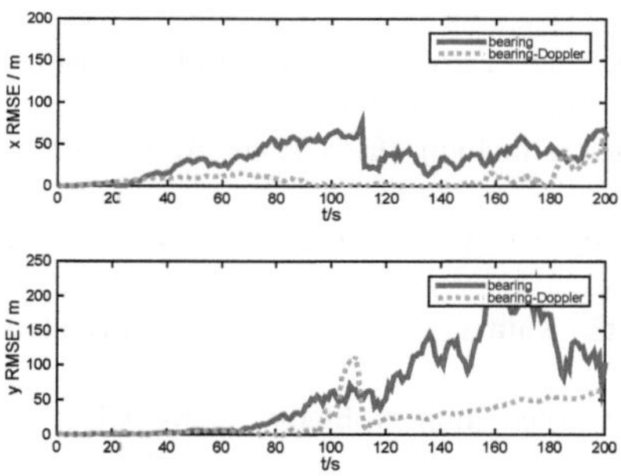

Fig. 2. RMSE of position

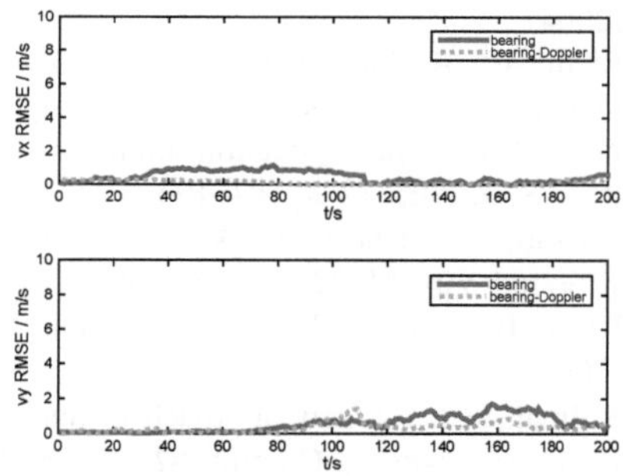

Fig. 3. RMSE of velocity

The true value, estimate value and measurement of bearings for the target are showed in Fig. 1. As is shown in Fig. 1, the true values of target's bearings for bearing-Doppler measurements system are more close to the estimate values than bearing-only system. This is because the bearing-Doppler system has one more measurement information than bearing-only system.

Figures 2 and 3 show the performance of bearing-only system and bearing-Doppler system in the sense of root mean square error (RMSE) of target position and velocity versus time scans. As seen in Figs. 2 and 3, the bearing-Doppler system exhibits a smaller RMSE in position than bearing-only system, and both two system have small RMSE in position. The RMSE in velocity are similar for both systems, and good tracking performance maintained over the simulation period. In addition, the computational load of the EKF algorithm is small.

4 Conclusion

To ensure the observability in passive underwater target tracking, we addressed the bearings-only and bearing-Doppler target tracking problem with single maneuvering observer, and extended Kalman filter algorithm was used for this problem. The computer simulations revealed that the EKF estimate yields good results and confirmed the effectiveness of the EKF in the tracking of underwater target under single maneuvering observer scenarios. Also the extended Kalman filter has lower computation complexity than the other nonlinear and non-Gaussian filter algorithms, such as unscented Kalman filter and particle filter.

Acknowledgments. This work was supported by the National Natural Science Foundation of China (grant No. 61703333) and the National Key Research and Development Program of China (grant No. 2017YFB1402103).

References

1. Arulampalam, M.S., Ristic, B., Gordon, N., Mansell, T.: Bearings-only tracking of maneuvering targets using particle filters. EURASIP J. Appl. Sig. Process. **15**, 2351–2365 (2004)
2. Ristic, B., Arulampalam, M.S.: Tracking a maneuvering target using angle-only measurements: algorithms and performance. Sig. Process. **83**, 1223–1238 (2003)
3. Foy, W.H.: Position-location solutions by Taylor series estimation. IEEE Trans. Aerosp. Electron. Syst. AES-12 **2**, 187–194 (1976)
4. Hassab, J.C.: Passive tracking of a moving source by a single observer in shadow water. J. Sound Vib. **44**, 127–145 (1976)
5. Ristic, B., Arulampalam, M.S., Gordon, N.: Beyond the Kalman Filter. Artech House, Boston (2004)
6. Kalman, R.E.: A new approach to linear filtering and prediction problems. Trans ASME-J. Basic Eng. Autom. Control. **82**, 35–45 (1960)
7. Li, X.H., Baum, M., Willett, P.: Evaluation of the PMHT approach for passive radar tracking with unknown transmitter associations. In: Proceedings of 17th International Conference on Information Fusion, Salamanca, pp. 1–7 (2014)
8. Song, T.L.: Observability of target tracking with bearings only measurements. IEEE Trans. Aerosp. Electron. Syst. **32**, 1468–1471 (1996)

A Motion-Driven System for Performing Art

Zizhao Wu, Feiwei Qin, Shi Li, and Yigang Wang(✉)

School of Media and Design, Hangzhou Dianzi University, Hangzhou, China
Yigang.wang@hdu.edu.cn

Abstract. In this paper, a motion-driven system was designed to combine the motion of human performers with physical simulations in order to generate aesthetic visual effects that respond to the performers in realtime. The system consists of two major components: the motion data acquisition and the visual effects feedback. We implement the motion data acquisition module based on infrared sensors which provides realtime performance with both 2D and 3D outputs. The visual effects feedback module is designed in charge of producing aesthetic effects based on the realtime motion data. We evaluated the effectiveness of our framework on several performing art shows. The results suggest that our system is capable of enhancing the traditional electronic art effects.

Keywords: Motion capture · Performing art

1 Introduction

Performing arts are a form of art in which artists use their voices or bodies, often in relation to other objects, to convey artistic expression. The performing arts range from dance, music, opera, drama and beyond. Recently, with the rapid development of human-computer interaction technologies, interactive arts has attracted great interests in the performing arts domain, which leads to a new perspectives to the creation of performing art works. For example, Dannenberg and Bates [2] describe several interactive artworks and show that there are strong similarities that transcend categories such as drama, music, and dance. Qian et al. [3] report a real-time gesture driven interactive system with multi-modal feedback for dance arts.

In this paper, we concern with the more common practice of using electronic and computer technology to facilitate the interactive dancing art based on the human-computer interaction technologies.

Our system consists of two major parts: the motion data acquisition module and the interactive visual feedback module. The motion data acquisition module is implemented to be scalable and adaptable to different physical situations, where full body motion data is captured and optimized, using commodity hardware devices like infrared sensors. A set of algorithms have been implemented in the system including image denoising, foreground extraction, skeleton extraction and so on, which lead to diverse kinds of motion data including the contour, skeleton, point clouds and so on. The full body motion data is then utilized to drive the visual effects feedback in an interactive manner. As a result, our framework can greatly liberate the shackles of the performers and enhance the integration of the virtual and real. We evaluated the effectiveness of

A. El Rhalibi et al. (Eds.): Edutainment 2018, LNCS 11462, pp. 245–248, 2019.
https://doi.org/10.1007/978-3-030-23712-7_33

our framework on several electronic art shows. The results suggest that our system is capable of enhancing the traditional electronic art effects.

2 Framework

Our system is designed for the performer acting on a stage with a screen behind the stage. Our system facilitates the stages in common use, especially when there is a center stage and a screen is located behind the stage. We use the infrared camera to capture the images of the stage, the layout arrangement is illustrated in the Fig. 1.

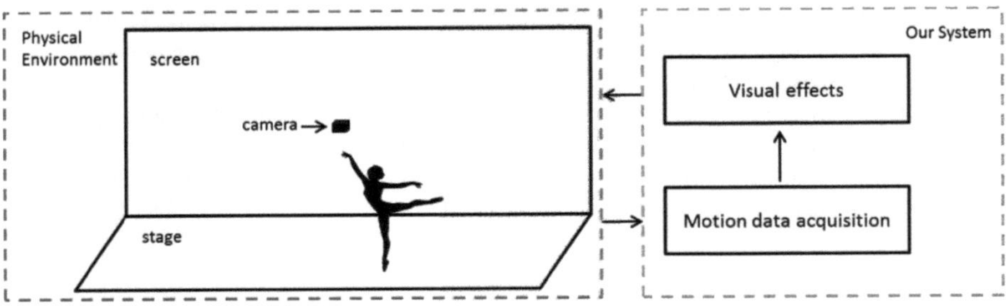

Fig. 1. This figure shows our system diagram.

Visual effect is displayed on the screen according to the performer's motion. All technologies behind them are provided by the framework, which consists of two main components: the full-body motion capture and the visual effect feedback.

2.1 Motion Data Acquisition

Data acquisition is the key to our framework, which supports understanding of the movements and shapes exhibited by the performers, and provides the necessary data for the following visual feedback. In our system, we provide multiple choices for capturing motion data depending on the stage environment.

For a small range of area, such as 5 $\times$ 5 m zone, our system directly introduce the Microsoft Kinect [1] as the input device, which is suggested to be a cheap and easy way to work with motion capture. For a large range of area, multiple infrared cameras are utilized to capture the original image data. Considering the efficiency for the computation, our framework utilizes the algorithms in high computation efficiency, such as the DirectShow SDK.

There may be some noise exists in the original data, caused by the real lighting environment. To alleviate this problem, we study to use the image filtering technologies to deal with it. More specifically, the mean filtering algorithm is employed, which is a simple sliding-window spatial filter that replaces the center value in the window with the average of all the pixel values in the window. Mathematically the mean filtering can be computed by:

$$h(i,j) = \frac{1}{M}\sum\nolimits_{(k,l)\in N} f(\mathrm{k},\mathrm{l}) \quad (1)$$

where $h(\mathrm{i},\mathrm{j})$ is the pixel value at point (x, y), M is the total number of pixels in the neighborhood N.

After denoising the original images, we employ the image binarization algorithm to replace all values to 1 s and 0 s with a thresholding operation. Finally, we can obtain the contour of human and motion directions based on comparing images of frames.

2.2 Visual Effects

Our system provides the visual feedback module to support the integration of the virtual and real. Thus, the movement of the performers will be amplified by the visual effects through inject motion elements into the virtual scenes, causing a number of projected digital particles to float above the projection surface.

In our system, the visual effects are mainly designed to be appeared in the form of particle system. Our particle system is specified by an absolute system position in three-dimensional space and a set of particles. Each individual particle is defined by its position, velocity, color, and size. Three sub-modules are developed to facilitate evolving a variety of common types of effects:

- the generic sub-module is devised to control the effects such as fire, smoke, explosions. Each particle has a position, velocity, color and size.
- the plane system is devised to warp individual particles into different shapes for bright flashes, lens flares, and engine exhaust effects.
- the trail sub-module is devised to compute trails of static particles behind each moving particle.

We utilize these particles to simulate the discretization of human bodies and their interaction effects. Various kinds of interaction techniques are provided, which include body interaction, hand interaction and speech interaction. For body interaction, we use the detected human contour to perform the collision detection. As the performer dances, the environment particles which are detected to collide with the performer are dynamically moved accordingly. For hand interaction and speech interaction, we use the open source solutions such as the Kinect SDK to support these kinds of operations.

3 Applications

Our system has been successfully applied in many public performances, including the Shanghai eArts Festival and the Meeting the Grande Canal shows, where both of them are big stage dramas. Our system obtains the motion of a performer via infrared cameras, and provides visual feedback with aesthetic visual effects. To some extent, our system fuses contemporary dance elements and physical theatre acrobatics with digital technology to explore the human relationship with physical and digital space.

For example, one effect of our system draws a chaotic image of swirling point clouds that appear around the dancer. Once the dancer move, the clouds may move following and then scattering. The second effect draws a 3D cube boundary swept out with the movement of the dancers on stage. The color of the surface is a gradient based on the activity of the dancer. The whole scene slowly dissolves away as it gets older, creating a colorful swirling, moving pattern that follows the dancer. We note that these kinds of online interactive scenarios can be set, altered, practiced and refined based on our system. All these demonstrate the usefulness of our system in a dance-orientated performing art (Fig. 2).

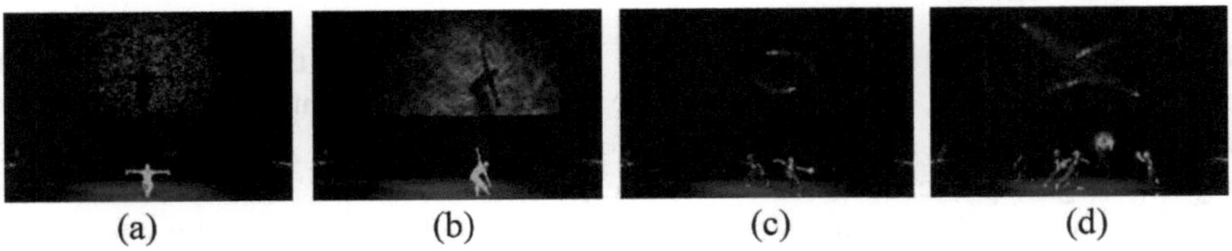

Fig. 2. One of dancing shows of our system, which mainly contains the motion data acquisition module and the visual effect feedback module.

4 Conclusion

In this work, we describe a creative system for performing art, our system automatically captures the dancer's performance and provides visual feedback in the form of aesthetic visual effects. The system acquires the motion of a performer based on infrared cameras, by analyzing the contour, the skeleton, the motion of the original data, our approach supports interaction with the virtual effect, lead to a high integration of the virtual and real. We have introduced some application scenarios which validate the usefulness and effectiveness of our system.

Acknowledgments. This work was supported in part by the National Natural Science Foundation of China (No. 61602139,61502129), the Open Project Program of State Key Lab of CAD&CG, Zhejiang University (No. A1803, A1817), and Zhejiang Province science and technology planning project (No. 2018C01030).

References

1. Kinect sdk. https://www.xbox.com/en-US/xbox-one/accessories/kinect
2. Dannenberg, R.B., Bates, J.: A model for interactive art. In: Proceedings of the Fifth Biennial Symposium for Arts and Technology, pp. 103–111 (1995)
3. Qian, G., Guo, F., Ingalls, T., Olson, L., James, J., Rikakis, T.: A gesture-driven multimodal interactive dance system. In: Proceedings of the 2004 IEEE International Conference on Multimedia and Expo, ICME 2004, 27–30 June 2004, Taipei, Taiwan, pp. 1579–1582 (2004)

Latent Topic Model Based Multi-feature Learning for PolSAR Terrain Classification

Junfei Shi(✉), Haiyan Jin, Yinghui Wang, Zhiyong Lv, and Lu Liu

School of Computer Science and Technology, Xi'an University of Technology, Xi'an 710048, Shaanxi, China
shijunfei@xaut.edu.cn

Abstract. The heterogenous areas of the polarimetric synthetic aperture radar (PolSAR) image are hardly to be classified into semantic homogenous regions due to the complex terrain structures. In order to overcome these disadvantages, a PolSAR image classification method is proposed based on the multi-feature learning and the topic model. The proposed method makes use of three kinds of features to formulate the visual codewords. Then, the higher level features are learned by the topic model for classification. Experimental results illustrate that the proposed method can obtain better performance than the state-of-art methods especially for the heterogenous areas.

Keywords: Polarimetric SAR classification · Topic model · Multi-feature learning · Visual codewords

1 Introduction

Polarimetric synthetic aperture radar (PolSAR) terrain classification is one of the most important tasks for SAR image processing. A number of unsupervised classification approaches were proposed by making full use of polarimetric information, which include scattering mechanism based methods [1,2], statistical distribution based approaches [3] and methods [4,5] by combining the scattering characteristics and statistical models. However, without considering the spatial and semantic information of an image, these pixel-based classification methods usually produce an inconsistent salt-and-pepper classification result. Recently, Topic model [6] is widely used as an efficient tool to establish a bridge between the low-level features and high-level semantic, and produces good classification results.

Inspired by the topic model, in this paper, a latent topic model-based multi-feature learning method is proposed for the PolSAR image classification, which has two characteristics as follows: (1) Three types of features are extracted to combine the scattering mechanism and polarimetric information. (2) Neighborhood information is used to obtain the sparse representation of each pixel, and a

A. El Rhalibi et al. (Eds.): Edutainment 2018, LNCS 11462, pp. 249–252, 2019.
https://doi.org/10.1007/978-3-030-23712-7_34

topic model is applied to learn semantic features. Experimental results illustrate the effectiveness of the proposed method.

The outline of this paper is organized as follows. In Sect. 2, the proposed method is described in detail. The experimental results are shown and discussed in Sect. 3. Finally, the conclusion is drawn in Sect. 4.

2 Proposed Method

In order to consider the spatial relationship and semantic information, a latent topic model and multi-feature learning based PolSAR image classification method is proposed. The main procedure is illustrated in Fig. 1. The detailed explanations are given below.

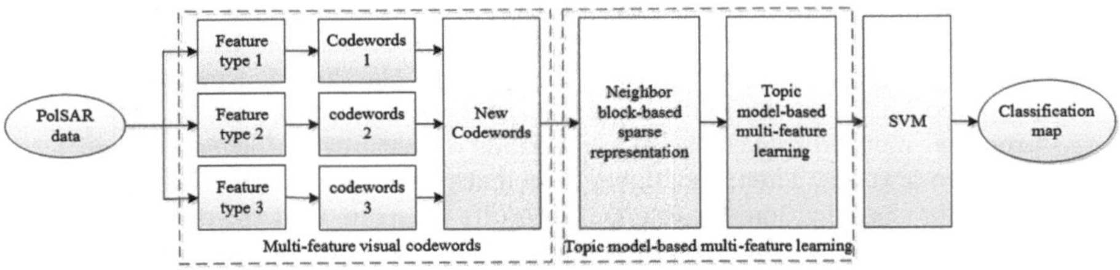

Fig. 1. The procedure of the topic model-based multi-feature learning method.

2.1 Multi-feature Visual Codewords

Feature Extraction from PolSAR Data: Three types of features (50 dimensions) are extracted from PolSAR data features in this paper.

(1) Features from original data (15 features)
(a) scattering matrix elements [1] (6 features);
(b) Coherency matrix elements [3] (9 features);

(2) Features from target decomposition (15 features)
(a) The Cloude and Pottier decomposition [2] (3 features): the entropy H, the anti-entropy A and the average of scattering angle α.
(b) The Freeman decomposition [3] (3 features): the surface, double-bounce and volume scattering power.
(c) Huynen decomposition [7] (9 features);

(3) features from PolSAR image (20 features)
(a) Gray-level co-occurrence matrix (GLCM) [8] features (4 features): contrast, energy, entropy and relativity.
(b) Contour features (16 features): Gaussian filters with three scales and 18 orientation are applied to three channels and SPAN images to compute the contour energy value respectively.

Construction of Visual Codewords: In this paper, three types of visual codewords are formulated respectively according to the three categories of features. Specifically, the extracted feature descriptors for each category is formulated as a feature vector. The feature vectors are normalized at first. Then, the k-means clustering method is used to obtain three set of visual words. Finally, a new set of codewords is formulated by combining three set of visual codewords extracted from three types of features.

2.2 Topic Model-Based Multi-feature Learning

According to the visual codewords, each pixel can be clustered to one visual word. In order to suppress speckle noises, a neighborhood block with 10×10 window size is used to represent the feature of a pixel. The sparse representation of each pixel is calculated by the histogram which is obtained by mapping all the pixels in the neighbor block to the codewords. Then, the topic model is utilized to learn the high-level features for each pixel. Finally, we use the Gaussian kernel support vector machine (SVM) to conduct nonlinear classification in this paper.

3 Experimental Study

In this section, the AIRSAR L band San Francisco area 4-look fully polarimetric data is used to test the effectiveness of the proposed method. During the experiment, 100 codewords are formulated for each kind of features. Three methods are used to compare their performance. They are the Wishart classification method, the Wishart MRF method and the multi-feature SVM method.

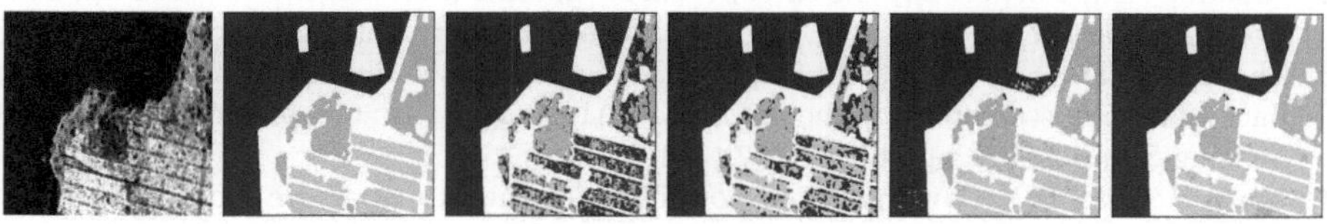

(a) (b) (c) (d) (e) (f)

Fig. 2. Classification results on San Francisco area. (a) Pauli image of San Francisco area. (b) Ground truth of (a). (c) Classification result by the Wishart method. (d) Classification result by the Wishart MRF method. (e) Classification result by the multi-feature SVM method. (f) Classification result by the proposed method. (Color figure online)

The PolSAR image of San Francisco area is used to test the proposed paper, and a subimage of San Francisco area is shown in Fig. 2(a) with the size of 512×512. The corresponding ground truth is given in Fig. 2(b). There are 3 categories in Fig. 2(b), which are *sea* in blue, the *forest* in cyan and the *buildings* in yellow. In addition, the other areas are the background areas which are labeled in white.

The classification results by Wishart, Wishart MRF and multi-feature SVM methods are shown in Fig. 2(c)–(e), and Fig. 2(f) is the classification result by the proposed method. It can be seen that the Wishart and Wishart MRF methods in Fig. 2(c)–(d) have many misclassifications in the *forest* and the *buildings*. The multi-feature SVM method in Fig. 2(e) also has misclassifications especially in the *buildings*. Compared with the three methods, the proposed method can obtain better performance in the *forest* and the *buildings* since high-level features can be learned by the topic model.

4 Conclusion

In this paper, a new method is proposed to learn high-level features by multi-feature learning. In addition, the neighbor block is utilized to reduce the speckle noises. Experimental results verify the effectiveness of the proposed method. Furthermore, how to select the numbers of visual words and topics adaptively will be exploited in the further work.

Acknowledgments. This work was carried out with the part-supports of the National Natural Science Foundation of China (Grant Nos. 61502382,61472204, and 61472319).

References

1. Zou, B., Lu, D., Zhang, L., Moon, W.M.: Eigen-decomposition-based four-component decomposition for polsar data. IEEE J. Sel. Top. Appl. Earth Obs. Remote Sens. **9**(3), 1286–1296 (2016)
2. Cloude, S.R., Pottier, E.: An entropy based classification scheme for land applications of polarimetric SAR. IEEE Trans. Geosci. Remote Sens. **35**(1), 68–78 (1997)
3. Zhao, L., Yang, J., Li, P., Shi, L., Xu, J.: Unsupervised classification of the weak backscattering scatterers by the use of PolSAR imagery. In: Geoscience and Remote Sensing Symposium, pp. 4714–4717 (2016)
4. Yang, S., Hao, H.X.: Unsupervised polarimetric synthetic aperture radar image classification based on sketch map and adaptive Markov random field. J. Appl. Remote Sens. **10**(2), 025008 (2016)
5. Liu, F., et al.: Hierarchical semantic model and scattering mechanism based PolSAR image classification. Pattern Recogn. **59**(C), 325–342 (2016)
6. Xing, H., Meng, Y., Hou, D., Song, J., Xu, H.: Employing crowdsourced geographic information to classify land cover with spatial clustering and topic model. Remote Sens. **9**(6), 602 (2017)
7. Huynen, J.R.: The stokes matrix parameters and their interpretation in terms of physical target properties. In: Proceedings of SPIE: The International Society for Optical Engineering, vol. 1317, pp. 195–207 (1990)
8. He, C., Li, S., Liao, Z., Liao, M.S.: Texture classification of PolSAR data based on sparse coding of wavelet polarization textons. IEEE Trans. Geosci. Remote Sens. **51**(8), 4576–4590 (2013)

E-Learning and Game

TLogic: A Tangible Programming Tool to Help Children Solve Problems

Xiaozhou Deng[1,2], Danli Wang[1(✉)], and Qiao Jin[1,2]

[1] The State Key Laboratory of Management and Control for Complex Systems, Institute of Automation, Chinese Academy of Sciences, Beijing, China
danli_wang@163.com
[2] School of Computer and Control Engineering, University of Chinese Academy of Sciences, Beijing, China

Abstract. In this paper, we present TLogic, a tangible programming tool for children aged 6–8. The tool contains two parts: tangible programming blocks and visual tasks with different difficulty levels. Children could use tangible programming blocks to complete visual tasks shown on computer screen. To evaluate our tool, a user study was conducted with 10 children. Results of user study show that the tool could reduce children's cognitive load while solving the tasks and children are more interested in challenging tasks than easy tasks in our tool.

Keywords: Tangible programming · Children · Edutainment

1 Introduction

Programming education has been proved positive for children's development in many aspects, not only in areas such as math and science, but also in language skills, creativity, and social emotional interaction [1]. Besides, learning programming is an efficient way to cultivate computational thinking which has been described as a fundamental skill for everyone, not only for computer scientists [2].

However, text-based programming is too difficult for young children due to the rigid syntax and complex programming environment [3]. To reduce the cognitive load of programming, researchers have designed a new interaction method: tangible user interfaces which could make programming easier for young children [4]. With tangible programming tools, children can write programs by assembling the physical objects without keystrokes, which is much easier to involve children in programming [5].

In this paper, we present a new tangible programming tool-TLogic, which contains two visual tasks with different difficulty levels. the reason we provide different visual tasks is that we want to explore children's preference on visual tasks while programming with tangible programming tool.

A. El Rhalibi et al. (Eds.): Edutainment 2018, LNCS 11462, pp. 255–262, 2019.
https://doi.org/10.1007/978-3-030-23712-7_35

2 Related Work

2.1 Tangible Programming Tools

There are many excellent tangible programming tools designed for children, which inspire our work a lot.

Electronic Block [6] uses building blocks to program. It consists of three types of building blocks: sensor blocks, logic blocks and behavior blocks. Each block is embedded with a processor and electronic parts. KIBO [7] is a robotics kit, with which children can construct robots with motors, sensors, and craft materials, and program the robots' actions with some wooden blocks. However, KIBO needs children to capture the programs using a camera manually which is inconvenient for children to use and learn. Tern [8] is a tangible programming language in which children could assemble some puzzle shaped blocks to program a virtual role or a real walking robot. Same as KIBO, Tern also needs children to manually capture the block sequence. Besides, the computer vision technology used in the tool was limited by illumination which might make children feel confused. Also limited by this problem, T-Maze [9] uses a camera to capture the programs that arranged by children and allows children play multi-level maze-escape games by programming. Additionally, real-time feedback is provided on the screen to show the path children have programmed for the characters in game. Strawbies [10] is a real-time tangible programming game designed for children age 5–10. It is an iPad app. Children can play it by constructing physical programs out of wooden tiles in front of an iPad. This work involved children in the design process and developed three different versions to explore different approaches for children easy to use the tool. This design method gave us inspirations.

Inspired by programming tools above, we find tools based on TUI can effectively provide children a programming environment.

2.2 Cognitive Development

Jean Piaget and Bruner's work show us the cognitive ability of children aged 6–8 [11]. According to their work, children aged 6–8 who are in pre-operation stage can't solve problem which contains plenty of intermediate states and complex logic. The theory of cognitive load indicates that real-time feedback which could reduce children's memory load is necessary [12].

The theory of cognitive development helps us make our system effective for children's programming learning and the theory of cognitive load helps us design our tool.

3 Design and Implementation

TLogic is a tangible programming tool with tasks of different complexity. TLogic consists of two parts: visual tasks presented by Unity3D and programming blocks. There would be a detailed rule statement before each task. And the tool provides children with real-time feedback and error massages while programming.

3.1 Visual Tasks

There are two tasks in TLogic. The first only contains sequential structure: two visual characters are on sides of a river. There is a suspension bridge on the river which could be dropped down by a controller. The controller needs to be activated by one of the characters. Children could use programming blocks to let the two characters meet each other. The picture of the first task is shown in Fig. 1.

Fig. 1. The two visual tasks.

The second task contains mutually exclusive objects and plenty of intermediate states. A visual character needs carry three objects, a tiger, a sheep and a grass cross a river. The character can only take one object, or nothing cross the bridge. But if the character is on the different side than the tiger and the sheep, there would be an error massage since the tiger would attack the sheep. It is same with the sheep and the grass. The picture of the second task is also shown in Fig. 1.

Considering the cognitive ability of children aged 6–8, we design these two tasks to make a comparison.

3.2 Programming Blocks

Programming blocks are made by 3 cm wooden brick cube with surface texture (Fig. 2). The semantics of blocks are directly corresponding to the operations in visual tasks. For example, in task two, there are four kinds of blocks which are matched with the four kinds way to cross the river in visual game. In our tool we use ReacTIVision framework [13] for real-time recognition of tangible programming blocks.

3.3 Feedback and Error Massage

The design of the feedback and the error massage is important, sometimes decisive to tangible user interface. During completing the second task, children often made some invalid operations while attempting to figure out the solution. For instance, they would try to carry object cross the river even if the object and the character weren't on the same side. It is necessary to make error massages clearly for these invalid operations.

Fig. 2. Programming blocks.

It is hard for children aged 6–8 remember intermediate states. Besides, the presentation of the intermediate states could also encourage children to carry on their programming. We provide children real-time feedback after each of their operation. The intuitionistic feedback reduces children's memory load of the process. Figure 3 show the intermediate state and the error massage.

Fig. 3. The intermediate state and the error massage.

4 User Study

To evaluate TLogic, we conducted a lab-based user study with children. In the user study, we were mainly concerned about whether TLogic could reduce children's cognitive load to help them complete more complex tasks and what kind of problems children like.

We have invited 10 children aged 6–8 (7 of them aged 7 and 4 of them are boys) to participate in our study. Experiments were conducted in a spacious room. To capture children's behaviors and voice, a video recorder was set up (Fig. 4).

During the experiment stage, firstly, we showed them how to control visual objects with programming blocks and the feedback on the screen. After these preparations, we let children program to solve the problems. Besides, once a child placed a valid programming block, the tool would log the time stamp.

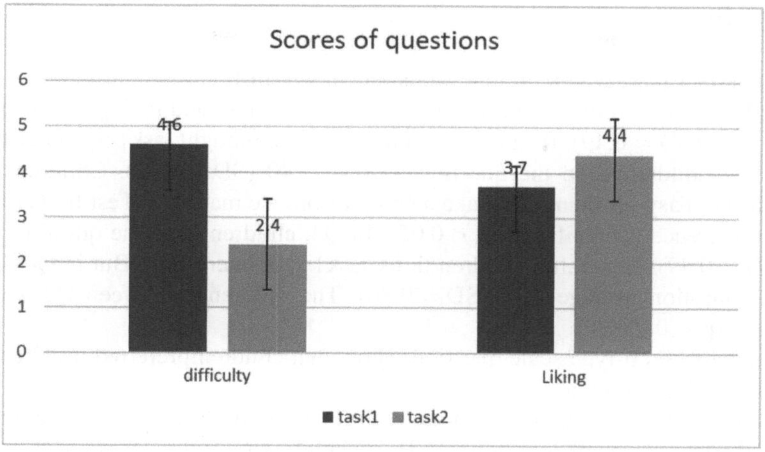

Fig. 4. Scores of Likert-type scale questions. The difficulty in the figure are corresponding to Q1 and Q2. And the liking in the figure are corresponding to Q3 and Q4.

Before programming, we made a short interview to get some basic information of children, such as age, gender and whether got involved with TUIs. After they completed the tasks, we made a brief interview which contains Likert-type scale questions and interview questions. The Likert-type scale is composed to 4 questions scored from one to five, where one means the minimum and five means the max score. The Likert-type scale questions are shown in Table 1.

Table 1. Likert-type scale questions.

Questions	Descriptions
Q1	Do you think the task1 is easy to learn?
Q2	Do you think the task2 is easy to learn?
Q3	How much do you like the task1?
Q4	How much do you like the task2?

The interview questions are shown in Table 2.

Table 2. Interview questions.

Questions	Descriptions
I1	Is there another block sequence of task 1?
I2	Is there another block sequence of task 2?
I3	Which block do you think is the key of task 2?
I4	Do you like this tool and which task do you like more?

5 Results

The results of Likert-type scale questions are shown in Fig. 4.

In Q1, children were asked how task1 is easy for them, and they gave the question average 4.60 (SD = 0.49). Results shown that children thought task1 was easy to them. As for Q2, children gave the question average 2.40 (SD = 1.02). Children thought task2 was not easy for them. To make a comparison, we made a T-Test for Q1 and Q2, and the difference is significant ($p < 0.05$). In Q3, children gave the question average 3.70 (SD = 0.49). Generally, children think task1 was interesting. But in Q4, children gave the question average 4.40 (SD = 0.80). The difference between Q3 and Q4 is significant ($p < 0.05$).

Results of Likert-type scale questions show that children preferred task2 and task2 was more difficult to children.

In order to find whether children did really understand how to solve the two tasks. We asked some interview questions. In I1, all children gave the correct answer. But in interview question I2, only three of them could tell us another block sequence of task2. As for the I3, half of them told us the key is carrying the sheep back. Considering the accidental solutions, we asked children who can't answer I2 and I3 to place the blocks for task2 again. All these kids could place the blocks properly and quickly again.

We have logged all the time stamps of children's valid operations and Fig. 5 shows the average finishing time. The average finishing time of task2 is longer that task1.

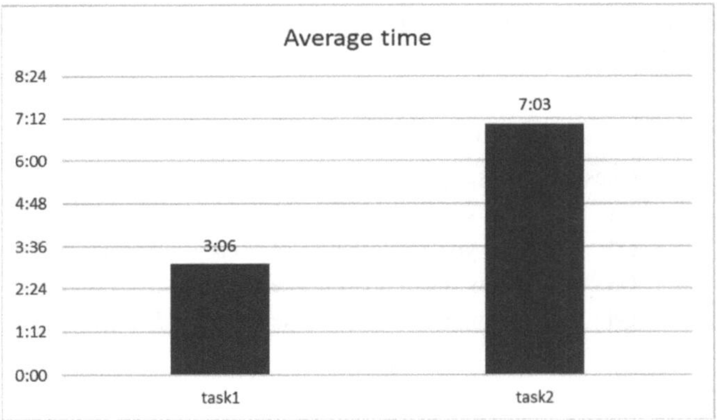

Fig. 5. The average finishing time (minute: second).

Considered all results above, we think TLogic could help children solve and understand the two visual tasks with tangible programming blocks. Besides, children like more difficult task while using TLogic.

6 Conclusions and Future Work

In this paper, we present a tangible programming tool designed for children aged 6–8 – TLogic, which could help children program in a physical form and execute the instructions to solve visual tasks.

According to the results user study, TLogic could reduce children's cognitive load for complex problems and children like challenges with this tool. Besides, after finishing task2 which is more difficult for children, they show self-affirmation and the joy of achievement. Furthermore, we found that children were enthusiasm to logic problems like task2.

To sum up, the design of the content is significant to tangible programming tools. Nowadays, more and more modern technology has provided more and more fantasy interfaces. Indeed, these new user interfaces could gain children's attraction. But we think the visual tasks is important for cognitive development and children may get interested in well-designed visual tasks.

In the future, this work can be improved in several ways. For example, real-time feedback is a significant factor to help children debug the program, so we will provide richer types of feedback. Besides, we need to find more tasks which is appropriate for children's education and apply them into our current work.

Acknowledgment. This research is supported by the National Key Research and Development Program under Grant No. 2016YFB0401202, and the National Natural Science Foundation of China under Grant No. 61672507, 61272325, 61501463 and 61562063.

References

1. Clements, D.H.: The future of educational computing research: the case of computer programming. Inf. Technol. Child. Educ. Ann. **1999**(1), 147–179 (1999)
2. Wing, J.M.: Computational thinking. Commun. ACM **49**(3), 33–35 (2006)
3. Cockburn, A., Bryant, A.: Leogo: an equal opportunity user interface for programming. J. Vis. Lang. Comput. **8**(5–6), 601–619 (1997)
4. Manches, A., O'Malley, C.: Tangibles for learning: a representational analysis of physical manipulation. Pers. Ubiquit. Comput. **16**(4), 405–419 (2012)
5. Horn, M.S.: Tangible interaction and learning: the case for a hybrid approach. Pers. Ubiquit. Comput. **16**(4), 379–389 (2012)
6. Wyeth, P., Purchase, H.C.: Programming without a computer: a new interface for children under eight. In: Australasian User Interface Conference IEEE (2000)
7. Sullivan, A., Elkin, M., Bers, M.U.: KIBO robot demo: engaging young children in programming and engineering. In: International Conference on Interaction Design & Children. ACM (2015)
8. Horn, M.S., Jacob, R.J.K.: Tangible programming in the classroom with tern. In: Proceedings of the CHI 2007 Extended Abstracts on Human Factors in Computing Systems, pp. 1965–1970 (2007)
9. Wang, D., et al.: E-block: a tangible programming tool for children. In: Adjunct ACM Symposium on User Interface Software & Technology. ACM (2011)

10. Hu, F., et al.: Strawbies: explorations in tangible programming. In: International Conference on Interaction Design & Children. ACM (2015)
11. Bruner, J.S., Lufburrow, R.A.: The Process of Education (1960)
12. Chandler, P., Sweller, J.: Cognitive load theory and the format of instruction. Cogn. Instruct. **8**(4), 293–332 (1991)
13. Kaltenbrunner, M., Bencina, R.: reacTIVision:a computer-vision framework for table-based tangible interaction. In: International Conference on Tangible & Embedded Interaction (2007)

School-Enterprise Cooperative Innovation and Entrepreneurship Courses and Case Library of Emerging Engineering Education

Kun Ma(✉), Yongzheng Lin, Kun Liu, Jin Zhou, and Jiwen Dong

Shandong Provincial Key Laboratory of Network Based Intelligent Computing, University of Jinan, Jinan 250022, China
{ise_mak,ise_linyz,ise_liuk,ise_zhouj,ise_dongjw}@ujn.edu.cn

Abstract. In response to the "Mass Entrepreneurship and Innovation", University of Jinan has built full-covered and hierarchical entrepreneurship and innovation education. In this paper, as a case of Computer Science and Technology of University of Jinan, the school-enterprise cooperative innovation and entrepreneurship courses and case library have been proposed under the support Entrepreneurship School. The course system considers both liberal and professional knowledge, improves interest in student participation, and reinforces school-government-enterprise cooperation. Some measures such as flipped classroom and achievement quality track have been taken to contribute innovation and entrepreneurship.

Keywords: Innovation · Entrepreneurship · School-enterprise · Emerging Engineering Education

1 Introduction

Recently, Chinese government has carried out several strategic matters including Innovation-Driven Development, Internet Plus, National Cyber Development. Against this background, Emerging Engineering Education (3E) is the industrial development direction of new engineering majors or new requirement of traditional majors [1,2].

Several universes set up courses of general education curriculum of innovation and entrepreneurship, and several universes reinforce practice ability training. Wuhan University has added 40 general courses including basic knowledge, basic ability, unique entrepreneurship, and practical experience [3]. Harbin Institute of Technology has added the required course of "Innovation and Entrepreneurship Education". This course affirms the course credit of scientific and technological achievements [4]. The development of this course makes students understand innovation and entrepreneurship methods. However, ubiquitous education ignore the professional ability of engineering. Zhenjiang University has setup

A. El Rhalibi et al. (Eds.): Edutainment 2018, LNCS 11462, pp. 263–267, 2019.
https://doi.org/10.1007/978-3-030-23712-7_36

professional innovation and entrepreneurship curriculum including professional general course, professional core course, and cutting-edge technology [5]. City University of Hong Kong has added courses of creativity guidance and business plan [6]. As a pilot, college of polytechnic has added result-driven innovation courses to improve the practical ability. Nowadays, the project-based method [7] is part of what is called authentic learning approaches in engineering case education. Students collaborate with each other to complete an authentic project. The improved project-based method is widely used [8]. In our previous study, the learning by doing method is such a typical case [9]. Universities strengthened the students' basis and improve their ability of practice using curriculum design, diploma project and cognitive learning in past few years. However, it gives insufficient weight to coordination skills in this way. On one hand, it massive work boosts pressure of students. On the other hand, duplicated task will efface the consciousness of innovation.

2 School-Enterprise Cooperative Innovation and Entrepreneurship Curriculum

Talent cultivation promotes entrepreneurship education and professional education to meet the needs of the society market. In computer science major of University of Jinan, we established School-Enterprise cooperative innovation and entrepreneurship course architecture. It includes basic course, professional course, and extra-curricular guidance. There are 3 layers of all courses. On the bottom, they are basic courses, including "Professional Career Guidance", "Innovation Thinking Training", "Innovation and Patent", "Demo China", and "Intellectual Property and Criterion of Academic Paper". Intermediately, they are professional courses, including "Program Development Foundation", "Database", "Software Engineering", and "Enterprise Software Development Process". On the top, it is extra-curricular guidance. Entrepreneurship School of University of Jinan provides expenditure and place support for students. Besides, some technical services such as entrepreneurship training, entrepreneurship incubation, entrepreneurship development are supported.

3 Innovations and Effects

3.1 Innovations

With the School-Enterprise cooperative project of Ministry of Education, University of Jinan collaborates with Amazon, Tencent, and Langchao to organize some technique sharing with our students. The software engineers help us appraise and elect excellent innovation project of students. The participation of domestic well-known enterprises gives students more incentive to learn knowledge. Besides, Entrepreneurship School is going to exploit Government-Enterprise cooperation to promote entrepreneurship. Enterprise R&D platform is introduced for students to do agile software development using user story, iteration plan, combustion diagram, and gated Launch. Students are converted into main subject of the class. The course teaching is innovated from class teaching and extra-curricular guidance. For class teaching, it takes multi-level combat exercise. Enterprise software engineers are invited to exchange experiences. For some courses, the project is from the engineering practice. Subject analysis, progress report, symposium are organized together. Entrepreneurship school helps us organize lectures and communications to foster entrepreneurship teams. Achievement are recognized as credits. The project is also extended to the final diploma project. For the team that has got finical support, we assess the progress of innovation and entrepreneurship. For entrepreneurship lectures, we invite professors, advanced engineers, and entrepreneur to participate the interaction.

3.2 Effects

From the year 2014, we begin to generalize School-Enterprise cooperative innovation and entrepreneurship courses and case library. We have made a survey on 4 kinds of students. Respondents are several graduates from 2016 to 2017. The number of graduates is 120, including 30 general graduates, 40 graduates who participate innovation and entrepreneurship, 40 graduates who are interested in tutorial system, 10 graduates who participate innovation only. The questionnaire was mainly distributed in the classroom, and the online questionnaire was supplemented by targeted email. 103 questionnaires were received, and the recovery rate was 85.8%. Table 1 is a survey of students' satisfaction with the innovation and entrepreneurship curriculum system. Four student types are #1 general graduates, #2 graduates who participate innovation and entrepreneurship, #3 graduates who are interested in tutorial system, and #4 graduates who participate innovation only. It is shown that the overall recognition of "Innovation and Entrepreneurship Courses and Case Library" is 82.5%. 13.6% of the students think "completely agree", 68.9% of the students think "basically agree", 13.6% of the students think "disagree", and 3.9% of the students think "completely disagree". It is shown that graduates who participate innovation and entrepreneurship has the highest satisfaction. These students are the beneficiary. It is also shown that graduates who participate innovation only has the lowest satisfaction. Therefore, it need to pay more attention to the students without success in entrepreneurship. Some students give us some suggestions: "Effect track of students", "Credit recognition of innovation and entrepreneurship prize and activity", and "Effect track of school-enterprise cooperation".

Table 1. Survey of students' satisfaction with the innovation and entrepreneurship.

Student type	Agree			Disagree			
	Completely agree	Basically agree	Subtotal	Disagree	Completely disagree	Subtotal	Total
1	2	19	21 (75%)	7	0	7 (25%)	28
2	9	27	36 (97.3%)	1	0	1 (0.7%)	37
3	2	23	25 (80.6%)	4	2	6 (19.4%)	31
4	1	2	3 (42.9%)	2	2	4 (57.1%)	7
Total	14 (13.6%)	71 (68.9%)	85 (82.5%)	14 (13.6%)	4 (3.9%)	18 (17.5%)	103

4 Conclusions

In response to the national strategy of innovation and entrepreneurship, we have proposed the solution of School-Enterprise cooperative innovation and entrepreneurship courses and case library of Emerging Engineering Education (3E). The course architecture includes basic courses, professional courses, and extra-curricular guidance. Case library increases the degree of participation. The results of several innovation and entrepreneurship achievements and results show that the scheme has achieved good results in innovation and entrepreneurship of University of Jinan.

Acknowledgments. This work was supported by the Industry-Academy Cooperative Education Project of Ministry of Education (201801002030 & 201701002017), the National Natural Science Foundation of China (61772231), the Guidance Ability Improving Program of Postgraduate Tutor in University of Jinan (YJZ1801), and the Teaching Research Project of University of Jinan (JZ1807).

References

1. Loh, E.Y.S., Ho, Y.H.: ICT implementation and its effect in engineering education. J. Emerg. Glob. Technol. **1**(2), 42–44 (2017)
2. Lucke, T., Dunn, P.K., Christie, M.: Activating learning in engineering education using ICT and the concept of 'Flipping the classroom'. Eur. J. Eng. Educ. **42**(1), 45–57 (2017)
3. Wang, Y., Li, Shanlin, Q.L.: Study on the design of the curriculum system of innovation and entrepreneurship in colleges and universities. In: 2017 Proceedings of Innovation and Entrepreneurship Education Annual Conference (2017)
4. Wang, Z.: Exploration and research on the construction of innovation and entrepreneurship curriculum system in Chinese universities. In: 2017 Proceedings of Innovation and Entrepreneurship Education Annual Conference (2017)
5. Chen, Y., He, M.: Data structure MOOC practice. China Univ. Teach. **2015**(12), 46–50 (2015)
6. Guo, W., Li, W., Zhong, C.: Program fight used for program design. Comput. Educ. **2012**(4), 55–58 (2012)

7. Kilpatrick, W.H.: The project method: the use of the purposeful act in the educative process, no. 3. Teachers College, Columbia University (1918)
8. Ma, K., Teng, H., Du, L., Zhang, K.: Exploring model-driven engineering method for teaching software engineering. Int. J. Continuing Eng. Educ. Life Long Learn. **26**(3), 294–308 (2016)
9. Ma, K., Teng, H., Du, L., Zhang, K.: Project-driven learning-by-doing method for teaching software engineering using virtualization technology. Int. J. Emerg. Technol. Learn. **9**, 26–31 (2014)

The Dilemma and Exploration of the Innovation of Internal Governance in Higher Education Institutions

Lei Sun[1(✉)] and Chunlin Li[2]

[1] School of Materials Science and Engineering, Northwestern Polytechnical University, Xi'an 710072, Shaanxi, China
sunlei@nwpu.edu.cn
[2] University Office, Northwestern Polytechnical University, Xi'an 710072, Shaanxi, China

Abstract. The construction of the world-class university and the world-class discipline makes a clear request to improve the system and ability of internal governance in higher education institutions. However, it is a common problems in colleges and universities in China, which the lag of institutional system, the serious imbalance between administrative power and academic power, the low efficiency of management. The negative list is an internationally accepted mode of foreign investment access management, which with the characteristics of law-based authority and responsibility, bottom-line management and shared governance. On the basis of clarifying the connotation and characteristics of the negative list, this paper gives some ideas for the introduction of negative list management in reform of internal governance in colleges and universities.

Keywords: The dilemma and exploration · Negative list management mode · Internal governance in higher education institutions

1 Introduction

In recent years, with the colligate reforms carried on in Chinese universities, new problems emerge because of the incompatibility of the fast development of universities and its old administration system. Therefore, there is an urgent demand to set up an internal governance system with clear responsibilities, complete supervision systems and scientific operations. It is believed that setting up this system is an inevitable choice to break the bottleneck of administration and to realize connotative development in "Double First Class Project". Negative list, a management tool and model in economics, takes a special position in improving the governance system. Currently, the research on negative list administration in universities is focusing on defining the range and responsibility of government and its sub-branches in administration, the ways to change the function of government in education management as well as how to increase autonomy of universities and etc. There is little study on negative list administration in university internal governance. Finding a solution to innovative

A. El Rhalibi et al. (Eds.): Edutainment 2018, LNCS 11462, pp. 268–274, 2019.
https://doi.org/10.1007/978-3-030-23712-7_37

improvement on internal governance of universities in reference with the idea and method of negative list administration is a topic worth exploring.

2 Problems and Difficulties Existing in Internal Governance of Universities

2.1 Regulative System Is Less Developed

Setting up a scientific regulative system is a primary requirement to strengthen the ability of university administration. On the one hand, the regulations on the national level could not specifically define the detailed structure and mechanism of internal governance in universities. On the other hand, in most Chinese universities, the systematic design of regulations is rather insufficient. Specific rules could not be made with the same pace of the national regulations. Some regulations could not realize their full functions. In addition, by influence of traditional model of administration, universities, to some extent, are still governed by men, but not by rules. Quite a number of universities are now managed by such force of "inertia".

2.2 Executive Power and Academic Power Are Out of Sync

Government has been used to adopting executive logic and bureaucratic management in governance of universities. Such administration has causes profound influence on the internal governance of universities. Administration should provide service and support for education, research, culture and innovation in universities. However, the idea "Official Rank Standard", (judging everything from the view of officials), which is very influential in reality usually causes the expansion of power in administration, but shrinking of power in academic issues. The academic organizations either on university level or on school level plays insufficient functions especially on academic issues. The students, the scholars and the academic issues are not given enough respect as cores of the university. Separate offices/divisions and their messy policies caused by bureaucratic management increase the cost of university operation and reduce the efficiency of management. In addition, some offices/divisions may extend their power by themselves to some extent, which caused coexistence of both "vacancy" and "offside" of power in administration.

2.3 Dominant Role of Schools Is Weak

Although schools, as organizations subordinated to universities, have some power in routine operation and finance issues, the main power is centralized on university level. Offices/divisions on behalf of the university possess the resources and have the power to evaluate the performance of schools. The offices/divisions of the university do not directly participate in teaching and research, but they possess the power to distribute teaching and research resources. It is schools that are organize the activities of teaching and research directly, while their power to deal with teaching and research resources is comparatively limited. Such "power and responsibility inversion" greatly influences the passion of schools to participate in administration and innovation [1].

3 Connotation and Feature of Negative List Administration

Negative list is an international popular administration model for foreign investment access. Its main idea is "to focus on the supervision after access, while the permit and approval before the access become supplementary". Such administration model simplifies or cancels the administrative approval system and adopts taking records system instead [2]. As a model of administration, making and running the negative list are helpful for regulators to have a clear boundary of their powers, and for the regulated to have a high efficiency and vitality in administration.

3.1 Change the Relationship Between Power and Responsibility from Ambiguity to Statutory

Governance by law is an important base for the modernization of administration system. It is also the primary meaning to improve administration ability. Compared with the executive mechanism (the executive power decides the qualification and the range of power that an organization possesses), negative list administration system takes laws and regulations as its unique standard to define the range of power and responsibilities [3].

3.2 Change Administration from "Versatile" Mode to "Bottom Line" Mode

The items marked with "red line" in negative list are the core interest of administrators in related areas and in certain time. This red line also sets the range for administrators—administrators should not interfere with the items outside the red line. Administrators on the one hand will streamline their authorities in condition that their core interests are guaranteed, on the other hand they should increase the supervision in and after the process of operation.

3.3 Change the Idea from Administration to Governance

During the time when planned economy is dominant, the relationship between regulators and the regulated appeared a kind of one way mode—"order and follow the order". In the frame of negative list administration, all the agents in the administrative group keep the relationship of "participation—joint governance". It is a multi-dimension interaction which requires coordination and conversation on mutual equal basis. Meanwhile, the loose regulative atmosphere in negative list administration brings all participants more sense of tolerance, which is the key to activating the governance system [3].

4 Functions and Mechanism of Negative List Administration in Internal Governance of Universities

4.1 It Is in Favor of Defining Power-Responsibility Relation and Maintaining Students, Scholars and Academic Issues in the Central Position

Administration power and academic power are two primary factors to internal governance in universities. They are also important pair-power in the operation of universities. Due to the traditional thought and the incomplete system, the place of academic power has been taken by administration power to a large extent. Making a negative list is a good way to define the range of power in administration. First sort out what items should be administrated and decided by universities (positive list). Then list in a negative way those items that administrators should not involve in or interfere with. And leave the items out of the range to the academic power. In this way, the academic power could be exerted independently. By taking the academic power back to the dominant position, the university will display its distinct characteristics as an academic organization.

4.2 It Is in Favor of Activating the Eagerness of Subordinated Units to Participate in Joint Governance

The reform of university-school double level administration refers to lowering the administrative center to set up a school-centered administration system by adjusting the distribution of the resources in universities and perfecting the power-responsibility relations [4]. The purpose of the reform is to make the responsibility of the university and it subordinated schools clear and to raise the efficiency and ability of administration. Although many universities are intended to set up the university-school double level administrative system, the problem that the power was still centralized on university level was not solved. The responsibilities which should be undertaken by schools were vacant. In negative list administration, university should define a "forbidden area" for schools. While in those "blank areas", those not in the "forbidden areas", schools have quite large freedom to exert their own powers. The university encourages the schools to explore the system boldly. Such administration could avoid either the power exceeding relative ranges or the reluctance to delegate powers. It also urges schools to innovate in management and realize its dominant position in administration based on its own characteristics and disciplines.

4.3 It Is in Favor of Raising Administrative Effectiveness and Service Ability

In the traditional administration, administrative goals are usually achieved by approvals, verifications and etc. to maintain the range of the power, to control the risks of the operation and to preserve the order of the organization. In the negative list administration, entry to administration becomes much easier and the process of approval and verification is simplified. The work of the offices/divisions changes from the approvals before the issue to the supervisions during and after the issue. It demands macro-adjustment and more concern on the problems above the bottom line. It not only enlarges the independent power of subordinated units, which makes them more active in the reform, but also changes the function of administrators from "managing" back to "serving". The administrators will have more time and energy to do the research and coordination in administration. The support and service to the subordinated units will become more specific and accurate.

5 Enlightenment of Negative List Administration to Internal Governance Innovation

5.1 Construct a Regulative System with Clear Power and Responsibilities Based on the University Charter

The university charter is the primary "law" of the university. It is the basis of defining the relationship between power and responsibility and of regulating all activities of the university. The first task to take the negative list administration is to clarify all the relations between the agents in universities. Therefore, all the regulations and rules should be examined to ensure that all the regulations and rules are in accordance with the university charter. The contents of the regulations and rules should be clear and standardized. At the same time, the university should strictly maintain the principal accountability under the leadership of Party committee. And the negotiating rules and process in Party committee, in the principal routine meetings and in the academic committees should be improved further. In order to construct a regulative system with clear power and responsibilities, other committees and leading groups should be removed or streamlined.

5.2 Clarify the Relationship Between Administration Power and Academic Power to Stress More Function of Academic Committees

According to the performance of the academic committees in universities as a whole, there are such problems as the academic committees not involving enough in academic activities; their execution of power being homogenous and the process of decision-making being for mere formality. Once the negative list administration is launched, all the academic evaluation activities and items in the respective offices/divisions will be publicized. All the criteria, process, conditions including the evaluators will be specified or explained in details. And all the "forbidden areas" for the offices/divisions in academic administration will be clearly defined. On the other side, the university will specify the responsibilities and limits of power of academic committees in developing disciplines, building academic spirit, evaluating academic activities and etc. The university shall pay more attention to the feasibility of the regulations to ensure the administration power has no or less influence on academic activities.

5.3 Define the Administrative Ranges of the University and Its Subordinated Schools to Consolidate the Dominant Position of Schools

Scientifically defining and separating the responsibilities and powers between the university and its subordinated schools are the preconditions of the university-school double level administrations and the core to improve the quality of administration in universities [5]. According to the negative list administration, there should be a clear separation of responsibilities and power between the university and the schools, in which the schools take the central position in university administration. The university will define, in a minimum principle, the "inaccessible areas" for the schools in the resources of human, financial, assets, and business areas. With more power goes to schools, schools will have more independence on the distribution of different resources [6]. The systems and regulations of schools should also be improved. More power will be catered to professors and scholars. The record system should be adopted, which means the schools could make their own policies in reforms and they only need to keep the record in related offices/divisions after the reforms. This is a way to increase the passion of schools to indulge in reforms. The offices/divisions should adjust their roles in administration. Their main task is to provide orientation and supportive service to schools to solve those problems emerging among all or most of the schools, therefore both the efficiency of administration and the service of offices/divisions could be fundamentally improved.

6 Conclusion

This paper explores the difficulty in the depth of internal governance of universities. It analyses the features and advantages of negative list administration. It is discovered that negative list is in favor of clarifying the boundaries of management, exerting powers scientifically, distributing power to schools, activating eagerness to participate in university governance. Negative list administration is good for the construction of a governance system which meets the requirement of modern universities to push the governance system and governance ability to higher modernization. This titanic and complicated process not only relies on the continuous improvement of the university external policy environment, but also requires that the university administrators should change from traditional methodology to modern ideology to push the reform of higher education system onto a higher stage.

References

1. Qin, D., Chen, X., Chen, W.: Some thoughts on promoting the modernization of China's University Governance Ability. J. Dong Hua Univ. (Soc. Sci.) (6), 55 (2014)
2. Zhou, G., Xu, M.: Reconstructing the relationship between university and government by introducing negative list administration. Chin. Univ. Sci. Technol. **11**, 9–10 (2014)
3. Zhang, S.: Interpretation of rule of law in negative list administration. Polit. Law **2**, 12 (2014)

4. Wang, H., Zhang, X.: Theory and practice of university-school two-level administration in universities. J. Chong Qing Jiaotong Univ. (Soc. Sci. Ed.) **2**, 100 (2010)
5. Chi, Y., Sun, Z.: Responsibilities and paths to realize university-school two-level administration under governance perspective. Educ. Explor. **4**, 63 (2016)
6. Yi, Y., Li, J.: Independent financial management: base of power in school substantialized universities. Jiang Su High. Educ. **5** (2001)

Interactive Web 3D Contents Development Framework Based on Linked Data for Japanese History Education

Chenguang Ma[1(✉)], Wei Shi[2], and Yoshihiro Okada[1,2(✉)]

[1] Graduate School of ISEE, Kyushu University, Fukuoka, Japan
okada@inf.kyushu-u.ac.jp
[2] Innovation Center for Educational Resources (ICER), Kyushu University, Fukuoka, Japan

Abstract. This paper treats Japanese history education as one of the activities of the center called ICER (Innovation Center for Educational Resources), Kyushu University. In this activity, one of the key challenges is the development of educational materials that attract students to Japanese history. As a first step, a database will be built that contains the Japanese history knowledge for the educational material development. So, the authors have already been building a database based on Linked Data. The other research agenda is to provide e-learning materials themselves using the database that attract students to Japanese history. The use of recent ICT (Information & Communication Technology) like 3D graphics enables e-learning materials to attract the students. In this paper, the authors propose interactive web 3D contents development framework based on Linked Data for Japanese history education.

Keywords: E-learning · Linked Data · Japanese history education · 3D graphics

1 Introduction

This paper discusses with one of the activities of our center called ICER (Innovation Center for Educational Resources). In this activity, we focus on Japanese history education and consider developing such educational materials like SPOC (Small Private Online Course), MOOC (Massive Open Online Course) and educational games. As a first step, we are building a database about Japanese history knowledge. If a database is built based on Linked Data, it becomes easy to update in terms of its contents and to share them easily with other researchers/educators. Therefore, we have already proposed the use of Linked Data in order to build a database about the IoT security information [1]. The next step is to provide e-learning materials about Japanese history using the database. Such materials should be attractive for students. The use of recent ICT (Information & Communication Technology) like 3D graphics enables e-learning materials to attract the students. We have already proposed a web-based interactive 3D educational contents development framework [2]. So, in this paper, we also propose the combinatorial use of this framework and the database of Japanese

A. El Rhalibi et al. (Eds.): Edutainment 2018, LNCS 11462, pp. 275–283, 2019.
https://doi.org/10.1007/978-3-030-23712-7_38

history knowledge realized as Linked Data, and introduce an interactive web 3D educational material for Japanese history education actually developed using the framework.

The remainder of this paper is organized as follows: Sect. 2 treats related work. In Sect. 3, we explain our Linked Data and implementation of RDF stores for Japanese history education, and introduce the overview of an authoring tool based on Linked Data for educational materials. Section 4 explains the web-based interactive 3D educational contents development framework and Sect. 5 introduces the interactive web 3D educational material for Japanese history. Finally, we conclude the paper and discusses our future work in Sect. 6.

2 Related Work

Berners-Lee coined the term Linked Data describing a set of best practices for publishing and connecting structured data on the Web [3, 4]. In the area of e-Learning, such data can be shared as learning objects (LO) or learning entities of any kind, respectively. Dicheva identifies three generations of Web-based educational systems [5]. The systems of the first generation provide a central entry-point for accessing learning materials and online course, e.g., LMS (Learning Management System) and educational portals. The systems of the second generation employ Web and AI technologies to support intelligently personalization and adaption. Such systems are called educational adaptive hypermedia systems. The third generation of Web-based educational systems is a class of ontology-aware software, using and enabling Semantic Web standards and technologies in order to grant scalability, reusability and interoperability of educational material that is distributed over the Web. Therefore, Linked Data technologies raise high expectations with respect to providing solutions in a field like e-Learning.

As for e-Learning material development systems supported by recent ICT like 3D graphics, there are many development systems and tools for 3D contents. Some of them are commercial products like 3D Studio Max, Maya, and so on. Although these products can be used only for creating 3D CG images or 3D CG animation movies, usually, these cannot be used for creating interactive contents. As a development system for 3D interactive contents, there is *IntelligentBox*, a constructive visual software development system for 3D graphics applications [6]. This system seems very useful because there have been many applications actually developed using it so far. However, it cannot be used for creating web-based contents. Although there is the web-version of *IntelligentBox* [7], it cannot be used for creating story-based contents. With *Webble World* [8], it is possible to create web-based interactive contents through simple operations for authoring and of course, possible to render 3D graphics assets. However, it does not have complete functionalities same as that of *IntelligentBox*.

There are some electronic publication formats like ePub, EduPub, iBooks and their authoring tools. Of course, these contents are used as e-Learning materials. However, basically, these do not support 3D graphics except iBooks. iBooks supports rendering functionality of a 3D scene and control functionality of its viewpoint. However, story-based contents cannot be created using it.

From the above situation, for creating web-based interactive 3D educational contents, we have to use any dedicated toolkit systems. The most popular one is Unity, one of the game engines, that also supports creating web-contents. Practically, using Unity, we have developed 3D educational contents [9, 10] for the medical course students of our university because Unity is a very powerful tool that supports many functionalities. However, the use of Unity requires any programming knowledge and skills of the operations for it. Therefore, it is impossible to use Unity for standard end-users like teachers. From the above reason, we proposed the framework [2] and extended it for supporting Linked Data [1].

3 Linked Data of Japanese History Knowledge

We stored the knowledge of Japanese history as Linked Data. We built up the RDF store for storing designed RDF data based on Apache Jena. Thereby, the integration and retrieval of Japanese history knowledge designed based on RDF by SPARQL, a query language for RDF store, are implemented.

3.1 Design of RDF Store for Japanese History Education

There are three steps in designing the Linked Data for Japanese history education. In the first step, we designed the schema of RDF store. An example of RDF store schema is shown in Fig. 1. As the figure shows, we designed a new prefix for Japanese history knowledge according to the RDF schema document. In the second step, an excel file of Japanese history knowledge is created according to the schema. In the third step, the excel file of Japanese history knowledge is converted to turtle format or RDF format by using OpenRefine, a free, open source, power tool for working with messy data.

3.2 Implementation of RDF Store for Japanese History Education

There are three steps for the implementation of RDF store of Japanese history education. In the first step, RDF store is built up based on Apache Jena, which is capable to store the integrated data as shown in Fig. 2. In the second step, the exported Turtle File of Japanese history knowledge is stored into the RDF store as shown in Fig. 3. In the third step, retrieval information of Japanese history through virtuoso (a server works as RDF store) by using the query language is able to be achieved as shown in Fig. 4.

3.3 Authoring Tool for Educational Materials of Japanese History

Figure 5 shows the screen image of our prototype system of an authoring tool [11]. By specifying a keyword 'kyuchu' (Imperial court) as the target of an educational material, the system retrieves text data, image data and video data related to the keyword from RDF stores. There are several candidate data for each of text, image and video so the user can choose one of them by the operation on [back], [next] buttons. In this way, by using the authoring tool, educational material developers are able to edit the contents of

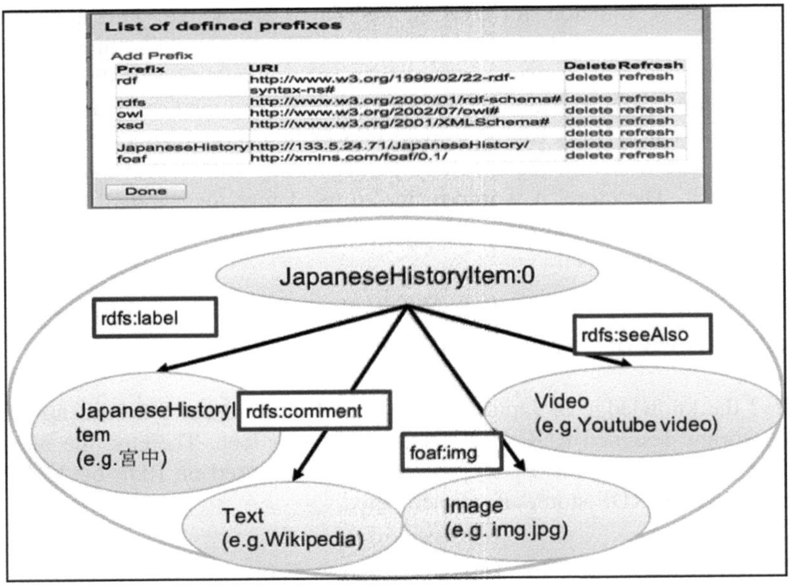

Fig. 1. RDF store schema for Japanese history education.

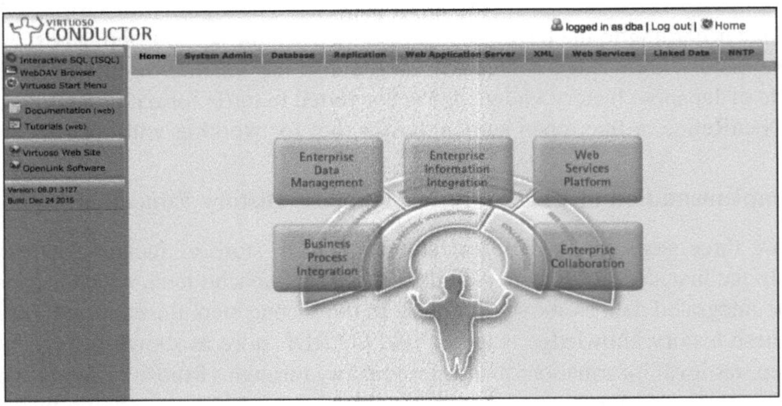

Fig. 2. Management of RDF data of Japanese history by virtuoso.

the material regarding Japanese history knowledge managed in RDF stores easily and efficiently.

After achieving the authoring of Japanese history educational materials, such educational materials are supposed to be shown as readable format like ePub/EduPub that facilitates the knowledge of Japanese history to be learned on the Web.

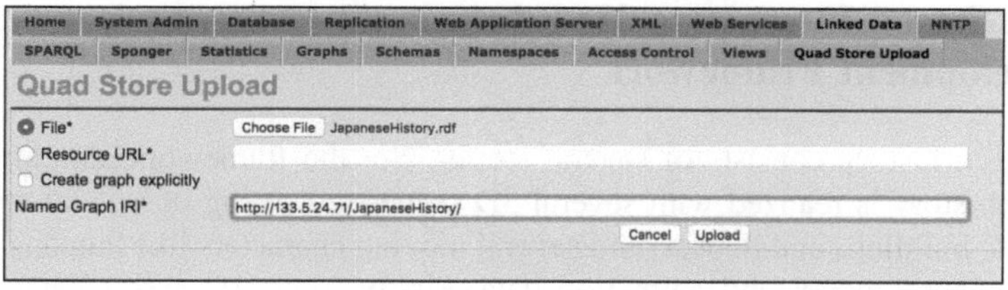

Fig. 3. Storage of RDF file.

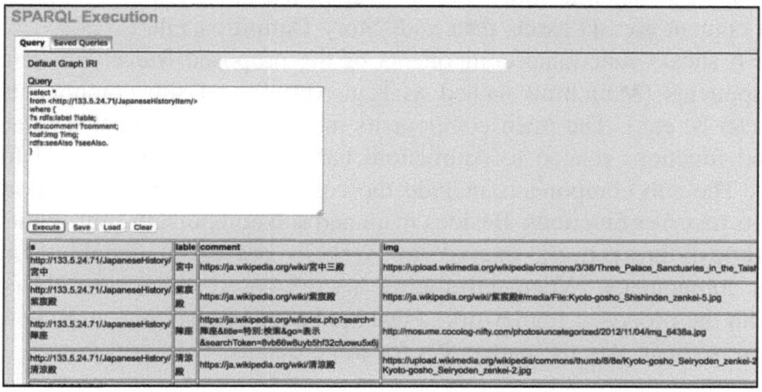

Fig. 4. Retrieval of RDF file.

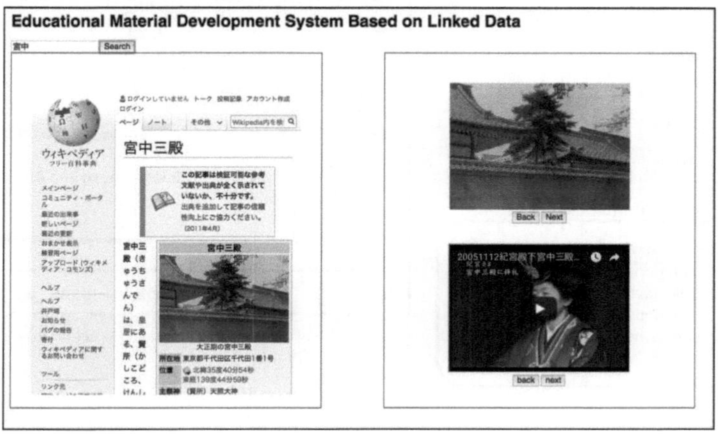

Fig. 5. Prototype system of authoring tool.

4 Web-Based Interactive 3D Educational Contents Development Framework

In general, a history consists of several stories. So, the framework should support a story. Each story is realized with several 3D scenes consisting of several architecture objects like buildings and houses, and several moving characters like humans who have their own shape model and animation data. Firstly, such 3D assets data should be prepared. Next, contents creators have to define a story for the content as one JavaScript file called 'Story Definition File', e.g., Kanso.js. 'Kanso' is a ceremony name was taken in the Imperial court. In our proposed framework, the requirements for creating a content are 3D assets data and 'Story Definition File'.

Figure 6 shows functional components of the proposed framework consisting of main components (Main.html named as Kanso.html) and sub components (AnimationCharacter.js, etc.). The main components include functions related to architecture objects and functions related to AnimationCharacter objects represented for moving characters. The sub components include the constructor of new AnimationCharacter class and its member functions. Besides main and sub components, our framework uses Three.js [https://threejs.org/], one of the WebGL based 3D Graphics Libraries as subsidiary components. When developing a story-based interactive 3D educational content with the proposed framework, a teacher has to prepare one story definition file and 3D assets for it. See the papers [2] for more details.

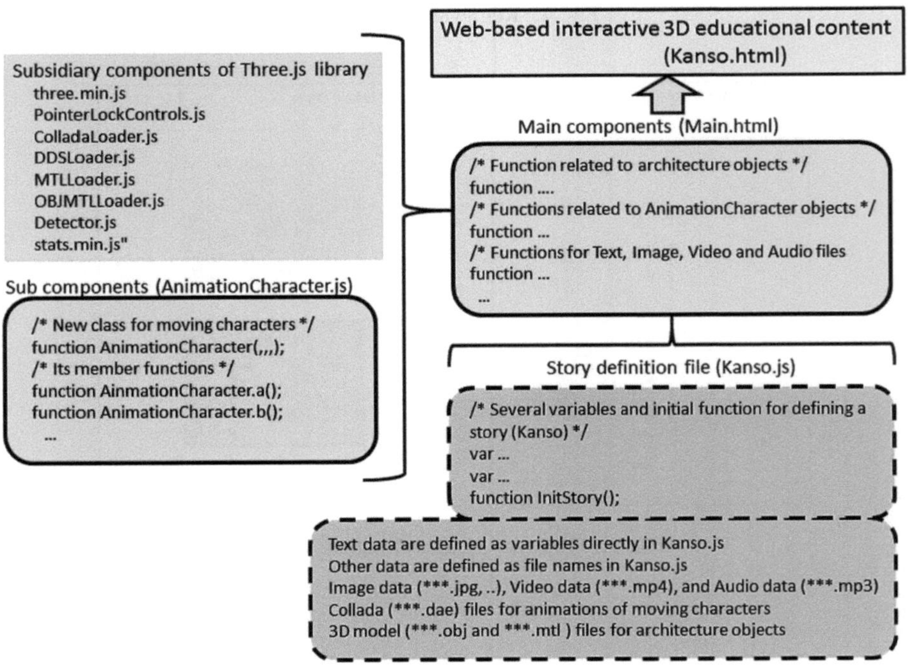

Fig. 6. Functional (Main and Sub) components of Framework about Kanso.html.

5 Interactive Web 3D Educational Material of Japanese History

As a case study, we have already developed an interactive web 3D educational material of Japanese history using the database of Japanese history knowledge realized as Linked Data and the development framework explained in Sect. 4. This is for teaching certain events and ceremonies taken in the Imperial court called 'Kyuchu', including ancient manners of the Emperor called 'Tennou' and Cabinet members called 'Daijin' and 'Daiben' and so on. Such ceremony is called 'Kanso'.

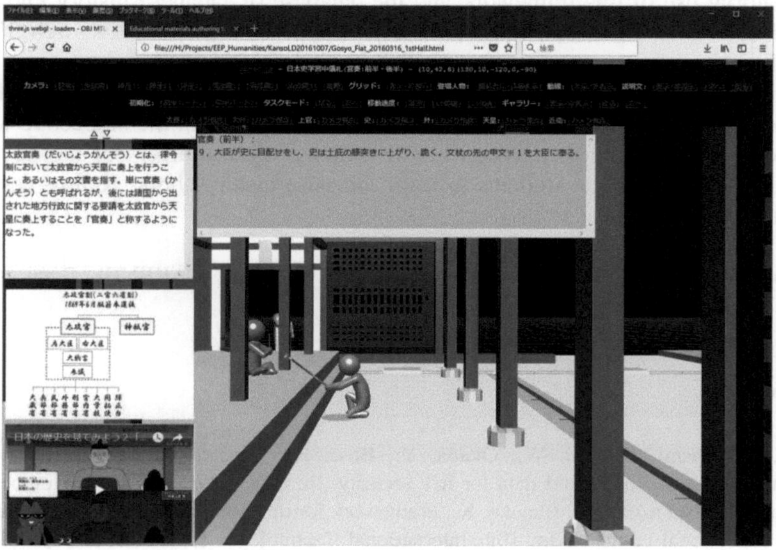

Fig. 7. A screenshot of the interactive web 3D educational material for 'Kanso'.

Figure 7 shows a screenshot of the interactive web 3D educational material for 'Kanso' executed on a PC browser. 'Kanso' includes various types of manners of 'Tennou' and 'Daijin, etc. In Japanese history education, students have to learn such manners by reading old documents about 'Kanso'. However, it is very difficult to understand the manners from the old documents because such documents written in an ancient calligraphy. With this interactive web 3D educational material of 'Kanso', it becomes easy for students to understand. Each moving characters are implemented as instances of AnimationCharacter class in JavaScript explained in Sect. 4. AnimationCharacter has its several animation data prepared as dae format files. For this content, we prepared around 100 dae format files. To reduce the cost to prepare these data files, we employ 3D human pictograms for the shapes of moving characters. Since their colors are different, it is possible to recognize each characters. The texts displayed in black color at the upper-middle position explain the behaviors of the moving characters. By reading the texts, the students can understand the manners in 'Kyuchu' more deeply with looking at the manners as 3D CG animations. If students click the mouse on any moving characters or architecture objects, its detail information will appear on the browser window as shown in the left part of the figure similarly to Fig. 5. In this way, the students will be able to learn 'Kanso' ceremony.

6 Conclusions

In this paper, we have treated a novel framework for the development of interactive web 3D educational materials about Japanese history. Especially, we proposed the combinatorial use of this framework and the database of Japanese history knowledge realized as Linked Data, and introduced a prototype of the interactive web 3D educational material for Japanese history.

As future work, we will complete the database as Linked Data for Japanese history education as soon as possible and will finish the development of the interactive web 3D educational material. Furthermore, we will evaluate the usefulness of the developed material by asking several students to learn Japanese history about 'Kanso' ceremony using it.

Acknowledgements. This research was supported by JSPS KAKENHI Grant Number JP16H02923 and JP17H00773.

References

1. Ma, C., Srishti, K., Shi, W., Okada, Y., Bose, R.: Educational material development framework based on linked data for IoT security. In: iCERi 2017, 16–18 November 2017
2. Okada, Y., Nakazono, S., Kaneko, K.: Framework for development of web-based interactive 3D educational contents. In: 10th International Technology, Education and Development Conference, pp. 2656–2663 (2016)
3. Berners-Lee, T.: Design issues for the World Wide Web. Architectural and "philosophical points" (1998)
4. Bizer, C., Heath, T., Berners-Lee, T.: Linked data - the story so far. In: Sheth, A. (ed.) Semantic Services, Interoperability and Web Applications: Emerging Concepts, pp. 205–227. IGI Global (2011). https://doi.org/10.4018/978-1-60960-593-3.ch008
5. Dicheva, D.: Ontologies and semantic web for e-learning. In: Adelsberger, H.H., Kinshuk, Pawlowski J.M., Sampson, D.G. (eds.) Handbook on Information Technologies for Education and Training. INFOSYS, pp. 47–65. Springer, Heidelberg (2008). https://doi.org/10.1007/978-3-540-74155-8_3
6. Okada, Y., Tanaka, Y.: IntelligentBox: a constructive visual software development system for interactive 3D graphic applications. In: Proceedings of Computer Animation 1995, pp. 114–125. IEEE CS Press (1995)
7. Okada, Y.: Web version of *IntelligentBox* (*WebIB*) and its integration with Webble World. In: Arnold, O., Spickermann, W., Spyratos, N., Tanaka, Y. (eds.) WWS 2013. CCIS, vol. 372, pp. 11–20. Springer, Heidelberg (2013). https://doi.org/10.1007/978-3-642-38836-1_2
8. Webble World

9. Sugimura, R., et al.: Mobile game for learning bacteriology. In: Proceedings of IADIS 10th International Conference on Mobile Learning, pp. 285–289 (2014)
10. Sugimura, R., et al.: Serious games for education and their effectiveness for higher education medical students and for junior high school students. In: Proceedings of 4th International Conference on Advanced in Information System, E-Education and Development (ICAISEED 2015), pp. 36–45 (2015)
11. Takubo, H.: Educational material development system based on linked open data. Graduation thesis. Faculty of Science, Kyushu University (2017). (in Japanese)

Collecting Visual Effect Linked Data Using GWAP

Shogo Hirai and Kaoru Sumi(✉)

Future University Hakodate, 116-2 Kameda, Hakodate-shi, Hokkaido, Japan
kaoru.sumi@acm.org

Abstract. We developed a game with a purpose (GWAP), which collects structured data corresponding to adjectives to build a visual effect dictionary. In this system, new semantic links can be acquired. Under the guise of a fighting game, the system encourages the user to vote on the commonsense knowledge associated with an object, because our previous research indicated that the rules of showing appropriate visual effect according to the adjective is related to commonsense knowledge of the target object. This system displays visual effects on the target object and the data structure is updated based on user's vote. This structured data underlies a new type of communication support system that continuously improves visual effects that modify adjectives and objects. In this paper, we discuss the structure of the visual effect dictionary through an experiment. Findings show that GWAP effectively improves the relationship between commonsense knowledge and objects, while creating new linkages via deduction.

1 Introduction

We introduce a game with a purpose (GWAP), which collects structured data corresponding to adjectives to build a visual effect dictionary. GWAP is a game that achieves a higher purpose with the by-product of game play. The purpose is to collect structured data recalled from a combination of adjectives and an object, while users play an enjoyable game. Even with the same adjective, visual effects differ, depending on the object it modifies. For example, in the case of the adjective, "delicious," "delicious apple" may recall a fruit with a glossy effect. However, "delicious ramen" may recall a ramen dish with a steam effect.

The system builds new links of the data, as well. From an impression evaluation experiment, the combination of the visual effects "steam" and "warm food," correlate to the expression of the word "delicious." Additionally, the visual effects, "glow" and "artifacts," correlate to the expression of the word "new" according to our previous research [1]. Therefore, when considering a visual effect expressing a modifier, commonsense knowledge, such as "warm," can be used to express the state of the related object. We developed a system to acquire commonsense knowledge about objects from users and to evaluate the validity of visual effects. However, because is difficult to acquire straightforward commonsense knowledge from humans, ingenuity was necessary. Thus, we developed a system that collects commonsense knowledge through a simple game interface.

A. El Rhalibi et al. (Eds.): Edutainment 2018, LNCS 11462, pp. 284–292, 2019.
https://doi.org/10.1007/978-3-030-23712-7_39

In this paper, we describe the proposed mechanism of GWAP, and we describe the experiment through a prototype.

2 Related Work

From visualization studies about converting words to visual objects, methods of converting text to pictures, text to scenes, and text to animations have been developed. Our research leverages a database of text-to-pictures conversions, with visual effects.

From the research of converting text to pictures and photos, the Story Picturing Engine [2, 3] converts a written story into a picture or a photo, displaying ranked images related to the nouns, adjectives, adverbs, and verbs as keywords. TTP [4] is a system that extracts common and proper nouns and adjectives from text and synthesizes new pictures, combining several images.

In the early studies of converting text to scenes, NALIG [5] and PUT [6] arranged 2D objects based on subjects, verbs, objects, etc. WordsEye [7] searches for and outputs objects, characters, and places related to common and proper nouns from a repository of 3-dimensional (3D) models. In this system, attributes (e.g., color) are modified by an adjective, and the action and pose of the 3D model are determined from the verb. AVDT [8] is a system that generates 3D scenes from natural language texts with detailed spatial explanations, including prepositions and several objects. Visualization of spatial relations is realized by assigning metadata expressing position to the preposition. There is also a system that visualizes implicitly related information [9–11]. For example, it is possible to output a desk from the expression, "there is a computer and a chair in the room."

In an early study about converting text to animation, SHRDLU moved building blocks around on a screen using natural language. This is now a well-known paradigm [12]. Kairai [13] is a system targeting more complicated movements and linguistic expressions. It expresses sound information as 3D objects. Kairai is a natural language understanding system that focuses on spoken words, such as "little" or "pretty" on a 3D space. Expressions about distances and colors, such as "far" and "blue," about adjective expressions are also possible. Anime de Blog [14–16] creates images by combining a character as a subject, character movements as its movements, 3D objects as word objects, and a background image as place information.

The visual expression of the modifier, as in this research, relates to the impression of the individual image. However, the expression method itself is difficult. In previous studies, adjective representation concerning the color of the object was handled, but there has been no research that uses the modifier as the main target.

Thus, to collect a semantic structure without conscious user intervention, a GWAP-like system, Open Mind Common Sense [17], was created to develop a commonsense knowledge base using input from thousands of people via the Web. ConceptNet [18] is a semantic network based on Open Mind Common Sense database information. Japanese Open Mind Common Sense, "*Na-ja to nazonazo*," is another GWAP-like model for collecting commonsense knowledge [19]. It is a game that teaches commonsense knowledge while offering quiz games with a female host. The goal is to attain Japanese ConceptNet data by acquiring commonsense knowledge possessed by

Japanese words. In that research, visual effects were developed to acquire commonsense knowledge. Using this structured data, it was possible to more clearly visualize Japanese with abstract expressions.

3 Visual Effect Dictionary System

We developed a visual effects dictionary that can express images of words, such as adjectives, by adding 3D objects to a visual effect. Figure 1 shows a screenshot of the visual effect dictionary system. The system converts given audio information into a visual effect and a 3D object. The recognized speech information is classified into "adjective" and "noun" by an NMeCab system. NMeCab is a morphological analysis engine of the .NET library. The IBM Watson Natural Language Classifier (NLC) classifies audio information using pre-trained classifiers. According to the classified information, the "adjective" is converted into a visual effect, and the "noun" is converted into a 3D object. It is known that the visual effect differs, depending on the object, but because this system does not have that knowledge, when the user changes only the noun with the same adjective, it is impossible to reflect the appropriate visual effect. Therefore, we developed GWAP to acquire linked data about the connection between adjectives and nouns for this dictionary.

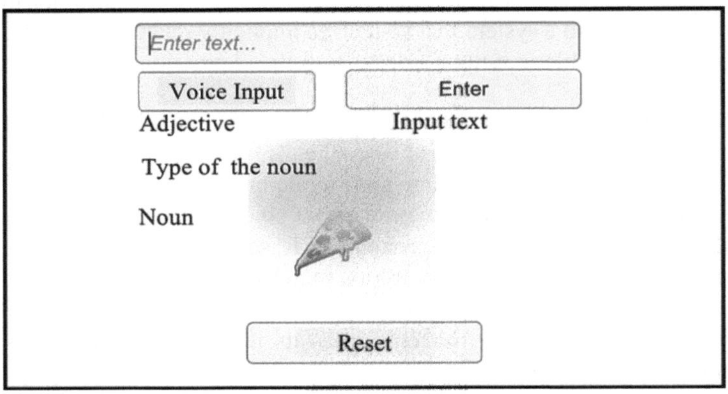

Fig. 1. Visual effect dictionary system

4 GWAP Collecting Linked Data

Figure 2 shows the flow of the system. According to the impression evaluation experiment, the combination of the visual effects, "steam" and "warm food," are correlated to the expression of the word "delicious," and the visual effects, "light" and "artifacts," are correlated to the expression of the word "new" [1].

Therefore, it is necessary to acquire commonsense knowledge from these correlations. However, it is a difficult task to have the user input commonsense knowledge in

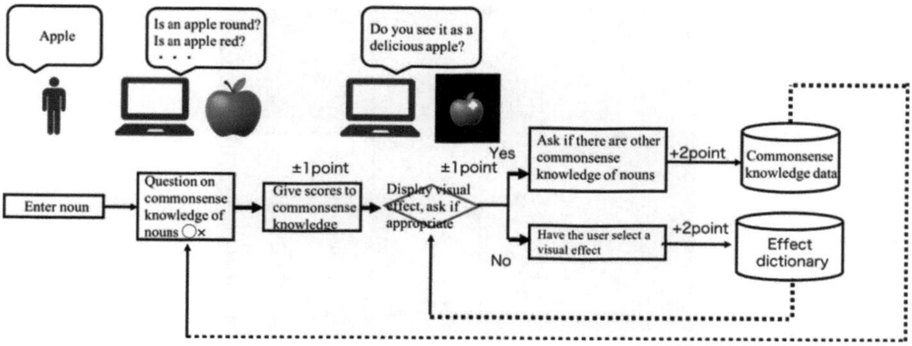

Fig. 2. System flow

a straight forward way. Thus, if there is an interface that can prompt the appropriate input while the user enjoys a game, we could motivate the user to provide the needed input. This research uses the data obtained from GWAP to create a link structure between a new visual effect and words that classify adjectives as abstract expressions.

In this example, the adjective "delicious" is targeted while the user plays the "Effect Game." First, the system presents "enter delicious food." The user inputs a specific noun corresponding to food. A 3D emoji object is used. Next, for the input noun, the system asks an ○/× question while showing the image of that noun. For example, "Is it a fruit?" The commonsense knowledge used for the question is of the following three varieties: (1) hypernym of WordNet [20], which is the broad meaning of a noun; (2) a combination of visual effects and adjectives obtained from experiments [1]; and (3) a new commonsense knowledge acquired from users. After the ○/× question is complete, the system selects a visual effect having a high score from those of commonsense knowledge of ○. There are nine types of visual effects. For the selection method, we select nine visual effects related to the image of the adjective "delicious," and we use input from the player to evaluate whether the visual effect seems to look delicious. The ○/× screenshot are shown in Fig. 3. Figure 4 shows a screenshot where the player defeated the enemy. Figure 5 shows examples of visual effects. The system asks the player, "Do you think the effect is appropriate?" in a Yes/No format. For example, when the player inputs "apple," the commonsense knowledge of "apple" is retrieved from the database. When the commonsense knowledge "round" is the highest score, the question is asked, "is the apple round?"

In this manner, the score of commonsense knowledge obtained from the user is also stored to the database. To ask whether the visual effect is appropriate, the system displays different visual effects, depending on the nouns. When "Yes" is selected, the data is saved as a score. Based on the score, it is possible to display different visual effects, depending on nouns, even for the same adjective. Therefore, by asking the user whether the selected visual effect is appropriate, a visual effect with many "Yes" selections results in an appropriate pairing with the noun. The data obtained for each question is as follows.

Fig. 3. The screen of O/× quiz

Fig. 4. The screen having defeated the enemy

- O/× Format: asking whether the combination of noun and commonsense knowledge is appropriate.
- Yes/No Format: asking whether the combination of visual effect and noun is appropriate.
  - In case of Yes: Acquiring a new commonsense knowledge possessed by a noun.
  - In case of No: Acquiring a new combination of visual effects from the player.

O/× and Yes/No formats are presented via the commonsense knowledge having the highest score. Thus, the problem is different every time the game is played. Table 1 shows the database format of the system.

Every time the user selects "O," the score is incremented by 1. In the case of "Yes," the system acquires unknown commonsense knowledge possessed by the noun. In the case of "No," the system acquires a new combination of visual effects provided by the player. Because these scores are evaluated directly by the player, two points are added.

The player must answer the quiz before the enemy arrives to the main character. If the answer to the quiz is not the same opinion as many users, the player cannot defeat

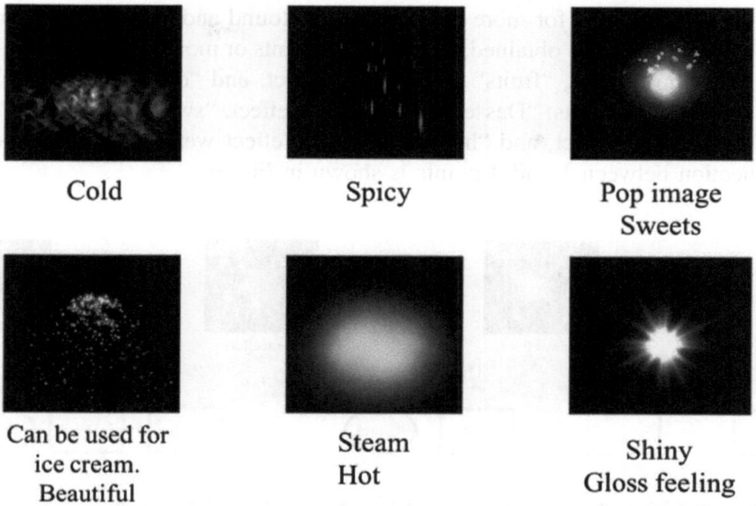

Fig. 5. Examples of visual effect

Table 1. System database format

O/× format	Food	Commonsense knowledge	Score
Yes/No format	Commonsense knowledge	Visual effect	Score

the enemy. If all the quiz questions are answered, the main character will emit an attack beam. The attack power of this beam is based on the ratio of O and × of the score of the combination of commonsense knowledge and effect. Thus, the higher the ratio, the stronger the attack. The intensity of the beam increases from 0 to 100, and it correlates to the percentage of O or ×. A player can defeat the enemy with a beam attack power of 90 or higher.

5 Experiment and Result

We provide the results of six people having played the GWAP. Each subject played the game by inputting the words, "apple," "orange," "cake," "dumplings," "pizza," "curry and rice," "ice cream," and "soft cream." In this experiment, we structured part of the data obtained from subjects. The structured data is shown in Fig. 6. Long red lines indicate more than 5 points. Gray dotted lines indicate between 1 and 4 points. Blue dotted and short lines indicate negative points. Squares indicate commonsense knowledge registered in the database. Round shapes indicate commonsense knowledge gained from users. With the O/× format, "fruits" and "apple," "fruits" and "orange," and "round" and "orange" all have more than 5 points. Additionally, regarding "dish," it was decided that "dish" and "pizza," "dish" and "dumpling," and "dish" and "curry and rice" were connected for more than 5 points. "Round and orange" and "spicy and curry rice" were new links obtained, each being 5 points or more. In the Yes/No format, "dish" and "shiny" effect, "fruits" and "shiny" effect, and "dish" and "steam" effect grew to more than 5 points. "Dessert" and "steam" effect, "sweet" and "steam" effect, "fruits" and "steam" effect, and "hot" and "shiny" effect were negative connections. The connection between 1 and 4 points is shown in Fig. 6.

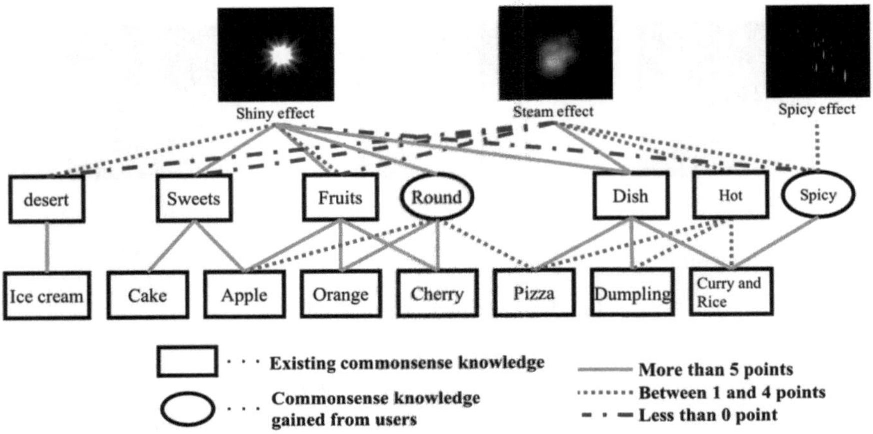

Fig. 6. Structured data from results (Color figure online)

6 Discussion

In this paper, we introduced the GWAP, which uses visual effects to acquire structured data and unknown commonsense knowledge. Experimental results suggested that there was a positive correlation with multiple commonsense knowledge related to the "shiny" effect. In WordNet, "curry" and "pizza" appeared under "dish," but there was no visual effect link. In our proposed effect dictionary, these are not only linked, the word "hot" is also linked to the "steam" effect. Additionally, in our system, commonsense knowledge, such as "hot" and "spicy" were newly obtained. In the case of "hot," the "steam" effect was appropriate, and in the case of "spicy," the "spicy" effect was appropriate. For "fruits," the "shiny" effect, "sweet" and "shiny" effect, and "round" and "shiny" effect were all positive associations suggested. The structure will be changed dynamically the more the player uses it.

In the future, by expanding the types of nouns, we can clarify the image and the structure of words to be remembered by adjectives. We believe that, by using the effect dictionary, communication support will be provided. For example, in cross-cultural communication, expressions of Japanese adjectives can be represented by subtle wording and visual effects.

There are some limitations in this system. When the player inputs unregistered noun information, the object will not be displayed. Unless an emoji is prepared for every noun, this problem cannot be solved. Additionally, there are not very many visual effects. To create more flexible visual effects for players to use, a mechanism (e.g., consumer generated media) is required.

References

1. Hirai, S., Sumi, K.: Visual-effect dictionary for converting words into visual images. In: Munekata, N., Kunita, I., Hoshino, J. (eds.) ICEC 2017. LNCS, vol. 10507, pp. 177–182. Springer, Cham (2017). https://doi.org/10.1007/978-3-319-66715-7_18
2. Joshi, D., Wang, J.Z., Li, J.: The story picturing engine: finding elite images to illustrate a story using mutual reinforcement. In: Proceedings of the 6th ACM SIGMM International Workshop on Multimedia Information Retrieval, pp. 119–126 (2004)
3. Joshi, D., Wang, J.Z., Li, J.: The story picturing engine—a system for automatic text illustration. ACM Trans. Multimed. Comput. Commun. Appl. (TOMM) **2**(1), 68–89 (2006). https://doi.org/10.1145/1126004.1126008
4. Zhu, X., Goldberg, A.B., Eldawy, M., Dyer, C.R., Strock, B.: A text-to-picture synthesis system for augmenting communication. In: AAAI 2007, vol. 7, pp. 1590–1595 (2007)
5. Adorni, G., Manzo, M.D., Ferrari, G.: Natural language input for scene generation. In: Proceedings of the First Conference on European Chapter of the Association for Computational Linguistics, pp. 175–182 (1983)
6. Clay, S.R., Wilhelms, J.: Put: language-based interactive manipulation of objects. IEEE Comput. Graphics **16**(2), 31–39 (1996). https://doi.org/10.1109/38.486678
7. Miller, G.: WordNet: An Electronic Lexical Database. Edited by C. Fellbaum. A Bradford Book, Cambridge (1998)
8. Spika, C., Schwarz, K., Dammertz, H., Lensch, H.P.A.: AVDT-automatic visualization of descriptive texts. In: VMV, pp. 129–136 (2011)
9. Chang, A., Savva, M., Manning, C.: Interactive learning of spatial knowledge for text to 3D scene generation. In: Proceedings of the Workshop on Interactive Language Learning, Visualization, and Interfaces, pp. 14–21 (2014)
10. Chang, A., Savva, M., Manning, C.: Semantic parsing for text to 3D scene generation. In: Proceedings of the ACL 2014 Workshop on Semantic Parsing, pp. 17–21 (2014)
11. Chang, A., Savva, M., Manning, C.D.: Learning spatial knowledge for text to 3D scene generation. In: Proceedings of the 2014 Conference on Empirical Methods in Natural Language Processing (EMNLP), pp. 2028–2038 (2014)
12. Winograd, T.: Understanding Natural Language. Academic Press, Cambridge (1972)
13. Tanaka, H., Tokunaga, T., Shinyama, Y.: Animated agents capable of understanding natural language and performing actions. In: Prendinger, H., Ishizuka, M. (eds.) Life-Like Characters. COGTECH, pp. 429–443. Springer, Heidelberg (2004). https://doi.org/10.1007/978-3-662-08373-4_18
14. Sumi, K.: Anime de blog: animation CGM for content distribution. In: Proceedings of International Conference on Advances in Computer Entertainment Technology (ACE2008), pp. 187–190 (2008)
15. Sumi, K.: Animation-based interactive storytelling system. In: Spierling, U., Szilas, N. (eds.) ICIDS 2008. LNCS, vol. 5334, pp. 48–50. Springer, Heidelberg (2008). https://doi.org/10.1007/978-3-540-89454-4_8
16. Sumi, K.: Capturing common sense knowledge via story generation. In: Common Sense and Intelligent User Interfaces 2009: Story Understanding and Generation for Context-Aware Interface Design, 2009 International Conference on Intelligent User Interfaces (IUI2009), SIGCHI ACM, February 2009

17. Singh, P., Lin, T., Mueller, E.T., Lim, G., Perkins, T., Li Zhu, W.: Open mind common sense: knowledge acquisition from the general public. In: Meersman, R., Tari, Z. (eds.) OTM 2002. LNCS, vol. 2519, pp. 1223–1237. Springer, Heidelberg (2002). https://doi.org/10.1007/3-540-36124-3_77
18. Speer, R., Havasi, C.: Representing general relational knowledge in ConceptNet 5. In: LREC, pp. 3679–3686 (2012)
19. OMCS: Japanese Open Mind Common Sense (2010). http://omcs.jp. Accessed 14 Feb 2018. (in Japanese)
20. Princeton University: About WordNet. https://wordnet.princeton.edu. Accessed 19 Dec 2017

E-learning Rhythm Design: Case Study Using Fighting Games

Shuo Xiong[1(✉)], Long Zuo[2(✉)], Zeliang Zhang[3], Shuo Zhang[3], and Hiroyuki Iida[3]

[1] School of Journalism and Information Communication, Huazhong University of Science and Technology, Wuhan, China
xiongshuo@hust.edu.cn

[2] School of Information Engineering, Chang'an University, Xi'an, China
zuolong@chd.edu.cn

[3] School of Information Science, Japan Advanced Institute of Science and Technology, Nomi, Japan
{zhangzeliang,zhangshuo,iida}@jaist.ac.jp

Abstract. Gamification and E-learning are the application of game-based elements and game design techniques. Many entertainment and learning platforms have applied gamification to increase motivation and engagement. Game refinement theory is a new game theory which concerns about the entertaining aspects of games using a game sophistication measure that is derived from a game progress model; it can judge the game quality. This paper analyzes the fighting game, which is a kind of video games where two on-screen characters fight with each other. The game refinement measure is employed for the assessment of the game sophistication of fighting games in different types. The analyzed results show the evolutionary changes of the fighting games. Also, it can show the experience of suitable E-learning rhythm. In the future, the human can use this method to design the target e-learning platform become more comfortable and reasonable.

Keywords: Game refinement theory · Fighting game · E-learning rhythm · Game design

1 Introduction

Gamification is a term that refers to the use of game-based elements such as mechanics, aesthetics, and game thinking in non-game contexts aimed at engaging people, motivating action, enhancing learning and solving problem [4]. In recent years, the gamification was commonly used in education or entertainment areas. Now we have an important research question is "How to make the education system more interesting or attractive", if the designer cannot control the rhythm well, the user may feel the system is too boring, what lost the value of gamification. On the other hand, if the game is too relax, the user may feel

A. El Rhalibi et al. (Eds.): Edutainment 2018, LNCS 11462, pp. 293–302, 2019.
https://doi.org/10.1007/978-3-030-23712-7_40

fewer challenge [15], seems like the complete leisure. Therefore, we have chosen one reliable mathematical measurement to design the system rhythm.

Duy Huynh has used the game refinement theory to analyze the E-learning system – Duolingo [4], which is one of the most popular language learning platforms by applying game refinement theory. Due to the lack of research on the gamification in the education domain, numerous questions arise as to clarify how gamification can be used and how it benefits us the most.

In Duy's paper "Analyzing Gamification of Duolingo with Focus on Its Course Structure", he highlights a gamification structure in each language course as the main aspect. The structure of language course is constructed by some core elements such as lesson and skill. Furthermore, Duy following the basic idea of game refinement theory to analyze the game progress by twofold elements, one is the goal of learners, which is to complete their study by getting all badges in the skill-tree. To archive a badge, users must complete all lessons in a skill. According to the analysis result, we can find the advantage and weakness of Duolingo E-learning system; the designer can study the analysis report to enhance the learning software. For the mechanism of game refinement theory in detail, we will introduce it in Sect. 2.

2 Mechanism and Method

We review the early work of game refinement theory from [5]. The decision space is the minimal search space without forecasting. It provides the common measures for almost all boardgames. The dynamics of decision options in the decision space has been investigated and it is observed that this dynamics is a key factor for game entertainment. Thus a measure of the refinement in games was proposed [6].

Later, the following works are sketched from [9,11] that expands the model of game refinement which was cultivated in the domain of boardgames into continuous movement games such as sports games and video games.

The game progress is twofold. One is game speed or scoring rate, while another one is game information progress with a focus on the game outcome. Game information progress presents the degree of certainty of a game's result in time or steps. Having full information of the game progress, i.e. after its conclusion, game progress $x(t)$ will be given as a linear function of time t with $0 \leq t \leq t_k$ and $0 \leq x(t) \leq x(t_k)$, as shown in Eq. (1). Then we get the derivation of this function by twice to get the accleration as Eq. (2).

$$x(t) = \frac{x(t_k)}{t_k}\, t \tag{1}$$

$$R = \frac{\sqrt{x(t_k)}}{t_k}\sqrt{n(n-1)} = C\frac{\sqrt{x(t_k)}}{t_k} \tag{2}$$

We show, in Table 1, measures of game refinement for various games [8,12,14]. From the results, we conjecture the relation between the measure of game refinement and game sophistication, as stated in Remark 1.

Remark 1. Sophisticated games have a common factor (i.e., same degree of informational acceleration value, say 0.07–0.08) to feel engaged or excited regardless of different type of games.

Table 1. Measures of game refinement for various types of games

Game	$x(t_k)$	t_k	R
Chess	35	80	0.074
Shogi	80	115	0.078
Go	250	208	0.076
Basketball	36.38	82.01	0.073
Soccer	2.64	22	0.073
Badminton	46.336	79.344	0.086
Table tennis	54.863	96.465	0.077
DotA ver 6.80	68.6	106.2	0.078
StarCraft II Terran	1.64	16	0.081

3 Analysis of Fighting Game

The fighting game is a video game sub-genre of action games, in which the player can find and control an favorite on-screen character and engages in exciting and thrilling close combat with an opponent which can be either an AI or controlled by another player. Because of its magnificent battle scenes, gorgeous battle stages and distinctive characters, it has even gained great popularity in the arcade period. But meanwhile in the fast game pace, it requires the players extremely difficult accuracy on the command inputting and rapid response to the opponent's action, so it is very hard to gain the entertainment for a new player and need players cost much time to practice on it. In this period of varieties of games compete and perform, the fighting game would soon be bored by the new players. So it loses its popularity gradually. The game refinement is a measurement of game sophistication. It was used in many papers reported recently to know the characteristic and evolutionary changes of the games in its history.

3.1 Historical Overview of Fighting Games

First of all, we overview the history of the fighting game as Table 2 shows, next we introduce the fighting game in details and then research the present popular fighting games using the Game Refinement Measure. At last we purpose the improvement and future perspective to the fighting game according to the present situation.

Table 2. A brief history of Fighting Games

Fighting Game	Year	Platform	Feature
Heavyweight Champ	1976	ARCADE	The first video fighting game
Karate Champ	1984	ARCADE	Establishing the one-on-one fighting game genre
Yie Ar Kung Fu	1985	FC	Player could perform up to sixteen different moves
Street Fighter	1987	ARCADE	Use the special moves and the game controls
Fatal Fury	1991	NEOGEO	Placed more emphasis on storytelling
Samurai Spirits	1993	NEOGEO	Famous for The warrior fought by weapons
Street FighterII	1991	SFC	Execute multi-button special moves reliably
Virtua Fighter	1993	SS	The first 3D fighting game
The King of Fighters '94	1994	NEOGEO	Crossover characters from SNK's fighting game
Mortal Kombat 3	1995	MD	Famous for its cruelty and bloody
The King of Fighters '97	1997	NEOGEO	Famous for its fierce rhythm
The King of Fighters '2002	2002	NEOGEO	The ninth game in The King of Fighters series
Virtua Fighter 5	2006	PS3	The fifth game in The Virtua Fighter series. First game in PS3
Dead or Alive 5	2012	PS3	The first DOA game to have multi-platform release
The King of Fighters XIV	2016	PS4	The first KOF game rendered entirely in 3D
TEKKEN 7	2017	PS4	The ninth game in the Tekken series

The earliest fighting games in the Japanese arcade scene were Sega's 1976 Heavyweight Champ, a boxing game, and a smattering of karate or kung-fu related games such as Karate Champ (1984) and Yie Ar Kung Fu (1985) that simulated realistic competitive martial arts [3]. 1979s Warrior is another title sometimes credited as one of the first fighting games. In contrast to Heavyweight Champ and most later titles, Warrior was based on sword fighting duels and used a bird's eye view [10]. Karate Champ from 1984 is credited with establishing and popularizing the one-on-one fighting game genre. In it, a variety of moves could be performed using the dual-joystick controls, it used a best-of-three matches format like later fighting games, and it featured training bonus stages [2].

Later, the release of Street Fighter II in 1991 is considered a revolutionary moment in the fighting game genre by Japanese company Capcom. Street Fighter II featured highly stylized characters, each with a repertoire of special techniques. It was also responsible for popularizing the combo mechanic, which came about when skilled players learned that they could combine several attacks that left no time for the opponent to recover if they timed them correctly [2].

The King of Fighters (KOF) series was a fighting game invented by SNK. KOF 97 has built the highest record of coin dropping in one week in Japan, what is not enough that it has an impressive impact in mainland of China and the hurl of this game is not evaded even right now. The player can choose the character to make the team, they also have special acting in other series of this game.

However, the Street Fighter or The King of the Fighters – and the many similar games it inspired across different developers and technology – are specifically what is known as "2D fighters". In a 2D fighter, there is no third dimension for on-screen action to move in. In order to compete with 2D fighting games, Sega created their Virtua Fighter games in 1993. Although they maintained many of the same aspects of Street Fighter that were critical – life gauges, special attacks, stylized characters, and a focus on 1-on-1 martial arts competition – the designers of Virtua Fighter used polygon rather than sprite-based graphics, producing 3D art rather than 2D art. Inside the game, players of Virtua Fighter could not only move left and right, but also around the battlefield itself. It became possible to win not just by knocking out one's opponent, but also by hurling them out of the proscribed arena, a type of win that would come to be known as a "ring out" [1]. For these games, we can find the sell volume and popularity as Table 3 shows.

Table 3. Sell volume for each game

Game	Sell volume
Tekken 3	8.5 million
Street Fighter II: The World Warriors	6.3 million
Mortal Kombat X	5 million
Street Fighter II Turbo	4.1 million
Mortal Kombat (2011)	4 million
Tekken	44 million
Street Fighter	39 million
Mortal Kombat	37 million
Soulcalibur	12 million

3.2 Mechanism of Fighting Games

Drawing on both the historical examples of fighting games, as well as the ways in which the genre is conceptualized, following definition have been made for a fighting game [3]:

- Close-quarters combat: For the most part, fighting games involve physical combat between the on-screen characters. Elements of that combat might involve projectile attacks – for example, the "Hadouken" signature projectile of SF series regular Ryu – but in general, as Wolf asserts, the focus of the game is not on out-shooting the opponent; projectiles are part of a broader context of enabling close combat [3].
- Standard techniques and special attacks: Characters in fighting games typically have two sets of "moves:" standard punches, kicks, and throwing techniques, and "special" moves that are performed through specific and more complex controller maneuvers [3].
- Quantifying of match parameters: Fighting games offer visual cues on the screen (commonly called the heads-up display or HUD) that quantify various aspects of the match. Vitality meters provide a color-coded expression of remaining health; a game clock ticks down the remaining seconds left in the match; markers identify how many rounds a player has won; and various gauges and meters measure other statistics depending on the game's individual 23 rule sets. For example, Super Street Fighter 2 Turbo added a "super gauge" which, when full, allowed the player access to a particularly powerful technique [3].
- Competitive: The goal of a fighting game match is to determine a winner. The common thread in all of the games considered above is that for an individual play session to end, a winner must be determined, either by knockout, ring out, or in extreme cases, the game clock running down to 0 [3].
- Allows for multiplayer competition: This is the primary difference between fighting games and the previously-described beat 'em ups. In playing against the CPU, the difference is mostly conceptual; both fighters and beat 'em ups involve moving through stages, using combat to defeat the enemy and progress. However, fighting games also allow for players to fight against each other competitively. While in many cases this is 1-on-1, the Smash series allows for a greater number of concurrent players [3].

3.3 Game Combo System

Game Combo System is the core part of the fighting games. It has much to do with expanding the ways to play the game and developing the entertainment. A skill has three stages – startup, active, and recovery. Note that some skills' recovery might have a cancelable period [7].

1st - Startup: After a given command is confirmed, the corresponding skill will be used. During this period, any other action cannot be used; the character will start to move, but still cannot make any damage to its opponent [7].

2nd - Active: These are the frames where an "attack hit box" (the red square in the first row of the above figure) appears. If the opponent character's "hit box" coincides the "attack hit box" of your character, the opponent character will be damaged. Note that in other games, the hit box is sometimes called the bounding box [7].

3rd - Recovery: The attack hit box disappears, and the character turns back to its normal status. In this example, there is a cancelable period, in which if there is a skill, say skill A that can cancel the current skill, skill A can be used. A cancelable frame means that if there is a skill can cancel the current skill's recovery time, it can be used during the cancelable frames [7].

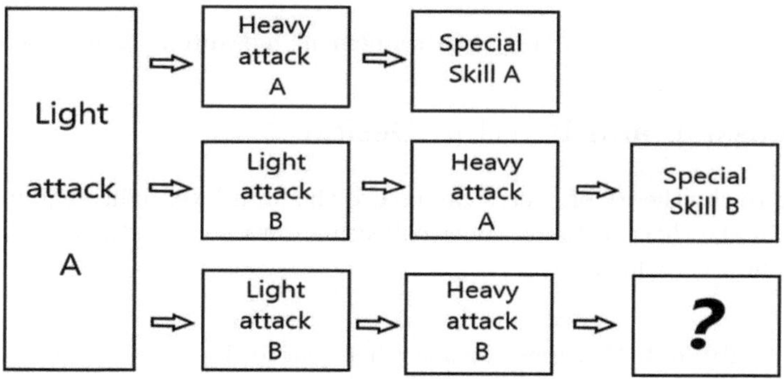

Fig. 1. The consist of a common combo

Through this frame figure, we could know the movements' details of the character. All of the attacks will give opponent's character a hit stun. And then we can combine the attacks into the combo to give our opponent big damage by leaving no time for his character to recovery. Certainly, the game will not let us cancel two or more skills all the time in an infinite loop. So between every attack there always exists a cancel level system. The action has high cancel level can connect behind the low one just like we showed in Fig. 1.

3.4 Game Refinement Progress of Fighting Games

We consider the progress of a fighting game. To find the game refinement measure, a reasonable game progress model is figured out by two factors: successful hit and attempt control. Players control the character to attack each other in the fighting games, some attack is valid, it means that hit opponent without defense, and make damage successfully. The other side, every attack is an attempt no matter successful or not, so in this condition, H stands for the average number of successful hit, and A is the average number of attack per game [13]. If one knows the game information progress, for example after the game, the game progress $x(t)$ will be given by Eq. 3.

$$x(t) = \frac{H}{A}\,t \tag{3}$$

A model of RPG information progress is given by Eq. 4.

$$x(t) = H(\frac{t}{A})^n \tag{4}$$

Here n stands for a constant parameter which is given based on the perspective of an observer in the game considered. Then acceleration of game information progress is obtained by deriving Eq. (4) twice. Solving it at $t = A$, the equation becomes

$$x''(T) = \frac{Hn(n-1)}{A^n}t^{n-2} = \frac{H}{A^2}n(n-1) \tag{5}$$

Hence we obtain Similarly, the game refinement measure as below: $GR = \frac{\sqrt{H}}{A}$.

4 Discussion and Rhythm Design

According to the theory of Sect. 3, we record the high-level fighting game competition and make their statistic. After collecting data and mathematical analysis, we get Table 4 as below.

Table 4. Measures of game refinement for Fighting Games

Title of Fighting Games	H	A	$R-value$
Yie Ar Kung Fu (1985)	11.6	52.3	0.065
Street Fighter II: The World Warriors (1991)	14.1	52.8	0.071
Samurai Spirits (1993)	13.1	38.8	0.093
Mortal Kombat 3 (1995)	41.2	73.3	0.088
The King of Fighters '97 (1997)	21.3	48.9	0.094
The King of Fighters 2002 (2002)	23.5	46.1	0.105
Virtua Fighter 5 (2006)	21.1	41.3	0.111
Dead or Alive 5 (2012)	31.2	44.7	0.125
The King of Fighters XIV (2016)	49.2	63.1	0.111
Tekken 7 (2017)	26.3	40.1	0.128

We made a polygonal line according to time's near and far, shows in Fig. 2. Axis x represents years, meanwhile axis y represents the value of R. We are able to observe the develop trend and the changing tendency of R *value* generally. We can find out in a directly way that in the earlier time R *value* of fighting games had always been in a low statement while R *value* of fighting games these years have grown higher and higher. We can tell in this illustrate that R *value* is increasing as time goes by years.

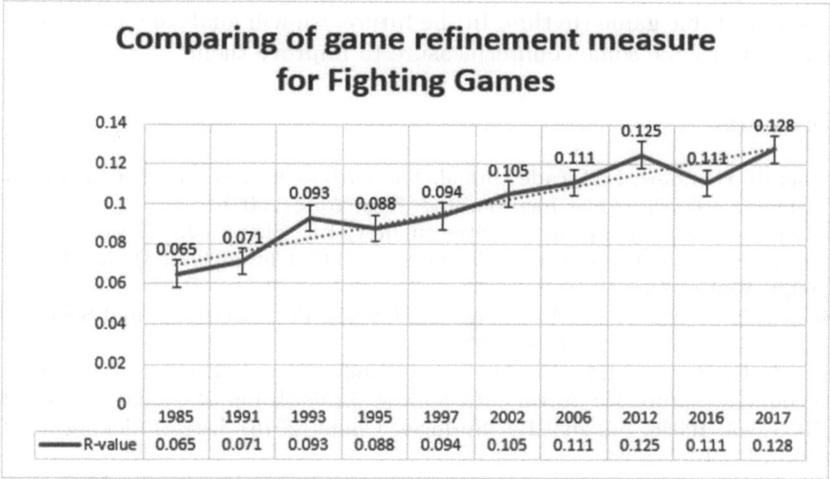

Fig. 2. Comparing of game refinement measure of Fighting Games

According to the players' experience and feeling, Super Street Fighter series have the slower game rhythm and nice balance between every character, while players attend a match, they need to focus on the psychological anticipation; The King of Fighters series has the higher game rhythm and excellent ornamental value, players need to focus on the combos. So refinement values of these two games should be different. Game refinement value of Super Street Fighter II is close to the traditional board games and sports games such as soccer, and The King of the Fighters has the exorbitant *R value* which means that the game is interesting and exciting and we can say this game is nice for watching but not so suitable for sports competition. The research result and experiment data fit the players' experience and audiences' feeling.

5 Conclusion

In this paper, we overview the past research of E-learning system and Duolingo, then we find the defeat point of E-learning system analysis. In order to solve the issue, we noticed the core idea of E-learning system is game rhythm, then we decided to choose the fighting game as the new research target. According to the research result, we found that fighting games in the earlier time are similar to gym games or board game. Moreover, refinement value is higher than before while era comes to middle 1990s until today, which means the fighting game become more relax and focus on the entertainment rather than competitiveness. Mainly fighting games in current era have a high speed of moving and processing with strong entertainment. Therefore, the evolution process of fighting game can show some genius and experience to the designer to develop their E-learning system with a comfortable game rhythm. In the future, we will analyze more E-learning systems and provide some countermeasure to improve them.

References

1. Ashcraft, B., Snow, J.: Arcade Mania!: The Turbo-Charged World of Japan's Game Centers. Kodansha Amer Incorporated, New York (2008)
2. Ferguson, C.J., Thompson, J., Streetfighter, I.I., Sherry, J.: Video Games: the Latest Scapegoat for Violence. Washington D.C, Chronicle of Higher Education (2007). Violent Games
3. Harper, T.L.: The Art of War: Fighting Games, Performativity, and Social Game Play. Ohio University, Athens (2010)
4. Huynh, D., Zuo, L., Iida, H.: Analyzing gamification of "Duolingo" with focus on its course structure. In: Bottino, R., Jeuring, J., Veltkamp, R.C. (eds.) GALA 2016. LNCS, vol. 10056, pp. 268–277. Springer, Cham (2016). https://doi.org/10.1007/978-3-319-50182-6_24
5. Iida, H., Takahara, K., Nagashima, J., Kajihara, Y., Hashimoto, T.: An application of game-refinement theory to Mah Jong. In: Rauterberg, M. (ed.) ICEC 2004. LNCS, vol. 3166, pp. 333–338. Springer, Heidelberg (2004). https://doi.org/10.1007/978-3-540-28643-1_41
6. Iida, H., Takeshita, N., Yoshimura, J.: A metric for entertainment of boardgames: its implication for evolution of chess variants. In: Nakatsu, R., Hoshino, J. (eds.) Entertainment Computing. ITIFIP, vol. 112, pp. 65–72. Springer, Boston, MA (2003). https://doi.org/10.1007/978-0-387-35660-0_8
7. Lu, F., Yamamoto, K., Nomura, L.H., Mizuno, S., Lee, Y., Thawonmas, R.: Fighting game artificial intelligence competition platform. In: 2013 IEEE 2nd Global Conference on Consumer Electronics (GCCE), pp. 320–323. IEEE (2013)
8. Nossal, T.N.: Expansion of game refinement theory into continuous movement games with consideration on functional brain measurement. Ph.D. thesis of Japan Advanced Institution of Science and Technology (2015)
9. Panumate, C., Xiong, S., Iida, H.: An approach to quantifying pokemon's entertainment impact with focus on battle. In: 2015 3rd International Conference on Applied Computing and Information Technology/2nd International Conference on Computational Science and Intelligence (ACIT-CSI), pp. 60–66. IEEE (2015)
10. Spanner Spencer: The tao of beat-'em-ups (2008)
11. Sutiono, A.P., Purwarianti, A., Iida, H.: A mathematical model of game refinement. In: Reidsma, D., Choi, I., Bargar, R. (eds.) INTETAIN 2014. LNICST, vol. 136, pp. 148–151. Springer, Cham (2014). https://doi.org/10.1007/978-3-319-08189-2_22
12. Xiong, S., Iida, H.: Attractiveness of real time strategy games. In: 2nd International Conference on Systems and Informatics (ICSAI), pp. 271–276. IEEE (2014)
13. Xiong, S., Peng, Y., Iida, H., Nordin, A.-B.: An approach to entertainment tuning in RPGs: case study using Diablo III and trails of cold steel. In: Bottino, R., Jeuring, J., Veltkamp, R.C. (eds.) GALA 2016. LNCS, vol. 10056, pp. 385–394. Springer, Cham (2016). https://doi.org/10.1007/978-3-319-50182-6_35
14. Xiong, S., Zuo, L., Chiewvanichakorn, R., Iida, H.: Quantifying engagement of various games. In: The 19th Game Programming Workshop 2014. Information Processing Society of Japan (2014)
15. Xiong, S., Zuo, L., Iida, H.: Possible interpretations for game refinement measure. In: Munekata, N., Kunita, I., Hoshino, J. (eds.) ICEC 2017. LNCS, vol. 10507, pp. 322–334. Springer, Cham (2017). https://doi.org/10.1007/978-3-319-66715-7_35

A Mobile Learning System with Multi-point Interaction

Jie Zhang[1](✉), Bingfang Qi[2], Yingpeng Zhang[2], Hui Zhao[3], and Toyohide Watanabe[4]

[1] Faculty of Computer Science and Engineering, Xi'an University of Technology, Xi'an, China
jiezhang1984@xaut.edu.cn

[2] SPKLSTN Lab, Department of Computer Science and Technology, Xi'an Jiaotong University, Xi'an 710049, Shaanxi, China
{moringq,yingpengzh}@stu.xjtu.edu.cn

[3] School of Computer Science and Technology, Xidian University, Xi'an 710071, Shaanxi, China
hzhao@mail.xidian.edu.cn

[4] Nagoya Industrial Science Research Institute, Nagoya 460008, Japan
watanabe@nagoya-u.jp

Abstract. Mobile learning have a capacity to respond to educational needs of learners dispersed across vast regions and cultures. Among a wide variety of popular mobile platforms. Android has become one of the optimal mobile operating systems. In this paper, we investigate the challenges of the mobile learning and propose a framework of mobile learning system. When the student log in for identification verification, they can select the recorded coursewares, join the real time class in various interactive learning methods including text, video and audio. A system with a user-friendly interface is designed, based on which experiments are performed to evaluate the effectiveness of the proposed system which can support 4 or 6 interactions at the same time.

Keywords: Mobile learning · Multimedia interaction · Android

1 Introduction

Mobile learning is concerned with a society on the move [1]. Mobile learning solutions, when designed and implemented successfully, have a capacity to respond to educational needs of learners dispersed across vast regions and cultures. Learning at a distance using mobiles has been accepted as beneficial both in developed and developing countries, particularly in settings where potential learners do not have direct access to education chances.

Using portable computing devices (such as iPads, laptops, tablet PCs, PDAs, and smart phones) with wireless networks enables mobility and mobile learning, allowing teaching and learning to extend to spaces beyond the traditional classroom. Within the classroom, mobile learning gives instructors and learners increased flexibility and new opportunities for interaction. There is much appreciation of learning principles,

A. El Rhalibi et al. (Eds.): Edutainment 2018, LNCS 11462, pp. 303–307, 2019.
https://doi.org/10.1007/978-3-030-23712-7_41

particularly suited to mobile learning. An appropriate framework, embraced by all participants, is needed for successful transcultural projects, including collaborative research studies.

To solve these challenges, we propose a solution named m-SkyClass based on WebRTC (Web Real-Time-Communications) to integrate real-time communications with massive course resources at web level. Based on the proposed framework, a prototype system with a user-friendly interface is designed. The experimental evaluation on the real lectures demonstrates the effectiveness and usefulness of the proposed system.

Our work can be summarized as follows:

- We propose a framework to support the Mobile learning system based on the Android system,
- We provide different learning methods online to support Q&A, thesis defense, and live broadcast mode by textual and multimedia interaction,
- We implement the Mobile Learning system based on the Kurento Media Server,
- We conduct experiments to evaluate the effectiveness and the usefulness of the proposed system.

This paper is organized as follows. Section 2 proposes a framework of the WebRTC based mobile learning system. Section 3 introduces the methods and technologies in the proposed system. Section 4 implements the framework and evaluate the system. Finally, Sect. 5 presents our conclusions and future work.

2 Conceptual Viewpoint with Framework

Due to the features of the mobile terminal device, we reserve the most central functions in traditional e-Learning system. There are five main function modules in the m-SkyClass system, the Main Page module, the VOD Study Page module, the Live Class Page module, the News Page module and the Settings Page module.

Next we describe these five page modules respectively.

Main Page Module. The main page is the front page when the student users log in the m-SkyClass system. In the main page, the students are provided with some videos of several chapters, which are parts of eight public courses for all students without chosen for the first learner.

VOD Study Page Module. The VOD study page mainly shows the selected courses in this semester for the current student user. Users can click on some course to enter the chapter video list. According to current learning progress, students can select the relevant sections to continue his study.

Live Class Page Module. The live class page module provide a real-time class for the students. In this page, there is a list of all the live classes. The list is displayed real-time, it shows not only the live courses, but also the scheduled courses to appear subsequently.

News Page Module. The news page mainly shows the related news from the School of Continuing Education at Xi'an Jiaotong University. Students can learn about the latest news and trends of the school, and click the interested news and read the details.

Settings Page Module. In the Setting Page module, there are several functions of personal information inquiry, including online consulting, course synchronization, application update user log out and so on.

3 Live Interaction Methods

In this section, we present the real time interaction methods for the Live Class Module proposed in Sect. 2. Figure 2 shows the different function modules for the live class. It is consisted of several modules, including the Login and register modules through the HTTP communications, the record will be read from the database for the identification verifications, and the register information will be write to the database for the log in next time (Fig. 1).

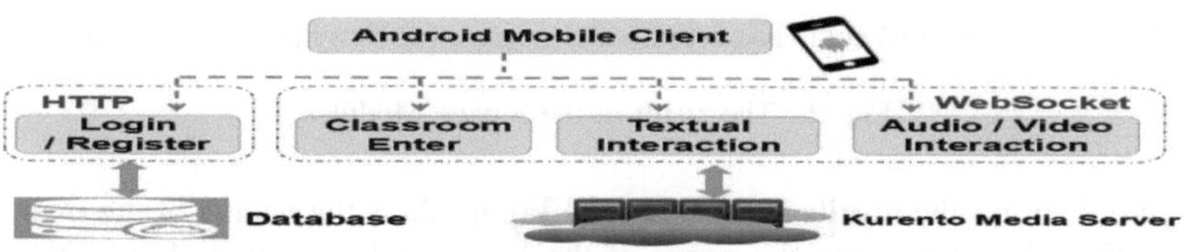

Fig. 1. The functional modules of the real-time interaction in the *Live Class Module*

Then we introduce these four function modules above respectively as follows.

Login and Register Methods. When the application starts, the student user enters the login activity firstly. There are two *EditText*s to enter the username and password respectively.

Class Entering Methods. After logging in the system successfully, the user will enter into the live classroom activity. After accessing to this activity, the client will first send a WebSocket request to establish the connection, and then the client will communicate with the server in real time through this connection.

Textual Interactive Methods. After users join the room successfully, they will enter the main activity. In this main activity, users can import the text message and click the send message button, the text message will be displayed in the text box at the bottom of the room page. They can send text messages at any time of the class as they wish to.

Video/Audio Interactive Methods. When users choose to interactive by video and audio stream in main activity, they will enter the P2P video activity. In this application scene, video interaction is implemented with the WebRTC. If users want to have multi-point interaction, they have to establish WebRTC connection channels between each other.

4 Experiments

We design an webRTC-based mobile learning system according to the proposed framework, integrated with the user-friendly interface. In this section, we evaluate the performance of the m-SkyClass, and report experiment results and our analyses.

Performance Evaluation. We report the experiment result in detail. First we will show the 5 pages of the m-SkyClass system mentioned in Sect. 2, and then present the interaction procedure in the live class mentioned in Sect. 3.

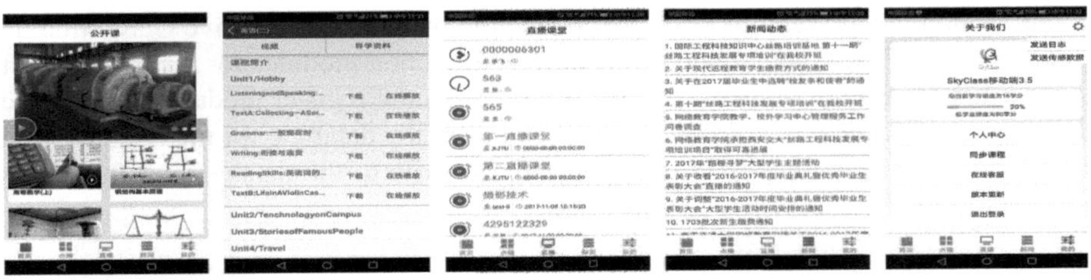

(a) Main page (b) VOD study page (c) Live class page (d) News page (e) Settings page

Fig. 2. The result of the 5 page Modules

Figure 2 shows the results of the systems. Figure 2a is the results of the main page module, Fig. 2b, c and d are the pages of the VOD study, the live classes, the news pages, the settings pages respectively.

The textual interaction scenes are shown in Fig. 3a–b and the multimedia interaction scenes are shown in Fig. 3c–d.

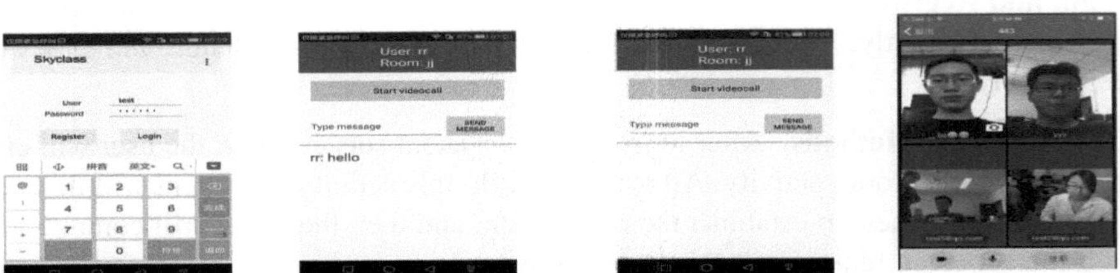

(a) Login/Register (b) Text interaction (c) Start multimedia interaction (d) 4 interactions

Fig. 3. The interaction scenes

System Evaluation. Compared to the existing mobile learning app AoPeng microschool, our system can also support the functions of VOD online study, message notification, credits and information inquiry, service consulting. Otherwise, our system has more functions like VOD offline study, live class, video download, studying log record and course BBS (Table 1).

Table 1. Detailed comparison with similar mobile learning systems

Name	VOD Class (Online)	VOD Class (Offline)	Live Class	Download	Study Log
m-SkyClass	✓	✓	✓	✓	✓
Open-Bar	×	×	×	×	×

Name	Message	Achievement Query	Cost Info Query	Exam Info Query	Customer Service
m-SkyClass	✓	✓	✓	×	✓
Open-Bar	✓	✓	✓	✓	✓

5 Conclusion and Future Work

In this paper, we proposed a framework to support the mobile learning system based on the Web browser; we provided different page modules to support the online and offline learning, as well as the textual and multimedia interaction methods in the live class for a better study experience. Our future work includes adding dynamic face recognition functions and accomplish more refined Virtual Reality. We devote to pursue more effective and high quality technologies to improve the interaction between the students and teachers.

Acknowledgments. This research was partly supported by the Research (#61702409, #61702400) from the National Natural Science Foundation of China, (#112-451116013, #112-451016023) from Xi'an University of Technology.

References

1. Zheng, Q., Chu, C.: A resource reservation and distribution system over satellite-terrestrial network. In: IEEE CSCWD, Xiamen, pp. 237–242 (2005)
2. Wang, Z., Zhang, J., Lian, Y., Zheng, Q.: A large scale distance learning system for IPv6/Ipv4 hybrid environment. In: International Conference on Computer Science and Software Engineering, pp. 532–535 (2008)
3. Balan, T., Stanciu, A., Surariu, S.: WebRTC based e-Learning platform. In: Conference Proceedings of e-Learning and Software for Education(eLSE), pp. 48–55 (2017)
4. Jing, Y., Craig, A.: A mobile learning framework for developing educational games and its pilot study for secondary mathematics education. In: The 15th World Conference on Mobile and Contextual Learning – mLearn, pp. 130–136 (2016)

Research on Mobile Learning System of Colleges and Universities

Hui Yu[1](✉) and Zhongqiu Zhang[2]

[1] School Office of Northwestern, Polytechnical University, Xi'an 710072, Shaanxi, China
yuhui@nwpu.edu.cn
[2] Mingde College of Northwestern Polytechnical University, Xi'an 710072, Shaanxi, China

Abstract. In recent years, with the rapid development of network communication technology and the widespread use of mobile devices. Mobile learning is getting more and more attention and research by scholars, becoming a new type of learning method. Students group is the highest popularization rate of smart phones, while college students also have strong ability to learn and accept new things quickly and so on. Therefore, under the new situation, colleges and universities should further study mobile learning and construct a mobile learning system that meets the needs of young students, which can provide a useful supplement for the current student education. The article introduces the research background and the status of mobile learning research. Then the article analyzes the characteristics of mobile learning and proposes a proposal for building a mobile learning system in colleges.

Keywords: Mobile learning · Smart phone · Student education · Mobile learning system

1 Introduction

According to the 40th "Statistical Report on the Internet Development in China" released by CNNIC. The number of mobile internet users in China reached 724 million. The proportion of mobile internet users increased from 95.1% at the end of 2016 to 96.3%. Mobile internet users online education reached 144 million users, accounting for 20% of the size of mobile internet users [1]. With the development of the internet and mobile communication technologies, and the widespread use of smartphones among university students, the dependence of university students on mobile phones has become increasingly stronger. As a new learning method, mobile learning is getting more and more attention from colleges and universities [2]. Constructing a mobile learning system is in line with the needs of social development, in line with the individual needs of young students, plays a positive role in promoting university student education. As a basic tool and learning carrier under the mobile learning mode, the mobile terminal has the characteristics of real-time, rapidity, and high efficiency, which promotes the speed of information exchange and improves the learning efficiency. In colleges and universities, smartphones and tablets have become the most

A. El Rhalibi et al. (Eds.): Edutainment 2018, LNCS 11462, pp. 308–312, 2019.
https://doi.org/10.1007/978-3-030-23712-7_42

commonly used mobile terminals for students. The popularization of mobile terminals has exerted an important influence on the traditional teaching mode and learning methods in colleges and universities, which also provided support for the construction of college mobile learning systems.

2 Research Situation of Mobile Learning

Mobile learning originated in Carnegie Mellon's Wireless Andrew research project in 1994. Since then, some Countries in Europe and North America have studied the two dimensions of theoretical study and practical application of mobile learning. The author uses mobile-learning and mobile-education as key words to find out that there are some researches on mobile learning in our country, including the theoretical research, empirical investigation and applied research of mobile learning. The research results include "the connotation, method and significance of distance learning of mobile learning", "Empirical study on influencing factors of continuous use behavior of mobile learning users", "Design and development of mobile learning resources for undergraduates based on smart phones" [3], and so on. Through these circumstances, we can see that the study of mobile learning at home and abroad already has a good foundation. With the development of mobile communication technology, the convenience of wireless technology applied to education and training is more and more large, and the potential of mobile learning is also growing. From digital learning to mobile learning, from simple mobile learning to complex mobile learning, mobile learning will get more and more applications. Therefore, to strengthen the study of mobile learning is very important. This article will combine the existing theoretical foundation and research experience to explore and construct the mobile learning system in universities and to put forward solutions.

3 Paper Preparation

Through the research, we found that there is not a unified definition of the concept of mobile learning at home and abroad at present. For example, some people think that "mobile learning is a new form of learning that refers to the use of wireless mobile communication network technology and wireless mobile communication devices to obtain educational information, educational resources and education services" [4]. As another example, some believe that "mobile learning is a new way of learning, which refers to the help of mobile terminal devices such as smart phones and the like, learners freely acquire learning information, learning resources anytime, anywhere according to their own individual needs, and communicate with teachers and other learners anytime, anywhere". The author favors the latter argument, emphasizing a learning method that can be used anytime, anywhere. Therefore, compared with other digital learning methods, mobile learning has some unique features:

3.1 The Openness of Learning

In the rapid development of information technology, smart phones have become one of the essential items for people to carry at any time, providing convenient and open learning anytime, anywhere for learners, bringing more learning resources and learning channels, expanding the learning space. This allows learning is no longer limited to classrooms and other physical space, promoting students to make full use of time to learn. Openness further encourages students to learn more autonomously, which greatly promotes learning efficiency.

3.2 The Immediacy of Learning

Compared with formal learning, the biggest advantage of mobile learning is to break through time and space constraints. Learners can learn when they really need it. And, by engaging with learners and teachers who share the same virtual learning community, to help learners solve problems or difficulties in a timely manner.

3.3 The Individuation of Learning

Compared with the traditional mode of teaching unified education, mobile learning learners can learn independently according to their own actual situation. For example, in their own smart phone terminal to install the learning software to meet their needs. For example, choose your favorite content to learn, and so on. These changes make learners better personalized learning.

4 Construction of Mobile Learning System in Colleges and Universities

The purpose of building a mobile learning system [5] in colleges and universities is to make a useful supplement to the traditional teaching and to provide an important platform for young students to make full use of the fragmentation time in daily study life. Through the analysis and research, the author thinks that the construction of mobile learning system in colleges and universities mainly includes the following aspects.

4.1 Building a Full Coverage of the Campus Network

Young students in the school to carry out anytime, anywhere to learn the basic premise is to have full coverage of the campus network. Colleges and universities should set up wireless routing terminals for students' study, living and scientific research to ensure the coverage of the network. In this regard, universities at home and abroad have done a lot of work, the vast majority of schools have achieved full wireless network coverage, which provides a good foundation for mobile learning for young people. At the same time, it also ensures the speed of network operation by improving technical aspects such as bandwidth, thus ensuring that young students will not be affected by the speed of the internet while carrying out mobile learning.

4.2 Building a Strong Interactive Information Platform

University mobile learning platform is a systematic project involving many departments within the university, especially with student education related departments. The exact requirement is to design and develop the basic premise of mobile learning platform. A deep understanding of student needs is the basic premise for research and design of mobile learning systems. Advanced software development technology is the platform guarantee. Currently, based on WAP, C/S, 3G, J2ME and other mobile learning system development technology is more mature. The learning platform developed based on these technologies is more interactive and flexible and has good application in the design and development of mobile learning platform. Therefore, the construction of interactive mobile learning platform must be done in two ways that one is to grasp the real needs of students and the second is to choose advanced software development technology.

4.3 Fostering Students' Awareness of Mobile Learning

Although students have a lot of free time at their disposal, they do not have the awareness of mobile learning that much time is wasted on purposeless browsing of useless web pages. The purpose of constructing mobile learning system in colleges and universities is to help students make full use of the fragmentation time outside the classroom and promote the improvement of individual learning of students. Therefore, colleges and universities should pay attention to the promotion of mobile learning awareness, so that more students participate in mobile learning based on smart phones. Specifically, you can take some measures, for example, Schools can publish information related to mobile learning on the school campus home page, school publications and other media to enhance students' understanding of mobile learning. As another example, a series of related activities based on mobile learning can be carried out to enable more students to understand mobile learning, which is represented by mobile learning of smart phones, so as to promote the full development of mobile learning. Only when students have the awareness of participation in mobile learning, mobile learning system will really play a role, and the mobile learning atmosphere in the school will be more and more concentrated.

4.4 Constructing the Guarantee Mechanism of Mobile Learning

In addition to the three aspects mentioned earlier, the promotion of mobile learning system in colleges and universities also need to have the appropriate mechanism to be protected. Through the study found that mobile learning is a personalized and emotional experience. Frustration of learners in the learning process will undermine their interest in mobile learning and reduce learning behavior. Therefore, a good incentive support mechanism to promote the development of mobile learning is very important, with the purpose of increasing learners' trust in mobile learning, and to stimulate and maintain learners' enthusiasm and initiative in learning. Specifically, the areas where mobile learning is practiced are common-sense, more interesting and less logical, with less intellectual input in learning areas. With the further development of mobile learning in colleges and universities, combined with the actual situation, expanding the field of mobile learning. At the same time, but also to establish learning incentives, such as for some mobile learning courses assigned credits. And establish the corresponding evaluation mechanism, objectively and impartially evaluate the learner's learning situation, truly reflect the learner's learning attitude, learning depth and learning outcomes.

5 Conclusion

Based on the above research, it is necessary to build a mobile learning system that meets the needs of students in order to promote the full use of fragmentation time for college students. The article puts forward four aspects of building a mobile learning system, which has certain reference value for specific practice. Moreover, some areas have practical applications in universities and have achieved certain results. Therefore, it has a certain practical promotion value.

References

1. China Internet Network Information Center: China internet development statistics report. http://www.cac.gov.cn/2017-08/04/c_1121427672.html
2. Li Yushun, M.: The current situation and trend of mobile learning. China Inf. Technol. Educ. (3), 9–11 (2008)
3. Ding, M.: A study on the status of college students' mobile learning based on smartphones. Nanchang University (2017)
4. Ying, W.: The research of mobile learning system design and development based on smart phone. Tianjin Normal University (2009)
5. Wang, W., Zhong, S.: An empirical research on college students' mobile learning. Res. Open Educ. (4) (2009)

A Study of Negative Emotion Regulation of College Students by Social Games Design

SiQi Xie, MengLi Shi, and Hong Yan(✉)

HaiNan University, Haikou 570228, China
yanhong@hainu.edu.cn

Abstract. There are numerous and complicated relationships among personal emotional, physiological reaction and cognitive evaluation. People can produce some negative emotions at any time and place. Especially, college students have a lot of stress such as study, interpersonal, competition, employment, so that negative emotional experience affects their common life. This article aims at the design of the interactive game on the intelligent terminal, pointing at the negative emotion of the college students. Through the combination of practice and theory at home and abroad to explore the role of interactive gameplay in emotional regulation. To provide users with a virtual platform outside real life, name it "Mood Robert." The emotional appeal is realized by adjusting the contradiction between "ego" and "super-ego." Sharing their emotions based on social network information communication to improve the ability to adjust themselves and reduce the impact of negative emotions on daily life.

Keywords: Social game · Emotion · College students

1 Introduction

Emotion is a complex psychological and physiological state produced by a variety of elements. In a broad sense, emotional expressions include action, language, expression, and so on. Rivera believes that emotions have two sides, both positive and negative. The atmosphere of positive emotions is positive; the atmosphere of negative emotions is negative. When positive emotions come into being, people will have an optimistic and confident attitude to do things more flexibly and efficiently. If user has negative emotion, it will reduce the enthusiasm of the user and affect his/her healthy life. When people brought the positive emotions into the group, the group efficiency will increase, and the negative emotions stop the pace. The emergence of Modern Psychology continues to affect the development of games. Researchers began to design research based on different theoretical paradigms. Nowadays, many games pay more attention to the integrity of the game than the previous one and the significance of its existence, and the objects concerned turn to explore the development of human emotion and learning.

Interaction theory is an important research category in social psychology. Wil-liamilliam James proposed that individuals interact with a variety of "typical others" with "typical self." Exploring the appropriate behaviors, intentions, and values of users have become the focus of the researchers' increasing attention. Therefore, the "interaction theory" extends the concept and connotation of the original games: social games

A. El Rhalibi et al. (Eds.): Edutainment 2018, LNCS 11462, pp. 313–317, 2019.
https://doi.org/10.1007/978-3-030-23712-7_43

pay more attention to users' emotions, increase user participation and attention and enhance communication between users. Especially for contemporary college students, because of social, family, academic and other factors, it is easy to produce negative emotions. There is a big gap in the way of interaction to regulate users' emotions.

Psychologist Maslow once put forward "human needs hierarchy theory." Game designers adjusted the game framework based on this theory. To a certain extent, it explains the reason which why Games attract us. Based on the personality structure of "id," "ego" and "superego" put forward by Freud, Users can achieve a sense of achievement in the game experience and meet the "superego" needs. At the same time, the game can spread the attention of the user, can bring the user's thinking into, absorb and learn the deep meaning of the game.

Therefore, negative emotions as an important part of people, and it not "ego" can be quickly resolved. However, through social games, we can share and discuss with others, immerse ourselves in "superego," and achieve the role of relieving emotions in this process. However, the game is virtual, and it does have a psychological adjustment. Users may take most of the time to use games as a tool for escapism. Therefore, exploring interactive games has important research value on the research of negative emotion regulation of college students. The purpose of this paper is to introduce game experience to a warm society from a cold mobile phone, from personal to social groups, to better share emotions and experience human feelings. We designed the social game called "Mood Robert," and aim to create a good interactive environment as an "intermediary," and user can appreciate expectation and be expected with communication.

2 Game Elements

With the development of mobile communication, the occupancy rate of intelligent mobile terminals is as high as 96%, which is becoming an indispensable dispensing for people's daily life. However, social games are more interesting, participation and emotional care for the users.

- Language Element

At present, there are dozens of branches in each game, forming a vast game family. The most famous MOBA (Multiplayer Online Tactical Competition) games, such as king glory, seldom communicate with each other, mostly on the fingertips, and increase user's emotion through the teamwork process of players. However, language is one of the most important means of communication in social interaction, and it is one of the ways to regulate its own emotions.

Language Element At present, there are dozens of branches in each game, forming a vast game family. The most famous MOBA (Multiplayer Online Tactical Competition) games, such as king glory, seldom communicate with each other, mostly on the fingertips, and increase user's emotion through the teamwork process of players. However, language is one of the most important means of communication in social interaction, and it is one of the ways to regulate its own emotions.

- Relation Element

Social games are belonging online game, usually two or more people play games together. There are relationships between users, unrelated (such as strangers), weak relationships (such as fans), and strong relationships (such as friends). These relationships are not static, which can further guide the interaction between the user and the user and establish the behavior of further relationships. Develop a positive sense of communication and teamwork ability.

- Interactive Element

The game does regulate our emotions, but the game is virtual, different from reality, and it is easy to cause the player to feel lost in the real world. A game is easy to addict to players and take up too much time by players. Players take most of the time to use games to escape reality, and at that time the game becomes a tool for people to escape from reality.

However, social games are to avoid the abuse of the game, in no small extent to eliminate the sense of loss and the heart of the player. Reduce the player's addiction to the game for other time; increase the interaction between players and promote communication between people.

- Psychical Element

The game affects the player fixedly. On the other hand, the player experiences the game in a different mood. When a user feels good about a game, and game developers are continually updating the set according to the player's experience, or at the very beginning, they catch the psychology of a small group of people. In the game, activities such as upgrading, chatting, and trade unions have met the needs of different levels of the experience. An uninterrupted drive drives him to continue to play, and players are dependent on the game.

3 Framework Design

According to the survey, more than half of the adults have a moderate degree of loneliness. The more severe the loneliness is, the more serious the adult's depression is; the positive emotion has a relatively positive influence on three aspects, including physical health, mental health, and social adjustment. "Robert" regulates the mood of the player in a relatively relaxed form of interactive games. Because our research is at initial stage, there are many shortcomings still need to be considered.

Firstly, "Mood Robert" is the first designed for college students when no listeners in a period, to provide an interactive platform for "Mood Robert" users to share their emotions, interact with other game players, to achieve the soothing effect, improve the ability to regulate user's emotion. Players can share their mood or recent events in their favorite scenes. Other players review their views in this scenario and hide them in the corner of the stage. Robert was selected according to the content of the commentators. The criteria for screening: the content of the commentary is positive or objective. After filtering, Robert will prompt the player to have comments, and use the curiosity of the players to drive the player to search in the scene. During the search, funny passages will appear randomly to adjust the player's mood. Players can communicate with their most satisfied commentators after they were found.

Secondly, the context is the most critical part of attracting players, conceiving a magical and exciting game world, interlude interactive related procedures into games, and let players unconsciously find themselves interacting with others. Social games will ultimately bring the sense of interaction to the players. The main component is the player, design, of course, role design. A functional role design can lead the experiences to interact with in the game. The player takes the role in the narrative context of the model, thus producing better interaction.

At last, the main set of rules are adjusting reward mechanism. Through the feedback to the game player's correct operation or illegal operation, the user can obtain the virtual gold or credits. Also, instant feedback was reflected in the activity motivation and activity motivation of communication participants, the interactive game just takes advantage of this mechanism, providing the same platform for different players to make better communication and interaction.

4 Design Prospect

Today, the level of social development has been greatly improved, people from the pursuit of material to the spiritual level of satisfaction. Our design of "Mood Robert" Research on the emotional adjustment of college students remains to be improved, and there is a lot of space for the game to intervene in psychological aspects. In addition, social game can be attached to more mature social platforms, such as WeChat small programs, micro-blog and so on. The purpose of our design is based on interaction and communication. In this process, college students' emotions are returned to the normal social life standard track from their emotional and behavioral aspects.

Acknowledgements. This work is supported by "Hainan Provincial Natural Science Foundation of China (Project Number: 619QN196)", "Hainan University Education and Teaching Reform Research Project (Project Number: HDJY1978)" and "Hainan University Research Research Initiation Fund Project (Project Number: KYQD(SK)1709)".

References

1. Wang, Y., Zhang, T., Li, W., Huang, B.: Research on framework elements of educational game design based on flow theory: a case study of speech learning game for special children. J. Distance Educ. **03**(32), 97–104 (2014)
2. Cooper, A.: About Face: The Essentials of Interaction Design, vol. 10, 4th edn, pp. 97–111. Industrial Press, Norwalk (2015). W. Ni's Translation
3. Dong, Y., Wang, Q., Xing, C.: Progress in the study of the relationship between positive emotion and physical and mental health. Psychol. Sci. (2012)
4. Levy-Gigi, E., Shamay-Tsoory, S.G.: Help me if you can: evaluating the effectiveness of interpersonal compared to intrapersonal emotion regulation in reducing distress. J. Behav. Therapy Experiment. Psychiatry **55**(Complete), 33–40 (2017)

5. Zhang, J., Zheng, Y.: How do academic stress and leisure activities influence college students' emotional well-being? A daily investigation. J. Adolesc. **60**, 114–118 (2017)
6. Hughes, C.M., Griffin, B.J., Worthington, E.L.: A measure of social behavior in team-based, multiplayer online games: the sociality in multiplayer online games (SMOG) scale. Comput. Hum. Behav. **69**, 386–395 (2017)
7. Manero, B., Torrente, J., Freire, M., Fernández-Manjón, B.: An instrument to build a gamer clustering framework according to gaming preferences and habits. Comput. Hum. Behav. **62**, 353–363 (2016)

Analysis of College Students' Employment, Unemployment and Enrollment with Self-Organizing Maps

Jie Kong(✉), Meng Ren, Ting Lu, and Congying Wang

School of Computer Science, Xi'an Shiyou University, No. 18 2nd Dianzi Road, Xian 710065, China
{jkong,mren,tlu,cywang}@xsyu.edu.cn

Abstract. The job-hunting and graduate school admission of college students are important tasks in universities. To investigate the impact of students' academic achievement to their graduation whereabouts, Self-Organizing Maps is introduced in this study. Through the analysis of experiment results, the features of academic performance in different students' graduation whereabouts segments are proposed. The findings could help educators better understand the relationship between academic performance and graduation whereabouts.

Keywords: Data mining · Self-Organizing Maps · Graduation whereabouts · Segmentation

1 Introduction

In China, most undergraduate students face the choice of employment or enrollment before their graduation. Unfortunately, some of the students are unable to be employed. The employment rate and enrollment rate of undergraduates are considered to be important indicators to assess the reputation of a university in China, which have an important significance for the administrators in university.

Data mining is a particular step in the process of discovering useful knowledge from data, and the application of specific pattern extraction algorithms [1]. In recent years, the application of data mining in education produced a new research direction named Educational Data Mining (EDM) [2]. So far, the existed works in EDM has covered the topics of student modeling, performance and behavior analysis, student support and feedback, etc. [3] However, to the best of our knowledge, only a few prior studies have tried to investigate features related to students' whereabouts. Piad et al. predict the employment of IT graduates using decision tree [4]. Verma tries to identify the admission criteria for master application using Chi-square test [5]. Huang applies rough set theory to the student enrollment data in order to draw some useful conclusions [6]. Jantawan and Tsai evaluate the effects of 5 classification algorithms for predicting graduate employment [7]. Most of these studies are based on supervised leaning approaches, which mainly focus on classify or predict tasks. However, studies based on unsupervised learning approaches, which could reveal the segmentation features of different student groups are still rare. Therefore, an unsupervised learning

A. El Rhalibi et al. (Eds.): Edutainment 2018, LNCS 11462, pp. 318–321, 2019.
https://doi.org/10.1007/978-3-030-23712-7_44

approach named Self-Organizing Maps (SOM) is used in this study to analyze the impact of students' academic achievement to their graduation whereabouts.

2 Basis of SOM

The SOM is an unsupervised neural network which could map the high-dimensional data onto a low-dimensional space, meanwhile, the topology of the input data in high-dimensional space is maintained in the low-dimensional representation [8]. There are two kinds of layers of nodes in SOM, namely the input layer and the Kohonen layer. The input layer is interconnected to the Kohonen layer. The connection strength between the node on each layer is denoted by a weight vector w.

The SOM learning process starts with randomly chosen weights for the nodes on the Kohonen layer. When receiving an input vector x, each node on the Kohonen layer will calculate the distance between its w and the vector x. The node with the shortest distance to x will be selected as the best matching unit. Next, the w of the best matching unit and its neighbor nodes will be adjusted so as to reduce the distance between their weight w and the input vector x. The w of the best matching unit' neighbor node (denoted as ΔW_i) is described in Eq. 1. In Eq. 1, N_m is the set of all neighbor nodes of the best matching unit. C_i is the coefficient which makes the neighbor nodes the further from the best matching unit receive less updating.

$$\Delta W_i = C_i(X_x - W_i^{old}), \quad \text{for} \quad i \in N_m \tag{1}$$

The above process is iterated for each input vector until the w has stabilized. At this time, the nodes in the Kohonen layer are arranged in order, the node in the input layer is clustered with the nodes which is similar to it, and the clustering result is mapped onto the Kohonen layer. Due to the space limitations, for detailed introduction of SOM training process, please refer to Kohonen's work [8].

3 Experiment Setting and Result Analysis

In this study, the SOM is adopted to map students' achievement records and the graduation whereabouts onto 2-dimensional representation. The training data is the achievement record of college students major in computer science in a Chinese university, as well as their graduation whereabouts, which contains 24542 records. To reduce the complexity, courses in the training data are grouped into 8 categories, including the courses related to Mathematics (MATH), Chinese (CHN), Ideological and Political (CIP), Physical Education (PE), English (ENG), Experiment and Practice (EP), Specialized Courses (SC), Specialized Basic Courses (SBC) and Optional Courses (OC). The score of each category is the average grade of all courses in such category. The graduation whereabouts are recorded in the STATUS attribute. Each student's scores about the 8 categories are treated as an input vector. Following the training process introduced in Sect. 2, the training result of SOM are shown in Fig. 1, which indicates the distribution of a single attribute among different segments. Blue represents for low value, red for high value. From Fig. 1, it's easy to identify 10 segments among the students, which are denoted as S1 to S10. The (i), (j) and (k) of Fig. 1 indicate that S7 is the segment of unemployed students, S8 and S9 for enrolled students, S1-S6 as well as S10 stand for employed students. Through the analysis of Fig. 1, some features of students can be identified.

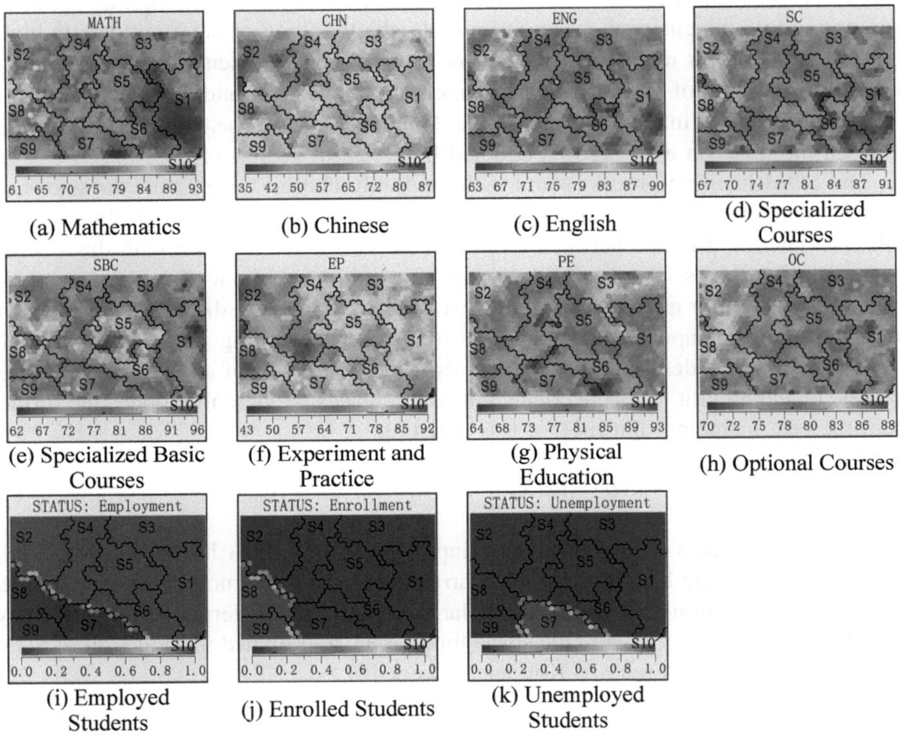

(a) Mathematics (b) Chinese (c) English (d) Specialized Courses
(e) Specialized Basic Courses (f) Experiment and Practice (g) Physical Education (h) Optional Courses
(i) Employed Students (j) Enrolled Students (k) Unemployed Students

Fig. 1. The training result of SOM (Color figure online)

Unemployed students (S7) have poor performance of the courses related to MATH, ENG, SC and PE. The first 3 categories of courses may play an important role in job-hunting. The performance of PE may indicate a student's positive altitude to the study and life. In general, which may have a positive impact on job-hunting.

The overall performance of **enrolled students** (S8 and S9) is better than the others. Specifically, students in S8 have obvious advantage of the courses related to MATH, CHN, and EP. In S9, some students' performance of the courses related to MATH and SC is not god enough, however, also be admitted to graduate school. This phenomenon deserves further investigation.

The academic performance of **employed students** (S1-S6, and S10) is generally between the group of unemployed and enrolled students, however, there are some noteworthy segments. E.g., comparing to S7, the performance of the courses related to

MATH, ENG, SC in S1 is also poor, but these students have succeeded in job-hunting. The reason for this contradiction needs further study. In S2, students have the similar level of performance to the enrolled students. However, they are good in EP, but poor in MATH. Good practical ability has a positive effect on job-hunting in IT industry, while poor Mathematics performance has a negative effect on the admission of graduate school in China, which may influence their decision making for the graduation whereabouts.

4 Conclusion

In this study, the impact of students' academic achievement to their graduation whereabouts is investigated through mapping the high-dimensional attributes into 2-dimensional representation by the SOM. The contribution of this study could help educators better understand the relationship between academic performance and graduation whereabouts. In addition, the data analysis method proposed in this study can also provide educators a new idea in understanding students' group characteristics.

Acknowledgments. This work is supported by the Science Research Project of Shaanxi Provincial Department of Education (Grant No: 17JK0614) and the Youth Innovation Fund of Xian Shiyou University (Grant No: 2013BS025).

References

1. Fayyad, U.M., Piatetskyshapiro, G., Smyth, P.: From data mining to knowledge discovery in databases. AI Mag. **17**(3), 37–54 (1996)
2. Baker, R.S.: Educational data mining: an advance for intelligent systems in education. IEEE Intell. Syst. **29**(3), 78–82 (2014)
3. Peña-Ayala, A.: Educational data mining: a survey and a data mining-based analysis of recent works. Expert Syst. Appl. **41**(4), 1432–1462 (2014)
4. Piad, K.C., Dumlao, M., Ballera, M.A., Ambat, S.C.: Predicting IT employability using data mining techniques. In: Third International Conference on Digital Information Processing, Data Mining, and Wireless Communications, pp. 26–30 (2016)
5. Verma, S.: Deciding admission criteria for master of computer applications program in india using Chi-Square test. In: International Conference on Information and Communication Technology for Competitive Strategies, pp. 103–106 (2016)
6. Huang, J.: Application of rough sets theory in graduate enrollment. Appl. Mech. Mater. **713–715**, 1640–1643 (2015)
7. Jantawan, B., Tsai, C.F.: The application of data mining to build classification model for predicting graduate employment. Int. J. Comput. Sci. Inf. Secur. **11**(10), 1–7 (2013)
8. Kohonen, T.: The self-organizing map. Neurocomputing **21**(1), 1–6 (1998)

Hands on Work Game: Neuro-Pedagogical Method to Improve Math Fraction Teaching

Manuel Ibarra[1(✉)], Ebert Gomez[1(✉)], Pablo Ataucusi[2(✉)], Vladimiro Ibañez[3(✉)], Eliana Ibarra[4(✉)], and Waldo Ibarra[5(✉)]

[1] Micaela Bastidas National University of Apurimac, Apurimac, Peru
manuelibarra@gmail.com, gomezintimpa@gmail.com
[2] COAR School, Challhuanca, Apurimac, Peru
elicoenal@gmail.com
[3] National University of Altiplano, Puno, Peru
viqibanezquispe@gmail.com
[4] San Pablo Psychological Center, Cusco, Peru
emic2705@gmail.com
[5] San Antonio Abad National University of Cusco, Cusco, Peru
ibarrazambrano@yahoo.es

Abstract. This research shows a new methodology to teach math fractions. It is based on a neuro-pedagogical approach where students have to create their own educational real-world game called "Hands on work" using recycled material. The experiments were done in two schools in Apurimac-Peru with 2 teachers and 36 students divided in two groups of 18 students. For this research we used two types of methodologies: Nominal Group for teacher's opinion and Direct Observation for student. The results show us that, according teacher's opinion the second stage called "Hands on Work" was the main activity to reinforce the student's knowledge. In the other hand, 17 students who use this methodology (real world game +software game) could get 70 points between 2.3 and 4.3 min, compared with the other style (only software game) in which 13 students get 70 points between 3 and 5.5 min.

Keywords: Math · Fraction · Neuroscience · Neuro-pedagogical · Learning · Teaching

1 Introduction

Mathematics is present in every field of study such as Engineering, Physics, Chemistry, Astronomy, Computer Science and other fields; Arithmetic, Algebra, Logic and Geometry are used in the daily life of human beings [1, 2]; not only to know how to perform mathematical operations, but rather to have a critical and reflective thought [3]. Mathematical learning disabilities and learning difficulties associated with persistent low achievement in mathematics are common and not attributable to intelligence [4]. Psychologists and pedagogues mention that the learning of mathematics depends on the context in which learns, the previous knowledge, skills and intrinsic motivation that the person possesses.

A. El Rhalibi et al. (Eds.): Edutainment 2018, LNCS 11462, pp. 322–326, 2019.
https://doi.org/10.1007/978-3-030-23712-7_45

Educators agree to say that the most important objective of mathematics teaching should be to develop students ability to "understand" rather than memorize formulas and operations [5]. The use of the computer is opening spaces for the student to live new experiences within the world of mathematics (difficult to achieve in traditional media such as blackboard, pen, paper, pencil), and allows the student to directly manipulate mathematical objects in an environment of exploration [6]. During the last years, researchers in the area of computation and didactics of mathematics have identified the need to find new strategies for teaching mathematics, focusing basically on doing it in a playful way, using computer animations, with visual representations and according to the context of students [7].

2 "Hands on Work" Methodology for Math Learning

After having reviewed the literature related to the teaching of mathematics, we will now describe the methodological proposal to teach math fractions, see Fig. 1.

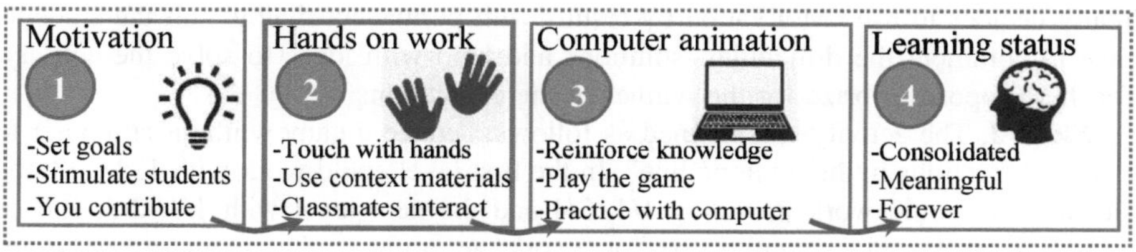

Fig. 1. Hands on work methodology

Level 1: Motivation. Motivation is the first step where the teacher has to be creative to motivate to students to achieve the goals set. All the students have to have a first conversation about the topic to be developed and each one of them must describe three important items: what problems do you have with math learning? How do you plan to solve the problem? and how can you help to others so solve problems?

Level 2: Hands on Work. Educational neuroscience is a new area of educational research that can be regarded as techniques, methods, frameworks or tools to solve educational problems related with the learning process [8]. In this stage, the teacher and students design an "Activity" to learn math fractions, for this purpose they create a didactic material. When the students create the didactic material (with recycled elements of the context) using their own hands, we called "hands on work", it has been observed that the neuronal activation for the recognition of quantities is greater than the only text explanation.

Level 3: Computer Animation. The activity created in the previous stage "hands on work", it has to be translated to a computer game animation, the elements elaborated in the previous activity must be designed and implemented considering cultural patterns of the regional environment and contextual elements (pictures, tools, persons and others). To play the game (previously designed by the students) to reinforce the knowledge about math, they can compare the real-world activity with the virtual game.

The motivation in this stage is natural, because students feel motivated when they play with computer games that they created previously [9].

Level 4: Learning status. In this final phase, the students consolidate their learning in a meaningful way and remember the topic developed permanently.

3 Experimental Results

To put in practice the proposed concepts for this new methodology of teaching fractions in mathematics, a case study has been carried out, for this purpose test cases were performed in two primary level schools of the rural area in Apurimac-Peru: "54461, Virgen del Carmen - Saywite - Curahuasi" and "50040, Asillo - Abancay" with modular code: "0200758" and "0237354" respectively. The participants were 36 students (10–12 years old) of 5th grade and 2 teachers.

Applying the 4 Stages of the Propose Methodology

Stage 1. The teacher starts selecting the "fractions" lesson to experiment the new methodology, then the teacher evaluates the strategies to motivate the students, and finally decides to use "Motivation by results with permanent dialog": all the students have to comment the difficulties, solutions and help with ideas to solve the activity. Teacher proposes a prize for the winner in the evaluation.

Stage 2. The activity was defined as follows: "create a game without computer to represent fractions in the numeric line". In the first level could work with 1, 1/2, 3; the second level could work including 1/4, 3/4 and the next level with 1/3, 2/3, and so forth. The teacher gives them a first homework: get a piece of wire and create circles and then spread it on the ground. Then, the teacher gives the next task: build a Cartesian plane to support at least 3 painted wooden circles each one fixed by a nail.

Stage 3. Computer animation game was developed to reinforce knowledge, it was directly related to transformation of fractions to Cartesian plane. The game was designed considering various levels, progressive difficulties and giving feedback about the progress of the player. The interface was designed according to the context of the Apurimac Region: mountains, clouds small houses, and other characteristics.

Stage 4. After having completed the previous stages, now the knowledge acquired is permanent because the brain stimulation was performed through an activity done by the person hands. We can also say that the learning was significant and the students have actively participated in this whole learning process.

Obtained Results

Results of the teachers' opinion. The most important results of the meeting are described as follows: Which of the stages do you think has been decisive for the student to obtain better results than before in the learning of fractions? the consensus answer was: *definitely the second one (Hands on Work), because before this methodology we explored with other games to teach math, but the students have a delay-time in exploring the meaning of the game or trying to understand the rules of the game.* How did you feel the student's attitude for this methodology? the answer was: *Throughout the process they were quite motivated, because they said they were building their own game and with materials from their environment.*

Results of Student's time-duration. The score data was released by 36 students in two groups, the score and time obtained by each student to make an analysis of progress and difficulties, taking into account the time and the score of each child (see Fig. 2A and B).

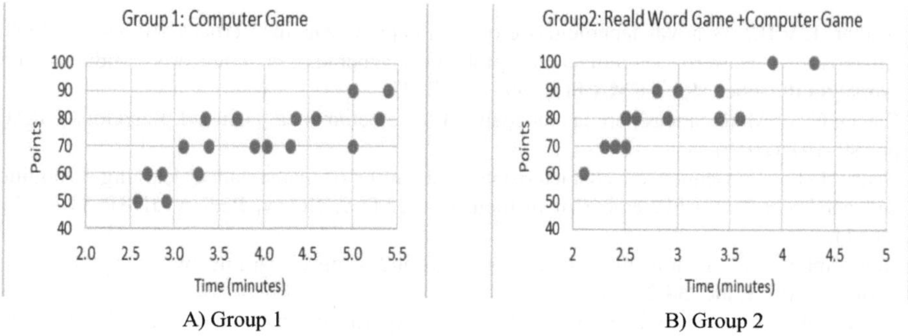

Fig. 2. (A) Group 1 (B) Group 2

Group 1: playing with: software game. Group 1 played directly with the computer-based software game.

Group 2: playing with: real word game +software game. Group 2 played first with the "real world game" built by their hands, and then they played with the "software game".

Figure 2A show us that the students of the first group that used software game, they get a score at least of 70 points between 3 and 5.5 min (13 students). The second group used the physical material built in the second stage (hands on work) and then the software game, reinforced its learning, they get a score at least 70 points between 2.3 and 4.3 min (17 students), as shown in Fig. 2B.

4 Conclusions

This article presents a new methodology to learn math fractions, based on four stages, where de second one is "Hands on Work" and is the most important to improve the teachers teaching process. According to teachers, this methodology improves the student's learning process, because they feel motivated and they built an extra activity using their hands and with materials according with the context. The experiments show us that 17 students who use this methodology (real world game +software game) could get 70 points between 2.3 and 4.3 min, compared with the other style (only with software game) in which 13 students get 70 points between 3 and 5.5 min. These results allow us to say that the manipulation of materials with the hands generates a brain activity that facilitates the understanding of the subject of fractions. As future work, we intend to analyze the relationship between the hands and other geometric figures like square and quadrilateral. We also need to probe this methodology in other context and regions of Peru.

References

1. Aguiar, E.V.B.: As novas tecnologias e o ensino-aprendizagem. Vértices **10**, 63–72 (2008)
2. Chamoso, J., Herrero, J.: Situaciones problemas generadas en contextos cotidianos: una estrategia didáctica. Rev. EMA **8**(1), 89–110 (2003)
3. Català, C.A.: Matemáticas para la ciudadanía. Educ. matemática y Ciudad. Barcelona GRAÓ, pp. 89–101 (2010)
4. Geary, D.C.: Consequences, characteristics, and causes of mathematical learning disabilities and persistent low achievement in mathematics. J. Dev. Behav. Pediatr. JDBP **32**(3), 250 (2011)
5. Newcombe, N.S.: Picture this: increasing math and science learning by improving spatial thinking. Am. Educ. **34**(2), 29 (2010)
6. Ibarra, M., Ataucusi, P., Ataucusi, E.: EducaApurimac una plataforma educativa con múltiples recursos digitales para enseñar en escuelas rurales sin acceso a internet. An. temporários do LACLO 2015 **10**(1), 26 (2015)
7. Ibarra, M.J., Soto, W., Ataucusi, P., Ataucusi, E.: MathFraction: educational serious game for students motivation for math learning. In: Latin American Conference on Learning Objects and Technology (LACLO), pp. 1–9 (2016)
8. Campbell, S.R.: Embodied minds and dancing brains: New opportunities for research in mathematics education. In: Sriraman, B., English, L. (eds.) Theories of Mathematics Education. AME. Springer, Berlin (2010). https://doi.org/10.1007/978-3-642-00742-2_31
9. Ibarra, M.J., Mamani, Y., Ataucusi, P.E., Palomino, C., Ibañez, V.: Raising students motivation for math learning using computer animation approach. In: Simposio Latinoamericano de Informática y Sociedad (SLIS-CLEI)-JAIIO 46, Córdoba (2017)

The Research on Serious Games in Social Skills Training for Children with Autism

Tingting Liu[1], Zhen Liu[2(✉)], Yanjie Chai[2], and Jin Wang[1]

[1] College of Science and Technology, Ningbo University, No. 505, Yuxiu Road, Zhuangshi, Zhenhai, Ningbo, Zhejiang, China
{liutingting, wangjin2}@nbu.edu.cn

[2] Faculty of Information Science and Engineering, Ningbo University, No. 818, Fenghua Road, Jiangbei, Ningbo, Zhejiang, China
{liuzhen, chaiyanjie}@nbu.edu.cn

Abstract. In recent years, the number of children with autism has risen sharply. It brings tremendous pain to their family. However, in many developing countries, for those autistic children, the number of rehabilitation agencies is rare, the training method is monotonous, and the rehabilitation cost is very high. Therefore, it has important practical significance to find a new effective and costless way for them. On the basis of summarizing the existing related work, this article develops a serious game prototype to assists social skills training for children with autism. The experimental results show that the emotional-based somatosensory game can significantly improve children's interests in learning. The serious game could be a new technical solution for the adjuvant treatment for children with autism.

Keywords: Autism · Serious games · Emotional model · Virtual character

1 Introduction

Autism is characterized by social-interaction difficulties. It usually occurs before the age of three. The children with autism will have abnormal social skills, communication skills, interests, and behavior patterns. They will have difficulty expressing emotions, and doing verbal and nonverbal communication. They can be identified by stereotyped and repetitive movements and behaviors.

Existing studies show that the symptoms of autism can be greatly alleviated by rehabilitation interventions. But not every autistic child will have the rehabilitation intervention. Currently, in many developing countries, for those autistic children, there are no sufficient rehabilitation agencies and high-level therapists. The training method is monotonous, and the rehabilitation cost is very high. To solve these problems, many countries have used serious game to assist the rehabilitation training. The serious game is a kind of computer game that can be used to do education and training. It can save a lot of money and will improve the social and emotional competence of children with autism. In order to enhance the effect of serious games, in this paper, an emotional model of social training has been proposed for children with autism. It will reduce the rehabilitation cost, attract the children and greatly improve therapeutic effect.

A. El Rhalibi et al. (Eds.): Edutainment 2018, LNCS 11462, pp. 327–330, 2019.
https://doi.org/10.1007/978-3-030-23712-7_46

2 Related Work

Although serious games have been used in autism treatment, lots of them are developed with two-dimensional graphics technology and traditional means of interaction. Developing games with three-dimensional virtual characters has been a new research direction. Hopkins et al. used an agent to help autistic children to recognize the facial expressions and develop social skills [1]. Kandalaft et al. constructed some real social scenes for social skill interventions for the high-functioning autism. Experimental results on eight high-functioning autism show that the serious games are a promising tool for social training [2]. The study of Kim et al. shows that the use of humanoid robots is more effective than the traditional touchscreen and is helpful to develop social skills [3]. Cai et al. developed a three-dimensional Serious Game that allowed autistic children to interact with a virtual dolphin through the Kinect. Children's different gestures (waving, etc.) can cause dolphin's different reactions. Studies about somatosensory games show that natural interaction will encourage patients to participate more in training, and will improve the effectiveness of the rehabilitation training [4]. Generally speaking, virtual characters in most of serious games are lack of autonomous emotional behaviors. We believe that emotional modeling of virtual characters plays an important role in improving human-computer interaction [5, 6].

3 Achieved Initial Results

By visiting relevant experts and autism rehabilitation institutions, we learned that autism is a social communication disorder that may be rehabilitated by training social skills. It should be noted that when social skills training is conducted, it is important to interact with the patient. To design an interactive serious game, we visited the volunteer organization for autistic children to find out the needs of those children. Scenes from daily life are constructed in a virtual community to develop those children's social skills. These scenes include a fruit shop, a barber shop, a toilet and so on. Figure 1(a) and (b) are screenshots of these scenes. While playing the game, the user can buy fruit at the fruit shop, cut hair at the barbershop, go to boys' or girls' toilet, and interact with other people in the community. Somatosensory interaction technology is used in our game. Children with autism can use gestures and fingers to interact with the computer, which enhances the fun of the game. In addition, there is a NPC character in the game,

Fig. 1. (a) The agent goes to the barbershop. (b) The user can grasp some bananas with the somatosensory interaction technology. (c) An autistic child is playing the game.

which can be a playmate to accompany the user to explore those virtual scenes. All interactive information of the game will be recorded and used to analyze the user's rehabilitation training.

Main innovations of the developed game are as follows:

(1) Develop virtual scenes of the community and its social life to train autistic children's social skills: The interactive scenes have been built in a three-dimensional virtual community. Gesture language suitable for children is defined to help children understand the meaning of the social actions. With these gestures, autistic children can interact with the computer, like say hello/goodbye and so on to virtual characters. Interactions in the game are designed for the social training of children with autism and can play a positive role in the rehabilitation of children with autism.
(2) Propose cognitive structure for virtual characters: A cognitive structure is proposed for the virtual character so that it can autonomously react to user's interaction in the game. The proposed structure contains perception, memory, motivation, goal, behavior, emotion, movement, social parameters and other modules. Among them, the emotion module contains emotional trigger, which will trigger emotions according to children's gesture language. With the proposed cognitive structure, virtual characters can respond to user's behavior. They will encourage the user and give tips of the task. These interactions will make the rehabilitation process to be interesting.
(3) Meet the needs of children with autism: The game is designed on the basis of the characteristics of children with autism and their parents' suggestions and feedbacks. It is an interesting educational game that has many special training scenarios. Users can choose the way they prefer from different interaction methods. Machine learning algorithm will be used to enhance the experience of the game in the future.

4 Conclusion

The number of children with autism is constantly growing. It is urgent to carry out rehabilitation training for those children. At present, the number of rehabilitation institutions is insufficient and rehabilitation measures are simple. Therefore, information technology can be used to improve the rehabilitation effect of children with autism. It will reduce the rehabilitation costs and benefit thousands of families.

In this paper, according to the rehabilitation needs of children with autism in speech expression, emotion recognition, and social interaction, some serious game-assisted autism rehabilitation technical solutions are proposed. A prototype system is developed for social training. Tests have shown that the game can help children become familiar with the community environment and improve their basic survivability. With the Kinect, user's body postures and facial expressions can be perceived by the camera. The autistic children can easily interact with the computer. In addition, an emotional interaction model is proposed to increase user's interest in the rehabilitation.

Our future work is to further improve the prototype system and investigate users to analyze the effectiveness of the game in improving social skills of the autism.

Acknowledgments. This work was sponsored by the Project of Medical and Health Science and Technology Plan in Zhejiang (2019PY077).

References

1. Hopkins, I., et al.: Avatar assistant: improving social skills in students with an ASD through a computer-based intervention. J. Autism Dev. Disord. **41**(11), 1543–1555 (2011)
2. Kandalaft, M., Didehbani, N., Krawczyk, D., Allen, T., Chapman, S.: Virtual reality social cognition training for young adults with high-functioning autism. J. Autism Dev. Disord. **43** (1), 34–44 (2013)
3. Kim, E., et al.: Social robots as embedded reinforces of social behavior in children with autism. J. Autism Dev. Disord. **43**(5), 1038–1049 (2013)
4. Cai, Y., Chia, N.K.H., Thalmann, D., Kee, N.K.N., Zheng, J., Thalmann, N.M.: Design and development of a virtual dolphinarium for children with autism. IEEE Trans. Neural Syst. Rehabil. Eng. **21**(2), 208–217 (2013)
5. Ortony, A., Clore, G.L., Collins, A.: The Cognitive Structure of Emotions. Cambridge University Press, New York (1988)
6. Picard, R.W.: Affective Computing. The MIT Press, Cambridge (1997)

A WebRTC e-Learning System Based on Kurento Media Server

Jie Zhang[1(✉)], Yingpeng Zhang[2], Bingfang Qi[2], Hui Zhao[3], and Toyohide Watanabe[4]

[1] Faculty of Computer Science and Engineering, Xi'an University of Technology, Xi'an, China
jiezhang1984@xaut.edu.cn

[2] SPKLSTN Lab, Department of Computer Science and Technology, Xi'an Jiaotong University, Xi'an 710049, Shaanxi, China
{yingpengzh, morinq}@stu.xjtu.edu.cn

[3] School of Computer Science and Technology, Xidian University, Xi'an 710071, Shaanxi, China
hzhao@mail.xidian.edu.cn

[4] Nagoya Industrial Science Research Institute, Nagoya 460008, Japan
watanabe@nagoya-u.jp

Abstract. WebRTC (Web Real-Time-Communications) enable blended learning in universities and support the "virtual universities". A primary challenges of the traditional technologies such as IPv4/IPv6 and TCP is the reliability. Besides, there is no free, high-quality and complete solution available that enables communication by the Web browser. In this paper, we investigate the problem of e-Learning system based on WebRTC, and propose the web-based Skyclass system on Kurento Media Server. Users may select the recorded courseware, join the real-time classroom in interactive learning methods by text, video and audio. A system with a user-friendly interface is designed, based on which experiments are performed to evaluated the effectiveness of the proposed system which can support up to 9 interactions at the same time.

Keywords: WebRTC · e-Learning system · Real-time communications

1 Introduction

The e-Learning is considered as an significant means to build continuing, lifelong and quality education [1, 2], which is starting to compete with traditional learning resource centres and enable the so-called "virtual universities" to offer a big range of specializations. There are three main ways to carry out the distance learning, including CATV, video conference and IP network [3]. But all the technology mentioned above rely on the client applications. Meanwhile, some certification programs, most vendors offer lectures "as-a-service" for training purpose (e.g. Cisco, Microsoft, VMware), but most of them are self-paced, so they miss the advantage of real-time communication and interaction with the teacher and other students. Most course providers are having their

A. El Rhalibi et al. (Eds.): Edutainment 2018, LNCS 11462, pp. 331–335, 2019.
https://doi.org/10.1007/978-3-030-23712-7_47

own implementations and methods for deploying personalized laboratory lessons, difficult to integrate with course content from other providers.

To solve these challenges, we propose a solution named web-Skyclass based on WebRTC (Web Real-Time-Communications) to integrate real-time communications with massive course resources at Web browser level [4]. The E-learning platforms become easily accessible from the browser without the need of any plug-in or any dedicated client (then, from any "thin client"), having all the communication back-end running in the cloud.

In this paper, we investigate the problem of E-learning system based on WebRTC, and propose the web-based Skyclass system. Users may select the recorded courseware, join the real-time classroom in interactive learning methods by not only text but also video and audio. Based on the proposed framework, a prototype system with a user-friendly interface is designed. The experimental evaluation on the real lectures demonstrates the effectiveness and usefulness of the proposed system which can support up to 9 interactions at the same time.

Our work can be summarized as follows:

- We propose a framework to support the E-learning system based on the Web browser,
- We provide different learning methods online to support Q&A, thesis defense, and live broadcast mode by textual and multimedia interaction.
- We implement the E-learning system based on the WebRTC.
- We preliminarily conduct experiments to evaluate the effectiveness and the usefulness of the proposed system.

This paper is organized as follows. Section 2 propose a framework of the WebRTC based online learning system. Section 3 introduce the methods and technologies in the proposed system. Section 4 implement the framework and evaluate the system. Finally, Sect. 5 presents our conclusion and future work.

2 Conceptual Viewpoint with Framework

We introduce the overview of the framework of our Skyclass system based on WebRTC. Users can open the browsers such as Chrome, Firefox or Opera on his PC to access our Skyclass system by Internet. There are three main function modes in the E-learning system, the question and answer (Q&A for short) mode, the thesis defense mode and the live broadcast mode, used by the administrator, the students and the teachers according to their different permissions.

Q&A Mode. The Question and Answer mode is used to answer the students' questions after class. As shown in Fig. 1, the teachers and students can use Skyclass at any time without geographic restriction. Merely a PC which supports web browser like Firefox, Opera and Chrome can satisfy all your requirements to use web-Skyclass.

Thesis Defense Mode. The thesis defense mode is made for students to graduate. In this mode, the process is basically similar to question and answer mode. Besides, there are another new functions, the desktop sharing and the face detection. The face detection function is very useful for the status identification to prevent indulge in corrupt practices.

Live Broadcast Mode. Live broadcast mode is used for online class, which is the basic and widely used all over the world. Not only distance education, but also the game videos are also shown in these platforms. All the student viewers merely have the priority to send textual message and watch the teachers' streams including audio, video and desktop screen.

3 Broadcasting Methods

In order to provide three different modes mentioned in Sect. 2, we have to broadcast the textual, audio, video and desktop screen streams in different methods. We name these broadcasting methods as 1 vs *n*, *n* vs *n* and *m* vs *n* accordingly. 1 vs *n* is the single-point to multi-point interaction for the basic live broadcast, *n* vs *n* is the multi-point to multi-point interaction such as the video conferencing, and *m* vs *n* is the shared interaction, which is suitable for the thesis defense mode.

***1* vs n Interaction.** The *1* vs *n* is the single-point to multi-point interaction for the basic live broadcast, which is the basic and widely used in the E-learning and online game broadcast applications all over the world as mentioned above.

***n* vs *n* Interaction.** The *n* vs *n* is the multi-point to multi-point interaction, the typical application is the online video conference system. In this interaction method, all the participants could share their textual, video, audio and desktop screen streams with the others. They can hand up to get the permission to send his voice any time all over this multi-point interaction.

***m* vs *n* Interaction.** The *m* vs *n* is the shared interaction, integrated the *1* vs *n* live broadcast and *n* vs *n* video conference features. The *m* vs *n* interaction is similar to the *n* vs *n* interaction. After the teachers and all the students pass the identity verification by traditional username-password and the face recognition, then participate in the online *m* vs *n* multi-point interaction. The only difference between them is that the content of the discussion can be shared with plenty of other audience viewers. Furthermore, the members' faces are detected in real time, consistent with the *n* vs *n* interaction. The audience viewers also has the merely textual priority in this interactive mode.

4 Experiments

We design an web-based E-learning system according to the proposed framework integrated with the user-friendly interface. In this section, we evaluate the performance of the web-Skyclass, report experiment results and our analyses.

Experiment Results. We show some experimental results first. Figure 1a is the 1 vs *n* broadcast method for the live classes. Figure 1b is the *n* vs *n* broadcast method for the online interaction conference mode. The main of the general appearance is the teacher's desktop screen, the lower right corner is the teacher's video stream, recorded 1 frame for desktop screen and 15 frames for the video per second separately.

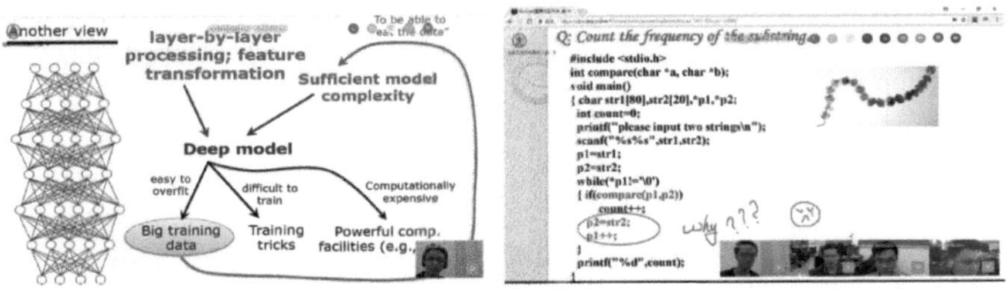

(a) 1 vs n broadcast for live class interaction (b) the n vs n broadcast for online

Fig. 1. The experimental results of the 1 vs n and the n vs n broadcast

Figure 2 show the process of the m vs n broadcast for the thesis defense mode. First, a respondent student and other audience students enter the conference room, the list of other audience students is shown on the left, and the respondent student send his audio and video stream in Fig. 2(a), as well as his desktop screen of his thesis defense presentation files, other experts in academic defense committee enter the conference mode subsequently in Fig. 2(b).

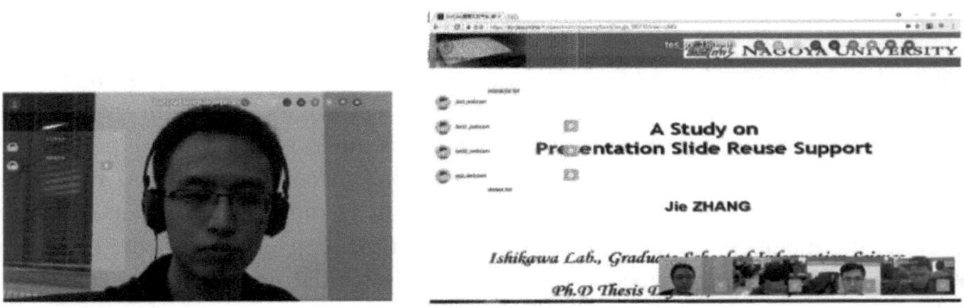

Fig. 2. The m vs n broadcast for thesis defense mode

System Evaluation. Compared to the training-course providers, such as Cisco, Microsoft, VMware, we not only provide massive multimedia coursewares to study and review, but also provide online interaction functions to discuss for a better understanding and mastery of the knowledge. As to the existing e-Learning client application, we can provide varies learning method without any client installing, only by the Web browser, all the users can access to our system, independent of his OS versions and other related software limitations. We have realized the functional implementation, and get satisfactory results, all the experiment participants are amazed by the convenience of our web-SkyClass. After some robustness evaluation on the system, which can support massive online access at the same time, our system will be employed on the website of the School of Continuing Education at Xi'an Jiaotong University (including the School of Vocational and Technical Education, and the School of Online Education) for massive access, further popularization and promotion.

5 Conclusion and Future Work

In this paper, we proposed a framework to support the E-learning system based on the Web browser, we provided different learning methods online to support Q&A, thesis defense, and live broadcast mode by textual and multimedia interaction. We implemented the E-learning system based on the WebRTC and preliminarily conduct experiments to evaluate the effectiveness and the usefulness of the proposed system.

Our future work includes designing a new way to add more dynamic face recognition functions and accomplish more refined VR. We devote to pursue more effective and high quality technologies to improve the interaction between the students and teachers. Another direction is to explore the system that can run on not only Chrome, Firefox, Opera but also other Web browsers to popularize our web-Skyclass system.

Acknowledgments. This research was partly supported by the National Natural Science Foundation of China (#61702409, #6172400), Xi'an University of Technology (#112-451116013, #112-451016023).

References

1. Zheng, Q., Chu, C.: A resource reservation and distribution system over satellite-terrestrial network. In: IEEE CSCWD 2005, Xiamen, pp. 237–242 (2005)
2. Zheng, Q., Guo, J.: A large scale interactive live teaching system over satellite and ground IP network. In: CSCWD 2005, pp. 1013–1017 (2005)
3. Wang, Z., Zhang, J., Lian, Y., Zheng, Q.: A large scale distance learning system for IPv6/Ipv4 hybrid enviroment. In: CCSE 2008, pp. 532–535 (2008)
4. Balan, T., Stanciu, A., Surariu, S.: WebRTC based e-Learning platform. In: Conference Proceedings of e-Learning and Software for Education (eLSE), pp. 48–55 (2017)
5. Ouya, S., Sylla, K., Faye, P.M.D., Sow, M.Y., Lishou, C.: Impact of integrating WebRTC in universities' e-learning platforms. In: 5th World Congress on Information and Communication Technologies (WICT), Marrakech, pp. 13–17 (2015)

A Plant Growing Game Based on Mobile Terminal and Embedded Technology

Jiwang Wang, Xiangyuan Lin, Jixuan Feng, Bin Wang, and Haiyan Jin(✉)

Faculty of Computer Science and Engineering, Xi'an University of Technology, P.O. Box 666, No. 5 South Jinhua Road, Xi'an 710048, China
jinhaiyan@xaut.edu.cn

Abstract. Usually, the reason that virtual plant growing games cannot attract players' attention is they cannot bring real game experience directly to players. In order to solve this problem, a plant growing game that combines virtuality with reality is designed and developed in this paper. Based on embedded hardware Arduino, Raspberry Pi and mobile terminals, game can change players' online operating instructions into real-world action, greatly improving the authenticity and fun of game. Experiments show that the game can run effectively.

Keywords: Plant growing game · Embedded system · Mobile terminal

1 Introduction

With the popularity of the Internet, online games become more and more people's favorite game. In recent years, the game about virtual plant cultivation has attracted many players, such as Alipay's Ant Forest. However, these games cannot give players real and interesting reality experience. The combination of virtual planting on the APP and planting cultivation in real life can greatly enhance the gaming experience and attract more players to participate. There are many virtual planting games on the APP nowadays, but there are fewer related games on how to combine virtuality with reality. This paper focuses on how to translate virtual operations on the APP into actions that handle the real world, and it gives a set of offline products that combine with virtual networks.

2 Related Equipment and Technology of Game

2.1 Related Equipment of Game

The hardware part of the game are mainly Arduino Board and Raspberry Pi, which can well analyze the data collected by the soil moisture sensor and upload data to the cloud server [1, 2].

This work is supported by National Natural Science Foundation (NNSF) of China under grant No. 61472204, and Industrial Science and Technology Project of Shaanxi Province (2016GY-140).

A. El Rhalibi et al. (Eds.): Edutainment 2018, LNCS 11462, pp. 336–340, 2019.
https://doi.org/10.1007/978-3-030-23712-7_48

The data collected by the soil moisture sensor need to be processed. This task can be well fulfilled with Arduino. Due to the limited ability of Arduino to process data, it is not convenient to upload data to the cloud server, Raspberry Pi is used to solve this problem. Through the serial port, it is easy to transfer data processed by Arduino to Raspberry Pi [3]. There are many versions of Raspberry Pi on the market, the third generation of Model B+ is utilized in this paper.

2.2 Related Technology of Game

In order to solve the problem that how to show the data of soil moisture to players and control the system to water plants remotely, an APP based on Android is designed and developed. Therefore, players can use it to control the watering system [4].

Material-Design style is utilized to design a unified and friendly user interface of APP [5], which can improve players' experience of operating APP. Taking into account the need to look over multiple groups of plants data, Fragment API was used in our design so that players can select the data they want to know.

No matter how far players are away from houseplants, they are able to know the data of soil moisture with APP. In order to achieve this goal, a cloud server is built to exchange data between APP and watering system. The main technologies to build it include Node.js, Express and MongoDB. Using these technologies, a server that has API of RESTful style can be built, which makes getting data stored on the server easier [6].

3 Structure of System

As shown in Fig. 1, firstly, the watering system obtains data of soil moisture collected by sensor and upload data to the cloud server over Wi-Fi. Then, APP can get data stored on cloud server. Finally, players can set the system into automatic mode through APP, and the system will determine whether to water plants or not based on the collected data. If the system operating mode is set to manual mode, players can manually control the system through the APP for watering plants.

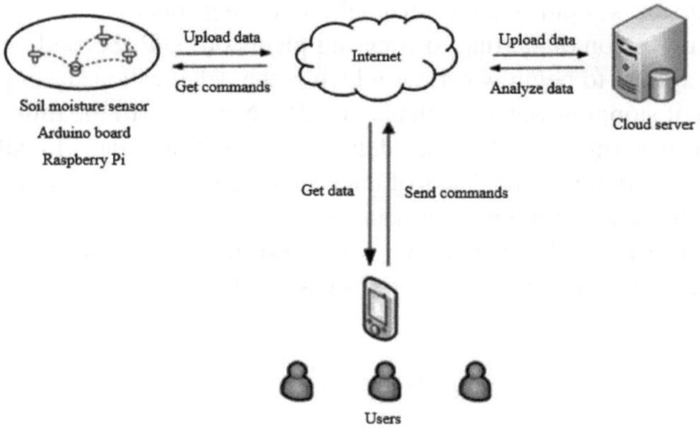

Fig. 1. Structure of system

The system is mainly composed of hardware part, which includes sensor, Arduino and Raspberry Pi, and APP. APP should be able to obtain real-time data collected by the hardware, and the hardware can receive commands sent by APP in time.

4 Research and Analysis of Experimental Results

Two kinds of experiments on house plants are designed to test the system. The first one is to analyze the delay existing in the process of collecting data by sensor. The remaining one is designed to analyze the delay, which is that when we use app for controlling system to water plants or stop watering.

4.1 Delay of Information Collection

If the value of data collected by sensor is lower than threshold, system will start to water plants. Otherwise, system will stop watering. There is delay when soil moisture sensor collect data. We wonder that if delay will have an impact on the sensitivity of the system, therefore the following experiment was done to find answer. (Make sure system is under automatic controlling mode)

First, place sensor of soil moisture in dry soil. Second, record the time it takes for the system to begin watering, which is the delay called information collection delay. Then, place sensor of soil moisture in wet soil. Next, record the time it takes for the system to stop watering, which is also information collection delay. Finally, repeat the previous steps for 25 times. Fifty data of delay are obtained because two delays can be gotten by repeating once.

As shown in Fig. 2, fifty delays were recorded. Experimental results showed that the average value of information collection delay is 1.75 s, which does not have a great bad effect on the system.

4.2 Delay of Starting and Delay of Ending

The following experiment was done to record the delay by utilizing APP to control system. (Make sure system is under manual controlling mode)

First, turn on button of starting to watering plants on APP. Second, record the time it took for the system to begin watering, which is the delay called starting delay. Then, turn on button of stopping watering plants on APP. Next, record the time it took for the system to stop watering, which is the delay called ending delay. Finally, repeat the previous steps for 50 times, and 2 sets of data can be gotten, one including fifty data for starting delay and one including fifty data for ending delay.

As shown in Fig. 3, the data above were recorded. Experimental results showed that the average value of starting delay is 2.46 s and the average value of ending delay is 2.51 s.

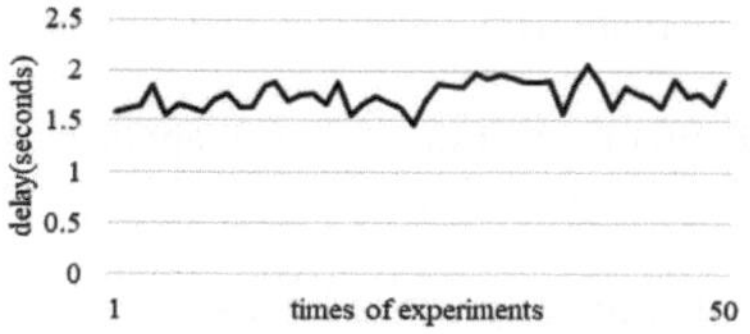

Fig. 2. Delay of information collection

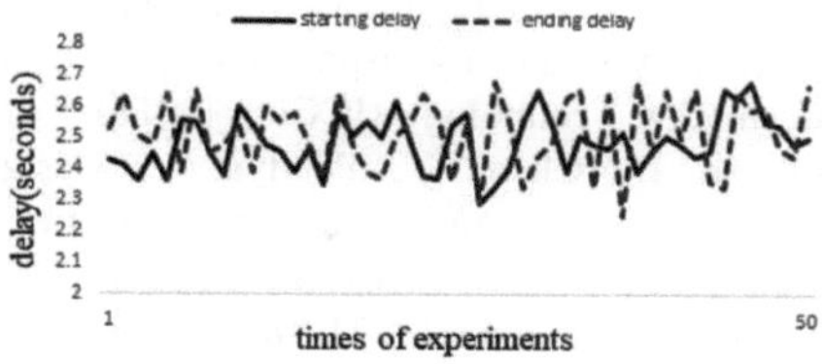

Fig. 3. Delay of starting and delay of ending

It is obvious that starting delay and ending delay are both a little longer than the information collecting delay, which is caused by network delay.

Due to the circuit, network and other factors, it is difficult to eliminate delay. Fortunately, the delay of system does not affect system badly. Therefore, we need not care too much about them. In other words, delays are so short that players can even ignore them.

5 Conclusion

Many people enjoy growing virtual plants on the APP. However, such games often do not give the player a real experience directly, rendering the game less attractive. Currently, there are fewer related games that combine virtuality with reality.

Intelligent Irrigation Game Based on Embedded Technology Arduino and Raspberry Pi are used to analyze the data collected by the soil moisture sensor and upload the data to the cloud server so that the player can remotely monitor the status of the actual plant. Players use the APP to grow plants, and they can see how their actions on the network affect plants in real life, which directly enhance the game experience.

However, the game still has some flaws, and there are some designs that make the game funnier. For example, we can add the sharing function to APP to attract more players to participate by ranking scores with other players. In addition, a surveillance camera module can be added to the game to see real-world plant status in real time. This solves the player cannot see the plant directly because of the long distance.

The game can also be developed into an educational game. We can add questions and answers to the game, which help players learn knowledge about plants, and players can apply it to grow plants in real life.

References

1. Krishna Kishore, K., Sai Kumar, M.H., Murthy, M.B.S.: Automatic plant monitoring system. In: International Conference on Trends in Electronics and Informatics (ICEI) (2017)
2. Gaja Priya, C., AbishekPandu, M., Chandra, B.: Automatic plant monitoring and controlling system over GSM using sensors. In: IEEE Technological Innovations in ICT for Agriculture and Rural Development (TIAR) (2017)

3. Imteaj, A., Rahman, T., Hossain, M.K., Zaman, S.: IoT based autonomous percipient irrigation system using raspberry Pi. In: The 19th International Conference on Computer and Information Technology (ICCIT) (2016)
4. Sullivan, D., Chen, W., Pandya, A.: Design of remote control of home appliances via Bluetooth and Android smart phones. In: IEEE International Conference on Consumer Electronics - Taiwan (ICCE-TW) (2017)
5. Hu, M., Xu, Z., Feng, L.: The research on user experience design of android system's control key. In: The 15th International Symposium on Parallel and Distributed Computing (ISPDC) (2016)
6. Wu, Z., Lei, Z., Zhao, K., Liu, Y.: The communication system between web application host computers and embedded systems based on Node.JS. In: The 10th International Congress on Image and Signal Processing, BioMedical Engineering and Informatics (CISP-BMEI) (2017)

Computer Vision in Edutainment

Static Gesture Recognition Method Based on 3D Human Hand Joints

Jingjing Gao and Yinwei Zhan(✉)

School of Computer, Guangdong University of Technology, Guangzhou 510006, China
ywzhan@gdut.edu.cn

Abstract. Depth cameras support working in a dark environment, and provide depth information from objects to cameras, hence have advantages over color cameras. So in this paper we adopt depth cameras to collect accurate gesture information for 3D modeling, in order to obtain accurate gesture recognition. On the depth map, we present methods of hand joint segmentation with random forest pixel classification and of gesture recognition with template matching, which provides accurate judgment for static gestures. Rotation may occur while the acquisition of hand data, so we conduct rotation correction by using SVD decomposition. Experimental results illustrate that this method provides more accurate joint segmentation, which is robust to hand rotation and achieves a recognition rate of 94.8% on ASL dataset.

Keywords: Hand gesture recognition · Deep map · Random forest · Singular value decomposition · Template matching

1 Introduction

Gestures provide a natural and effective way of non-verbal communication with the computer interface. Therefore, gestures can be used as a natural and effective interactive language in many aspects of daily life, such as family entertainment, medical treatment and education.

Vision based hand gesture recognition methods can deal with both motion and static gesture recognition. We focus in this paper on static gesture recognition. From the current literature [1–3], methods of static gesture recognition can be roughly classified into two categories: (1) gesture recognition based on 2D images; (2) gesture recognition based on 3D images.

In general, there are several underlining problems in 2D static gesture recognition: (1) how to deal with environmental noise that causes difficulties in detecting hand gesture images; (2) how to correct scale, rotation, and perspective changes that lead to variations of images of the same gesture; (3) how to settle complex gestures. In [1], several low-level color descriptors on 2D images that only make use of some local characteristics of a hand are developed to partly overcome illumination and rotation problems. But it's still hard to provide a compact representation for the articulated objects such as the hand.

A. El Rhalibi et al. (Eds.): Edutainment 2018, LNCS 11462, pp. 343–351, 2019.
https://doi.org/10.1007/978-3-030-23712-7_49

A depth image contains the distance information between the related object and the sensor in three-dimensional space. Compared with color images, depth images have color invariance and are not sensitive to light source types, light intensity and reflection of an object surface. Due to the distance information, depth images can simplify the contour extraction of target objects, and improve the efficiency of target detection. Guo et al. [2] extracts finger and fingertip region in the segmented precise hand region by the pixel classification. Then fingertip points are accurately obtained by the method of ellipse fitting. Ye et al. [3] uses hierarchical PSO to forces the kinematic constraints to the results of the CNNs for hybrid hand pose estimation, which is computationally expensive and time consuming. These methods do not take rotation correction into consideration.

If a gesture is not parallel to the XY plane, it should be rotated to a certain angle. In order to further improve rotational invariance and increase computing efficiency in the static gesture recognition, we try to use singular value decomposition (SVD) [4] to calculate the rotation matrix in 3D joint model. The complexity of the rotation matrix in 3D joint model is smaller than that of the whole hand by using SVD. At the same time, we use the combination of color images and depth images for hand segmentation. This trick cannot only cope with the rotation and deformation of the sample to a certain extent, but also has the robustness of illumination change and skin color interference.

2 Hand and Component Segmentation

2.1 Hand Joint Model

Joint motions include translations and rotations and each is called a degree of freedom (DOF). A human hand is a skeleton structure of hinged joints with 26 DOFs [5]. The DOFs of hand joint model is illustrated in Fig. 1(a). Gesture modeling using 3D model, benefitted from sufficient DOFs, could adapt to scale and rotation changes of gestures in different images.

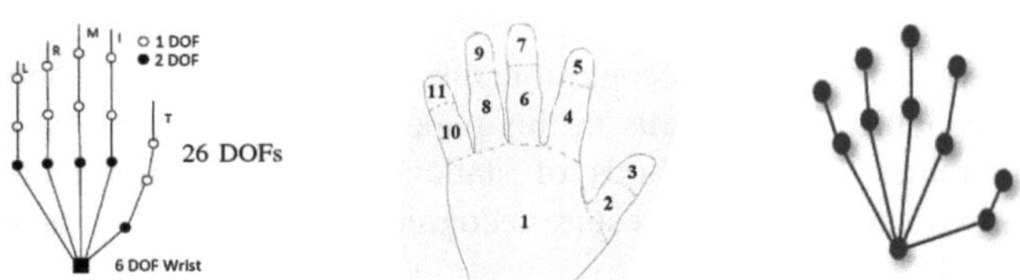

(a) Hand DOFs (b) A simplified hand model (c) Joint model

Fig. 1. Different hand models.

In practice, the joint points are often extracted by means of the simplified parts [6] as illustrated in Fig. 1(b). The joint model composed of 11 joint points for template matching is as Fig. 1(c). Each joint point represents a 3D point in the space. The lines between points mean the kinematic constraint of the hand. The simplified model has the ability to increase joint and finger distance, reduce some occlusion effect, and simplify calculation.

2.2 Background Segmentation

There are many challenges in separating a hand from a complex environment. First of all, the background is not static; it may be affected by light changes and other parts of the body interference. In addition, a hand is not independent of the connected wrist. Therefore, in order for a hand to be separated from the background, we combine both the depth image and the color image in YCrCb space (cf. [7]).

Using the combination of the nearest point gray value and the fixed threshold segmentation method directly [8] has a positive effect on the situation that the gesture parallel to the camera. For the situation that there is a tilt between the hand and camera or the distance between the hand and the body is too small, we use the maximum inter class variance with a fixed threshold for hand segmentation. The larger the variance between the foreground and the background, the greater the difference between the two parts of the image; here the hand is foreground and the other parts of the body are background.

For an RGB-D image $I(I_C, I_D)$ captured by an RGB-D camera, the depth image I_D: $S \to \mathrm{R}$ and the color image I_C: $S \to \mathrm{R}^3$ are of the same domain S. Suppose the skin color region S_B is obtained by skin color detection from I_{Cr}: $S \to \mathrm{R}$, the Cr chrominance component of I_C. Now we further find the hand region S_H from I_D, i.e.

$$S_H(t) = \{x \in S_B | I_D(x) > d\} \tag{1}$$

with a suitably chosen threshold d.

2.3 Adaptive Depth Comparison Feature

After the hand region segmentation, to separate the components of the hand becomes a pixel classification problem. Shotton *et al.* [9] put forward the depth comparison feature. For each pixel x in S_H, its depth comparison feature f_θ along the direction $\theta = (u, v)$ can be computed as

$$f_\theta(x) = I_D(x + \frac{u}{I_D(x)}) - I_D(x + \frac{v}{I_D(x)}) \tag{2}$$

where $1/I_D(x)$ ensures the features being depth invariant.

Depth comparison features are translation invariant and depth invariant, which can effectively solve the influence of light, brightness and other environmental factors on the collection of gesture samples. In [10, 11] which has good effects on human body posture recognition.

Due to the diversity of human hand gestures and the large number of training data, randomly selecting the offset vectors is of low efficiency. Therefore, Liang *et al.* [6] proposed a depth comparison feature of distance-adaptive sampling scheme. They use a kernel function of the Gauss distribution to determine the location of each context point in the hand region. Figure 2 illustrates the distribution of feature points based on a conventional method and distance-adaptive sampling scheme respectively.

(a) (b)

Fig. 2. Depth comparison feature and distance adaptive depth comparison feature.

In order to simplify the calculation, the offset vector pair is taken in the square centered at x of size $2r + 1$. For simplicity, we focus the discussion on one dimension, for the sampling scheme is symmetric. Take a non-increasing quadratic function $h(s)$ as the adaptive sampling function with s the horizontal or vertical distance from the current pixel x to its context point. The coordinate of the context point can be obtained by solving

$$\int_0^s h(s)ds = j, \qquad j = 1, 2, \ldots, r. \tag{3}$$

From the two kinds of sampling methods in Fig. 2, we see that the sampling in (b) is more intensive near the center and retains more details of the hand region, so these feature points can provide more accurate basis for pixel classification.

2.4 Component Segmentation

Random forest classifier is put forward by Breiman *et al.* [12], which is a rapid and stable method of machine learning. It is a strong classifier by the combination of multiple weak classifiers, using the method of bagging to overcome overfitting. Based on the depth comparison features, a random forest classifier is trained to label the hand parts by per-pixel classification. The objective is to assign for each pixel $x \in S_H$ a label $c(x) \in L = \{1, 2, \ldots, 11\}$.

In the testing stage, the input pixel x is first processed by each tree in the random decision forest that has T trees in total. For each tree with index t, the posterior probability $Pt(c|x)$ is obtained by starting at the root and recursively assigned to the left or the right child based on the tree node test result until it finally reaches a leaf node. Finally the target category $P(c|x)$ is obtained by

$$P(c|x) = \frac{1}{T}\sum\nolimits_{t=1}^{T} P_t(c|x). \tag{4}$$

The final classification results of the random forest are decided by the classification results of each tree. Every pixel $x \in S_H$ of the hand region will vote for a single shape label for the hand images

$$c^* = \arg\max_c P(c|x). \tag{5}$$

3 Gesture Recognition

3.1 Joint Point Location

In Sect. 2, the segmentation result generates the probability distribution $P(c|x)$ of each pixel x belonging to a tag c. It must be pointed out that this pixel level classification method may have some pixels misclassified. For this, we adopt mean-shift model technique. For discrete hand joint pixels, the center of the density is calculated iteratively to serve as the actual location of the joint point. For a pixel x initialized by the random forest's probability distribution center of the pixels, take its neighborhood pixels $\{x_i, i = 1, \ldots, N\}$ in the searching window. Then the mean-shift vector

$$m(x) = \frac{\sum_{i=1}^{N} K(x_i, x)x_i}{\sum_{i=1}^{N} K(x_i, x)} \tag{6}$$

is defined with Gauss kernel functions

$$K(x_i, x) = P(c|x_i)I_D(x_i)^2 \exp(-\sigma||x - x_i||^2). \tag{7}$$

Here σ is the bandwidth of the Gauss function related to the size of the component and $I_D(x_i)^2$ is used to estimate the area of pixel point in the world coordinate system, which is related to the distance of the object to the camera.

The above defined $m(x)$ always points toward the direction of maximum increase of the density of $\{x_i, i = 1, \ldots, N\}$. Iteratively update x via $x \leftarrow m(x)$ until $||m(x) - x|| < \lambda$, with λ a small nonnegative value, and take the final x as the expected joint position.

3.2 Rotation Correction of Skeleton Model

In order for the geometric correction of the input gesture, SVD is used to calculate the rotation matrix between the input gesture and the template gesture in joints model, which can effectively improve the recognition rate and reduce the computational complexity. Suppose the set of input joints is $P = \{p_1, p_2, \ldots, p_n\}$, the c-th template of joint points is $O_c = \{o_1, o_2, \ldots, o_n\}$. To calculate the rigid transpose information of P and O_c, we introduce the rotation matrix M_R and shift matrix M_T, take $\bar{p}$ and $\bar{o}$ as the gravity center of P and O_c, and make the two plane of the gravity center coincide by translation. Then minimize the distance between P and O_c by

$$F(M_{\mathrm{R}}, M_{\mathrm{T}}) = \underset{M_{\mathrm{R}}, M_{\mathrm{T}}}{\arg\min} \sum\nolimits_{i=1}^{n} ||(M_{\mathrm{R}} p_i + M_{\mathrm{T}}) - o_i||^2, \tag{8}$$

and equivalently, by making the partial derivative of the sum with M_{T} being zero, i.e. $M_{\mathrm{T}} = \bar{o} - M_{\mathrm{R}}\bar{p}$,

$$F(M_{\mathrm{R}}, M_{\mathrm{T}}) = \underset{M_{\mathrm{R}}, M_{\mathrm{T}}}{\arg\max}\, \mathrm{tr}(M_{\mathrm{R}}(P - \bar{p})(O - \bar{o})^T) + e \tag{9}$$

where e is a constant. Using SVD, we have $(P - \bar{p})(O - \bar{o})^T = U \sum V^T$. Hence the rotation matrix $M_{\mathrm{R}} = UV^T$.

3.3 Gesture Recognition Based on Template Matching

To complete the gesture recognition task, the minimum Euclidean distances between the input gesture skeleton P and the template skeletons O_c, $c \in L$, is calculated, and the related index is $c' = \arg\min_c ||P - O_c||$. If the minimum distance $||P - O_{c'}||$ is smaller than a prescribed threshold, then the gesture falls into class c'.

4 Experiment

4.1 Experimental Data

In the detection stage, we use the American Sign Language (ASL) data set, which contains 72000 hand gesture depth images and color images collected by Kinect, reflecting skin color disturbances, background changes, and light changes. We select 10 of English alphabet gestures from A to K, in which all but J are *static* gestures; see Fig. 3. This subset of ASL dataset includes 500 pictures randomly selected from each gesture, totally 5000 pictures, and is taken as experiment data, in which 100 pictures are selected for each gesture as test data.

Fig. 3. Gestures A-I and gesture K in ASL data set.

4.2 Process and Result Analysis

As for the sample sizes as discussed in Sect. 2.3, we choose r = 10 to collect u-v vector pairs, so the number of depth comparison features is $(2r + 1)2 - 1 = 440$. Experiment suggests that the best parameters for segmentation with random forest are $T = 4$ for the number of decision tree and maxDepth = 19 for the maximum depth of decision tree.

Yao *et al.* [13] propose a method of component segmentation based on 3D hand contour extraction of depth image. This method does not rely on a large number of training data in the classification, and can achieve real-time effect. The experiment show that our method performs much better than Yao's. See Table 1.

Table 1. Segmentation and recognition rate.

Parts	Thumb T	Thumb	Index T	Index	Middle T	Middle	Ring T	Ring	Small T	Small
Contour Segm.	41.2%	39.6%	40.5%	30.8%	28.1%	39.3%	32.2%	32.9%	36.7%	36.1%
Ours method	70.5%	74.6%	88.9%	71.3%	88.2%	81.9%	84.1%	83.9%	78.3%	79.8%

Dong *et al.* [14] use the adaptive depth comparison features as the basis in classification, use mean-shift to cluster joint locations, and distinguish different signs according to the relationship between the joint angles. Without dealing with the rotation angle of the hand, they can only obtain an average accuracy rate at 85.3%. In our method, we not only produce accurate position of joint points, but also propose the method to correct the non-standard input gesture before matching the standard template, which achieves an average accuracy of 94.8% (Table 2).

Table 2. Recognition rates on ASL data sets (%).

	A	B	C	D	E	F	G	H	I	K	AVG
Dong's	83.7	88.2	90.6	93.5	81.3	91.1	76.4	83.2	91.5	78.6	85.3
Ours	94.9	96.4	95.5	97.4	92.3	96.7	89.6	95.9	96.5	92.5	94.8

This set of gestures can be used to design commands to control a player's operation, for scenarios like classroom teaching and home entertainment. According to the player's functions, we choose the first letter of the eight words naming the control instructions. See Table 3.

Table 3. A set of gestures and their actions.

Gesture	Command	Activity	Description	Gesture	Command	Activity	Description
	E	Enter	Enter the player		K	Ok	Start to play
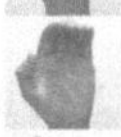	C	Close	Close the player		H	Hold	Play pause
	A	Advance	Former song		I	Increase	Increase the volume
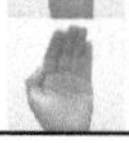	B	Back	Next song		D	Decrease	Decrease the volume

5 Conclusion

Static gesture recognition has been widely investigated in literature, whereas there still remain some challenges like higher recognition rate and robustness in illumination change. So we designed an algorithm for static hand gesture recognition with 3D hand joint model from RGB-D data. Skin region is first obtained from the color component of the input RGB-D image and the hand region is further segmented from the depth component. Then the joint positions in 3D model are found through random forest and mean-shift. Here the 3D joint model is of benefits to represent complex gestures and reduce computational costs. We also invoke SVD transform to deal with rotation variation. This hybrid strategy, according to experiments, is able to deal well with the changes of illumination, skin color and rotation, at a recognition rate of 94.8% on the ASL data set. It should be noted that we do not consider the case of self-occlusion of fingers. The hidden parts of fingers would be induced by the structural logics of fingers or kinematical constraint or modeled with multi-view RGB-D images, which becomes our further focus. Efforts should also be put on the real-time implementation of the proposed method so that applications on education will be well conducted.

Acknowledgments. This work was supported by Project of Science and Technology Program of Guangzhou (grant no. S201604016034), Project of Science and Technology Program of Guangdong (grant no. 2017B010110015).

References

1. Feng, Z., Yang, B., Chen, Y., et al.: Features extraction from hand images based on new detection operators. Pattern Recognit. **44**(5), 1089–1105 (2011)
2. Guo, S., Zhang, M., Pan, Z., et al.: Gesture recognition based on pixel classification and contour extraction. In: International Conference on Virtual Reality and Visualization, pp. 93–100. IEEE (2015)
3. Ye, Q., Yuan, S., Kim, T.-K.: Spatial attention deep net with partial PSO for hierarchical hybrid hand pose estimation. In: Leibe, B., Matas, J., Sebe, N., Welling, M. (eds.) ECCV 2016. LNCS, vol. 9912, pp. 346–361. Springer, Cham (2016). https://doi.org/10.1007/978-3-319-46484-8_21
4. Klema, V., Laub, A.J.: The singular value decomposition: its computation and some applications. IEEE Trans. Autom. Control **25**(2), 164–176 (1980)
5. Kuch, J.J., Huang, T.S.: Vision based hand modeling and tracking for virtual teleconferencing and telecollaboration. In: International Conference on Computer Vision, p. 666. IEEE Computer Society (1995)
6. Liang, H., Yuan, J., Thalmann, D.: Parsing the hand in depth images. IEEE Trans. Multimed. **16**(5), 1241–1253 (2014)
7. Dhruva, N., Rupanagudi, S.R., Sachin, S.K., et al.: Novel segmentation algorithm for hand gesture recognition. In: International Multi-Conference on Automation Computing Communication Control and Compressed Sensing, pp. 383–388. IEEE (2013)
8. Hachaj, T., Ogiela, M.R., Piekarczyk, M.: Dependence of Kinect sensors number and position on gestures recognition with gesture description language semantic classifier. In: Computer Science and Information Systems, pp. 571–575. IEEE (2013)

9. Shotton, J., Fitzgibbon, A., Cook, M., et al.: Real-time human pose recognition in parts from single depth images. In: IEEE Conference on Computer Vision and Pattern Recognition, pp. 1297–1304. IEEE Computer Society (2011)
10. Rafi, U., Gall, J., Leibe, B.: A semantic occlusion model for human pose estimation from a single depth image. In: Computer Vision and Pattern Recognition Workshops, pp. 67–74. IEEE (2015)
11. Ionescu, C., Carreira, J., Sminchisescu, C.: Iterated second-order label sensitive pooling for 3D human pose estimation. In: Computer Vision and Pattern Recognition, pp. 1661–1668. IEEE (2014)
12. Breiman, L.: Random forests. Mach. Learn. **45**, 5–32 (2001)
13. Yao, Y., Fu, Y.: Real-time hand pose estimation from RGB-D sensor. In: IEEE International Conference on Multimedia and Expo, pp. 705–710. IEEE Computer Society (2012)
14. Dong, C., Ming, C.L., Yin, Z.: American sign language alphabet recognition using Microsoft Kinect. In: Computer Vision and Pattern Recognition Workshops, pp. 44–52. IEEE (2015)

A Combined Deep Learning and Semi-supervised Classification Algorithm for LS Area

Xiaofeng Wang[1(✉)], Guohua Geng[1], Na Wang[1], Qiannan Song[1], Ge He[1], and Zheng Wang[2]

[1] Information Science and Technology, Northwest University, Xi'an 710127, China
xfwang@nwu.edu.cn
[2] School of Computing and Communications Infolab21, Lancaster University, Lancaster, UK

Abstract. In real world, there are many areas with **L**arge images but only **S**mall labelled (we called **LS area**), in there supervised and unsupervised algorithm can't work well, but semi-supervised technology exploiting patterns both in labelled and unlabeled data to get labels can work well. The classification accuracy directly depends on the features extracted from the images. Recently, with the emergence and successful deployment of deep learning techniques for image classification, more research on getting features is directed to deep learning techniques. This paper proposes a combined semi-supervised classifier and pre-trained deep CNN model algorithm—**CDLSSC** (**C**ombined **D**eep **L**earning and **S**emi-**S**upervised **C**lassification) for LS area. The transfer learning that has been tested and verified in some areas is used to extract features in this algorithm. The method **CDLSSC** is evaluated on three image datasets and achieves superior performance. We apply it to the Terra-Cotta Warriors image classification area and get super results, which means that it can be used in cultural relic's area successfully.

Keywords: LS area · Feature extract · Semi-supervised classifier · Transfer learning · Image classification

1 Introduction

Image classification is an important task for computer vision. The task of image classification has been investigated in a supervised learning paradigm for a long time, which is bound by the number and the quality of the training instances. But with the emergence of large image collections and vigorous development of the Internet, the available labelled images are usually inadequate for training a supervised classifier. Furthermore, in real-world applications, collecting and annotating huge amount of domain-specific data is time consuming and expensive, and labelling more images will incur high time and monetary costs. To address this problem, semi-supervised image classification has been developed to explicitly exploit the information revealed by both limited labelled images and sufficient unlabelled images [1], so automatic image

A. El Rhalibi et al. (Eds.): Edutainment 2018, LNCS 11462, pp. 352–360, 2019.
https://doi.org/10.1007/978-3-030-23712-7_50

labelling or semi-supervised image labelling can scale up the training instances, but it requires having a set of high-quality features to capture the essential characteristics of the input image.

Existing approaches rely on handcrafted features generated through a combination of expert domain knowledge and extensive human involvement [2]. However, due to drastic efforts required in feature engineering, the obtained features can only target a small class of images and can't exactly represent the original images, which makes the semi-supervised images' labels hard to generalize. Now the deep learning introduces the concept of end-to-end learning by using the trainable feature extractor followed by a trainable classifier [3, 4], which reveals the remarkable progress for image classification. The deep learning model, such as Convolutional Neural Networks (CNNs) [5] and Deep Belief Networks (DBNs) [6] have been widely used for image classification and object recognition. Especially, they have good performance on feature learning [7–9]. However, a new deep learning model contains millions of parameters, training one model requires huge amount of data, high computational resources, and long time—several hours even several days. It doesn't suitable for the small data area. But transfer learning can control this problem, it mainly employs two approaches: (1) preserving the original pre-trained network and updating the weights based on the new training dataset. (2) using pre-trained network for feature extraction, and representation followed by a generic classifier for classification [10]. The second approach has been successfully applied for many recognition and classification tasks [11]. Our proposed technique for image classification also falls under the second category. We investigate the recently proposed benchmark deep models such as AlexNet [12], GoogleNet [13], Inception, VGG, ResNet, and so on. Base on the experimentations, we select the AlexNet as source model for building a target model for the image classification task. AlexNet (Fig. 1) has demonstrated excellent classification results on the ImageNet competition.

The input is 227 × 227 pixels RGB images and the network has 5 convolutional layers (from C1 to C5) and 3 fully connected layers (Fc6 to Fc8). The source model has been used for feature extraction and representation followed by a semi-supervised classifier for less labelled image data classification.

2 Related Works

In this section, we review some representative existing literature of semi-supervised image classification, deep learning and transfer learning on image classification, as they are related to this work.

A. Semi-supervised Image Classification

Semi-supervised learning (SSL) has been studied for a long time, which aims to classify the data that has a massive number of unlabelled data only with a few labelled. Although the massive unlabelled examples do not have explicit labels, they convey the distribution information of the entire data, which can be exploited for accurate classification. With respect to its application to image classification, Kuznietsov [14] proposed a novel approach to depth map prediction from monocular images in a semi-supervised way, in the experiments the author demonstrated superior performance in depth map prediction from single images. Zhang [15] investigated the usage of semi-supervised learning (SSL) to obtain competitive detection accuracy with very limited training data.

B. Deep learning and transfer learning on Image Classification

Deep learning refers to a class of computing machines that can learn a hierarchy of features by establishing high-level features from low-level ones and is pioneered by Fukushima [16]. One of these models is the convolutional neural network (CNN) developed by Lécun [5], which comprises several deep layers to learn an information hierarchy by building high-level information from low-level data and can automatically get discriminative information. Murthy [18] presented a generic framework to build an efficient deep learning network that significantly improves the performance. Ghazi [19] used deep convolutional neural networks to identify the plant species captured in a photograph and evaluated different factors affecting the performance of these networks. In machine learning, utilizing the previously learnt knowledge for solving a new task is known as transfer learning or knowledge transfer [16], which is very helpful for training the model with limited size dataset because CNN is prone to overfitting with a small dataset, and is used to fine-tune the pre-trained models. Shao [20] analyzed on the adjust hyper-parameters method and provided insights and a deeper understanding of different deep learning algorithms for RGB-D feature extraction and fusion. Ding [7] designed task-driven deep structures for better knowledge transfer combining classifier and deep Neural Net structures to generate a more discriminative non-linear features optimized for the classifier and got good results.

So we compare these methods and apply them to semi-supervised area, and propose our Combined Deep Learning and Semi-Supervised Classification Algorithm (CDLSSC).

3 CDLSSC Algorithm

In this paper, we combine the merits of AlexNet and semi-supervised classifiers to propose the CDLSSC Algorithm (Fig. 1), which is for the LS area that contains huge images and only with less labelled images.

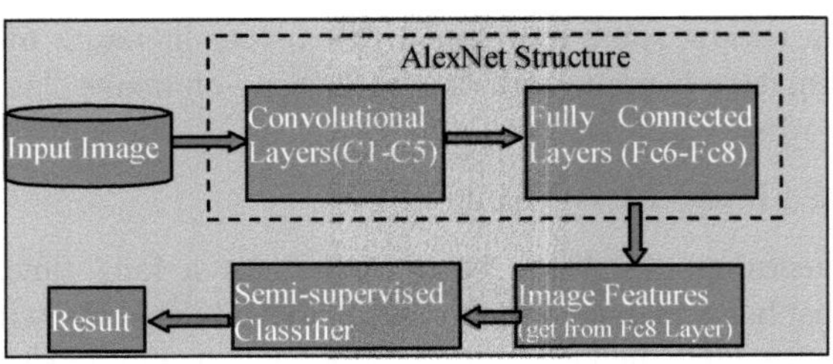

Fig. 1. CDLSSC method structure

First, we use AlexNet as the feature extractor to extract the useful features. Second, we use semi-supervised classifier for image classification.

About the semi-supervised classifier, the notations are defined as following. Suppose the number of labelled and unlabelled samples is L and U respectively.

The set of labelled pairs is denoted as $\left\{\left(x^{(m)}, y^{(m)}\right)\right\}_{m=1}^{L}$, and the set of unlabelled samples is denoted as $\left\{x^{(m)}\right\}_{m=L+1}^{L+U}$ where $x^{(m)} \in R^{N\times 1}(\mathrm{N} = \mathrm{L} + \mathrm{U})$, $y^{(m)} \in \{1, 2, \cdots, K\}$, and N is the total number of samples. The goal of classification is learning a model which assign labels to unlabelled samples.

Conventional semi-supervised image classification is usually conducted on a weighted similarity graph $\mathrm{G} = \ <\mathrm{V}, \varepsilon>$, where V is the node set representing all images, and ε is the edge set encoding the pairwise similarities between these images. The target is iteratively propagating the labels from L to U so that all the elements in U can be precisely classified. This method works on each node, if the data is huge, there will be a large amount of calculation.

So, we improve the algorithm by adding KNN cluster to class the data into different groups, and the method gives them labels based on the groups, which greatly reduces the amount of calculation.

The details of the semi-supervised classifier are shown in Fig. 2.

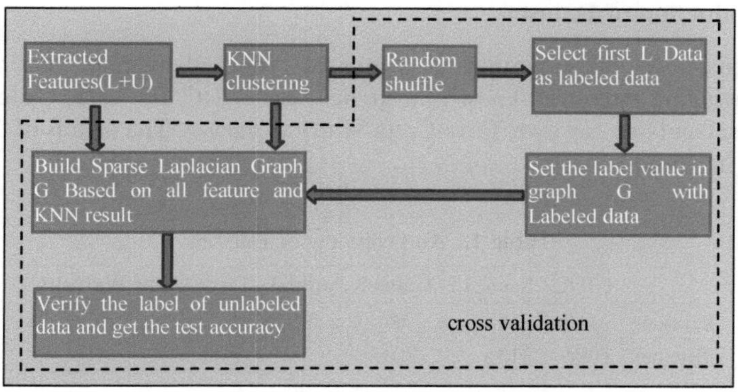

Fig. 2. Semi-supervised application structure

The algorithm is as following:

Step 1: Using transfer learning and AlexNet extract features of all images, including Labelled and Unlabelled $(\mathrm{L} + \mathrm{U})$ images.

Step 2: Compute K-Nearest Neighbors (KNN) for each data point (the point itself is also included in the list), and get each data point's indices of its nearest neighbors, in this step the parameter k defines the amount of the data point's nearest neighbors.

Step 3: Based on KNN results build Laplacian Graph L using Gaussian Kernel (1).

In this step there is one parameter σ.

$$k(\|x - xc\|) = \exp\left\{-\frac{\|x - xc\|^2}{2 * \sigma^2}\right\} \tag{1}$$

Step 4: Randomly shuffle all images' features and select R images as labelled data, so the rest images are unlabelled data. Then based on Graph L and labelled images R we build a sparse curvature-aware Laplacian Graph G .

Step 5: Using graph G and Labelled data get the labels of the unlabelled images, and the accuracy of the model by comparing the labels getting from the algorithm and true labels of unlabelled images. We use two methods to test the algorithm (introduced in Sect. 4.2).

Step 6: Continue to do Step 4 and Step 5 for 10 times (10-fold cross verify), and then we can get the average correct accuracy and the time cost.

Step 7: Change value of parameter R in the experiments to get the different classification accuracy results based on different labelled images.

4 Experimentations and Results

4.1 Introduction of Dataset

This section shows the experimental results of proposed method working on four datasets, including three well-known image datasets: UIUC, Scene15, Caltech Animal image dataset and one our own Terra-Cotta Warriors dataset. The details of the datasets are shown in Table 1.

Table 1. An Overview of Datasets

	UIUC	Scene15	Caltech Animal	Terra-Cotta Warriors
#classes	8	15	9	6
#images	1096	3135	720	1800

Terra-Cotta Warriors dataset (Fig. 3) is collected by ourselves. It contains one whole model's 6 parts: leg, foot, dress, above the waist, hand and leg. Each part has 300 images, so totally we have 1800 images.

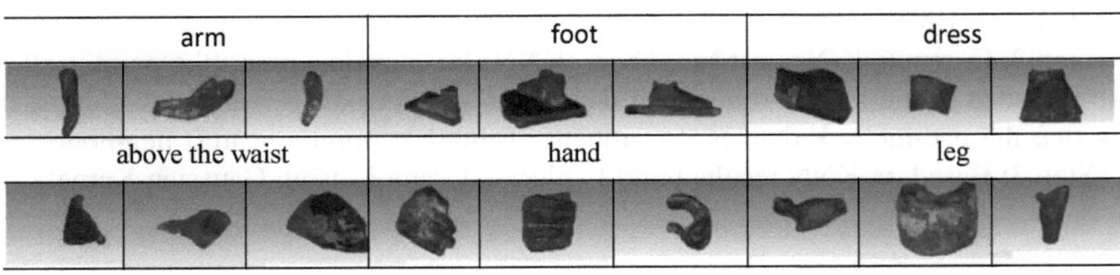

Fig. 3. Terra-Cotta Warriors dataset

4.2 Experiments of CDLSSC Algorithm on Datasets

For the graph-based semi-supervised classification algorithm, there are two ways to get the classification accuracy of test images. One is using test and train images together to reconstruct the graph, and then the labels of test images are got by label transfer technology. Another one is adding some other additional forecasting mechanisms, such as using train images (include labeled and unlabeled) to train a classification such as SVM model to predict the labels of test images. In this paper, we use first one method to test accuracy, and we adopt two solutions to evaluate the algorithm, one is treating all unlabeled images as test images, and another one is randomly selecting 40% of all images (include labeled and unlabeled) as test images.

There are three parameters k, σ and R in the program effecting the classify accuracy, k specifies the size of nearest neighbors for each data point, and σ is the parameter for the weight function in building the graph Laplacian, and R indicates the number of labeled images. We tune the parameters using cross-validation, and do numerous experiments to compare the accuracy, and find that σ influence the accuracy and k influence the time spent mainly. Based on the experiments we get suitable values of k and σ, which are 20 and sample variance respectively. For different dataset there are different amount of labelled images, so we use different numerical value R to test the algorithm and use 10-fold cross verify method to get average accuracy.

1. Evaluation on three well known dataset

There are many works on three well known image datasets [3], and different methods get different results (Fig. 4). Our proposed method CDLSSC is also used on datasets, and getting the results (Tables 2, 3 and 4), which are precede other works [3]. So from Fig. 4 and Tables 2, 3 and 4, we get the information that the method CDLSSC is better than the methods in state of art.

Table 2. The accuracy of UIUC dataset using CDLSSC methods (proposed in the paper)

Labeled images	80	240	400	560	720
Accuracy (all unlabeled images as test data)	0.85	0.91	0.92	0.92	0.92
Accuracy (40% all images as test data)	0.73	0.90	0.93	0.94	0.96

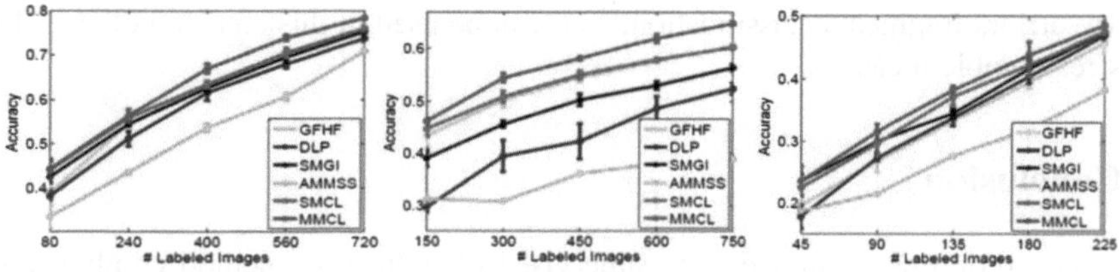

(a)UIUC dataset (b)Scene15 dataset (c) Caltech Animal dataset

Fig. 4. Comparison results of three datasets in the paper [3]

Table 3. The accuracy of Scene15 dataset using CDLSSC methods

Labeled images	150	300	450	600	750
Accuracy (all unlabeled images as test data)	0.53	0.62	0.68	0.73	0.75
Accuracy (40% all images as test data)	0.73	0.78	0.83	0.88	0.90

Table 4. The accuracy of Caltech Animal dataset using CDLSSC methods

Labeled images	45	90	135	180	225
Accuracy (all unlabeled images as test data)	0.44	0.65	0.71	0.75	0.77
Accuracy (40% all images as test data)	0.39	0.61	0.66	0.74	0.81

2. Evaluation on Terra-Cotta Warriors Fragments dataset

In society there is a strong need for Computer-Aided automatic reassembling in broken cultural relics and protection work. The Terra-cotta warrior models are very complex, and there are huge number of fragments need to reassemble. Directly reassembling them is very hard and need to do many matching works, so we first classify the fragments into different parts to reduce the number of reassemble pieces and then reassemble them. Most fragments of them are unlabeled, so we use the semi-supervised method in the cultural relic reassembly area and classify the Terra-Cotta Warriors fragments into different body parts. The results are shown in Table 5, which shows that CDLSSC has good effect in the Terra-Cotta Warriors dataset.

Table 5. The accuracy of Terra-Cotta Warriors dataset using CDLSSC method

Labeled images	200	300	600	800	1000	1200	1500
Accuracy (all unlabeled images as test data)	0.77	0.82	0.88	0.91	0.91	0.92	0.94
Accuracy (40% all images as test data)	0.79	0.84	0.92	0.95	0.96	0.97	0.99

From all the results, we get the conclusion that our method can achieve higher semi-supervised classification rate than other methods due to the features extracted by deep learning. And we also find that the CDLSSC method has good effect in Terra-Cotta Warriors fragments classification, so it can be used in this area and other cultural relics reassemble areas.

5 Conclusion

This paper proposes an image semi-supervised classification method combined with transfer learning technology. The transfer learning technology is used as a feature extractor and the semi-supervised classification is used to classify the image data with only a few labeled images in the LS area. It demonstrates that transfer learning can successfully utilize the already learned knowledge to the new task and is very useful in the data insufficient area. The performance of the CDLSSC is tested on UIUC, Scene15 and Caltech Animal images three well-known datasets, and the results are better than other methods [3]. The comparative analysis confirms that the proposed methods outperforms the similar state-of-the-art methods. In addition to this, it also confirms that semi-supervised classification with features extracted by deep learning net has an advantage over the hand-craft features in boosting the accuracy of the recognition system. In this paper, we also use the method to classify the Terra-Cotta Warriors fragments and get great effect, which indicates that the CDLSSC method can extend to the cultural relics reassemble area. In future, we would like to extend this method for more complex data.

Acknowledgments. We thank the National Natural Science Youth Foundation of China (Number: 61602380, 61802311), National Natural Science Foundation of China (Number: 61673319, 61772421, 61731015) and Shaanxi Provincial Education Special foundation of China (Number: 12JK0730).

References

1. Liu, X., Guo, T., He, L., et al.: A low-rank approximation-based transductive support tensor machine for semi-supervised classification. IEEE Trans. Image Process. Publ. IEEE Signal Process. Soc. **24**(6), 1825–1838 (2015)
2. Gong, C., Tao, D., Maybank, S.J., et al.: Multi-modal curriculum learning for semi-supervised image classification. IEEE Trans. Image Process. Publ. IEEE Signal Process. Soc. **25**(7), 3249 (2016)
3. Zhu, F., et al.: From handcrafted to learned representations for human action recognition: a survey. Image Vis. Comput. **55**, 42–52 (2016)
4. Sargano, A.B., Angelov, P., Habib, Z.: A comprehensive review on handcrafted and learning-based action representation approaches for human activity recognition. Appl. Sci. **7** (1), 110 (2017)
5. Lécun, Y., Bottou, L., Bengio, Y., et al.: Gradient-based learning applied to document recognition. Proc. IEEE **86**(11), 2278–2324 (1998)
6. Hinton, G.E., Osindero, S., Teh, Y.-W.: A fast learning algorithm for deep belief nets. Neural Comput. **18**(7), 1527–1554 (2006)
7. Ding, Z., Nasrabadi, N.M., Fu, Y.: Task-driven deep transfer learning for image classification. In: IEEE International Conference on Acoustics, Speech and Signal Processing, pp. 2414–2418. IEEE (2016)
8. Gao, X., Li, W., Loomes, M., et al.: A fused deep learning architecture for viewpoint classification of echocardiography. Inf. Fusion **36**, 103–113 (2016)
9. Yu, S., Wu, Y., Li, W., et al.: A model for fine-grained vehicle classification based on deep learning. Neurocomputing **257**, 97–103 (2017)
10. Zeiler, M.D., Fergus, R.: Visualizing and understanding convolutional networks. In: Fleet, D., Pajdla, T., Schiele, B., Tuytelaars, T. (eds.) ECCV 2014. LNCS, vol. 8689, pp. 818–833. Springer, Cham (2014). https://doi.org/10.1007/978-3-319-10590-1_53
11. Sharif Razavian, A., et al.: CNN features off-the-shelf: an astounding baseline for recognition. In: Proceedings of the IEEE Conference on Computer Vision and Pattern Recognition Workshops (2014)

12. Krizhevsky, A., Sutskever, I., Hinton, G.E.: ImageNet classification with deep convolutional neural networks. In: Advances in Neural Information Processing Systems (2012)
13. Szegedy, C., et al.: Going deeper with convolutions. In: Proceedings of the IEEE Conference on Computer Vision and Pattern Recognition (2015)
14. Kuznietsov, Y., Stückler, J., Leibe, B.: Semi-supervised deep learning for monocular depth map prediction (2017)
15. Zhang, Z., Xing, F., Shi, X., et al.: SemiContour: a semi-supervised learning approach for contour detection. In: Computer Vision and Pattern Recognition, pp. 251–259. IEEE (2016)
16. Aytar, Y.: Transfer learning for object category detection. University of Oxford (2014)
17. Wang, S., Ren, D., Chen, L., et al.: On study of the binarized deep neural network for image classification (2016)
18. Murthy, V.N., Singh, V., Chen, T., et al.: Deep decision network for multi-class image classification. In: Computer Vision and Pattern Recognition, pp. 2240–2248. IEEE (2016)
19. Ghazi, M.M., Yanikoglu, B., Aptoula, E.: Plant identification using deep neural networks via optimization of transfer learning parameters. Neurocomputing **235**, 228–235 (2017)
20. Shao, L., Cai, Z., Liu, L., et al.: Performance evaluation of deep feature learning for RGB-D image/video classification. Inf. Sci. Int. J. **385**(C), 266–283 (2017)

A Novel Feature-Based Pose Estimation Method for 3D Faces

Ye Li[1(✉)], YingHui Wang[1(✉)], Jing Liu[1], Wen Hao[1], and Liangyi Huang[2]

[1] Institute of Computer Science and Engineering, Xi'an University of Technology, No. 5 South Jinhua Road, Xi'an 710048, China
{liye, wyh}@xaut.edu.cn

[2] School of Engineering and Applied Science, George Washington University, Washington DC 20052, USA

Abstract. A novel feature-based pose estimation method for 3D faces is described in this paper. Depending on the salient crest lines which describe the rough sketch of prominent convex regions on a 3D face, the nose tip and the nose bridge are determined and used to estimate face pose without manual initialization, modeling, and training. The experimental results demonstrate that the proposed method can provide accurate, continuous and autonomous pose estimation of six degrees of freedom (DOF) for 3D faces with large pose rotation and self-occlusion.

Keywords: 3D face · Pose estimation · Feature-based · Nose tip · Nose bridge

1 Introduction

Head pose estimation plays an important role in many real-world applications, such as human computer interaction, driver attentiveness monitoring, face recognition, and gesture recognition. Most of the head pose estimation methods in the existing literature are traditionally performed on two-dimensional (2D) images or videos. These methods get impressive results and can meet the most needs of applications in human–computer interaction, driver attentiveness monitoring and gesture recognition. However, in the application of face recognition across poses, the pose estimation results based on 2D data are still heavily affected by the changes of illumination and viewpoint under uncontrolled environment especially for single-sample problem. Fortunately, three-dimensional (3D) capturing process is becoming cheaper and faster in recent years, and 3D facial models can provide a lot of useful geometric information for pose estimation, which is illumination and viewpoint independent.

2 Related Work

Notable head pose estimation methods from 3D data can be categorized into three types, classifier-based methods, registration-based methods and feature-based methods.

A. El Rhalibi et al. (Eds.): Edutainment 2018, LNCS 11462, pp. 361–369, 2019.
https://doi.org/10.1007/978-3-030-23712-7_51

Among the classifier-based methods, Faneli et al. [1] proposed an approach for real time face pose estimation based on random regression forests. The regression forests are trained on a large dataset of synthetically generated examples and the face pose parameters are estimated from all surface patches within a regression framework. Moreover, in their follow-up work [2], the approach is used on significantly noisier data provided by a Kinect sensor. Tulyakov et al. [4] presented a new approach for head pose estimation using cascaded tree classifiers. Papazov et al. [3] developed a 3D head pose and facial landmark estimation method using a novel triangular surface patch descriptor from RGB-D image. As the accuracy of classifier-based methods depends on the amount of training examples, these methods require extensive training with large datasets and the generating of datasets is a key issue. Moreover, the classifier trained on one 3D sensor usually does not generalized very well to others.

Registration-based methods treat the task of 3D head pose estimation as a registration problem and usually register a 3D head model to the measured data using the rigid/non-rigid ICP algorithm. Weise et al. [5] employed precise morphable model fitting to enable any user to control the facial expressions of a digital avatar. To ensure robustness to expressions, they only selected less deformable regions of the face in the reference model. Martin et al. [6] presented an accurate approach for 3D head pose estimation. They registered 3D head models with the iterative closest point (ICP) algorithm and used the features detection technique to determine the initial pose. In Ref. [7], using a combination of particle swarm optimization (PSO) and the iterative closest point (ICP) algorithm, Meyer et al. performed pose estimation by registering a morphable face model to the measured depth data. Most of registration-based methods are used in pose tracking or facial animation. They assume that the face pose is initially known in order to track the pose in subsequent frames. So these methods usually require offline and manual initialization of key points to create the subject-specific reference models. When landmarks detection is not precise and the absolute pose of the reference face is unknown, these methods can only provide rough estimations.

Feature-based methods exploit the configuration of several key facial features to estimate pose. In a 3D coordinate system, three or more suitably chosen facial features are sufficient to estimate a face pose. Curbuz et al. [8] presented a stereovision-based and model free 3D head pose estimation system. Using the face plane together with eye locations, the "head pose matrix" uniquely describing the orientation and position of a face is formed and used to compute head pose. Peng et al. [9] proposed a training-free nose tip detection method on 3D face and applied it to coarsely estimate head pose. Li et al. [10] proposed a 3D face pose estimation method based on central profile. Cai et al. [11] proposed an automatic method to locate 3D nose tip and estimate head pose. Breitenstein et al. [12] presented a real-time and automatic algorithm to estimate the 3D face pose in a single range image. Malassiotis et al. [13] proposed an approach of robust real-time 3D face pose estimation by applying robust knowledge-based 3D feature detection and localization techniques.

Compared with the methods of other categories, feature-based methods are simpler because they can obtain decent pose estimation with only a few facial features. It is especially applicable to pose estimation for face recognition on single sample. Furthermore, the facial features obtained during pose estimation can be well utilized to face recognition. As the detection of facial features may suffer from head rotations, expressions, and occlusions in most cases, it is important to select stable geometrical relationship between facial features to form the criterions of pose estimation. Because the detection of the features from eyes and mouth, is intrinsically difficult under varying facial expressions, head rotations and partial occlusions (e.g. eye-glasses, beard, hair etc.), the pose estimation methods based on features extracted from nose region have more advantages. As is known to all, the shape of nose is almost not affected by facial expressions and is visible in a wide range of head rotations. However, most of the existing methods which based on the features from nose are sensitive to large rotations. In Ref. [9], because the location of nose tip relies on the accurate and complete 2D Left-and-Right-Most face profiles, it is sensitive to rotation of Z-axis and likely to fail in self-occlusion faces caused by large pose variation. In Ref. [10], as the detection of the central profile highly depends on the protrusion and symmetry degree of face profiles, it is error-prone due to large roll and the impact of hair. In Ref. [13], the nose tip is located in the point which is closest to a local surface minimum. The method cannot estimate large head pose rotations accurately, e.g. pure profile poses. Moreover, many of the existing methods estimate pose rotation angles roughly and discontinuously. In Ref. [11], the experimental result shows that the algorithm is not accurate enough and is only suitable to establish an initial rough matching location. In Ref. [12], as the estimation result is obtained by comparing the input face with all reference pose range images which are corresponding to the hypotheses of head poses, it cannot provide a full range and continuous of head motion estimation.

To obtain an accurate and continuous estimation result on single sample with a large rotation and self-occlusion, a novel feature-based pose estimation method depending on the localization of the nose tip and the nose bridge from 3D faces is presented in this paper. According to the salient geometry shape of nose, our method detects the nose tip and the nose bridge based on the distinct convex crest lines, which are closely connected with the facial skeletons of convex regions. Since all features are detected only relying on surface curvatures, the proposed method is invariant to rigid transformation of head. And due to the distinct and protruding shape of nose, the detection of those features is insensitive to the self-occlusions caused by large rotations. Compared with some methods only based on key points detection, our method which depends on both key point and key line detection are more stable to self-occlusion and noise. It can provide an autonomous, continuous estimation of six DOFs for a 3D face without initialization, modeling and training. We test the proposed method on 3D synthetic faces with various rotation angles and 3D real faces from two publicly available 3D face databases (ie. BU-3DFE, GavaDB). It achieves best-in-class performance for 3D faces with large rotations and self-occlusion.

Figure 1 sketches the main steps of the proposed method.

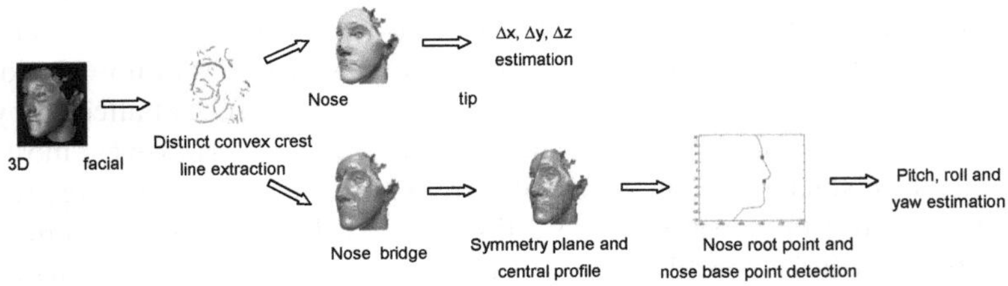

Fig. 1. Schema of the proposed pose estimation method

3 The Proposed Pose Estimation Method

3.1 Distinct Convex Crest Lines Extraction

As we know, the nose region sticks out from the rest of facial surface obviously. The nose tip is the highest point of the convex nose region and the facial surface bends sharply along the nose bridge. In Mathematics, ridge points are the sharp variation points of the surface normal which can be described via extrema of the surface principal curvatures along their corresponding lines of curvature in local region. The crest lines can be obtained by connecting the salient ridge points.

The extraction of ridge points and convex crest lines on a 3D face is accomplished through the following steps. For each mesh vertex, the normal vector is computed from weighted facet normal firstly. Then by fitting the region of each mesh vertex in the k-ring ($k = 1, 2, 3\ldots$) neighborhoods with a local cubic surface, the principal curvatures are computed. Next, we use the method of Ohtake [14] to detect ridge points and convex crest lines on the whole facial mesh model.

Due to the remarkable geometry of nose, the convex crest lines corresponding to nose are more salient than the others. Therefore, three measures are taken to remove the inessential convex crest lines in the process of detecting distinct convex crest lines. Since the ridge points detected in very small local regions will bring lots of inessential crest lines and is error-prone because of the noise, the first measure in our method is to select a proper larger k-ring neighborhood for fitting local surface during detecting the ridge points (k is empirically selected as 6 in our experiment). For the number of the ridge points on a salient ridge line is significantly greater than the number of ridge points on an inessential one, the second measure is to abandon the crest lines on which the number of ridge points below the mean value. The third measure is to use a parameter RS (Ridge Strength to select the convex crest lines which have more strong ridge feature. The formula of the RS is:

$$RS = \sum_{i=1}^{k-1} \delta_i \frac{k_{\max}(p_i) + k_{\max}(p_i + 1)}{2} \|p_i - p_{i+1}\| \tag{1}$$

$$\delta_i = \frac{1}{1 + \left| \frac{k_{\max}(p_i) + k_{\max}(p_{i+1})}{2} - \frac{1}{n}\sum_{i=1}^{n} k_{\max}(p_i) \right|} \tag{2}$$

where p_i is one ridge point on a convex crest line and n is the number of ridge points on this crest line, $k_{\max}(p_i)$ is the maximal principal curvature at the ridge point p_i, δ_i is a stability factor at the ridge point p_i.

3.2 Nose Tip and Nose Bridge Localization

Since the region surrounding nose tip has the higher Gaussian curvature and dome-like shape (approximately spherical), we locate the nose tip on the distinct convex crest lines based on Gaussian curvature distribution characteristic of spherical surfaces. More detailed introduction of the nose tip detection process can be seen in our previous work [15].

As the nose bridge is the intersection of two plane-like nose wings and runs horizontally across the top part of the nose, we detect it from the distinct convex crest lines based on its position relation to nose tip and its characteristic of linear regression. According to its position relation to nose tip and in consideration of possible data missing caused by self-occlusion, the candidates of nose bridge are detected in a spherical neighborhood of the nose tip and the radius of the sphere is experimental set to 15 mm. The distinct convex crest lines are selected as the candidates of nose bridge if a portion of them are within the spherical neighborhood. The selected candidates of nose bridge are composed mainly of the true nose bridge and the outlines of nose wings. Due to its characteristic of linear regression, we use the least square method to fit each nose bridge candidates with a straight line L, which through the nose tip P_t (x_t, y_t, z_t). Since the ridge points far away from the nose tip have only limited effects for fitting and sometimes may cause loss of precision, the ridge points which distance from the nose tip are bigger than 30 mm are removed from the nose bridge candidates. The equation of the line L in standard form is

$$\frac{x - x_t}{t_1} = \frac{y - y_t}{t_2} = \frac{z - z_t}{t_3} \tag{3}$$

where t_1, t_2, t_3 are the three parameters of L to be determined. And a parameter LS (Line Strength) is used to evaluate the approximation degree between a nose bridge candidate and a real straight line. LS is calculated as

$$LS = \frac{1}{\sqrt{\frac{1}{m}\sum_{i=1}^{m}\left[x_{pi} - (az_{pi} + b)\right]^2 + \frac{1}{m}\sum_{i=1}^{m}\left[y_{pi} - (cz_{pi} + d)\right]^2}} \tag{4}$$

$$a = \frac{t_1}{t_3}, b = x_t - \frac{t_1}{t_3}z_t, c = \frac{t_2}{t_3}, d = y_t - \frac{t_2}{t_3}z_t \tag{5}$$

where m is the number of ridge points on the nose bridge candidate and p_i is one of these ridge points. The nose ridge candidate with the largest *LS* is selected as the true nose bridge and meanwhile the three parameters t_1, t_2, t_3 of L are determined.

3.3 Pose Estimation

After the nose bridge is detected, a rough estimation of pitch, yaw and roll can be obtained according to the normal vector of nose tip and the nose bridge line. Nevertheless, this rough estimation results can not meet the higher accuracy requirements for face recognition. In order to achieve the more precise pose rotations, the symmetry plane and central profile are detected in the following step.

Depending on the nose bridge line L and the mean of normal vector of all ridge points on L, the normal vector of the symmetry plane can be calculated. Based on the normal vector of the symmetry plane and the position of nose tip, the symmetry plane can be obtained. And by cutting a 3D face with its symmetry plane, the central profile is obtained. After the symmetry plane and the central profile have been determined, the rotation angles of roll and yaw can be estimated. It is obvious that the direction of normal vector is the *X*-axis of the frontal face, the angle between the symmetry plane and the *Y*-axis is the roll rotation angle, and the angle between the symmetry plane and the *Z*-axis is the yaw rotation angle.

At last, the pitch is estimated according to the angle between the *Y*-axis and the line which connects the nasal root point and the nasal base point. To locate the nasal root point p_r, the intersection points of L and the central profile are obtained firstly. Then, the point whose distance to the nose tip is farthest in all intersection points is selected as the nasal root point. For the nasal base point p_b is a conspicuous turning point lying on the central profile beneath the nose tip, we search for p_b alone the central profile, starting at the nose tip p_t and away from the nasal root p_r. The first inflection points detected on this portion of the profile curve is determined as the nasal base point. According to the angle between the *Y*-axis and the reference line, the value of pitch angle α can be obtained as the following formula:

$$\alpha = a\tan\left(\frac{z_{pr} - z_{pb}}{\sqrt{(x_{pr} - x_{pb})^2 + \sqrt{(y_{pr} - y_{pb})^2}}}\right) \tag{6}$$

where (x_{pr}, y_{pr}, z_{pr}) are the coordinates of the nasal root point p_r, and (x_{pb}, y_{pb}, z_{pb}) are the coordinates of the nasal base point p_b. The central profile of a 3D face and the reference line which connects p_r and p_b are shown in Fig. 2.

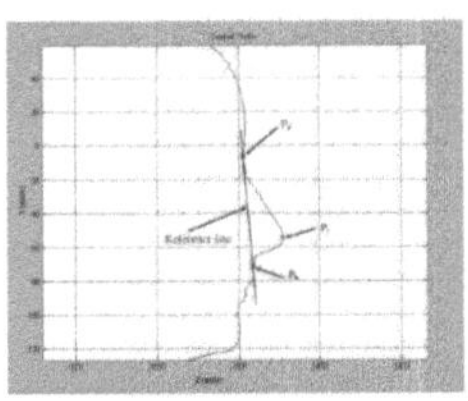

Fig. 2. Central profile and the reference line between p_r and p_b

4 Experiments and Discussion

To evaluate the robustness of our method to real faces with self-occlusion, we select all 3D facial models in GavabDB [16] as testing set. GavabDB contains 549 3D images of facial surfaces. The database provides systematic variations with respect to the pose, including large rotations. For examples, each subject in GavabDB has a face of pure profile pose, i.e. the yaw rotation of the face is 90°. All non-frontal faces in GavabDB are with self-occlusion. Examples of the nose tip and the nose bridge detection results on 3D faces with self-occlusion are shown in Fig. 3. Because the proposed method fuses the high-order curvatures with the low-order ones to detect the nose tip, and the high-order curvatures have the stable characteristic on global facial surface while the low-order ones have the stable characteristic on local facial surface, it can detect the nose tip accurately for various poses with pitch, yaw and roll rotations. Though the detection of the crest line corresponding to the nose bridge are slightly affected by self-occlusion, mostly caused by large pitch rotation, due to the stable line characteristic of the nose bridge and the distinct protruding shape of nose, the nose bridge can be determined correctly.

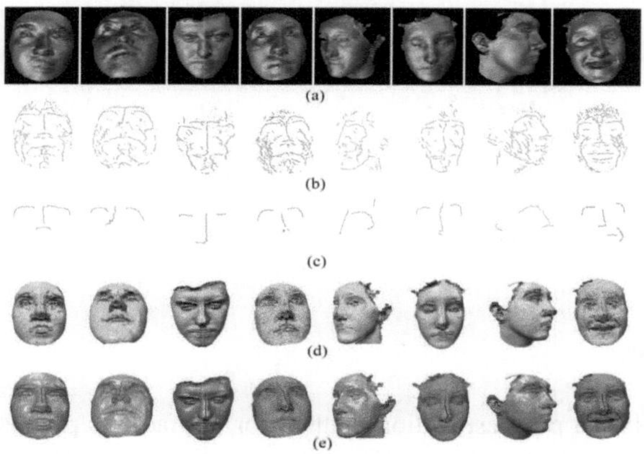

Fig. 3. The detection result of crest ridge lines, nose tip and nose bridge on real face models (a)3D face models (b) convex crest lines (c) Distinct convex crest lines (d) Nose tip (e) Nose bridge

To demonstrate the effectiveness of the proposed method, we compare it with other feature-based pose estimation methods [9–13], which all mainly depend on the features from nose region, for the accuracy rate of the nose tip localization and all pose angles estimations. We manually select the benchmark of nose tip on each 3D face and compare all the detected nose tips with their ground truth points in our experiment. To annotate each face with ground truth pose, we compute the three pose angles by manually marking the positions of nose tip, nasal root point and the nasal base point. The comparisons of pose estimation results are given in Table 1. Among all algorithms in Table 1, the results of Peng et al. [9] and Li et al. [10] are both achieved on FRGC datasets, in which almost all of 3D real faces are in frontal or near-frontal poses. Though the algorithm proposed by Cai et al. [11] performs experiments on the faces with large rotations and self-occlusions, for original intention of their algorithm is only to estimate an initial rough matching location for other matching algorithms, such as ICP, the pose estimation is not accurate enough and no actual concrete experimental result is mentioned in their paper. Despite including large rotations and self-occlusions, the faces in testing dataset of Breitenstein et al. [12] does not contain roll rotation. The algorithm proposed by Malassiotis et al. [13] is only tested on the faces under small rotations and without self-occlusions. The proposed method, which including both the large rotations of three directions and self-occlusions, is more comprehensive and archives an encouraging performance.

Table 1. Comparison of pose estimation results on 3D real faces

Algorithm	Testing set		Nose tip detection accuracy rate (%)		Angle estimations accuracy rate (%)			
	Large rotation	Self-occlusion	Error in 10 mm	Error in 20 mm	Error in	Pitch	Yaw	Roll
Peng et al. [9]	No	Yes	95.89	99.44	—	—	—	—
Li et al. [10]	No	Yes	98.16	99.84	12°	72.6	98.2	100
Cai et al. [11]	Yes	Yes	95.15	—	—	—	—	—
Breitenstein et al. [12]	Yes	Yes	—	100	10°	80.8	80.8	—
Malassiotis et al. [13]	No	No	100	100	10°	100	100	100
Our algorithm	Yes	Yes	100	100	10°	85.1	95.8	96.2

5 Conclusion

A novel feature-based pose estimation method for 3D faces is proposed in this paper. Compared with other feature-based 3D pose estimation methods, our method can be applied well for 3D faces with large pose rotation and self-occlusion. The accuracy of achieved estimations both in rotation angles and the nose tip position are comparable or superior to the state of the art. The main contribution of this paper is presenting a new feature-based 3D pose estimation method based on rotation independent features localization by combination of precise point features with stable line features, and its application on 3D faces with large pose rotation and self-occlusion. Future work will focus on the application in pose-invariant face recognition.

Acknowledgments. This work is supported in part by the National Natural Science Foundation of China under Grants No. 61472319, 61872291, 61871320 and No. 61602373, and in part by the Dr. Start-up fund of Xi'an University of Technology, and in part by Shaanxi Science Research Plan under Grant No. 2017JQ6023.

References

1. Fanelli, G., Gall, J., Gool, L.V.: Real time head pose estimation with random regression forests. In: IEEE Conference Computer Vision and Pattern Recognition IEEE, pp. 617–624. IEEE Press, Washington, DC (2011)
2. Fanelli, G., Weise, T., Gall, J., Van Gool, L.: Real time head pose estimation from consumer depth cameras. In: Mester, R., Felsberg, M. (eds.) DAGM 2011. LNCS, vol. 6835, pp. 101–110. Springer, Heidelberg (2011). https://doi.org/10.1007/978-3-642-23123-0_11
3. Papazov, C., Marks, T.K., Jones, M.: Real-time 3D head pose and facial landmark estimation from depth images using triangular surface patch features. In: IEEE Conference on Computer Vision and Pattern Recognition, pp. 4722–4730. IEEE Press, Boston (2015)
4. Tulyakov, S., Vieriu, R.L., Semeniuta, S., Sebe, N.: Robust real-time extreme head pose estimation. In: 22nd International Conference on Pattern Recognition, pp. 2263–2268. IEEE Press, Stockholm (2014)
5. Weise, T., Bouaziz, S., Li, H., Pauly, M.: Realtime performance-based facial animation. ACM Trans. Graph. **10**(4), 76–79 (2011)
6. Martin, M., Van De Camp, F., Stiefelhagen, R.: Real time head model creation and head pose estimation on consumer depth cameras. In: 2nd International Conference on 3D Vision, pp. 641–648. IEEE Press, Tokyo (2014)
7. Meyer, G.P., Gupta, S., Frosio, I., et al.: Robust model-based 3D head pose estimation. In: IEEE International Conference on Computer Vision, pp. 3649–3657. IEEE, Santiago (2015)
8. Gurbuz, S., Oztop, E., Inoue, N.: Model free head pose estimation using stereovision. Pattern Recognit. **45**(1), 33–42 (2012)
9. Peng, X., Bennamoun, M., Mian, A.S.: A training-free nose tip detection method from face range images. Pattern Recognit. **44**(3), 544–558 (2011)
10. Li, D., Pedrycz, W.: A central profile-based 3D face pose estimation. Pattern Recognit. **47** (2), 525–534 (2014)
11. Cai, Y., Huang, Y., Zhang, S.: A method for nose tip location and head pose estimation in 3D face data. In: International Conference on Automatic Control and Artificial Intelligence, pp. 115–118. IET, Xiamen (2012)
12. Breitenstein, M.D., Kuettel, D., Weise, T., et al.: Real-time face pose estimation from single range images. In: IEEE Conference on Computer Vision and Pattern Recognition, pp. 1–8. IEEE Press, Anchorage (2008)
13. Malassiotis, S., Strintzis, M.G.: Robust real-time 3D head pose estimation from range data. Pattern Recognit. **38**(8), 1153–1165 (2005)
14. Ohtake, Y., Belyaev, A., Seidel, H.P.: Ridge-valley lines on meshes via implicit surface fitting. ACM Trans. Graph. **23**(3), 609–612 (2004)
15. Li, Y., Wang, Y.H., Wang, B.B., Sui, L.S.: Nose tip detection on three-dimensional faces using pose-invariant differential surface features. IET Comput. Vis. **9**(1), 75–84 (2015)
16. Moreno, A.B., Sanchez, A.: GavabDB: a 3D face database. In: 2nd COST Workshop on Biometrics on the Internet: Fundamentals, Advances and Applications, Vigo, pp. 77–82 (2004)

Humanoid Robot Control Based on Deep Learning

Bin Guo[1], Pengfei Yi[1(✉)], Dongsheng Zhou[1(✉)], and Xiaopeng Wei[2]

[1] Key Laboratory of Advanced Design and Intelligent Computing, Dalian University, Ministry of Education, Dalian 116622, China
{yipengfei, zhoudongsheng}@dlu.edu.cn
[2] College of Computer Science and Technology, Dalian University of Technology, Dalian 1160243, China

Abstract. The direct control of humanoid robot by human motion is an important aspect of current research. Most of these methods are based on additional equipments, such as Kinect, which are usually not equipped on robot. In order to avoid using these external equipments, we explored a robot controlling method only using the low-resolution camera on robot. Firstly, a stacked hourglass network is employed to obtain the accurate 2D heatmap containing positions of human joints from RGB image captured by camera on robot. Then, 3D human poses including coordinates of human body joints are estimated from 2D heatmaps by a method aiming to reconstruct 3D human poses from 2D poses. Finally, the rotation angles of robot are computed according to these 3D coordinates and are transmitted to the robot to reconstruct the original human pose. Using the NAO robot as an example, the experimental results show that the humanoid robot can imitate motions of different human actors in different scenes well while applying our method.

Keywords: Deep learning · Human pose estimation · Humanoid robot control

1 Introduction

Humanoid robots integrates many science and technology domains, including mechanics, electronics, computer, sensor, control technology, artificial intelligence, etc. Its design and manufacture needs the knowledge of body structure, humanoid motion, learning ability, thinking intelligence and so on. Since the advent of humanoid robot, a large number of researchers have been devoted to the study of motion control, human-computer interaction, sys architecture, etc.

In the field of humanoid motion control, it is almost impossible to control the robot directly because of its high degrees of freedom. Recently, Abdallah et al. [1] and Guo et al. [2] have broken through the previous traditional research methods, combined pose-sensing techniques with humanoid robot, and used the Kinect to collect the human joints data and mapped them to the corresponding joints of the robot to achieve the motion imitation. Although this method is much simpler and easier to implement than other traditional methods of controlling humanoid robot, which avoids the complex programming of low-level motion controls, Kinect is an external device for robot, which is always unavailable on robots. This reduce the generality of the method.

A. El Rhalibi et al. (Eds.): Edutainment 2018, LNCS 11462, pp. 370–377, 2019.
https://doi.org/10.1007/978-3-030-23712-7_52

To avoid using external equipments, we propose a method to drive robots directly via cameras equipped on themselves, employing the latest research in the field of computer vision. Firstly, 2D image data are obtained from the robot's own camera. Secondly, 3D poses of human are estimated by a deep network and a 3D pose estimating procedure. Finally, the rotation angles of the corresponding joints in 3D poses are calculated to drive the robot to imitate the human motion.

2 Related Work

Human pose estimation has a wide range of applications in various tasks such as motion understanding [3–5], monitoring [6], human-computer interaction [7] and motion capture. The process of estimating 3D human poses from 2D RGB images can be divided to two steps: generating 2D heatmaps of 2D joints from input images and estimating 3D human poses from 2D joints.

2.1 2D Heatmap Generation

Previous studies of human joints estimating were based on classical image models [8–10] until Toshev et al. [11] replaced the model by deep networks in his research. After that, the accuracy of the human pose estimation has been greatly improved. The convolutional pose machines (CPM) method proposed by Wei et al. [12] adapts convolution neural network (CNN) to obtain the human body joint locations of the heatmaps. They use the component response graph to express the spatial constraints among the components. The response graph and the feature map as data are passed together in the network, and there is supervisory training [13] at each stage, which can avoid the problem difficult to optimize because the network is too deep. The stacked hourglass networks method proposed by Newell et al. [14] uses repeated pooling down and upsampling process to learn the spatial distribution. It extracts the features of the joints from the human body on different scales in the image and eventually integrates into a complete human feature. The subsequent hourglass module allows these high-level features to be re-processed to further evaluate and reevaluate high-order spatial relationships, which is similar to the relay supervisory optimization methods [12, 13] used in other pose estimation.

In the MPII pose analysis contest, the stacked hourglass network method defeat the CPM with 90.9% PCKh on MPII dataset [15] where CPM is 88.5%. At the same time, the stacked hourglass networks method adopts modular design, which make the network has the advantages of simplicity, easy understanding and modification.

2.2 3D Human Pose Estimation

The 3D human pose from 2D RGB images is considered to be more difficult than the 2D pose estimation due to the 3D pose's larger space, greater ambiguity, and incorrect problems caused by irreversible perspective projection. At present, the most advanced method can be divided into two types: methods treated the pose estimation task as the regression problem of a joint position from the input image [11, 16–18] and the others used the CNN architecture to detect the body parts [19–21], and then the 2D spatial relationship among the body parts is usually treated as a follow-up step [17, 22]. Zhou et al. [23] employed the EM algorithm after a preliminary estimate of 2D pose to find the best matching pose from the 3D human dictionary, which was proven more accurate. Compared with other 3D reconstruction methods [24, 25], the proposed approach considers an arbitrary pose uncertainty.

According to the above analysis, we will apply the CNN-based stacked hourglass network method [14], which is the near-state-of-the-art method, to accomplish the current 2D pose estimation, and the method proposed by Zhou et al. [23] to estimate the 3D human poses for its ability of processing arbitrary poses with uncertainty, which is helpful for increasing the robustness of our method.

3 Method

In this section, we will describe our method in detail, The overall schematic diagram and the flow chart of our system is shown in Fig. 1.

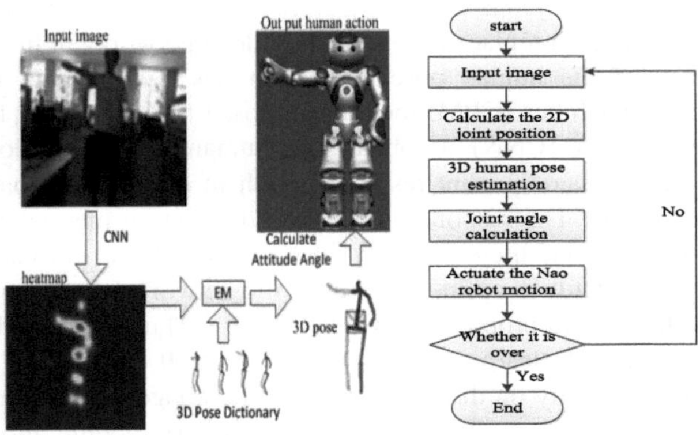

Fig. 1. The overview and flow chart of our system.

Firstly, one input image is an RGB image captured by robot's camera containing human bodies, then a 2D heatmap including 2D joints position is generated by a CNN-based stacked hourglass network (Sect. 3.1), the heatmap represents a mapping from the image to a probability distribution of the joint location, and a 3D pose is estimated by the EM algorithm with a 3D pose dictionary (Sect. 3.2), among which the heatmap is as input, and 16 three-dimensional coordinate data of the human body joint is output. Finally, the rotation of robot's joints is calculated from the three-dimensional coordinate data of the human body joint (Sect. 3.3). The rotation angle of the computed radian is used to drive the robot to correspond to the joint motion. Among them, heatmap, 3D human pose estimation and attitude angle calculation are realized on a remote workstation, and image acquisition and driving joint motion are performed directly on the robot. Data are transmitted by the TCP/IP network between them. By repeating the loop, human motions can be imitated by robot pose by pose.

The implementation of our method is described in detail as following:

3.1 Generating 2D Heatmaps from RGB Images

We use the stacked hourglass networks method to generate the heatmaps, the network is a CNN model trained on the MPII dataset under the deep learning framework of torch 7. Although this model is suitable for estimating arbitrary human motion, the input image to the network should have the target figure centered in the appropriate proportion. In order to obtain accurate 2D heatmaps from images with different resolutions, we modify the coordinate transform in [14] to regularize the inputs as follows:

$$\begin{bmatrix} x \\ y \\ 1 \end{bmatrix} = \begin{bmatrix} 1 & 0 & \Delta x \\ 0 & 1 & \Delta y \\ 0 & 0 & 1 \end{bmatrix} \begin{bmatrix} x_0 \\ y_0 \\ 1 \end{bmatrix}$$

Where (x_0, y_0) represents the pixel coordinates of the original image, (x, y) represents the pixel coordinates of the image after transformation, and $(\Delta x, \Delta y)$ represents the translation in the horizontal and vertical direction.

3.2 Estimating 3D Human Poses from 2D Heatmaps

We use the 3D pose reconstruction method described above [23] for pose estimation. The relationship between a 3D pose and its 2D pose is modeled with a weak perspective camera model. The algorithm in [17] is used to learn the 3D pose dictionary from human3.6M dataset [26]. For non-specific action cases [23], the size of the dictionary is set to K = 128.

3.3 Human Joints Data Processing

To represent the pose of the robot, Euler angles are used to indicate the rotation angle of the robot joints in each direction. We first define the initial position of the robot body, then the coordinate system is established, and then the rotation angle of parts such as shoulder joints and elbow joints can be calculated one by one. Let $\mathbf{R}_x$, $\mathbf{R}_y$ and $\mathbf{R}_z$ represent the rotation matrices of coordinate axis respectively. We take the *X*-axis as an example to set up the coordinate system, and the rotation angle of the shoulder joint around the coordinate axis is calculated as follows:

$$\mathbf{R}_x \mathbf{R}_y \mathbf{R}_z v_0 = v$$

Where v_0 is the vector of the original position, v is the vector of the current position. These vectors are in the same coordinate system. When the order of rotation axes is considered, the rotation angles can then be calculated. The rotation angles of child joints can then be calculated according to the following:

$$\mathbf{R}_x \mathbf{R}_y \mathbf{R}_z v_0 = \mathbf{R} v$$

Where $\mathbf{R}$ is the rotation matrix of the child joint under the coordinate of the parent joint.

4 Experiments

In this paper, we take NAO robot as an example. Although we can extract the data of 16 joints from the human body, due to the balanced problems of lower limb movement, we only use the data from human upper body to drive the robot upper limbs to imitate human motion in this experiment to protect the robot.

We test our method in different scenes, to evaluate the effectiveness of our method. 5 groups of experiments are designed in which we choose a few motions with large differences. In all of the following figures of results, from left to right, each row includes the original image, heatmap, 3D pose, robot imitation motion.

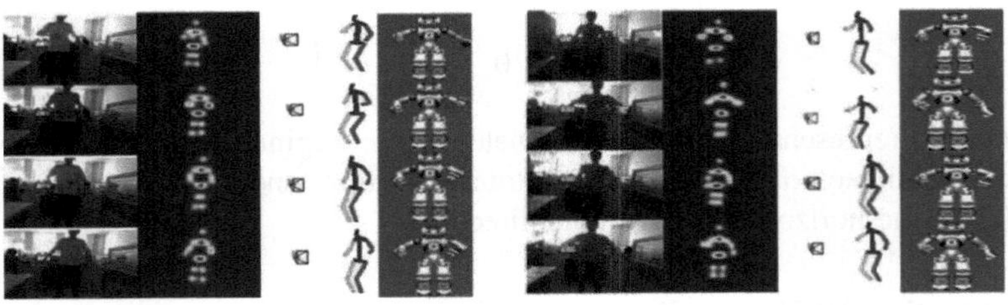

Fig. 2. Results with different body heights, different clothes same background under same natural lighting.

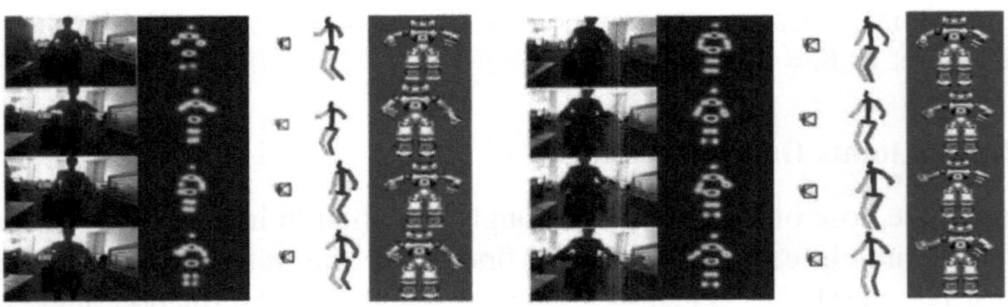

Fig. 3. Results with same person, different shape, different clothes, same background under same natural lighting.

According to results showed in Figs. 2 and 3, one can easily found that our method performs no matter how body size, body shape and clothing of the participants change, under same background and natural lighting.

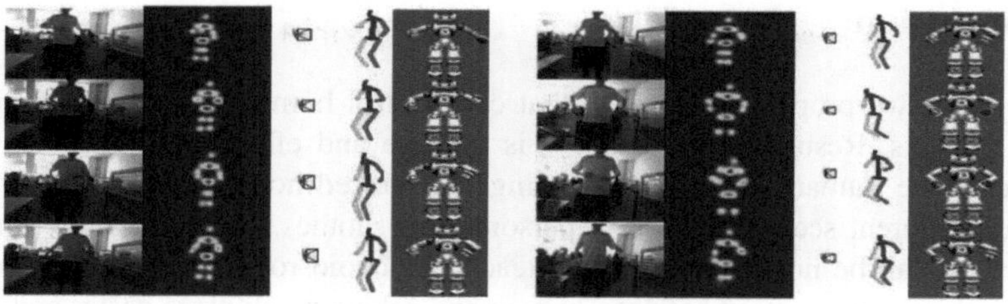

Fig. 4. Results with same person, same clothes, same background, under different lightings of natural lighting and mixed light (natural light and light).

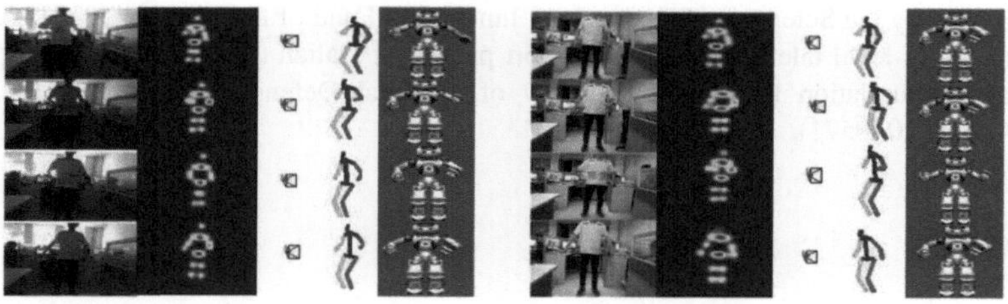

Fig. 5. Results with same clothes, same background, under different lightings of natural lighting and unnatural light.

According to results showed in Figs. 4 and 5, one can found that our method can make the robot imitate human actions well, no matter how illumination changes.

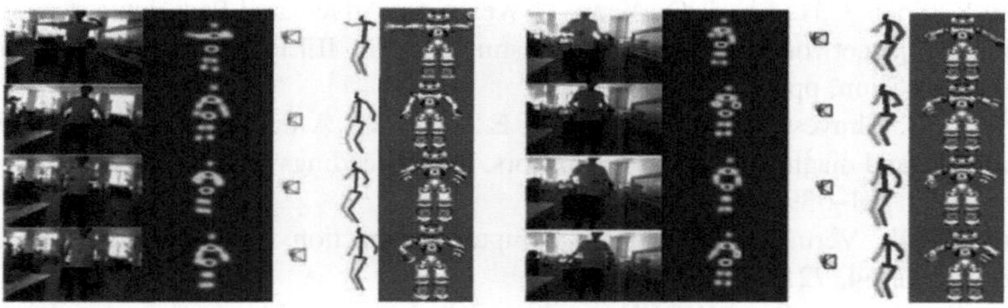

Fig. 6. Results with same person, clothes under natural light and different backgrounds.

As showed in Fig. 6, one can found the robot can imitate the human motion very well if the human's motion are in the range of the robot's joint, not influenced by the background change.

In summary, we can conclude that the proposed method of controlling humanoid robots from human motions is robust when applied on different shape, different clothing, different backgrounds and different illumination.

5 Conclusion

In this paper, we proposed a method that can control humanoid robots directly from human motions. Results showed that it is feasible and effective to make humanoid robots estimate human well. By combining the stacked hourglass network, it is also robust on different scenes differed in personalities, clothes, shapes and environments. The method can be not only applied to teach humanoid robots by human actors, but also to make the interaction between human and robots much more easier and natural.

Acknowledgment. This work is supported by the Liaoning Distinguished Professor, the Liaoning Province Doctor Startup Fund (No. 201601302); the Hunan Provincial Natural Science Fund Project (No. 2015JJ6028); Excellent Youth Project of Hunan Education Department (No. 16B065); by the Science and Technology Innovation Fund of Dalian (No. 2018J12GX036), and by the High-level talent innovation support project of Dalian (No. 2017RD11); Equipment Pre-research Foundation for Key Laboratory of National Defense Science and Technology (No. 614222202040571).

References

1. Abdallah, I.B., Bouteraa, Y., Rekik, C.: Kinect-based sliding mode control for Lynxmotion robotic arm. Adv. Hum.-Comput. Interact. **2016**, 1–10 (2016)
2. Guo, M., Das, S., Bumpus, J., Bekele E., Sarkar, N.: Interfacing of kinect motion sensor and NAO humanoid robot for imitation learning. Young Scientist (2013)
3. Nie, B.X., Xiong, C., Zhu, S.: Joint action recognition and pose estimation from video. In: Computer Vision and Pattern Recognition, pp. 1293–1301 (2015)
4. Simonyan, K., Zisserman, A.: Two-stream convolutional networks for action recognition in videos. In: Neural Information Processing Systems, pp. 568–576 (2014)
5. Chen, Y., Shen, C.H., Liu, L.Q., Yang, J., Wei, X.S.: Adversarial PoseNet: a structure-aware convolutional network for human pose estimation. In: IEEE International Conference on Computer Vision, pp. 1221–1230 (2017)
6. Alwasel, A., Elrayes, K., Abdel-Rahman, E., Haas, C.: A human body posture sensor for monitoring and diagnosing MSD risk factors. In: Proceedings of the 30th ISARC, Montreal, Canada, pp. 531–539 (2013)
7. Sharma, R.P., Verma, G.K.: Human computer interaction using hand gesture. Procedia Comput. Sci. **54**, 721–727 (2015)
8. Sapp, B., Taskar, B.: MODEC: multimodal decomposable models for human pose estimation. In: IEEE Conference on Computer Vision and Pattern Recognition, pp. 3674–3681 (2013)
9. Pishchulin, L., Andriluka, M., Gehler, P.V., Schiele, B.: Strong appearance and expressive spatial models for human pose estimation. In: International Conference on Computer Vision, pp. 3487–3494 (2013)
10. Yang, Y., Ramanan, D.: Articulated human detection with flexible mixtures of parts. IEEE Trans. Pattern Anal. Mach. Intell. **35**, 2878–2890 (2013)
11. Toshev, A., Szegedy, C.: DeepPose: human pose estimation via deep neural networks. In: IEEE Conference on Computer Vision and Pattern Recognition, pp. 1653–1660 (2014)
12. Wei, S., Ramakrishna, V., Kanade, T., Sheikh, Y.: Convolutional pose machines. In: IEEE Conference on Computer Vision and Pattern Recognition, pp. 4724–4732 (2016)

13. Pfister, T., Charles, J., Zisserman, A.: Flowing ConvNets for human pose estimation in videos. In: International Conference on Computer Vision, pp. 1913–1921 (2015)
14. Newell, A., Yang, K., Deng, J.: Stacked hourglass networks for human pose estimation. In: Leibe, B., Matas, J., Sebe, N., Welling, M. (eds.) ECCV 2016. LNCS, vol. 9912, pp. 483–499. Springer, Cham (2016). https://doi.org/10.1007/978-3-319-46484-8_29
15. Andriluka, M., Pishchulin, L., Gehler, P., Schiele, B.: 2D human pose estimation: new benchmark and state of the art analysis. In: IEEE Conference on Computer Vision and Pattern Recognition, pp. 3686–3693 (2014)
16. Li, S., Chan, A.B.: 3D human pose estimation from monocular images with deep convolutional neural network. In: Cremers, D., Reid, I., Saito, H., Yang, M.-H. (eds.) ACCV 2014. LNCS, vol. 9004, pp. 332–347. Springer, Cham (2015). https://doi.org/10.1007/978-3-319-16808-1_23
17. Zhou, X., Zhu, M., Leonardos, S., Daniilidis, K.: Sparse representation for 3D shape estimation: a convex relaxation approach. IEEE Trans. Pattern Anal. Mach. Intell. **39**, 1648–1661 (2017)
18. Tekin, B., Rozantsev, A., Lepetit, V.: Direct prediction of 3D body poses from motion compensated sequences. In: Computer Vision and Pattern Recognition, pp. 991–1000 (2016)
19. Chen, X., Yuille, A.: Articulated pose estimation by a graphical model with image dependent pairwise relations. In: Neural Information Processing Systems, pp. 1736–1744 (2014)
20. Tompson, J., et al.: Joint training of a convolutional network and a graphical model for human pose estimation. In: Advances in Neural Information Processing Systems, pp. 1799–1807 (2014)
21. Yasin, H., Yasin, H., Iqbal, U., Kruger, B., Weber, A., Gall, J.: A dual-source approach for 3D pose estimation from a single image. In: Computer Vision and Pattern Recognition, pp. 4948–4956 (2016)
22. Zhu, Y., Huang, D., De La Torre, F., Lucey, S.: Complex non-rigid motion 3D reconstruction by union of subspaces. In: Computer Vision and Pattern Recognition, pp. 1542–1549 (2014)
23. Zhou, X., Zhu, M., Leonardos, S., Derpanis, K.G., Daniilidis, K.: Sparseness meets deepness: 3D human pose estimation from monocular video. In: Computer Vision and Pattern Recognition, pp. 4966–4975 (2016)
24. Akhter, I., Black, M.J.: Pose-conditioned joint angle limits for 3D human pose reconstruction. In: Computer Vision and Pattern Recognition, pp. 1446–1455 (2015)
25. Ramakrishna, V., Kanade, T., Sheikh, Y.: Reconstructing 3D human pose from 2D image landmarks. In: Fitzgibbon, A., Lazebnik, S., Perona, P., Sato, Y., Schmid, C. (eds.) ECCV 2012. LNCS, vol. 7575, pp. 573–586. Springer, Heidelberg (2012). https://doi.org/10.1007/978-3-642-33765-9_41
26. Ionescu, C., Papava, D., Olaru, V., Sminchisescu, C.: Human3.6M: large scale datasets and predictive methods for 3D human sensing in natural environments. IEEE Trans. Pattern Anal. Mach. Intell. **36**, 1325–1339 (2014)

Improved Modular Convolution Neural Network for Human Pose Estimation

Zhengxuan Zhang[1], Jing Dong[1(✉)], Dongsheng Zhou[1(✉)], Xiaoyong Fang[3], and Xiaopeng Wei[2]

[1] Key Laboratory of Advanced Design and Intelligent Computing, Dalian University, Ministry of Education, Dalian 116622, China
{dongjing, zhoudongsheng}@dlu.edu.cn
[2] School of Computer Science and Technology, Dalian University of Technology, Dalian 1160243, China
[3] Research Institute of Human, Factors and Safety Engineering, Hunan Institute of Technology, Hengyang 421002, Hunan Province, China

Abstract. Human pose estimation in image is an important branch of computer vision and graphics research. In this paper, an improved modular convolution neural network is proposed to solve the problem of human pose estimation in static 2D images. A cascaded three-stage full convolutional network (FCN) can learn the non-linear mapping from image feature space to human pose space in an end-to-end way. In order to improve the accuracy of predicting joints, the method of multi-feature source fusion is adopted to improve the estimation process of the human body posture. The first two stages of the network focus on learning local image features and joints neighborhood pixel features, and these features are merged in the third stage of the network. Finally, the coordinates of human joints are obtained by regression of the merged features. In our experiments, using the strict PCP criteria on the full body pose dataset LSP, the average prediction accuracy of our method is 79.3%. In addition, using the PCKh standard on the upper body pose dataset FLIC, our method achieves an average prediction accuracy of 93% without additional training.

Keywords: Human posture estimation · Full convolution neural network · Structural prediction · Feature fusion

1 Introduction

Articulated pose estimation is one of the fundamental challenges in computer vision. Progress in this area can immediately be applied to important vision tasks such as human tracking [1], action recognition [2] and video analysis. Despite the long history of efforts, it is still a challenging problem. The large variation in limb orientation, clothing, viewpoints, background clutters, truncation and occlusion makes the localization of body joints still difficult and challenging.

Previous pose estimation works can be divided into two groups, (1) traditional model-based approach and (2) more powerful feature learners such as convolution neural networks. The former is dedicated to design complex and sophisticated features,

A. El Rhalibi et al. (Eds.): Edutainment 2018, LNCS 11462, pp. 378–388, 2019.
https://doi.org/10.1007/978-3-030-23712-7_53

such as SIFT or HoG, as input. These features are used by specific algorithms to estimate the position of human joints. The latter is committed to designing a clever convolution neural network architecture which automatically learns the relationship between the characteristics and human joints.

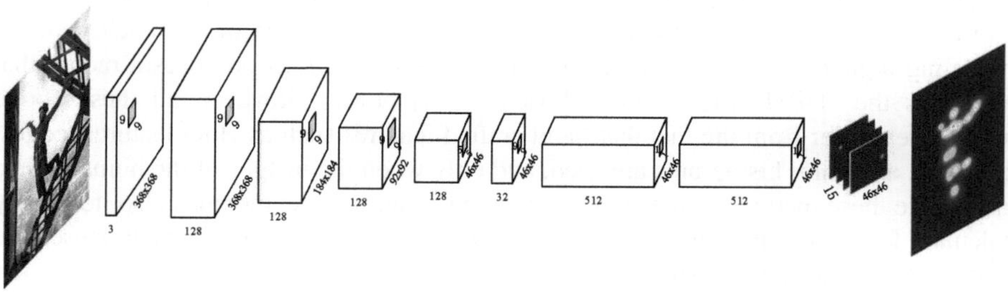

Fig. 1. Our pipeline for pose estimation.

Based on the design of the *Pose Machine* [3] and *Convolution Pose Machine* [4], a three-stage convolution neural network architecture is proposed with the method of multi-feature source fusion to improve the estimation process of the human body posture. The network can continue operate the belief maps generated by the previous stage. Estimations of part positions are increasingly refined without the need for explicit graphical modeling inferences.

The data pipeline is a schematic diagram of the first phase of our network processing, where the leftmost image represents the input image and the rightmost image represents the predicted results of the network on this image. As can be seen from the Fig. 1, the input image is cropped to a size of 368×368 and then convolved with convolution kernels of 9×9, 5×5 and 1×1 size. The output is 15 two-dimensional vector images of 46×46 size, which are referred to as belief maps for short. The 15-dimensional belief map represents, in turn, the sum of the projections of all 14 joint points and 1 all joint points of the human body. Finally, we obtain the position coordinate of the human joint through the operation of summing the maximum value and the up-sampling interpolation of the belief map, and complete the process of human pose estimation.

2 Related Works

In unconstrained image domains human pose estimation is an important and challenging problem, the corresponding extraction, learning and understanding of the entire body features have been proposed. In general, many approaches to this problem fall into two broad categories: (1) Representing the body parts or joints with the graph node and optimizing hand-crafted features and human joints location by pictorial inference; (2) Using deep convolution neural network (DCNN) to automatically learn the relationship between human joints and images.

In the traditional graph model approach, Ramanan et al. [5] use a combination of local detectors and structural reasoning for coarse human tracking. Felzenszwalb et al. [6] make this approach tractable with "Deformable Part Models (DPM)". Subsequently a large number of related models and algorithms are invented [7–9] to model more complex joint relationships. Yang et al. [10] use a flexible mixture of templates modeled by linear SVMs. Johnson and Everingham et al. [11] use a cascade of body part detectors to obtain more discriminative templates. Most recent approaches aim at modeling higher-order part relationships. Pishchulin et al. [12] proposes a model that augments the "DPM" model with "Poselet" [13] priors. However, all these above approaches suffer from the fact that hand crafted features such as HoG features, edges, contours, and color histograms are used, and only when the images of the human joints are visible these methods can achieve very good results. These methods also iteratively calculate features, especially when these features are miscalculated, which causes the failure of human joint recognition.

The best performing algorithms for human pose estimation are based on DCNN. Ouyang et al. [14] propose a multi-source deep model for constructing the non-linear representation from multiple information sources. Jain et al. [15] use a multi-resolution DCNN and adopt motion features to improve the accuracy of body parts localization. Tompson et al. [16] propose spatial pooling to overcome the reduced localization accuracy caused by pooling operations. Chen et al. [17] use a DCNN to learn the conditional probabilities for the presence of parts and their spatial relationships. They further propose flexible compositions of object parts [18] to handle significant occlusions in images. Pfister et al. [19] use a network module with large receptive field to capture implicit spatial models.

3 Our Method

Based on the work of Wei et al. [4], this paper introduces the method of multi-feature source fusion to improve the estimation process of the human body posture. The first two stages of the network focus on learning local image features and joints neighborhood pixel features, and these features will be merged in the third stages of the network. Finally, the coordinates of human joints are obtained by regression of the fused features. In order to ensure that multi-source features can be effectively transmitted between stages, this paper uses the confidence map to describe the propagation of this non-parametric encoded information in the network.

This chapter will focus on our network architecture and network characteristics, the definition of the global objective function and belief maps transmission in the multi-stage.

3.1 Architecture

Our network architecture is shown in Fig. 2, after 3 times 9×9 size convolution kernel and 3×3 size maximum pooling, the data flow into branches (the branch number equals to the number of stages) to make regression with human joints in an end to end way. By using the global objective function, the network can automatically learn image local features and contextual features.

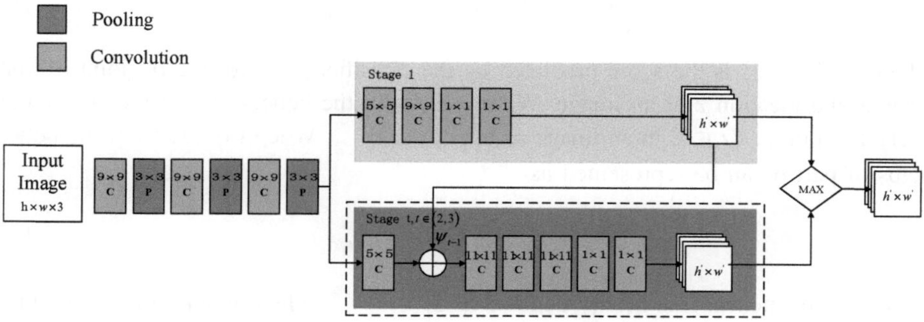

Fig. 2. Architecture of our multi-stage CNN. Each stage predicts P + 1 dimensions $h' \times w'$ size belief maps (i.e. confidence score maps) in which P represents 14 human joints belief maps and 1 is for the sum of all belief maps. In the next stage, the network can continually operate on the belief maps to make regression with joints position.

In the first stage, the network predicts part beliefs only from local image evidence. The image is a local feature because at this stage the network uses 9×9, 5×5 and other large convolution kernels with sliding steps to cut the input image into many small pieces. Then these small pieces are putted into the network to make regression with human joints coordinates. The receptive field of the first stage network is constrained to a small patch around the output pixel location, so that our network can automatically learn the local features of images.

In the second or subsequent stage of the network, the belief maps generated by previous stage will be inputted to the next stage along with the local features extracted to make regression with human joints. In this stage, the network not only calculates local features of the image, but also learns neighborhoods pixel features of the joints location predicted by the previous stage. By this way, some easily detectable joints such as the head, neck and shoulders can be used as auxiliary information to help identify the positions of some joints which are hardly detected due to occlusion, blur and posture distortion in the subsequent stage.

3.2 Confidence Maps for Part Detection

We denote Y_P and $p \in (1, 2, 3, \ldots, 14)$ represents the pixel location of the pth joint of human body. $Y_P \in \mathbb{Z}$, where $\mathbb{Z}$ is the set of all (u, v) locations in an image. Our goal is to predict the image locations $Y = (Y_1, Y_2, Y_3, \ldots, Y_P)$ for all body joints.

Our network can be thought of as a series of multi-level predictors. $g_t(.)$. In each stage $t \in \{1, 2, 3\}$, these predictors $g_t(.)$ predict belief maps for assigning a location to each part $Y_P = z, \forall z \in \mathbb{Z}$. Based on the features extracted from the image at the location $z \in \mathbb{Z}$ denoted by x_z and contextual information from the preceding predictors in the neighborhood around each Y_P, the predictor $g_t(.)$ in the first stage t = 1, produces the following belief values:

$$g_1(x_z) \rightarrow \{b_1^p(Y_p = z)\}_{p \in \{1,2,\ldots,14\}} \tag{1}$$

where $b_1^p(Y_p = z)$ is the score predicted by the classifier $g_1(.)$ for the pth joint in first stage at the location z of an image. We represent all the beliefs of part p evaluated at every location z, $\forall z \in \mathbb{Z}$ in an image as $b_1^p(Y_p = z)_{\forall z \in \mathbb{Z}}$. When $t \in \{1, 2, 3\}$, the belief maps of part p can be represented as

$$b_t^p[u, v] = b_t^p(Y_p = z)_{\forall z \in \mathbb{Z}} \tag{2}$$

For convenience, it is briefly denoted as $b_t^p \in \mathbb{R}^{w \times h}$, where w and h are the width and height of an image. The collection of belief maps for all parts can be represented as $b_t \in \mathbb{R}^{w \times h \times (P+1)}$, where P is 14, the number of human body joints, and 1 is the sum of all belief maps.

In the subsequent stages, these predictors $g_t(.)$ predict belief maps for assigning a location to each part $Y_P = z, \forall z \in \mathbb{Z}$ based on features of the image data x_z^t and contextual information $\psi_t(z, b_{t-1})$ from the previous classifier in the neighborhood around each Y_P. It is represented as:

$$g_t(x_z^{\prime}, \psi_t(z, b_{t-1})) \rightarrow \{b_t^p(Y_p = z)\}_{p \in \{1,2,\ldots,14\}} \tag{3}$$

where $\psi_{t>1}(.)$ is a mapping from the beliefs b_{t-1} to context features.

3.3 Objective Function

Each stage of our network is trained to produce the belief maps repeatedly for the locations of each part. An objective function is defined at the output of each stage t. It uses the L_2 distance as $\|x\|_2 = \sqrt{\sum_{i=1}^{N} x_i^2}$ to minimize the differences between the predictions and ideal belief maps for each part, and is given by:

$$f_t = \sum_{p=1}^{14} \sum_{z \in \mathbb{Z}} \|b_t^p(z) - b_*^p(z)\|_2^2 \tag{4}$$

Where $b_t^p(z)$ is the belief map for the pth joint in the stage t, and the $b_*^p(Y^P = Z)$ is the ideal belief maps for the pth joint in the stage t, which is created by putting Gaussian peaks at ground truth locations of each body part p. The overall objective for the full architecture is obtained by adding the losses at each stage t, and is given by:

$$\mathrm{F} = \sum_{t=1}^{3} f_t \tag{5}$$

It is worth noting that the coordinates of the joint location Y_p are the values with the smallest global objective function F, therefore that is:

$$Y_p = argmin \sum_{p=1}^{14} \sum_{z \in \mathbb{Z}} \|b_t^p(z) - b_*^p(z)\|_2^2 \tag{6}$$

4 Experiment

4.1 Datasets and Evaluation Metrics

In this section, the datasets used in our experiments training and evaluation are introduced to lay the foundation for the next experimental evaluation. This experiment uses three public datasets MPII[1], FLIC[2], LSP[3,4] which are commonly used in human pose estimation research. In order to avoid over-fitting, about 18 K images in the training set of MPII dataset were added to the LSP training dataset by normalizing 14 body joints location coordinates as ground truth for training. But in the network prediction and evaluation stage, only the results on LSP dataset and FLIC dataset were compared. The primary reason is that MPII dataset does not provide ground-truth label for test set as other datasets. In this paper, the experimental results were evaluated with three evaluation metrics strict PCP [20] (Percentage of Correct Parts), PCKh (Probability of Correct Keypoint) and PDJ (the curve of Percentage of Detected Joints).

4.2 Implementation Detail

In this section, a brief overview of our data augmentation methods, network training details, running platforms and time efficiency are provided.

Data Augmentation

Our model implementation and network training code are based on the framework of *Caffe* [21] and part of the implementation code are referred to *Convolution Pose Machine* [4]. The training network used normalized size of 368 $\times$ 368 images. In order to have the normalized input samples, the images were firstly roughly resized into the same scale, then were cropped or padded according to the center positions or the rough scale estimations provided by the datasets. In some datasets such as LSP, there is not the rough scale estimation information, and they can be estimated according to joint positions or image sizes.

[1] http://human-pose.mpi-inf.mpg.de/.

[2] https://bensapp.github.io/flic-dataset.html.

[3] http://sam.johnson.io/research/lsp.html.

[4] http://sam.johnson.io/research/lspet.html.

For testing, similar resizing and cropping or padding were performed, but the estimations of center position and scale were not given. In addition, the belief maps from different scales (perturbed around the given one) were merged for final predictions to decrease the inaccuracy of the given scale estimation.

Settings
Our experimental host is the HP Z840 Workstation (with 2 Intel® Xeon® CPUs 2.4 GHz 12-core, 64G memory, 2T hard drives and 1 nvidia Quadro K6000 with 12 GB of Graphics memory). Testing a single picture usually takes an average of 130 ms.

4.3 Benchmark Results and Compare

In this section, the evaluation results are given by using of the Strict PCP, PCKh and PDJ standards on LSP, FLIC datasets. Then the compared results with others by use of PCK and PDJ standard on the LSP datasets are shown. Finally, the prediction examples and error analysis are given.

Table 1. Our Benchmark results, use of PCKh, PDJ metrics on LSP and FLIC datasets.

LSP Dataset

Method	Ankle	Knee	Hip	Wris	Elbo	Shou	Head	Mean	AUC
PCKh	75.2	82.8	87.2	73.3	80.5	88.3	96	83.3	58.9
PDJ@0.10	66.5	73.8	62	63.1	70.4	76.2	84.5		
PDJ@0.20	75.2	82.7	87.2	73.4	80.5	88.3	96		

FLIC Dataset

Method	Head	Shou	Elbo	Wris	Hip	Mean	AUC
PCKh	98	92.5	88.3	92.3	96.3	93	68.3
PDJ@0.10	58.5	43.9	32.6	38.5	65.7		
PDJ@0.20	87.8	74.4	60.7	67.4	86.5		

Using the PCKh and PDJ evaluation methods, our benchmark results can be divided into two parts in Table 1 from top to bottom: one is on the LSP datasets and the other is on FLIC datasets. In general, our network model's evaluation results on the FLIC datasets are better than the results on LSP datasets. In the case of LSP datasets alone, it can be seen that using the PCKh evaluation method (the bigger, the better), the Head joint has the highest score value and it means this joint is easily to be predicted correctly. The rest is followed by the order of Shou, Hip, Knee, Elbo, Ankle and Wirs. It's also consistent with common sense that the Head joint's motion range is smaller

Table 2. The results comparison on LSP datasets use of strict PCP metric.

Paper	L.legs	U.legs	L.arms	U.arms	Head	Torso	Mean
Wang and Li, CVPR'13 [22]	55.8	56.0	32.1	43.1	79.1	87.5	54.1
Tompson, NIPS'14 [23]	61.1	70.4	51.2	63.0	83.7	90.3	66.6
Fan, CVPR'15 [24]	69.8	77.7	49.1	62.8	86.6	**95.4**	70.1
Yang, CVPR'16 [25]	71.8	78.5	61.8	72.2	83.9	**95.6**	74.8
Ours	**75.0**	**84.3**	**65.5**	**77.8**	**93.1**	94.4	**79.3**

than other human body joints, so it's can be more easily detected (Table 2).

For most human body joints, our method has significantly improved Yang's result [25] in CVPR'16 years of work, but the prediction accuracy of the Torso joint is not as good as Fan's results [24] and Yang et al.

In Fig. 3, Our results are compared with the results of Wang, Tompson, Fan and Yang's work by use of the PCKh evaluation method on the LSP dataset. The compared raw data results come from the official website of the MPII dataset[5]. Note that: Person-Centric was used to annotate LSP datasets and 10,000 images in the LSP extension dataset were for training. It also can be seen more obviously that our results (marked by black color line) are better than others.

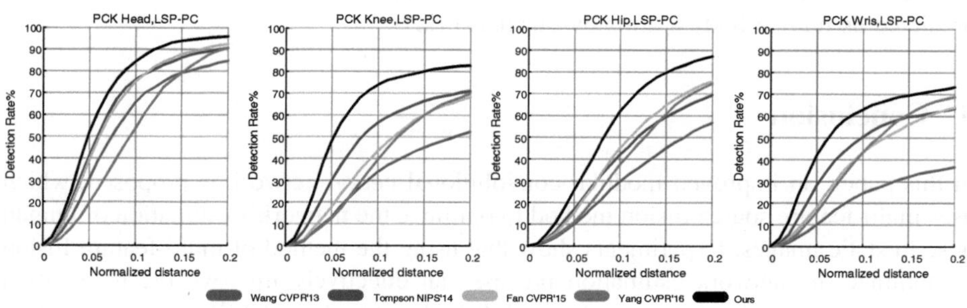

Fig. 3. Our results compared with others by use of PCKh metrics in single joint.

Figure 4 shows some samples of the predicted results on the LSP and FLIC test datasets. In most cases, the proposed network can achieve excellent predictions on the LSP dataset. But in some cases of special human posture, symmetrical joint or when

[5] http://human-pose.mpi-inf.mpg.de/#related_benchmarks.

the color of background is similar with the color of people's clothes, our network output is not good at predicting, which is more obvious in upper body pose datasets FLIC. It is expected that expanding the size of the training set will improve the accuracy of these difficult situations.

Fig. 4. Qualitative results of our method on FLIC and LSP datasets respectively.

In the last line, some error prediction examples (the first five are from the LSP dataset and the last five are from the FLIC dataset) are usually due to the occlusions and distractions from clothing or overlapping people. There is a special example in the 8th picture of the error line (from left to right), the windshield and front cover of a car are predicted as human body's arms by our network.

5 Conclusion

In this paper, an improved modular convolutional neural network is proposed, which uses multi-feature source fusion method to optimize the network's estimation of human pose in static images. Experiments show that using the method of multi-feature fusion to optimize the network estimation process can effectively improve the recognition accuracy of human joint points. On the full body pose dataset LSP, the average prediction accuracy of our method by using the strict PCP criteria is 79.3%. In the future, we will try to apply this method to solve the problem of multi-person posture recognition in still images.

Acknowledgments. This work is supported by the National Natural Science Foundation of China (Nos. 61603066), Program for the Liaoning Distinguished Professor, the Hunan Provincial Natural Science Fund Project (No. 2015JJ6028); Excellent Youth Project of Hunan Education Department (No. 16B065); by the Science and Technology Innovation Fund of Dalian (No. 2018J12GX036), and by the High-level talent innovation support project of Dalian

(No. 2017RD11); Equipment Pre-research Foundation for Key Laboratory of National Defense Science and Technology (No. 61422202040571).

References

1. Cho, N., Yuille, A.L., Lee, S.: Adaptive occlusion state estimation for human pose tracking under self-occlusions. Pattern Recogn. **46**(3), 649–661 (2013)
2. Wang, C., Wang, Y., Yuille, A.L.: An approach to pose-based action recognition. In: Proceedings of the IEEE Conference on Computer Vision and Pattern Recognition (2013)
3. Ramakrishna, V., Munoz, D., Hebert, M., Andrew Bagnell, J., Sheikh, Y.: Pose machines: articulated pose estimation via inference machines. In: Fleet, D., Pajdla, T., Schiele, B., Tuytelaars, T. (eds.) ECCV 2014. LNCS, vol. 8690, pp. 33–47. Springer, Cham (2014). https://doi.org/10.1007/978-3-319-10605-2_3
4. Wei, S., et al.: Convolutional pose machines. In: Proceedings of the IEEE Conference on Computer Vision and Pattern Recognition (2016)
5. Ramanan, D., Forsyth, D.A., Zisserman, A.: Strike a pose: tracking people by finding stylized poses. In: IEEE Computer Society Conference on Computer Vision and Pattern Recognition, CVPR 2005. IEEE (2005)
6. Felzenszwalb, P., McAllester, D., Ramanan, D.: A discriminatively trained, multiscale, deformable part model. In: IEEE Conference on Computer Vision and Pattern Recognition, CVPR 2008. IEEE (2008)
7. Eichner, M., Ferrari, V., Zurich, S.: Better appearance models for pictorial structures. In: BMVC 2009 (2009)
8. Yang, Y., Ramanan, D.: Articulated pose estimation with flexible mixtures-of-parts. In: 2011 IEEE Conference on Computer Vision and Pattern Recognition (CVPR). IEEE (2011)
9. Dantone, M., et al.: Human pose estimation using body parts dependent joint regressors. In: Proceedings of the IEEE Conference on Computer Vision and Pattern Recognition (2013)
10. Yang, Y., Ramanan, D.: Articulated human detection with flexible mixtures of parts. IEEE Trans. Pattern Anal. Mach. Intell. **35**(12), 2878–2890 (2013)
11. Johnson, S., Everingham, M.: Learning effective human pose estimation from inaccurate annotation, pp. 1465–1472 (2011)
12. Pishchulin, L., et al.: Strong appearance and expressive spatial models for human pose estimation. In: Proceedings of the IEEE International Conference on Computer Vision (2013)
13. Bourdev, L., Malik, J.: Poselets: body part detectors trained using 3D human pose annotations. In: 2009 IEEE 12th International Conference on Computer Vision, pp. 1365–1372. IEEE (2009)
14. Ouyang, W., Chu, X., Wang, X.: Multi-source deep learning for human pose estimation. In: Proceedings of the IEEE Conference on Computer Vision and Pattern Recognition (2014)
15. Jain, A., et al.: Learning human pose estimation features with convolutional networks. arXiv preprint arXiv:1312.7302 (2013)
16. Tompson, J., et al.: Efficient object localization using convolutional networks. In: Proceedings of the IEEE Conference on Computer Vision and Pattern Recognition (2015)
17. Chen, X., Yuille, A.L.: Articulated pose estimation by a graphical model with image dependent pairwise relations. In: Advances in Neural Information Processing Systems (2014)
18. Chen, X., Yuille, A.L.: Parsing occluded people by flexible compositions. In: Proceedings of the IEEE Conference on Computer Vision and Pattern Recognition (2015)

19. Pfister, T., Charles, J., Zisserman, A.: Flowing convnets for human pose estimation in videos. In: Proceedings of the IEEE International Conference on Computer Vision (2015)
20. Pishchulin, L., et al.: Articulated people detection and pose estimation: reshaping the future. In: 2012 IEEE Conference on Computer Vision and Pattern Recognition (CVPR). IEEE (2012)
21. Jia, Y., et al.: Caffe: convolutional architecture for fast feature embedding, pp. 675–678 (2014)
22. Wang, F., Li, Y.: Beyond physical connections: tree models in human pose estimation, pp. 596–603 (2013)
23. Tompson, J., et al.: Joint training of a convolutional network and a graphical model for human pose estimation. In: Advances in Neural Information Processing Systems (2014)
24. Fan, X., et al.: Combining local appearance and holistic view: dual-source deep neural networks for human pose estimation. In: Proceedings of the IEEE Conference on Computer Vision and Pattern Recognition (2015)
25. Yang, W., et al.: End-to-end learning of deformable mixture of parts and deep convolutional neural networks for human pose estimation. In: Proceedings of the IEEE Conference on Computer Vision and Pattern Recognition (2016)

Using Face Recognition to Detect "Ghost Writer" Cheating in Examination

Huan He[1,4(✉)], Qinghua Zheng[1,2], Rui Li[4], and Bo Dong[3,4]

[1] SPKLSTN Lab, Xi'an Jiaotong University, Xi'an 710049, China
{hehuan, qhzheng}@mail.xjtu.edu.cn
[2] School of Electronic and Information Engineering, Xi'an Jiaotong University, Xi'an 710049, China
[3] National Engineering Lab of Big Data Analytics, Xi'an Jiaotong University, Xi'an 710049, China
dong.bo@mail.xjtu.edu.cn
[4] College of Distance Education, Xi'an Jiaotong University, Xi'an 710049, China
lrvberg@mail.xjtu.edu.cn

Abstract. Cheating in examinations of the online distance education is a serious problem which may damage the fairness of exam and further undermine the credibility and reputation of certificates. In order to detect the "Ghost Writer" cheating strategy that existed in both online and offline exams, we propose the Student Identification by Face Recognition (SIFR) framework, a three layers architecture based on face recognition technique and micro-service principle, to detect the ghostwriter who takes the exam for others. In addition, we implement a prototype system based on open source projects and public cloud services. To evaluate the system, an experimental test was conducted with public data. The results indicated that the SIFR framework is feasible and the accuracy of detection is directly affected by the performance of face recognition service, which can be upgraded or replaced with better facial feature extraction module.

Keywords: Online distance education · Ghost writer · Cheating detection · Face recognition · Micro-service architecture

1 Introduction

Honesty is the cornerstone of all success, and there is no exception in education. With the rapid development of internet technologies, online distance education (ODE) plays an important role in promoting lifelong learning and providing foundation for long-term personal development [1, 2]. However, as the scale of enrollment increases, the problem of academic dishonesty becomes more apparent in online learning environment [3]. Especially, the problem of cheating in exams has been a major concern in ODE schools [4, 5], which not only damaged the fairness of examinations seriously, but also undermined the credibility and reputation of ODE certificates.

Present studies of cheating are focused on the following aspects: detection of cheating practices by analyzing multiply accounts' submission [6] or learning behavior

A. El Rhalibi et al. (Eds.): Edutainment 2018, LNCS 11462, pp. 389–397, 2019.
https://doi.org/10.1007/978-3-030-23712-7_54

and performance [7, 8]; motivations and environmental factors related to cheating [9–11]; and prevention methods [12, 13]. In order to detect and prevent cheating in online learning, technologies such as data mining and statistical methods were used to analyze students' learning behaviors or submissions [6–8]. In addition, with the development of deep learning related technologies, face recognition has gradually become a mature technology provided as public cloud service on internet [14] and has been applied in educational environment to authenticate students [15] and to evaluate engagement by recognizing their facial expressions [16]. Since the literature has clearly highlighted the importance of the identification of cheating and feasibility of applying face recognition technology in online learning, we further add to this by proposing a technical framework to detect a typical cheating strategy in ODE examination context.

The major contributions of this paper are summarized as follows:

First, the "Ghost Writer" cheating strategy in ODE examinations is analyzed. And we summarized the challenges of anti-ghostwriter.
Second, the Student Identification by Face Recognition (SIFR) framework is proposed to address the challenges in detecting ghostwriters.
Third and last, a prototype system based on SIFR framework is implemented and experimental validated.

The rest of this paper is structured as follows: Sect. 2 describes the current examination system in ODE and analyzes the "Ghost Writer" cheating strategy. Section 3 proposes the SIFR framework for detecting the ghostwriter. Section 4 demonstrates the prototype system and discusses the experimental results. Section 5 concludes.

2 The "Ghost Writer" Cheating Strategy

Due to the wide geographical distribution of students, ODE schools usually commissioned learning centers located in various regions to recruit students and organize examinations. There are currently two types of examinations in ODE, entrance exams and course exams. Entrance exams are offline written examinations. Students must pass the entrance exams before starting online learning. Course exams are combinations of online and offline examinations. Some courses require students to take a written examination to test students' mastery of knowledge (e.g., engineering drawing, mechanical design, etc.) or include hands-on examinations (e.g., computer programming language, electrical and electronic technology, etc.), so only offline examinations can be used. Due to the huge size of enrollment and large number of course exams, it is a great challenge to maintain the fairness in the large-scale examinations.

In offline exams, due to the limitation in the number of examiners and their attention, it is difficult to monitor all activities in exam completely. Although cheatings such as "paging receiver" and "wireless earphone" have been prevented by metal detectors, some students still use the "Ghost Writer" cheating strategy in exams. They attempt to pass exams and earn credits by hiring ghostwriters to take the exam for them.

Before the exam begins, the examiner will inspect whether the photo on ID provided by the student is the same as that of himself/herself one by one. In order to pretend to be the student and pass the inspection, the ghostwriter merged student's photo and his/her own photo to make a fake photo indistinguishable from the student and further counterfeit documents. They may also change their appearance (e.g., using glasses, fake beard, make-up, changing hair style, etc.) to make examiners difficult to judge immediately. In addition, it's a great pressure for examiners to check thousands of students in detail during exam season. Therefore, this cheating strategy has been implemented in some exams and has not been identified. The situation in online exams may be more serious. Since student's identity is validated only by username and password when login into exam system, which makes identifying ghostwriters more difficult.

By analyzing the above cheating practices of the "Ghost Writer" strategy and the difficulty in detecting and preventing this cheating strategy, we summarized three challenges of anti-ghostwriter as follows:

- Accurate detection in both online and offline exams. Although online examinations have become more prevalent in ODE, there are still many courses that have to adopt offline exams due to course content characteristics or technology limitations. Therefore, the solution of anti-ghostwriter should not only be able to support online exam, but also support the offline exams.
- Scalable for large-scale detecting. Since there are a large population of enrollment in ODE school every year and lots of courses provided to students, the solution of anti-ghostwriter should support horizontal expansion and contraction on demand.
- Affordable for learning centers and students. There are several technologies can provide reliable student identification such as handwriting matching, fingerprint recognition and iris recognition, etc. However, these technologies require the purchase of specialized equipment and software with trained personnel to operate, which would be a large investment and needs to be upgraded in hardware and software over time. It is unacceptable for ODE school to make additional large-scale investments in this respect. Especially for students, purchasing extra set of equipment only for online exams is impractical. As a result, the solution of anti-ghostwriter must be affordable for both ODE school and students.

3 The Proposed Framework

To detect and further prevent the "Ghost Writer" cheating strategy described above, we propose the Student Identification by Face Recognition (SIFR) framework for administrators and teachers to support anti-cheating in both online and offline ODE examinations. This framework depends on the following key technologies/services.

First, face recognition. As introduced in Sect. 1, face recognition has become a proven technology in many typical scenarios. With photo taken by a standard camera on mobile device or web camera on computer, this technology can provide facial feature detection and comparison at enough accuracy in typical scenarios without further investment in hardware. Not only does the industry have a large number of companies that offer related services, but there are also several open source projects published by companies, organizations or individuals, which provide solid foundation for establishing internal, private and customized services. *Second*, micro-services architecture. In the framework designed based on micro-services architecture, the key technologies or services can be packaged as web-based APIs for external system to use. Without affecting external service access, the underlying implementation can be replaced, upgraded or expanded smoothly.

With the supports of above key technologies/services, the SIFR framework is presented in Fig. 1. We will describe each layer of the SIFR framework in the following subsections.

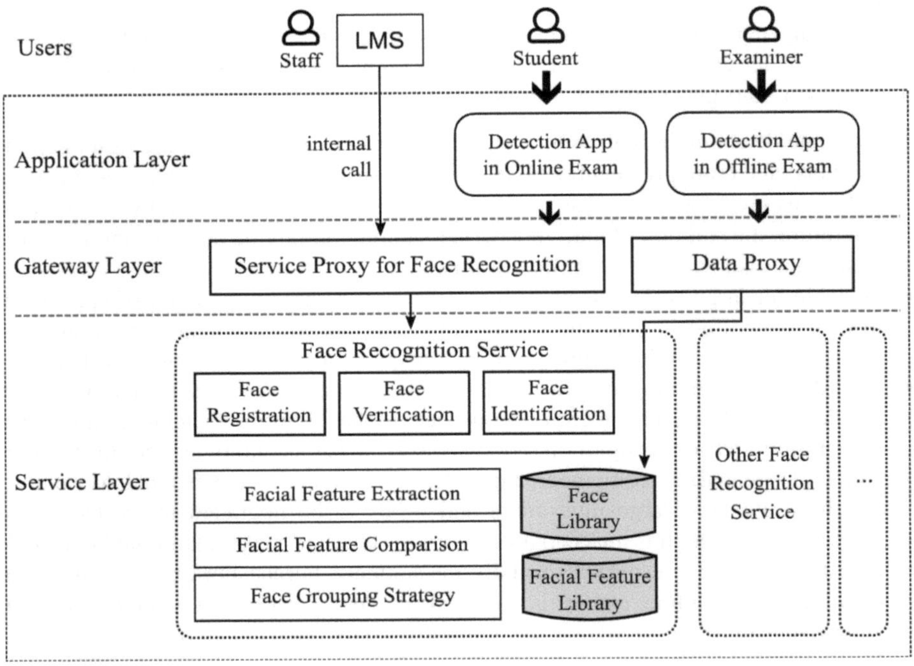

Fig. 1. The architecture of the SIFR framework.

3.1 The Service Layer

In this layer, there are two key technologies and one strategy to provide core support for face recognition service. *First*, the facial feature extraction is the most important function in this layer, it extracts a few basic measurements from the face in photo. *Second*, the facial feature comparison function calculates the difference of facial features between two faces. Small difference may indicate that two faces belong to the same person. *Third and last*, the grouping strategy is used to organize faces into groups to reduce computation load when identifying a specified face. Faces can be identified accurately even without grouping if the size of facial feature library is small. Nevertheless, as the number of faces increases, the possibility that several students have similar facial features will increase and the accuracy of face recognition may reduce. Therefore, it is necessary to design suitable grouping strategy in advance.

Based on the above three functions, we further summarize three core generic interfaces to meet the requirements of anti-ghostwriter.

- Face Registration. According to the principle of face recognition, a grouped facial feature library must be pre-built in order to provide base data for face comparison. As the basic interface at this layer, photos of all students will be imported through this interface into photo library, further processed and saved in facial features library by invoking key technology of facial feature extraction and specified grouping strategy. Because every student must submit a passport-style photo when they register in ODE school, the photo library and facial feature library can be built with this interface as soon as he/she submit it. The input of this interface includes a student ID, a group ID and a photo which belong to this student.
- Face Verification. This interface checks that weather the input photo belongs to a specified student by invoking the facial feature extraction and the facial feature comparison. If the photo belongs to the student, the verification is passed. The input of this interface includes a student ID and a photo to be verified.
- Face Identification. Similar to the function of face verification, by invoking the facial feature extraction and multi-times of facial feature comparison, this interface checks the input photo against a group of faces to find the student whom the photo may belong to. The input of this interface includes a group ID and a photo to be identified.

3.2 The Gateway Layer

In order to provide the scalable student identification service and related photo data to examiners, two types of proxies are required. As shown in Fig. 1, the data proxy provides students' photo files to apps which help examiners to further identify students on their own. The service proxy connects to all services and exports the specified interfaces to users. In addition, the service proxy balances the work load from requests of apps to different workers. With the increasing requests of face recognition from users, single worker of face recognition service may not handle all of the computations. Therefore, more workers can be combined together, and the service proxy will distribute requests to them.

When the service provided in service layer is unavailable, upgrading or removed, the service proxy can switch to workable service in order to avoid interruption. On the other hand, heterogeneous services with same interfaces from different providers can be integrated into the service layer and provide face recognition service together. With this feature, any third-party AI service can be imported as a module in this framework to increase performance and accuracy of detection.

3.3 The Application Layer

Due to the differences in scenarios, the application of interfaces differs. The user in online exam scenario is student himself/herself, so the target student is clear for the app. Therefore, the app only need to use the interface of face verification. While in offline exam scenario, examiners may use both interfaces of face verification and face identification to detect a student with student ID or an unknown student. Besides, the face registration interface will be invoked by LMS when staff in ODE school register student for exams.

4 The Implementation and Discussion

To verify the technical feasibility and workflow of the proposed SIFR framework, we implemented a prototype system based on open source projects and public cloud services. Details about each module used in each layer is listed in Table 1.

Table 1. The modules used in the prototype system of the SIFR framework.

Layer	Module	Implementation
Application layer	App in online exam	A plugin for exam system written in JavaScript
	App in offline exam	A HTML5 mobile app for Android smart phone
Gateway layer	Service proxy	Nginx with a proxy server written in Python
	Data proxy	Nginx web server
Service layer	Face recognition	A private service based on open source project: face_recognition and Flask in Python A public cloud service from Baidu Inc. [14]
	Data storage	Hadoop DFS as the photo library Redis database as the facial features library

In the application layer, we create a HTML5 mobile app for Android smart phone to help examiners in classroom and a plugin which is inserted in web page of exam system. The user interfaces of both apps are shown in Fig. 2. With these apps the detection of "Ghost Writer" cheating strategy in both online and offline exams can be achieved without further investment in specialized devices. In addition, our private service and a public cloud service were both integrated in the prototype system. To further validate the performance of the SIFR framework, we tested the face identification interface by the mobile app of the prototype system with a small-scale face recognition dataset PubFig83 as students (made up of more than 100 images for each of 83 persons) [17], and other photos from internet as ghostwriters.

As listed in Table 2, all ghostwriters were correctly identified. On average, more students were wrongly identified as other students by our private service than public cloud service. The results indicate that the proposed SIFR framework is feasible and the performance of face recognition may be acceptable with public cloud service.

Although our private face recognition service is functional available, the accuracy is relative lower than public cloud service. This result may be due to small size of

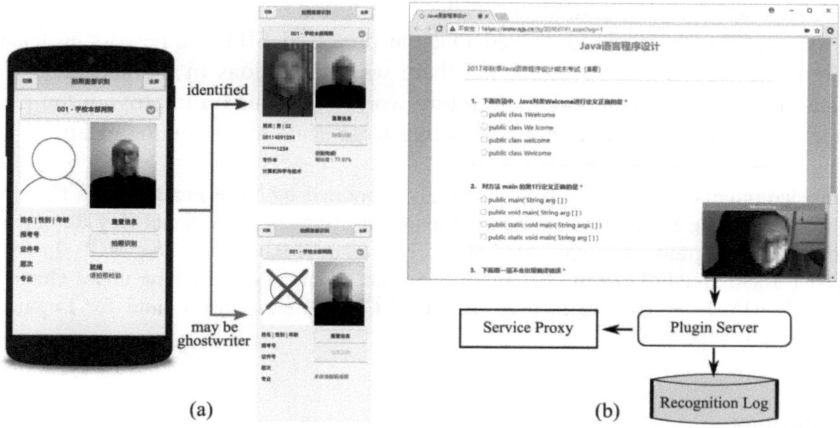

Fig. 2. The apps created for examiners and students. (a) The mobile app on Android. Examiners can use this app to identify students with two steps: (1) select the face group, (2) take photo. This app will automatically send photo and identify the person. (b) The plugin in exam system. After student login to the system, the plugin will request to authorize access to the camera and stay in background if permission is granted. During the exam, the plugin will randomly take photo and send back for detection. The recognition results will be saved for further analysis.

Table 2. The experimental results. (83 faces in one face group and 17 ghostwriters.)

Service	Student		Ghostwriter		Accuracy	Precision
	Correct	Incorrect	Correct	Incorrect		
Private service	75.9	7.1	17	0	92.90%	91.45%
Public cloud service	78.9	4.1	17	0	95.90%	95.06%

training sample and generic facial feature model. Besides, both the training sample size and hardware acceleration equipment used in public cloud service are far beyond ours, which also contributes to their accuracy. As a result, the facial feature extraction of our private service should be upgraded in order to achieve better performance. As mentioned in Sect. 2, ghostwriters may make their appearance difficult to identify by applying makeup or other means (e.g., pretending to be injured by wrapping gauze). In this situation, the facial features may not be detected properly, which indicates that there are still limitations in technical means, and further research is required not only in technologies but also in regulations and execution.

5 Conclusion

In order to detect the "Ghost Writer" cheating strategy in ODE examinations, we proposed a framework with face recognition to identify students in both online and offline exams. A prototype system was developed, which implemented two face recognition services. In addition, the system was tested on a small-scale public dataset, and the experiment results indicated that the proposed SIFR framework is feasible. Whereas the results also revealed that there were limitations in the accuracy of our private face recognition service. The future work will focus on improving the performance of our private service and conducting large-scale test in online exams.

Acknowledgments. This research was partially supported by "The Fundamental Theory and Applications of Big Data with Knowledge Engineering" under the National Key Research and Development Program of China with Grant No. 2016YFB1000903, the MOE Innovation Research Team No. IRT17R86, the National Science Foundation of China under Grant Nos. 61721002, 61502379, 61532015, and Project of China Knowledge Centre for Engineering Science and Technology.

References

1. Ding, X., Niu, J., Han, Y.: Research on distance education development in China. Br. J. Educ. Technol. **41**, 582–592 (2010)
2. Hu, F.: Return to education for china's return migrant entrepreneurs. World Dev. **72**, 296–307 (2015)
3. Corrigan-Gibbs, H., Gupta, N., Northcutt, C., Cutrell, E., Thies, W.: Deterring cheating in online environments. ACM Trans. Comput.-Hum. Interact. **22**, 1–23 (2015)
4. Arnold, I.J.M.: Cheating at online formative tests: does it pay off? Internet High. Educ. **29**, 98–106 (2016)
5. Keresztury, B., Cser, L.: New cheating methods in the electronic teaching era. Procedia – Soc. Behav. Sci. **93**, 1516–1520 (2013)
6. Alexandron, G., Ruipérez-Valiente, J.A., Chen, Z., Muñoz-Merino, P.J., Pritchard, D.E.: Copying@Scale: using harvesting accounts for collecting correct answers in a MOOC. Comput. Educ. **108**, 96–114 (2017)
7. Sabonchi, A.K.S., Görür, A.K.: Plagiarism detection in learning management system. In: 2017 8th International Conference on Information Technology (ICIT), pp. 495–500 (2017)
8. Salhofer, P.: Analyzing student behavior in CS courses: a case-study on detecting and preventing cheating. In: 2017 IEEE Global Engineering Education Conference (EDUCON), pp. 1426–1431 (2017)
9. Kalhori, Z.: The relationship between teacher-student rapport and student's willingness to cheat. Procedia – Soc. Behav. Sci. **136**, 153–158 (2014)
10. Toki, E.I., Tafiadis, D.C.: Identification of plagiarism by Greek higher education students. Do I cheat? In: 2014 International Conference on Interactive Mobile Communication Technologies and Learning (IMCL2014), pp. 364–367 (2014)
11. Turner, S.W., Uludag, S.: Student perceptions of cheating in online and traditional classes. In: 2013 IEEE Frontiers in Education Conference (FIE), pp. 1131–1137 (2013)
12. Awad, M.K., Zogheib, B., Alazemi, H.M.K.: A penalty scheme for academic dishonesty. In: Proceedings of 2013 IEEE International Conference on Teaching, Assessment and Learning for Engineering (TALE), pp. 580–584 (2013)
13. Kaur, N., Prasad, P.W.C., Alsadoon, A., Pham, L., Elchouemi, A.: An enhanced model of biometric authentication in e-learning: using a combination of biometric features to access e-learning environments. In: 2016 International Conference on Advances in Electrical, Electronic and Systems Engineering (ICAEES), pp. 138–143 (2016)
14. Baidu Face Recognition of AI Platform. http://ai.baidu.com/solution/faceprint

15. Zhao, Q., Ye, M.: The application and implementation of face recognition in authentication system for distance education. In: 2010 International Conference on Networking and Digital Society, pp. 487–489 (2010)
16. Whitehill, J., Serpell, Z., Lin, Y.C., Foster, A., Movellan, J.R.: The faces of engagement: automatic recognition of student engagement from facial expressions. IEEE Trans. Affect. Comput. **5**, 86–98 (2014)
17. Pinto, N., Stone, Z., Zickler, T., Cox, D.: Scaling up biologically-inspired computer vision: a case study in unconstrained face recognition on Facebook. In: CVPR 2011 Workshops, pp. 35–42 (2011)

Texture Image Segmentation Based on Stationary Directionlet Domain Probabilistic Graphical Model

Zhenguo Gao, Shixiong Xia(✉), and Jiaqi Zhao

School of Computer Science and Technology,
China University of Mining and Technology,
No. 1, Daxue Road, Xuzhou 221116, Jiangsu, China
shixiongxia.cumt@outlook.com

Abstract. In this paper, a stationary directionlet (SD) domain probabilistic graphical model (PGM) for texture image segmentation is proposed. Hidden markov chain (HMC) is a good tool to capture the persistence and clustering properties of the coefficients of SD transform. The homogeneous property of texture image is described by markov random field (MRF). Combining HMC and MRF in SD domain result in SDPGM. Image segmentation based on SDPGM, which is denoted as SDPGMseg, involves inferring the maximum a posterior (MAP) solution to class labels on the coefficients of SD transform. The segmentation result can be obtained by minimizing an energy function. Experiment results show that SDPGMseg can obtain better performance especially in homogeneous regions and boundaries of different regions.

Keywords: Image segmentation · Directionlet transform · Hidden Markov chain · Markov random field · Probabilistic graphical model

1 Introduction

Image segmentation is a key technology in the area of image understanding and interpretation [1]. The objective of image segmentation is to divide an image of different regions based on certain attributes such as intensity, texture, context information and so on. A texture is a set of texture elements occurring in some regular or repeated pattern, it is very rich in images [2]. Texture analysis plays an important role in images segmentation, ranging from remote sensing images [3] to medical images [4]. To extract and represent the texture information about images effectively helps a lot for image segmentation.

In the past decades, many methods have been proposed and a dense literatures are available for texture image segmentation [5]. Wavelet transform has been a useful tool for image processing in many areas, such as image denoise, image reconstruction, image fusion and so on. Wavelet transform based methods have been used for image segmentation in many literatures [6]. In many

A. El Rhalibi et al. (Eds.): Edutainment 2018, LNCS 11462, pp. 398–405, 2019.
https://doi.org/10.1007/978-3-030-23712-7_55

works, wavelet transform is used to extract the texture feature, such as channel variances features, wavelet histogram and wavelet co-occurrence feature, mean energies of sub-bands, local energy histograms of all the wavelet sub-bands and so on.

Hidden markov tree (HMT) model was applied to describe the statistical distribution of wavelet coefficient in [7], and the model was successfully used for image denoise. Image segmentation method based on HMT (HMTseg) was proposed in [8], in which HMT model was used to describe the clustering and persistence across scale of wavelet coefficient and context based fusion model was used to fusion the segmentation results in different scales. However, HMTseg is a supervised image segmentation method, to train the model different types of image patches should be selected manually. The HMTseg can be implemented in unsupervised way by taking clustering methods of pre-segmentation. Fuzzy c-means clustering algorithm (FCM) [9] was applied for pre-segmentation in order to select samples of each class before HMT model parameters training.

Many multi-scale geometric analysis (MGA) tools have been developed for image processing, such as contourlet transform, directionlet transform, curvelet transform and so on [10]. Similarly with wavelet transform the MGA is also very useful for texture analysis. The contourlet domain HMT model for image segmentation method (CHMTseg) was proposed in [11], in which a new weighted neighborhood background model was designed to fuse multiple scales results. The directionlet domain HMT model for image segmentation method (DHMT-seg) was proposed in [10], which obtained segmentation results much better than HMTseg and CHMTseg. However, HMT model cannot capture the neighborhood semantic information for image segmentation. In this paper, we propose stationary directionlet domain probabilistic graphical model (SDPGM), which combines HMT and MRF together, not only can describe texture information clearly, but also can capture semantic information for image segmentation.

The remainder of this paper is organized as follows. The details of SDPGMseg are described in Sect. 2. Section 3 presents discussion of performance evaluation results of the proposed algorithm. Section 4 provides conclusions.

2 Image Segmentation Based on SDPGM

2.1 Image Segmentation in SD Domain

The objective of image segmentation in SD domain is to find Maximum an approximate (MAP) estimation of a label configuration X when given the SD coefficients D, and the solution can be formulated as Eq. 1.

$$\widehat{X} = \underset{X \in \Omega}{argmax}\, P(X|D) \tag{1}$$

where, $\widehat{X}$ is the real segmentation result, Ω is the solution domain. According to the theory of Bayesian rule, the problem can be formulated as Eq. 2.

$$P(X|D) = \frac{P(X)P(D|X)}{P(D)} \tag{2}$$

where $P(X|D)$ is the posterior probability distribution, $P(D)$ is the density of SD coefficient, which is a constant for an image. $P(D|X)$ is the likelihood estimation, $P(X)$ is prior probability. Then the MAP estimate equivalently with Eq. 3.

$$\widehat{X} = \underset{X \in \Omega}{argmax}\, P(X)P(D|X) \tag{3}$$

To solve this problem, SD domain PGM (SDPGM) is proposed, in which SD domain HMC model is used to calculate the likelihood term $P(D|X)$, and MRF model is used to describe the prior term $P(X)$. The details of SDPGM will be discussed in the next part.

2.2 PGM in SD Domain

In this paper, HMC and MRF are combined together in SD domain, result in SDPGM. HMC is used to transfer the information between different layers of SD coefficients of an image, MRF is used to capture homogeneous properties of images. The sketch map of SDPGM is show in Fig. 1. In the Figure the black nodes on the map represent the SD coefficients of a sub-band, and the nodes in different planes represent coefficients in different layers. The links between the vertical direction represent the chain of HMC, which transfers information between different layers of SD coefficients in the same position. The links between horizontal direction represent the description of MRF, which is used to model the neighbor prior that describes local homogeneity in an image.

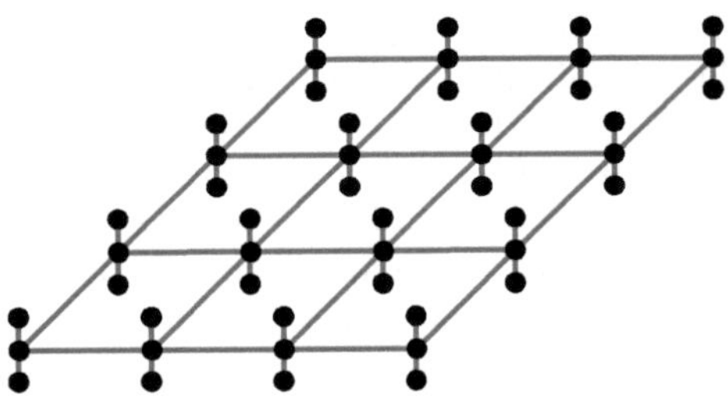

Fig. 1. The sketch map of SDPGM.

2.3 The Framework of SDPGMseg

The framework of SDPGMseg is shown in Fig. 2. The process of image segmentation is divided into two stages: initialization stage and SDPGMseg stage.

Initialization Stage. The algorithm of the initialization stage is shown in Algorithm 1. Initial segmentation result and examples for each texture class will be used for fine segmentation by SDPGMseg method, the details will be introduced in the next part.

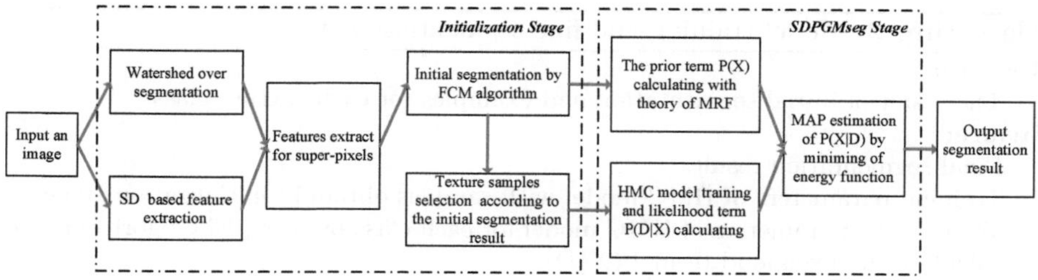

Fig. 2. The image segmentation framework of SDPGMseg

Algorithm 1. Initialization stage

Require:
An image for segmentation.
Ensure:
The initial segmentation result and examples for each texture category.
1: Watershed over segmentation.
segment the input image by watershed method, build watershed mapping and add datum indexed to image mapping.
2: SD features extraction and normalization.
3: Extracting features of superpixels
4: Initial segment the image by FCM algorithm, via clustering the SD features which are created in previous step.
5: Select 10% high membership patches as examples for each class based on the result obtained in previous step.
6: **return** Initial segmentation result and examples for each texture class.

Fine Segmentation Stage. Image segmentation is formulated as an MAP estimation, which is described by SDPGM. The object function is given in this part. By combining MRF and HMC model the MAP estimation can be formulated as Eq. 4.

$$P(X|D) \propto P(X)P(D|X) \tag{4}$$

The objective function for image segmentation can be considered as an energy minimization problem. Recently, the Graph cuts have been widely used in computer vision community. There are many advantages for the Graph cuts algorithm, such as practical efficiently, global optima, and the ability to fusion a wide range of image cues. In [12] Boykov proposed an energy minimum framework and a fast Graph cuts algorithm, and multi-labels problem can be solved in [13]. In this paper, Graph cuts is adopted to optimize the object of SDPGMseg. The algorithm of the fine segmentation stage is shown in Algorithm 2. Experimental results will be discussed in the next section.

Algorithm 2. Model training and fine segmentation stage

Require:
The result of initial segmentation and examples for each texture class.
Ensure:
Final segmentation result.
1: Training parameters of HMC model with samples obtain in initialization stage.
To train the parameters of HMC model for each class by using EM algorithm, and calculate the likelihood term $P(X|D)$.
2: Building MRF model for the initial segmentation result obtained in initialization stage.
The segmentation result in initialization stage can provide prior information as $P(X)$.
3: Minimization the objective function by Graph cuts.
4: **return** Final segmentation result.

3 Experimental Results and Analysis

To study the performance of the new proposed SDPGMseg algorithm, several synthetic texture images are tested in this section. Besides, three other algorithms: HMTseg, CHMTseg, and DHMTseg are used to compare with the proposed algorithms. The source codes for these algorithms are programmed based on the Matlab code of HMTseg which can be downloaded from the website (http://www.dsp.rice.edu/software). All of the experiments run on a HP Pro 3380 PC with Intel(R) i5-3470, 4G memory and Windows 7 operating system.

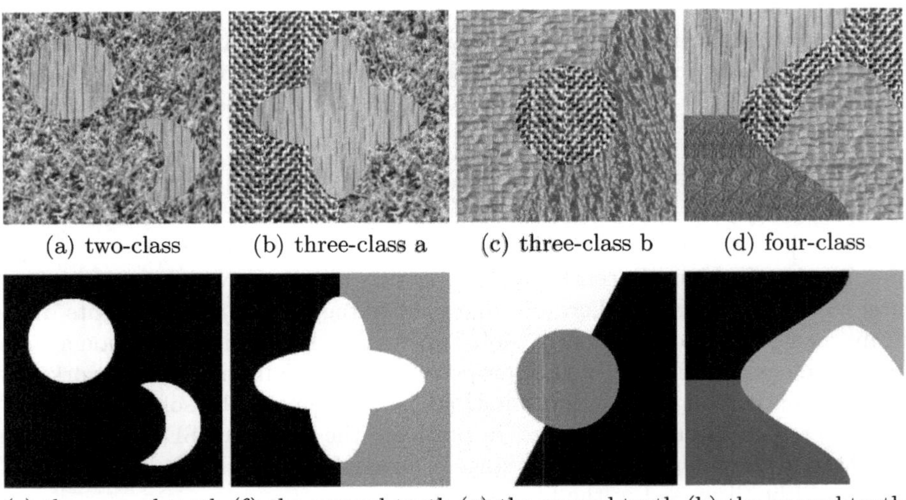

(a) two-class (b) three-class a (c) three-class b (d) four-class

(e) the ground truth of (a) (f) the ground truth of (b) (g) the ground truth of (c) (h) the ground truth of (d)

Fig. 3. Four texture images and the corresponding ground truth from Brodatz album.

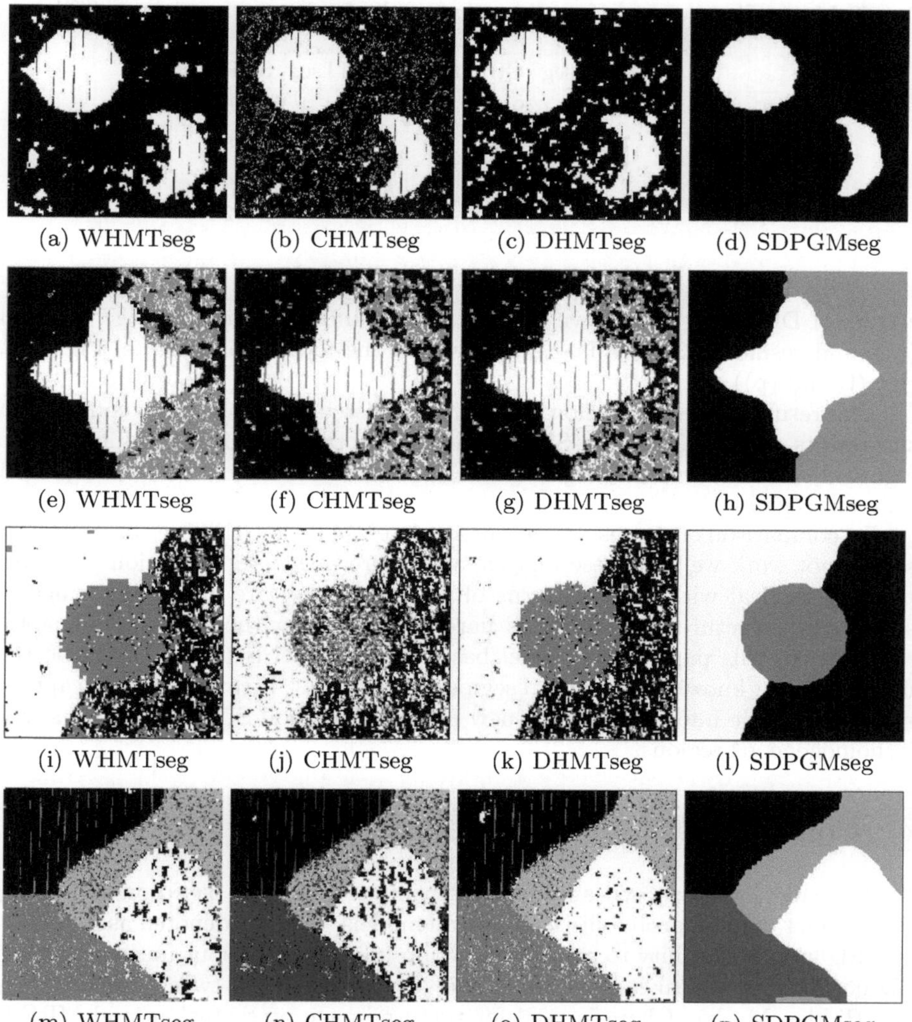

Fig. 4. Segmentation results of four texture images.

Four synthetic texture images have two three, and four categories from the Brodatz album [14]. The original images and standard segmentation results of these images are given in Fig. 3. The size of all these texture images is 256×256.

For texture image segmentation, we compare results of segmentation and the segmentation correct rate to evaluate the performance of every algorithm. The segmentation results of all algorithms are shown in Fig. 4. In the Figure, results of HMTseg are shown in the first column (i.e. Fig. 4(a), (e), (i) and (m)), results of CHMTseg are shown in the second column (i.e. Fig. 4(b), (f), (j) and (n)),

Table 1. The accuracy of segmentation results for four texture images (%).

	HMTseg	CHMTseg	DHMTseg	SDPGMseg
Texture (a)	93.55	91.83	90.79	**96.59**
Texture (b)	79.21	72.25	79.54	**95.94**
Texture (c)	81.74	69.89	85.13	**97.89**
Texture (d)	86.49	81.71	89.77	**96.24**

results of DHMTseg are shown in the third column (i.e. Fig. 4(e), (g), (k) and (o)), and results of SDPGMseg are shown in the fourth column (i.e. Fig. 4(d), (h), (l) and (p)).

The results of segmentation accuracy are listed in Table 1. By comparison the results we can find that SDPMGseg can obtain the best results of these algorithms, not only in homogeneous regions but also can detect boundaries of different regions.

By comparison of the results we can see that HMTseg, CHMTseg and DHMT-seg do not work well on these images, as texture image segmentation is a hard problem to deal with. The patterns of texture images are in varying range of scales, the structure of patterns is hard to describe without spatial semantic methods. In this paper, super-pixel based MRF model is used to describe the neighbor prior knowledge of initial segmentation result, it can effectively capture spatial semantic information. The new proposed method SDPGMseg plays well in homogeneous regions.

4 Conclusions

In this paper, we proposed an image segmentation method based on stationary directionlet domain probabilistic graphical models, which is denoted as SDPGM-seg. SD has good ability to capture direction information about images, and the SD coefficients of real images are sparse and continuity between different layers. Hidden Markov Chain is used for texture image presentation, and MRF is built to capture context information of images, the prior knowledge is provided by the initial segmentation result. Experimental results of texture images show that SDPGMseg can obtain better performance in homogeneous regions and boundaries than other compared methods.

Acknowledgment. This work was partially supported by the National Natural Science Foundation of China (No. U1610124, 61772530 and 61572505), and the National Key Research and Development Plan (No. 2016YFC0600908), and the National Natural Science Foundation of Jiangsu Province (No. BK20171192).

References

1. Maninis, K.K., Pont-Tuset, J., Arbelaez, P., Gool, L.V.: Convolutional oriented boundaries: from image segmentation to high-level tasks. IEEE Trans. Pattern Anal. Mach. Intell. **PP**(99), 1 (2017)
2. Qian, P., et al.: Knowledge-leveraged transfer fuzzy c-means for texture image segmentation with self-adaptive cluster prototype matching. Knowl.-Based Syst. **130**, 33–50 (2017)
3. Min, H., et al.: An intensity-texture model based level set method for image segmentation. Pattern Recogn. **48**(4), 1547–1562 (2015)
4. Devi, C.N., Chandrasekharan, A., Sundararaman, V., Alex, Z.C.: Neonatal brain MRI segmentation: a review. Comput. Biol. Med. **64**, 163–178 (2015)
5. Masood, S., Sharif, M., Masood, A., Yasmin, M., Raza, M.: A survey on medical image segmentation. Curr. Med. Imaging Rev. **11**(1), 3–14 (2015)
6. Shankar, T., Yamuna, G., Suman, G.: Segmentation of natural colour image based on colour-texture features. In: 2013 International Conference on Communications and Signal Processing (ICCSP), pp. 455–459. IEEE (2013)
7. Crouse, M.S., Nowak, R.D., Baraniuk, R.G.: Wavelet-based statistical signal processing using hidden Markov models. IEEE Trans. Sig. Process. **46**(4), 886–902 (1998)
8. Choi, H., Baraniuk, R.G.: Multiscale image segmentation using wavelet-domain hidden Markov models. IEEE Trans. Image Process. **10**(9), 1309–1321 (2001)
9. Bezdek, J.C., Ehrlich, R., Full, W.: FCM: the fuzzy c-means clustering algorithm. Comput. Geosci. **10**(84), 191–203 (1984)
10. Bai, J., Zhao, J., Jiao, L.: Image segmentation using directionlet-domain hidden Markov tree models. In: 2011 IEEE CIE International Conference on Radar (Radar), vol. 2, pp. 1615–1618. IEEE (2011)
11. Sha, Y., Cong, L., Sun, Q., Jiao, L.: Unsupervised image segmentation using contourlet domain hidden Markov trees model. In: Kamel, M., Campilho, A. (eds.) ICIAR 2005. LNCS, vol. 3656, pp. 32–39. Springer, Heidelberg (2005). https://doi.org/10.1007/11559573_5
12. Boykov, Y., Kolmogorov, V.: An experimental comparison of min-cut/max-flow algorithms for energy minimization in vision. IEEE Trans. Pattern Anal. Mach. Intell. **26**(9), 1124–1137 (2004)
13. Delong, A., Osokin, A., Isack, H.N., Boykov, Y.: Fast approximate energy minimization with label costs. Int. J. Comput. Vis. **96**(1), 1–27 (2012)
14. Brodatz, P.: Textures: a photographic album for artists and designers. Department of the University of Central Florida

Hand Pose Estimation Using Convolutional Neural Networks and Support Vector Regression

Yufeng Dong, Jian Lu(✉), and Qiang Zhang(✉)

Key Laboratory of Advanced Design and Intelligent Computing, Dalian University, Ministry of Education, Dalian 116622, China
{lujian, zhangq}@dlu.edu.cn

Abstract. In order to improve the accuracy of hand pose estimation from a depth image, a method based on convolutional neural network (CNN) is proposed in this paper. First of all, we modify the structure of traditional CNN to recognize the 3D joint locations from a depth image. By appending some shortcuts between layers, the proposed network increases the correlation between the front and back layers. This structure can avoid the information loss caused by the simple layer-by-layer transmission, and can improve the estimation accuracy effectively. Afterwards, the estimated joint locations continue to be inputted into a support vector regression (SVR) phase. The use of SVR can introduce the constraint of local joint information, which can get rid of those abnormal estimations further. Extensive experiments show that our method enables significant performance improvement over the-state-of-arts in the accuracy of hand pose estimation.

Keywords: Convolutional neural network · Hand pose estimation · Support vector regression

1 Introduction

Gesture plays an important role in applications of human-computer interface (HCI) with high operational efficiency and pleasant operating experience. However, because of many disadvantages such as high complexity, high degree of freedom and serious self-occlusion in this field, there are some difficulties for accurate estimation of hand pose [1, 2].

Recent studies based on the depth map mainly divide into two categories. The first approach is the model-based generative method. It fits the hand model to the observed images [3, 4]. The second approach is discriminative. It directly predicts the locations of the joints. [5, 6] mainly used random forests to obtain joint locations directly. Besides, with the emergence of the convolutional neural network (CNN), hand pose estimation would be brought to a new stage [7–9].

Discriminative model based on CNN has become one of the focuses. [10] combined CNN of 5 convolutional layers with restraint of kinematics formulas to estimate

A. El Rhalibi et al. (Eds.): Edutainment 2018, LNCS 11462, pp. 406–413, 2019.
https://doi.org/10.1007/978-3-030-23712-7_56

hand joint. [11] estimated hand pose by CNN with multiple cascade convolutional layers and fully connected layers.

In essence, hand pose estimation is a serious non-linear problem. Thus, it is usually difficult to obtain satisfactory results depending on a single CNN. Therefore, the output of the deep network needs some correction. For example, [8] got the initial results of hand pose estimation through a CNN and then another CNN refined hand joint position. [12] first used CNN to classify hand pose, then amended joint position by multiple cascaded random forests. In [7], the authors used the feedback loop CNNs consisting of Predictor, Synthesizer and Updater to iteratively correct hand pose.

Based on the existing methods, in this paper, CNN and SVR are used to estimate the 3D joint locations from a depth map, to achieve accurate estimation. As shown in Fig. 1, our approach consists of two phases:

In the first phase: the preliminary estimation of the hand pose is obtained by CNN. To reduce the loss of hand characteristics in transmission, we increase the local path to keep more useful information on hand pose in SqueezeNet [13].

In the second phase: support vector regression (SVR) [14] corrects the preliminary estimation of the hand pose. Rough estimation is then locally sampled and vectorized (Local vectorization) according to the rough estimation, to use SVR to correct joint position. After correction, there is a smaller distance between the estimated result (light grey line) and the actual result (dark grey line) than before. It shows that SVR further utilizes the local depth information, reducing the abnormal estimates of the first phase.

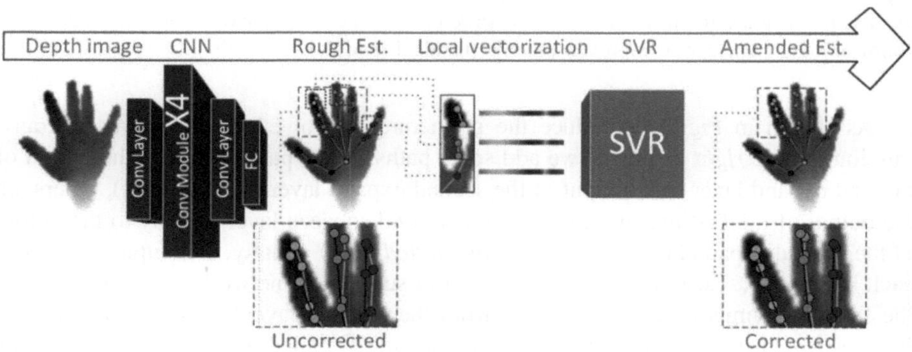

Fig. 1. Two stages of hand pose estimation. The *depth image* is input to *CNN* to obtain the preliminary estimation result. Then, it is locally sampled and vectorized (*Local vectorization*) according to the initial position of the joint, to use *SVR* to correct joint position.

In the remainder of the paper, improved CNN to recognize hand joints is introduced in Sect. 2. Then, correcting positions by SVR is introduced in Sect. 3. Section 4 shows the comparison with classical methods, followed by the conclusion in Sect. 5.

2 Hand Pose Estimation Using Convolutional Neural Network

This part mainly introduces the first phase of our method. First, we introduce how to build the local network module. Then, we introduced the overall structure of hand pose estimation network. Finally, we demonstrate the improvement of results.

2.1 Residual Module

Considering the requirement of speed and accuracy in hand pose estimation, this paper decides to adopt SqueezeNet [13] as the basis of network structure.

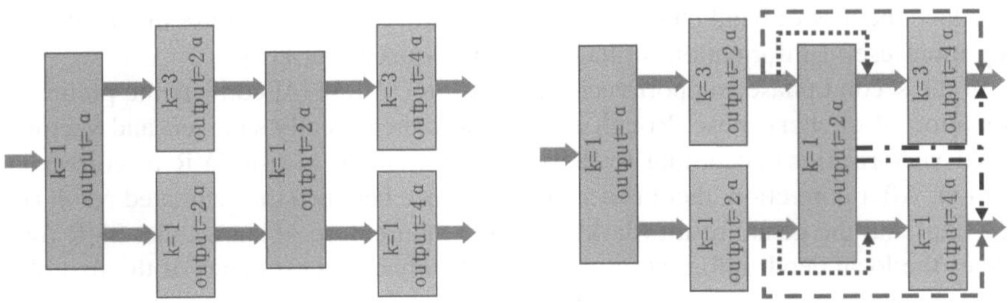

Fig. 2. *Left* is SqueezeNet module (Actually, there are two SqueezeNet modules. On the one hand is to facilitate the description of the structure, on the other hand do not let readers feel confused) and *right* is our improved module (residual module).

As shown in Fig. 2, to reduce the premature loss of effective features in transmission, on the *right* of Fig. 2, we add some paths. Some paths are from the output of the first expand layer to the input of the second expand layer (*dashed lines*), others are the output of the first expand layer and the second squeeze layer directly to the output of the second expand layer (*chain lines and dotted lines*). Finally, the output features of each layer are cascaded together as the input of subsequent network modules. It allows the follow-up units to get information from the shallow layers. And it reduces valid features lost in the network. This network module is called as *residual module*. The improvements will be demonstrated in Sect. 2.3.

2.2 Network Structure

In the previous, we introduce the residual module. Next, we will describe how to connect modules to build a complete network for hand pose estimation.

The network structure is shown in Fig. 3. The parameters k and α denote the size and number of filters respectively. In addition, J denotes the number of hand joints. First, conv1 loads the depth maps and extracts features with 64 filters. Next, followed by 4 residual modules, coefficients α are 32, 48, 64, and 96. After residual modules, there are 1000 outputs from conv6 and avgpool6. Finally, J joint positions with 3 dimensions will be obtained through fc7. In addition, the network fits max-poolings with a stride of 2 and 3 × 3 filters after conv1 and the first three residual modules. All of convolutional layers use Rectified Linear Unit activation functions.

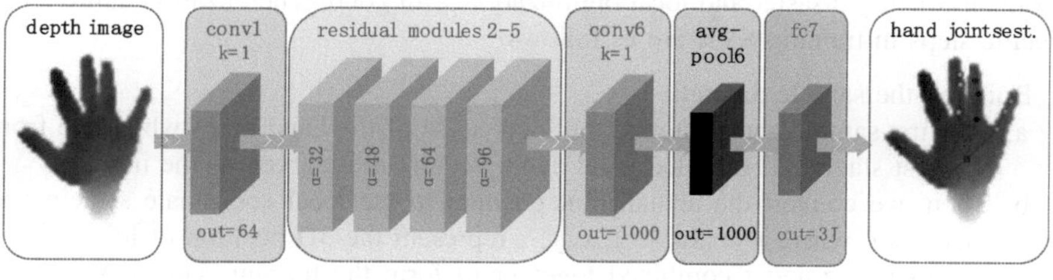

Fig. 3. Our whole network structure used in estimations.

2.3 Experiment Evaluation

To demonstrate the effectiveness of our change. We show four experiments. The first three groups of experiments compare the structural changes to the improvement of the estimation. The fourth experiment increases the number of filters in the module to further enhance the recognition effect.

Experiments with different modules use the same architecture as Fig. 3. In the first group, modules are shown on the *left* of Fig. 2. Based on the first group, the second adds the path which is the *dotted lines* on the *right* of Fig. 2. The third further adds other paths which are the *dashed* and *chain lines.* These three networks are labeled SqueezeNet, One Path and All Paths, with α 16, 24, 32, 48.

Table 1. Comparison of mean error and speed of hand pose estimation in different networks.

Networks	SqueezeNet	One path	All paths	Ours
Error (mm)	9.8	9.5	9.3	8.5
FPS (frames per-second)	410.8	402.1	400.0	362.3

Table 1 shows the mean error and speed at hand pose estimation in ICVL [6]. As shown in Table 1, the average error gradually drops from 9.8 mm to 9.3 mm. The network is effectively enhancing the effect of hand pose estimation.

In addition, number of filters is in relation to the ability of extracting valid features from the network. The fourth experiment increases the parameters α to 32, 48, 64, 96, which is introduced in Sect. 2.2. With the increase in network paths and convolutional kernels, our network can still obtain 8.5 mm with 362.3 FPS.

3 Hand Pose Correction Using Support Vector Regression

This part introduces the correction based on support vector regression (SVR) [14]. We introduce how to train SVR models and demonstrate the result.

Hand pose estimation is a nonlinear mapping problem with a high degree of freedom, self-occlusion and noise, thus there are some difficulties to directly estimate hand pose with a CNN. Therefore, this paper attempts to use SVR to correct the estimation. SVR adopts structural risk minimization and effectively solve the problem of dimensionality disaster and local optimization with good generalization ability. The specific steps in training SVR are as follows:

1. Building the sample dataset:
   a. We first sample and vectorize the local areas of the hand maps which are from the first stage. All sampled local depth vectors are marked as the input a.
   b. Then, we convert the actual joint position to the local coordinate system and mark as t, where $t = (x, y, z)$, x, y, z represent the 3D position of joint.
   c. Parameters a and t combined together to form the training sample set (a, t). Then, it is divided into: $(a, x), (a, y), (a, z)$ according to the dimension of t.
2. Training SVR models:
   a. Setting hyper-parameters in SVR: loss function parameter ε, regularization parameter C and kernel function.
   b. The training sample sets: $(a, x), (a, y), (a, z)$ are respectively fed into three groups of SVR models for obtaining trained models.

In order to show improvements, the experiment shows mean error of each position before correction (CNN) and after correction (CNN + SVR) on ICVL [6] and NYU [15] datasets. As shown in Fig. 4, the abscissa represents each hand joint, the ordinate represents the average error at each joint. After being corrected by SVR, most of the joint error have a significant decline.

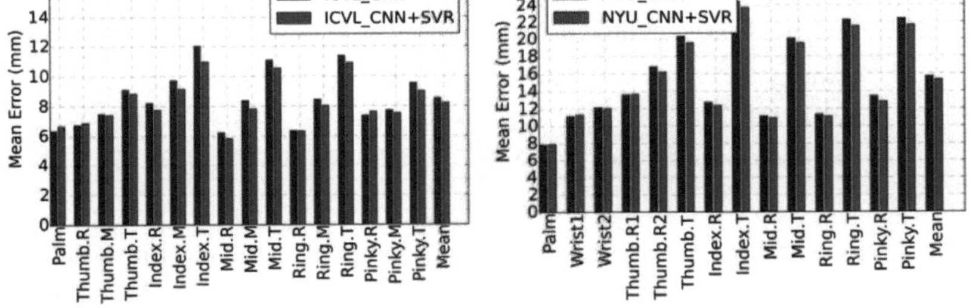

Fig. 4. Mean error in each joint whether or not SVR is used on ICVL (*left*) and NYU (*right*).

4 Experiments

To compare with the classical method, all 16 joints in ICVL [6] are used in this experiment. And we use the same 14 joints as DeepPrior [8] in NYU [15]. CNN described in Sect. 2.2 is implemented within Caffe [16]. We use a workstation with Core i7-7700 processors and a Nvidia GTX1080 GPUs for CNNs training. The networks are trained using Adaptive Moment Estimation (ADAM) with a batch size of 64 for 300000 iterations. The learning rate starts from 0.0001 and is divided by 10 after every 60000 iterations. In addition, SVR is implemented by Scikit-learn [17], and set the insensitive parameter ε to 0.1, the regularization parameter C to 1.0, and the kernel to radial basis function. In addition, 1% and 2% samples are respectively divided from training sets of ICVL and NYU to train SVR. And size of the local image (*Local vectorization* in Fig. 1) is 10 × 10 pixels.

To demonstrate the effectiveness of our proposed method, we compare it against several classical methods.

In Fig. 5, the *left* image shows mean error of each joint on the ICVL dataset. Comparing the proposed method with LRF [6], DeepPrior [8] with refinements and DeepModel [10], our method achieves the smallest error. The *right* image shows the fraction of frames where all joints are within a maximum distance from the ground truth. It can also be seen from the figure that the corresponding curve of our method is the larger than others. It shows that in the ICVL dataset, the number of test samples that can meet certain accuracy requirements is higher than others.

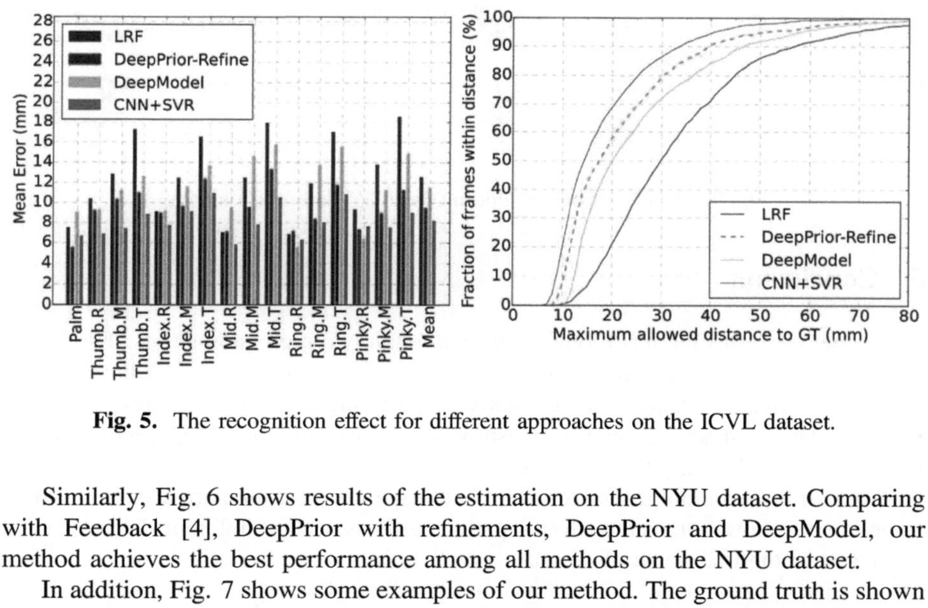

Fig. 5. The recognition effect for different approaches on the ICVL dataset.

Similarly, Fig. 6 shows results of the estimation on the NYU dataset. Comparing with Feedback [4], DeepPrior with refinements, DeepPrior and DeepModel, our method achieves the best performance among all methods on the NYU dataset.

In addition, Fig. 7 shows some examples of our method. The ground truth is shown in dark grey line, estimated results in light grey line. The first and second lines represent the identification results on the ICVL and NYU datasets. It can be seen that our method can well identify complex hand poses.

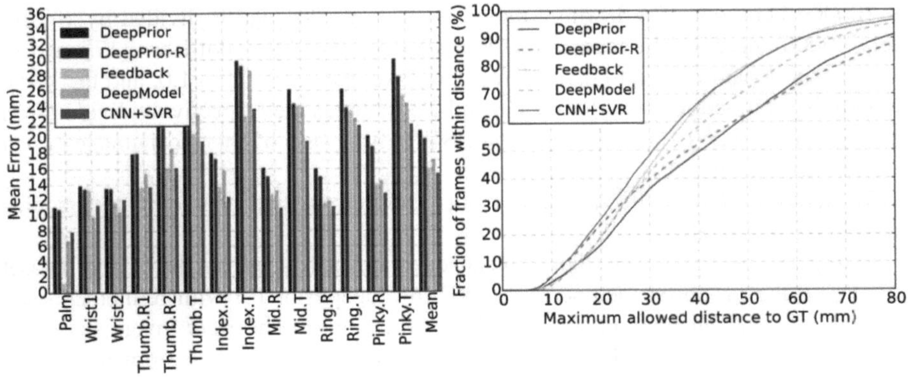

Fig. 6. The recognition effect for different approaches on the NYU dataset.

Fig. 7. Results of our method on the *ICVL* and *NYU* datasets.

5 Conclusion

This paper estimates the hand joint position through two regression stages. The first is performed by a CNN. Based on the SqueezeNet module, this paper adds three groups of network paths. It reduces the cumulative superposition of valid features lost in the network. The accuracy of hand pose estimation is also improved. The second is performed by a SVR. Using the local depth information of the joint, it effectively corrects the estimation deviation generated in the first stage and obtains more accurate results. Experiments show our method has superior performance on different datasets when compared to the traditional methods.

Acknowledgments. This work is supported by the Liaoning Provincial Natural Science Foundation of China (20170540039).

References

1. Ueda, E., Matsumoto, Y., Imai, M., Ogasawara, T.: A hand-pose estimation for vision-based human interfaces. IEEE Trans. Industr. Electron. **50**, 676–684 (2003)
2. Yin, X., Xie, M.: Estimation of the fundamental matrix from uncalibrated stereo hand images for 3D hand gesture recognition. Pattern Recogn. **36**, 567–584 (2003)

3. Tagliasacchi, A., Schr, M., der Tkach, A., Bouaziz, S., Botsch, M., Pauly, M.: Robust articulated-ICP for real-time hand tracking. In: Proceedings of the Eurographics Symposium on Geometry Processing, pp. 101–114. Eurographics Association (2015)
4. Taylor, J., et al.: Efficient and precise interactive hand tracking through joint, continuous optimization of pose and correspondences. ACM Trans. Graph. **35**, 1–12 (2016)
5. Li, P., Ling, H., Li, X., Liao, C.: 3D hand pose estimation using randomized decision forest with segmentation index points. In: 2015 IEEE International Conference on Computer Vision (ICCV), pp. 819–827 (2015)
6. Tang, D., Chang, H.J., Tejani, A., Kim, T.-K.: Latent regression forest: structured estimation of 3D articulated hand posture. In: 2014 IEEE Conference on Computer Vision and Pattern Recognition, pp. 3786–3793. IEEE Computer Society (2014)
7. Oberweger, M., Wohlhart, P., Lepetit, V.: Training a Feedback loop for hand pose estimation. In: 2015 IEEE International Conference on Computer Vision (ICCV), pp. 3316–3324 (2015)
8. Oberweger, M., Wohlhart, P., Lepetit, V.: Hands deep in deep learning for hand pose estimation. Computer Science (2015)
9. Ge, L., Liang, H., Yuan, J., Thalmann, D.: Robust 3D hand pose estimation in single depth images: from single-view CNN to multi-view CNNs. In: 2016 IEEE Conference on Computer Vision and Pattern Recognition (CVPR), pp. 3593–3601 (2016)
10. Zhou, X., Wan, Q., Zhang, W., Xue, X., Wei, Y.: Model-based deep hand pose estimation. In: Proceedings of the Twenty-Fifth International Joint Conference on Artificial Intelligence, pp. 2421–2427. AAAI Press (2016)
11. Madadi, M., Escalera, S., Baro, X., Gonzalez, J.: End-to-end global to local CNN learning for hand pose recovery in depth data. arXiv e-prints, pp. 1–11 (2017)
12. Yang, H., Zhang, J.: Hand pose regression via a classification-guided approach. In: Lai, S.-H., Lepetit, V., Nishino, K., Sato, Y. (eds.) ACCV 2016. LNCS, vol. 10113, pp. 452–466. Springer, Cham (2017). https://doi.org/10.1007/978-3-319-54187-7_30
13. Iandola, F.N., Han, S., Moskewicz, M.W., Ashraf, K., Dally, W.J., Keutzer, K.: SqueezeNet: AlexNet-level accuracy with 50x fewer parameters and <0.5 MB model size. arXiv e-prints, vol. 1602, pp. 1–13 (2016)
14. Smola, A.J., Schölkopf, B.: A tutorial on support vector regression. Stat. Comput. **14**, 199–222 (2004)
15. Tompson, J., Stein, M., Lecun, Y., Perlin, K.: Real-time continuous pose recovery of human hands using convolutional networks. ACM Trans. Graph. **33**, 169 (2014)
16. Jia, Y., et al.: Caffe: convolutional architecture for fast feature embedding. In: Proceedings of the ACM International Conference on Multimedia - MM 2014, pp. 675–678. ACM (2014)
17. Pedregosa, F., et al.: Scikit-learn: machine learning in python. J. Mach. Learn. Res. **12**, 2825–2830 (2011)

Author Index

Abdulazeez, Sarmad A. 177
Aguilera-Canon, Mara Catalina 30
Álvarez, Luis Alejandro 84
Ataucusi, Pablo 322

Buitrago, Diego Fernando Loaiza 84

Cai, Lei 211
Cao, Mingliang 69
Chai, Yanjie 79, 161, 327
Chang, Jian 169
Chen, Bo 149
Chen, Tang 132

Dai, Shijun 35
Deng, Xiaozhou 255
Dong, Bo 389
Dong, Jing 378
Dong, Jiwen 263
Dong, Yufeng 406
Duque, Diego Fernando 84

El Rhalibi, Abdennour 177

Fan, Jinsong 69
Fan, Yuling 231
Fang, Xiaoyong 378
Feng, Jixuan 336

Gao, Jingjing 343
Gao, Zhenguo 398
Geng, Guohua 352
Gomez, Ebert 322
González, Carolina 26
Guo, Bin 370
Guo, Fenggen 203

Hao, Wen 140, 361
He, Ge 352
He, Huan 389
Hirai, Shogo 284
Huang, Liangyi 115, 123, 192, 361

Ibañez, Vladimiro 322
Ibarra, Eliana 322
Ibarra, Manuel 322
Ibarra, Waldo 322
Iida, Hiroyuki 53, 293

Jiang, Hao 13
Jin, Haiyan 3, 145, 154, 249, 336
Jin, Qiao 255
Jin, Yao 169
Junjun, Pan 21

Kong, Jie 318

Li, Bing 132
Li, Chengyang 169
Li, Chunlin 268
Li, Lu 236
Li, Peng 132
Li, Rui 389
Li, Shi 245
Li, Xiaohua 241
Li, Xiuxiu 3, 140, 145, 241
Li, Ye 361
Liang, Wei 140, 154
Lin, Wentao 3
Lin, Xiangyuan 336
Lin, Yongzheng 263
Liu, Feng 107
Liu, Haibo 35
Liu, Huan 3
Liu, Jing 361
Liu, Kun 263
Liu, Lu 140, 154, 249
Liu, Rui 219
Liu, Shaohua 13, 35
Liu, Tingting 79, 161, 327
Liu, Xiaotong 99
Liu, Zhen 79, 161, 327
Lu, Jian 406
Lu, Ting 318
Lv, Ke 115, 123, 192
Lv, Zhiyong 91, 249

Ma, Chenguang 275
Ma, Jie 91
Ma, Kun 263
Mao, Tianlu 13, 35
Marquez, Carlos 84

Nait-Charif, Hammadi 30
Nasr Eddine, Amira 21
Navarro-Newball, Andres A. 84
Ning, Xiaojuan 91, 115, 123, 192

Okada, Yoshihiro 275
Ortiz, Andrea 26

Pan, Huaxian 211

Qi, Bingfang 303, 331
Qi, YuTao 236
Qin, Feiwei 245

Ren, Meng 318

Saint-Priest, Yana 84
Segovia, Patricia 84
Shakouri, Farbod 39
She, Lvjie 69
Shi, Junfei 154, 249
Shi, Liwen 145
Shi, MengLi 313
Shi, Min 13
Shi, Wei 275
Shi, Zhenghao 115, 123, 132
Song, Dan 169
Song, Qiannan 352
Song, Xiyuan 13, 35
Sumi, Kaoru 61, 284
Sun, Lei 268

Tian, Feng 39
Tobar, Hendrys 26
Tong, Ruofeng 169

Vitery, Cristian 26

Wainwright, Tom 30
Wang, Bin 3, 336
Wang, Congying 318
Wang, Danli 255
Wang, Heng 99
Wang, Jin 79, 161, 327
Wang, Jing 107
Wang, Jiwang 336
Wang, Lijuan 192
Wang, Lu 149
Wang, Meili 231
Wang, Na 352
Wang, Ningna 115, 123, 192
Wang, Tongtong 169
Wang, Xiaofeng 99, 352
Wang, Yigang 245
Wang, Yinghui 91, 115, 123, 132, 140, 192, 249
Wang, YingHui 361
Wang, Zheng 352
Wang, Zhichao 53
Watanabe, Toyohide 303, 331
Wei, Xiaopeng 370, 378
Wu, Qihui 219
Wu, Zizhao 203, 245

Xia, Shixiong 398
Xiao, Zhaolin 3, 145
Xie, SiQi 313
Xiong, Shuo 53, 293
Xu, Qingzheng 91

Yabuki, Keigo 61
Yan, Hong 313
Yang, Dongsheng 231
Yang, Xiaosong 30
Yang, Xiuhong 140
Yi, Pengfei 370
Yu, Hui 308
Yu, Jusheng 236
Yu, Xiangchuan 149

Zhan, Yinwei 343
Zhang, Hongwei 35
Zhang, Jie 107, 303, 331
Zhang, Jiulong 241
Zhang, Qiang 219, 406
Zhang, Shuang 149
Zhang, Shuo 293
Zhang, Yingpeng 303, 331
Zhang, Zeliang 293
Zhang, Zhengxuan 378
Zhang, Zhongqiu 308
Zhao, Chenxu 241

Zhao, Hui 107, 303, 331
Zhao, Jiaqi 398
Zhao, Minghua 115, 123, 132
Zhao, Tong 35
Zhao, Yanni 115, 123
Zheng, Qinghua 389
Zhou, Dongsheng 219, 370, 378
Zhou, Jin 263
Zhou, Pengbo 99
Zuo, Long 53, 293

MIX
Papier aus verantwortungsvollen Quellen
Paper from responsible sources
FSC® C105338

If you have any concerns about our products,
you can contact us on
ProductSafety@springernature.com

In case Publisher is established outside the EU,
the EU authorized representative is:
Springer Nature Customer Service Center GmbH
Europaplatz 3, 69115 Heidelberg, Germany

Printed by Libri Plureos GmbH
in Hamburg, Germany